Criminological Theories

To Jodi, my best friend, and Richard and Sharon, my parents, for giving me the support, understanding, and encouragement necessary to edit and compile this anthology.

Criminological Theories

Bridging the Past to the Future

Suzette Cote

California State University, Sacramento *Editor*

SAGE Publications
International Educational and Professional Publisher
Thousand Oaks ▪ London ▪ New Delhi

For information:

Sage Publications, Inc.
2455 Teller Road
Thousand Oaks, California 91320
E-mail: order@sagepub.com

Sage Publications Ltd.
6 Bonhill Street
London EC2A 4PU
United Kingdom

Sage Publications India Pvt. Ltd.
M-32 Market
Greater Kailash I
New Delhi 110 048 India

Printed in the United States of America

Library of Congress Cataloging-in-Publication Data

Main entry under title:
 Criminological theories: Bridging the past to the future / edited by Suzette
Cote.
    p. cm.
Includes bibliographical references and index.
 ISBN 0-7619-2502-3 (c)
 ISBN 0-7619-2503-1 (p)
 1. Criminology. I. Title.
HV6018 .C68 2002
364--dc21

                          2001005393

This book is printed on acid-free paper.

02 03 04 05 10 9 8 7 6 5 4 3 2 1

Acquisitions Editor:	Jerry Westby
Editorial Assistant:	Vonessa Vondera
Copy Editor:	Rachel Hile Bassett
Production Editor:	Denise Santoyo
Typesetter:	Siva Math Setters, Chennai, India
Indexer:	Teri Greenberg
Cover Designer:	Michelle Lee

CONTENTS

PREFACE

WHY THEORY?

A student in my undergraduate criminal justice course, Crime and Punishment, once asked, mid-semester, why she needed to know *why* the offender "did what he did" instead of just learning about how to prevent future crimes and how to punish the offenders once they've committed their crimes. I chuckled (to myself), took a deep breath, and explained that by having an understanding of why the offender became deviant and committed a crime, the criminal justice system can better respond with improved prevention and sanctioning strategies. I firmly concluded by saying that despite the bad name it's gotten, theory really is important to the study of crime, punishment, and criminal justice. Unfortunately, my response was met with very little enthusiasm. In fact, my response was met with very little emotion, period. I sighed quietly as my gaze absorbed the blank stares and puzzled expressions on my students' faces.

I am not breaking new ground when I say that theory has become synonymous with Latin for many current undergraduate, and even some graduate, students, in many criminology and criminal justice programs. As Simpson (2000) laments in the preface of her text, *Of Crime and Criminality: The Use of Theory in Everyday Life:*

> Typically, most [undergraduate students] find [theory] obtuse and irrelevant to their everyday lives. This is particularly true for more traditional theories which many tend to find overly simplistic and non-inclusive. . . . Students often suggest that the social circumstances that give rise to these theories no longer exist. Consequently, they fail to see how the ideas, explanations, and predictions developed in the past are relevant to life at the dawn of the new millennium. (p. xiii)

Perhaps this view reflects the larger American view and attitude toward theory. In Chapter 2, Ineke Haen Marshall, comments on the uniqueness of America's relationship to pragmatism and, I will add, action. Readers should consult her article for the full development of her ideas, but a few points she raises are worthy of mention here. She writes, "The mainstay of American scientific thought is very much coloured by pragmatism" (p. 19, this volume). She adds that "in the view of many American interpreters, Americans have often been hostile to theory, be it in literature, philosophy or science" (p. 19, this volume). Essentially, the belief is that if ideas (i.e., theories) do not change current circumstances or people's behaviors, then ideas are pointless. Perhaps we can add criminal justice to that list! Consequently, many students feel a disconnection between theory (the abstract) and practice (the reality).

These attitudes also permeate the walls of the academy, filtering into the thoughts and attitudes of the very professionals who supposedly develop and promote the frameworks within which action, or *research* in this case, can occur. Bernard similarly bemoans in Chapter 1 the lack of theoretical development and scientific progress in the field of criminology. He asks,

> Why do most researchers specialize to the exclusion of theorizing, but few theorists specialize to the exclusion of researching? My answer is that there are systematic pressures that drive criminologists and other social scientists toward research and away from theory. . . . The ultimate result of those pressures is the failure to make scientific progress. (p. 12, this volume)

In addition to the disconnection felt by many undergraduates, many graduate students and professionals feel that time would be better spent focusing on the consequences of crime rather than its origins. Additionally, these students claim that most of the "old theories" no longer make sense, and they cannot see how those theories make contributions today by synthesizing with other theoretical perspectives.

Why spend all of this time explaining the general (negative?) attitudes toward theory? First, to demonstrate the present state of affairs in which theory has found itself and, more important, to illustrate the importance, necessity, and relevance of theory not only to research but to problem solving (i.e., in the world of criminal justice professionals) and even to everyday life. Therefore, based on a variety of experiences and conversations with students and criminal justice professionals, my own research in terms of this project, and the need for a greater emphasis on the often-ignored critical perspectives and more recent theoretical developments, I approach this project with three broad objectives:

1. To demonstrate the importance and necessity of theory in the criminological and criminal justice enterprise and to show how theory—criminological theories in particular—informs criminal justice policies and crime prevention practices

2. To present the full spectrum of criminological theories that have been developed over the past century and today

3. To give attention to novel integrated theories of crime and frequently neglected criminological perspectives

I feel that it is critical that students, academicians, and professionals alike obtain a comprehensive understanding of not only why theory is important to the field and the criminal justice profession but how learning from theories of the past helps to inform and shape theories of the present and future. To further that end, I include three articles that will demonstrate the importance of theory and theorizing in criminology as well as in the criminal justice discipline and field.

This anthology includes a number of unique features that will distinguish it from other readers currently on the market. Although some article selections overlap with existing readers, many of the articles chosen have never been included in a reader and, most important, offer a distinctive perspective that deserves recognition in the broadest possible manner. More specifically:

1. The selections are from top-rated peer-reviewed journals, providing comprehensive coverage of all major criminological theories.

2. There is a strong emphasis on the most recent theoretical developments.

3. There is a greater emphasis on issues of gender, race, and class within criminological theories and criminality.

4. The anthology includes and expands on topics typically neglected in other texts, namely white-collar crime; criminology and the Holocaust/genocide; developmental criminology; new penology; postmodern and constitutive theories; and integrated theories that consider genetics, psychology, and environmental approaches.

5. The readings provide insight into ways of theorizing about criminology and criminal justice.

THEORETICAL SCOPE OF THE BOOK

This book will address numerous topics dealing with crime, criminology, and, to a lesser extent, criminal justice. The scope and breadth of the topics further substantiate my belief that many readers from various academic disciplines and professions will benefit greatly from this interdisciplinary approach. This book will be most useful to students, researchers, and professionals in the fields of criminology, criminal justice, and sociology. Although I have attempted to include a variety of classics in the book where appropriate, I may not have included as many as some readers may have liked. Because of space limitations, it was impossible to include every article and text excerpt that I felt was appropriate for the book. The text and article selection process for this book was difficult and arduous, to say the least!

Moreover, the original articles have been substantially edited and abridged to make them more accessible to students, because journal articles are typically written for a professional audience and not for students. However, I attempted to retain the structural and conceptual core of the articles and texts as best I could without eroding the seminal points raised in the authors' arguments. Therefore, if readers have further questions or feel that the edited versions leave questions unanswered, they should consult the original article or text.

Within these limitations, the book stands strong in its original premise and scope. I placed more emphasis on new theoretical developments in the field and on theories that have not received as much coverage in other texts. To that end, I feel that more attention needs to be given to "less mainstream" perspectives, including critical, postmodern, constitutive, and feminist theories of crime. Although a vast majority of criminology theory readers include these perspectives (Cullen & Agnew, 1998; Henry & Einstadter, 1998; Paternoster & Bachman, 2000; Williams & McShane, 2001), the present book will provide examples of the more recent theoretical developments in these areas. For example, David Shichor's article (Chapter 27, this volume) demonstrates how the new penology can be used as a framework for explaining a controversial criminal justice policy, the three-strikes legislation. Brannigan's article (Chapter 5, this volume) on the Holocaust and criminology highlights an often-ignored area of criminality, genocide and xenophobia, that deserves attention, especially in light of past and present tragedies in Nazi Germany, Bosnia, and Rwanda.

Furthermore, these current theoretical developments expand upon the classics in a variety of interesting and insightful ways. Developmental criminology and Tittle's control balance theory provide good examples of the ways in which elements of earlier theories (i.e., psychological, biological, and control theories) can be modified and enhanced to explain criminality (Loeber and Stouthamer-Loeber, Chapter 33, this volume; Braithwaite, Chapter 16, this volume; Tittle, Chapter 17, this volume). Consequently, this book contains several articles that address integrated approaches as well as interdisciplinary perspectives on crime and criminality. For example, in Chapter 36, Anthony Walsh unites behavior genetics and strain theory. He offers a novel way of explaining how the environment and genetics play a role in shaping how individuals

adapt to and cope with the strain they may face in their surroundings. Students of criminology, as well as academicians and professionals, can only benefit from exposure to and insights from other academic disciplines.

I divided the book into six main sections, some of which have a number of subsections. Each broad section represents a particular approach to crime and criminality, with the first section highlighting the important nexus between criminology and criminal justice theory and practice. Generally, this book will provide a unique, comprehensive, interdisciplinary approach to classic and novel theoretical developments in the field of criminology. In order to explain to readers the essentials of the theoretical perspective of each text covered, the book includes a brief introduction to each of the six sections. These introductions provide readers with a comprehensive overview of the individual articles, highlighting important themes, intellectual developments, and unique contributions to the field. Additionally, a brief introduction precedes each of the 36 chapters. By highlighting the key issues on which readers should focus, these introductions make the excerpts more understandable and accessible.

Last, my book also includes discussion questions at the end of each chapter that will encourage students, especially, to reflect on the readings in an individual and holistic manner. These questions may also be used as a catalyst for class discussions. The questions may provide academicians and researchers with important insights into issues that they may not yet have considered. Although I provide some context for the reader with the inclusion of the general and section introductions, this text is designed to be used in conjunction with or as a supplement to a theory text. My hope is that all readers will find it to be a beneficial and informative resource for understanding and appreciating criminological theory.

ACKNOWLEDGMENTS

Although I had the responsibility of selecting articles and text excerpts for this book, I could not have done it without the help of others. The reviewers commissioned by Sage offered wonderful advice and suggestions, especially in terms of evaluating articles and texts I had selected and encouraging me to look at others. Although I did my best to respond to everyone's comments, that task is an impossibility.

The original table of contents that the reviewers saw underwent a number of revisions before the final article and text selections were made. Additionally, several changes were made with respect to the classification of theories and the development of additional categories. I would like to thank Timothy Ireland and David Kauzalrich in particular for providing further insight into the organization of the theoretical categories and placement of certain readings.

Second, I would like to thank the staff at Sage for their patience with my schedule and for pushing the book through so it could be marketed and available for use in a short period of time. Jerry Westby deserves exceptional thanks and praise not only for speaking with me and encouraging me to submit a proposal—and subsequently approving it—but also for helping me to develop a collection of readings that would be accessible to readers and that address the central themes of the book. Additionally, I want to recognize the expert assistance from the staff at Sage, namely editorial assistant Vonessa Vondera. Thanks also to Denise Santoyo, the production editor, and Rachel Hile Bassett, the copy editor.

I also wish to thank the office staff in the Division of Criminal Justice at California State University, Sacramento (CSUS). They provided me with access to equipment that enabled me to scan many of the articles and texts onto a computer disk, saving me hours of time. Additionally, their support, encouragement, and company are always much appreciated. I would also like to thank those colleagues in the Division who provided me with resources, insight, advice, and technological assistance. Last, I want to thank the reference librarians and library assistants in the CSUS library for assisting me in the early stages of this project and for allowing me to borrow library journals for an extended period of time. Specific thanks go to the following people at CSUS for their assistance, support, and encouragement on this project: Ben Amata, Cecil Canton, Phyllis Donovan, Karen Edgerly, Kall Loper, Debra Mullin, Thomas Phelps, Alicia Snee, James Summerfield, Miki Vohryzek-Bolden, Stephanie Whitus, and Maria Wihren.

REFERENCES

Cullen, F. T., & Agnew, R. (Eds.). (1998). *Criminological theory: Past to present, essential readings*. Los Angeles: Roxbury.

Henry, S., & Einstadter, W. (Eds.). (1998). *The criminology theory book*. New York: New York University Press.

Paternoster, R., & Bachman, R. (Eds.). (2000). *Explaining criminals and crime: Essays in contemporary criminological theory*. Los Angeles: Roxbury.

Simpson, S. S. (2001). *Of crime and criminality: The use of theory in everyday life*. Thousand Oaks, CA: Pine Forge Press.

Williams, F. P., III, & McShane, M. D. (Eds.). (2001). *Criminology theory: Selected classic readings* (2nd ed.). Cincinnati, OH: Anderson.

INTRODUCTION

Crime is a controversial, complex phenomenon that often raises more questions than it answers. Nonetheless, crime and criminality demand that answers be given when any type of crime occurs, whether it be the theft of a bicycle from a garage, a robbery of the local 7-Eleven, or a school shooting incident. The explanations for crime embody a number of challenges. Although many public commentators contend that most of the answers to the crime problem can be found by simply using common sense, criminologists and others heavily involved in the discipline of crime and criminality know that the explanations run deeper than that. The challenge of explaining crime requires that we set aside our biases about certain people and learn to approach the problem slowly and holistically. By holistically, I am referring to that process by which we consider all sides of an issue and all possibilities in our search for an answer.

But how easy is that? Simply put, it's not. We live in a very public world in which every decision that a politician, a criminologist, or a criminal justice official makes is scrutinized and frequently criticized. Politicians, in their quest for reelection, must not appear "soft on crime." Even criminologists must be wary of being mistaken as racist, sexist, classist, or heterosexist when they provide explanations of crime that involve difficult issues such as the racial and gendered distributions of crime in certain geographic areas of an urban community. These concerns often lead to the sacrificing of a scientifically rigorous, and perhaps unpopular, explanation of crime for one that appeals to the broad moral center of the populace. To this end, many public commentators and even criminologists find themselves supporting crime prevention and crime control measures that posture a "tough on crime" stance, despite the fact that many of these programs and strategies have been unproven or have been found to be unsuccessful.

THE COMPLEXITY AND EXTENT OF CRIME

Despite the controversy that surrounds crime and the various explanations for criminality, the study of crime remains a daunting necessity. Crime exists everywhere, but the extent to which it exists often becomes distorted and sensationalized by public officials and the media. Both the media and public analyses of crime paint a frightening picture of criminality. The primary image is that most of the crimes that occur are of a brutally violent nature, causing widespread injuries to all victims involved; a secondary image is that most Americans live in constant fear of crime, imprisoning themselves behind locked doors and within gated communities. Although there may be some elements of truth in these explanations, most Americans never directly experience or even witness a violent assault or murder, and although many people take security precautions—whether in the form of simply locking the doors of one's home at night, installing security alarm systems, or purchasing a gun—most people feel relatively safe in and around their residences and neighborhoods (Beckett & Sasson, 2000). Studies have shown that media consumption remains more strongly correlated to the fear of social violence than to fear of personal victimization; more to fear of unknown or nonlocal places than to fear of known, local places; and more to fear of urban areas than to fear of nonurban areas (Beckett & Sasson, 2000; Surette, 1998).

Regardless of the concerns raised in the media and by public officials, crime remains an important and serious matter that warrants thorough analysis and understanding. Although many of us can live our lives relatively free from crime and victimization, many Americans do not, and many living in urban areas face the potential for victimization every day. Statistics—which have their own set of limitations—reveal an interesting, yet disturbing, picture as well. Each year, the Federal Bureau of Investigation (FBI) releases the Uniform Crime Reports (UCR), in which the FBI lists the number of crimes that have become known to police departments. Police departments typically gather this information from citizens' reports, and the findings and figures are submitted voluntarily to the FBI (FBI, U.S. Department of Justice, 2000). According to a preliminary report for the first six months of 2000, index crime decreased by 0.3% compared with figures reported for the same period of the preceding year. The UCR combines violent and property crimes to measure index crime. The Crime Index comprises both violent crimes (murder and nonnegligent manslaughter, forcible rape, robbery, and aggravated assault) and property crimes (burglary, larceny theft, motor vehicle theft, and arson). The preliminary report shows that violent and property crime both declined by 0.3% compared with the same data for the same period in 1999. More specifically, murder declined by 1.8% and robbery by 2.6%. However, both rape and aggravated assault increased by 0.7%. The changes with respect to property crime revealed mixed results. Arson and burglary showed decreases of 2.7% and 2.4%, respectively, while larceny theft and motor vehicle theft showed increases of 0.1% and 1.2%, respectively (FBI, U.S. Department of Justice, 2000).

Crime Index trends by population group and area as well as geographic region showed interesting results. It appears that the Crime Index fell in cities with populations of more than 250,000; however, the Crime Index increased in cities with all other population groups under 250,000 and in suburban and rural counties. In terms of geographic region, the overall Crime Index dropped in the Northeast by 1.9%, in the West by 0.9%, and in the Midwest by 0.7%. Conversely, the Crime Index increased in the South by 1.2%. Startling statistics reveal an increase in murder of 5.5% in the Northeast, and the West shows an increase of 4.5% in motor vehicle theft (FBI, U.S. Department of Justice, 2000).

Although the UCR provides us with very important information in terms of crime trends for violent and property crimes, the UCR captures only a small frame of the nation's overall crime problem. Many people do not report crimes to the police, thus rendering their voices, and victimization, statistically silent. Although figures in the National Crime Victimization Survey (NCVS), a nationwide study that asks citizens to describe their experiences with different types of crime, also reveal an overall decrease in the number of crimes committed against individuals between 1997 and 1998, the NCVS does show a 7.1% increase in the rate of rape and sexual assault and a 20% increase in the rate of sexual assault (*Sourcebook of Criminal Justice Statistics,* 1999, p. 172). Because many people do not report these experiences to the police, the NCVS data reveal a much higher level of criminal victimization than do the UCR data.

Recently, confusion has arisen as to whether the crime rate is actually up or down in the United States. Just two weeks after the FBI issued its report, highlighting a decade-long decline in crime rates, the U.S. Bureau of Justice Statistics (BJS) released a separate report concluding that violent crime had taken a nosedive by 15% in 2000 (Lichtblau, 2001). This figure represents the largest single drop in the BJS's 27-year history of studying crime rates, but the divergence in the results confounds criminologists.[1] Despite the disparity, the BJS researchers found that crime rates fell for almost every demographic group under consideration, regardless of gender, race, ethnicity, geography, age, and income (Lichtblau, 2001).

It is well-known that the UCR and NCVS, and other studies as well, provide contradictory information regarding trends in criminal victimization for several reasons. Primarily, the UCR and NCVS do not measure identical crimes or cover identical time periods. For example, the UCR includes statistics only on serious street crime despite our realization that minor crimes—theft and simple assaults, for example—are much more common and occur with greater frequency. Therefore, comparisons of these data must consider these methodological differences (Beckett & Sasson, 2000; FBI, U.S. Department of Justice, 2000; Lilly, Cullen, & Ball, 1995). Additionally, "self-report" surveys, which ask respondents whether and how many criminal offenses they have committed, indicate that illegal acts are much more rampant among various types of people than is captured in the UCR or even in the NCVS (Lilly et al., 1995).

Regardless of the differences between the UCR and the NCVS, both reveal that overall, crime is on the decline in the United States. To many, that is extremely good news. Several explanations for this decline assert that "get tough" policies regarding drugs, the use of handguns, and mandatory sentencing policies have led to the decrease in the number of crimes (Merlo & Benekos, 2000). Other explanations for the decrease in crime center on community-based prevention programs, a stronger economy, and a general change in attitude among youth:

> The decline reflects, in part, a subtle cultural shift among the young, especially minority youths—a growing turn away from violence against their peers, driven by revulsion against the destructiveness of the epidemic that had destroyed the lives, bodies, and futures of so many of their relatives and friends. (Currie, 1998, p. 188, quoted in Merlo & Benekos, 2000, p. 173)

As Merlo and Benekos (2000) comment, the explanations for this reduction in crime remain as complex as the explanations for the prevalence of crime and the reasons for why crime occurs in the first place!

Despite these complexities, despite the existing statistics, and even despite the drop in the crime rate, the fact remains that crime prevails as a prominent issue in our society today. As research suggests, violence is higher in the United States than in any other industrialized nation (Messner & Rosenfeld, 2001). Although it is sometimes difficult to make cross-cultural comparisons of crime rates because definitions of illegal behavior and data collection methodologies may differ (Lilly et al., 1995), there is something unique about the United States, as a modern, industrialized nation, that contributes to its excessively high crime rate (Messner & Rosenfeld, 2001). Messner and Rosenfeld tackle this issue later in this book.

But for now, questions remain about the problem of crime and criminality in the United States. Why is crime so prevalent? Why is it prevalent in some neighborhoods but not in others? Why do some people seem predisposed to criminality while others in similar circumstances lead crime-free lives? Are there differences between the poor and the affluent in the reasons why they commit criminal acts? How do we explain all of these variations in criminality among offenders, victims, places, and times? Is there any one particular explanation that is better than another? How do these explanations inform policy?

These and other questions will be addressed in some manner by the various articles and text excerpts contained in this book. Although the book does not and cannot offer any definitive answers to the problem of crime, one goal of the book is to provide a context for thinking about and addressing the current crime problems and thoughts in the fields of criminology and criminal justice.

CONFRONTING THE CRIME PROBLEM: BEGINNING WITH THEORY

Americans are concerned about crime, regardless of its recent decline, and most have little difficulty identifying the circumstances that they believe cause individuals to engage in deviant behavior. When asked for an opinion about what causes crime in certain situations, although some may respond that they have no opinion because they do not know enough about the crime or the case, usually most people will come up with a reason. Whatever reason they offer, most people, in general, have developed certain views as to why crime occurs. Therefore, it is fair to say that we all have a "theory" of criminal behavior. A variety of factors—social, economic, political, cultural, legal, and historical—shape the manner in which we view crime, but most people cannot ground their views in anything more than their own world experiences and what they might read or see on TV (Lilly et al., 1995). Unfortunately, much of this talk or "theorizing" gets transformed into popular crime myths or stereotypes, one of the most common being that African American males commit most violent crimes.

But for those who study crime professionally, theory, or the theory-making process, emerges as a systematic, scientifically based statement about the relationships between observable phenomena (Vold, Bernard, & Snipes, 1998). For example, some theories make statements about the relationship between the social characteristics of an individual (i.e., where a person lives) and the likelihood that the person will engage in delinquent behavior. Other theories examine the relationship between a person's race and his or her treatment by police officers.

Theory has been a cornerstone of criminology since its inception, although in recent years some claim that advances in criminological theory making have been on the decline. Criminology needs "something to breathe fresh life into it" (Walsh, Chapter 36, this volume, p. 347), or at least revision, with more attention paid to the falsification of theories rather than further explanation of verified approaches (Bernard, Chapter 1 in this volume; Vold et al., 1998) and consideration of "subterranean" work of criminological theorists (Rock & Holdaway, 1998) who may be theorizing "in a different voice, undertaken behind the scenes so to speak, yet moving forward in a deliberate and systematic manner from project to project" (Shearing, 1998, p. 16). Simply put, theory matters to the world of crime control; what many students of criminology and, perhaps, professionals sometimes fail to recognize is that having an understanding of why crime occurs is frequently a precursor to developing strategies to control the behavior.

The Role of Criminology

Before delving into the issue of what role criminology plays in the study and control of crime, it might be wise to define it first. Sutherland and Cressey's (1955) widely cited definition of criminology states that "criminology is the body of knowledge regarding crime as a social phenomenon. It includes within its scope the processes of making laws, of breaking laws, and of reacting toward the breaking of laws" (p. 3). Most criminologists would likely agree with this general statement. Some might add that "criminology is the scientific study of crime as a social phenomenon" (Sheley, 2000, p. 1). Still others may counter that controversy surrounds the content and scope of criminology: Is it scientific? Is it an autonomous discipline, independent of sociology, its most closely related disciplinary

relative? Is it without biases? Is its application to social problems critical (Henry & Einstadter, 1998)? Answers to these questions have become muddled by a number of factors, including disciplinary fragmentation, failure to develop effective crime reduction policies (Henry & Einstadter, 1998), stagnation in theory development (Bernard, Chapter 1, this volume), and, as I believe, a waning consensus—politically, professionally, and on the societal level—on the importance of theory in its application to policy.

Although criminology aims to accomplish many goals regarding crime and crime prevention, the criminological enterprise during the 20th century has focused largely on the discovery of causes of law-breaking, though much discord exists about the scope of this endeavor. Some question how wide the criminological umbrella should spread in terms of its disciplinary reach (i.e., does it also include victimology or the sociology of law?), but for purposes of this reader, criminology is treated as a separate discipline, influenced by many. Likewise, the field of criminal justice defines itself as a discipline in its own right, struggling with the same theoretical and methodological issues that plague all of the social sciences (Bernard & Engel, Chapter 3, this volume). Despite these controversies, criminology seeks to identify and explain the causes of criminality, mainly through rigorous, scientific, theory-research interaction. In this sense, criminology is as much about "thinking" about crime as it is about "doing something" about the problem. This continuous knowledge-production process further supports the scientific premises on which the field was first developed.

The Nature of the Criminological Discipline and Theory

The lack of agreement over its disciplinary scope has likely contributed to the vast breadth of theories that have been developed by criminologists in the 20th century. Criminological theories emerged from a multidisciplinary framework—a blessing or a curse, depending on which side of the issue you favor—and, as a multidisciplinary social science, criminology borrows from various other fields in its attempts to explain crime and criminality. It derives its theories from fields as varied as biology, economics, political science, law, sociology, history, anthropology, geography, and linguistics. This colorful patchwork of theoretical development demonstrates the complexities of the crime problem and the significant effort by criminologists to consider nearly all perspectives in order to explain crime and criminality.

On the other hand, this multidisciplinary nature undermines criminology's disciplinary integrity: Does diversity in theoretical scope constitute criminology as an independent discipline with various subdisciplines, or does the amalgam of perspectives establish criminology as an interdisciplinary field, which suggests complete integration of subdisciplines into a unified whole? No clear answer exists, and this anthology does not attempt to resolve the debate! Nonetheless, the point can be made that the disciplinary core of criminology lies somewhere between multidisciplinary and interdisciplinary. Recent theoretical development over the past 20 years suggests that criminology is moving toward integration, though it very much retains a multidisciplinary constitution (in this volume, see Elliott, Ageton, & Canter, Chapter 34; Thornberry, Chapter 35; and Walsh, Chapter 36).

The importance of the multidisciplinary nature of criminology lies in the manner in which it has sustained theoretical development over the past century. Theories of old are not discarded in favor of new models; rather, they are rehashed, transformed, and shaped to apply appropriately to today's conditions and problems. Breathing life into previous theories demonstrates how theoretical perspectives that shaped and informed the discipline earlier in the 20th century should—and do—inform and shape it today, while still allowing it room to grow.

For example, biological theories thrived at the turn of the 20th century and for the next 20 years, eventually falling under heavy criticism for racist and eugenic overtones and prescriptions for social policy. Within the past 15 years or so, sociobiology, life-course psychology, developmental criminology, and behavior genetics have all stepped into the limelight. Though these more recent, sophisticated approaches have not received as much support as their sociological counterparts, they do make important, insightful contributions that merit careful and serious consideration. Although distinct from their biological predecessors, the theories incorporate some of the original thoughts of the early theorists: that biology and psychology, to varying degrees, may play a role in criminality.

Currently, no overarching theory exists in criminology that explains all of the complexities of crime. The roots of crime run deep. The arguments for either a single, general theory of crime versus an integrated approach will undoubtedly continue for as long as criminology exists, though it is difficult to ignore the fact that because crime is not a naturally occurring concept or fact but a socially and legally constructed one imposed on certain behaviors, and because our society is heterogeneously constituted in terms of difference, it becomes increasingly difficult, if not altogether impossible, to claim that one general theory of crime can apply to all facts of crime and criminality under all circumstances. As this reader illustrates, some theories may have more powerful explanatory power than others but only under certain social conditions of law-breaking. Therefore, criminology may retain its disciplinary integrity not by attempting to do it all or to develop a "one-size-fits-all" approach, but rather by appreciating and encouraging its rich and diverse theoretical expanse. The following section attempts to provide a brief overview of the development of criminological theories. For complete consideration of the theorists and their respective works, readers should consult the original source.

The Scope of Criminological Theories

European Influences

In the 19th century, criminology focused primarily on finding a single cause of crime, though this notion was quickly discarded in favor of multiple explanations because of the acknowledged complexities inherent in criminality. The roots of criminology stem from the era of 18th-century Enlightenment, with Cesare Beccaria (1735-1795) and Jeremy Bentham (1748-1832) as the predominant figures of the time, though current debate exists as to whether Beccaria's work truly exemplified and advanced a classical position.[2] Best known for his intellectual advancements in classical criminology, Bentham was a British utilitarian social philosopher who focused on legal and penal reform rather than on formulating and advancing explanations of criminal behavior (Akers, 2001). Both Beccaria and

Bentham asserted that criminals were rational individuals who, through their own free will, consciously violated society's laws.

Concerned with penal and legal reform, Bentham condemned the arbitrary and capricious nature of the European justice system. At that time, punishments were handed down in an unreasonable, uncertain fashion. In contrast, Bentham favored a legal system that was more rational and fair. He argued that, to motivate citizens to obey the laws of a society, penal sanctions should be certain, swift, and severe enough to ensure the principle of proportionality: Let the punishment fit the crime, and do no more. This affirms the idea of maximum utility: People will avoid crime if they know the pain (i.e., punishment) they will surely receive if they engage in that behavior. Many of the classical school's legal reforms proposed at the time were later incorporated into the American system of government and law. Additionally, this theory of crime remains relevant for criminologists and criminal justice professionals today, especially in terms of their contribution to contemporary deterrence and rational choice theories (in this volume, see Cornish & Clarke, Chapter 30, and Felson, Chapter 31).

The classical school of criminology remained the dominant force in the study of crime until the end of the 19th century. By the 1870s, classical theory began to give way to biological "positivism," which proposed that crime was not a rational endeavor chosen freely by individuals, but rather a result of inborn abnormalities. Positivists such as Cesare Lombroso, Raffaele Garofalo, and Enrico Ferri of the Italian School argued for the scientific study of crime and criminals. Positivists argued that the certainty and severity of punishment under classical theory would have no impact on "natural-born" criminals, because their crimes were caused by an innate biological constitution immune to law.[3] Other European positivists who followed in this tradition included psychoanalytic theories, which were heavily Freudian in application and scope.

American Criminology

In the early part of the 20th century, American criminology shared, to varying degrees, this biologically based theoretical ground, though American criminology has been (and will likely continue to be) predominantly influenced by sociology. The emergence of sociology, and subsequently criminology, occurred within a whirlwind of circumstances during the first 20 years of the 20th century, which historians identify as the Progressive Era. Mainly middle-class citizens from a variety of backgrounds, the Progressives expressed concerns about the harsh social consequences of urbanization and industrialization that were destroying the nation. Their efforts aimed at providing assistance for those living in poverty, rehabilitating offenders, and providing humane treatment for the insane (Gibbons, 2001).

American sociology, and later criminology, emerged against this Progressive backdrop. Although these individuals helped shape sociological thought, sociology, like criminology, did not gain disciplinary stature until much later. In the early part of the 20th century, efforts focused instead on the pathological nature of social problems and individuals, which the Progressives saw as a consequence of modern industrial life.

Criminological theories that emerged at this time in the United States reflected this near obsession with the pathology of crime. Evolving from a strong belief in the notion that scientific methods should be used to solve problems of human behavior, the positivist school of criminology in the United States reached its full potential when Progressive reformers proposed that offenders should be individually diagnosed and subsequently treated scientifically. For example, in my own research on sexual psychopaths and the laws that were enacted to control them, I found that the transformation of the psychopath into a violent, male, sexual offender represented an emerging trend in the fields of criminology and psychiatry that was primarily caused by the expansion of psychiatry beyond the walls of mental hospitals and into courts and prisons (Cote, 2000). As a result, new explanations for criminal behavior and definitions of the criminal slowly emerged.[4] American criminologists began using psychiatric diagnoses in the late 1920s partly because of the dominant theory of the time, which maintained a strong correlation between "mental defect" and "feeblemindedness" and criminal predisposition (Cote, 2000).

By the 1930s, many of the biological and psychological theories had begun to wane because of the new theoretical advances from sociology and because of increased moral and social concern regarding the underlying objectives of these approaches.[5] Therefore, by the middle of the 20th century, the sociological approach had begun to monopolize the study of crime and criminality. The early work of the Chicago School cultural ecology theorists, Robert Park and Ernest Burgess, in the 1920s enabled sociology to secure and then expand its disciplinary roots. Criminology became part of this expansion with the publication of Edwin Sutherland's (1924) classic text, *Criminology.*

Chicago School sociologists demonstrated that biological explanations alone cannot account for why certain geographical areas of the city reflected persistent and consistent crime patterns even when populations shifted. Clifford R. Shaw and Henry D. McKay's important study (Chapter 6 in this volume) became the foundation for a social disorganization theory of crime, which maintains that delinquency is a cultural tradition in some urban areas.

By the 1940s and 1950s, several sociological theories of crime had emerged. These approaches included the Durkheim-influenced *strain* or *anomie* theory of crime developed by Robert K. Merton (Chapter 9, this volume), which viewed crime as an illegitimate response to an unequal distribution of resources. Other significant contributions during the period between 1940 and 1960 include Edwin Sutherland and Donald Cressey's (1955) social learning theory of differential association; Thorsten Sellin's (1938) theory about culture conflict; and the voluminous body of work on subcultural theories of delinquency from Albert Cohen (1955), Richard Cloward and Lloyd Ohlin (1960), and Walter Miller (1958).

These sociologically based theories formed the foundation for "mainstream criminology," which dominated the field from 1945 to 1970 (Gibbons, 2001). In different ways, these sociological theories each demonstrate that crime involves more than mere individual choices (i.e., free will) influenced by the external threat of penal sanctions or individual variations in biological or psychological constitution. Rather, these theories view crime as resulting from structural, sociocultural, and organizational forces (Henry & Einstadter, 1998).

The 1960s witnessed the slow demise of structural and cultural explanations of crime. The challenges to these mainstream approaches mirrored the social turmoil that began to tear the fabric of traditional American social values. During this era, criminological theories assumed a social psychological approach, which emphasized active social processes over both structural and deterministic influences. The work of Albert Bandura (1973, 1977), borrowing from Gabriel Tarde's (1886) imitation theory, established social learning theory as a primary explanatory framework for criminal violence. Bandura's work expanded upon B. F. Skinner's (1953) operant conditioning model and Eysenck's (1964) criminal personality theory. Robert Burgess and Ronald Akers (1966) proposed a full reformulation, explaining criminal behavior in their differential association-reinforcement theory, which retained the principles of differential association and combined them with, and restated them in terms of, the principles of operant and respondent conditioning (Akers, 2001). Akers (Chapter 13, this volume) developed his own social learning theory by fully integrating principles of differential association and operant conditioning models with an additional feedback component.

The 1960s also witnessed the emergence and rise of the neutralization theory of delinquency of Sykes and Matza (Chapter 14, this volume) and the control theory of delinquency of Hirschi (1969). These theories supported the idea that socialization processes could be powerful enough to negate the importance of conformity to social norms and laws under any circumstances. In this vein, Hirschi's social bonding theory seeks answers to the question of why we all don't commit crime. This Hobbesian query stresses the importance of the socialization process in a variety of environments, namely the family.

Labeling theories of the late 1960s and 1970s made important contributions to criminology, but they have had little empirical success. Drawing on the early work of Frank Tannenbaum (1938), labeling theorists proposed that the crime problem worsened because of criminal justice agencies' attempts to control it. In other words, the extremely negative effects the system could have on a person's self-identity actually limited the system's ability to do something to curb the problem. Theories of deviance by Edwin Lemert

(1951, 1967), Howard Becker (1963), Edwin Schur (1965), and to a certain extent Erving Goffman (1963) demonstrated how deviant careers evolved over time, mainly from the effects of being labeled by and then processed through the criminal justice system.

A logical offshoot of the labeling perspective assumed an even more critical approach to crime control. Conflict, radical, and critical criminology, largely reflected in the works of Austin Turk (1966), William Chambliss (1964), Richard Quinney (1973, 1977, 1980), and Ian Taylor, Paul Walton, and Jock Young (Chapter 24 in this volume) extended the previous Marxist works of Willem Bonger (1916) to proclaim not only that criminal justice agents and agencies were contributing to the crime problem but that the entire capitalist system fostered a criminogenic ideology. The "new criminology," discussed in Taylor, Walton, and Young's text excerpt in this volume, asserted that the powerful social classes, including the capitalist state, committed crimes such as corporate corruption, fraud, pollution, and bribery that were at times more serious than street and property crimes, although they were punished to a lesser extent if at all.

Contemporary Approaches: Theoretical Integration

The 1980s and 1990s reflected a period of new theoretical growth, testing, and integration. Though the theories of the 1970s were not entirely discarded, the ideas in them were fairly limited and more philosophical than scientific in nature. The theoretical development in this later period reflects the elaboration of earlier approaches into several interesting and informative approaches, many of which are included in this volume. More contemporary theoretical perspectives resurrect some of the theories of the past and combine them in unique ways with new developments. For example, the rational choice theory of Derek B. Cornish and Ronald V. Clarke (Chapter 30, this volume) incorporates elements of classical deterrence theory into its framework. Incidentally, rational choice theory has been merged into the routine activities framework by Marcus Felson (Chapter 31, this volume). Other rational choice elements have been adopted and modified by Michael Gottfredson and Travis Hirschi (Chapter 22, this volume) in their

development of a general theory of crime, although the theory recognizes the importance of family socialization in the development of self-control.

The Importance of Integrated Theories to This Reader

A word or two about theoretical integration is necessary here. Akers (2001) contends that there are three principle ways in which theories can be evaluated and developed: (a) evaluation of a single theory on its own merits; (b) evaluation of two or more theories, which he refers to as "theory competition"; or (c) theory integration (Akers, 2001). Each is not without its problems and limitations. Evaluating evidence from a single theoretical perspective rarely leads to falsification of that theory, a problem highlighted by Bernard in Chapter 1 of this volume. Second, theory competition, or critiquing one theory from the perspective of another, has revealed, generally, that very few of the current criminological theories have generated strong empirical support, with the exception of social learning theory (Akers, 2001).

That leaves the third method of assessing and constructing theories: integration. According to Akers (2001), the goal of theory integration is to "identify commonalities in two or more theories to produce a synthesis that is superior to any one theory individually" (p. 238). Theoretical integration often involves deliberate attempts to fuse together two closely related approaches, but integration may also emerge out of theory competition. Although some have argued that theoretical integration is nothing more than "oppositional theories in disguise" (Hirschi, 1989, pp. 41-42, as quoted in Akers, 2001), if done correctly, theoretical integration and elaboration can account for important compatibilities among different perspectives.

Although empirical testing of single theories and theory competition continue, integrated theories seem to dominate the current theoretical landscape of the 1990s and today in criminology. Notwithstanding the concerns raised by Akers (2001), theoretical integration seems to be one way in which advances in criminological theory making might be made. Although this anthology is not the context within which I would like to develop that proposition, several of the works selected for this volume do reflect this novel integrative approach. In fact, great efforts were made to ensure that a vast majority of the articles connected to one another in some way, whether in terms of theoretical elaboration or further empirical testing. In this way, the reader establishes and maintains a sense of cohesiveness that may otherwise be lacking. I believe that this issue of theoretical integration lies at the forefront of future criminological theory making, and this reader reflects some of the most recent advances of that thinking.

Examples of these newly integrated approaches include seminal integrative works by Delbert S. Elliott, Suzanne S. Ageton, and Rachelle J. Canter (Chapter 34, this volume) and by Terence P. Thornberry (Chapter 35, this volume). Additionally, assumptions about rational choice, biological predisposition, and personality have been combined with other behavioral and social science perspectives in James Wilson and Richard Herrnstein's (1985) approach.[6] Robert Agnew's (Chapter 11, this volume) general strain theory has been incorporated into Walsh's (Chapter 36, this volume) analysis of the biosocial perspective of behavior genetics to suggest that crime is a product of biological, psychological, and genetic as well as environmental factors.

Social disorganization and social ecology theories have also been revised, with communities once again becoming the central focus of criminological research (Bursik & Grasmick, 1993; Rose & Clear, Chapter 7, this volume; Sampson & Groves, 1989). Additionally, feminist criminology, building upon early critical work, has made significant advances in terms of understanding the intersection of gender, race, and class in the criminological and crime control enterprises. The work of Kathleen Daly (Chapter 29, this volume) and Daly and Meda Chesney-Lind (Chapter 28, this volume) has raised awareness of the importance of these forces and how they shape and are shaped by crime and criminal justice. Lastly, another unique area of integration that stems from the labeling, conflict, and social constructionist perspectives involves Stuart Henry and Dragan Milovanovic's (Chapter 25, this volume) constitutive criminology. Combining elements of critical, radical, postmodern, and linguistic theory, they focus on the central role that power and difference play in constituting crime.

The Criminological Theory/ Criminal Justice Policy Nexus

Many people frequently dismiss theory as empty musings about abstract ideas that have no relevance or consequence to the practicality of everyday life. This notion could not be farther from the truth! Clarifying the underlying nature of crime as harm against others and society, analyzing its causes, and acknowledging the various disciplinary influences on the field of criminology are extremely important endeavors for criminologists because, in two words, theory matters. Theory matters because criminological theories have vast implications for social policy created to deal with the crime problem (Lilly et al., 1995).

Even Sutherland and Cressey (1955) understood the importance of criminological theory to crime control policies and the practical application of knowledge:

> While experimentation may increase theoretical knowledge and thereby contribute to ultimate improvements in policies, it is necessarily wasteful unless it can be directed by the best organized and critical thought available. . . . Organized and critical thinking in this field is therefore peculiarly difficult and also peculiarly necessary. (p. 4)

Although the necessity of this difficult task is obvious, the link between theory and policy is not always so clear-cut. Theories are not constructed in a vacuum but are developed and fostered in a historical, social, political, economic, and cultural context. Theories typically reflect the existing ideologies, beliefs, and laws of the time and society. They emerge from particular schools of thought that may be more popular at one time or another. The point here is that the context within which the theories are developed limits the growth of theoretical possibilities. To put it more simply, there may be a dozen ways to explain crime, but depending upon what is proposed as the reason for illegal behavior—and who the audience is that hears it—certain criminal justice policies will appear rational and in concordance with a particular theoretical framework, and others will seem fairly unreasonable.

To illustrate, during the 1970s and 1980s, crime rates escalated to fearful heights. Ideas that centered on the rehabilitative ideals of the earlier part of the 20th century began to fade as retributivist ideas of justice fell into the "law and order" limelight. By the mid-1970s, the rehabilitative ideal had fallen out of favor with policymakers and the public alike; dissatisfaction stemmed from the fact that penal policy goals of lower crime rates and a changed criminal failed miserably. Many critics contended that the efficacy of the rehabilitative approach was overblown (Cote, 2000). In response, policymakers launched a more retributive, "just desserts" attack, whereby state legislatures enacted tough mandatory sentencing laws to create a reduction in judicial discretion and greater consistency and certainty in sentencing (Cote, 2000). In this context, the criminological and penological theories at the time were fairly consistent with the criminal justice policies in effect to control crime.

Today, most criminal justice policies embody the same punitive, "just desserts" mentality, even in the face of declining crime rates. The "three-strikes" laws provide an excellent example of criminal justice policies that represent social, political, and organizational responses to a high-profile, traumatic crime that had very little to do with current theorizing. The law satisfies the insatiable appetites of a public desirous of a quick, punitive reaction, but the policies lack theoretical substance. Evidence suggests that these laws have done very little to affect the crime rate or control dangerous offenders (see Shichor's article [Chapter 27, this volume] for an analysis and critique of the three-strikes law in California).

Despite this complicated relationship between theory and policy, theories do shape and even challenge existing conditions and crime control strategies. For instance, feminist criminologists and legal scholars expressed concern over the manner in which victims of domestic violence had been dealt with by law enforcement and the courts. Research and the development of theoretical frameworks, such as Lenore Walker's (1979) *learned helplessness,* and Widom's (1992) *cycle of violence,* had led to the development and implementation of mandatory arrest laws in many communities throughout the United States.

To reiterate a point I made earlier, the typical theory-policy link emerges when politicians want a "quick fix" to an immediate problem, which is usually designed to appease a demanding public rather than to develop a long-term solution. However, it is absolutely critical that we not lose sight of the fact that theory and practice are inextricably linked, as one often informs the other in an interactive process. To varying degrees, the readings in this volume demonstrate the importance of that nexus. Although some may not understand my decision to include articles that attempt to address this nexus, my hope is that the readings will, at a minimum, trigger thoughtful consideration and discourse about how a particular theory can be applied in a practical manner.

ORGANIZATION OF THE READINGS

I organized the readings in this anthology according to the various theoretical classifications into which they fall. I view these categories fluidly, and readers should also consider them as flexible groupings with mobile boundaries. It certainly would have been possible to place some of the selections into other categories. In fact, a number of articles moved around several times before I found a satisfactory theoretical "home" for them! Nonetheless, as I have presented them, I feel strongly that they effectively represent the scope of theoretical development from the early days of the discipline, through the present, and into the future. As the title of the text suggests, the readings presented within these pages are not designed to be the final word on criminological theory. Rather, they are a bridge to the next theoretical innovations that will emerge in the future. Conceptualized in this manner, the text—like theory making and theory application—is dynamic; it was designed with the intention of engaging readers in a critical, thought-provoking exercise not only within themselves but also in interaction with each other. The questions at the end of each excerpt provide a catalyst for critical discourse among all students of criminology.

Last, I would like to point out that, like all learning tools and processes, this anthology is necessarily incomplete and inconclusive, just as theory itself is incomplete and frequently inconclusive. Therefore, you should use this book as an additional map to guide you to further understanding of crime and criminality; use it as a launching pad into further inquiry and reading. My hope is that even if you disagree with some of the readings included in this anthology, or even with the inclusion of the particular article or text excerpt itself, you will come away after having delved into it with a fuller comprehension and better appreciation for the richly diverse landscape of criminological theory.

NOTES

[1] Concerned about the validity and reliability of their numbers, researchers at BJS ran their numbers a second time; both sets of analyses confirmed the 15% decline. What did the researchers find? The report, based on U.S. Census Bureau surveys that asked nearly 160,000 residents ages 12 and older whether they had been victims of crime in the past year, estimated that nearly 26 million crimes were committed in the United States in 2000. That figure came down from 28.8 million in 1999 and represents the lowest rate on record with BJS in its 27-year history of tracking crime rates. At that time, an estimated 44 million offenses were committed (Lichtblau, 2001).

[2] In his review and analysis of Beccaria's key classical text, *Dei delitti e delle pene* [*Of Crimes and Punishments*], Piers Beirne (1991) points out the persistent misrepresentations of Beccaria's famous treatise. Beirne asserts that, in contrast to conventional wisdom, Beccaria's thesis in his treatise regards the application of crime and penality to the "science of man," a deterministic discourse that is clearly at odds with conventional assumptions of the humanist and discretionary premises of classical criminology (Beirne, 1991).

[3] Incidentally, Charles Goring (1913) tested Lombroso's theory with English convicts and found no support for it.

[4] The following example illustrates how theory affects subsequent policy and influences the ways in which certain offenders are defined. In 1911 Massachusetts enacted the Briggs Law, the first American psychopathy legislation that recognized defective delinquents as a distinct class of criminals. In later years, many of the prisoners who could not be diagnosed as "mentally defective" individuals were labeled "psychopathic." These newly created classifications of "mentally defective" individuals broadened the category of insanity and aided the development of the "psychopath," a new deviant population (Cote, 2000).

[5] Although eugenic philosophies dominated Nazi Germany in Europe during the 1920s and 1930s, culminating in the 1940s with the extermination of millions of Jews, gypsies, and homosexuals, eugenic practices occurred in the United States as well. For example, it was not uncommon for those deemed "feebleminded" or "mentally defective" to undergo sterilization procedures, which were even upheld under legal scrutiny (*Buck v. Bell,* 1927).

[6] Although Wilson and Hernnstein's (1985) work was not selected for inclusion in this volume, it speaks to the importance of recognizing the psychological and biological perspectives.

REFERENCES

Akers, R. (2001). *Criminological theories: Introduction, evaluation, and application* (3rd ed.). Los Angeles: Roxbury.

Bandura, A. (1973). *Aggression: A social learning analysis.* Englewood Cliffs, NJ: Prentice Hall.

Bandura, A. (1977). *Social learning theory.* Englewood Cliffs, NJ: Prentice Hall.

Becker, H. S. (1963). *Outsiders: Studies in the sociology of deviance.* New York: Free Press.

Beckett, K., & Sasson, T. (2000). *The politics of injustice: Crime and punishment in America.* Thousand Oaks, CA: Pine Forge Press.

Beirne, P. (1991). Inventing criminology: The "science of man" in Cesare Beccaria's *Dei delitti e delle pene* (1764). *Criminology, 29,* 777-820.

Bonger, W. (1916). *Criminality and economic conditions.* Boston: Little, Brown.

Buck v. Bell, 274 U.S. 200 (1927).

Burgess, R. L., & Akers, R. L. (1966). A differential association-reinforcement theory of criminal behavior. *Social Problems, 14,* 128-147.

Bursik, R. J., Jr., & Grasmick, H. G. (1993). *Neighborhoods and crime: The dimensions of effective community control.* New York: Lexington Books.

Chambliss, W. (1964). A sociological analysis of the law of vagrancy. *Social Problems, 11,* 67-77.

Cloward, R. A., & Ohlin, L. E. (1960). *Delinquency and opportunity: A theory of delinquent gangs.* New York: Free Press.

Cohen, A. (1955). *Delinquent boys: The culture of the gang.* Glencoe, IL: Free Press.

Cote, S. (2000). *Modernity, risk, and contemporary crime control strategies as risk management: An analysis of sex offender statutes and the shift toward a risk society* (Doctoral dissertation, State University of New York at Buffalo, 2000). *UMI Dissertation Abstracts,* 99-58253.

Eysenck, H. J. (1964). *Crime and personality.* London: Routledge & Kegan Paul.

Federal Bureau of Investigation, U.S. Department of Justice. (2000, December 18). UCR crime index trends. *Press Release 2000.* Retrieved April 28, 2001, from the World Wide Web: http://fbi.gov/pressrel/pressre100/ucrcit2000.htm

Gibbons, D. C. (2001). Criminology, criminologists, and criminological theory. In S. S. Simpson (Ed.), *Of crime and criminality* (pp. xvii-xxxiii). Thousand Oaks, CA: Pine Forge Press.

Goffman, E. (1963). *Stigma: Notes on the management of spoiled identity.* Englewood Cliffs, NJ: Prentice Hall.

Goring, C. (1913). *The English convict: A statistical study.* London: HMSO.

Henry, S., & Einstadter, W. (1998). Criminology and criminological theory. In S. Henry & W. Einstadter (Eds.), *The criminology theory reader* (pp. 1-13). New York: New York University Press.

Hirschi, T. (1969). *Causes of delinquency.* Berkeley: University of California Press.

Lemert, E. M. (1951). *Social pathology: A systemic approach to the theory of sociopathic behavior.* New York: McGraw-Hill.

Lemert, E. M. (1967). *Human deviance, social problems and social control.* Englewood Cliffs, NJ: Prentice Hall.

Lichtblau, E. (2001, June 14). Experts puzzled by crime trend reports. *Sacramento Bee,* p. A7.

Lilly, R. J., Cullen, F. T., & Ball, R. A. (1995). *Criminological theory: Context and consequences* (2nd ed.). Thousand Oaks, CA: Sage.

Merlo, A. V., & Benekos, P. J. (2000). *What's wrong with the criminal justice system: Ideology, politics, and media.* Cincinnati, OH: Anderson.

Messner, S., & Rosenfeld, R. (2001). *Crime and the American dream* (3rd ed.). Belmont, CA: Wadsworth.

Miller, W. G. (1958). Lower class culture as a generating milieu of gang delinquency. *Journal of Social Issues, 14,* 5-19.

Quinney, R. (1973). *Critique of the legal order.* Boston: Little, Brown.

Quinney, R. (1977). *Class, state, and crime.* New York: David McKay.

Quinney, R. (1980). *Class, state, and crime: On the theory and practice of criminal justice* (2nd ed.). New York: David McKay.

Rock, P., & Holdaway, S. (1998). Thinking about criminology: "Facts are bits of biography." In S. Holdaway & P. Rock (Eds.), *Thinking about criminology* (pp. 1-13). Toronto, Ontario, Canada: University of Toronto Press.

Sampson, R. J., & Groves, W. B. (1989). Community structures and crime: Testing social disorganization theory. *American Journal of Sociology, 94,* 774-802.

Schur, E. M. (1965). *Crimes without victims: Deviant behavior and public policy.* Englewood Cliffs, NJ: Prentice Hall.

Sellin, T. (1938). *Culture, conflict, and crime.* New York: Social Science Research Council.

Shearing, C. (1998). Theorizing—*sotto voce.* In S. Holdaway & P. Rock (Eds.), *Thinking about criminology* (pp. 15-33). Toronto, Ontario, Canada: University of Toronto Press.

Sheley, J. (2000). A brief introduction to criminology. In J. Sheley (Ed.), *Criminology* (3rd ed., pp. 1-9). Belmont, CA: Wadsworth/Thomson Learning.

Skinner, B. F. (1953). *Science and human behavior.* New York: Macmillan.

Sourcebook of criminal justice statistics: 1994-1998 annual editions [CD-ROM]. (1999). U.S. Department of Justice, Bureau of Justice Statistics. NCJ 178912.

Surette, R. (1998). *Media, crime, and criminal justice: Images and realities* (2nd ed.). Belmont, CA: West/Wadsworth.

Sutherland, E. (1924). *Criminology.* Philadelphia: J. B. Lippincott.

Sutherland, E., & Cressey, D. (1955). *Principles of criminology* (5th ed.). Chicago: J. B. Lippincott.

Tarde, G. (1886). *La criminalite comparee.* Paris: Alcan.

Tannenbaum, F. (1938). *Crime and community.* New York: Ginn.

Turk, A. T. (1966). Conflict and criminality. *American Sociological Review, 31,* 338-352.

Vold, G. B., Bernard, T. J., & Snipes, J. B. (1998). *Theoretical criminology* (4th ed.). Oxford, UK: Oxford University Press.

Walker, L. (1979). *The battered woman.* New York: Harper & Row.

Widom, C. S. (1992). *The cycle of violence* (National Institute of Justice Research in Brief, NCJ 136607). Washington, DC: Government Printing Office.

Wilson, J. Q., & Herrnstein, R. (1985). *Crime and human nature.* New York: Simon & Schuster.

PART I

CRIME, CRIMINOLOGY, AND CRIMINAL JUSTICE

This first section of readings is a unique feature of this anthology, and, in this regard, it distinguishes the anthology from other criminological theory collections. Unlike other anthologies, which typically open with a collection of readings on the biological or psychological theories, this section opens with three readings that speak generally to the problems with theorizing and theories in criminology, particularly in the American criminological enterprise.

Although at first glance, this approach may seem confusing or out of line with the objectives of a criminological theory reader, I view it—and have constructed it—as a point of clarification of the wider disciplinary and professional concerns with respect to theorizing about crime. Just as we cannot understand how to control crime without first constructing and consulting a critical framework for analysis of that problem, we cannot fully understand theory and its importance—in both criminology and criminal justice—without first considering the broader disciplinary (and, to some extent, ideological) concerns that pervade and influence the theory-construction process. In other words, in order to make progress, we should take stock of where we've been and where we're going.

I will frame my general overview of the readings in this section around three broad theoretical concerns raised by each of the authors:

1. A theoretical crisis in criminology

2. The overt emphasis of pragmatism over theory in American criminology

3. A need for theory in the practical arena of criminal justice

My understanding of these primary concerns is that theory needs to be brought out of the subterranean landscape so that it may be revived, reconsidered, and revised. To that end, scholars and professionals alike need to engage in critical discourse and interactive practices that demonstrate the importance of theory to the crime problems that exist not only in our own communities but also around the world.

THEORETICAL CRISIS?

As I discussed in the introduction to the text, many scholars within criminology and other social sciences assert that theory is experiencing a crisis. It seems that over the past 20 years or more, quantitative research has expanded tremendously in criminology (Bernard, Chapter 1, this volume). Although this research tests a variety of theories, some theories have been falsified, whereas others have shown positive results to the point where criminologists no longer need question them. In Chapter 1, Bernard states that scientific progress occurs when the assumed base of accumulated knowledge expands through the results of prior research and future research builds on more exact lines of inquiry. He adds that to the extent that researchers do not agree on what knowledge has been accumulated, then no accumulated base exists that researchers can assume and advance beyond.

Not able to find verifiable knowledge in any of the theories and research he has reviewed, Bernard finds that criminological theory is at a standstill, with little consensus in the field itself about the most basic facts of crime. Therefore, as Bernard argues, because it is difficult to identify a theory that has been falsified, it is increasingly difficult to maintain that criminology has made any scientific progress in terms of theory. He claims that although his controversial position may appear dismal, he offers a range of suggestions for criminologists to make scientific progress a reality.

Primarily, he begins with the critical "chicken and egg" claim that neither research nor theory came first: All research must be based on theory and all theory must be based on research, regardless of whether the two endeavors seem implicit, illogical, or scattered. He adds that science progresses slowly and carefully: "Theory interprets the results of past research and charts the direction of future research. Both theory and research are necessary for scientific progress to occur" (p. 8, this volume). Currently, the lack of scientific progress in criminology arises from a failure of theorists to interpret the results of past research and chart a future research agenda. A reason for this failure, Bernard contends, is that research efforts over the past 20 years have been scattered rather than focused, and there has been no accumulation of verified knowledge that criminologists can assume and move beyond.

In his chapter, Bernard offers six suggestions for ways in which theorists can make scientific progress, but I want to concentrate on two of them because of their relevance to my own purpose in this section. First, he claims that a problem arises when theory is viewed as an "all or nothing" enterprise in which you either present a new and complete explanation or you present nothing at all. In contrast, he argues that by focusing on falsification, theory can be viewed as a cumulative and developmental process in which long-range progress is accomplished by a large number of steps.

Another important suggestion addresses what Bernard sees as the source of the problem: the manner in which theorists are groomed and nurtured in criminology graduate school programs. Essentially, he claims that theory and theoretical training have been sacrificed for the ever-increasing demands to produce empirical research, acquire grants, submit empirical research results for publication, and continue the research process over and over in order to ensure job security—tenure.

The controversial and perhaps unpopular stance of Bernard's contribution notwithstanding, I believe his premises and suggestions warrant serious consideration. In a variety of ways, Bernard's preoccupations with these issues speak to concerns among many criminologists. For example, British criminologists Rock and Holdaway (1998) claim that the increased emphasis on empirical research rather than theoretical criminology is the result of a "triple onslaught of brute facts":

1. the dramatic rise in crimes recorded by police, which demanded attention from criminologists;

2. victim surveys, which demanded that other types of crimes and social problems, including poverty, discrimination, inadequate housing, unemployment, etc., receive attention as well; and

3. the research environment itself, which was generated by successive governments professing practicality, efficacy, and value [in research] for money. (Rock & Holdaway, 1998, pp. 7-9)

As a consequence, criminological theorizing persisted, but it became a subterranean endeavor for many criminologists "who are simply too pressed, too preoccupied with the empirical, too dependent on funding agencies uninterested in speculation, or too jaded to conduct their theorizing publicly and as a main pursuit" (Rock & Holdaway, 1998, p. 10).

Bernard (Chapter 1), like other theorists such as Rock and Holdaway (1998), makes important points about the decline in theoretical productivity and analysis among criminologists. As these authors suggest, criminological theory certainly needs to be revisited and reformulated in order for us to progress scientifically within the discipline. The second reading selection in this section, by Haen Marshall, addresses and reaffirms this point.

OVERT EMPHASIS OF PRAGMATISM OVER THEORY IN AMERICAN CRIMINOLOGY

In Chapter 2, Haen Marshall echoes the concerns of the other theorists, which compares European criminology to the criminological enterprise in the United States. The article not only raises important points of comparison between these criminologies but also highlights the exceptional influence of American criminology on Western criminology as a whole. Most important, at least in terms of the purposes of this section of readings, Haen Marshall draws attention to the overtly powerful emphasis the United States, in general, places on pragmatism and policy making at the expense of abstract speculation on the crime problem. Again, in the same vein as Rock and Holdaway (1998), Haen Marshall notes that although American scholars do play a role in this critical, self-reflexive process of theorizing, it represents a somewhat marginalized approach.

This relative lack of theorizing in American criminology reflects the larger cultural concern with the American way of "doing science." More specifically, Haen Marshall claims that pragmatism characterizes American research endeavors primarily because of the fact that Americans define scientific progress mainly in terms of a researcher's ability to apply the scientific method to a particular problem and solve it. To a certain extent, Bernard (Chapter 1, this volume) would define scientific progress in this manner as well; however, he tempers his contentions with recognition of the important role that critical self-reflection plays in framing and conducting research.

Haen Marshall indicates that the emphasis on pragmatism involves several beliefs that have permeated the American philosophical spirit and that can be used for a comparative understanding of the way in which the United States approaches the study of crime, law, and justice. These beliefs include the following:

1. Thinking is an activity aimed in response to a concrete situation and at solving problems.

2. Theories must be "cutting edge" or make a difference in people's behavior or the environments in which they live, or else there is no point in considering them.

3. Problems can be solved by applying knowledge to social problems.

These beliefs make up the primary mindset of the scientific method in the United States—a practical problem focus and a need for ideas or theories with practical application.

In criminology, the American way of *doing science* emerges through the way in which crime, law, and justice are studied and the policies are enacted. By forgoing the important contributions that theory can make, many laws that have been enacted today have little, if any, theoretical substance or relationship to the problem they purport to resolve. In the American criminal justice system, and in the minds of students and professionals alike, thinking about crime should be focused not on timeless, universal problems of crime and punishment but on the here and now. Crime rates, victims' voices, and money for research demand action—now.

But there is clearly a problem with what some have called this anti-intellectual way of thinking, which Haen Marshall and the other authors in this section point out. The example of current punitive policies enacted in the United States in the 1990s effectively illustrates Haen Marshall's points. The laws regarding the registration and notification of sex offenders—Megan's Laws—enacted in the mid-1990s reflect this quick-fix, *do-something* mentality of the American justice system. In response to the sexual assault and murder of Megan Kanka, for whom the law was named, by a twice-convicted sex offender, and the ensuing moral panic that erupted around the nation during the period of 1994 to 1996, all 50 states and the federal government enacted versions of Megan's Law that contain provisions for registration and notification of sex offenders, to varying degrees and scope (Cote, 2000).[1] Because agents of social control, including criminal justice officials and politicians, do not want those moral panics to get out of control, they respond with policies, campaigns, or laws that pay lip service to the do-something mentality that characterizes the modern American social control agencies and decision-making processes. In sum, they employ principles of science (i.e., pragmatism) to solve the problem of the violent sex offender. They make risk assessments, calculate the factors, control the damage, and contain the fallout (Cote, 2000, p. 81).

Many crime control policies enacted in the United States in the past decade, including Megan's Law, lack theoretical substance mainly because of the fact that theory building—a critical process of reflexivity—takes time, and issues external to the problem itself—emotional public outrage, political and organizational legitimacy—cannot (or refuse to) wait for a more informed response. The legitimacy of the criminal justice system and the perceived competency of politicians depend on prompt responses to traumatic events. In the case of Megan's Law, failure to react to the problem of sexual offending would be nothing short of political and institutional suicide. These external pressures to act become more important than the substance of the criminological issue itself.[2] Simply put, with the absence of critical reflection, "act now, clean up later" seems to characterize the crime control enterprise in the United States today.

THE NEED FOR
CRIMINAL JUSTICE THEORY

The inclusion of Bernard and Engel's work (Chapter 3) completes the points raised in regard to the criminology/criminal justice theory nexus. Although this anthology concerns itself mostly with criminology theory making and not criminal justice theory, as Bernard and Engel indicate, there is much that criminology can offer to criminal justice in terms of developing a solid theoretical framework within which to analyze the problems of crime and crime control.

Most important, the chapter—and the points raised in the other two readings in this section—confirms the importance of theory's place even in a practitioner-based, policy-oriented discipline such as criminal justice. As all of these authors point out, theory can be used to better understand the relationships among different variables of crime, law-breaking, and crime control, thereby better informing and shaping future research in both criminology and criminal justice. Last, with more consideration and credence given to theoretical contributions in these fields, our crime control policies can be more effective in their efforts at resolving the ever-present problem of crime.

NOTES

[1] For example, not all states have notification requirements in their statutes, but all states require sex offenders to register with their local law enforcement agencies following release from prison.

[2] These laws received widespread public and legal support despite the fact that considerable debate arose, and continues, around the effectiveness and necessity of these punitive policies in light of declining crime rates.

REFERENCES

Cote, S. (2000). *Modernity, risk, and contemporary crime control strategies as risk management: An analysis of sex offender statutes and the shift toward a risk society* (Doctoral dissertation, State University of New York at Buffalo, 2000). *UMI Dissertation Abstracts,* 99-58253.

Rock, P., & Holdaway, S. (1998). Thinking about criminology: "Facts are bits of biography." In S. Holdaway & P. Rock (Eds.), *Thinking about criminology* (pp. 1-13). Toronto, Ontario, Canada: University of Toronto Press.

1

Twenty Years of Testing Theories

What Have We Learned and Why?

Thomas J. Bernard

EDITOR'S INTRODUCTION—Thomas Bernard's article opens this reader with a provocative thesis regarding the problems inherent in testing (criminological) theories. He makes a somewhat surprising argument that researchers in the field of criminology have made very little scientific progress in the sense of falsifying some theories and accumulating verified knowledge in the context of others.

Bernard contends that the problem lies with theory itself, which he maintains is often conceptualized in terms of an "all or nothing" endeavor aimed at explanation. In contrast, he proposes a new conception of theorizing as a cumulative, iterative, developmental exercise directed toward falsification. Falsification of theories, Bernard contends, extends knowledge of the issues under study, whereas accumulation of verified knowledge results in scientific stagnation, where "science might be better viewed merely as a social activity that employs increasing numbers of people" (p. 6, this volume). Last, Bernard adds that the source of these problems lies with faulty theory construction among criminologists as well as with the manner in which graduate students are academically trained and professionally groomed in graduate programs in criminal justice disciplines.

Despite the surprising nature of these claims, Bernard's essay merits thoughtful consideration. Primarily, it offers, if nothing else, a thorough analysis of the scientific method and the manner in which it can be properly used in conducting scientifically sound research. Second, and more important, it calls attention to the significant role that theory plays in scientific progress. In other words, researchers can no longer turn a blind eye to the role that theory construction plays in their research. Otherwise, just as Bernard maintains, what good is it to realize something that we already know to have been positively demonstrated?

He stresses the need for criminologists and criminal justice scholars to move away from the idea that theory is an "all or nothing" enterprise in which researchers either make contributions to the field or they do not. Instead, Bernard asserts that if theory were conceived of as a developmental enterprise aimed at falsification, the small contributions to the field could be "worth" something down the road.

The past 20 years have seen a vast expansion of quantitative research in criminology. Twenty years ago, there were fewer journals and they published a greater variety of articles, including quantitative and qualitative research, theoretical and policy arguments, and even polemical pieces (Wolfgang, Figlio, & Thornberry, 1978). Today, there are more journals and they mainly publish quantitative research. All research tests theories of one sort or another (see Bernard & Ritti, 1990), so we have had 20 years of increasingly intense theory testing in criminology. If we compare the state of criminology theory today with its state 20 years ago, we should be able to identify what has been learned in that time period.

The results of research can be either favorable or unfavorable to the theory being tested. In the past 20 years, some theories (whether formally stated or not) may have accumulated unfavorable results to the point where they are no longer taken seriously. Such theories can be said to have been falsified (Popper, 1968). Other theories may have accumulated favorable findings to the point where criminologists no longer question those findings. New research therefore simply assumes those findings and is organized to move beyond them to add to the depth and breadth of knowledge in the context of that theory. This is the process that Kuhn (1970) described as "normal science."

In this chapter, I define "scientific progress" in terms of the accumulation of research findings in the context of theories. This definition assumes that science is associated with learning over time and that such learning can be either negative (falsification of some theories) or positive (accumulation of verified knowledge in the context of other theories). If neither negative nor positive learning takes place in science, then scientific progress is not a meaningful concept. In that case, science might be better viewed merely as a social activity that employs increasing numbers of people (e.g., Barnes, 1985).

Negative Learning:
The Falsification of Some Theories

Despite the enormous volume of quantitative research, there has been no substantial progress in falsifying the criminology theories that existed 20 years ago. Twenty years ago, Hirschi's (1969) control theory had already been published. Burgess and Akers (1968) already had published the first article in what would become social learning theory. Cloward and Ohlin's (1960) theory had already reached the peak of its policy influence in the War on Poverty, along with Cohen's (1955) theory. Lemert (1967) had already published his labeling theory of secondary deviance, Quinney (1970) and Turk (1969) had published their non-Marxist conflict theories, and Marxist criminology (e.g., Quinney, 1974; Taylor, Walton, & Young, 1973) was about to emerge. Eysenck (1964) had already published his theory linking crime to low autonomic nervous system functioning, and modern classical theories had already appeared in the form of econometric studies (e.g., Becker, 1968) and deterrence theory (e.g., Andenaes, 1966, 1968; Zimring & Hawkins, 1968). Highly respected and well-established senior theories in the field included those of Shaw and McKay (1942), Merton (1938), Durkheim (1951, 1965), and Sutherland (1947). None of these theories has been falsified in the past 20 years. One can question the extent to which these theories have been tested. . . .

I have argued (Bernard, 1987a) that Merton's strain theory has never been tested, despite the fact that it is over 50 years old. I derived falsifiable propositions from the theory that could form the basis for such a test and presented similar arguments for Cohen's (1955) and Cloward and Ohlin's (1960) theories, which are now over 30 years old. These theories have not been falsified, but that may be because they have not ever been tested. At the broadest level, I could argue that no theoretical approach to crime has ever been falsified in the history of criminology. In Vold and Bernard's (1986) book, each chapter began at the historic point where a particular approach to crime emerged. It then described the revisions and modernizations that allow each approach to remain viable today. In the over 30 years since the first edition of that book, no theoretical chapters have been dropped but six new ones have been added. This suggests that, broadly construed, there is no falsification of theories at all in criminology, only the addition of new theories.

Bernard, T. J. (1990). Twenty years of testing theories: What have we learned and why? *Journal of Research in Crime and Delinquency, 27,* 325-347.

Several criminologists suggested to me that labeling theory, as an approach to crime, has been falsified. It is true that research has consistently shown that labeling by criminal justice agencies does not produce the negative effects hypothesized by the theory (e.g., Wellford, 1987). However, a more complex approach to labeling as a cause of crime is still viable (e.g., Farrington, Ohlin, & Wilson, 1986, chap. 5), and labeling theory as a general theoretical framework is also viable (e.g., Hagan, 1989). Labeling theory has been modified, but it has not been falsified. . . .

POSITIVE LEARNING: THE ACCUMULATION OF VERIFIED KNOWLEDGE IN THE CONTEXT OF OTHER THEORIES

Knowledge is considered accumulated when it forms a "taken for granted" base for the entire scientific discipline (Kuhn, 1970). Scientists then assume that base and organize their research to move beyond it. Progress occurs as the base expands through the results of past research and as future research focuses on more precise questions. To the extent that researchers do not agree on what knowledge has been accumulated, then there is no accumulated base at all, since there is nothing that researchers can simply assume and move beyond.

I have difficulty identifying any "verified knowledge" that has been "accumulated" in criminology in this sense. For example, Hirschi's (1969) probably has been the most heavily researched theory over the past 20 years, and there are numerous assertions of its extensive empirical support (e.g., Agnew, 1985, p. 47; LaGrange & White, 1985, p. 19; LeBlanc, 1983, p. 40). Of the four elements of the social bond, the most heavily researched has been attachment, and of the three types of attachment, the most heavily researched has been attachment to parents. Rankin and Wells (1990) reviewed research on attachment and other family factors and concluded that it shows that "as a group, numerous family factors are inextricably related to delinquency. However, the sheer number of these factors makes it difficult to specify, in precise terms, the exact causal paths" (p. 141). Thus it is not possible to simply assume a causal connection between parental attachments and delinquency, as asserted by Hirschi's (1969) theory. There are numerous conceptual and empirical reasons for this (Wells & Rankin, 1988), but the point is that we have not yet accumulated verified knowledge in the context of Hirschi's theory on the relation between delinquency and parental attachments. . . .

Part of the problem is that, to some extent, verification is an inverse of falsification: A theory is verified if, under rigorous testing, the theory is not falsified (Bernard & Ritti, 1990; Popper, 1968). If no combination of research results is sufficient to falsify a theory, then no combination of research results will be sufficient to verify a theory. To the extent that we cannot falsify anything in criminology, we cannot verify anything either. . . . [T]he failure to accumulate verified knowledge in the context of specific theories should not be surprising. There is almost nothing in criminology that researchers can simply assume and move beyond when they organize new research.

SCIENTIFIC PROGRESS IS POSSIBLE

Thus far, I have argued that criminology has failed to make scientific progress in the past 20 years in the sense of falsifying some theories and accumulating verified knowledge in the context of other theories. Now I assert, without supporting arguments, that such scientific progress actually is possible within criminology. My position contrasts with those who argue that the lack of falsification and accumulation is an inevitable characteristic of all social sciences (e.g., Ritzer, 1975). It also contrasts with the more common position that scientific progress is possible and that such progress has actually occurred in criminology in the past 20 years (e.g., Gottfredson & Hirschi, 1987; Laub, 1987).

My argument that criminology *can* make scientific progress but *has failed* to do so in the past 20 years implies that something is drastically wrong in our field. This is a threatening and challenging argument, one that is unlikely to be readily accepted. I believe that it would be unproductive to defend this argument further, and so I turn to an analysis of what might be wrong in criminology. A critique of the past 20 years provides the basis for thoughts about how scientific progress might be facilitated in the future.

THEORY, RESEARCH, AND SCIENTIFIC PROGRESS

Scientific theory and research are like the chicken and the egg—each comes from the other but neither comes first. All research must be based on theory, even if it is implicit rather than explicit and illogical rather than coherent. All theory must be based on research, even if empirical observations are scattered rather than systematic and the analysis of those observations is crude rather than sophisticated. Science progresses through careful alternation between theory and research (Bernard & Ritti, 1990). Research demonstrates convergence or divergence between existing theory and empirical observations. Theory interprets the results of past research and charts the direction of future research. Both theory and research are necessary for scientific progress to occur.

At the present time, the lack of scientific progress in criminology arises from a failure of theorists to adequately interpret the results of past research and to chart the direction of future research. As a result of this failure, research efforts in the past 20 years have been scattered rather than focused, and there has been no accumulation of a "taken for granted" base of verified knowledge that criminologists can assume and move beyond. Various ways in which theorists can better accomplish their tasks in the generation of scientific progress are discussed here. This discussion is based on the following general arguments.

First, theory focuses on explaining the phenomenon under investigation, and theorists in the past have devoted most of their efforts to this task. I argue that theorists instead should devote most of their efforts to falsifying theories, since it is only through falsification that scientific progress can occur. Second, theory generally has been viewed as an "all or nothing" enterprise in which either you present a new and complete explanation or you present nothing at all. This "all or nothing" view has limited the number of criminologists engaged in theorizing and limited the variety of their contributions. By focusing instead on falsification, theory can be viewed as an iterative, cumulative, developmental enterprise in which long-range progress is accomplished by a large number of small steps. This is comparable to the way that research is viewed today. It would allow a greater number of criminologists to contribute to theorizing and a greater variety of contributions from those criminologists.

Third, research is expensive, while theory (as a form of "talk") is cheap. Because it is cheap,

the contribution of theory toward the solution of a particular problem always should be maximized before any scarce research resources are applied to that problem. Fourth, theory contributes to scientific progress by guiding research away from questions that ultimately turn out to be unproductive and toward questions that ultimately turn out to be crucial. This guidance can be provided only by explicitly stated theories (Bernard & Ritti, 1990). Research that does not test such theories should . . . not [be] funded or published. Fifth, there may be many explanations of a phenomenon, but only falsifiable explanations are scientific (Bernard & Ritti, 1990). In addition to explaining their theories, theorists should make a brief but precise statement about how the theory can be falsified. Theories that do not include such statements should not be published. Sixth, the role of the theorist needs to be "nurtured" in criminology through practical changes in graduate education, in publication decisions in refereed journals, in the awarding of grants, in the tenure and promotion process, and in the hiring of faculty in prominent graduate schools.

TASKS FOR THE CRIMINOLOGICAL THEORIST

In this section, five specific tasks are described for the criminological theorist. These are not intended to be a definitive list but an illustration of how theory can be viewed as a cumulative, iterative, developmental enterprise directed toward falsification. . . . The first two tasks focus on how to falsify new and existing theories, while the third focuses on analyzing relations among theories so that comparative tests can be made. At present, these tasks are performed by researchers who test theories. I suggest that they be performed by theorists and that outlets for publishing these efforts be expanded.

The fourth task involves constructing formal statements of the definitions and propositions in an existing theory. Theories that do not make such formal statements are intuitively appealing but unclear about what they actually assert, so that it is difficult to know how to test them. In addition, definitions and propositions can be merged when they are not formally stated, which results in tautologies that are inherently unfalsifiable. Both conditions inhibit scientific progress.

The fifth task involves eliminating value orientations embedded in language systems of theories. Values are not falsifiable, and to the extent that a theory embeds values, the theory is not falsifiable either. This is related to the preceding task because values necessarily are eliminated when a theory is formally stated in falsifiable propositions. These two tasks are not often performed by anyone at present and are likely to be more controversial.

Constructing New Theories

How can we explain the lack of falsification of criminology theories, given the enormous volume of quantitative research over the past 20 years and the fact that all scientific theories make falsifiable predictions? There are three possible explanations:

1. Criminology theories do not really make falsifiable predictions and therefore are not really scientific.

2. These theories make falsifiable predictions, but researchers have been incompetent in their attempts to test them.

3. What the theories predict is not clear.

I believe that most of the problem lies with the third point.

In my opinion, the lack of clarity arises because of a natural tendency for theorists to emphasize explanation in presenting their theories. Researchers, however, need to know what will falsify the theories. That is, theorists naturally emphasize the positive side of their theories, but researchers need to know the negative side. Theorists generally let researchers translate their glowing prose into falsifiable propositions, but researchers often simplify complex theoretical arguments because of the difficulties of the research task (Blalock, 1984). As a result, essential arguments in the theory may be distorted and the ensuing research may seem only marginally applicable to the theory being tested. Those who like the results of the research accept them, but those who do not like the results claim that they are invalid. Consequently, no "taken for granted" base of verified knowledge is accumulated.

Analyzing how to falsify a theory is not a research task and therefore not a task that researchers can be expected to perform well. In addition to explaining their theory, theorists should be required to explain how to falsify it. That is, the theory should contain a clear statement of the specific research findings that would result in the theory being discarded.

For example, I recently presented a "theory of angry aggression" (Bernard, 1990). The theory links two types of cognitions (constitutive and regulative rules of anger) to extreme violence associated with trivial conflicts and insults. It also links those same cognitions to social structural conditions that generate increased levels of physiological arousal, including urban environments, low social position, and racial and ethnic discrimination. Thus the theory uses biological and psychological research on anger and aggression to explain the social distribution of a certain type of violent crime. The biological and psychological arguments in this theory are supported by existing research, and further similar research could falsify the theory at that level. The social arguments link broader constitutive and more aggressive regulative rules to the likelihood of engaging in a certain type of violence. Those rules of anger are cognitions that can be measured through survey research, and the violence can be measured by official or self-reported data. The social arguments also link broader constitutive and more aggressive regulative rules to certain social conditions, which can be tested by comparing the rules of people who experience those conditions with the rules of those who do not.

The theory would be falsified if individual-level research determined that the probability of engaging in angry aggression is not associated with the breadth of constitutive rules or the aggressiveness of regulative rules of anger. It also would be falsified if aggregate-level research determined that the breadth and aggressiveness of those rules are not associated with particular social conditions, such as urban environments, low social position, and racial and ethnic discrimination. Thus the theory of angry aggression asserts positive relations among measurable variables and is readily falsifiable.

While the theory of angry aggression . . . can be falsified, many theories in criminology cannot (Gibbs, 1985a). Consider, for example, Cohen and Machalek's (1988) evolutionary ecological theory of expropriative crime. The strength of the theory is that it uses relatively parsimonious concepts from behavioral ecology and evolutionary biology to derive a large number of hypotheses found in standard theories of crime causation and to generate additional hypotheses that are testable but not derivable from the standard theories.

This theory could provide a conceptual framework for understanding past theory and research and could act as a guide for generating an enormous variety of future research. Such a role would be comparable to that achieved by differential association theory in the 1940s and 1950s, which acted as an "organizing principle" for the field (Cressey, 1960) and generated an enormous range of testable predictions (DeFluer & Quinney, 1966). The problem with differential association theory was that there is no apparent way to falsify it (Gibbs, 1985a; Hirschi & Gottfredson, 1980). Interest in the theory has waned in recent years, but it is still viable as a theory (e.g., Orcutt, 1987). Similarly, it is not apparent to me how Cohen and Machalek's (1988) theory can be falsified. The authors conceded that "definitive empirical tests are difficult" and suggested computer simulations, mathematical models, or multiple laboratory or natural experiments. These suggestions are vague and do not state the precise research findings that would result in this theory being discarded.

My argument is that, as a condition of publication, Cohen and Malachek (1988) should have been required to state in precise terms the set of research findings that would result in their theory being discarded. If they were unable to do so, then I would not publish the theory at all. My reasons would be twofold. On a theoretical level, I regard falsification as the criterion of science (Bernard & Ritti, 1990) and would not publish a theory that cannot demonstrate its scientific nature by stating the conditions under which it would be falsified. On a practical level, I do not believe that it is useful to add more untestable criminology theories to the pile we already have (cf. Gibbs, 1985b). While authors should be required to state how their theory can be falsified, they should stop presenting massive amounts of research to support their theory. Such efforts serve no scientific purpose. . . .

Analyzing an Existing Theory

. . . Because theories are separate from the theorists who create them, an important role for other theorists is to analyze existing theories. This analysis should be directed toward and part of the broader effort to falsify the theory. It would supplement the analysis provided by the author of the theory who, after all, has a vested interest in not having the theory falsified. Criminology theories often are so complex that they cannot be falsified by a single observation. This is particularly true with social (as opposed to biological or psychological) theories. Analysis of such theories should break the theories into separate falsifiable propositions, each of which is clearly stated. In general, the falsification of any one of those will not falsify the others. Thus the theorist should describe the impact on the theory that the falsification of a given proposition would have.

I have done this with the three major structural strain theories. Four separate falsifiable propositions were identified in Merton's theory, eight in Cohen's, and five in Cloward and Ohlin's (Bernard, 1987a). After identifying a falsifying pattern of observations, I analyzed the precise impact on the theory if that pattern occurred.

For example, Merton's (1938) theory was said to contain four falsifiable propositions:

1. There is cross-cultural variation in the value placed on monetary success, that is, in the link between monetary success and status or prestige.

2. Cross-cultural variation in the value placed on monetary success is positively related to rates of utilitarian, profit-oriented criminal activity.

3. Within a given society, rates of utilitarian criminal behaviors in different groups are inversely related to the access those groups have to legal means of acquiring wealth.

4. Within a given society, access to the legal means of acquiring wealth varies according to social structural location. Specifically, in American society there is a positive relation between access to legal means of acquiring wealth and social class position, with the lowest social class having the least access and the highest social class having the most access.

In general, I argue that (a) Propositions 1 and 2 constitute a cultural argument whereas Propositions 3 and 4 constitute a structural argument; (b) the cultural argument can be falsified without affecting the structural argument; (c) within the structural argument, Proposition 4 can be falsified without falsifying Proposition 3; and (d) the theory should be discarded if Proposition 3 is falsified. . . .

In an ideal world, there would be a number of competing analyses, each of which would focus on how to falsify the theory. A dialogue would take place in scholarly journals among criminologists, including the author of the theory, eventually resulting in considerable clarity about the exact falsifiable propositions asserted by the theory. Only after this theoretical process had taken place would research be funded and conducted to test the theory. Because of widespread disagreements in criminology, there may be theories about which such clarity cannot be achieved. Research related to such theories should not be funded or conducted. If there is no clarity beforehand on what is to be tested, there will be no agreement afterward on what the results mean. That being the case, the research will not result in scientific progress.

Analyzing the Relations Among Existing Theories

A related role for theorists is to analyze relations among existing theories. These analyses should be directed toward the efficient use of scarce research resources in setting up comparative tests of theories.

I suggest that journal editors invite a wider variety of these interchanges but that they require them to analyze the relations between the theories with the goal of determining how a comparative test might be formulated. Funding sources should direct funds to the issues that emerge from such interchanges. . . . Funds distributed without such prior interchanges often fail to generate scientific progress. . . .

There are empirical issues between [Hirschi's and Merton's theories] that can be the subject of comparative research. For example, the drive to crime in Merton's theory lies in culture, while in Hirschi's, it lies in human nature. This issue can be tested through cross-cultural research on whether the prestige and status attached to

monetary success is constant or variable (Bernard, 1989). Research instead has addressed whether the drive to crime within a given culture is constant or variable. This is irrelevant to a comparative test because both theories describe that drive to crime as constant.

Separating Definitions From Propositions

An additional type of analysis of existing theories involves the separation of definitions from propositions. Definitions specify how terms are used, while propositions make empirical assertions about those definitions. Failure to explicitly state definitions and propositions can result in confusion about the content of the theory. . . .

A more serious problem can arise when definitions and propositions are not explicitly stated. It is easy to cross the line between the two, which results in tautologies that are impossible to falsify (Burgess & Akers, 1966). The major point of my article (Bernard, 1987b) was that Hirschi crossed the line between definitions and propositions in his arguments about commitment, which resulted in a tautology. In my view, *commitment* is properly defined as a structural variable that is conceptually and empirically antecedent to the other variables. This structural interpretation contrasts with Hirschi's social psychological interpretation in which attachment is the most important variable.

Such a radical reconceptualization might seem a violation of Hirschi's "proprietary" rights to his theory, but I would respond that I treat Hirschi's theory in the same way that researchers treat Hirschi's research. Other researchers do not simply accept the results of Hirschi's research. Rather, they conduct additional research and publish their results whether Hirschi agrees with them or not. That is, Hirschi's research is viewed as the beginning of a research enterprise, not as the final word on the matter. . . .

Eliminating Value Orientations

Central to the definition of a scientific theory is that it must be falsifiable, but central to the definition of a value is that it cannot be falsified. Values may affect theorists in numerous ways without affecting the ability to falsify the resulting theory. But if theorists embed values in the arguments of the theory itself, it renders that portion of the theory unfalsifiable and therefore (in my view) unscientific. To the extent that the competition among criminology theories is a competition over embedded values, that competition cannot be resolved through empirical research, and research funds devoted to that effort are wasted. I make these assertions despite expected disagreement from across the political spectrum. . . .

I agree that most theories contain implicit values, but I do not agree that they *necessarily* contain those values. Rather, I argue that the assertions of a theory must be value-free or they cannot be falsified, that falsification is the criterion of science, and that the lack of scientific progress in criminology is intimately connected to the lurking presence of values in criminology theories. In my view, two specific value statements are frequently embedded in the assertions of a theory, making those portions of the theories unscientific. Those value statements involve nonfalsifiable assumptions about human nature and the ideal society (Bernard, 1983, 1985). For example, Hirschi's (1969) theory begins with nonfalsifiable Hobbesian assumptions about human nature: If left alone, people naturally would engage in a war of each against all. These assumptions underlie Hirschi's explanation of crime as a breakdown of social controls and imply a nonfalsifiable vision of an ideal society in which the Hobbesian human nature has been fully controlled through social forces. This vision of the ideal society then provides the basis for a value judgment about our own society: It is pretty good because it controls human nature fairly well, but it could be better because human nature is not fully controlled.

Contrast this to a Marxist theory, such as Quinney's (1977). He also began with nonfalsifiable assumptions about human nature: If left alone, people naturally would live in peace and harmony with each other. These assumptions underlie Quinney's explanation of crime as a product of social structural arrangements, since it cannot be explained by the harmonious human nature. Quinney's view of human nature then implies a nonfalsifiable vision of an ideal society in which people live in peace and freedom, consistent with their essential natures. This vision of the ideal society then provides the basis for a value judgment about our own society: It is pretty bad because it generates all of this unnatural crime.

These value judgments would be eliminated if each theory were expressed as falsifiable propositions, since views of human nature and visions of the ideal society cannot be expressed in these terms. Visions of the ideal society are value judgments that are not falsifiable at all. Views of human nature are empirical propositions, but at present, they are not falsifiable because we do not have the research to reach a conclusion one way or the other.

THE ORIGIN OF THE PROBLEM

All researchers must know theory or their research will be meaningless, and all theorists must know research or their theories will be ridiculous. But most researchers do not engage in theorizing as a scientific activity. In contrast, most theorists engage in researching as a scientific activity, in addition to their theorizing. Why do so few researchers engage in theorizing when so many theorists engage in researching?

. . . Why do most researchers specialize to the exclusion of theorizing, but few theorists specialize to the exclusion of researching? My answer is that there are systematic pressures that drive criminologists and other social scientists toward research and away from theory. Those pressures begin and end in doctoral education. The ultimate result of those pressures is the failure to make scientific progress. Compare the way in which theory and research are taught in doctoral programs. Students are required to *learn about other people's research,* but this is only the beginning of their research education. Regardless of their interests, all students are required to learn the basics of *how to be a researcher,* that is, how to engage in researching as a scientific activity. They typically are required to take a series of courses in statistics and methodology, followed by a comprehensive evaluation of their research abilities.

The requirements and opportunities for learning to be a researcher are not matched by comparable requirements and opportunities for learning to be a theorist. Students are required to *learn about other people's theories,* just as they are required to learn about other people's research. But where this is the beginning of their education on research, it is the end of their education on theory. . . .

In addition to the lack of formal requirements and opportunities to learn to be a theorist, there also may be informal pressures that direct students away from theory and toward researching. Most faculty in doctoral programs are researchers. Like anyone else, they may prefer to teach classes and "mentor" students in their areas of competence. The idea of teaching students to become theorists, in contrast, may sound alien and even threatening. Students who are initially interested in being theorists may end up as researchers if they are sensitive to faculty preferences.

The pressures toward research do not end in graduate education. Students who emerge from graduate programs as theorists move into academic positions and attempt to gain tenure. That decision is strongly affected by publications in refereed journals, but editors and referees of those journals often view theory as an "all or nothing" enterprise directed toward explanation. Given this standard, the normal result of a "blind review" process is to publish relatively few theoretical articles, mainly authored by those who are more senior in the field. For young, untenured faculty, the practical way of accumulating the publications necessary for tenure is to do research. Most theorists, therefore, obtain tenure by producing research articles. Pressures toward research also originate in the funding of grants, which are highly valued in academia in general and in tenure decisions in particular. There are very few grants given for theoretical projects and almost all of those are given to prominent senior theorists. Young, untenured theorists who are under pressure to obtain grants normally abandon their theorizing and turn to research.

These pressures continue after the theorist obtains tenure. Grants and publications are the major criteria for yearly salary increases and for promotion to senior rank. But research articles are more readily accepted for publication than are theoretical articles, and research grants are more readily funded than are theoretical grants. . . . Finally, prominent graduate programs (which train most of the future criminologists) hire prominent criminologists for their faculty. These are criminologists with extensive and prestigious publication and grant records who turn out to be researchers. These researchers then "nurture" the research role among their graduate students, since it is the role they know best. Thus the circle is complete.

The lack of scientific progress in criminology is a direct result of this state of affairs. Scientific progress requires a balance between theory and research. If progress is to be made, systematic pressures toward research and away from theory must be counterbalanced. Theorizing must be nurtured as researching presently is nurtured: in graduate education, in refereed journals, in the funding of grants, in tenure, promotion, and salary decisions, and in the hiring of faculty in prominent graduate schools.

Conclusion

. . . The central problem, in my opinion, comes from the view of theory as an "all or nothing" enterprise directed toward explanation. . . . If theory could be conceived as an iterative, cumulative, developmental enterprise directed toward falsification, then many different theorists could make many different, small but significant contributions that add up in the long run.

Discussion Questions

1. Why does Bernard feel that little scientific progress has been made in the field of criminology over the last 20 years?

2. How would falsification of theories contribute to the body of theoretical knowledge?

3. According to Bernard, how can theorists better accomplish their tasks in the generation of scientific progress? What are the five tasks he has outlined for the criminological theorist?

4. Where is the origin of this problem, and what seems to be perpetuating it?

2

THE CRIMINOLOGICAL ENTERPRISE IN EUROPE AND THE UNITED STATES

A Contextual Exploration

INEKE HAEN MARSHALL

EDITOR'S INTRODUCTION—Ineke Haen Marshall's article provides a welcomed contribution to any criminological theory reader, most of which tend to focus exclusively on theories and research from American criminologists (which, not coincidentally, tend to focus on the crime problem in the United States!). Marshall proposes three basic objectives: "(1) to highlight how the criminological enterprise in North America (in particular the US) differs from Europe; (2) to interpret some of these differences in the light of unique American socio-cultural national characteristics; and (3) to speculate about the degree to which these national differences will colour the criminological enterprise of the future" (p. 15, this volume).

Marshall begins her article by pointing out the "exceptionalism," or unique features, that characterize American society and culture and how these differ from Europe and other Western countries, especially in terms of politics, economy, culture, religion, education, public policy, and the manner in which the United States interacts with other societies. With respect to criminology, American criminology differs from that in Europe. Marshall indicates that American criminologists tend to focus exclusively on American theories and professional conferences, whereas European criminologists are more apt to spread their scholarly wings into other countries, thereby "internationalizing" their scope.

What are the main differences between American and European criminology, and where do they lie? Primarily, Marshall suggests that although differences exist within European criminology itself, the influence of American criminology is much stronger and more pronounced. She contends that primary differences exist with respect to the *history* of the development of criminology in America and Europe; the *scale*, or size, of the criminological enterprise in America as compared to Europe; the *accessibility* of American publications and research; the *diversity* in theory and method in terms of the roots of criminological frameworks; and, last, with respect to *focal research questions*.

Marshall goes on to illustrate these differences in an interpretive analysis of how the American intellectual context has shaped both the method and focus of criminology in the United States. She first examines the unique ways in which American researchers emphasize a "practical problem focus" almost to the exception of theoretical pursuits. Next, she examines the American justice system, noting the ideological struggles with respect to crime control (i.e., due process vs. crime control models and punitive policy making). Last, Marshall points out the exceptional nature of America's high crime rate and the fact that much of American theorizing has centered on America's street crime problem. Marshall concludes her essay by claiming that the current criminological enterprise is really "Eurocentric" and ignores other non-Western criminologies and voices.

As she notes, focusing on America's "exceptionalism" compared to what is happening in Europe involves the danger of overlooking the fact that America's boundaries and influence transcend its geographical limits. Although American criminology has made positive contributions to the field and study of crime, its policy-oriented, methodologically driven, lackluster theoretical development and diversity (if perceived to be true), place fear in the minds of many scholars, who sense that the "Americanization" of European criminology and other criminologies may become a reality. It will become even more important for criminologists in all regions of the world to recognize the importance of the globalization of criminology.

A rose is a rose by any other name . . ." so reads one of Shakespeare's most famous lines. A rose has a delicious fragrance, prickly thorns and velvety leaves regardless of whether you hold it in Amsterdam, Rome, Shanghai or New York. The same is not true of the thing called—by lack of a better name—the "criminological enterprise" as it exists in the different regions of the world. There are as many criminologies as there are nations in the world. National social factors permeate the practice of science deeply. The sociology and philosophy of science and the history of ideas are replete with examples which demonstrate the social and contingent nature of knowledge (Smith 1975; Glick 1987; Goetzman 1992; Goonatilake 1998). Science and technology practices vary, "depending upon such factors as the country's history, funding sources, research and developmental allocations, and coordinatory mechanism . . ." (Goonatilake 1998, p. 17). Criminology is no exception to this observation. There are many criminologies, but among the most significant are those in Europe and the US.

The purpose of this article is to (1) highlight how the criminological enterprise in North America (in particular the US) differs from Europe; (2) to interpret some of these differences in the light of unique American socio-cultural

national characteristics; and (3) to speculate about the degree to which these national differences will colour the criminological enterprise of the future.

Why Europe *Versus* the United States?

Does it make sense to attempt sweeping comparisons between one particularly large nation-state (the US) and an aggregate of individual nation-states (Europe)? Comparing Europe *versus* the US is in many ways like comparing apples and oranges, yet we do it all the time. Such comparison builds on a long and well-established tradition, emphasising American "exceptionalism" (the phrase is De Tocqueville's). Almost since its very foundation, it has been believed that America is unique, and that it in crucial ways is different and distinct from other Western countries (Lipset 1991, p. 1). The US was created differently, and thus has to be understood differently— essentially on its own terms and within its own context, or so the belief goes (Shafter 1991). . . . The American uniqueness is typically contrasted with 'Europe' conceived as a cultural entity, where the whole (that is, Europe) is more than the sum-total of the individual nation-states. For many purposes, it is obviously appropriate to treat European culture as a distinct entity.

Marshall, I. H. (2001). The criminological enterprise in Europe and the United States: A contextual exploration. *European Journal on Criminal Policy and Research, 9,* 235-257.

However, in many instances it would be misleading to overlook the fact that Europe (unlike the US) is made up of a number of separate individual nations, each with a distinct history, socio-political culture, and language. These deep-seated national differences within Europe remain of crucial importance, rendering sweeping Europe *versus* US comparisons problematic. This point is best illustrated by the case of the United Kingdom, a nation which explicitly and self-consciously distinguishes itself from continental Europe in many of its writings and other contexts. For a variety of purposes, the UK is lumped together with other English-speaking countries (including the US) as representing Anglo-Saxon culture. The heterogeneity of (continental) Europe is further emphasised by the prevalent use of several well-established regional country clusters within Europe (Scandinavia or the Nordic countries, Southern Europe, former socialist countries, and so on). Even within hese more homogeneous clusters, individual countries vary significantly in many ways (for example Sweden and Norway, or Switzerland and Germany). Of course, the US is not a culturally homogeneous entity either. Individual American states also differ significantly from each other in many ways. Alabama is quite different from North Dakota, New York or California. At the same time, the US does have a shared language, history, and overarching federal political and legal system, [and] the level of internal cultural and socio-political heterogeneity is in no way comparable to that of Europe. Van Swaaningen gets at the heart of the issue by stating: "[. . .] the similarities between Western European nations are perhaps only evident in terms of their contrast with America" (1997a, p. x). He continues that "[. . .] nowhere in the First World does such a diversity occur in such small geographical area. A multiplicity of nations with differing political systems, legal cultures and social structures exist next to each other" (1997a, pp. x-xi).

European Criminology
Versus American Criminology?

If you were to ask an American criminologist to define the essence of the 'American' criminological enterprise, s/he may be hard-pressed for an answer. Many will never have thought about it. This may reflect the ethnocentric orientation typical for those who are not brought into daily contact with other cultures. With notable exceptions, American criminologists tend to interact primarily within their own English-speaking world, where there is no need to be explicit about the essence of the 'American' criminological enterprise. Not surprisingly, for most American scholars, criminology is *American* criminology. That is what they do, that is what they know. It is reflected in the courses they teach, the publications they read, and the congresses they attend. On the other hand, to speak in terms of 'European criminology' is much more precarious. 'European criminology' is distinct from criminology in Europe. Although there is no question that criminology as a discipline emerged in Europe (Beirne 1993; Rock 1994), in the past 'European criminology' was primarily another way of identifying one or more of the more prominent national developments in Europe (the Italian positivists, or the French environmentalists). This is also the most common approach taken by American textbooks and histories of criminology.

Criminology in Europe has never been entirely constrained by national boundaries, or practised within a country entirely by its own nationals (Shapland 1991, p. 15). . . . This is a natural by-product of the internationalisation of society, possibly also reflecting the belief that this is needed to provide a counterweight to the apparent dominance of American criminology. . . .

DIFFERENCES BETWEEN THE USA AND EUROPE WITH REGARD TO THE 'CRIMINOLOGICAL ENTERPRISE'

What are the main differences between American criminology and criminology in Europe? As I just mentioned, for purposes of comparison I approach European criminology simply as the subtotal of the efforts by those involved in the study of law, social order and crime in Europe. Such broad comparison is not without pitfalls. There exist[s] a wide diversity in the criminological enterprises within Europe; the fact that in some countries, the American influence is quite pronounced (such as the Netherlands, the UK), further muddles the US/Europe comparison.

History

The history of criminological thought in Europe far predates [that of] the US. The systematic and scientific search for the causes of crime and criminality began in Europe in the 1800s, and by the end of the 1800s, the European tradition in criminology was firmly established (Willis et al., 1999, p. 227; but see Rock (1994) for interpretations that go back much earlier in history). Moreover, and importantly, whereas the US only has one history of the development of criminology, Europe knows multiple histories of the study of crime, law and social order. Each nation has its own history, very much shaped by its unique cultural, social and political conditions (compare Italy and the Netherlands, or the UK and Germany).

Scale

Stated very simply: 'size does matter!' The popular expression that everything is larger in the US, has a kernel of truth. The American criminological enterprise is the largest in the world. Measured by the number of people who focus on the study of crime, law and social control, the number of university courses, the number of scholarly and professional publications and books, the number of research projects and the amount of funding, there is no question that the US takes the cake. . . . The product of the sum total of these efforts is a huge number of studies (admittedly of varying quality), more so than in any European country where considerably fewer scholars are involved in the study of crime and justice. . . .

Degree of Institutionalisation

European countries differ widely in the degree in which the study of criminology has been institutionalised (Van Swaaningen, 2001). Many European countries do have scholars who are involved in the criminological enterprise broadly defined (education, research), but without the American level of crystallisation as a clearly defined and well-institutionalised field of study. . . . The high level of institutionalisation is the fruit of decades of focused investment by the American national government in higher education and research in the areas of crime and crime control.

Crime and crime control have been a high political priority on the American agenda since the late 1960s, with considerable resources allocated to this issue. . . . The distinction between criminology and criminal justice is not that one is abstract and the other applied, but rather in the scope of its study. The study and higher education with respect to law, crime and crime control in the US is—after several decades of focused development—now deeply and soundly entrenched in universities and research institutes, with large numbers of students, professors and researchers. Criminal justice is seen as a respectable and recognised profession, with thousands of bachelors' degrees, and hundreds of advanced graduate degrees offered by American universities. There exists a clearly defined criminal justice professoriat, with large and active professional organisations, hundreds of peer-reviewed publications, several national and regional annual congresses. Although scholars in European countries focus on many comparable issues related to crime, police, courts, and prisons, there is not—within one single country—a comparable level of crystallisation as a well-defined independent academic field of study.

Accessibility

Often it seems that American criminologists believe that the really significant (recent) works on crime are produced primarily in the US. There may be one simple explanation for that: language! . . . Since many foreign language publications are not accessible to Americans, it also means that the flow of information has been heavily biased: Europeans may know what is going on on the other side of the Atlantic, but Americans remain largely ignorant of the activities in the different European criminological enterprises. I am undoubtedly not the first to speculate about the important role of the UK as an intermediary between the US and continental Europe in this regard. The increasing use of English as a world language is likely to increase the accessibility of the body of criminological knowledge to more scholars.

Diversity in Theory and Method

The history of criminology in Europe may be traced back to a diversity of fields (biology, psychology, history, law, social statistics, and sociology). In the US the theoretical development of criminology drew its inspiration mainly from sociology (Willis et al., 1999, p. 227). The historical diversity continues to resonate in contemporary times. Although there is no European country in which only one model of criminology exists, there are cultural traditions of criminology "which render its practice and theoretical enquiry different in different countries" (Shapland 1991, p. 14). . . .

In the United States, there are a relatively large number of individuals and organisations which focus on the study of crime and justice, but they operate within the boundaries of a relatively narrow range of theoretical perspectives and methods. Allowing for a certain amount of bias, the American critical criminologist Currie seems to get at the essence of the American criminological enterprise:

> there is a large, rather technocratic, 'middle' contingent, the 'mainstream,' which often produces quite useful work, but is only rarely engaged in the public arena and shies away from sticking its neck out; there is the small but extremely effective right wing that has an extraordinary amount of presence and influence, less within the profession than in the media and among politicians [. . .]; and there is a self-defined 'radical' contingent, complete with its own separate organizations and subsections of organizations [. . .] (Currie 1999, pp. 17-18)

Bernard and Engel (2001, p. 14) state that large-scale quantitative studies have become "the bread and butter" of criminal justice research (in the US). The point is not that there is no diversity within American criminology, but rather, that there is, proportionally, dominance of the sociological approach (with some role for biological and psychological factors), with a methodological emphasis on sophisticated quantitative analysis of large data sets.

Critical and Self-Reflexive Stance

This point—although already referred to in Currie's characterisation of the American criminological enterprise—deserves to be singled out. European countries differ significantly in the extent to which their study of law, crime and social control is characterised by a critical, self-reflexive stance (for example, compare France

and the UK with the Netherlands, see Van Swaaningen 1997a). A comparative perspective (which is more likely to be taken by European scholars because of the context in which they operate) tends to be more conducive to the development of a critical, macro-level view on law and social control. This is one possible explanation. Another explanation may be found in the presumed American disdain for the importance of abstract speculation (discussed in the next section). . . .

Focal Research Questions

A recent overview of the criminological enterprise in nine Western European countries (Van Outrive and Robert 1999) suggests that a large number of the research topics (victims, public and private police, judicial decision-making, juvenile delinquency, organised crime) are similar to those studied in the US (often using similar methods). There is no doubt that many questions related to crime and law transcend national boundaries. Yet, the particular intensity and focus is shaped by the unique national context. . . .

The American Way of 'Doing Science'

I have already alluded to the notion of American exceptionalism. Literally thousands of scholarly and literary works have attempted to get at the essence of the American identity. Shafter's analysis presented in the book, *Is America Different?* (1991) may serve as a fairly typical illustration of what the 'American model' entails. In his view, the American model is characterised by four central themes: populism, individualism, democratisation, and market-making (p. 233). *Populism* is the doctrine that all members of society should be conceived of as social equals. *Individualism* is the doctrine that the single and independent members of society have a right to construct their personal lives according to their own preferences. *Democratisation* is the notion that major social institutions should be run so as to be directly responsive to the wishes of the public. Finally, *market-making* is the notion that organised alternatives—in products and services, but also in occupations, entertainments, and even lifestyles—ought to appear or disappear as there is (or is not) sufficient demand to sustain them (Shafter 1991, pp. 234-235).

These themes, closely interwoven with a host of other historical, intellectual, political and social influences, have provided the context for the 'American model' of science (including the study of law, crime and social control).

A well-accepted view among sociologists of knowledge and historians of science is that America from its very beginnings has been "permeated by the culture of science" (Goetzman 1992, p. 414). . . . Pragmatism is one of the key themes of American scientific culture. Scholars have attempted to associate pragmatism with a package of characteristic American traits (Moyer 1992, p. 206). Pragmatism is important because it reflects "Americans' preconceptions about and aspirations for a modern, scientific culture" (Moyer 1992, p. 207). . . .

Foreign observers (but Americans also) have typified the historical American attitude toward science and scientific research with the so-called "indifference theme" (Glick 1987, p. 6). Thus, while there was a great deal of activity devoted to inventions and the creation of practical implements, Americans were indifferent to basic science and basic research (Glick 1987, p. 5), or so it was argued. A later reinterpretation is that—rather than doing pure or fundamental research as a search for knowledge for its own sake—Americans tended to do pure research for economic profit, practical application, and technological progress. A main element of pragmatism is its fixation on "the process of inquiry itself rather than the actual acquisition of knowledge" (Moyer 1992, p. 207). The "scientific habit of mind" was supposed to rescue civilisation from detrimental trends (Moyer 1992, p. 207). The pragmatic principle tends to accentuate the scientific method of inquiry. Thus, the American pragmatists (Peirce, James, and Dewey) all proclaimed in one form or another "the scientific method itself, unfettered by traditional absolutes, as the ideal guide to a public philosophy for the nation" (Goetzman 1992, p. 414). This has [led] to the characterisation of a 'scientistic' America.

The mainstay of American scientific thought is very much coloured by pragmatism. . . . In the view of many interpreters, Americans often have been hostile to theory, be it in literature, philosophy or science. A case in point is the recently published account of the philosophical and literary "theory wars" (between the French and the Americans) (Mathy 2000). In order to interpret the cross-Atlantic tensions, Mathy makes reference to Hofstadter's (1970) often-cited "anti-intellectualism" in the United States, and its implied resistance to theory in particular in American culture.

In *Essays on American Intellectual History,* Smith (1975) defines the three focal beliefs through which the American philosophical spirit over the last 100 years can be articulated. . . . Firstly, the belief that thinking is primarily an activity in response to a concrete situation and that this activity is aimed at solving problems. Secondly, the belief that ideas and theories must have a 'cutting edge' or must make a difference in the conduct of people who hold them and in the situation in which they live. This feature has long been regarded as the essence of the American character (Smith 1975, p. 476). . . . Americans believe that their total intellectual energy should be focused on 'here and now' issues and that there is no time for dealing with problems of a generalised nature which have no clear focal point in time (Smith 1975, p. 476). Closely connected with this focus on specific problems is the belief that intellectual activity is justified to the extent to which its results are translated into action. . . . Thirdly, the American belief that the earth can be civilised and obstacles to progress overcome by the application of knowledge.

In sum, American intellectual thought embodies the primary importance of the scientific method, a practical problem focus (rather than on abstract issues), and a need for ideas (theories) with practical implications. The particular American way of 'doing science' finds its reflection in the American criminological enterprise. Besides the scientific culture of a country, there are many other political and socio-cultural factors which shape the way law, crime and social control are studied. Of central importance are those aspects of society which have a direct (substantive) impact on the criminological enterprise: namely, the administration of justice (including the legal tradition on which these practices are based) and the nature of the crime problem.

The American Way of 'Doing Justice'

Legal factors—both principles and practices—are of critical importance in shaping the nature of the criminological enterprise. Since the mainstay of American intellectual thought is a pragmatist problem- and action-orientation, it is to be expected that perceived problems related to law and justice have guided American criminology and criminal justice studies.

Many scholarly works have analysed the differences between the American common law system, which differs from most of Europe with the continental (or inquisitorial) system (see Reichel 1996; Terrill 1999). That is not the only— or even the main—difference, however; after all, the British (among others) obviously also have a common law tradition[;] that is where the Americans got it from. It seems that the role of law in American society differs significantly from the European (including the British) situation. The characteristics of the adversarial system of common law are pushed to the extreme in the United States. . . . The juridical principle: absolute respect for the rules of procedure is a basic principle governing American life; due process is not just an ideological substrate of American life; it expresses itself in a number of concrete practices and procedures (Crozier 1984, p. 103). . . .

The American 'due process model' has been contrasted with the 'crime control model,' more common in Europe which focuses on the maintenance of law and order, and is less protective of the rights of the accused and of individuals generally (Lipset 1991, p. 33). Contrasting the American (common law) due process model with the European (inquisitorial or continental law) crime control model is one way of looking at the implications of different legal traditions cross-nationally. Ironically, however, within the US the friction between the ideal of due process and the reality of crime control has turned out to be the major impetus for the development of criminal justice research and theory in the USA.

In a recent article, 'Conceptualizing criminal justice theory,' the American criminologists Bernard and Engel (2001) provide a most interesting interpretative analysis of the historical development of the academic field of criminal justice in the US. One important point is that the scholarly focus on the functioning of the criminal law in the US was initiated in the 1950s by a practical concern of 'reform commissions' who were concerned with bringing the 'law in practice' into greater conformity with 'the law on the books.' The realisation that there was a gap between the ideal and the real in criminal justice runs like a connecting thread through much of the criminal

justice research in the US. The single event most responsible for the development of criminal justice as an academic field was the realisation based on several observational studies in the 1960s, that pervasive discretion—although often conflicting with the requirements of due process expressed in the 'law on the books' was an inevitable reality in the daily 'law in practice.' The field began to acknowledge that a certain amount of legitimate exercise of discretion was not necessarily incompatible with the notion of due process. Gradually, criminal justice research shifted from qualitative (observational) to quantitative and systematic large-scale studies, examining contextual influences on individual decision-making and focusing entirely on describing and explaining what criminal justice agents were actually doing (Bernard and Engel 2001, p. 13). The research implicitly compares the practice of criminal justice against a normative ideal (equality, due process). These studies focused strongly on the effects of race, gender, class and demeanour—that is, non-legal, and therefore unacceptable factors conflicting with the due process model—on decisions in the criminal justice process.

Another characteristic of the American system of justice is its relative harshness and punitiveness, and its reliance on the criminal law (incarceration) as a means to maintain social control. . . . Concern about growing prison populations and market-thinking focus on effectiveness and efficiency, have inspired many studies on the incapacitating effects of incarceration, as well as the deterrent effect of punishment. Crime control and safety is now 'big business' in the US; the market-based approach is reflected in the application of business management principles in the streamlining of criminal justice processing, as well as institutionalised scientific evaluation of processes and results. This type of research provides the 'bread and butter' of an ever-growing number of private and public research and training institutes in the USA.

Bernard and Engel (2001, p. 25) conclude their interpretative analysis of the historical development of the academic discipline of criminal justice in the US with the observation that

[C]riminal justice [as an academic field] [. . .] originated as descriptive research, in which theory, insofar as it existed at all, was highly specific and focused on the particular topic at hand. Over the last 50 years, criminal justice [as an academic discipline] has been working its way, with difficulty, towards theory.

They contrast this with the development of criminological theory (in the US): "criminology originated as sweepingly discursive general theories [. . .] and has worked its way, with difficulty, towards phrasing these theories in such a way that research could test them adequately" (p. 25). The pragmatic resistance toward abstract theorising notwithstanding, American scholars have indeed developed several discursive (middle range), abstract crime theories. It is very clear, however, that the focus and content of these theories reflect the practical problems which America experiences with crime. This is briefly discussed in the next section.

The American Way of 'Doing Crime'

Crime—in particular serious violent crime—has been defined as one of the major social problems in the US since the 1960s. Countless observers have noted that the US—compared to Europe—suffers much higher crime rates. This difference has begun to level off during the last few years (Blumstein and Wallman 2000). This recent decline, in conjunction with the high levels of violence in Eastern Europe over the last several years, challenges the popular view of the USA as the most violent nation in the industrialised world. Still, serious (gun-related) violence continues to be a problem in the US. On the positive side, crime and crime control have been a major concern for academics in the US for several decades, considerable funding for crime-related research has been available, and a lot of knowledge has been developed. Some of this knowledge may be transferable to Europe, whereas some . . . may be tied to uniquely American conditions.

The focus of criminological theorising and research reflects—to a large degree—the realities of the American crime problem. Allowing for a certain degree of media-hype and social construction of criminality, it cannot be denied that there have been real problems with street crime, the central theme of American criminological theory. . . .

Violence, in particular gun-related violence, has also ranked high on the agenda of American criminologists (e.g. Wolfgang and Ferracuti's subculture of violence, 1967). With the rise of the serious inner-city violence in the mid-1980s, the link between drugs, guns, and violence became a central concern (e.g. Blumstein and Wallman 2000). The focus on street crime, drugs and violence has placed the role of race and ethnicity in the American crime picture centre stage (e.g. Sampson and Wilson 1995; Short 1997). White collar crime has also been a focus of American scholarly inquiry, albeit in much lesser degree (e.g. Sutherland 1940; Coleman 1989; Shover and Bryant 1993). This is not surprising in view of the fact that the US is a capitalist society par excellence, with a well-documented problem with corporate and occupational crime. The problems with organised crime in the US have also, quite understandably, been the subject of scholarly exploration (Albini 1971; Ianni 1973; Abadinsky 1981; Block and Chambliss 1981; Ianni and Reuss-Reuter et al., 1983; Jacobs and Gouldin 1999). This is but a handful of the more obvious examples of the problem-based focus of the American criminological enterprise. . . .

Theoretical explanations of crime in the US typically have been tied to American exceptionalism, both by American and non-American scholars. Large-scale crime is seen as a natural by-product of American culture (Bell 1953; Lipset 1991). . . . The high level of violence in the US is typically explained by reference to the American 'culture of violence.' The American 'culture of violence' is viewed as a natural product of America's unique violent history: the frontier tradition, the influence of slavery, lynchings, the Indian Wars (see Butterfield 1995; Brown 1991). It is assumed that America's violent history has formed the essence of the modern American identity, a violent identity. Criminal violence is viewed as a spillover of socially accepted violence. . . .

Inspired by practical issues or not, there is no question that American scholars have contributed important theoretical insights to the field of criminology. However, it seems that the heydays of creative criminological (sociological) theory development in the US are long gone. . . . The current focus on crime prevention and risk management together with deep dissatisfaction about the practical utility of (sociological) crime theories has resulted in a gradual turning away from trying to develop etiological theories of crime. Efforts to develop so-called integrated theories are an important exception to this trend (e.g. Sampson and Laub 1993; Vila 1994; Tittle 1995; Bernard and Snipes 1996). The relatively new kid on the block, life course and developmental crime theory, with its focus on identification of risk factors and implications for crime prevention is the product of collaborative efforts between American researchers and researchers from other countries (see Farrington 1994). . . .

CONCLUSION

Although there is a growing criminology in Latin America, South Africa, India, and other parts of the world (see Willis et al. 1999; Del Olmo 1999; Shank 1999), the criminological enterprise remains—for the time being at least—eurocentric. Criminologists in Europe, the United States, Canada, Australia, New Zealand all use what the philosopher Richard Rorty has called "the conversation of the West." Focusing on the uniqueness or 'exceptionalism' of (the criminological enterprise of) the United States compared to what is going on in Europe, has the danger of overlooking the fact that intellectual life in America is a part of a larger civilisation that encompasses the national cultures of European countries as well as that of the United States (Hollinger 1985, p. 176). . . .

However, if one defines the essence of American criminology as being policy-oriented, methodologically driven, and lacking theoretical lustre, diversity, and short of a critical edge, then the fear of 'Americanisation' of European criminology is well-placed. 'Americanisation' refers to fundamental developments of modernity as cultural homogenisation ('McDonaldisation'), and degeneration. "America so conceived may exist outside of the United States and involve no actual Americans [. . .]" (Ceasar 1997, p. 2). It is no longer the criminological enterprise of the US *per se,* but rather an idea or symbol, called 'Americanisation' which is really at issue here. If increasing cultural (including legal) convergence and homogenisation across the countries of the world means growing American dominance (and it should be noted that there are conflicting views

on this issue, see Held et al., 1999), then it is reasonable to speculate that American criminology will gain more applicability in 'Americanised' Europe. However, regional criminologies will always retain their significance (Haen Marshall 1998). Furthermore, the growing realisation that many different and valuable ways of thinking about crime, law and social control exist outside North America and Western Europe is bound to enrich the conceptual and methodological toolbox of the criminological enterprise (Willis et al., 1999).

A final thought: Internationalisation of crime and crime control makes it inevitable that the future of the criminological enterprise will centre more and more around questions that transcend national boundaries. The need for a transnational or global criminology is no longer to be denied (see e.g. Findlay 1999). Such worldwide criminology can only prosper through the joint efforts of criminologists from all the continents and regions of the world.

DISCUSSION QUESTIONS

1. What is American "exceptionalism," and why is it important in Marshall's comparison of Europe and European criminology with the United States and its criminology?

2. What are the main differences between the United States and Europe with regard to the "criminological enterprise"?

3. Discuss the American ways of (a) doing science; (b) doing justice; and (c) doing crime. What are the strengths of these strategies, and what are the potential problems or limitations that may arise as a result of the "American Way"?

4. What does Haen Marshall mean by the term *Americanization*? Is that something people in European and other nations should fear?

3

CONCEPTUALIZING CRIMINAL JUSTICE THEORY

THOMAS J. BERNARD AND ROBIN SHEPARD ENGEL

EDITOR'S INTRODUCTION—The inclusion of this very recent article by Thomas J. Bernard and Robin Shepard Engel illustrates the importance of how theory can be used to inform practice. In this essay, the authors attempt to advance the development and generalization of criminal justice theory as a whole, but rather than proposing an entirely new and comprehensive approach that attempts to describe and explain the entire criminal justice *system*, they examine the history and development of the academic field of criminal justice itself.

Initially, the authors briefly describe previous attempts to classify and generalize criminal justice theories, discuss the problems associated with these theoretical attempts, and assess the reasons why they have been relatively unsuccessful as frameworks for organizing the field. Recognizing the limitations of these approaches—which are essentially too narrow in scope, limiting comparison across criminal justice organizations and hindering theory development—the authors propose a new conceptual framework, which argues that

1. "A meaningful categorization of criminal justice theories must cut across the components of the criminal justice system: police, courts, and corrections."

2. The classification of theories should be able to incorporate content similarities found in theories across those components and be able to facilitate generalization and testing of theories.

3. Categories must include considerable detail and specificity in order to be useful and should not be so broad and general that the entire criminal justice field is divided into only two or three categories." (p. 26, this volume)

Therefore, the authors propose that criminal justice theories should be classified first on their dependent variables and then according to their independent variables. In their rich, interpretive analysis of the historical development of the academic field of criminal justice, Bernard and Engel contend that the three broad types of dependent variables include a focus on individual behavior of criminal justice agents (i.e., the behavior of police officers); the behavior of criminal justice organizations (i.e., behavior of court organizations); and last, the characteristics of the overall criminal justice system and its components (i.e., police killings and "get tough" sentencing policies). Classification of theories in this manner increases conceptual clarity in discussions of criminal justice theory.

In the interpretive history, which comprises the bulk of the authors' contribution, Bernard and Engel argue that criminal justice theories and research have explicitly or implicitly incorporated "prescriptive ideals that are used to assess the legitimacy of what criminal justice agents and organizations should be doing" (p. 26, this volume). The authors acknowledge that the idealism that underlies the reformist tendencies of scholarly research has always existed in academic criminal justice. The subsequent goals of many early criminal justice scholars aimed at closing the gap between the ideal and the real—the "law on the books" and the "law in action"—in order to change the prescriptive ideal to fit more closely the reality of criminal justice practices. The gap eventually closed when studies began to consider the concept of discretion in their analyses of organizational legitimacy.

It is against this backdrop of legitimacy that Bernard and Engel argue that criminal justice scholars should acknowledge their work explicitly. In other words, the field of criminal justice cannot be understood fully without recognition of its prescriptive elements. The authors offer some lessons from the field of criminology in terms of theory building; although the fields differ in terms of their theoretical roots and approaches to the study of crime and crime control, criminology theory making provides a viable framework that can be modeled and implemented by criminal justice scholars.

The academic field of criminal justice originated in the 1950s with observational research on criminal justice organizations. The diversity and complexity of those organizations led to diversity and complexity in the resulting theories, which then did not easily generalize into something that could properly be called "criminal justice theory." After 50 years, a great deal of research has accumulated along with an increasing number of relatively specific theories to interpret that research. Despite some movement to generalize the theories, little progress has been made in formulating criminal justice theory per se (e.g., Hagan, 1989).

It may be that the criminal justice system as a whole is so diverse and complex that meaningful theories spanning the system are impossible to formulate. It may even be that its major components (police, courts, corrections, and juvenile justice) are too diverse to be the subject of meaningful theories. Alternatively, something called "criminal justice theory" may be not only possible but also necessary for the further progress of criminal justice as an academic and scientific discipline. In this paper we explore the possibilities for developing such theory.

Rather than proposing a new and comprehensive theory that attempts to describe and explain the entire criminal justice system, our methodology is to examine the history and development of the academic field of criminal justice itself.

To determine what "criminal justice theory" is, we examine the actual theories that have developed within the field of criminal justice since it was founded. First, we briefly describe earlier attempts to classify and generalize criminal justice theories, discuss the problems accompanying each of these attempts, and assess the reasons why they generally have not been successful as frameworks for organizing the field. We then propose a new conceptual framework for classifying and generalizing criminal justice theories. Next we present an interpretive analysis of the historical development of the academic field of criminal justice in order to demonstrate how the field can be organized within that framework. We conclude with a description of lessons about theory learned in the field of criminology and apply these lessons to the field of criminal justice.

ORGANIZING AND CLASSIFYING CRIMINAL JUSTICE THEORIES

Earlier Classifications of Theories

The field of criminal justice has accumulated a large body of knowledge based on much empirical testing; it has also accumulated a variety of rather specific theories. Some attempts have been made to organize and classify those theories. The three most common bases for

Bernard, T. J., & Engel, R. S. (2001). Conceptualizing criminal justice theory. *Justice Quarterly, 18,* 1-30.

classification are (1) type of organization within the criminal justice system (e.g., police, courts, corrections); (2) underlying theoretical assumptions (e.g., consensus, conflict); and (3) predictor variables (e.g., individual, situational, organizational, community). Although each of these classification schemes presents a way to conceptualize the research, each has weaknesses.

The simplest and most straightforward way to organize theory in criminal justice is to categorize it by component of the criminal justice system. Dividing criminal justice theory into police, courts, and corrections has become the standard, [and] many criminal justice researchers identify themselves primarily with one of these three areas. This approach to organizing material impedes theoretical development in criminal justice for a number of reasons. First, some topics (e.g., juvenile justice, gun control, systemic discrimination) do not fit neatly into any one particular category. Second, this classification limits comparisons across components, hindering development of theory regarding the relationships between organizations and how they work together to accomplish their respective tasks. Furthermore, it is difficult to describe and explore the similarities and differences among the components. Finally, it is difficult to conceptualize the criminal justice system as a single entity when research is continually divided into three areas. Although the criminal justice system is marked by decentralized and fragmented parts with inconsistent goals (some observers argue that it is not even a "system" in the true meaning of the word), the relationships that do exist among and between these parts are obscured by such a classification.

A second type of classification focuses on the underlying assumptions and propositions of particular theories. Scholars generally move toward this type when they attempt to break out of categorization by criminal justice component. For example, Scheingold (1984) acknowledged that there are many individual differences among theories but suggested that they can be classified most appropriately as belonging to one of three groups: mainstream, Marxist, or conflict. Similarly, Hagan (1989) categorized criminal justice theory and research as based on either consensus or conflict theory. He then noted the limitations of having only two predominant theories of criminal justice available, and

suggested an alternative approach for theoretical development.

This approach presents certain problems. Such a broad classification obscures differences among theories and research while doing little to increase clarity. Unlike other "pure" academic disciplines, the field of criminal justice is multidisciplinary, applying theoretical propositions from sociology, criminology, economics, political science, psychology, and anthropology. Describing theories on the basis of such general theoretical assumptions further limits theory that should consider the propositions and assumptions of many of these disciplines. Therefore we believe that classifying theories according to their underlying theoretical assumptions is not useful.

A third attempt to organize the literature involves grouping research by dependent and independent variables. Unlike classification by underlying theoretical propositions, which generally is an attempt to move "upward" from classification by system components, classification by dependent and independent variables generally is a move "downward" in the sense that it has occurred only in particular components of the system. The leading example is Sherman's (1980) review of research on police behavior. Sherman described the different types of police behavior (e.g., arrest, use of force, detection, and service) that were the dependent variables. Primarily, however, he focused on the conceptual grouping of the independent variables that explained these various types of police behavior (e.g., individual, situational, legal, organizational, and community). Riksheim and Chermak (1993) later updated this review, and Worden (1986) adopted a similar approach to categorize research on police use of force.

This approach provides a useful way of organizing the vast amount of research on police behavior, and is a significant improvement over the previous classification schemes. It has not yet been used, however, to organize research across the system components. Indeed, we are aware of such classification only in regard to police, and do not know whether it has been applied to courts or corrections. In addition, because this approach focuses on one particular type of dependent variable, namely police behavior, the classification scheme concentrates on organizing the independent variables.

Our Proposal for Organizing Criminal Justice Theory

We believe that a meaningful categorization of criminal justice theories must cut across the components of the criminal justice system: police, courts, and corrections. It cannot simply organize theories and research within each separate component. We also believe that such a classification must be able to incorporate the similarities in content found in theories across those components, and to facilitate generalization and competitive testing of the theories. Finally, we believe that categories must be able to include considerable detail and specificity in order to be useful; they cannot be so broad that the entire field is divided into only two or three categories.

We propose that *criminal justice theories should be grouped or classified first on their dependent variables, and then according to their independent variables.* This approach is essentially similar to Sherman's (1980) and Riksheim and Chermak's (1993) approach to classifying empirical police research, although much broader. As stated above, Sherman took police officers' individual behavior as the dependent variable. That general category included a number of more specific dependent variables: arrest, use of force, detection, and service. After grouping the theories on their dependent variables, Sherman grouped them on the basis of their independent variables: individual, situational, legal, organizational, and community. He reported research findings on the basis of independent variables, whereas Riksheim and Chermak, in their update of Sherman's review, reported findings on the basis of dependent variables.

We propose expanding this approach to the entire field of criminal justice. In our interpretation of the history of criminal justice, as described below, we suggest that there are three broad types of dependent variables; the first two encompass most of the theory and research in the field. The first type focuses on the *individual behavior of criminal justice agents* (e.g., the behavior of police officers, courtroom officials, correctional officers). The second focuses on the *behavior of criminal justice organizations* (e.g., the behavior of police departments, court organizations, correctional organizations). The third type of dependent variable focuses on the *characteristics of the overall criminal justice system*

and its components (e.g., police killings, "get tough" sentencing, incarceration rates). This type operates at the aggregate level with theories and research that examine the relationship between societal-level characteristics and the rates and distributions of criminal justice system behaviors.

Each general type of dependent variable would include a variety of more specific dependent variables. And for each dependent variable, whether more general or more specific, a variety of independent variables would be expected to have at least some causal effect, especially because multivariate models now are used routinely in criminal justice research that incorporate different types of independent variables within one model. By categorizing all theory and research on the basis of the dependent variable, one can compare and contrast research on the basis of the perceived influence of various independent variables. This approach allows generalization and competitive testing of criminal justice theory and research across system components.

Our scheme does not classify theories according to underlying assumptions, such as consensus versus conflict theories. In our view, these underlying assumptions represent types or categories of *independent* variables. Thus classification on these variables would occur only after the theories had been classified on their *dependent* variables. When classified on their dependent variables, most conflict-type theories are found to be aggregate-level: the dependent variables are either the entire criminal justice system or an entire system component such as policing or corrections. At that point, the issue of consensus versus conflict is empirical rather than theoretical: how much variation in the dependent variable is explained by conflict-type independent variables, and how much is explained by consensus-type independent variables.

Finally, in the interpretive history presented below, we argue that criminal justice theories and research historically have incorporated, either explicitly or implicitly, prescriptive ideals that are used to assess the legitimacy of what criminal justice agents and organizations should be doing. This idealism underlies the reformism tendencies that have always been present in criminal justice as an academic field, in which the reality of criminal justice practices moved closer to the prescriptive ideal. We suggest that, for all three types of dependent variables, prescriptive ideals in the form of discussions of legitimacy should be made explicit rather than left implicit. This step forms the basis of any reformist implications for criminal justice theory and research.

CRIMINAL JUSTICE AS AN ACADEMIC FIELD

The following description of the history of criminal justice as an academic field is presented as a concrete representation of how our proposed framework can organize the academic field of criminal justice so as to facilitate both the competitive testing and the generalization of theories. This interpretive history, however, should not be taken too literally. Any attempt to sort material into conceptual boxes is always a matter of opinion, and no classification system is completely fair to its subject matter. In addition, although we present a particular sequence that suggests progression over time, the time periods overlap considerably. Nevertheless, and despite whatever flaws might be apparent, we believe that our proposed framework is useful for organizing the academic field of criminal justice.

The ABF [American Bar Foundation] Studies: A Shift in the Attribution of Legitimacy

Before 1960, all but a very few empirical studies of criminal justice organizations were undertaken in the context of periodic "reform commissions" (Remmington, 1990; Walker, 1992). These commissions did not define their task as purely descriptive research, but rather in language taken from the critical legal studies movement, as bringing the "law in practice" into greater conformity with the "law on the books." That is, they examined actual criminal justice practices to determine how much those practices deviated from some prescriptive ideal. The deviation itself was assigned a negative moral evaluation: it was said to reflect corruption and/or incompetence. The goal of the reform commissions was to minimize deviations between real criminal justice practices and the prescriptive ideal, and thereby maximize the legitimacy of those practices.

The pre-ABF reform commissions attributed legitimacy entirely to the prescriptive ideal (the "law on the books"). The ABF studies were controversial and significant because they attributed some (but not all) legitimacy to actual criminal justice practices, even when those practices deviated from the ideal. The studies therefore posited two simultaneous and largely incompatible sources for legitimacy of criminal justice practices: the "law on the books" and pervasive discretion. The positing of a second source of legitimacy generated hostility and resistance, but it also opened the door to the study of criminal justice practices in their own right.

Closing the Gap Between Ideal and Real

Despite the shift in attribution of legitimacy, significant continuities existed between the pre-ABF reform commissions and the post-ABF academic field of criminal justice. The most significant was the overall goal of closing the gap between the ideal and the real in criminal justice. . . . [T]he goal of the pre-ABF reform commissions was to bring the real into greater conformity with the ideal. The ideal was viewed as an independent and stable reference point that defined legitimacy; thus the real was viewed as illegitimate insofar as it deviated from the ideal. Thus, for the pre-ABF reform commissions, closing the gap between the ideal and the real was to be accomplished *entirely by changing the reality of criminal justice practices to make them more like the ideal.* In contrast, the ABF interpretation of real criminal justice practices implied that the "law-in-practice" could have its own legitimacy and could deviate from the "law on the books" without necessarily being illegitimate and needing reform. Thus the "ideal" in criminal justice no longer was defined solely in terms of the "law on the books." Rather, it incorporated elements of the real world of criminal justice, the actual practices of criminal justice organizations.

Although the goal of the ABF studies still was to close the gap between the ideal and the real, they attempted to accomplish this *by changing both the ideal and the real in order to make each more like the other.* In part, like the earlier reform commissions, the ABF studies attempted to change the reality of criminal justice practices by bringing them into greater conformity with the ideal. Also in part, however, these studies attempted to change the prescriptive ideal to fit more closely the reality of criminal justice practices. That ideal was broadened to include the legitimate exercise of discretion, a concept taken from the reality of criminal justice practices. The gap between the ideal and the real would close when the two eventually met in the middle.

Polarization Theories: Official Conceptions Versus Actual Practices

In the 50 years since the ABF studies were conducted, the field of criminal justice has focused strongly on the real in criminal justice, and the ideal was faded into the background. But at least initially, in the years following the ABF studies and at least partially in response to the studies, the focus remained more on the gap between the real and the ideal, or on the relationship between the two, rather than on the real itself.

Specifically, in a number of theories that followed the ABF studies, the prescriptive ideal was transformed into something like 44 "official conceptions" of how criminal justice organizations are supposed to operate. These conceptions more or less described how criminal justice agents and administrators, as well as politicians, *described criminal justice practices in public discourse.* Therefore they also described, more or less, how the public thought criminal justice agents and organizations were supposed to behave. "Official conceptions" diverged markedly from the real practices of those agents and organizations: the real practices were concealed from the public and shrouded in secrecy. Criminal justice agents and politicians who publicly presented these "official conceptions" generally knew all about the real practices, so the secrecy had elements of a conspiracy.

A number of early theories that followed the ABF studies maintained the ABF position that both "official conceptions" and the reality of criminal justice practices had their own legitimacy. . . . In these theories, the argument was that both of the polarized conceptions were necessary for an understanding of criminal justice as a social phenomenon. Compared with the ABF studies, these studies placed greater emphasis on understanding the two sides of criminal justice and the gap between them, and less emphasis on the overt goal of closing that gap, despite an implicit sense that a thorough understanding eventually could lead to reduction or closure of the gap.

Observational Studies of Criminal Justice Organizations

"Polarization" theories were fairly global: they tended to encompass either the entire criminal justice system or at least entire component parts (e.g., police). The academic field of criminal justice moved rather quickly from these core global theories and began to focus on the more particular. The emphasis shifted from broad explanation to close observation and description. With this shift on focus, the goal of closing the gap between the ideal and real faded into the background, and attention moved strongly toward understanding the extraordinary complexity of criminal justice. Usually somewhere in the background was an unspoken assumption that a thorough understanding of the reality of criminal justice would lead to a reconciliation of the real with the ideal.

Initially most of these investigations were qualitative, observational, descriptive case studies of individual criminal justice organizations. [Researchers at the time] viewed the prescriptive ideal—"official conceptions" conveyed in public discourse on what was legitimate for criminal justice agents and organizations—as a greater problem than the reality of criminal justice practices. . . . Criminal justice scholars came down on the side of the real as opposed to the ideal, thus reversing the stance of the pre-ABF reform commissions. Yet the prescriptive ideal did not entirely disappear in these qualitative studies, as might be expected in a purely scientific endeavor. Rather, it remained in the background as a standard against which to hold the complex descriptions of the reality. . . . The studies both examined the reality of criminal justice practices and considered appropriate standards for legitimacy, given the complexity of that reality. Thus the field of criminal justice became increasingly complex both in its descriptions of reality and in its discussions of the prescriptive ideal.

Early Theories: Structure/Culture Socialization Versus Individual Typologies

The descriptive studies of criminal justice organizations introduced themes and posed questions that were the source of much later research and theory in criminal justice. One particular theoretical argument that emerged from these early observational studies can be described as a structure/culture/socialization argument. This argument proposed a structural explanation of organizational culture. The organizational culture in turn explained the characteristics of the criminal justice organization, while socialization into the culture explained the behavior of criminal justice agents.

This argument essentially explained why the reality of criminal justice practices diverged so much from the "official conceptions" of those practices. The answer, according to the argument, lay in the structured conditions of the work environment. Organizational realities faced by individual criminal justice agents tended to generate work practices that differed from the "official conceptions" but were similar to practices of other criminal justice agents. Those organizational realities and the resulting work practices generated similar patterns of thought among criminal justice agents; these then were shared and transmitted interpersonally, and became subcultural. The result was a cohesive community in which secrecy was used to conceal the gap between actual work practices and the "official conceptions" of those practices. Finally, socialization processes developed for incorporating new criminal justice agents into this secrecy-based community. These structure/culture/socialization arguments typically offered vague suggestions about how to close the gap, but primarily they described and explained the reality of criminal justice practices.

Quantitative Studies of Criminal Justice Agents' Behavior

Over time, criminal justice research became systematic and quantitative. Much larger numbers of observations were collected more systematically, often from several similar organizations (e.g., several police departments), and the data [were] analyzed quantitatively rather than interpreted in qualitative, descriptive fashion. . . . With systematic observation and quantitative analysis, the focus shifted to *the behavior of the individual criminal justice agent,* particularly decision making. . . . The research task now was to describe the complexity of the contextual influences on individual decision making. The criminal justice organization then became one of several types of variables that influenced the individual agent's behavior. . . .

These quantitative studies became the "bread and butter" of criminal justice research. . . . These quantitative studies seemed to abandon all "official conceptions" of what criminal justice agents *should be* doing and to focus entirely on describing and explaining what they actually *were* doing. Therefore they seemed to be purely descriptive and to bear little relation to the reformism that characterized the field at its beginning. Even so, prescriptive ideals about what criminal justice agents should be doing remained in the background of these studies, providing implicit value judgments about the legitimacy of what was observed and described.

Also important for our purposes, these studies reveal a continuing but quite subtle development in the complexity of the prescriptive ideal. The ABF studies had set that ideal in motion, so that it no longer was a static and unchanging "law on the books," but instead interacted with the reality of criminal justice practices. In the later polarized theories about the two sides of criminal justice and in the later observational studies of criminal justice organizations, the prescriptive ideal was made even more complex and more firmly grounded in reality, and yet (it was hoped) still capable of attributing legitimacy in public discourse. The systematic quantitative research studies on criminal justice agents' behavior continued that trend. While describing real criminal justice practices, the researchers asked, at least implicitly, "In the light of the complex realities they face, what *should* criminal justice agents and organizations be doing? What constitutes legitimacy in criminal justice?" The answers became increasingly complex.

The Explicit Return to Reformism

Armed with a large number of systematic observations of criminal justice agents' real behavior, as well as with complex and sophisticated interpretations of criminal justice organizations' functioning, criminal justice scholars proposed various entirely new conceptions of criminal justice practice that differed from the "official conceptions" and from the actual practices that were current at the time. These scholars essentially argued that their reform proposals were both realistic and legitimate. The reforms, they said, were realistic approaches to criminal justice that actually could be implemented.

Criminal justice agents no longer would be influenced by structural workload conditions to act in one way, and then pressured by highly divergent "official conceptions" to hide behind the secrecy of the occupational subculture. At the same time, these reforms were said to be legitimate enough to function as "official conceptions" for the purposes of public discourse by criminal justice agents and administrators, as well as politicians. Thus the new proposals were offered as ways to close the gap between the ideal and the real. They were offered as a way to make criminal justice practices more legitimate. Other arguments explaining the failure of reforms were primarily cultural. Studies associated with these arguments typically found no relationship between workload pressures and work practices. Instead the explanations for failure focused on the social norms of the occupational work groups. . . .

Aggregate-Level Studies of the Criminal Justice System and Its Components

Almost from the founding of the discipline, some studies in criminal justice have linked societal-level characteristics to the rates and distributions of criminal justice behaviors. This is a very different type of study than those which focus either on the behavior of individual criminal justice agents or on the behavior of the criminal justice organization as a functioning entity. . . . At an even broader level, many theories have focused on characteristics of the entire criminal justice system rather than on components of that system. Chambliss and Seidman (1971) presented a theory of "the law in action," using a conflict perspective. They suggested that law "can be understood only by considering the total social milieu of the persons whose behavior is supposed to conform to the rules and thus achieve the higher goals implicit in the rules" (p. 4).

Other aggregate-level theoretical arguments focus on criminal justice policy. In an examination of street crime and public policy, Scheingold (1984) described the influence of politics over policy making within the criminal justice system. He argued that divisions in society produce conflicts of both interest and value, and that these conflicts generate cleavages, resulting in the development of subcultures. Within the criminal

justice system, Scheingold's theory explains the political nature of policy making by describing organizational differences, changes in the political environment, and differences in criminal justice actors' attitudes and beliefs.

Also operating at the aggregate level but proposing even more complex independent variables, Hagan (1989) suggested that the lack of theory in criminal justice was due in part to the nature of the criminal justice system, which he and other scholars characterized as "loosely coupled" (Glassman, 1973; Meyer & Rowan, 1978). Hagan further suggested that theories of criminal justice should focus on the structure of criminal justice organizations, and the environments in which they operate. He provided a framework for a theory of criminal justice system operations that stresses the importance of examining political power and organizational forms through a set of premises and propositions.

Although all of these studies appear to be descriptive, they exist against the backdrop of prescriptive ideals that define legitimacy in one way or another. Studies linking imprisonment rates to aggregate-level economic characteristics such as unemployment or labor surplus are interesting precisely because such a linkage has the appearance of being illegitimate. Thus variables are interesting even if they explain relatively small portions of the variance. The prescriptive ideal is that imprisonment rates should be determined solely by legally relevant variables such as crime rates.

Discussion

Classifying theories first on the dependent variable and then on the independent variables increases conceptual clarity in discussions of criminal justice theory, allows different theories to be compared and contrasted with each other, and facilitates theory building through generalization. Some theories explain criminal justice agents' behavior by focusing on the individual characteristics of the agents themselves, including police officers (Broderick, 1977; Muir, 1977; White, 1972), attorneys (Carter, 1974; Jack & Jack, 1989; Mather, 1979), and correctional agents (Irwin, 1980; Kauffman, 1988; Rosecrance, 1988). These theories are comparable across criminal justice system components because one particular type of dependent variable (the behavior of individual agents) is explained by one particular type of independent variable (individual characteristics). Other theories explain individual criminal justice agents' behavior as socialized adaptations to the work environment (Blau, 1974; Blumberg, 1967; Cole, 1970; Feeley, 1973; Lipsky, 1980; Prottas, 1978; Skolnick, 1966). Again, these theories are comparable because one type of dependent variable (individual agents' behavior) is explained by one type of independent variable (socialization into a work environment).

This type of classification facilitates competitive testing and generalization across system components for these types of dependent and independent variables. In addition, competitive testing could address the relative explanatory power of the two types of independent variables: individual characteristics versus work socialization. Finally, such testing enables various kinds of theory building. . . .

The second type of dependent variable in our proposed organizational scheme is the behavior of criminal justice organizations as functioning entities. Classifying theories on this type of dependent variable allows comparisons based on the independent variables. For example, many theories explain criminal justice organizations' behavior in terms of the occupational cultures in those organizations. Police scholars generally recognize the work done in the area of police culture (Brown, 1981; Herbert, 1998; Manning, 1977; Skolnick, 1966; Westley, 1953, 1970), but this work is rarely linked to similar developments in courtroom work groups (Church, 1985; Eisenstein & Jacob, 1977) or to work describing the occupational culture of prison officials (Duffee, 1975; Hepburn, 1985; Lombardo, 1981; Marquart, 1986; Philliber, 1987; Toch & Klofas, 1982). In all of these theories, occupational cultures are said to arise from structural factors such as workload pressures or work conditions. Essentially these cultures are used to explain the behavior of organizational units such as police departments or courtroom work groups. Categorizing theories by dependent and independent variables, as opposed to the standard categorization by system components, would allow these theories to be generalized across system components, and would facilitate competitive testing of specific independent variables within this overall category.

Theories that explain organizational behavior in terms of occupational cultures obviously are similar to individual-level theories that explain the behavior of individual criminal justice agents in terms of socialization into the occupational culture. The difference between these two types of theories lies in differences in the dependent and the independent variables rather than in any contradiction or competition between the theories. In the individual-level theory, the dependent variable is the behavior of the individual agent; socialization into an occupational culture is the independent variable. In the organizational-level theory, the dependent variable is the behavior of the organizational unit, the intervening variable most often is the occupational culture (although sometimes this is the independent variable), and the independent variable most often is the set of structural conditions associated with the work.

Particularly with these two types of theories, the attempt to create a comprehensive picture of criminal justice realities leads some scholarly works to move back and forth among the various dependent variables. Although this practice is intuitively appealing, it can lead to confusion when the researcher is attempting to compare, competitively test, or generalize theories. In Wilson's (1968) study of police organizations and DiIulio's (1987) examination of prisons, for example, organizational behavior seems to be the primary dependent variable. At the same time, both of these theories explain criminal justice agents' behavior as a consequence of working for particular organizations. These theories also have implications about the overall characteristics of criminal justice components at the societal level, and to that extent they include aggregate-level as well as individual- and organization-level dependent variables. Recognizing that some theories can be applied across two or more types of dependent variables adds conceptual clarity and allows more specific comparison of research findings across theories and system components.

Additional confusion arises when the dependent variable is not distinguished clearly from the independent variable. In several theories that are described as theories of criminal justice, for example, criminal behavior is the dependent variable and criminal justice is the independent variable (e.g., Gorecki, 1979; Gross, 1971). We exclude these theories from the present analysis because we regard them as theories of criminal behavior rather than as theories of criminal justice.

In general, our proposed organization captures and organizes most of the theory and research described above in the interpretive history of criminal justice as an academic field. A continuing theme throughout that history, however, is the role of the prescriptive ideal in defining legitimacy for criminal justice. This ideal is more explicit in the earlier studies, but even in the later studies it exists in the background as a standard for measuring real criminal justice practices. Criminal justice scholars, we recommend, must recognize that their discipline inevitably includes a prescriptive dimension, which itself is always undergoing change in an interactive relationship with real criminal justice practices. Thus we suggest that this dimension be included explicitly for each type of dependent variable.

By acknowledging and making explicit the prescriptive dimension, we can incorporate into the field of criminal justice various other theories that focus exclusively on that dimension. For example, numerous scholars have advanced theories that describe and analyze the concept of justice as a philosophical orientation and explain the moral and social components of justice within societies (i.e., Barry, 1989; Gross, 1971; Rawls, 1971, 1999). These theories provide the grounding for prescriptive ideals related to aggregate-level characteristics of the criminal justice system overall. Similarly, theories of the philosophy of punishment (e.g., Hudson, 1996; Tunick, 1992) focus on the nature and content of prescriptive ideals for correctional systems.

CONCLUSION: LESSONS FROM CRIMINOLOGY

We believe that the best way to organize criminal justice theory is to categorize it on the basis of the dependent variable. There are three general types of dependent variables: the individual behavior of criminal justice agents, the organizational behavior of criminal justice organizations, and the aggregate behavior of the criminal justice system and its components as a whole. Once theories have been classified on the basis of their dependent variables, it is possible to sort and organize by independent variables. This organization of theory promotes conceptual clarity, allows generalization across system components, and permits competitive testing of theories in criminal

justice; all of these benefits will advance criminal justice as a scientific enterprise.

Our approach is similar to the approach to criminology theory taken by Bernard and Snipes (1996; also see Vold, Bernard, & Snipes, 1998). According to Bernard and Snipes, the scientific process provides that theory will always exist in a context of research, [and] the ultimate criterion for theory is usefulness to research, just as the ultimate criterion for research is usefulness to theory. Theory can achieve utility for research more successfully by conceptualizing its goal as identifying variables and recognizing the order and organization among these variables. In a more policy-oriented phrase, the utility of theory is best achieved by identifying the sources of independent variation for precise dependent variables.

Bernard and Snipes therefore argue that the most important variable is the dependent variable, and that it should be the basis for sorting and classifying theories of criminology. Conceptual confusion arises when criminologists classify or categorize theories by the independent variables (e.g., biology, psychology, economics, social disorganization, strain, control, learning), even though this approach is intuitively appealing. The problem is that classifying theories on the independent variables implicitly assumes a single dependent variable, whereas in fact criminology involves multiple dependent variables. Bernard and Snipes describe three types of variables in criminology: individual criminal behavior, the rates and distributions of criminal behavior in social units, and the behavior of criminal law. Each type includes many quite specific variables, all of which can be linked to particular independent variables and to particular orders or organizations of those variables. For each dependent variable, multiple causal factors are described by multiple theories that compete with one another over explained variation. This approach is highly integrative as compared with standard interpretations, in which different theories contradict each other, so that only one theory can survive competitive testing while the others are falsified on the basis of statistical significance. In our approach, because the competition concerns explained variation, theories are not falsified, although they may be found to possess so little utility (account for so little variation) that they can be discarded.

All of these points, in our view, apply to criminal justice theory. We believe, however, that criminology and criminal justice theories differ in two major respects. First, criminology originated as sweepingly discursive general theories (Gibbs, 1985) and has worked its way, with difficulty, towards phrasing those theories in such a way that research could test them adequately. Criminal justice, on the other hand, originated as descriptive research, in which theory, insofar as it existed at all, was highly specific and focused on the particular topic at hand. Over the last 50 years, criminal justice has been working its way, with difficulty, towards theory.

The second difference, we believe, is that criminal justice theories retain implicit or explicit prescriptive ideals. Criminal justice scholars should acknowledge explicitly that their work exists against a backdrop of attributions of legitimacy. This legitimacy standard is not a disembodied, static entity but is constructed in a constant, interactive relationship with the reality of criminal justice as revealed by our research. Our field has been both descriptive and prescriptive since it was founded; it cannot be understood fully without an acknowledgment of its prescriptive elements.

Discussion Questions

1. Why has developing a sound, cohesive theory of criminal justice been so problematic?

2. What are some ways in which the field of criminal justice can be organized within a historical framework?

3. Why do the authors feel that classifying the theories first on the dependent variable and then on the independent variable will better facilitate criminal justice theory making in general?

4. What can criminal justice scholars learn from the field of criminology?

PART II

Biological and Psychological Theories of Crime

Biological Theories

Although the classical theories of Bentham and Beccaria helped shape criminal justice policy in Europe in the late 18th and 19th centuries, they did little to affect the ever-rising crime rates. Crime statistics became available in France in 1827 and demonstrated a fairly consistent rate of crime with slight community variation (Vold, Bernard, & Snipes, 1998). Although the consistency in the crime rates countered the notion of free will, which might have led to some rate fluctuations, it supported the classical theorists' claim that crime is influenced by a combination of free will and societal factors. The hope of these theorists was that if they changed these factors, crime rates would decline.

But this was not the case, as the statistics illustrated. Although the crime rate remained constant, it did not go down. In response to the inability of the classical policy to control crime, a new approach to studying crime—positivist criminology—emerged. The goal of positivism was to study the causes of crime at the individual and societal levels.

In the realm of criminology, positivism sought to discover what it was about individuals that caused them to commit crimes. Although positivism centered mainly on individuals, it also applied to society-level factors as they contributed to criminality. Biological theories emerged primarily in the 1870s, although positivist roots stem back to the beginning of the 19th century through the work of Andre-Michel Guerry (1802-1866) and Adolphe Quetelet (1796-1874), whose focus on statistics shaped future empirical approaches to crime. Shortly after the publication of the first modern national crime statistics in 1827, Guerry, a lawyer and later director of criminal statistics for the French Ministry of Justice, published what many consider to be the first work in "scientific criminology" (Vold et al., 1998). In his work, Guerry used shaded ecological maps that represented differing crime rates as they related to a variety of social factors (Vold et al., 1998). Guerry's main contributions to criminology centered on his study of the relationships between poverty and crime and between a lack of education and crime. He found that, in terms of poverty, the key factor was opportunity. The crime rates were higher in the wealthiest areas of France because those areas offered more to steal (but those areas also had a lot of poverty). In terms of education, he found interesting results, which suggested that areas with the highest education levels also had the highest crime rates, whereas the opposite was true for the lowest education levels.

Quetelet, a Belgian mathematician and philosopher, incorporated the use of *social mechanics,* or statistical techniques, to analyze social data such as the number of births and deaths in a given year. In general, Quetelet maintained that crime was an inevitable feature of social organization; he identified different areas of France that increased or decreased the likelihood of criminal behavior. His findings did not differ very much from Guerry's. He also concluded that the propensity to engage in criminal behavior was really a reflection of one's moral character. Although Quetelet felt that to a large extent individuals freely choose to behave in certain ways, he held on to the view that crime was basically caused by "moral defectiveness" (Vold et al., 1998, pp. 31-32). He argued further that moral defectiveness revealed itself in biological physiology, thereby laying the groundwork for another important biological determinist, Cesare Lombroso (1835-1909) of the Italian School.

Biological approaches were the dominant theories of crime at the turn of the 20th century, led primarily by Lombroso. Heavily influenced by Darwin's theory of evolution, Lombroso argued that criminals were genetic throwbacks, or *atavistic*. They were primitive people in a modern era. In his study of the cadavers of inmates in the Italian penal system, Lombroso, a physician there, extended the traditions of physiognomy and phrenology by studying all of the anatomical features of the human body, not solely the face and shape of the skull. Lombroso found that all of the inmates he examined possessed a significant number of characteristics that resembled those of primitive people. These features included mainly a swollen head and face, unusually small ears, protruding lips, abnormal teeth, excessive hair and wrinkling over their bodies, long arms (disproportionate to their height), extra fingers or toes, and asymmetry of the brain (Vold et al., 1998). Based on his findings, he claimed that these atavistic individuals were "born criminals."

Lombroso's theory and other early biological theories were relatively simplistic: "Atavistic," abnormal physiology will lead directly to crime. But the theory generated powerful reactions, both favorable and unfavorable. Challengers subjected the findings to rigorous scientific review several years later, with researchers comparing the traits of criminals with carefully matched noncriminals. However, such comparisons yielded little support for biological theories of crime. In addition, there was concern for the policy implications of these approaches, such as selective breeding, sterilization, and support for eugenic policies, and therefore biological theories of crime fell into disrepute and eventual decline.

In an interesting theoretical twist, the core elements of biological theories were subsequently modified and diffused into more acceptable multicausal theories of crime, namely social causes. These elements later emerged through the work of criminal anthropologists, in physical constitution theories, and later in the notions of "feeblemindedness" and "mental defect," which linked delinquency with delayed mental capacities (offenders were labeled "defective delinquents").

A recent interest in biological theories has developed within the past 15 years or so, but these new approaches distinguish themselves from earlier approaches in a number of ways. First, the most recent biological theories focus on a vast spectrum of biological factors, including genetic inheritance, environmental factors (i.e., head injuries and toxins such as lead poisoning), and reproductive conditions. Second, these theories do not claim that biology leads to crime or that a "crime gene" exists. Instead, the theories assert that biological factors influence crime, to the extent that individuals learn to behave, by shaping the development of particular traits that are more conducive to crime than others. Last, biological theories recognize the importance of the social environment in relation to individual development. These theories maintain that the social environment shapes the development of certain traits and determines whether these traits will lead to crime.

The selection by Diana H. Fishbein (Chapter 4, this volume) provides an excellent overview of the various recent biological theories of crime. She asserts that data being generated from various biological sciences, such as behavioral genetics, physiological psychology, psychopharmacology, and endocrinology, indicate that biological factors do play a significant role in the development of antisocial behavior and merit serious evaluation.

In sum, contemporary biological theories recognize the importance of social and psychological variables in the shaping of criminal or noncriminal behavior. In a related section of this anthology, readers should direct their attention to the contributions by those writing in the area of developmental criminology (Loeber & Stouthamer-Loeber, Chapter 33, this volume; Moffitt, Chapter 32, this volume) as well as the selection by Walsh (Chapter 36, this volume) in the integrated theories subsection. Although they all could have been placed within a "biological theories" category, I feel that those articles stand better on their own in their respective subsections. This decision was based, in part, on the newly emerging area of developmental criminology and the highly integrated approach that Walsh takes in his work.

PSYCHOLOGICAL THEORIES

Psychological approaches gained popularity at the turn of the 20th century, but like biological theories, they were quickly overshadowed by the dominance of sociological theories of crime. The development of a psychological theory in relation to crime originated with the notion of uncovering hidden unconscious forces within a person's psyche. Although he produced little work on crime and criminals, Sigmund Freud (1856-1939) is frequently cited as the founder of this approach to crime. Freud was interested in explaining all types of behaviors, including crime. He is best known for his invention of "psychoanalysis." Psychoanalysis is centered on the concept of free association, in which the patient talks freely about whatever comes to mind (Vold et al., 1998). Freud thought that this process of free association would tap into the patient's unconscious and enable the patient to reconstruct events of the past. Once aware of these earlier events, patients could gain an understanding of and control over their present circumstances (Vold et al., 1998).

The main idea is that all behavior is motivated and aimed at a distinct purpose. Because not all behaviors are socially approved, they need to be repressed into the subconscious for the preservation of moral decency and social order. Freud outlined the ensuing tensions within the id, a source of biological and psychological urges; the ego, the source of conscious control; and the superego, which acts as a self-criticizing mechanism, keeping the person's behavior in line with appropriate moral and social standards. Under the psychoanalytic theory, crime is the expression of inner tensions and urges each person has but that the criminal fails to restrain.

A number of Freud's colleagues used his psychoanalytic theory in their research on criminals and delinquents. For example, Alexander and Healy (1935) explained criminality in terms of attempts to relieve guilt; overcompensation for perceived inferiority; negative, spiteful feelings toward mothers; and a focus on instant gratification (Lilly, Cullen, & Ball, 2001).

Aichorn (1936) also wrote that certain children never matured because of a failure in their ability to develop an ego and a superego that would make them conform to age-related expectations (Lilly et al., 2001). Finally, Friedlander (1949) examined the behavior of children and asserted that some children develop antisocial behavior, which makes them prone to delinquency.

The psychoanalytic theory and its application to crime have been criticized in a number of different ways. One criticism concerns the theory's untestability, although some psychoanalysts claim that Freud's ideas can be formulated into testable hypotheses (Vold et al., 1998). A second criticism lies with the fact that a psychoanalytic explanation of a person's behavior is highly subjective. A more specific criticism concerns the application of this theory to crime and criminality. The theory contends that crime is caused, in part, by unconscious tensions that develop in a family environment at different stages of development. This explanation may fit crimes that stem from irrational behavior, but most crimes emerge out of a conscious, rational thinking process. Consequently, psychoanalysis has not been very successful in helping people to understand criminality (Vold et al., 1998).

Since Freud, psychology has diverged along numerous and varied paths. Psychology repeatedly acknowledges the importance of environmental influences on learning, interpretation, and analysis of complex information. For example, Pavlov and B. F. Skinner's theories of classical and operant conditioning shaped behavioral and situational learning approaches to crime and delinquency. Based on the idea of "learning by association," the objective was to see whether an accumulation of positive or negative responses resulting from past learning influenced a person's present behavior.

Like biological theories, psychological theories are enjoying a resurgence in popularity, though two strains of psychological theory remain dominant today: theories that focus on individual traits and those that emphasize the processes by which individuals learn to behave under certain circumstances. Because this anthology does not directly address these psychological approaches, for thorough overviews of these perspectives, readers should consult the works of Allport (1937), Andrews and Bonta (1994), Blackburn (1993), Cleckley (1976), Farrington (1994), Feldman (1993), Glueck and Glueck (1950), Hollin (1989, 1992), Redl and Toch (1979), Schuessler and Cressey (1950), and Shoham and Seis (1993).

Special Focus: Evolutionary Psychology

This anthology takes a different turn once again to focus on a newly emerging approach to psychology, evolutionary psychology. This approach uses knowledge and principles from modern Darwinian theories in research on the human psyche. According to this perspective, the mind consists of a "rich array of information-processing mechanisms that were designed by natural selection to solve adaptive problems that were recurrent in hominid evolution" (Rode & Wang, 2000, p. 926). In general, the primary objective of evolutionary psychology is to explain psychological processes as biological adaptations (de Jong & van der Steen, 1998). For instance, evolutionary psychologists would contend that our thoughts and feelings evolved from certain mechanisms that have, over time, enhanced human survival. These survival-enhancing traits include personality, love and affection, parental care, social behavior and the origins of morals, and reasoning and decision-making skills (de Jong & van der Steen, 1998). Proponents of this perspective extol it as an extension of evolutionary biology, bringing psychology within the growing body of integrated approaches toward explaining human thought processes and behavior, although there is some debate as to whether evolutionary psychology provides satisfactory or appropriate integration with biology (de Jong & van der Steen, 1998).

A brief discussion of the historical background of evolutionary psychology merits consideration. Two major periods of history have been influenced by biological thought, especially Darwinian evolutionary theory. The first period, identified as "social Darwinism," lasted from 1850 to 1914, and the second wave, referred to as "sociobiology," began in the 1970s. Another label that characterizes this general approach includes "neo-social Darwinism," which draws parallels between the two movements (Dawson, 1999). In the early 20th century, social Darwinism lost much of its popularity because of the critical

acceptance of Mendelian genetics, which discredited the idea that acquired traits might be heritable. At this time, biologists also became fully aware of the problems associated with group selection and altruistic behaviors. They found it increasingly difficult to explain group behavior in classical Darwinian terms (i.e., principles of natural selection, which encourage behaviors and processes that work to promote the fitness of *individuals* and *organisms* for survival and reproduction) because behaviors that lead individuals to sacrifice themselves for the benefit of the group are, or should be, anti-Darwinian (Dawson, 1999). History has documented numerous times when the fittest humans exhibited extreme altruism (i.e., warfare).

The reaction against social Darwinism began with sociologists, namely Emile Durkheim, who argued that social phenomena constitute a system completely autonomous from other natural phenomena and can only be explained in terms of other social phenomena. Anthropologists defined *culture* in Durkheimian terms and promoted the idea of *cultural determinism* over that of *biological determinism*. This notion later formed the basis for the "standard social science model" (SSSM), because it became so pervasive in the social sciences, humanities, and cultural theory for much of the 20th century.

Despite the reign of the SSSM, social Darwinism emerged again in the 1970s under the term *sociobiology*. At this time, a neo-Darwinian synthesis emerged that made it possible to explain group selection and the evolution of animal, and human, social behavior. At this time, William Hamilton, a British biologist, developed a theory that demonstrated the operation of *inclusive fitness*, which stipulates that natural selection promotes the survival and reproduction not only of individuals but also of their close relatives, who share much of the same genetic legacy (Dawson, 1999). Hamilton based his theory on the study of social insects (who demonstrate peculiar cooperative behavior), but his approach was applied in other contexts as well in order to demonstrate that genealogical relatedness is not required for group selection, especially in the more intelligent species. In other words, mechanisms for social reciprocity can evolve between unrelated organisms and even unrelated species. In terms of the fate of altruists, who according to classical Darwinian theory of natural selection should die off, they can flourish by associating with other altruists. In other words, a population may evolve a system of rewards and punishments to encourage altruistic traits. The benefits of altruism would then be reaped without incurring the costs, thereby demonstrating natural selection or group selection.

Evolutionary psychology has been used recently to explain a number of phenomena, including warfare and group selection (Dawson, 1999). For example, Dawson explains that *ethno-centricity*, which means that humans have a tendency to form exclusive groups that close their ranks against outsiders, is a heritable trait that is at the root of warfare and that is the principal catalyst in human evolution. This notion of the "genetic seeds of warfare" suggests that human beings are strongly predisposed to respond with unreasonable hatred to external threats and to escalate their hostility to such a degree that it overwhelms the sources of the threat by a sufficient buffer of safety. This notion contradicts psychological theories of behavior and the SSSM, which both essentially maintain that nearly all of our traits and behaviors are learned (i.e., culturally based), not preprogrammed.

Evolutionary psychologists propose an alternative model of inherited psychological mechanisms of adaptation, or thinking of the mind as "an intricate network of functionally dedicated computers" with specialized mechanisms and cues that evolved to handle certain adaptive problems of the various epochs. Suggesting a distinction between "adopted culture" and "evoked culture," an evolutionary psychology model proposes that a certain body of mental content is learned and reconstructed in our minds (adopted culture), whereas other mechanisms lie dormant in the mind until brought forth when needed (evoked culture) (Dawson, 1999).

Evolutionary psychology has also been used to better understand the issues of genocide and xenophobia. The reading selection in this section by Augustine Brannigan (Chapter 5) applies the principles of evolutionary psychology to the problems of genocide and xenophobia. More specifically, Brannigan uses the evolutionary psychology framework to examine issues surrounding the Holocaust. Raising similar issues as Dawson (1999), Brannigan suggests that ethnocentrism and xenophobia have evolved as adaptive scripts among certain groups. He asserts that

the collective act of genocide that occurred in Nazi Germany emerged as a result of a pervasive and elaborate racist belief system about human differences that evolved over time and that revealed itself during the 1930s and 1940s. As Brannigan points out, evolutionary psychology provides a unique framework for criminologists to use to explore crime, especially those crimes in which violence and aggression play a significant role, as well as in terms of the widespread collective violence that is occurring presently in our world.

REFERENCES

Aichorn, A. (1936). *Wayward youth*. New York: Viking.

Alexander, F., & Healy, W. (1935). *Roots of crime*. New York: Knopf.

Allport, G. (1937). *Personality: A psychological explanation*. New York: Holt.

Andrews, D. A., & Bonta, J. (1994). *The psychology of criminal conduct*. Cincinnati, OH: Anderson.

Blackburn, R. (1993). *The psychology of criminal conduct*. Chichester, UK: Wiley.

Cleckley, H. (1976). *The mask of sanity*. St. Louis, MO: C. V. Mosby.

Dawson, D. (1999). Evolutionary theory and group selection: The question of warfare. *History and Theory, 38*, 79-100.

de Jong, H. L., & van der Steen, W. J. (1998). Biological thinking in evolutionary psychology: Rockbottom or quicksand? *Philosophical Psychology, 11*, 183-205.

Farrington, D. P. (Ed.). (1994). *Psychological explanations of crime*. Dartmouth, UK: Aldershot.

Feldman, P. (1993). *The psychology of crime*. Cambridge, UK: Cambridge University Press.

Friedlander, K. (1949). Latent delinquency and ego development. In K. R. Eissler (Ed.), *Searchlights on delinquency*. New York: International University Press.

Glueck, S., & Glueck, E. (1950). *Unraveling juvenile delinquency*. New York: Commonwealth Fund.

Hollin, C. (1989). *Psychology of crime*. London: Routledge.

Hollin, C. (1992). *Criminal behavior: A psychological approach to explanation and prevention*. London: Falmer Press.

Lilly, R. J., Cullen, F. T., & Ball, R. A. (2001). *Criminological theory: Context and consequences* (3rd ed.). Thousand Oaks, CA: Sage.

Redl, F., & Toch, H. (1979). The psychoanalytic perspective. In H. Toch (Ed.), *Psychology of crime and criminal justice* (pp. 183-197). New York: Holt, Rinehart & Winston.

Rode, C., & Wang, X. T. (2000). Risk-sensitive decision making examined within an evolutionary framework. *American Behavioral Scientist, 43*, 926-939.

Schuessler, K. F., & Cressey, D. R. (1950). Personality characteristics of criminals. *American Journal of Sociology, 55*, 476-484.

Shoham, S. G., & Seis, M. (1993). *A primer in the psychology of crime*. New York: Harrow and Heston.

Vold, G. B., Bernard, T. J., & Snipes, J. B. (1998). *Theoretical criminology* (4th ed.). Oxford, UK: Oxford University Press.

4

BIOLOGICAL PERSPECTIVES IN CRIMINOLOGY

DIANA H. FISHBEIN

EDITOR'S INTRODUCTION—Starting in the early 1920s, biological theories of crime began to fade into the shadows of the growing popularity of sociological perspectives. Never completely disappearing, biological theories of causality existed on the theoretical periphery, sometimes emerging with intriguing findings of crime causality, ranging from chromosomes (XYY) to hormones as culpable inner forces that supposedly drive people to commit crime. Nonetheless, the most prominent biological theorists today tend to focus on a wide array of potential forces, namely genetic, typically using studies of twins and adoptees to demonstrate genetic effects.

The article by Diana H. Fishbein illustrates the fact that contemporary biological theorists are taking a more sophisticated approach to the issue of crime and its biological and genetic roots, suggesting not only that genes interact with the environment to affect human behavior, but that even when they do make an impact, they only account for part of that effect. In her extensive review of a variety of theoretical and methodological contributions, Fishbein examines and assesses the contributions of biological "markers" in shaping the behavior of the most vulnerable or persistent antisocial offenders. She determines that biological contributions alone cannot satisfactorily explain these effects. Rather, she argues for a multidisciplinary approach that considers data being generated from numerous biological sciences, such as behavioral genetics, physiological psychology, psychopharmacology, and endocrinology, which are making significant contributions to the understanding of the role of biosocial and genetic factors in criminality.

Fishbein couches her theoretical assessment in terms of particular theoretical and methodological parameters that she says are critical to the framing of the issues in biological research. More specifically, she states that the four requirements for multidisciplinary investigation in criminology, which are contingent on the assumptions of the research, include (a) the establishment of the relevancy of biology to the study of crime; (b) the development of the groundwork for including biological data in criminological theories; (c) the design of research projects that use compatible measurement instruments, data sets, and statistical techniques; and (d) the determination of the boundaries of practical applications of biological findings, mainly in the criminal justice arena. Issues pertinent to biological theorists include "nature versus nurture, free will versus determinism, identifying relevant behavioral disorders and subject populations, assumptions and conceptual framework, and finally, methodological considerations" (p. 43, this volume).

Readers will likely find Fishbein's contribution to be extremely important and relevant to their understanding of further developments in this area, especially with respect to other works included later in this volume that address biological theoretical concerns (i.e., Moffitt [Chapter 32] on life-course psychology and adolescent-persistent and -nonpersistent antisocial behavior; Loeber & Stouthamer-Loeber [Chapter 33] on developmental criminology; and Walsh [Chapter 36] on behavior genetics and anomie/strain theory).

Wilson and Herrnstein (1985) recently published a massive evaluation of the implications of biological data for topics of interest to criminologists. Their message is that insufficient consideration has been given to biological and social interactions in criminological studies. Consistent observations that a small percentage of offenders are responsible for a preponderance of serious crime (Hamparin et al., 1978; Moffitt et al., 1989; Wolfgang [et al.], 1972) suggest that particular forces produce antisocial behavior in particular individuals. Further, much research shows that violent criminals have an early history of crime and aggression (Loeber & Dishion, 1983; Moffitt et al., 1989). The possibility that biological conditions may play a role in the development of antisocial and criminal behavior is accentuated by these reports and has spurred a search for biological markers in "vulnerable" subgroups (Mednick et al., 1987).

In the past, theories of the biological aspects of criminal behavior were marked by a general lack of knowledge regarding the human brain and by serious methodological shortcomings (see, e.g., Glueck & Glueck, 1956; Goddard, 1921; Hooten, 1939; Jacobs et al., 1965; Lombroso, 1918; Sheldon, 1949). Indeed, "biological criminology" was eventually discredited because findings were largely unscientific, simplistic, and unicausal. Biological facts were globally rejected due to the inability of theorists to posit a rational explanation for the development of criminal behavior. More recently, biological aspects of criminal behavior have been investigated by numerous behavioral scientists employing a multidisciplinary approach that promises to enhance substantially the rigor of the findings. Scientists in such fields as genetics, biochemistry, endocrinology, neuroscience,

immunology, and psychophysiology have been intensively studying aspects of human behavior that are relevant to the criminologist and the criminal justice practitioner. Due to the highly technical and field-specific language of much of this research, findings generated from these works are not usually included in the literature reviews of criminologists. The relative lack of interdisciplinary communication has resulted in a lack of awareness of data pertinent to the study of crime and criminal behavior. This chapter is a small step toward filling that gap.

The primary purpose of this article is to present an overview of biological perspectives on the study of crime. Once acquainted with the parameters and findings of biological research, criminologists may begin to incorporate reliable biological aspects of criminal behavior into their theoretical and applied frameworks. Specific findings in biology are presented for criminologists to consider. Although the paper provides only an initial, condensed introduction to the vast amount of work accomplished in the behavioral sciences, it may help develop a sound, scientific, and pragmatic framework for future criminological research with a multidisciplinary orientation.

THEORETICAL AND METHODOLOGICAL PARAMETERS

Several critical issues must be addressed in order to (1) establish the relevancy of biology to the study of crime, (2) develop the groundwork for including biological data in criminological theories, (3) design research projects using compatible measurement instruments, data sets, and statistical techniques, and (4) determine the boundaries of practical applications of biological findings. These four requirements for

Fishbein, D. H. (1990). Biological perspectives in criminology. *Criminology, 28,* 27-72.

multidisciplinary investigation in criminology are contingent on the assumptions and paradigm of the researcher, which have yet to be set forth adequately in the criminological literature. Pertinent issues include nature versus nurture, free will versus determinism, identifying relevant behavioral disorders and subject populations, assumptions and conceptual framework, and finally, methodological considerations. The discussion of these issues that follows may be opposed or modified by other criminologists with a biological orientation. This discussion [is] not intended as the last word, but rather as one of the first.

NATURE OR NURTURE?

The first issue that must be addressed before the parameters of biological research in criminology can be established is the age-old question of whether human behavior is a product of nature or nurture. Theoreticians of the past generally espoused one or the other viewpoint. Those who claim that nature contributes predominantly to an individual's behavior have been affiliated in the past with conservative political ideologies and were known as "hereditarians." In this circle, behavior was primarily attributed to inherited predispositions, and genetic influences were considered responsible for most of the variance in complex human behaviors. . . . These opposing views are reflected in past political and social movements, such as *radical behaviorism* and *social Darwinism,* many of which have had devastating social and scientific consequences. The concept of *predatory ethics,* couched in the possibility of the state's punitive sanctioning of "unacceptable" or merely predicted future behaviors, eventually contributed to a complete rejection of biological perspectives by many scientists and their sponsors. The threat of "control and oppression by science" was realized and feared. Few behavioral scientists today adhere to either of these extreme views [i.e., that behavior is determined solely by nature or nurture]. A consensus has been emerging over the past 10 to 15 years that the "truth" lies somewhere in between—a "nature plus nurture" perspective (see Plomin, 1989).

Evidence for an interaction between nature and nurture comes from both animal and clinical studies, which demonstrate the strength and importance of the dynamic link between biological and acquired traits. . . . [A]s evidence for a substantial genetic influence grows we must be cautious not to replace environmental explanations with biological deterministic views. Instead, a more accommodating, balanced approach will carry more empirical weight.

FREE WILL OR DETERMINISM?

The acceptance of biological explanations for human behavior has been thought by many to preclude the possibility of free will. This fundamental fear has resulted in a pervasive rejection of biological contributions to behavior. Although some behavioral scientists are deterministic in their views, attributing behavior to everything from socioeconomic conditions to neurochemical events, most individuals prefer to credit their own free will for their behavior. A compromise reflecting a more accurate position on the forces behind human behavior is widely accepted, however—the theory of "conditional free will" (see Denno, 1988, for discussion of "degree determinism," a related view). . . .

. . . . The principle of conditional free will does not demand a deterministic view of human behavior. Rather, it postulates that individuals choose a course of action within a preset, yet to some degree changeable, range of possibilities and that, assuming the conditions are suitable for rational thought, we are accountable for our actions. Given "rational" thought processes, calculation of risks versus the benefits, and the ability to judge the realities that exist, the result is likely to be an adaptive response, that is, the behavior will be beneficial for the individual and the surrounding environment.

This theory of conditional free will predicts that if one or more conditions to which the individual is exposed are disturbed or irregular, the individual is more likely to choose a disturbed or irregular course of action. Thus, the risk of such a response increases as a function of the number of deleterious conditions. For example, a child with a learning disability may function well in society. With the addition of family instability, lack of appropriate educational programs, and a delinquent peer group, however, the learning-disabled child may be more prone to maladaptive behavior, which may, in turn, result in actions society has defined as criminal. The child's range of possible decisions has, in other words, been altered.

IDENTIFYING BEHAVIORS AND POPULATIONS FOR STUDY

. . . . The term *criminality* includes behaviors that do not necessarily offend all members of society, such as certain so-called victimless acts, and it excludes behaviors that may be antisocial or illegal but that are not detected by the criminal justice system. *Maladaptivity* includes antisocial behaviors that are costly to citizens and society overall. Such behaviors do not necessarily violate legal norms or come to official attention, however. Individuals who display maladaptive behavior do have a high probability of being labeled as delinquent or criminal, but being so labeled is not a sufficient criterion to be identified as maladaptive. . . . Criminal behavior is not exclusively maladaptive or dysfunctional behavior; thus, biological theories are differentially relevant to various forms of criminality. Biological findings in behavioral research are of particular interest for the study and management of maladaptive behaviors, both criminal and undetected behaviors that are detrimental to individuals so affected or their milieu. This paper focuses on maladaptive behaviors that may place an individual at risk for criminal stigmatization, in particular violent criminal behavior.

CONCEPTUAL FRAMEWORK

. . . . Individuals are not inherently criminal, nor do they suddenly become homicidal maniacs (except under unusual circumstances). Antisocial behavior has many precursors. Manifestations of a problem are frequently observed in childhood when innate tendencies toward antisocial behavior or other risk factors are compounded by suboptimal environmental and social conditions (Denno, 1988; Lewis et al., 1979, 1985; Mednick et al., 1984). These early seeds of maladaptive behavior are commonly ignored, inappropriately treated, or not recognized as complications that warrant intervention. In such cases, the severity of the condition and resultant behaviors are well advanced by adolescence and adulthood. According to this "developmental course" model of human behavior, criminal behavior is

virtually always secondary to an underlying problem(s) . . .

One straightforward example of this process, which pervades the criminological literature, is the link between IQ or learning disabilities and delinquent/criminal behavior. Children with conduct disorders tend to have lower IQ scores than nondeviant controls (Huesmann et al., 1984; Kellam et al., 1975; Lewis et al., 1981; Robins, 1966). Several investigators (Huesmann et al., 1984; Kellam et al., 1975; Olweus, 1979; Richman et al., 1982) have reported that an antecedent factor(s) contributes to both difficulties independently. Probable conditions that may antedate both low IQ and conduct disorder are parental psychopathology, temperamental disturbances, neurological problems, genetic susceptibilities, and disadvantageous environmental influences (Shonfeld et al., 1988). . . . Although low IQ or a learning disability is not inherently criminogenic, in the absence of proper intervention the child may become frustrated attempting to pursue mainstream goals without the skills to achieve them. . . .

Once the individual attracts the attention of the criminal justice system, the problem is already significantly compounded and difficult to treat, and the costs to society are exorbitant. Evidence for the existence of a developmental phenomenon in antisocial behavior highlights the dire need for early detection and intervention. The earlier the intervention, the more favorable the outcome (Kadzin, 1987). The learning process as it contributes to behavior cannot be underestimated in this model because, fundamentally, both biological and social behavior are learned. Biological traits and proclivities are not stationary characteristics; they are reinforced or, in some cases, altered through social learning processes. . . .

Humans are equipped with the innate biological capacity to learn as a product of their genetic blueprint, which is physically expressed in the structure of the brain. When an individual is exposed to a stimulus from the internal (biological) or external (social) environment, permanent changes occur in the neural structure and biochemical function of the brain. This process is referred to as "memory," experiences coded and stored for retrieval in the form of chemical transformations. . . . When stimuli are received and remembered, all future behaviors are modified, and perception will be subsequently altered. Thus, humans interrelate current experiences with information previously learned, and the future response to an equivalent stimulus may be different. The integrity of each of the above activities determines whether the learning experience will result in accurately encoded memories to produce an appropriate behavioral response.

The learning process of comparing new information with memories to produce a response frequently results in "behavioral conditioning." There is an innate foundation for learning in our biological structure that sets contingencies for behavioral conditioning in an individual, consistent with the premise of conditional free will. Consequently, behavioral sequences are neither programmed nor innate; they are acquired. The two forms of behavioral conditioning, classical and instrumental, both directly involve biological mechanisms. Classical conditioning refers to the response elicited by a neutral stimulus that has been associated with the acquisition of a reward or the avoidance of harm; for example, a white laboratory coat is associated with food and elicits salivation or viewing drug paraphernalia elicits craving for a drug.

When an individual is instrumental in causing a stimulus to occur, operant or instrumental conditioning is at work. The stimulus being elicited either satiates a drive or permits one to avoid a noxious result. . . . Certain behaviors are reinforced when the following conditions exist: (1) the behavior and the stimulus occur together in time and space (continuity), (2) repetition of the association strengthens the conditioned response, (3) the result either evokes pleasure or relieves pain, and (4) there is no interference, as in the form of new experiences, to weaken or extinguish the response. The concept of deterrence is founded on these principles.

In general, the criminal justice system relies on the association made between specific, in this case illegal, behaviors and the application of a painful or punitive sanction, which generally involves the removal of certain freedoms and exposure to unpleasant living conditions. The painful stimulus must be temporally associated with the behavior, consistently applied, and intense enough to prevent further such behaviors. According to the fourth condition listed above, the individual must not learn that the intrinsic reward properties of the behavior are greater or

more consistent than the punishment. And finally, opportunities for preferred modes of behavior must be available. Due to the prevalence of low clearance rates, trial delays, inconsistently applied dispositions, legal loopholes, the learning of improper reward and punishment contingencies, and a lack of available legitimate opportunities, the criminal justice system and society at large have been unable to meet the criteria set above for deterrence and prevention.

The experience of a painful consequence being associated with a behavior is encoded into memory, and when we calculate the consequences of performing that behavior in the future we are deterred by the possible negative response. The impetus for such behavioral change resides in our nervous system. We feel anxiety when the threat of a negative repercussion exists because of the learned association between the behavior and its likely consequence. . . . Theoretically, psychopaths do not sufficiently experience the discomfort of anxiety associated with a proscribed behavior because they have a hypoaroused automatic nervous system, and thus, they are not easily conditioned or deterred (Hare & Schalling, 1978; Lykken, 1957). They make a rational choice based on the calculation that the benefits of the act (e.g., monetary gain) outweigh the costs (e.g., anxiety and detection). Accordingly, one would expect that psychopaths encountered by the criminal justice system would be resistant to most deterrence programs. Rewards and punishments influence behavior directly through brain mechanisms. Centers responsible for pain and pleasure are located in a section of the brain known as the limbic system. Not surprisingly, memories are encoded, stored, and retrieved in this same system. . . .

In sum, social behavior is learned through the principles of conditioning, which are founded on biological and genetic dictates in accord with stimulus response relationships. Social rewards remain secondary to biological rewards; our desire for money is social, but it is secondary to being a means for obtaining food and shelter. Thus, social behavior satisfies biological needs and drives by providing adaptive mechanisms for reproduction, mating, rearing, defense, and numerous other biological functions. Even though these strategies are fundamentally biological, how we behave to satisfy them relies heavily on learning.

Measurement and Methodological Issues

Research findings from various behavioral sciences that are relevant to the criminologist can be evaluated in the context of the parameters described above. The next section discusses selected studies that may have bearing on criminological research. A summary critique accompanies discussion of the studies. As a prelude to the discussion, this section examines some of the weaknesses common to such studies.

First, studies of incarcerated populations present obvious problems regarding the generalizability of findings in that any observed effect or correlation may be due to the effects of institutionalization rather than to the variable(s) of interest. Many studies that used institutionalized offenders as subjects did not attempt to measure or control for prison conditions and influences. Also, prisoners are a selective group, and thus their study does not include individuals outside that population with the trait of interest. Second, many forms of bias in selecting subjects are evident in some studies. For example, several studies focus on criminal offenders and ignore pervasive illegal behaviors in undetected samples. There is a strong possibility that apprehended or incarcerated subjects differ from those who avoid detection in terms of their characteristics and the impact of criminal justice procedures.

Third, the use of control subjects is frequently neglected or inappropriate controls are examined. Unmatched controls or subjects with psychopathology (e.g., schizophrenics) are used all too often as comparison *subjects*. Fourth, widely divergent conceptual and methodological principles are, at times, applied across studies, which makes it difficult to compare and replicate findings. Concepts such as psychopathy, antisocial personality, aggression, criminal behavior, and so on, are inconsistently defined and measured. Also, biological parameters are not uniformly identified, for example, electroencephalographic studies employ different measures of brain activity. Measurement instruments differ among studies and interpretations of findings are variable.

Fifth, several points of caution are particularly relevant to interpretation of studies of psychopathic subjects. The widespread use of self-report and retrospective data is problematic generally, but additional problems arise when these data sources are used to examine offenders, a population notorious for falsifying records. Psychopaths, who are depicted as crafty deceivers, offer especially unreliable data. Yet, self-report measures are frequently used to select and categorize subjects. Not all criminals are psychopaths and vice versa. Moreover, psychological, behavioral, and physiological traits characterizing psychopathy occur along a continuum; psychopathy is not a binary phenomenon. Thus, both personality traits and actual behaviors must be carefully assessed before assigning subjects to groups. Last, the terminology used to describe individuals exhibiting psychopathic behavior is often inexact, confusing, and inconsistent (Blackburn, 1988). . . .

Finally, of immediate importance, the majority of so-called multidisciplinary studies have examined only a few variables in isolation, without accounting for interactive effects between biological and socioenvironmental conditions. A truly collaborative research project, examining an extensive data set and incorporating the sophisticated methodological and statistical techniques of sociologists, would hold the promise of yielding more informative results regarding the nature of bio-socio-environmental influences on antisocial behavior. (See Mednick et al., 1987, for detailed critiques of biological approaches to the study of criminal behavior). . . .

Selected Studies of the Biology of Maladaptive Behavior

Evolutionary Dictates

. . . . Most behaviors have some adaptive significance (i.e., they reflect an attempt to adapt to environmental conditions) and, thus, can be studied in an evolutionary context. Aggression is one form of behavior that has been extensively studied with respect to its adaptive significance. For example, "abnormal" environmental conditions have been associated with a display of extreme, overt aggression because they are perceived as threats to survival. . . . Abnormal environmental conditions characterize prisons and may contribute to the incidence of overt aggressive behavior among inmates; they may also partially explain the relationship between contacts with the criminal justice system (e.g., amount of time incarcerated) and recidivism rates. Also, the prevalence of abnormal environmental conditions has increased with the ever-increasing breakdown of the family structure, community disorganization, disparity between public policy and biological needs, crowding, learned help-lessness, and other frequently cited characteristics of U.S. urbanization (Archer and Gartner, 1984, pp. 98-117; Larson, 1984, pp. 116-141). Investigation of how these deleterious conditions exacerbate maladaptive behavioral mechanisms may eventually lead to socioenvironmental programs to enhance, rather than detract from, adaptive capabilities. . . .

Genetic Contributions

Genetic studies of criminal behavior specifically have been even more severely criticized (Mednick et al., 1987; Plomin et al., 1990; Rowe & Osgood, 1984; Walters & White, 1989; Wilson & Herrnstein, 1985). This research suffers from a high level of abstraction because "criminal behavior" is a legalistic label, not descriptive of actual behavior. This weakness is not unique to genetic research, however. Criminal behavior, as a single phenomenon, is far too variable and subject to individual and cultural judgments to be defined for reliable and valid investigation. Instead, research should be predicated on dis-aggregated behaviors that are reflective of actual acts that can be consistently and accurately measured and examined. Accordingly, genetic studies that focus on criminal behavior per se may be inherently flawed; as criminal behavior is heterogeneous, genetic effects may be more directly associated with particular traits that place individuals at risk for criminal labeling. . . . As a rule, what is inherited is not a behavior; rather, it is the way in which an individual responds to the environment. It provides an orientation, predisposition, or tendency to behave in a certain fashion. Also, genetic influences on human behavior are polygenic—no single gene effect can be identified for most behaviors.

Numerous studies have attempted to estimate the genetic contribution to the development of criminality, delinquency, aggression, and anti social behavior. Each has used one of three methods designed to assess the relative contributions of environment and heredity to various aspects of human behavior: family, twin, and adoption studies. Overall, many of these behavioral genetic studies suffer from one or more of the methodological weaknesses discussed earlier. . . .

Family Studies

The family study seeks to identify genetic influences on behavioral traits by evaluating similarities among family members. Cross-generational linkages have been reported for personality and behavioral attributes related to criminal behavior. . . . Despite conclusions . . . that genetic effects are largely responsible for criminal behavior, this method of study does not directly assess genetic contributions. Environmental influences on measures of behavior may be common to parents and offspring, and thus, large environmental correlations among relatives cannot be accounted for. Diet, environmental toxins, neighborhood conditions, and television-viewing habits are only a few examples of environmental factors that similarly influence family members. Family studies also suffer from many of the weaknesses listed above. At this point, one may only conclude that the incidence of criminal and related behaviors appears to have a familial basis. The relative influences of genetics and environmental conditions cannot, however, be estimated.

Twin Studies

The classic twin design involves the testing of identical (monozygotic or MZ) and fraternal (dizygotic or DZ) twins. MZ twins share genetic material from the biologic parents and are thus considered genetically identical. DZ twins are approximately 50% genetically alike, as are regular siblings. The extent to which MZ resemblances with respect to a characteristic are greater than DZ resemblances provides evidence for a genetic influence on the variable. To the extent that there is still some degree of DZ resemblance after genetic influences have been accounted for, there is evidence for the influence of common family environment on the variable. For example, if a sample of MZ twins is 60% similar for IQ and a matched sample of DZ twins is 25% similar for IQ, one can conclude that IQ is largely a function of heredity. . . .

. . . . Twin studies commonly suffer from a number of unique methodological weaknesses

(Plomin et al., 1980). First, MZ twins are selected more frequently due to their visibility, and study group sizes thus become disproportionate. Second, sampling techniques may favor the selection of MZ pairs that are similar in relevant behavioral traits, which biases the results. Third, MZ twins tend to share more similar environments than do DZ twins because of their similar appearance (DZ twins look no more alike than regular siblings). Because environmental assessments are not commonly conducted, such similarities cannot be estimated to determine their relative influence. In favor of the validity of the twin method, however, is evidence that physical and environmental similarities among MZ twins do not bias studies of personality (see DeFries & Plomin, 1978, p. 480; Plomin & Daniels, 1987).

Fourth, only recently have researchers employed biochemical tests to verify the zygosity of the twins. The bulk of genetic studies were performed prior to the ready availability of such tests, and thus, the genetic influence may have been underestimated. Fifth, measurement errors may further increase the tendency to underestimate genetic influences. On the other side of the coin, the twin method can only examine the level of genetic contribution over and above environmental influence. Thus, there is contamination from an unknown amount of environmental contribution and the influence of heredity may be overestimated. No definitive conclusions can be drawn from twin studies of aggressiveness or criminal behavior because no consistent pattern of genetic influence emerges. Nevertheless, twin studies of criminal and related behaviors fairly consistently provide some intriguing evidence for a genetic effect, and genetic influences warrant continued, but more rigorous, study.

Adoption Studies

Adoption studies examine individuals who were raised from infancy by nonrelated adoptive parents rather than biological relatives. To the extent that subjects resemble the biological relatives and not the nonbiologic relatives, heredity is thought to play a contributory role. The adoption study method promises to provide unambiguous evidence for the relative contribution of heredity as a cause for behavioral traits and for genetics-environment interactions. Nevertheless, the method has some weaknesses

(see Walters & White, 1989, for examples). First, due to difficulties in locating subjects, sample sizes tend to be small, which reduces the power of the results. Second, selection bias may be introduced in the adoption process because assignment to adoptive parents may not be random with respect to biological parent characteristics. Third, a primary criticism of a majority of adoption studies on criminality is the inadequacy and inconsistency of the methods used to operationalize and measure the dependent variable (see Plomin et al., 1990; Walters & White, 1989). Fourth, researchers should ensure that the duration and type of biological parenting [are] similar among all subjects to avoid contamination. Ideally, infants should have been adopted within a few weeks of birth so that the age of adoption does not relate to subsequent criminal behavior (see Mednick et al., 1984). . . .

. . . . Adoption studies highlight the importance of gene-environment interactional models (Rowe & Osgood, 1984). Mednick et al. (1984) proposed that having a criminal adoptive parent most profoundly affects those with a genetic propensity for criminality. In other words, those who inherited certain antisocial personality and temperamental traits are more likely to manifest criminal behaviors in the presence of deleterious environmental conditions (e.g., criminal parents). Even though these conditions interact to produce antisocial behavior, many researchers attest that environmental and genetic factors differentially influence behavior and that their relative contributions may be measurable (see Plomin et al., 1990). . . .

Biological Contributions

Biochemical Correlates

A number of biochemical differences have been found between controls and individuals with psychopathy, antisocial personality, violent behavior, conduct disorder, and other behaviors associated with criminal behavior. . . . Current investigations of biochemical mechanisms of aggressiveness focus on the study of central neurotransmitter systems. . . . [S]tudies indicate that serotonin functioning is altered in some types of human aggressiveness and violent suicidal behavior. Thus, a decrease in serotonergic activity may produce disinhibition in both brain mechanisms and behavior and result in increased aggressiveness or impulsivity.

Findings of reduced serotonergic activity among individuals with impulsivity and aggressivity are well supported by behavioral and personality studies of animals and humans. Nevertheless, this research is relatively new to the area of antisocial behavior and frequently suffers from theoretical and methodological inadequacies (see Soubrie, 1986). First, categorizing subjects according to their behavioral attributes has been inconsistent across studies, and group assignment within studies is, in some cases, controversial. Second, because aggression is not a unitary phenomenon it is important to determine whether serotonergic activity levels are specific to types of aggression or whether they globally regulate aggression. Third, psychopathy or antisocial personality is frequently used to describe subjects without respect to the presence of trait anxiety (see above), which is known to involve serotonergic systems (Soubrie, 1986). . . . And fourth, serotonergic activity is all too often studied in isolation of other interacting biological systems. Thus, these studies have not been able to identify precisely the neural mechanisms for regulating aggression. They do, nevertheless, bring us closer to identifying neurobiological mechanisms for aggression, impulsivity, and antisocial behavior.

There is a noticeable absence of research on female criminality in general, and reports that do exist are largely sociological or anecdotal. Widom (1978) wrote that biological factors contributing to individual differences in temperament, arousal, or vulnerability to stress may be important in the etiology of female criminal behavior. Different socioenvironmental influences may differentially interact with biological sex differences to produce variations in male and female criminality (see, e.g., Ellis & Ames, 1987). There is evidence that high levels of the male sex hormone testosterone may influence aggressive behavior in males (Kreuz & Rose, 1971; Olweus et al., 1988; Rada et al., 1983; Schiavi et al., 1984), although discrepant studies exist (Coe & Levine, 1983). It has been further suggested that sex hormones may also contribute to antisocial behavior in some women. . . . [Despite methodological shortcomings,] there remains a general impression among investigators and clinicians that a small number of women

appear to be vulnerable to cyclical changes in hormonal levels, which causes them to be more prone to increased levels of anxiety and hostility during the premenstrual phase (Carroll & Steiner, 1987; Clare, 1985). . . .

[Additionally], [e]xposure to toxic trace elements is yet another factor that has been shown to interfere with brain function and behavior. Chronic or acute exposure to lead, for example, has a deleterious effect on brain function by damaging organ systems, impairing intellectual development, and subsequently interfering with the regulation of behavior. . . .

Psychophysiological Correlates

Psychophysiological variables, for example, heart rate, blood pressure, attention and arousal levels, skin conductance, brain waves, and hormone levels, are quantifiable indices of nervous system function. These measurable conditions directly reflect emotional responses and can be experimentally manipulated in human populations. Studies of criminal behavior, aggression, and psychopathy have repeatedly found psychophysiological evidence for mental abnormality and central nervous system disturbances as putative markers for criminal behavior. For example, psychopaths have been found to differ from nonpsychopathic controls in several physiological parameters. These indices include (a) electroencephalogram (EEG) differences, (b) cognitive and neuropsychological impairment, and (c) electrodermal, cardiovascular, and other nervous system measures. . . .

Psychopharmacological Inducements

Psychopharmacology is the study of the psychological and behavioral aspects of drug effects on brain metabolism and activity. Aggression, for example, can be elicited or extinguished by the administration of a pharmacologic agent. In fact, the pharmacologic treatment of aggressive and violent behavior has become increasingly popular and its efficacy in many cases has been demonstrated (Kuperman & Stewart, 1987; Lion, 1974, 1979; Yudofsky et al., 1987). Certain drugs, particularly many of the illicit drugs, are reported to increase aggressive responses, for example, amphetamines, cocaine, alcohol, and phencyclidine (PCP). The actual expression of aggressive behavior depends on the dose, route of administration, genetic factors, and type of aggression. . . .

. . . . "Vulnerability" studies suggest that certain personality types may be more at risk for drug abuse than other types (Brook et al., 1985; Deykin et al., 1986; Kellam et al., 1980; McCardle & Fishbein, 1989). This does not mean, however, that these individuals will inevitably become drug abusers due to a natural predisposition. More recent studies provide evidence for the substantial contribution of family support systems in the final determination of whether an individual with a vulnerable personality type will, in fact, abuse drugs (Tarter et al., 1985, pp. 346-347). . . .

IMPLICATIONS FOR CRIMINAL JUSTICE PRACTICES

At this stage of scientific inquiry in the biological sciences, researchers have yet to determine the significance of biological disorders in criminal populations. Nor are they able to speak of a causal link between biological abnormalities and specific behavioral disorders. They are beginning to identify putative correlates or markers of antisocial behavior using biological tests (e.g., EEG slowing, body lead burden, neurotransmitter imbalance). Some of those correlations may prove to be spurious, but at present, which ones [are spurious] cannot be identified. Seen in this light, it would be premature to apply biological findings routinely to criminal justice procedures. Demands for evaluation of causal relationships are made in decisions regarding the granting of bail, release on personal recognizance, competency, guilty pleas, sentencing options, proba-tion and parole, and proclivity to recidivate. Conclusions and prognoses regarding the role of biological factors in an offender's behavior, however, are not definitive at this time, regardless of the informational source.

To further establish the relevance of biology to criminology, researchers must demonstrate the ability to predict antisocial behavior reliably using a combination of biological and social variables. The central question thus becomes, can more of the variance in the incidence of antisocial behavior be explained with an integrated approach than with a unidisciplinary perspective? Many mental health professionals and researchers have reached a tentative consensus that predicting antisocial behavior with social or legal variables is inherently unreliable (Cocozza & Steadman, 1974; Gottfredson, 1986; Monahan, 1981; Wenk et al., 1972). Is it possible that prediction studies incorporating biological measures into sociological databases will facilitate the isolation of significant predictors of antisocial behavior and enhance explanatory power?

In the introduction of Brizer and Crowner's recent text (1989) on the prediction of violence, Brizer aptly notes that the actual study of predictive ability suffers from methodological limitations, and thus, one cannot conclude that valid prediction is impossible. Studies reviewed in their text indicate that the inclusion of biological variables (e.g., integrity of central nervous system function) may, indeed, enhance predictive ability if dispositional (temperament and other features considered "innate") and situational factors are considered as interacting forces. . . .

Denno (1988) conducted a fairly comprehensive study of the effects of numerous environmental and biological variables on criminal behavior, juvenile delinquency, and disciplinary problems. The model was able to predict 25% of future adult criminality among males and 19% of future adult criminality among females. Denno drew the following conclusions:

> Biological and environmental variables exert strong and independent influences on juvenile crime . . . . [and] crime appears to be directly related to familial instability and, most important, a lack of behavioral control associated with neurological and central nervous system disorders (p. 659).

She cautions, however, that behavior should be predicted in terms of a series of probabilities of expected behavior, not in terms of cause and effect. Perhaps an approach that neither neglects nor places undue emphasis on socioenvironmental or biological features of behavior provides considerable promise as the direction of future research into practical problems in criminology.

The final stage of scientific inquiry requires that researchers be able to manipulate and control antisocial behavior, in this context with biological variables. Reliable behavioral changes attributable to biological treatments have yet to be demonstrated in this field, however. Biological intervention studies and programs render mixed and controvertible results, which indicate that the biology of antisocial behavior is under preliminary stages of investigation and requires further study before it can be applied to criminal justice practices. One particularly visible example of the controversial application of biological data is the pharmacologic treatment of sex offenders. Antiandrogen agents (e.g., Depo-Provera), which compete with male hormones believed to be responsible for sexual deviance, are administered in some clinics to suppress sex drive and, consequently, sex offending. . . . [This approach has been criticized] because of (1) the equivocal findings that provide empirical support, (2) the fact that the behaviors resurface when the drug is discontinued, (3) its strictly experimental nature, (4) the issue of forced compliance, and (5) evidence that only nonviolent sex offenders respond to antiandrogen treatment (see Demsky, 1984). Such biological management techniques require further scientific support and, even more important, time for the legal system to become acquainted with their premises in order to establish appropriate guidelines.

It is perhaps unreasonable to expect dramatic behavioral improvements following a biological treatment, even when a disorder has been properly diagnosed. One of the central tenets of this article is that behavior is a result of a dynamic interaction among many diverse social and biological conditions. The appropriate administration of a medication or other treatment may certainly be warranted for some individuals with identifiable pathology. However, this approach undermines the proposal that multiple factors are responsible for behavior. One cannot manipulate biological variables and expect behavior to change without attending to other interacting contributions. Once an individual has entered the criminal justice system, behavioral problems are substantially compounded and the treatment of only one condition does not yield adequate therapeutic results.

Findings of biological involvement in antisocial behavior have, in a few studies (e.g., Lewis et al., 1979, 1981, 1985, 1986, 1988), disclosed measurable abnormalities, but in a number of studies, measurements do not reach pathologic levels. In other words, many studies show group differences between violent and nonviolent subjects, but the biological values do not necessarily exceed normal limits and would not alarm a practicing physician. Findings of this type do not

have intrinsic clinical significance, and they indicate that individual intervention programs should not be globally implemented based on current information.

Nevertheless, at the very least, the inclusion of biological measures holds promise of explaining individual variation within a social context. Why is it, for example, that not all children exposed to child abuse become violent as adults? Research into individual differences may be interpreted to suggest that whether child abuse contributes to violent behavior partially depends on the presence of brain damage or other central nervous system disorder (Lewis et al., 1979). Perhaps abused children without concomitant or resultant brain damage would be less aggressive and more in control of their impulses. Research yet to be conducted may also show that individuals with biological "disadvantages" respond with more violent or criminal behavior in a criminogenic environment than those equipped with biological "insulators," for example, high intelligence or adequate serotonergic activity.

Statistically significant findings generated to date show biological involvement in antisocial behavior only with respect to populations. Thus, society is closer to enacting prevention programs aimed at populations who are at risk for exposure to biological and socioenvironmental hazards that are known to increase the incidence of behavioral problems. Factors that may prove to be important contributors to relevant behavioral disorders (e.g., toxic element concentrations, child abuse/neglect, poor prenatal care, neurological impairments, substance abuse, and learning disabilities) could subsequently be manipulated on a wide scale to prevent the onset of behavioral or forensic disorders in the general population. Early detection programs could be implemented by school systems, and parents could be educated to recognize signs of an impairment. Screening clinics, regulating environmental toxins, programs, prenatal care facilities, and public educational programs are only a few of the preventative measures possible. The number of "risk" factors could, in essence, be reduced or minimized. . . .

DISCUSSION QUESTIONS

1. What are the four parameters for understanding biological theories of crime that Fishbein

outlines in her article? What is the significance behind a multidisciplinary approach to biological theories of crime?

2. Discuss the four issues that are relevant to biological considerations of crime.

3. In terms of the various approaches to the study of maladaptive behavior, what are the contributions from evolutionary, genetic, and biological approaches? Which seem(s) the most promising in terms of strong empirical support?

4. What are the implications for criminal justice practice and policy?

5

CRIMINOLOGY
AND THE HOLOCAUST
Xenophobia, Evolution, and Genocide

AUGUSTINE BRANNIGAN

EDITOR'S INTRODUCTION—Brannigan's article offers readers an insightful analysis into an often-overlooked aspect of criminal behavior: genocide. Brannigan makes it clear that modern theories of crime and delinquency tend to be individualistic in their level of analysis and tend to be consensus oriented in their definition of criminality. Consequently, the phenomenon of ethnic genocide is virtually impossible to examine within such parameters. Traditional criminological theories are not very useful in understanding and explaining situations such as the Holocaust during World War II, or the more contemporary tragedies in Bosnia and Rwanda, where the crimes, though sometimes committed one-on-one, were collective acts of extreme violence and hatred.

Recent histories of the Holocaust by Christopher Browning and Daniel Goldhagen shed new light on the nature of the Holocaust and the motivational and institutional dynamics without which the Holocaust likely would not have occurred. These historians suggest that the Holocaust was carried out by ordinary citizens who supported its objectives, not by dysfunctional psychopaths. Nor was it carried out by individuals intimidated by powerful authority structures. Because of the inability of criminology to explain this and more recent genocidal phenomena, Brannigan undertakes the task of reviewing the evidence from these new historiographies and proposes a theory of genocide based on theories of xenophobia that have been developed in recent accounts of evolutionary psychology.

The first part of Brannigan's essay consists of a historical account of the rampant racism that emerged during the rise of Hitler and Nazi ideology in the 1930s and a discussion of Goldhagen's examination of "exterminationist anti-Semitism." However, Brannigan maintains that the evidence provided in Goldhagen's text fails to account for the larger picture of the origins of the crimes that occurred at that time. Some of the evidence Goldhagen provides suggests that the Germans felt justified in committing the heinous acts of murder. If this is true, Brannigan points out the necessity to determine *how* the human psyche could be open to collective acts that would reflect insanity if they were the behavior of an individual. In other words, Brannigan maintains that a larger perspective is required in order to capture how the appetite for anti-Semitism was stimulated and reinforced and how genocide remains such a predictable aspect of human intergroup competition.

It is with this question that he explicates the theory of the evolutionary psychology of genocide. Brannigan cites research that has found that the evolution of sociability, altruism, and the instincts for coalitions goes hand in hand with hostility toward outsiders. Noting that humans often revel collectively in opposition and confrontation, Brannigan states that this phenomenon is "at the heart of our sociability as a species and is the root of xenophobia" (p. 60, this volume). Anti-Semitism has been the leading case of out-group hatred in many Christian nations, but what made it reach such virulent heights in Nazi Germany was the elaborate racist belief systems about human differences that motivated ordinary people to kill their fellow neighbors and the institutional abilities to carry out the violence on such an unprecedented scale. Brannigan's theory of xenophobia has important implications for criminologists, who need to examine more closely these genocidal crimes against humanity.

The Problem of Genocide in Criminological Theory

Modern criminology, like sociology itself, is marked by a proliferation of theoretical perspectives and paradigms. These are typically best as competing mutually exclusive accounts of crime, each independent and capable on its own of explaining all the major trends. Gottfredson and Hirschi's self-control theory (1990) is a good example of this approach. They argue that common crimes such as robbery, murder, and theft, as well as upper world crimes like embezzlement and tax evasion, are equally amenable to an explanation based on impulsiveness. By contrast, at other times one gets the feeling that the apparent plurality of approaches to criminology results from the fragmentation of complex social processes, each piece of which is captured to some extent by what are misperceived as mutually exclusive theories. . . .

[If] criminologists have difficulty coming to terms with such phenomena as "garden variety" juvenile delinquency and crime, it is hardly surprising that they have virtually nothing to say about the most lethal crimes of the century: "racial-ethnic conflict crimes." Gibbons (1997, p. 361) notes that, in contrast to garden variety crimes, "racial-ethnic conflict crime rarely receives attention in the criminological literature." Ethnic cleansing in the former Yugoslavia, and in Rwanda, the systematic use of rape and murder to advance group "purity" in a racially mixed territory, receive little theoretical attention.

According to Gibbons (1997, p. 362), "there is relatively little in the way of an overarching theory of racial-ethnic conflict."

In control theory, crime is defined as the use of force or fraud in the pursuit of self-interest. Like many other theories in mainstream criminology, it is individualistic in its level of analysis and consensus oriented in its definition of criminality. How useful are these approaches to situations such as the Holocaust during World War II? On the face of it, not very useful, particularly in that the crimes of the Holocaust, though sometimes committed one on one, were collective acts of virulent and lethal hatred. In recent years, a debate has emerged in Holocaust studies that sheds new light on its nature and the motivational and institutional dynamics without which it would not have happened. This debate is found particularly in the writings of historians Christopher Browning (1992) and Daniel Goldhagen (1997). In light of criminology's inability to explain collective crime, their work may have some relevance to criminologists. This essay reviews this work, contrasts it to the contemporary explanations of the Holocaust in social science, and explores the possibility of an overarching theory of such collective, predatory crime in terms of a theory of xenophobia.

Hitler's Racist State

In 1933, after remarkable advances in popular support for the National Socialists, Adolf Hitler negotiated a political coalition that put him into the role of the Chancellor of the German

Brannigan, A. (1998). Criminology and the Holocaust: Xenophobia, evolution, and genocide. *Crime & Delinquency, 44*, 257-278.

Reichstag. Within months he had declared an emergency decree expropriating the buildings and property of communists and trade unionists. Following a fire at the Reichstag building set surreptitiously by the Nazis (Shirer, 1990, p. 268), new rules were passed justifying "protective custody" for the enemies of the National Socialists, a step that permitted indiscriminant imprisonment without warrant or trial. By March, thousands of critics of the regime had been imprisoned at the newly constructed "concentration camp" at Dachau, near Munich (Gilbert, 1985, p. 2). Public beatings of individual Jews and destruction of Jewish property (Einzelo-perationen or "individual actions") by Nazi Storm troops began almost at once (p. 33). The Nazi government enacted the racially exclusionary laws and policies that they had promoted for over a decade. Jewish stores were looted and boycotted. Jewish professionals in every line of work were excluded from public life. Lawyers were barred from the courts. Civil servants, teachers, professors, and medical doctors were fired. Musicians and playwrights were forced out of work. By the end of July, 26,000 Germans, many of them Jews, had been taken into protective custody or put into Gestapo prisons. Discipline was arbitrary and summary execution common. European diplomats were stunned, but the racial policies were only beginning to come into effect.

In 1934, the Nazis promoted a campaign to create "Jew-free" villages and towns, and laws were adopted to expropriate Jewish businesses and force them into "Aryan hands." By 1935, the Nuremburg laws stripped Jews of German citizenship and forbade intermarriage. The euthanasia program, based on doctrines of racial purity, led German doctors to take the lives of 70,000 Germans with mental and/or physical infirmities. The attempt of the Nazis to force a unification of all the Germanic speaking peoples of Europe led to the outbreak of the war in 1939, and the onset of the war provided the operational cover for the systematic murder of some 6 million Jews, noncombatants, men, women, and children, out of a total European population of approximately 8 million Jews (Gilbert, 1985, p. 18).

Conventional wisdom holds that this unprecedented genocide was primarily the work of a vanguard of psychopathic Nazis and their sadistic counterparts in the SS and other military and quasi-military organizations. But, the recent historiography suggests another view. Browning's *Ordinary Men: Reserve Police Battalion 101 and the Final Solution in Poland* (1992) stresses that it was "ordinary men," not psychopaths, who paved the way to the Holocaust. Browning points out that in the spring of 1942, some 75 to 80 percent of all the victims of the Holocaust were still alive, but 11 months later, most had been killed. "At the core of the Holocaust was a short, intensive wave of mass murder" (1992, p. xv). But most of the Polish Jews lived in small villages in scattered communities. At the time of active military campaign on the Eastern front, the Germans had to invest tremendous resources in personnel and material to uproot, "re-settle," concentrate, transport, and deliver millions of people to sites to be gassed, shot, or worked or marched to death. In the process, "the grass-roots perpetrators became 'professional killers'" (p. xvii). . . . Police Battalion 101 was composed of middle-aged policemen too old for normal combatant service, but they and other battalions were responsible for the shootings of hundreds of thousands of civilian Jews.

Daniel Goldhagen's more recent book, *Hitler's Willing Executioners: Ordinary Germans and the Holocaust* (1997), makes more of the particular animosity of the Germans toward the Jews. Goldhagen stresses that the elimination of European Jewry was only possible because hundreds of thousands of ordinary Germans were complicit in the slaughter and participated because they thought that it was an appropriate thing to do. Indeed, without their participation, it would never have happened. Also, had the Nazis not been defeated, the toll would probably have been the annihilation of the 8 million Jews from every corner of Europe. The euthanasia program was stopped because ordinary Germans objected to it. But regarding the Jews, the Germans neither viewed their actions as criminal nor did they shrink from opportunities to inflict suffering, humiliation, and death—openly, knowingly, and zealously upon their victims. As Goldhagen comments on some recent examples: "Who doubts that the Tutsis who slaughtered Hutus in Burundi or the Hutus who slaughtered Tutsis in Rwanda . . . that the Serbs who have killed Croats or Bosnian Muslims, did so out of conviction in the justice of their actions? Why do we not believe the same for the German perpetrators?" (p. 14).

GOLDHAGEN'S CRITIQUE
OF MILGRAM'S PSYCHOLOGY

Previous attempts to explain the Holocaust have centered on specific psychological mechanisms that presumably prevented ordinary citizens from acting decently. The main account comes from Milgram, whose *Obedience to Authority* (1974) suggests that people in bureaucratic structures simply were forced to comply [with] the orders of superiors. By contrast, Goldhagen (1997) observes that any explanation that does not get at the mind-set of the ordinary perpetrators and their anti-Semitic attitudes basically misconceives the nature of the problem. . . . [His book] eschews the ahistorical, universal social psychological explanations—such as the notions that people obey all authority or that they will do anything because of peer pressure—that are typically reflexively invoked when accounting for the perpetrator's actions. By contrast, the book stresses the individuality and humanity of the actors whose personal anti-Semitic attitudes were a reservoir of scapegoating and hate on which the Nazis could initiate the Holocaust as a kind of "national project" (p. 477).

In his introduction, "Reconceiving Central Aspects of the Holocaust," Goldhagen reviews some of the unfounded beliefs about the situation in German Europe after the start of the war. "It has been a widespread conviction (again until recently) that had a German refused to kill Jews, then he himself would have been killed, sent to a concentration camp or severely punished" (1997, p. 10). A second explanation characterizes the perpetrators as "having been blind followers of orders," a compulsiveness sometimes associated with "a peculiarly German reverence for and propensity to obey authority."

According to Goldhagen (1997, p. 12), "a third explanation holds the perpetrators to have been subject to tremendous social psychological pressure, placed upon each one by his comrades and/or by the expectations that accompany the institutional roles that individuals occupy." A fourth explanation emphasizes the self-interest of petty bureaucrats who promoted the Final Solution "with a callous disregard for the victims" in a large impersonal bureaucracy that undermined personal responsibility, whereas a fifth explanation stresses the fragmentation of the process of killing, which diluted and minimized the individual contributions to and apprehension of the consequences of the overall eliminationist program.

All these explanations "assume a neutral or condemnatory attitude on the part of the perpetrators" (Goldhagen, 1997, p. 13). They are premised on the notion that forces had to be in place to make the perpetrators do what they believed inwardly to be reprehensible. They paint the perpetrators as ineffectual agents who could be manipulated by their circumstances to act against their conscience, as "beings moved solely by external forces or by transhistorical and invariant psychological propensities," as people who were themselves the victims of the Nazi bureaucracy. These explanations assume that such forces could be understood as though "inducing people to kill human beings is fundamentally no different from getting them to do any other unwanted or difficult task" and that the identity of the victims—Jews—was beside the point.

Goldhagen's thesis is quite the opposite. The perpetrators participated because they thought the Jews ought [to] die, that the annihilation of the Jews was socially desirable, that the Jews were a particularly inferior form of subhumans. The killing of the men, the women, and the children, although often nauseating in its particulars, was consistent with the form of anti-Semitism that had come to dominate Germany (and other Central European countries) for decades (if not centuries) before the Holocaust and that came to a head during the period of the Third Reich. When Hitler's *Mein Kampf* called for a solution to the Jewish problem, he was preaching to the converted. . . . The Holocaust was the culmination of "exterminationist anti-Semitism," and the religious sentiments of devout German Catholics and Lutherans, with one or two notable exceptions, failed to blunt Hitler's murderous policies. Viewed in this light, Milgram fails to understand the nature of the problem. . . .

GOLDHAGEN'S EVIDENCE
FROM THE HOLOCAUST

. . . The early part of [*Hitler's Willing Executioners*] reviews the proliferation of anti-Semitism during the 1930s. . . . Matters came to a head on the night of November 9-10, 1938—Kristallnacht—when Germans in hundreds of cities, towns, and villages were awakened to systematic Nazi mob destruction of Jewish businesses, synagogues, and private property. Approximately 100 Jews were murdered and 30,000 were hauled off to concentration camps (p. 100). If anyone had illusions about the state's plans for the Jews—and certainly the Nazis did not disguise their commitment to a "solution" to the Jewish problem—it became clear that Kristallnacht was a clarion call, but most Germans were more affronted by the lack of decorum in the violence than by the proposition that the Jewish menace needed attention. Thus, when the authorities began systematic deportation of German Jews to the East in 1941, few could doubt that their fate was bleak. By that time, the destruction of Polish and Russian Jews was already well under way following the occupation of the conquered territories.

What evidence does Goldhagen adduce that challenges the passive role ascribed to the conduct of ordinary Germans in previous accounts? The most convincing evidence comes from the accounts of the key exterminationist institutions established in the East immediately following the occupation of Poland. These included the actions of German Police Battalions . . . the creation of work camps, and the forced marches at the end of the war.

POLICE BATTALIONS AND OTHER INSTITUTIONS OF EXTERMINATION

In the . . . ghetto clearing at Lomazy in August [1942], the Battalion rounded up 1,600 Jews after shooting those who were not mobile. The photographs show the police patrolling the assembled victims, whips in hand, standing proudly on guard. They took pictures and recorded the details on the reverse side: "condemned Jews/ Lomartzie 18 Aug 42/1600." The photos were mailed back to policemen's families without any sense of the horror of the operation. A pit was excavated by some of the Jewish men, and small groups of people were taken and shot by the policemen and their Polish collaborators in the pit. However, the Germans humiliated the

old Jews by making them crawl through the dirt before entering the pit to be massacred. They cut their beards, making photographs of their humiliation. Thousands of victims sat in the town square under the hot sun for hours, skin burning, and listened to the screams and gunshots before their own deaths were appointed. And, in forcing them to the pit, the Germans made the victims run a gauntlet of whips and rifle butts. The death pit itself was filling with water, and many of the victims were only wounded before being covered by later bodies and buried alive with dirt by the final detail of Jews before the latter were dispatched. Sixteen hundred victims were shot at close range in a scene from hell. What Goldhagen notes in this episode is the extreme cruelty over and above the horrific fact of execution, and the obvious pleasure that the executioners took in their assignment once they had worked out a routine for doing it more or less efficiently.

The point of the exercise was not merely to "cleanse" Poland of its Jews, but to symbolically humiliate and to mark them as socially dead before turning them into corpses. After the day's work, the police would return to their barracks, join their wives, attend poetry and band performances, and continue living "normally". . . .

The work camps similarly reveal volumes about the German attitudes to the Jews. The camps were almost never effective economic enterprises, especially in regard to the Jews. The Jews were whipped and starved by their male and female captors, frequently required to engage in pointless, debilitating "make-work" before being beaten to death or dispatched by gas. Why didn't the Germans exploit the skilled Jewish slave labor more effectively, particularly as the tide was turning against the Reich? Goldhagen argues that, again, humiliation was a more important motive to the Germans on a personal level than was economic production. . . .

And finally, the forced marches of camp inhabitants over hundreds of miles in the last days of the war were meant to kill Jews, even though the guards knew that the German war effort was lost. Goldhagen reports that when Himmler ordered local commanders to desist from the marches because they were compromising terms of surrender with the Americans, the local commanders persisted in walking their emaciated hostages to death through exhaustion, starving them, killing those who attempted escape, and preventing local people from offering them food. The destruction of the Jews did not derive from structures of higher authority but from the close and cruel handiwork of thousands of ordinary Germans operating within an exterminationist anti-Semitic culture. . . .

IS EXTERMINATIONIST ANTI-SEMITISM A CAUSE?

How sound is the explanation? Was "exterminationist anti-Semitism" the causal linchpin of the terrible Holocaust against the European Jews—or was it the phenomenon we are trying to explain? That the Germans as well as other Europeans were anti-Semitic and brimming with hatred for their Jewish neighbors is not in doubt. But the proposition that this attitudinal mind-set was the cause of the Holocaust may be as tautological in Goldhagen's account as the agentic state was in Milgram's. What is the evidence that the attitude of Germans was "exterminationist" aside from the outcome? At what point did the long-standing historical animosity of anti-Semitism become exterminationist? And how could this powerful psychological mind-set disappear so remarkably after the war (if indeed it did)?

There are grounds for believing that wars tap deep psychological instincts, based on xenophobia, racism, and invidious hatreds (Ridley, 1996, pp. 171-95). In the prosecution of the war by the Nazis, racial considerations were always paramount. The act of making war, particularly offensive campaigns, as was the case of the Germans in Europe, was expedited by the aggressors casting themselves as victims of their racial opponents, thereby justifying preemptive retaliation. Certainly, Germans were humiliated by the terms of peace forced upon them by the treaty of Versailles in 1919 following World War I. Hitler's mission was ostensibly to repair this injury. . . . With the declaration of armed conflict, the prospect of potential mutual annihilation was used to justify, as in all wars, extraordinary measures. If the war appears just to the citizens, and particularly where the enemies are already objects of deep suspicion, contempt, and hatred, the measures of offense become total. Even before the details of the Final Solution were

worked out, Hitler was clear that in the event of war, the European Jews would die. . . The future victims were cast as though they were the cause of the war, and the cover of war would permit their annihilation, even though they were noncombatants.

Although Hitler's cynical plans for the murder of European Jewry are covered well by Goldhagen, he pays little attention to how the cover of war also permitted Hitler to plan the virtual annihilation and subjugation of the Slavs, particularly the Russians. This can be illustrated from several observations, starting with the treatment of Russian POWs after "Operation Barbarossa," which referred to the invasion of Russia that began on June 22, 1941. It resulted in stunning tactical victories and the capture of some 3,800,000 Russian prisoners by December before winter ended the German advantage. In mid-winter, when the SS explored the possibility of enlisting the Russian POWs in German industries, it was determined that only several hundred thousand remained healthy enough to perform slave labor. What happened to the others? Before Operation Barbarossa was finally over, 5,750,000 Russian soldiers fell under German control, but barely a million survived the war (Shirer, 1990, p. 1241). Two million were starved to death or died from exposure in open camps during the bitterly cold Russian winter of 1942-1943, whereas another million were never accounted for and may have died from similar circumstances and from mass executions at the hands of the SS. In some camps, all the Asian POWs were screened and shot (Shirer, 1990, p. 1242).

. . . A last point that is pertinent in terms of the Nazi exterminationist mentality was the occupation policy with respect to food. The Russian invasion was certain to produce economic ruin and privation among civilians, but the German administration of occupied territories was expressly enjoined from feeding civilians. "The workers and their families in these regions would simply be left to starve" (Shirer, 1990, p. 1092). Nazi strategists estimated that "many millions of persons will be starved to death if we take out of the country the things necessary for us" (p. 1093).

In the longer term Nazi plans, the eastern territories were to become Germany's breadbasket and a zone of Aryan expansion. The displacement of the existing population was inevitable. In this regard, the actions of the Germans were calculated to bring about massive annihilation, whether of soldiers or of civilians. How are these plans to be explained? Do they reflect "exterminationist racism" or "exterminationist anti-Bolshevism"? And in what respect were these different from "exterminationist anti-Semitism?"

Goldhagen writes as though the treatment of the Jews arose from a distinctive mental construct restricted to the relationship of Germans to Jews—exterminationist anti-Semitism—but, when viewed in the context of the other exterminationist policies of the Germans, hatred of Jews appears to have been part of a hierarchy of hatreds and animosities. And while it may be true that the Jews were selected out for the most brutal treatments, the policies toward Russian civilians and POWs were also murderous state policies, similarly activated under the pretext of a just war and carried out by ordinary men. It should also be recalled that there was an intense escalation of public hatred of the Jews throughout the Nazi period by deliberate propaganda policies designed to vilify them and blame them for the postwar misery of the Germans. From this point of view, the escalation of racial hatred to collective murder under the cover of war was a function of propaganda used to forge racial in-group solidarity and to undermine the normal inhibitions against killing out-group strangers, particularly nonthreatening and weak strangers.

The matter is all the more complicated because if the evidence is that ordinary people thought they were acting with justice, in what sense are they culpable of homicide? Goldhagen equivocates. At points he stresses that the ordinary Germans did not seem to appreciate the nature and quality of their acts—they beamed as old men were humiliated, and they snapped souvenir photographs of wanton slaughter. . . . [T]he German perpetrators during the war did not view the Jews as human beings. . . . The theories of racial purity proposed in the leading schools of racial hygiene made the Jew a threat to Aryan purity and group survival.

Goldhagen identifies other evidence that suggests that the police were frequently a dignified lot. Preoccupied with animal welfare, they showed a decency that required the humane treatment of cows overcrowded in the same cattle cars used to ship the Jews to gas camps and a concern for the care of German shepherds, which were dramatically at variance to their insensitivity to the Jews. . . . In view of the evidence of their decency on other matters, we might say that the Germans appear to have been suffering from something that, if exhibited in an individual, would be viewed as a delusion or temporary insanity and that might undermine the specific capacity to commit murder. Goldhagen calls this "exterminationist anti-Semitism" and says that the carriers of this orientation suffered from "nazified minds." If we accept temporary insanity in the case of battered wives or persons suffering from delusions, why not in the case of delusional nations and their members?

. . . If interracial slaughter is typically righteous and undertaken with a sense of justice, then this requires us to determine how the human psyche could be open to collective acts that mirror what we might describe as insane were the behavior unique to an individual. Goldhagen's case for exterminationist anti-Semitism ultimately falls short of the mark. We need a larger perspective to capture how the appetite for anti-Semitism was stimulated and reinforced, and how genocide remains such a predictable feature of human intergroup rivalry. How can we explain this?

THE EVOLUTIONARY PSYCHOLOGY OF GENOCIDE

In his analysis *The Origins of Virtue*, Matt Ridley (1996) observes that an unexpected by-product of the evolution of cooperative society is group prejudice. Ridley is one of the most recent members of a new generation of evolutionary theorists who are attempting to explain complex social conduct in terms of "fitness mechanisms," but his approach has long enjoyed support (see Hamilton, 1975; Alexander, 1987; Richards, 1987; Wright, 1994; de Waal, 1996). In their view, the human psyche is an evolved organ with specific appetites and inclinations that are context sensitive and highly moralistic. Whereas Lombroso's Darwinism was reductionistic, the new evolutionary psychology presupposes a theory of action, that is, human decision making is based on choices, moral conflicts, and dilemmas—not mechanical causation or reflex action. However, the "appetites" are not socially constructed but, like the evolved gustatory ability to distinguish salt, sugar, and fats in our food supplies, we have evolved social capacities to recognize honesty, trustworthiness, reciprocity—and foreignness. But how does this illuminate the question of genocide?

There is persuasive evidence that the human species exhibits xenophobia and, like chimpanzees, practices murderous competition and out-group exclusion. . . . Indeed, chimps raid neighboring troops for females and stalk male competitors from neighboring bands—as do the Yanomamo of Venezuela, a modern stone-age people. The instinct for coalition formation appears to have evolved in the context of sexual selection pressures. Coalitions by males in ape and dolphin societies expedite male access to sexually receptive females. . . . [E]vidence suggests that the same occurs in human hunter and gatherer societies. . . .

The coalitionist or "tribal" instinct is at the core of human nature. We cooperate to compete. But the dark side of this sociability is group prejudice and an intolerance for out-groups (Reynolds, Falger, & Vine, 1987). In fact, the maintenance of group boundaries is premised on instinctual hatred of the Other. Whereas selection pressures at the level of kin probably fostered the development of altruistic and nepotistic instincts (Trivers, 1971), the same is not true at the level of larger, genetically diverse groups (Williams, 1966). . . . [C]ulture may provide social cohesiveness in spite of the group's genetic diversity.

What makes human beings different is culture. Because of the human practice of passing on traditions . . . there is a whole new kind of evolution going on in human beings—a competition not between genetically different individuals or groups, but between culturally different individuals or groups. One person may thrive at the expense of another not because he has better genes, but because he knows or believes something of practical value.

According to Herbert Simon (1990), the most adaptive strategy in group-mediated survival is "conformism". . . . Surprisingly, the facts suggest otherwise. The ordinary men who carried out the program of racial hygiene were simply reflecting the views of Jewish racial inferiority already advocated by leading German race scientists. . . . Nazi race policies "were based not on ignorant race prejudices nor on the paranoid delusions of a madman, but rather on the findings of what was at the time considered to be rigorous and authentic research" by respectable scientists.

In summary, the evolution of sociability, altruism, and the instincts for coalitions goes hand in hand with hostility to outsiders. . . . The belligerence arises from our coalitionist nature, and we often revel collectively in opposition and confrontation. . . . This is at the heart of our sociability as a species and is the root of xenophobia. Anti-Semitism has arguably been the leading case of out-group hatred in Christian countries, but what made it more virulent in Nazi Germany was the elaborate racist belief systems—both lay and professional—about human differences that motivated ordinary people to kill their neighbors and the technological and institutional abilities to carry out the violence on an unprecedented scale. . . . [T]his does not mean there is a gene for genocide. But genocide thrives through a combination of cultural animosities, forces that are proximal, and our instinctual legacy for groupishness, forces that are distal.

Was Lombroso on the Right Track?

The single most influential study of crime in the 19th century appeared in 1876—Cesare Lombroso's *L'Uomo Delinquente* (*Criminal Man*). In this work, Lombroso brought the study of crime under a Darwinian framework, the new science of "criminal anthropology." In Lombroso's view, criminals were not made by culture but were biologically impelled to "a life of crime" at birth. According to Lombroso, criminals were atavists—throwbacks to a more primitive human race—and as such, in Lombroso's view, the criminal exhibited a distinct physical type with telltale cranial, facial, and bodily characteristics. The search for these physical anomalies in populations of incarcerated offenders lasted almost a century. But as we all know, the search ultimately proved fruitless. No evidence of atavism was ever observed.

What then is the point of asking whether Lombroso was on the right track? Clearly, in specific terms, the evidence suggests emphatically that he was not. But if we abandon the idea of physical atavism and examine the potential of evolutionary theory, we find an emphasis on psychological atavism in much Darwinian psychology. Whereas Darwin's "dangerous idea"

(Dennett, 1995) became the intellectual bedrock of the natural and physical sciences, criminology, particularly in the last two decades, appears to have been returning to Bentham and his rather simplistic notions of appetites (see Wilson & Herrnstein, 1985; Gottfredson & Hirschi, 1990). Evolutionary psychology opens the question of appetites and desires to adaptive mechanisms and instincts and may explain some peculiarities of criminal behavior that are anomalous within a Benthamite frame of reference, for example, inter-male murders arising from "trivial altercations" and the compulsiveness of male sexual jealousy associated with stalking. . . .

NOT QUITE BACK TO ATAVISM

First, within criminology, evolutionary theories of crime are still theories of action. We still are concerned with saints and sinners and with individual responsibility for behavior. The sphere of action is human decision making, choices, moral conflicts and dilemmas, and the conditions under which such choices are exercised. What evolutionary theories of criminal action suggest is why certain appetites or desires—such as racial hatreds—would have the appeal they sometimes have and their probable evolutionary origins, but unlike Lombroso's Darwinism, the perspective remains voluntaristic.

Second, Lombroso juxtaposed crimes that arose from nature (atavism) and crimes that arose from culture or society (crimes of passion). In our view, this is a false distinction. Evolution may have created numerous appetites and instincts, but cultures are mechanisms for both switching them on and exciting other "instincts" or mechanisms that can curb them or switch them off. The Nazis may have played to instinctual out-group animosities in the reign of terror from 1933 to 1945, but the postwar peace process and the trial of war criminals orchestrated the innate moral instincts to reduce racial bigotry in Germany. . . .

Third, the adoption of an evolutionary perspective does not entail acceptance of heredity as fate. Or does it? This is a tricky question, and the attraction of the new evolutionary thinking as a voluntaristic perspective hangs to some extent in the balance. In *The Evolution of Desire*, Buss (1994, p. 17) [offers optimistic advice]: "We are the first species in the known history of three and a half billion years of life on earth with the capacity to control our destiny."

Certainly, we can learn to curb our appetites for salty, sweet, and high-fat foods and expressions of sexual jealousy. However, this ability seems to borrow in spades from the mechanisms central to sociological criminology—high levels of self-control and social control, conditions that are acquired to various degrees during early childhood socialization. It is at this point that we see a convergence of the interests of evolutionists and control theorists.

I offer a final point. Much of the writing in evolutionary psychology is curiously preoccupied with an aversion to our nature. Like Lombroso, Buss, as well as Daly and Wilson and Ridley, theorize about "vestiges" akin to psychological atavism, as though our nature contained considerable surplus baggage that is not quite human. For example, Daly and Wilson (1988, p. 219) write: "The man who hunts down and kills a woman who has left him has surely lapsed into futile spite, acting out of his vestigial agenda of dominance to no useful end." The other side of the picture involves all of those evolved mechanisms such as the capacity for language, representation, music, loyalty, the moral sense, cheater detection, cooperation, and so on—all the many and varied aspects of our nature that contribute positively to our lives and that we should never dream of "designing out" of our experience. In some cases, there seems to be a vision of a post-evolutionary future, as though selection pressures would wither in the designed society, just as Marxists believed in the withering of the class struggle with the rise of socialism. I suggest that xenophobic behavior—and its management—are here for the long haul. . . .

DISCUSSION QUESTIONS

1. Contrast the traditional explanations for German citizens' participation in the extermination of the Jews with Goldhagen's thesis. What is so striking about Goldhagen's proposition?

2. What evidence from the Holocaust does Goldhagen provide to support his thesis?

3. What is *exterminationist anti-Semitism* as defined by Goldhagen? Why does Brannigan

feel that Goldhagen's case "falls short of the mark"?

4. What does the evolutionary psychology of genocide framework offer to Brannigan's argument and construction of a theory of xenophobia? Why might this theoretical development and research be especially relevant and pertinent for criminologists?

PART III

SOCIAL STRUCTURAL THEORIES OF CRIME

Social structural theories of crime comprise a large number of individual theories of crime that have been subsumed under the wider category of sociological approaches to crime. Social structural theories of crime, in contrast to the other group of sociological theories—the social process theories—emphasize that environmental factors, such as social order, structural organization, individuals' relations to social norms and values, and the level of community solidarity in terms of these norms and values, play the most important role in determining whether crime will ensue. The three theoretical frameworks considered in this section, namely social disorganization, subcultural theories, and anomie/strain theories, emphasize the importance of social structural "arrangements" and order in communities in terms of their relationship to crime and delinquency.

Despite the fact that social disorganization and anomie/strain theories of crime evolved from different theoretical and research backgrounds, they are included together in this part of the anthology primarily because they share a common theme. Both theories suggest that social order, stability, and social and cultural integration with the large community foster conformity, whereas disorder and a failure to integrate lead to crime and deviance. Social systems, or communities, achieve social order and integration if members of the community can arrive at a consensus regarding the community's norms and values, if a strong sense of cohesion binds members, and if social interaction among members carries on in an orderly fashion (Akers, 2001). In contrast, the social system is anomic or disorganized if interaction and social order become disturbed, if a breakdown in social control occurs, or if an overwhelming sense of normlessness pervades the entire system itself.

Both social disorganization and anomie/strain theories propose that the less cohesive or integrated a community becomes, the more likely it is to become fertile ground for delinquent behavior. Additionally, each approach attempts to explain the high rates of delinquency within ethnically mixed lower-class groups. Moreover, subcultural theories of crime also take this approach to delinquency and attempt to incorporate elements of both approaches in their theoretical premises. In an interesting theoretical twist, at times, social disorganization and anomie/strain theories focus specifically on delinquent gangs and subcultures! Subcultural theories of crime attempt to answer the question of why there appear to be high rates of delinquency and crime among particular groups and in particular areas or regions. Like social disorganization and anomie/strain theories, subcultural theories examine the degree to which members of a subculture adhere to the dominant society's norms and values and how they negotiate these norms and values within the normative value structure of their subculture.

SOCIAL DISORGANIZATION AND CRIME

The prominent sociologist Emile Durkheim, often considered to be one of the founders of modern sociology, maintained in his anomie theory that rapid social change was linked with increased crime rates because of the breakdown of social controls in the community. This idea formed the basis of the newly emerging sociological theories of delinquency, which were first developed in the 1920s by members of the Department of Sociology at the University of Chicago in their attempts to specify certain environmental conditions associated with crime and to determine the relationships among those factors.

In contrast to Durkheim's societal approach to anomie, these theorists focused on crime and disorder within neighborhoods. It is important to keep in mind that at this time, both the United States and Europe were undergoing major social changes with respect to urbanization and industrialization. Cities were growing at unprecedented rates, which frequently contributed not only to problems associated with criminality but also to other social problems related to the surge in immigration, the migration of rural American farmers to large urban centers, public health and welfare, education, and the use of child labor in the workplace.

Chicago, like other large cities at this time, was not immune to this social upheaval. The researchers at the University of Chicago began to treat Chicago as a natural laboratory teeming with a variety of social maladies and conditions that required examination and diagnosis.

Human Ecology and the Concentric Zone Theory

The original Chicago School sociologists, Robert Park and Ernest Burgess, based much of their research on the image of communities taken from plant ecology (Burgess, 1925/1967). Subsequently, their ideas became known as the Chicago School of Human Ecology. Within plant ecology, ecologists study a vast web of interrelationships and interdependencies among organisms in order to reveal the forces that characterize the roles and activities of each part (Vold, Bernard, & Snipes, 1998). Park and Burgess likened the growth of the city to these ecological processes among plant life, stressing the significance of competition over land use as the population grew and as the city expanded its boundaries. They asserted that this competition process led to adaptations, which resulted in

cooperation in a state of balanced community equilibrium. But in this process, they found that certain areas of the city underwent changes that subsequently left social institutions completely ineffective. This condition was labeled *social disorganization* (Krohn, 2001).

Burgess proposed that Chicago was growing in a series of concentric circles, or zones, beginning in the center of the city and growing outward to the residential suburbs. The residential, commercial, and industrial pattern of urban settlement and activity characterized these zones. Directly adjacent to the city's commercial and business core of the city was a "zone in transition," which was beginning to shift away from residential to commercial. Burgess found that this zone generated the highest rates of delinquency.

Physical decay, poor housing, broken families, high rates of illegitimate births, and an unstable and heterogeneous population characterized this zone (Akers, 2001). The residents tended to occupy the lowest rungs of the educational, occupational, and social ladder. Plagued with high rates of delinquency, this zone also became an area ripe for mental illness, alcoholism, drug addition, and prostitution. Burgess concluded that all of these forms of deviance and crime resulted simply from the high level of social disorganization within this particular urban area.

A significant theoretical point emerged out of this research. These residents of Chicago at the time of the research did not suffer from any biological or psychological abnormalities. Instead, the deviance and lawlessness in that area was a normal reaction by normal people to abnormal social conditions, namely disorganization. Furthermore, under these conditions, criminal and delinquent traditions developed over time and later became an intergenerational phenomenon. In sum, the Chicago sociologists concluded that industrialization, urbanization, and other social changes in modern society caused social disorganization by disrupting the normative social order and control mechanisms that typically kept everything in check.

Shaw and McKay's Restatement of Social Disorganization

Shaw and McKay (Chapter 6 of this volume) extended Park and Burgess's research regarding the concentric zones, focusing mainly on Zone II, the zone in transition. Shaw and McKay felt that Burgess's theory of the city might give them direction in terms of their research on juvenile delinquency in Chicago. If Burgess's propositions and findings were indeed correct, then, Shaw and McKay asserted, rates of juvenile delinquency should be highest in the inner-city areas. The intersection of a wide variety of conditions such as persistent poverty, rapid population growth and changing composition (i.e., culture conflict), and a transient population base (i.e., mobility) combined to disrupt the core social institutions of society, such as the family. However, instead of focusing on any one of these specific conditions, they introduced the term *social disorganization* "to describe the intervening mechanism between the social conditions described and the rates of crime" (Krohn, 2001, p. 375). Shaw and McKay claimed that delinquency would be higher in these communities and lower in neighborhoods that were more organized or stable.

In their 1942 study of juvenile delinquency, Shaw and McKay found that the combined effects of an absence of resources, a highly mobile population, and cultural uncertainty produced inadequate and unstable social institutions in these areas, which suggested that these individuals were not being socially integrated into the larger social institutions or with each other. This lack of integration led to an inability on the part of social control agents to control the behavior of these individuals.

Shaw and McKay's finding that crime rates in particular areas were relatively stable over time led them to conclude that the characteristics of the areas themselves, not the values of the individuals living in them, were what regulated the level of delinquency in those areas. They observed that even though the dominant ethnic and racial composition of such areas was in perpetual motion, the crime rates remained persistently high. In order to explain this persistence of crime, Shaw and McKay developed a mixed model of delinquency. In this model, they stressed that the lack of opportunities, or strain, that these people experienced by living in these areas and the cultural deviance were being transmitted from one generation to the next.

Recent Reformulations of Social Disorganization Theory

Although Shaw and McKay's theory of social disorganization found an important place among criminologists in the years following its introduction to the research community, the theory had lost its appeal by the 1960s. Other theories being addressed at that time gained more prominence. Nonetheless, beginning the 1980s, their theory has received recent attention and interest. Although a number of these theories addressed a renewed interest in ecological research (Blau & Blau, 1982), many of the more recent approaches have attempted to use Shaw and McKay's theory to explain crime in today's society. For example, Sampson (1986) argued that inner cities have high crime rates because the residents have lost their ability to exercise "informal social control." Sampson found that living in a community characterized by a high number of single-parent homes created an environment in which control could not be exercised effectively (Sampson, 1986).

In this volume, Rose and Clear (Chapter 7) offer another extension of social disorganization theory. In their reformulation, they contend that even though areas plagued with high levels of social disorganization may be conducive to delinquency, efforts to restore social order to communities may nevertheless exacerbate the problem. They build on Bursik and Grasmick's (1993) recursive model by including a reciprocal component that takes into account these public controls. Rose and Clear use the example of incarceration as the primary factor with respect to this problem. Their theoretical expansion of social disorganization provides important insight not only for criminologists but for criminal justice professionals as well, in terms of using alternative methods of control, such as community policing, which may help to empower residents, increase cohesion and integration, and restore social order (Rose & Clear, Chapter 7).

ANOMIE/STRAIN AND SUBCULTURAL THEORIES OF CRIME

For purposes of clarity and brevity, these subsections in the anthology will be collapsed. This anthology makes a point of distinguishing anomie/strain and subcultural theories namely to point out to readers the primary theoretical thrust of the article or text excerpt. Strain theory, also known as anomie theory, broadly encompasses both psychological and sociological concerns in its explanation of crime and delinquency. The history of the theory extends back to Durkheim, who used the term *anomie* to refer to a state of normlessness or lack of social regulation in modern society as one condition that promotes high crime rates. In other words, when societal equilibrium becomes disrupted, individuals no longer have the normative guidance necessary to enable them to "fit" themselves into the whole of their community. Amid this lack of social cohesion or integration, crime rates may escalate. Durkheim also recognized that capitalism produced certain social and economic conditions that were also conducive to high crime rates. He concluded that this type of society, by encouraging desires and appetites while providing no way to feed them, caused anomic strain within the community.

Merton's Theory of Anomie and Its Application to Subcultural Theories of Crime

Merton (Chapter 9, this volume) applies this Durkheimian approach to the condition of modern industrial states, namely the United States. Merton claims that crime and deviance may be a natural response in egalitarian societies, where cultural goals are established for everyone to achieve (i.e., monetary success) but where the legitimate means to achieve those goals are not made universally available.

Merton's stipulation formed the essential core of strain theory, although it has been modified substantially over the years and applied to a number of different circumstances of crime. For instance, early social disorganization theorists such as Shaw and McKay (Chapter 6, this volume) promptly adopted the basic anomie concept of the disparity between success goals and legitimate means (Akers, 2001). Additionally, subcultural theories have been conceptualized largely in terms of anomie/strain theory. Subcultural theories of crime argue that certain groups or subcultures in our society approve of crime or hold values that are conducive to crime. Individuals who interact with members of such a subculture may eventually adopt the criminal values held by the group and may subsequently engage in criminal behavior. For example, individuals who shoplift may do so because they have learned from others that shoplifting is OK, or that it is at least allowed.

Subcultural theories assert that individuals typically do not feel strained or frustrated, and therefore strain is not the likely source of the delinquent behavior. Sutherland's theory of differential association (Chapter 12, this volume) provides the general context within which subcultural criminality can be understood. Therefore, subcultural theories assert that "criminal behavior is learned in interaction with others who approve of crime or who hold values conducive to crime" (Agnew, 2001, p. 357).

Many of the various subcultural theories advanced during the 1950s and 1960s borrowed heavily from Merton. In terms of subcultural theories of crime, Cohen (1955) and Cloward and Ohlin (1960) used Merton's approach in their research on gangs in lower-class areas. Cloward and Ohlin observed that strain emerged as a result of the perceived or actual inability to achieve the cultural goal of monetary success. Altering Merton's anomie/strain formula, Cloward and Ohlin proposed a differential opportunity model of subcultural delinquency, which argues that just as legitimate opportunities to achieve goals may not be available, *illegitimate* opportunities to these goals are also socially structured. Their theory combines anomie, differential association, and social disorganization theories to explain deviant adaptations in terms of a person's position in both the legitimate and illegitimate opportunity structures. Where both types of opportunities are blocked, delinquency becomes the norm.

This theory was criticized for being too simplistic in its conception, but Hagedorn's (1994) article elaborates on their theoretical premises. Hagedorn's Milwaukee, Wisconsin, study of male adult gang members who are involved with drug dealing and occasional participation in conventional employment shows that only a few of these individuals could be considered "committed long-term participants" in the drug economy. His typology of gang members suggests that only one type has completely rejected conventional values, whereas the other types continue to struggle with their desires to "be legit" while participating in the drug subculture on an irregular basis. His findings have powerful implications for social policy regarding the drug economy and drug enforcement policies. Additionally, Hagedorn's findings suggest some similarities with earlier research on subcultural delinquency and gangs.

Another earlier subcultural theory proposed by Cohen (1955) focused on the goal of middle-class status. Cohen's version of anomie theory is in basic agreement with Merton's theory, but for Cohen, it is not the inability to gain material success but the inability to achieve status and acceptance in conventional society that produces strain among lower-class youth. Cohen's theory is sometimes referred to as the "lower-class boy, middle-class measuring rod" approach. According to this theory, delinquency results from a conscious rejection of middle-class standards, which many of these lower-class youth feel are not attainable and cause them severe frustration.

Other theorists have used the concept of subculture in order to explain violence. For example, Wolfgang and Ferracuti (Chapter 8, this volume) relate the violence of lower-class, young, and disproportionately African American males to a subculture of violence. They contend that the typical homicide usually results from a cultural system of values and beliefs that has become more favorable to the use of violence than is the wider dominant culture.

A Reformulation of Merton's Approach: Institutional Anomie Theory

All of the examples discussed above demonstrate the correlation of crime with social class as a test of anomie. This conceptualization of Merton's original formulation of anomie/strain theory suggests that his anomie theory is a theory of social organization, not a theory of individuals' criminal impulses. Consequently, a proper test of the empirical validity of anomie theory lies with the determination of the social structural correlates of rates of crime (Akers, 2001). Messner and Rosenfeld (Chapter 10 of this volume) suggest that "the impact of anomie fostered by economic inequality is conditional on the strength or weakness of non-economic social institutions that provide normative restraints against achieving material success by deviant means" (Akers, 2001, p. 151). In their "institutional theory of anomie," Messner and Rosenfeld claim that the excessive emphasis placed on the "American Dream" of monetary success undermines the ability of the family, school, religion, law, and the polity to control the use of deviant means. Likewise, the use of legitimate means to achieve these goals is also undermined by poor social integration of cultural ends and social means.

Recent Reformulation and Elaboration of Strain Theory

Strain theory has undergone substantial revision and extension over the past decade. Robert Agnew's (2001) *general strain theory* embodies the most significant modification and recent elaboration of strain theory. He argues that the general strain theory of crime and delinquency can overcome prior criticisms of the theory, which centered on the overly deterministic nature of the theory, the lack of consideration for human agency, and the narrow definition of legitimate goals in terms of financial success. According to Agnew's theory, crime and delinquency provide an adaptation to stress, whatever the source of that stress may be. In his theory, he identifies three major types of deviant-producing strain, namely the failure to achieve positively valued goals, the removal of positively valued stimuli, and confrontation with negative stimuli.

REFERENCES

Agnew, R. (2001). Sources of criminality: Strain and subcultural theories. In J. Sheley (Ed.), *Criminology* (3rd ed., pp. 349-371). Belmont, CA: Wadsworth/Thomson Learning.

Akers, R. (2001). *Criminological theories: Introduction, evaluation, and application* (3rd ed.). Los Angeles: Roxbury.

Blau, J. R., & Blau, P. (1982). The cost of inequality: Metropolitan structure and violent crime. *American Sociological Review, 47*, 114-129.

Burgess, E. W. (1967). The growth of the city: An introduction to a research project. In R. E. Park & E. W. Burgess (Eds.), *The city* (pp. 47-62). Chicago: University of Chicago Press. (Original work published 1925).

Bursik, R. J., Jr., & Grasmick, H. G. (1993). *Neighborhoods and crime: The dimensions of effective community control*. New York: Lexington.

Cloward, R. A., & Ohlin, L. E. (1960). *Delinquency and opportunity: A theory of delinquent gangs*. New York: Free Press.

Cohen, A. (1955). *Delinquent boys: The culture of the gang*. Glencoe, IL: Free Press.

Hagedorn, J. M. (1994). Homeboys, dope fiends, legits, and new jacks. *Criminology, 32*, 197-219.

Krohn, M. (2001). Sources of criminality: Control and deterrence theories. In J. Sheley (Ed.), *Criminology* (3rd ed., pp. 373-399). Belmont, CA: Wadsworth/Thomson Learning.

Sampson, R. J. (1986). Crime in cities: The effects of formal and informal social control. In A. J. Reiss & M. Tonry (Eds.), *Communities and crime* (pp. 271-311). Chicago: University of Chicago Press.

Vold, G. B., Bernard, T. J., & Snipes, J. B. (1998). *Theoretical criminology* (4th ed.). Oxford, UK: Oxford University Press.

6

Delinquency Rates and Community Characteristics

Clifford R. Shaw and Henry D. McKay

EDITOR'S INTRODUCTION—This contribution by Clifford R. Shaw and Henry D. McKay reflects and extends the early classical work of social disorganization theory originally developed in the 1920s by Robert Park and Ernest Burgess of the Chicago School of Sociology. In this seminal work, the authors focused on the importance of the urban setting as a factor affecting delinquency rates.

In their study, *Juvenile Delinquency and Urban Areas*, Shaw and McKay focus on "the geographic distribution of delinquent or alleged delinquent boys and the manner in which rates of delinquent boys vary from area to area in Chicago" (Shaw & McKay, 1969, p. 43). Shaw and McKay present data that serve as a means of indicating the pattern of the distribution of delinquent behavior in Chicago and the extent to which this pattern has changed or remained the same throughout a 40-year period. Their findings suggest that community breakdown, or "social disorganization," led to increases in juvenile delinquency.

In the chapter included in this volume, "Delinquency Rates and Community Characteristics," the authors attempt to answer the question about what unique quality of modern city life produces delinquency. Specifically, they ask, "Why do relatively large numbers of boys from the inner urban areas appear in court with such striking regularity, year after year, regardless of changing population structure or the ups and downs of the business cycle?" (p. 70, this volume). This chapter extends their analysis in previous chapters of their book by comparing the series of distributions of truants and other criminals with other community characteristics—median rentals, families on relief, and infant mortality rates. In other words, they wanted to know the extent to which these two sets of data were related.

In drawing comparisons to rates of delinquency, Shaw and McKay examined the following factors: (a) the location of major industrial and commercial developments and population increases; (b) economic status, including percentage of families on relief, median rentals, and home ownership; and (c) population composition, including the percentage of "foreign-born" and "Negro" heads of families. Their findings indicate a high degree of association between rates of delinquency and other community characteristics when correlations are computed on the basis of values in square-mile areas and a closer association by large zones or classes of areas.

What they find in later chapters in their book highlights the importance of even more subtle differences among community members, namely values, standards, attitudes, traditions, and institutions. For a fuller understanding of their study, readers should consult the main text.

DELINQUENCY RATES
AND COMMUNITY CHARACTERISTICS

The question has been asked many times: "What is it, in modern city life that produces delinquency?" Why do relatively large numbers of boys from the inner urban areas appear in court with such striking regularity, year after year, regardless of changing population structure or the ups and downs of the business cycle? In preceding chapters different series of male delinquents were presented which closely parallel one another in geographical distribution although widely separated in time, and the close resemblance of all these series to the distribution of truants and of adult criminals was shown. Moreover, many other community characteristics—median rentals, families on relief, infant mortality rates, and so on—reveal similar patterns of variation throughout the city. The next step would be to determine, if possible, the extent to which these two sets of data are related. How consistently do they vary together, if at all, and how high is the degree of association?

Where high zero-order correlations are found to exist uniformly between two variables, with a small probable error, it is possible and valid to consider either series as an approximate index, or indicator, of the other. This holds true for any two variables which are known to be associated or to vary concomitantly. The relationship, of course, may be either direct or inverse. In neither case, however, is there justification in assuming, on this basis alone, that the observed association is of a cause-and-effect nature; it may be, rather, that both variables are similarly affected by some third factor. Further analysis is needed. Controlled experimentation is often useful in establishing the degree to which a change in one variable "causes" or brings about a corresponding change in the other. In the social field, however, experimentation is difficult. Instead, it is often necessary to rely upon refined statistical techniques, such as partial correlation, which, for certain types of data, enable the investigator to measure the effects of one factor while holding others relatively constant. By the method of successive redistribution, also, the influence of one or more variables may be held constant. Thus, it is possible to study the relationship between rates of delinquents and economic status for a single nationality group throughout the city or for various nationality groups in the same area or class of areas. This process may be extended indefinitely, subject only to the limitations of the available data. In the analysis to be presented, both of the latter methods have been used in an attempt to determine how much weight should be given to various more or less influential factors.

Several practical considerations prevent the neat and precise statistical analysis which would be desirable. The characteristics studied represent only a sampling of the myriad forms in which community life and social relationships find expression. The rate of delinquents must itself be thought of as an imperfect enumeration of the delinquents and an index of the larger number of boys engaging in officially proscribed activities. Not only will there be chance fluctuations in the amount of alleged delinquency from year to year, but the policy of the local police officer in referring boys to the juvenile Court, the focusing of the public eye upon conditions in an area, and numerous other matters may bring about a change in the index without any essential change in the underlying delinquency-producing influences in the community or in the behavior resulting therefrom. If the infant mortality rates or the rates of families on relief are looked upon as indexes of economic status or of the social organization of a community, it is obvious that they can be considered only very crude indicators at best. The perturbing influence of other variables must always be considered.

Certain exceptional conditions are known to limit the value of other variables chosen as indicators of local community differentiation. Median rental has been used widely because of its popularity as an index of economic status, although in Chicago such an index is far from satisfactory when applied to areas of colored population. The Negro is forced to pay considerably higher rents than the whites for comparable housing—thus his economic level is made to appear higher on the basis of rental than it actually is. Similarly, rates of increase or decrease of population are modified in Negro areas by restrictions on free movement placed upon the

Shaw, C. R., & McKay, H. D. (1969). Delinquency rates and community characteristics. In C. R. Shaw & H. D. McKay, *Juvenile delinquency and urban areas* (2nd ed., pp. 140-169). Chicago: University of Chicago Press.

Negro population. Thus, in certain areas the population is increasing where it normally would be expected to decrease if there were no such barriers. Likewise, the percentage of families owning homes is not entirely satisfactory as an economic index in large urban centers, where many of the well-to-do rent expensive apartments. It is, however, an indication of the relative stability of population in an area.

Correlation of series of rates based on geographical areas is further complicated by the fact that magnitude of the coefficient is influenced by the size of the area selected. This tendency has been noted by several writers, but no satisfactory solution of the problem has been offered. If it be borne in mind that a correlation of area data is an index of geographical association for a particular type of spatial division only, rather than a fixed measure of functional relationship, it will be apparent that a change in area size changes the meaning of the correlation. Thus, an *r* of .90 or above for two series of rates calculated by square-mile areas indicates a high degree of association between the magnitudes of the two rates in most of the square miles but does not tell us the exact degree of covariance for smaller or larger areas.

With these limitations clearly in mind, a number of correlation coefficients and tables of covariance are presented. The statistical data characterizing and differentiating local urban areas may be grouped under three headings: (1) physical status, (2) economic status, and (3) population composition. These will be considered, in turn, in relation to rates of delinquents.

INDEXES OF PHYSICAL STATUS
IN RELATION TO RATES OF DELINQUENTS

The location of major industrial and commercial developments, the distribution of buildings condemned for demolition or repair, and the percentage increase or decrease in population by square-mile areas were presented in chapter 2 as indications of the physical differentiation of areas within the city. Quantitative measures of the first two are not available, but inspection of the distribution maps shows clearly that the highest rates of delinquents are most frequently found in, or adjacent to, areas of heavy industry and commerce. These same neighborhoods have the largest number of condemned buildings. The

only notable exception to this generalization, for Chicago, appears in some of the areas south of the central business district.

There is, of course, little reason to postulate a direct relationship between living in proximity to industrial developments and becoming delinquent. While railroads and industrial properties may offer a field for delinquent behavior, they can hardly be regarded as a cause of such activities. Industrial invasion and physical deterioration do, however, make an area less desirable for residential purposes. As a consequence, in time there is found a movement from this area of those people able to afford more attractive surroundings. Further, the decrease in the number of buildings available for residential purposes leads to a decrease in the population of the area.

Population Increase or Decrease. Increase or decrease of population and rates of delinquents, by square-mile areas, do not exhibit a linear relationship. A relatively slight difference in rate of decrease of population, or of rate of increase for areas where the increase is slight, is generally associated with a considerable change in rates of delinquents; while for large differences in rates of increase of population, where increase is great, there is little or no consistent difference in rates of delinquents. Thus, areas increasing more than 70 per cent show no corresponding drop in rates of delinquents, although the relationship is clear up to this point. . . .

[T]here is a similarity between the pattern of distribution of delinquency and that of population growth or decline. The data do not establish a causal relationship between the two variables, however. The fact that the population of an area is decreasing does not impel a boy to become delinquent. It may be said, however, that decreasing population is usually related to industrial invasion of an area and contributes to the development of a general situation conducive to delinquency.

POPULATION COMPOSITION
IN RELATION TO RATES OF DELINQUENCY

In Chicago, as in other northern industrial cities, as has been said, it is the most recent arrivals—persons of foreign birth and those who have migrated from other sections of this country—who find it necessary to make their homes in neighborhoods of low economic level. Thus the newer European immigrants are found concentrated in certain areas, while Negroes from the rural South and Mexicans occupy others of comparable status. Neither of these population categories, considered separately, however, is suitable for correlation with rates of delinquents, since some areas of high rates have a predominantly immigrant population and others are entirely or largely Negro. Both categories, however, refer to groups of low economic status, making their adjustment to a complex urban environment. Foreign-born and Negro heads of families will therefore be considered together in order to study this segregation of the newer arrivals, on a city-wide scale.

Percentage of Foreign-Born and Negro Heads of Families.[1]

When the rates of delinquents in the 1927-33 series are correlated with the percentage of foreign-born and Negro heads of families as of 1930, by 140 square-mile areas, the coefficient is found to be .60 ± .03. Similarly, when the 1917-23 delinquency data are correlated with percentages of foreign-born and Negro heads of families for 1920, by the 113 areas into which the city was divided for that series, the coefficient is .58 ± .04. When rates of delinquents are calculated for the classes of areas . . . wide variations are found between the rates in the classes where the percentage of foreign-born and Negro heads of families is high and in those where it is low. . . . Since the number of foreign-born heads of families in the population decreased and the number of Negroes increased between 1920 and 1930, the total proportions of foreign-born and Negro heads of families in each class do not correspond. The variation with rates of delinquents, however, remains unchanged.

While it is apparent from these data that the foreign born and the Negroes are concentrated in the areas of high rates of delinquents, the meaning of this association is not easily determined. One might be led to assume that the relatively large number of boys brought into court is due to the presence of certain racial or national groups were it not for the fact that the population composition of many of these neighborhoods has changed completely, without appreciable change in their rank as to rates of delinquents. Clearly, one must beware of attaching causal significance to race or nativity. For, in the present social and economic system, it is the Negroes and the foreign born, or at least the newest immigrants, who have least access to the necessities of life and who are therefore least prepared for the competitive struggle. It is they who are forced to live in the worst slum areas and who are least able to organize against the effects of such living.

In Chicago three kinds of data are available for the study of nativity, nationality, and race in relation to rates of delinquents. These data concern (1) the succession of nationality groups in the high-rate areas over a period of years; (2) changes in the national and racial backgrounds of children appearing in the juvenile Court; and (3) rates of delinquents for particular racial, nativity, or nationality groups in different types of areas at any given moment. In evaluating the significance of community characteristics found to be associated with high rates of delinquents, the relative weight of race, nativity, and nationality must be understood. . . .

It appears to be established, then, that each racial, nativity, and nationality group in Chicago displays widely varying rates of delinquents; that rates for immigrant groups in particular show a wide historical fluctuation; that diverse racial, nativity, and national groups possess relatively similar rates of delinquents in similar social areas; and that each of these groups displays the effect of disproportionate concentration in its respective areas at a given time. In the face of these facts it is difficult to sustain the contention that, by themselves, the factors of race, nativity, and nationality are vitally related to the problem of juvenile delinquency. It seems necessary to conclude, rather, that the significantly higher rates of delinquents found among the children of Negroes, the foreign born, and more recent immigrants are closely related to existing differences in their respective patterns of geographical distribution within the city. If these groups were found in the same proportion in all local areas, existing differences in the relative number of boys brought into court from the various groups might be expected to be greatly reduced or to disappear entirely.

It may be that the correlation between rates of delinquents and foreign-born and Negro heads of families is incidental to relationships between rates of delinquents and apparently more basic social and economic characteristics of local communities. Evidence that this is the case is seen in two partial correlation coefficients computed.

Selecting the relief rate as a fair measure of economic level, the problem is to determine the relative weight of this and other factors. The partial correlation coefficient between rate of delinquents and percentage of families on relief, holding constant the percentage of foreign-born and Negro heads of families, in the 140 areas, is .76 ± .02. However, the coefficient for rates of delinquents and percentage of foreign-born and Negro heads of families, when percentage of families on relief is held constant, is only .26 ± .05. It is clear from these coefficients, therefore, that the percentage of families on relief is related to rates of delinquents in a more significant way than is the percentage of foreign-born and Negro heads of families.

It should be emphasized that the high degree of association between rates of delinquents and other community characteristics, as revealed in this chapter, does not mean that these characteristics must be regarded as causes of delinquency, or vice versa. Within certain types of areas differentiated in city growth, these phenomena appear together with such regularity that their rates are highly correlated. Yet the nature of the relationship between types of conduct and given physical, economic, or demographic characteristics is not revealed by the magnitude either of zero-order or partial correlation coefficients, or of other measures of association.

A high degree of association may lead to the uncritical assumption that certain factors are causally related, whereas further analysis shows the existing association to be entirely adventitious. This is apparently the case with the data on nativity, nationality, and race. . . . That, on the whole, the proportion of foreign-born and Negro population is higher in areas with high rates of delinquents there can be little doubt; but the facts furnish ample basis for the further conclusion that the boys brought into court are not delinquent *because* their parents are foreign born or Negro but rather because of other aspects of the total situation in which they live. In the same way, the relationship between rates of delinquents and each associated variable should be explored, either by further analysis, by experimentation, or by the study of negative cases.

Summary

It has been shown that, when rates of delinquents are calculated for classes of areas grouped according to rate of any one of a number of community characteristics studied, a distinct pattern appears—the two sets of rates in each case varying together. When values of these other community characteristics, in turn, are calculated for classes of areas grouped by rate of delinquents, the same consistent trends appear. . . . The data . . . indicate a high degree of association between rates of delinquents and other community characteristics when correlations are computed on the basis of values in square-mile areas or similar subdivisions, and a still closer general association by large zones or classes of areas. . . .

Discussion Questions

1. Provide an answer to Shaw and McKay's question: "Why do relatively large numbers of boys from the inner urban areas appear in court with such striking regularity, year after year, regardless of changing population structure or the ups and downs of the business cycle?" (p. 70, this chapter)

2. What factor plays the greatest role in contributing to the problem of delinquency?

3. Although the information is not presented in this volume, how might values, attitudes, standards, traditions, and institutions affect rates of delinquency perhaps more than physical and economic status and population composition?

Note

1 The categories "foreign born" and "Negro" are not compat[i]ble, since the former group is made up primarily of adults, while the latter includes all members of the race. The classification "heads of families" has been used, therefore, foreign-born and Negro family heads being entirely comparable groupings. The census classification "other races" has been included—a relatively small group, comprising Mexicans, Japanese, Chinese, Filipinos, etc.

Reference

Shaw, C. R., & McKay, H. D. (1969). *Juvenile delinquency and urban areas* (2nd ed.). Chicago: University of Chicago Press.

INCARCERATION, SOCIAL CAPITAL, AND CRIME

Implications for Social Disorganization Theory

DINA R. ROSE AND TODD R. CLEAR

EDITOR'S INTRODUCTION—Dina R. Rose and Todd R. Clear offer an insightful approach to the problem of crime within disorganized and crime-prone communities. They postulate that formal state controls, namely the criminal justice system, *negatively* affect the functioning of family and neighborhood controls. In other words, at the community, or even neighborhood, level, the side effects of policies intended to fight crime by removing individual offenders may *exacerbate*—not minimize—problems that originally lead to crime. Although the authors assert that some will see their argument as obviously plausible, they initiate their analysis from the counterintuitive nature of their position.

The first part of their work involves a consideration of the theoretical framework of social disorganization theory, which maintains that "some communities are unable to effectively self-regulate due to the damaging effects of certain environmental characteristics" (p. 76, this volume). Rose and Clear cite important contributions from Sampson (1987), Sampson and Groves (1993), and Bursik and Grasmick (1993), who all, in their respective studies, extended social disorganization theory to show how factors in communities and neighborhoods influence different dimensions and levels of control.

In their basic systemic model of crime, Bursik and Grasmick (1993) focus specifically on different levels of control and "merge systemic and social disorganization theories to examine the mediating role of private, parochial, and public controls" (p. 76, this volume). But as Rose and Clear demonstrate, this recursive model, which suggests that communities that experience less social disorganization experience less crime, limits a full consideration of the public controls that feed back upon the other elements in the basic model. Rose and Clear's nonrecursive model "specifies a reciprocal relationship between public social control and human and social capital and between public social control and . . . socioeconomic status, residential stability, and racial/ethnic heterogeneity through levels of incarceration" (p. 79, this volume).

The remainder of their work discusses the reciprocal effects of incarceration on communities. Rose and Clear find that, contrary to some widely held beliefs, incarceration of predominantly minority (mainly African American) males strongly affected communities on familial, economic, and political levels. As they note in a section not included here, "high levels of incarceration undermine social, political, and economic systems already weakened by low levels of human social capital produced under conditions of high rates of poverty, unemployment, and crime" (Rose & Clear, 1998, p. 467). The authors conclude with several suggestions for policy change with respect to crime control. A greater emphasis on neighborhood-based approaches, such as community policing, might give residents a greater sense of personal control within their neighborhoods and, perhaps, a better quality of life in their neighborhoods.

It is commonly accepted that in the absence of effective controls, crime and disorder flourish. Controls can operate at the individual, family, neighborhood, and state levels; and the safest neighborhoods are thought to be those in which controls work at each of these levels. This study is a theoretical exploration of the impact of state social control on the functioning of family and neighborhood social controls. We argue that state social controls, which typically are directed at individual behavior, have important secondary effects on family and neighborhood structures. These, in turn, impede the neighborhood's capacity for social control. Thus, at the ecological level, the side effects of policies intended to fight crime by controlling individual criminals may exacerbate problems that lead to crime in the first place.

We recognize that to some readers our argument is entirely plausible, perhaps even obvious. "After all," they might say, "everyone knows that current socioeconomic policy produces structural damages to the poor, creating a permanent underclass." Yet other readers will find our argument curious or even counterintuitive. How can it be bad for neighborhood life to remove people who are committing crimes in those very neighborhoods? We discuss a topic on which today's informed observers hold opposing views and on which there is little direct empirical evidence. We argue that a substantial body of indirect evidence exists on the expected social impacts of high incarceration rates, and that this evidence is well established within ecological frameworks of neighborhood life. To develop this theoretical line of reasoning, we move from the individualist paradigm that dominates contemporary thought about crime and crime policy, as exemplified by "criminal careers" and "criminal incapacitation" (see Blumstein et al., 1986; and Zimring & Hawkins, 1995) to a more inclusive ecological model of crime, crime control, and neighborhood life.

Ecological theories of crime seek to explain spatial variations in urban crime rates by exploring differences in the capacity for control across areas. Social disorganization theory, for example, attributes crime and disorder to impaired local controls at the neighborhood level. As a result, some communities are unable to self-regulate. In their study of neighborhood-level control, social disorganization theorists have largely ignored the impact of public, or state control, on processes of neighborhood organization and subsequent opportunities for crime. This is because formal public controls are thought of as responses to crime. Yet, there is clearly a relationship between the use of local and public controls. When local controls are impaired, communities must rely more heavily upon the controls of the state. Partly this is because there is more crime in these areas so the communities need the added strength of formal law enforcement in their response to crime. However, it may be that increased state efforts shift control resources from local to public, thus making state efforts more necessary. For instance, in high-crime neighborhoods, a concentration of police efforts removes large numbers of residents from the neighborhood. It is assumed that measures taken by the state, such as arresting and imprisoning offenders, will make communities safer by

Rose, D. R., & Clear, T. R. (1998). Incarceration, social capital, and crime: Implications for social disorganization theory. *Criminology, 36,* 441-480.

removing dangerous residents and by enabling those remaining to shore up their local controls. This may not always be the case. Rather, these practices may undermine the kinds of networks that form the basis of local control. Inherent in our analysis is the view that offenders have complex relationships to the networks in which they are embedded. They may contribute both positively and negatively toward family and neighborhood life. Their removal in large numbers alters those networks both positively and negatively. In highly organized communities, where levels of crime are low, reaction by the criminal justice system may enhance neighborhood networks overall by fostering ties between residents who now feel safer. In highly disorganized areas, however, action by the criminal justice system may damage neighborhood structure by disrupting network ties of offenders and nonoffenders and fostering alienation among residents and between the neighborhood and the state. In the latter case, the impact on local social control of the removal of residents is similar in nature (though different in kind) to Wilson's (1987) observation that communities experience a loss of control due to the out-migration of middle-class families. In this study we explore the hypothesis that an overreliance on formal controls may hinder the ability of some communities to foster other forms of control. As a result, these communities may experience more, not less, social disorganization.

Social Disorganization Theory, Social Control and Crime

In the search to explain spatial variation in crime rates, social disorganization theorists have explored the structural characteristics associated with crime. Shaw and McKay's (1942) social disorganization theory, and more recently work done by Bursik (1986, 1988), Sampson (1985, 1986a, 1986b, 1986c, 1987), and others, focuses on group adaptations to social processes such as urbanization and shifting patterns of economic growth, rather than concentrating on individual criminality. The essence of this theory is that some communities are unable to effectively self-regulate due to the damaging effects of certain environmental characteristics. This condition leads to a disrupted neighborhood organizational structure, which subsequently attenuates residents' ties to each other and to the community. As a result, some residents no longer submit to normative social controls.

Disorganized communities are unable to realize the common values of their residents and are unable to solve commonly experienced problems (Kornhauser, 1978) because they cannot establish or maintain consensus concerning values, norms, roles, or hierarchical arrangements among their members (Kornhauser, 1978; Shaw & McKay, 1942). As a control theory, social disorganization theory assumes that one common goal residents in all neighborhoods share is the desire to live in an area that is safe to inhabit (Bursik & Grasmick, 1993, p. 15). We assume all residents desire this since even offenders do not wish to be victimized. Researchers working within this theoretical domain have focused their efforts on identifying which ecological conditions are most associated with crime. Attention has commonly been centered on such variables as poverty, residential mobility, ethnic heterogeneity, population, and structural density. The state of disorganization remains latent, only to be inferred by the existence of these destabilizing factors.

Recently, attempts have been made to explore the "black box" of disorganization. Sampson (1987) and Sampson and Groves (1989) have investigated the mediating effects of guardianship, community attachment, and informal social control. They have shown that integration and social ties are important mediators between social conditions and crime. For instance, Sampson (1988) finds that integration *is* indicated by individuals' local friendships, their attachment to the community and their participation in local activities. Integration fosters participation, which fosters deeper integration. Whereas these scholars focus their efforts on identifying *dimensions* of control, Bursik and Grasmick (1993) have identified different *levels* of control. They merge systemic and social disorganization theories to examine the mediating role of private, parochial, and public controls. Bursik and Grasmick's extension of disorganization theory shows how ecological factors influence different levels of control. Social control, they argue, represents an effort by neighborhood residents to regulate the behavior of both locals and outsiders to achieve the goal of a safe living

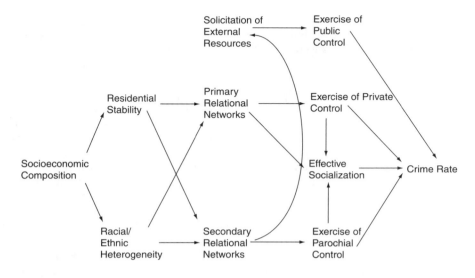

Figure 7.1   Bursik and Grasmick's Basic Systemic Model of Crime

environment. Figure 7.1 shows their "Basic Systemic Model of Crime." This is a model of the structure of social resources that produce crime. It is composed of three panels of theoretical effects. The first panel is derived from the work of Shaw and McKay (1942) and contains the traditional social disorganization constructs: socioeconomic composition, residential stability, and racial/ethnic heterogeneity. The second panel comprises external resources and primary and secondary relational networks. It is an amalgam of the human/ social capital construct derived from Wilson's work (1987, 1996). This panel represents the interplay between local familial and voluntary groups and forces external to the neighborhood that may affect neighborhood life. The final panel, drawn from Hunter's work (1985), is a classification of the levels of social control by which communities carry out self-regulation.

Private control occurs among intimates and primary groups, such as family members or very close friends. Control stems from the allocation or threatened withdrawal of sentiment, social support, and mutual esteem. Parochial controls are the kinds of supervision and surveillance of places that occur naturally within communities, as people interact in normal day-to-day routines (see Felson, 1996). They encompass the broader, local, interpersonal networks, including the relationship among local institutions, such as

stores, schools, and churches. For instance, Sampson et al. (1997) identified several examples of informal community control tactics, such as willingness to intervene to prevent truancy or street-corner loitering by teenagers or confrontation of individuals who are damaging public property or disturbing the neighborhood. Control is located in the effectiveness of these groups and in the capacity of neighbors to supervise each other. Public controls involve the networks developed between the neighborhood and outside agencies, including those operated by the criminal justice and other governmental systems. Control is a function of the ability of the neighborhood to secure public goods and services from sources outside the neighborhood (Bursik and Grasmick, 1993, pp. 16-17).

These efforts by Sampson (1987), Sampson and Groves (1989), and Bursik and Grasmick (1993) highlight the significance of networks in neighborhood control. Sampson and Sampson and Groves primarily focus their efforts on components of the primary and parochial levels. They recognize that the extent to which individual residents are integrated and tied to the neighborhood influences its capacity to self-regulate. Conversely, when residents' ties are attenuated, when they feel anonymous and isolated, local control is difficult to achieve. Social control becomes compromised because there is a lack of community interaction and shared obligation. As a result, the community is weakened and can no longer intervene on behalf of the neighborhood (Sampson, 1987). Bursik and Grasmick add to this the idea that public control plays a role in neighborhood regulation to the extent that relations between the community and the state determine the type and quality of services and resources provided. We would add that networks between these actors influence the community's receptivity to coercive controls and determine whether the two engage in a largely cooperative or adversarial relationship. While it is tempting to think about these as three distinct levels of control, they are implicitly linked because they are interdependent. . . .

. . . . Black (1976) was one of the first to suggest a relationship between formal and informal controls as part of his larger theory about the quantity and style of law. His work recognizes the distinction between governmental and nongovernmental control and proposes the importance of both for effective regulation. He argued, as we do, that as informal social controls deteriorate, formal controls increase. We note that empirical results have provided only mixed support for Black's hypothesis. Leesan and Sheley (1992) recently attributed this to the fact that most studies (Braithwaite & Biles, 1980; Gottfredson & Hindelang, 1979; Kruttschnitt, 1980-81; Massey & Myers, 1989; Myers, 1980; Smith, 1987) have been conducted at the microsociological level. Their macrosociological level study, however, fared little better.

The lack of support found for the link between informal and formal controls might be attributed to the way in which control is conceptualized. Black considered informal control to be primarily familial and intimate. Lessan and Sheley (1992) use homicide and suicide rates as an indicator of the loss of community nongovernmental control over its members because they assumed these acts occur in the context of familial and intimate violence. This operationalization only vaguely connects to the broader ideas of informal social control, and it omits the role of parochial controls, which we view as essential. The interplay among all three types of control is important for effective community self-regulation, and a simple, recursively linear model is insufficient to test these relationships.

An overreliance on public controls may diminish the capacity of private and parochial controls as communities learn to rely on outsiders. While it is assumed that neighbors who call the police to control excessive noise have summoned public controls to shore up private and parochial controls, they actually may have replaced parochial with public control. Perhaps more significantly, policies and practices of public control agencies can directly attack the functioning of lower levels of control by disrupting the networks of association and the resources on which private and parochial controls rely. For instance, in 1996, President Clinton announced that the federal government would be funding community-based policing, through neighborhood crime watches and foot patrols, as part of community revitalization efforts. Although these programs are community based, they are often thinly veiled, "top-down" policy models in which the formal social control agencies assign duties and sanctions for the neighborhood group to impose on its members. When the focus of community policing derives from the biases of the formal control agency, tensions among residents of the neighborhood escalate, as does the hostility between the community and the police (Goetz, 1996). This is particularly true in disorganized communities, where the relationships among the levels of control are fragile.

The Nonrecursive Model

In its current form, the Bursik and Grasmick model is recursive, suggesting the traditional form of the crime control relationship: Communities that experience less social disorganization experience less crime. Our argument is that the public controls (the third panel) feed back upon most of the elements of the Basic Systemic Model. Thus, we argue for a reciprocal model in which public control influences the exogenous variables in the model. Figure 7.2 is a revision of Bursik and Grasmick's Basic Systemic Model illustrating our idea. It incorporates a feedback loop into a theory of the impact of crime control on neighborhood structures and its subsequent impact on self-regulation. It also subsumes primary and secondary relational networks and the solicitation of external resources under the heading "human and social capital." We return to this point below.

Our model specifies a reciprocal relationship between public social control and human and social capital and between public social

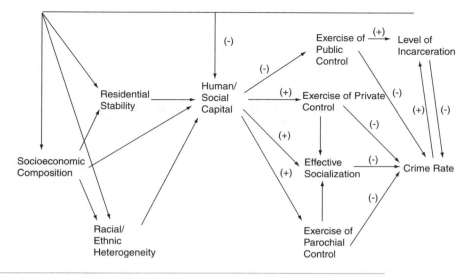

Figure 7.2   A Nonrecursive Model of Crime Control, Social Disorder, and Crime

control and the endogenous variables socio-economic status, residential stability, and racial/ethnic heterogeneity through levels of incarceration. Bursik and Grasmick make the argument that residential mobility and racial/ethnic heterogeneity affect the relational networks that are the basis of control because both conditions make it difficult for residents to establish and maintain ties within the neighborhood. Further, both decrease the ability and willingness of individuals to intervene in criminal events on behalf of their neighbors due to individual anonymity and alienation and, possibly, due to hostility or mistrust between different groups. In addition, mobility and heterogeneity potentially impair the socialization of youths, who are presumably exposed to multiple standards and forms of behavior rather than to one, unified code (Bursik and Grasmick, 1993, pp. 35-36).

Traditionally, Shaw and McKay (1942) believed that the key factor influencing residential mobility and ethnic heterogeneity was the socioeconomic composition of the neighborhood. Shaw and McKay believed poor neighborhoods were multiethnic and transient because they were the first stopping ground of new immigrants, who tended to move on when they were financially able. Today, although contemporary researchers tend to model all three variables as equally exogenous, they continue to subscribe to

the idea that disorganized communities are ethnically heterogeneous and residentially mobile because they are poor. Current work on the urban underclass, poverty, and residential segregation questions the chances of upward mobility for certain segments of the population (Anderson, 1990; Massey, 1990; Wilson, 1987). Thus, economic opportunities may not be driving residential mobility trends in some of today's poorer neighborhoods. Rather, other forces may be at work, forces producing entrenched deficits in social capital.

Our modification of Bursik and Grasmick's Basic Systemic Model is aligned with recent attempts by researchers to move beyond simple recursive models of crime to incorporate the nonrecursive or systemic features of the phenomenon. For the most part, work on nonrecursive models has dealt with the causes and effects of crime. For instance, Cook (1986, pp. 6-19) describes a "feedback loop" in which individuals limit their exposure to potential victimization as a result of their assessment of the likelihood of their being victimized, and in so doing, reduce the number of criminal opportunities. This takes the form of a market in which the volume of crime is partly determined by an interaction between potential victims who adapt their self-protection efforts based upon the probability of victimization and potential criminals who adapt their rate of offending based upon the overall quality of criminal opportunities. Skogan (1986, 1990) argues that levels of crime increase fear, which results in psychological and physical withdrawal from the neighborhood. This in turn weakens informal control, damages the organizational life and mobilization capacity of the neighborhood, and deteriorates business conditions. Wilson (1996) has argued that these forces also lead to the economic abandonment of inner cities, which produces further deterioration. These changes result in more crime and lead to a change in the composition of the population.

Within the social disorganization tradition, researchers have begun to examine the reciprocal relationship between community structure and crime rates with the understanding that social disorganization produces crime, which then produces more disorganization. Sampson et al. (1997) found that in very disadvantaged neighborhoods, decreases in collective efficacy (informal social controls and social cohesion within a neighborhood) result in a significant decrease in residential stability, which in turn increases the poverty of those neighborhoods. The so-called "broken windows" thesis (Wilson & Kelling, 1982), for example, is that the visible existence of minor criminal events conditions beliefs about more basic public safety and softens potential offenders' self-controls against criminal conduct. Likewise, Rose's (1995) analysis of crime and neighborhood organization in Chicago identified a reciprocal model in which neighborhood organizations affect opportunities for crime, the existence of which influences the need for renewed organizational efforts, which in turn alters subsequent opportunities for crime. Gottfredson and Taylor (1988) have shown that neighborhood characteristics affect individual arrest probabilities of prison releasees, even after their personal characteristics are controlled. The import of this line of inquiry is that crime trends are not independently linear, but must be understood contextually within local communities, especially with regard to other forms of self-regulation (see Bursik and Grasmick, 1993). In this vein, a recent paper by Taylor (1997) shows how the parochial controls described by Bursik and Grasmick are mediated by street-block characteristics.

Bursik and Grasmick (1993, pp. 57-59) note that their systemic model may be incomplete because of a failure to incorporate the degree to which crime and delinquency affect a neighborhood's capacity for social control. We add that it may be incomplete because of its failure to incorporate the feedback effect of the key systemic feature of public social controls. The nonrecursive nature of the relationship between crime and community suggests that a simple recursive model of removing offenders to improve neighborhood life fails to consider the feedback effect of public social control on the system of communities and crime. To the degree the feedback effects weaken community structure, there would then be unintended consequences of crime control strategies that damage neighborhood self-regulation.

We argue that one of those forces is incarceration, for it affects the three disorganizing factors originally identified by Shaw and McKay (1942). First, incarceration alters the socioeconomic composition of the neighborhood by influencing vital local resources, such as labor and marriage markets. (We consider these and other impacts of incarceration in more detail below.) Second, in many areas penal practices are a key factor influencing mobility in and out of the neighborhood. Every entrant into prison is someone exiting a neighborhood; every release from prison returns someone to a neighborhood. Finally, incarceration influences heterogeneity. Shaw and McKay, and others since them, have examined the impact of racial and ethnic heterogeneity on social organization because of the assumption that different ethnic groups represent different norms and values. Today, in many poor communities, there is racial homogeneity (these areas often are primarily black) but a heterogeneity of norms and values still exists (see Anderson, 1990, for a review of this argument). Not only do incarceration trends open opportunities for entrance of newcomers (with potentially different norms and values) into the neighborhood, but they increase opportunities for individuals to be socialized into prison subcultures. One might think that the removal of offenders would increase the cultural homogeneity of the neighborhoods they leave behind. However, well over 90% of prison admissions are eventually released after an average prison stay of about two years (Clear & Cole, 1997). Upon their return to the community, the stronger deviant orientation of prison releasees increases local cultural heterogeneity, thereby increasing disorganization.

The Reciprocal Effects of Incarceration

Since 1973, the incarceration rate has grown from about 90 per 100,000 to over 400 per 100,000; prisoners have increased from 350,000 to more than 1.5 million. Though the accumulation of additional prisoners has been gradual, the net impact of this profound shift in the collective experience of incarceration is important to understand. Growth in imprisonment has disproportionately affected the poor and people of color. When controlling for age and social class, it has been estimated that a minimum of 10% of *underclass* African-American males aged 26 to 30 were incarcerated in 1986 (Lynch & Sabol, 1992)—a number that has certainly grown with the prison population's growth (about double) since that time. In 1992 alone, 1 in 27 African-American males aged 16 to 34, living in metropolitan areas and contiguous counties, was admitted to prison (Lynch & Sabol, 1997). In 1994, approximately 9% of all African-Americans were under some form of correctional supervision (incarcerated or on probation or parole) (Bureau of Justice Statistics, 1996). Approximately 7% of all African-American males aged 20 to 50 are currently in prison (Bureau of Justice Statistics, 1995). Overall, the lifetime probability of an African-American male going to state or federal prison is 29% (Bonczar & Beck, 1997). The residential segregation of African-Americans in urban communities means that some of their neighborhoods have suffered war-level casualties in parenting-age males during the increase in imprisonment since 1973, when far fewer African-American males were incarcerated.

Our view builds on Wilson (1987), who argues that the out-migration of the middle class has resulted in neighborhoods without sufficient economic and social foundations for effective social control. These communities, he argues, are characterized by "joblessness, lawlessness, low-achieving schools" and increasing social isolation from mainstream society (Wilson, 1987, p. 58). Further, it is the impact of joblessness on social isolation that is crucial to understanding the underclass. Without a financially stable middle class (and no way to create a new one), these communities have neither the residents who socialize their youngsters to conventional norms and values, nor the ability to sustain local institutions.

The goal of Wilson's analysis was to account for the growth of severe poverty, and he begins by examining the events that disrupt a fully functioning community. Our analysis begins where he left off; it examines events that disrupt low-functioning neighborhoods. Communities hardest hit by incarceration are already depleted and each resource is vital. Compared to healthy neighborhoods, ones with sufficient supplies of human and social capital, disorganized areas most likely suffer exponentially with each additional network disruption. We expect, then, the same type of effect on communities from the out-migration of residents (even those who offend) as did Wilson, but with greater magnitude because of the fragile nature of the neighborhood.

A great deal depends, of course, on whether the active offender is viewed as a neighborhood asset or a liability. It is logical to assume that the loss of criminal males benefits communities simply because they are residents who are committing crimes. Their removal, then, could be seen as a positive act by the state: Criminals are gone, communities are safer and informal controls are now free to blossom. But if offenders are not solely a drain—if they are resources to some members of the community and if they occupy roles within networks that form the basis for informal social control—their removal is not solely a positive act, but also imposes losses on those networks and their capacity for strengthened community life. Research shows offenders represent both assets and liabilities to their communities. . . .

. . . . Studies confirm that some active offenders whose crimes make them eligible for incarceration are financial assets to their families and their communities. They contribute directly to the welfare of their families and other intimates in the same way noncriminal males do, although perhaps they provide fewer total dollars. This contribution helps explain why a study conducted a generation ago (Clear et al., 1971) found that over half of a sample comprised of one month's admissions to the Indiana Department of Corrections reported that their families went onto public assistance immediately following their imprisonment. Other street ethnographies show how young male offenders often live within tight associational networks of families and children, and they act as resources to those networks (e.g., McCall, 1994; Shakur, 1993). Recent research on gangs (Jankowski, 1991; Venkatesh, 1997) shows gang members in multidimension[al] roles—some detrimental and some beneficial to the neighborhood.

Our point is not that offenders be romanticized as "good citizens," but rather that they not be demonized. A view of them as "merely bad" is a one-sided stereotype that not only ignores the assets they represent to the networks within which they live, but also fails to account for the benefits they contribute to their environments. It also fails to recognize the damage done to other relational networks when they are incarcerated, networks often consisting of nonoffending family members, relatives, and friends. One reason disorganized communities are disorganized is because they do not have the strong bonds and dense social relationships that are important to social control (Kornhauser, 1978, p. 45). This makes the fragile linkages in those areas even more important. To say that offenders contribute to their communities is not to say they are ideal relatives and neighbors. It does recognize, however, [that] their contribution exists, and in disorganized areas with low levels of control partly due to weak ties, the contribution of offenders may not be that much less than [that of] their nonoffending neighbors.

Socially organized areas have sufficient assets and resources to overcome the loss of an offender's asset in order to remove the offender's liability from the neighborhood. In socially disorganized areas, however, assets are already sufficiently depleted that the neighborhood feels the loss of the asset just as it rejoices in the loss of the liability. Further, bouts of incarceration tend to produce individuals more hostile to legal legitimacy, less willing to work, and less able to get a job—conditions that increase that individual's role as a liability and diminish him as an asset. Add to this mix potentially hostile and antagonistic relations with the police and the state and incarceration trends may serve to exacerbate a neighborhood's social isolation. The question is, To what degree is this true? To respond to this question, we first consider the role of social and human capital in building informal social control.

SOCIAL AND HUMAN CAPITAL: THE IMPORTANCE OF PLACE

Social disorganization theory is implicitly based upon the notions of social and human capital, even if the terms have not been explicitly adopted. Social capital refers to the social skills and resources needed to effect positive change in neighborhood life. It is the aspect of structured groups that increases the capacity for action oriented toward the achievement of group goals (Hagan, 1994). Goals are accomplished by transforming resources gathered in one forum, for one purpose, into resources for another forum and for another purpose (Coleman, 1988). The essence of social disorganization theory is that disruptions of both formal and informal processes of social control impede a neighborhood's ability to self-regulate (Bursik, 1988). Social capital is the essence of social control for it is the very force collectives draw upon to enforce order. It is what enables groups to enforce norms and, as a result, to increase their level of informal control. Disorganized communities, then, suffer from crime and other negative conditions partly because they have insufficient supplies of social capital.

In Bursik and Grasmick's Basic Systemic Model, the solicitation of external resources and both primary and secondary relational networks (the three factors directly influencing the three levels of control) are elements of social capital. We discuss them in terms of this broader category in order to emphasize the idea that socially organized communities need integrated networks at many different levels for effective self-regulation. In socially organized areas resources accumulated at one level can become resources for control at another level. This does not occur so readily in socially disorganized areas.

Social capital works by facilitating certain actions and constraining others. It stems from a sense of trust and obligation created through interaction among community members and serves to reinforce a set of prescriptive norms. Thus, social capital effectively unites individuals within a neighborhood, thereby initiating and enhancing a sense of collectivity (Coleman, 1988). . . . It follows that communities rich in social capital also will experience relatively low levels of disorganization and low levels of crime. It has been shown, for instance, that immigrant groups rich in human and social capital are more able to promote self-employment than their more capital-poor counterparts (Sanders & Nee, 1996). This, then, insulates the neighborhood from the link between unemployment and crime.

Social capital relies upon (and in turn promotes) human capital. Human capital refers to the human skill and resources individuals need to function effectively, such as reading, writing, and reasoning ability. It is the capital individuals acquire through education and training for productive purposes (Hagan, 1994). In a sense, social capital contextualizes human capital (and vice versa) because neighborhoods rich in social capital exert more control over individual residents, thus helping to produce more highly educated, employable, and productive members of the community. Neighborhoods deficient in social capital are areas conducive to crime because they are characterized by many individuals who are undereducated, unemployed, and more likely to be criminal. Thus, communities rich in social capital also are communities rich in human capital. Conversely, those without one, tend also to be without the other. Recent research provides evidence to support these relationships. . . .

What this amounts to is that where people live greatly affects their lives. By providing an environment either rich or deficient in resources, place of residence affects tangibly the quality of day-to-day life (Sullivan, 1989). Place of residence also influences the range of opportunities people find available because area affects the quality and extent of their personal networks. Environments rich in human capital promote the development of social capital (and vice versa), and these are the areas in which residents, both individually and collectively, are able to solve problems. Neighborhoods are the focal point for satisfying daily needs through informal support networks. . . .

. . . . Not much is known about the networks so fundamental to social capital and social control. On the individual level, research has explored the impact of network disruption on the quality of life. For instance, Kessler and McLeod (1984) and Conger et al. (1993) show that women suffer psychological distress from "network" events, life events that do not occur to them but to members of their networks, and that men are more distressed by work and financial events. . . . In this study, we ask: How much disruption can networks sustain before they fail to function?

. . . . [A]t the community level a minimum number of healthy networks is needed for the neighborhood to function effectively. When a sufficient number of individual networks [are] disrupted, the community is disrupted too. We do not speculate on what that number is, though it can be answered empirically. There may even

be a tipping point; that is, a small number of offenders may be removed with little ill effect because remaining networks are minimally affected. But after some point of removing males, the remaining networks have taken sufficient hits that their capacity to function in ordinary social controls is severely dampened. Indeed, this threshold may be lower in the most disorganized communities, where networks may be thin to begin with and thus more vulnerable to disruption. In other words, social capital contextualizes the impact of network disruption through incarceration. Not only do disorganized communities have more networks disrupted through incarceration, the impact may be stronger in these neighborhoods because they have a lower threshold due to depleted supplies of social capital.

Legitimate Systems of Neighborhood Order

The potential for unintended consequences of imprisonment is made plain by a "systems" model in which criminals are seen as embedded in various interpersonal, family, economic, and political systems. While there are many networks and systems at work in the community, our point is best illustrated by exploring three important legitimate systems of neighborhood order: family, economic, and political. Familial systems are the most important source of private social controls. Economic and political systems set the context within which parochial social controls flourish or wane. We investigate these systems as direct ways in which incarceration affects a neighborhood's capacity for informal social control. In addition, we also propose ways in which incarceration influences illegitimate systems within the community.

Familial Systems

Communities that contribute higher rates of members to incarceration experience higher rates of family disruption, single-parent families, and births to young, single adults (Lynch & Sabol, 1992). The close association between these factors and the removal of high rates of young males from these underclass, racial-minority communities suggests a plausible hypothesis that one is, in part, a product of another (or at least that they are mutually reinforcing phenomena). What are the implications of this pattern?

It is well established that children suffer when parents are removed from the home. What is less clear is the nature and extent of disruption that follows an incarceration. Studies of this problem have tended to focus on mothers (Gabel, 1992), but there have also been a few attempts to document the impacts of imprisonment of fathers (Brodsky, 1975; Carlson & Cervera, 1992; Fishman, 1990; King, 1993; Lowenstein, 1986). The studies show that the negative psychological and circumstantial impact on children from the removal of a parent for incarceration is similar in form though not in degree to that produced by removal due to divorce or death. . . . Children's internalization of social norms may also be disrupted by high levels of incarceration. Changes in parental working conditions and family circumstances are known to affect children's social adjustment and norm transmission across generations (Parcel & Menaghan, 1993). . . . [I]f a parent is incarcerated, and the stability of the family is thus jeopardized, the remaining parent has less time for interaction with the children or the school, increasing the chances of dropout.

At a most basic level, the absence of males restricts the number of adults available to supervise young people in the neighborhood. While it is commonly assumed that criminally active adults are less capable or willing guardians, there is no evidence to support this. . . . [However], the presence of large numbers of unsupervised youth is predictive of serious crime at the neighborhood level (Sampson & Groves, 1989). A recent study (Carlson & Cervera, 1991) shows women had to rely on family and friends to fill the role of their incarcerated husbands in terms of money, companionship, and babysitting. . . . However, one would be unwise to assume, and it would contradict current wisdom on child development, that the absence of such a parent improves the child's situation. Unfortunately, research on the parenting skills of offenders, either pre- or post-incarceration, does not exist to our knowledge. The incarceration of large numbers of parent-age males also restricts the number of male partners available within the neighborhood. This means that mothers find more competition for partners and parents for their children. In the context of more competitive parental situations, mothers may feel reluctant to end relationships that are unsuitable for children partly because prospects for a suitable replacement are perceived as poor. . . . [Additionally], [i]t is known that abusive relationships with parents contribute to later delinquency. . . . This chain of negative effects on the family—the socialization unit of private social control—contributes to the gradual reduction of social capital within a community. None of these changes by itself "causes" delinquency, but such disruptions are associated with earlier and more active delinquent careers. Their effects would be expected to be additive and, in more extreme levels of removal of males, interactive.

Economic Systems

Fagan's (1997) exhaustive review of legal and illegal work illustrates that it is simplistic to view offenders as solely illegally employed. Research shows that many, if not most, criminals also have legal employment so that their removal from the neighborhood removes a worker from the local economy. Fagan recognizes the argument that removing a single offender who held a legal job frees that position for another (potentially non-offending) resident. However, in local areas where a high proportion of residents engage in both legal and illegal work, Fagan notes that removing many individuals may devastate the local economy. . . . The result [of incarceration] is that numerous household units suffer specific losses and the community suffers a net loss. . . . Incarceration removes from the neighborhood many of the men who provide some type of support to these women. Prior to incarceration, most prisoners are an economic resource to their neighborhoods and immediate families. . . . What happens to a neighborhood that experiences a steady growth in these transfers of its wealth? Economic hardship is one of the strongest predictors of crime rates. . . . Therefore, it is reasonable to assume that a neighborhood experiencing economic loss as a result of incarceration will experience an increase in crime (Wilson, 1987).

Imprisonment not only has an economic effect on the community that was home to the prisoner, it also affects the prisoner's level of human capital directly. . . . Individuals suffering from insufficient supplies of human capital are destined to have low-level jobs, which not only do not pay well, but offer no vision for the future. Individuals whose jobs hold no future have less of a stake in conformity and are more likely to engage in criminal activity (Crutchfield, 1997). . . .

In addition, to the extent incarceration primarily removes young men from the neighborhood, it also increases the likelihood of single-parent families being headed by women. . . .

The macroeconomics of crime policy also damage inner-city communities by shifting government funding priorities away from those communities toward penal institutions. The harsh budgetary politics of the 1990s has corresponded to equally harsh punitive politics in which correctional expenditures have grown by billions of dollars annually while money to support schools, supplement tuition, provide summer jobs for teens, and so forth all received cuts. The latter provide meager supports for communities already hard hit by crime and justice, and they become even more meager still. Whatever role these social programs play in propping up informal networks of social control is eliminated with the depletion of their funding. In addition, these policies may even motivate the communities hardest hit by budget cuts to accept or *encourage criminal* behavior in order to sustain what little *sense of* community remains. . . .

Political Systems

. . . . Communities vary in their desire and their capacity to organize. The extent to which a neighborhood has developed a network of political and social institutions prior to the occurrence of a specific threat helps to determine whether the community will be able to mobilize collective action against the threat (Henig, 1982).

Bursik and Grasmick's (1993:52) systemic model of social control shows that it is the interrelationship between community institutions and between community organizations and outside agencies that draws upon and produces social capital. Areas with well-developed networks are able to acquire externally based goods and services that enhance their ability to fight crime locally. Communities without such programs may not have extensive connections to the wider community or may not know how to obtain external funding and other necessary resources (Bursik & Grasmick, 1993, p. 15). In addition, most successful programs build upon existing networks, and disrupting these networks may damage already fragile programs. . . .

. . . One factor determining participation in local political structures is belief in their efficacy.

In disorganized communities there is reason to suspect residents do not believe that the state's justice agencies work on their behalf. Most minority children can tell stories of racism in the criminal justice system, and the validation of these tales is apparent to the eye. One-in-three African-American males in his twenties is under some form of formal justice system control; in many cities, half of this group are subjects of the system (Mauer, 1995). Many are casualties of the war on drugs. Instituted at the national level, this war was fought at the local level. In a comprehensive review of drug policy, Goetz (1996) points out that policy is often driven by the conscious political strategy of politicians rather than by levels of crime. Further, the spatial impact of this war has been a concentrated increase in criminal justice activity in lower income, inner-city neighborhoods. . . . [D]rug offenders eventually [return] to the community further criminalized by prison experiences. Moreover, the alienation of otherwise law-abiding residents who no longer feel part of a society that is so hostile to the drug economy (one dimension of Wilson's social isolation) leaves them less likely to participate in local political organizations or to submit to the authority of more formal ones. . . .

There is another level at which this negative political impact may operate: It may reduce deterrence. . . . Part of the deterrent power of the prison may be strengthened by the mystery that surrounds it. Once experienced, prison, no matter how harsh, is transformed from an awful mystery to a real-life ordeal that has been suffered and survived. High recidivism rates are consistent with the idea that prison experiences fail to deter. Fear of prison (especially among the middle class who have not experienced it) may be most potent when it is an unacquainted fear. In minority communities, prison is a part of life. A black 10-year-old is likely to have at least one (and likely more) ex-cons among his fathers, uncles, brothers, and neighbors. The lesson is that prison is not awesome, but is survivable. Widespread use of prison is tantamount to a widespread reassurance that prison is "normal." Thus, the politics of imprisonment may be a combination of increasing resentment and decreasing marginal gain. Turning dominant cultural symbols upside down, there is even the claim that inner-city residents accrue street status from surviving prison (Shakur, 1993).

Illegitimate Systems

To this point we have discussed only the legitimate components of neighborhood structure that promote self-regulation. But high levels of incarceration also affect illegitimate local activity in unintended ways—to mangle Tip O'Neill's famous observation about politics, we might say that "all street crime is local." By saying this, we mean that with the exception of some rare instances of violent crime, all criminality is contextual, embedded in interpersonal and group relations. These relations may be seen as illegitimate systems that operate at the neighborhood level, also subject to the effects of incarceration.

Crime is often a group phenomenon (see Reiss, 1988). Young males commit much of their street-level acquisitional crime in groups—muggings, burglaries, robberies, and so forth. Nearly all drug crime, from sales to consumption, is a group activity. . . . [W]hat happens when the criminal justice system removes one member of a criminal group[?] The hope is that the disruption will be sufficient to end the activities of the group and/or that the general deterrent effect will be sufficient to dissuade others from participating. It may often be, however, that the group continues its criminal activity as before. . . .

DISCUSSION

This extension of social disorganization theory has important theoretical and policy-related implications. Theoretically, it means that simple recursive studies of disorganization may be inadequate. The growing body of evidence suggests that communities are embedded in a system that reflects and continually reproduces levels of disorganization. It also means that one must look to additional sources of disorganization. Clearly, empirical research should be conducted to test the central tenets of this study.

Our hypotheses could be tested directly by investigating the linkages between the effects of a concentration of high incarceration rates and the net impact on family and social life, analyzed at the neighborhood level. For instance, if communities suffering from the removal of a large number of adult males through incarceration could be shown to suffer subsequently from higher rates of single-parent families, more out-of-wedlock births, an increase in residential mobility for the remaining family members, and higher crime, that would begin to provide empirical evidence supporting our theoretical case that a reliance on incarceration is one of the social conditions leading to crime. This is a conclusion other researchers (see Lynch & Sabol, 1992, for example) have already begun to draw.

To develop fully an empirical test of a nonrecursive process requires data organized by neighborhoods, and such data are not yet currently available. (For an explication of the lack of such data and a description of the problems in collecting them, see Bursik & Grasmick, 1993.) A further testing of our argument awaits the availability of suitable data. If our hypothesis has some value, it raises enormous implications for social policy on crime. For one thing, it confirms the common aphorism about prison construction, that society cannot build its way out of the crime problem. . . . A crime control strategy that looks only to coerce compliance from members of communities and that ignores the ways in which it can strengthen the neighborhood's internal mechanism of social control is worse than neutral. It is self-defeating.

There is reason to think this pattern applies primarily (perhaps even exclusively) to the most resource-poor communities. These areas suffer from the most crime partly because they lack enough social and human capital in the first place. As a result, they suffer the most from incarceration and its unintended consequences. Stronger communities produce fewer offenders because they suffer from fewer of the environmental conditions conducive to crime. Also, because stronger communities have larger supplies of human and social capital, they have stronger foundational structures and, as a result, suffer from less crime. Incarceration is a crime control strategy that works for these communities because there are fewer offenders. Of these, few are removed (most stay within local formal control systems such as probation) and the disruption caused by their absence is minimal.

By contrast, high-crime neighborhoods are also high-incarceration neighborhoods. In these places, children are more likely to experience family disruption, lack of parental supervision, property devoid of effective guardians, and all other manner of deteriorated informal social controls that otherwise deflect the young from criminal behavior. . . The prison can never be a substitute for absent adults, family members, and neighbors in making places safe.

We emphasize that our position does not suggest a wholesale rejection of incarceration; we do not believe in instituting policies that leave communities at risk. . . . Our position is that society must consider the relationships among various forms of control so that it can employ practices that maximize the effectiveness of each level of control. . . .

DISCUSSION QUESTIONS

1. What are the differences between the recursive and the nonrecursive models of crime presented in this chapter? How does Rose and Clear's model extend and enhance the model developed by Bursik and Grasmick (1993)?

2. What are social and human capital? How do they contribute to the importance of "place" in terms of whether one will turn to criminality?

3. In what ways does incarceration influence legitimate systems of neighborhood order— familial, economic, and political—and illegitimate systems?

4. What implications does Rose and Clear's model have for social policy?

REFERENCES

Bursik, R. J., Jr., & Grasmick, H. G. (1993). *Neighborhoods and crime: The dimensions of effective community control.* New York: Lexington Books.

Rose, D. R., & Clear, T. R. (1998). Incarceration, social capital, and crime: Implications for social disorganization theory. *Criminology, 36,* 441-480.

Sampson, R. J. (1987). Communities and crime. In M. R. Gottfredson & T. Hirschi (Eds.), *Positive criminology.* Beverly Hills, CA: Sage.

Sampson, R. J., & Groves, W. B. (1993). *Crime in the making: Pathways and turning points through life.* Cambridge, MA: Harvard University Press.

8

THE SUBCULTURE OF VIOLENCE

MARVIN E. WOLFGANG AND FRANCO FERRACUTI

EDITOR'S INTRODUCTION—In their 1967 text, *The Subculture of Violence*, Wolfgang and Ferracuti present an explanation of homicide and other crimes of violence. They draw on Sutherland's differential association theory, as well as other approaches, to explain why certain groups have higher rates of violence. Their "subculture of violence" thesis is that the "typical" homicide results most frequently from a cultural system of values and beliefs that views violence as a more appropriate, or even required, response to a wide variety of provocations and insults.

In this excerpt, Wolfgang and Ferracuti present a general version of this subculture of violence thesis. They begin by presenting a variety of propositions that constitute the thesis, ranging from psychoanalytic theories of aggression, medical and biological studies, the frustration-aggression hypothesis, containment theory, child-rearing practices, and social learning and conditioning propositions. They do point out that the subculture of violence does not entirely contradict the dominant, normative culture. Additionally, they argue that a subculture of violence does not approve of violence unconditionally and that violence is not necessarily supported by all members of the "subsociety."

This type of subculture tends to be most prominent among young adults. The subculture defines violence as an expected response to various situations—a broader range of situations than is recognized by the larger culture of which the subculture is a part. Violence, then, can be thought of as being required only in certain sets of circumstances. Wolfgang and Ferracuti employ Sutherland's differential association theory when they claim that the subculture is learned in interaction with others, and it also involves a process of differential learning, association, or identification with the values of the subculture. In other words, members of the subculture who wholly assimilate the subculture of violence will react differently to certain situations than will those persons who do not completely assimilate the behaviors. To illustrate, someone who has completely assimilated the values may react with violence to a minor verbal offense, whereas someone who has not completely absorbed the values may merely ignore it.

It is important to note that whereas earlier theories incorporated the notion of "culture" into their theories, Wolfgang and Ferracuti brought it forth as a central component of their thesis. For instance, Wolfgang and Ferracuti's theory of a subculture of violence has been widely used to explain why certain regions or cities have higher rates of homicide than others do. The argument is that regions or other places where this subculture is heavily concentrated will likely have higher rates of homicide than other areas.

We believe that despite the plethora of acts, tendencies to act, feelings, thoughts, attitudes, despite the multitudinous values, norms, prescriptions and proscriptions of conduct, and despite the variability of personality and behavior, an effort to locate dominant values in a culture and in its subcultural components, to classify and to measure them, should and can be made. While the individual may be unique as a composite, he and his values can be clustered with other individuals and values. One of the functions of science is to distinguish regularities, patterns, configurations, and classifications. And this function serves the additional one of prediction. If individuals may be grouped on the basis of certain likenesses, so may value-orientations and value-laden and norm-demanding situations. It is in the pursuit of this goal that the parameters of a subculture and, concomitantly, the collection of individuals constituting a subculture, may be located. It is doubtful whether a subculture requires formal social organization or even highly structured roles; therefore the absence of formal means of communication may be noted without damage to the thesis of the existence of a specified subculture. But values shared in similar rank order and with similar intensity would seem to be the critical elements in the definition and precision of the meaning of subcultures.

THE THESIS OF A SUBCULTURE OF VIOLENCE

This section examines the proposition that there is a subculture of violence. . . . It is necessary to build upon previous related research and theory in order to extend a theoretical formulation regarding the existence of subcultures in general if we are to hypothesize a particular subculture of violence. It would be difficult to support an argument that a subculture exists in relation to a single cultural interest, and the thesis of a subculture of violence does not suggest a monolithic character. It should be remembered that the term itself—subculture—presupposes an already existing complex of norms, values, attitudes, material traits, etc. What the subculture-of-violence

formulation further suggests is simply that there is a potent theme of violence current in the cluster of values that make up the life-style, the socialization process, the interpersonal relationships of individuals living in similar conditions.

The analysis of violent aggressive behavior has been the focus of interest of many social and biological researches, and psychology has attempted to build several theories to explain its phenomenology, ranging from the death-aggression instinct of the psychoanalytic school to the frustration-aggression hypothesis. The present discussion is the result of joint explorations in theory and research in psychology and in sociology, using the concept of subculture as a learning environment. Our major area of study has been assaultive behavior, with special attention to criminal homicide . . . [S]ome of the main trends in criminological thinking related to this topic must now be anticipated for the proper focus of the present discussion.

Isolated sectional studies of homicide behavior are extremely numerous, and it is not our intention to examine them in this chapter. There are basically two kinds of criminal homicide: (1) premeditated, felonious, intentional murder; (2) slaying in the heat of passion, or killing as a result of intent to do harm but without intent to kill. A slaying committed by one recognized as psychotic or legally insane, or by a psychiatrically designated abnormal subject involves clinical deviates who are generally not held responsible for their behavior, and who, therefore, are not considered culpable. We are eliminating these cases from our present discussion, although subcultural elements are not irrelevant to the analysis of their psychopathological phenomenology.

Probably fewer than five per cent of all known homicides are premeditated, planned intentional killings, and the individuals who commit them are most likely to be episodic offenders who have never had prior contact with the criminal law. Because they are rare crimes often planned by rationally functioning individuals, perhaps they are more likely to remain undetected. We believe that a type of analysis different from that presented here might be applicable to these cases. Our major concern is with the bulk of

Wolfgang, M. E., & Ferracuti, F. (1967). The subculture of violence. In M. E. Wolfgang & F. Ferracuti, *The subculture of violence* (pp. 140-161). London: Routledge Publishers.

homicides—the passion crimes, the violent slayings—that are not premeditated and are not psychotic manifestations. Like Cohen, who was concerned principally with most delinquency that arises from the 'working-class' ethic, so we are focusing [on] the preponderant kind of homicide, although our analysis . . . will include much of the available data on homicide [in] general.

Social Learning and Conditioning

Studies of child-rearing practices in relation to the development of aggressive traits lead us to consider briefly one important theoretical development from the field of general and social psychology which, in our opinion, provides the theoretical bridge between an individual's violent behavior and his subcultural value allegiance. We are referring to what is generally included under the heading of 'social learning.' Issues which arise in any analysis of the structure and phenomenology of subcultures are the process of transmitting the subculture values, the extent of individual differences in the strength of allegiance to those values, and the fact that not all the individuals with ecological propinquity share value and motive identity with the surrounding culture. The process of social learning, through a number of mechanisms ranging from repetitive contacts to the subtler forms of imitation and identification, involves the acquisition of value systems in early childhood and their integration in the complex personality trait-value-motive system, which makes up the adult global individuality.

A recent paper by Jeffery summarizes a number of theoretical statements accepting the general principle that criminal behavior can be explained as learned behavior if conceptualized as operant behavior and reinforced through reward and immediate gratification. However, the complexity of learning theory and the serious uncertainties that still plague its core concepts have thus far produced an heuristic deficiency in transferring from theory and experimental laboratory research to field applications. The same may be said about transferring to diagnostically oriented studies of the differential psychology of violent offenders. Admittedly, the transposition from laboratory and animal experimentation to the street corner and the prison is not easy, is somewhat speculative, and may prove impossible until the social-learning approach can produce

measurable, economical, and valid diagnostic instruments.

An interesting beginning towards such a development in criminology has been made by Eysenck and his collaborators. A general restatement of the theory can be found in Trasler, and earlier statements appear in Mowrer, for example. Bandura's rich production follows a social-learning approach, and his recent books with Walters provide a detailed discussion of mechanisms, patterns, and implications for the application of a behavioristic learning approach to analysis of personality development.

Indoctrination into a subculture can take place through early-infancy learning processes. However, not only does this indoctrination prove difficult to reconstruct in an individual diagnostic process, or impossible to demonstrate in the laboratory, but it is confused with individual differences. These differentials in the imitation and identification processes beg the central question of why equally exposed individuals terminally behave differently and exhibit values and norms that resist attempts to classify them into discrete, yet uniform categories. Eysenck has approached this problem through introduction of the concept of individual differences in conditioning, including, by extension, social conditioning. This approach assumes that, whereas introverts are easier to condition and therefore more readily absorb socialized values, extroverts are resistant to conditioning and dominated by anti-social impulsive reactions. The conceptualization can be extended to include social learning of whole antisocial value systems. These notions, if logically followed, would postulate two types of violent offender: (1) the introversive, who are socialized into a subculture of violence through conditioning, and are frequent in specific ecological settings; (2) the extroversive, impulsive, unsocialized types, who cut across social, cultural, and subcultural strata. Both types can exhibit violent behavior, but the etiology and the probability of such behavior vary along with basic psychological make-up, i.e. a set of inherited characteristics which, in Eysenck's terms, dichotomize individuals according to biological determinants that place them in a given position on the introversion-extroversion continuum. Only modest confirmation is so far available for this far-reaching conceptualization. An extension of the behavioristic learning theory into therapy has been proposed by Bandura and Walters and analyzed by several others. The advisability of granting scientific status to an approach which is still highly experimental has been seriously questioned.

Although the social-learning approach still awaits confirmation, it does provide a conceptually useful bridge between the sociological, the psychological, and clinical constructs which we have discussed in the preceding pages. It also furnishes us with the possibility of utilizing two other personality theories which have a definite place in the transposition of the concept of subculture from sociology to psychology. Dissonance theory, as one of these, constitutes an elegant, if unproved, link between the cognitive aspects of subcultural allegiance, the psychoanalytic mechanism of projection, and the internal consistency (with consequent reduction of the anxiety level) which constitutes the differential characteristics of members of the subculture. No dissonance is experienced so long as the value system of the individual is not confronted by different or certainly conflicting values. The treatment implications of the concept of cognitive dissonance in relation to subculture allegiance are obvious, and point to the need to fragment and rearrange antisocial group alliances. The utilization of cognitive dissonance in this way in the prevention of international conflict has been advocated, for example, by Stagner and Osgood. Stagner has, however, carefully analyzed the importance of perceptual personality theory to individual and group aggression. A subculture allegiance entails an organization or reorganization of the process of personality formation as a process of learning to perceive objects, persons, and situations as attractive or threatening, in accordance with subcultural positive and negative valences.

The general psychological contributions from conditioning, learning theory, cognitive dissonance, perceptual personality theory, are indeed far from providing a total theoretical system as a counterpart to the sociological notions about subcultures. However, we are convinced that these behavioral constructs of social learning not only are the most directly related to subculture theory but also are capable of generating an integrated theory in criminology.

The Cultural Context

Like all human behavior, homicide and other violent assaultive crimes must be viewed in terms of the cultural context from which they spring. De Champneuf, Guerry, Quetelet early in the nineteenth century, and Durkheim later, led the way toward emphasizing the necessity to examine the *physique sociale,* or social phenomena characterized by 'externality,' if the scientist is to understand or interpret crime, suicide, prostitution, and other deviant behavior. Without promulgating a sociological fatalism, analysis of broad macroscopic correlates in this way may obscure the dynamic elements of the phenomenon and result in the empirical hiatus and fallacious association to which Selvin refers. Yet, because of wide individual variations, the clinical, idiosyncratic approach does not necessarily aid in arriving at Weber's *Verstehen,* or meaningful adequate understanding of regularities, uniformities, or patterns of interaction. And it is this kind of understanding we seek when we examine either deviation from, or conformity to, a normative social system.

Sociological contributions have made almost commonplace, since Durkheim, the fact that deviant conduct is not evenly distributed throughout the social structure. There is much empirical evidence that class position, ethnicity, occupational status, and other social variables are effective indicators for predicting rates of different kinds of deviance. Studies in ecology perform a valuable service for examining the phenomenology and distribution of aggression, but only inferentially point to the importance of the system of norms. Anomie, whether defined as the absence of norms (which is a doubtful conceptualization) or the conflict of norms (either normative goals or means), or whether redefined by Powell as 'meaninglessness,' does not coincide with most empirical evidence on homicide. Acceptance of the concept of anomie would imply that marginal individuals who harbor psychic anomie that reflects (or causes) social anomie have the highest rates of homicides. Available data seem to reject this contention. Anomie as culture conflict, or conflict of norms, suggests that there is one segment (the prevailing middle-class value system) of a given culture whose value system is the antithesis of, or in conflict with, another, smaller segment of the same culture. This conceptualism of anomie is a useful tool for referring to subcultures as ideal types, or mental constructs. But to transfer this norm-conflict approach from the social to the individual level, theoretically making the individual a repository of culture conflict, again does not conform to the patterns of known psychological and sociological data. This latter approach would be forced to hypothesize that socially mobile individuals and families would be most frequently involved in homicide, or that persons moving from a formerly embraced subvalue system to the predominant communal value system would commit this form of violent deviation in the greatest numbers. There are no homicide data that show high rates of homicides among persons manifesting higher social aspirations in terms of mobility. It should also be mentioned that anomie, as a concept, does not easily lend itself to psychological study.

That there is a conflict of value systems, we agree. That is, there is a conflict between a prevailing culture value and some subcultural entity. But commission of homicide by actors from the subculture at variance with the prevailing culture cannot be adequately explained in terms of frustration due to failure to attain normative-goals of the latter in terms of inability to succeed with normative-procedures (means) for attaining those goals, nor in terms of an individual psychological condition of anomie. Homicide is most prevalent, or the highest rates of homicide occur, among a relatively homogeneous subcultural group in any large urban community. Similar prevalent rates can be found in some rural areas. The value system of this group, we are contending, constitutes a subculture of violence. From a psychological viewpoint, we might hypothesize that the greater the degree of integration of the individual into this subculture, the higher the probability that his behavior will be violent in a variety of situations. From the sociological side, there should be a direct relationship between rates of homicide and the extent to which the subculture of violence represents a cluster of values around the theme of violence.

Except for war, probably the most highly reportable, socially visible, and serious form of violence is expressed in criminal homicide. Data show that in the United States rates are highest among males, non-whites, and the young adult ages. Rates for most serious crimes, particularly against the person, are highest in these same groups. In a Philadelphia study of 588 criminal homicides, for example, non-white males aged 20-24 had a rate of 92 per 100,000 compared with 3:4 [3.4] for whites males of the same ages. Females consistently had lower rates than males in their respective race groups (non-white females, 9:3 [9.3]; white females, 0:4 [0.4], in the same study), although it should be as we shall discuss later that non-white females have higher rates than white males.

It is possible to multiply these specific findings in any variety of ways; and although a subcultural affinity to violence appears to be principally present in large urban communities and increasingly in the adolescent population, some typical evidence of this phenomenon can be found, for example, in rural areas and among other adult groups. For example, a particular, very structured, subculture of this kind can be found in Sardinia, in the central mountain area of the island. Pigliaru has conducted a brilliant analysis of the people from this area and of their criminal behavior, commonly known as the *vendetta barbaricina*. . . .

. . . . We suggest that, by identifying the groups with the highest rates of homicide, we should find in the most intense degree a subculture of violence; and, having focused on these groups, we should subsequently examine the value system of their subculture, the importance of human life in the scale of values, the kinds of expected reaction to certain types of stimulus, perceptual differences in the evaluation of stimuli, and the general personality structure of the subcultural actors. In the Philadelphia study it was pointed out that:

> . . . the significance of a jostle, a slightly derogatory remark, or the appearance of a weapon in the hands of an adversary are stimuli differentially perceived and interpreted by Negroes and whites, males and females. Social expectations of response in particular types of social interaction result in differential "definitions of the situation." A male is usually expected to defend the name and honor of his mother, the virtue of womanhood . . . and to accept no derogation about his race (even from a member of his own race), his age, or his masculinity. Quick resort to physical combat as a measure of daring, courage, or defense of status appears to be a cultural expression, especially for lower socioeconomic class males of both races. When such a culture norm response is elicited from an individual engaged in social interplay with others who harbor the same response mechanism, physical assaults, altercations, and violent domestic quarrels that result in homicide are likely to be common.

The upper-middle and upper social class value system defines subcultural mores, and considers many of the social and personal stimuli that evoke a combative reaction in the lower classes as "trivial." Thus, there exists a cultural antipathy between many folk rationalizations of the lower class, and of males of both races, on the one hand, and the middle-class legal norms under which they live, on the other.

This kind of analysis, combined with other data about delinquency, lower-class social structure, its value system, and its emphasis on aggression, suggest the thesis of a violent subculture, or, by pushing the normative aspects a little further, a *subculture of* violence. Among many juvenile gangs, as has repeatedly been pointed out, there are violent feuds, meetings, territorial fights, and the use of violence to prove 'heart,' to maintain or to acquire 'rep.'

Physical aggression is often seen as a demonstration of masculinity and toughness. We might argue that this emphasis on showing masculinity through aggression is not always supported by data. If homicide is any index at all of physical aggression, we must remember that in the Philadelphia data non-white females have [homicide] rates often two to four times higher than the rates of white males. Violent behavior appears more dependent on cultural differences than on sex differences, traditionally considered of paramount importance in the expression of aggression. . . .

. . . It appears valid to suggest that there are, in a heterogeneous population, differences in ideas and attitudes toward the use of violence and that these differences can be observed through variables related to social class and possibly through psychological correlates. There is evidence that modes of control of expressions of aggression in children vary among the social classes. Lower-class boys, for example, appear more likely to be oriented toward direct expression of aggression than are middle-class boys. The type of punishment meted out by parents to misbehaving children is related to this class orientation toward aggression. Lower-class mothers report that they or their husbands are likely to strike their children or threaten to strike them, whereas middle-class mothers report that their type of punishment is psychological rather than physical; and boys who are physically [punished] express aggression more directly than those who

are punished psychologically. As Martin has suggested, the middle-class child is more likely to turn his aggression inward; in the extreme and as an adult he will commit suicide. But the lower-class child is more accustomed to a parent-child relationship which during punishment is for the moment that of attacker and attacked. The target for aggression, then, is external; aggression is directed toward others.

The existence of a subculture of violence is partly demonstrated by examination of the social groups and individuals who experience the highest rates of manifest violence. This examination need not be confined to the study of one national or ethnic group. On the contrary, the existence of a subculture of violence could perhaps receive even cross-cultural confirmation. Criminal homicide is the most acute and highly reportable example of this type of violence, but some circularity of thought is obvious in the effort to specify the dependent variable (homicide), and also to infer the independent variable (the existence of a subculture of violence). The highest rates of rape, aggravated assaults, persistency in arrests for assaults (recidivism) among these groups with high rates of homicide are, however, empirical addenda to the postulation of a subculture of violence. Residential propinquity of these same groups reinforces the socio-psychological impact which the integration of this subculture engenders. Sutherland's thesis of 'differential association,' or a psychological reformulation of the same theory in terms of learning process, could effectively be employed to describe more fully this impact in its intensity, duration, repetition, and frequency. The more thoroughly integrated the individual is into this subculture, the more intensely he embraces its prescriptions of behavior, its conduct norms, and integrates them into his personality structure. The degree of integration may be measured partly and crudely by public records of contact with law, so high arrest rates, particularly high rates of assault crimes and rates of recidivism for assault crimes among groups that form the culture of violence, may indicate allegiance to the values of violence.

We have said that overt physical violence often becomes a common subculturally expected response to certain stimuli. However, it is not merely rigid conformity to the demands and expectations of other persons, as Henry and Short seem to suggest, that results in the high probability of homicide. Excessive, compulsive, or apathetic conformity [of] middle-class individuals to the value system of their social group is a widely recognized cultural malady. Our concern is with the value elements of violence as an integral component of the subculture which experiences high rates of homicide. It is conformity to *this* set of values, and not rigid conformity *per se,* that gives important meaning to the subculture of violence. . . .

It is not far-fetched to suggest that a whole culture may accept a value set dependent upon violence, demand or encourage adherence to violence, and penalize deviation. . . . Homicide, it appears, is often a situation not unlike that of confrontations in wartime combat, in which two individuals committed to the value of violence come together, and in which chance, prowess, or possession of a particular weapon dictates the identity of the slayer and of the slain. The peaceful non-combatant in both sets of circumstances is penalized, because of the allelomimetic behavior of the group supporting violence, by his being ostracized as an outgroup member, and he is thereby segregated (imprisoned, in wartime, as a conscientious objector) from his original group. If he is not segregated, but continues to interact with his original group in the public street or on the front line that represents the culture of violence, he may fall victim to the shot or stab from one of the group who still embraces the value of violence. . . .

. . . . We have said that overt use of force or violence, either in interpersonal relationships or in group interaction, is generally viewed as a reflection of basic values that stand apart from the dominant, the central, or the parent culture. Our hypothesis is that this overt . . . (and often illicit) expression of violence (of which homicide is only the most extreme) is part of a subcultural normative system, and that this system is reflected in the psychological traits of the subculture participants. In the light of our discussion of the caution to be exercised in interpretative analysis, in order to tighten the logic of this analysis, and to support the thesis of a subculture of violence, we offer the following corollary propositions:

1. *No subculture can be totally different from or totally in conflict with the society of which it is a part.* A subculture of violence is not entirely an expression of violence, for there must be interlocking value elements shared with the dominant culture. . . .

2. *To establish the existence of a subculture of violence does not require that the actors sharing in these basic value elements should express violence in all situations.* The normative system designates that in some types of social interaction a violent and physically aggressive response is either expected or required of all members sharing in that system of values. . . .

3. *The potential resort or willingness to resort to violence in a variety of situations emphasizes the penetrating and diffusive character of this culture theme.* The number and kinds of situations in which an individual uses violence may be viewed as an index of the extent to which he has assimilated the values associated with violence. . . .

4. *The subcultural ethos of violence may be shared by all ages in a sub-society, but this ethos is most prominent in a limited age group, ranging from late adolescence to middle age.* . . . [T]he known empirical distribution of conduct, which expresses the sharing of this violence theme, shows greatest localization, incidence, and frequency in limited sub-groups and reflects differences in learning about violence as a problem-solving mechanism.

5. *The counter-norm is nonviolence.* Violation of expected and required violence is most likely to result in ostracism from the group. . . .

6. *The development of favorable attitudes toward, and the use of, violence in a subculture usually involve learned behavior and a process of differential learning, association, or identification.* Not all persons exposed—even equally exposed—to the presence of a subculture of violence absorb and share in the values in equal portions. Differential personality variables must be considered in an integrated social-psychological approach to an understanding of the subcultural aspects of violence. . . .

7. *The use of violence in a subculture is not necessarily viewed as illicit conduct and the*

users therefore do not have to deal with feelings of guilt about their aggression. Violence can become a part of the life style, the theme of solving difficult problems or problem situations. . . . [W]hen the attacked see their assaulters as agents of the same kind of aggression they themselves represent, violent retaliation is readily legitimized by a situationally specific rationale, as well as by the generally normative supports for violence. . . .

DISCUSSION QUESTIONS

1. According to Wolfgang and Ferracuti, for which groups are homicides most likely within a "subculture of violence" framework?

2. How might someone explain the origin of a subculture of violence?

3. What are the seven propositions of the theory? How would you know if someone had completely assimilated the values of the subculture? What might you try to find out about that person?

4. Can you think of alternative explanations for the excessively high rate of homicides in the South or among lower-class African American males?

9

SOCIAL STRUCTURE AND ANOMIE

ROBERT K. MERTON

EDITOR'S INTRODUCTION—In Merton's widely read article, he challenged previously held biological theories of crime, which held that crime results from innate "biological drives," or "natural appetites" that are not adequately constrained by society. In contrast, Merton argued that many of the appetites in individuals are not "natural" but originate in the "culture" or American society. He also asserted that the "social structure" of the American society limits the ability of members of certain groups to satisfy these appetites. This constraint puts pressure on some individuals in society to resort to nonconformist rather than conforming behavior to satisfy them.

Merton's theory comprises two components: anomie and strain. The first component derives from Emile Durkheim's theory of anomie, which Merton later revised into what became known as *strain theory*. Durkheim analyzed anomie as a breakdown of the ability of a society to regulate the natural drives of individuals in the face of rapid social change. In *The Division of Labor,* Durkheim (1895/1933) found that, to the extent that a society is "mechanical," which characterizes a society with relatively little division of labor; a highly uniform system of law (one penal code); and isolated, self-sufficient social groups, that society derives its solidarity from pressure for conformity from the diversity of its members. Criminalizing certain behaviors is a normal and necessary part of this conforming process. Conversely, if a society is "organic," meaning that the different segments of society depend on one another in a highly organized and specialized division of labor, then the function of the law is to regulate all of these different interactions of the various components as a whole. If this regulation is inadequate, a variety of social ills emerge, including crime. Durkheim referred to this state of normlessness, or inadequate regulation, as *anomie.*

Durkheim argued that the rapid social changes that characterize organic societies lead to this state of anomie. The anomie theory of crime seeks to explain why some societies have higher crime rates than others do. Merton adapted some of Durkheim's views, but he shifted the focus away from rapid social change. Instead, he argued that certain relatively stable social conditions existed that tended to be associated with higher overall crime rates in American cities, as well as with the higher crime rates that plagued the lower classes. Merton used the term *social structural strain* to describe these social conditions.

The anomie theory centers on the relative emphasis placed on cultural goals and institutional means of achieving those goals. Merton indicates that each society's culture defines certain goals that are "worth striving for," and although many of these goals may exist in every society, they vary from culture to culture. The most prominent goal in American society is to acquire wealth. Durkheim maintains that this goal may be perceived as a "natural aspiration," but American culture encourages this goal beyond any intrinsic rewards the goal itself might have. Because accumulated wealth is often equated with personal value and worth, a high degree of prestige, and high social status, even those individuals who have personal characteristics which may be valued elsewhere, may feel degraded if they do not have money.

Additionally, cultures also specify approved norms, or appropriate institutional means, for achieving those goals. These means are based on the values of the particular culture, many of which include hard work and honesty or what most would consider "middle-class values." Merton found that because not all persons can be expected to achieve the prescribed goals of a given culture, it becomes critical that the culture emphasize the importance of institutionalized means and the necessity of following them. But sometimes, the emphasis on the goal overshadows the importance of following the rules, which translates into de-emphasis on the rewards provided by the task itself, such as a job. When this situation occurs, the institutional means are subjected to severe strain and are minimally rewarding in themselves, because they do not enable the individual to achieve the goal.

Merton found that societies that placed a lot of emphasis on monetary success and accumulated wealth and a low emphasis on the norms and rules for attaining these goals have higher crime rates. These societies are subject to states of normlessness because the goal-seeking behavior of individuals is not regulated. Consequently, individuals use "any means necessary," the most efficient and expedient method, to achieve their goals. Merton also adds that certain individuals and groups find themselves subject to increased social pressures for crime. Although everyone is encouraged to achieve the American Dream of monetary success, lower-class persons are frequently prevented from achieving such results through legitimate networks. As a result, once under strain, they find they must adapt their behaviors in order to attain their goals. Merton outlines five possible modes of adaptation in his work, and many of these adaptations involve crime. He goes on to discuss why certain individuals are more likely to respond to strain with crime than others are.

Merton's theory, which extends and adapts Durkheim's approach, has laid the foundation for research and further consideration. Though his strain theory has never been directly tested, it has formed the basis for an intriguing analysis and discussion of institutional anomie in the work of Messner and Rosenfeld (Chapter 10, this volume) and in Agnew's (Chapter 11, this volume) general strain theory of crime.

There persists a notable tendency in sociological theory to attribute the malfunctioning of social structure primarily to those of man's imperious biological drives which are not adequately restrained by social control. In this view, the social order is solely a device for "impulse management" and the "social processing" of tensions. These impulses which break through social control, be it noted, are held to be biologically derived. Nonconformity is assumed to be rooted in original nature. Conformity is by implication the result of a utilitarian calculus or unreasoned conditioning. This point of view, whatever its other deficiencies, clearly begs one question. It provides no basis for determining the nonbiological conditions which induce deviations from prescribed patterns of conduct. In this paper, it will be suggested that certain phases of social structure generate the circumstances in which infringement of social codes constitutes a "normal" response.

The conceptual scheme to be outlined is designed to provide a coherent, systematic approach to the study of socio-cultural sources of deviate behavior. Our primary aim lies in discovering how some social structures *exert a definite pressure* upon certain persons in the society to engage in nonconformist rather than conformist conduct. The many ramifications of the scheme cannot all be discussed; the problems mentioned outnumber those explicitly treated.

Among the elements of social and cultural structure, two are important for our purposes. These are analytically separable although they merge imperceptibly in concrete situations. The first consists of culturally defined goals, purposes, and interests. It comprises a frame of aspirational reference. These goals are more or less integrated and involve varying degrees of prestige and sentiment. They constitute a basic, but not the exclusive, component of what Linton aptly has called "designs for group living." Some

Merton, R. K. (1938). Social structure and anomie. *American Sociological Review, 3,* 672-682.

of these cultural aspirations are related to the original drives of man, but they are not determined by them. The second phase of the social structure defines, regulates, and controls the acceptable modes of achieving these goals. Every social group invariably couples its scale of desired ends with moral or institutional regulation of permissible and required procedures for attaining these ends. These regulatory norms and moral imperatives do not necessarily coincide with technical or efficiency norms. Many procedures which from the standpoint of particular *individuals* would be most efficient in securing desired values, e.g., illicit oil-stock schemes, theft, fraud, are ruled out of the institutional area of permitted conduct. The choice of expedients is limited by the institutional norms.

To say that these two elements, culture goals and institutional norms, operate jointly is not to say that the ranges of alternative behaviors and aims bear some constant relation to one another. The emphasis upon certain goals may vary independently of the degree of emphasis upon institutional means. There may develop a disproportionate, at times, a virtually exclusive, stress upon the value of specific goals, involving relatively slight concern with the institutionally appropriate modes of attaining these goals. The limiting case in this direction is reached when the range of alternative procedures is limited only by technical rather than institutional considerations. Any and all devices which promise attainment of the all important goal would be permitted in this hypothetical polar case. This constitutes one type of cultural malintegration. A second polar type is found in groups where activities originally conceived as instrumental are transmuted into ends in themselves. The original purposes are forgotten and ritualistic adherence to institutionally prescribed conduct becomes virtually obsessive. Stability is largely ensured while change is flouted. The range of alternative behaviors is severely limited. There develops a tradition-bound, sacred society characterized by neophobia. The occupational psychosis of the bureaucrat may be cited as a case in point. Finally, there are the intermediate types of groups where a balance between culture goals and institutional means is maintained. These are the significantly integrated and relatively stable, though changing, groups.

An effective equilibrium between the two phases of the social structure is maintained as long as satisfactions accrue to individuals who conform to both constraints, viz., satisfactions from the achievement of the goals and satisfactions emerging directly from the institutionally canalized modes of striving to attain these ends. Success, in such equilibrated cases, is twofold. Success is reckoned in terms of the product and in terms of the process, in terms of the outcome and in terms of activities. Continuing satisfactions must derive from sheer participation in a competitive order as well as from eclipsing one's competitors if the order itself is to be sustained. The occasional sacrifices involved in institutionalized conduct must be compensated by socialized rewards. The distribution of statuses and roles through competition must be so organized that positive incentives for conformity to roles and adherence to status obligations are provided for every position within the distributive order. Aberrant conduct, therefore, may be viewed as a symptom of dissociation between culturally defined aspirations and socially structured means.

Of the types of groups which result from the independent variation of the two phases of the social structure, we shall be primarily concerned with the first, namely, that involving a disproportionate accent on goals. This statement must be recast in a proper perspective. In no group is there an absence of regulatory codes governing conduct, yet groups do vary in the degree to which these folkways, mores, and institutional controls are effectively integrated with the more diffuse goals which are part of the culture matrix. Emotional convictions may cluster about the complex of socially acclaimed ends, meanwhile shifting their support from the culturally defined implementation of these ends. As we shall see, certain aspects of the social structure may generate countermores and antisocial behavior precisely because of differential emphases on goals and regulations. In the extreme case, the latter may be so vitiated by the goal-emphasis that the range of behavior is limited only by considerations of technical expediency. The sole significant question then becomes, which available means is most efficient in netting the socially approved value? The technically most feasible procedure, whether legitimate or not, is preferred to the institutionally prescribed conduct. As this process continues, the integration of the society becomes tenuous and anomie ensues.

Thus, in competitive athletics, when the aim of victory is shorn of its institutional trappings and success in contests becomes construed as "winning the game" rather than "winning through circumscribed modes of activity," a premium is implicitly set upon the use of illegitimate but technically efficient means. The star of the opposing football team is surreptitiously slugged; the wrestler furtively incapacitates his opponent through ingenious but illicit techniques; university alumni covertly subsidize "students" whose talents are largely confined to the athletic field. The emphasis on the goal has so attenuated the satisfactions deriving from sheer participation in the competitive activity that these satisfactions are virtually confined to a successful outcome. Through the same process, tension generated by the desire to win in a poker game is relieved by successfully dealing oneself four aces, or, when the cult of success has become completely dominant, by sagaciously shuffling the cards in a game of solitaire. The faint twinge of uneasiness in the last instance and the surreptitious nature of public delicts indicate clearly that the institutional rules of the game *are known* to those who evade them, but that the emotional supports of these rules are largely vitiated by cultural exaggeration of the success-goal. They are microcosmic images of the social macrocosm.

Of course, this process is not restricted to the realm of sport. The process whereby exaltation of the end generates a *literal demoralization,* i.e., a deinstitutionalization, of the means is one which characterizes many groups in which the two phases of the social structure are not highly integrated. The extreme emphasis upon the accumulation of wealth as a symbol of success in our own society militates against the completely effective control of institutionally regulated modes of acquiring a fortune. Fraud, corruption, vice, crime, in short, the entire catalogue of proscribed behavior, becomes increasingly common when the emphasis on the *culturally induced* success-goal becomes divorced from a coordinated institutional emphasis. This observation is of crucial theoretical importance in examining the doctrine that antisocial behavior most frequently derives from biological drives breaking through the restraints imposed by society. The difference is one between a strictly utilitarian interpretation which conceives man's ends as random and an analysis which finds these ends deriving from the basic values of the culture.

Our analysis can scarcely stop at this juncture. We must turn to other aspects of the social structure if we are to deal with the social genesis of the varying rates and types of deviate behavior characteristic of different societies. Thus far, we have sketched three ideal types of social orders constituted by distinctive patterns of relations between culture ends and means. Turning from these types of *culture patterning,* we find five logically possible, alternative modes of adjustment or adaptation by *individuals* within the culture-bearing society or group. These are schematically presented in Figure 9.1, where (+) signifies "acceptance," (−) signifies "elimination" and (±) signifies "rejection and substitution of new goals and standards."

Our discussion of the relation between these alternative responses and other phases of the social structure must be prefaced by the observation that persons may shift from one alternative to another as they engage in different social activities. These categories refer to role adjustments in specific situations, not to personality *in toto.* To treat the development of this process in various spheres of conduct would introduce a complexity unmanageable within the confines of this paper. For this reason, we shall be concerned primarily with economic activity in the broad sense, "the production, exchange, distribution and consumption of goods and services" in our competitive society, wherein wealth has taken on a highly symbolic cast. Our task is to search out some of the factors which exert pressure upon individuals to engage in certain of these logically possible alternative responses. This choice, as we shall see, is far from random.

In every society, Adaptation I (conformity to both culture goals and means) is the most common and widely diffused. Were this not so, the stability and continuity of the society could not be maintained. The mesh of expectancies which constitutes every social order is sustained by the modal behavior of its members falling within the first category. Conventional role behavior oriented toward the basic values of the group is the rule rather than the exception. It is this fact alone which permits us to speak of a human aggregate as comprising a group or society.

Conversely, Adaptation IV (rejection of goals and means) is the least common. Persons who

	Culture Goals	Institutionalized Means
I. Conformity	+	+
II. Innovation	+	−
III. Ritualism	−	+
IV. Retreatism	−	−
V. Rebellion	+/−	+/−

Figure 9.1

"adjust" (or maladjust) in this fashion are, strictly speaking, *in* the society but not *of* it. Sociologically, these constitute the true "aliens." Not sharing the common frame of orientation, they can be included within the societal population merely in a fictional sense. In this category are some of the activities of psychotics, psychoneurotics, chronic autists, pariahs, outcasts, vagrants, vagabonds, tramps, chronic drunkards and drug addicts. These have relinquished, in certain spheres of activity, the culturally defined goals, involving complete aim-inhibition in the polar case, and their adjustments are not in accord with institutional norms. This is not to say that in some cases the source of their behavioral adjustments is not in part the very social structure which they have in effect repudiated nor that their very existence within a social area does not constitute a problem for the socialized population.

This mode of "adjustment" occurs, as far as structural sources are concerned, when both the culture goals and institutionalized procedures have been assimilated thoroughly by the individual and imbued with affect and high positive value, but where those institutionalized procedures which promise a measure of successful attainment of the goals are not available to the individual. In such instances, there results a twofold mental conflict insofar as the moral obligation for adopting institutional means conflicts with the pressure to resort to illegitimate means (which may attain the goal) and inasmuch as the individual is shut off from means which are both legitimate *and* effective. The competitive order is maintained, but the frustrated and handicapped individual who cannot cope with this order drops out.

Defeatism, quietism and resignation are manifested in escape mechanisms which ultimately lead the individual to "escape" from the requirements of the society. It is an expedient which arises from continued failure to attain the goal by legitimate measures and from an inability to adopt the illegitimate route because of internalized prohibitions and institutionalized compulsives, *during which process the supreme value of the success-goal has as yet not been renounced.* The conflict is resolved by eliminating *both* precipitating elements, the goals and means. The escape is complete, the conflict is eliminated and the individual is asocialized.

Be it noted that where frustration derives from the inaccessibility of effective institutional means for attaining economic or any other type of highly valued "success," that Adaptations II, III, and V (innovation, ritualism and rebellion) are also possible. The result will be determined by the particular personality, and thus, the *particular* cultural background, involved. Inadequate socialization will result in the innovation response whereby the conflict and frustration are eliminated by relinquishing the institutional means and retaining the success-aspiration; an extreme assimilation of institutional demands will lead to ritualism wherein the goal is dropped as beyond one's reach but conformity to the mores persists; and rebellion occurs when emancipation from the reigning standards, due to frustration or to marginalist perspectives, leads to the attempt to introduce a "new social order."

Our major concern is with the illegitimacy adjustment. This involves the use of conventionally proscribed but frequently effective means of attaining at least the simulacrum of culturally defined success—wealth, power, and the like. As we have seen, this adjustment occurs when the individual has assimilated the cultural emphasis on success without equally internalizing the morally prescribed norms governing means for its attainment. The question arises, Which phases of our social structure predispose toward this mode of adjustment? We may examine a concrete instance, effectively analyzed by Lohman, which provides a clue to the answer. Lohman has shown that specialized areas of vice in the near north side of Chicago constitute a "normal" response to a situation where the cultural emphasis upon pecuniary success has been absorbed, but where there is little access to conventional and legitimate means for attaining such success. The conventional occupational opportunities of persons in this area are almost completely limited to manual labor. Given our cultural stigmatization of manual labor, and its correlate, the prestige of white collar work, it is clear that the result is a strain toward innovational practices. The limitation of opportunity to unskilled labor and the resultant low income can not compete *in terms of conventional standards of achievement* with the high income from organized vice.

For our purposes, this situation involves two important features. First, such antisocial behavior is in a sense "called forth" by certain conventional values of the culture *and* by the class structure involving differential access to the approved opportunities for legitimate, prestige-bearing pursuit of the culture goals. The lack of high integration between the means-and-end elements of the cultural pattern and the particular class structure combine to favor a heightened frequency of antisocial conduct in such groups. The second consideration is of equal significance. Recourse to the first of the alternative responses, legitimate effort, is limited by the fact that actual advance toward desired success-symbols through conventional channels is, despite our persisting open-class ideology, relatively rare and difficult for those handicapped by little formal education and few economic resources. The dominant pressure of group standards of success is, therefore, on the gradual attenuation of legitimate, but by and large ineffective, strivings and the increasing use of illegitimate, but more or less effective, expedients of vice and crime. The cultural demands made on persons in this situation are incompatible. On the one hand, they are asked to orient their conduct toward the prospect of accumulating wealth and on the other, they are largely denied effective opportunities to do so institutionally. The consequences of such structural inconsistency are psycho-pathological personality, and/or antisocial conduct, and/or

revolutionary activities. The equilibrium between culturally designated means and ends becomes highly unstable with the progressive emphasis on attaining the prestige-laden ends by any means whatsoever. Within this context, Capone represents the triumph of amoral intelligence over morally prescribed "failure," when the channels of vertical mobility are closed or narrowed *in a society which places a high premium on economic affluence and social ascent for all its members.*

This last qualification is of primary importance. It suggests that other phases of the social structure besides the extreme emphasis on pecuniary success, must be considered if we are to understand the social sources of antisocial behavior. A high frequency of deviate behavior is not generated simply by "lack of opportunity" or by this exaggerated pecuniary emphasis. A comparatively rigidified class structure, a feudalistic or caste order, may limit such opportunities far beyond the point which obtains in our society today. It is only when a system of cultural values extols, virtually above all else, certain common symbols of success for the population at large while its social structure rigorously restricts or completely eliminates access to approved modes of acquiring these symbols for a considerable part of the same population, that antisocial behavior ensues on a considerable scale. In other words, our egalitarian ideology denies by implication the existence of noncompeting groups and individuals in the pursuit of pecuniary success. The same body of success-symbols is held to be desirable for all. These goals are held to transcend class lines, not to be bounded by them, yet the actual social organization is such that there exist class differentials in the accessibility of these common success-symbols. Frustration and thwarted aspiration lead to the search for avenues of escape from a culturally induced intolerable situation; or unrelieved ambition may eventuate in illicit attempts to acquire the dominant values. The American stress on pecuniary success and ambitiousness for all thus invites exaggerated anxieties, hostilities, neuroses and antisocial behavior.

This theoretical analysis may go far toward explaining the varying correlations between crime and poverty. Poverty is not an isolated variable. It is one in a complex of interdependent social and cultural variables. When viewed in such a context, it represents quite different states of affairs. Poverty as such, and consequent limitation of opportunity, are not sufficient to induce a conspicuously high rate of criminal behavior. Even the often mentioned "poverty in the midst of plenty" will not necessarily lead to this result. Only insofar as poverty and associated disadvantages in competition for the culture values approved for *all* members of the society is linked with the assimilation of a cultural emphasis on monetary accumulation as a symbol of success is antisocial conduct a "normal" outcome. Thus, poverty is less highly correlated with crime in southeastern Europe than in the United States. The possibilities of vertical mobility in these European areas would seem to be fewer than in this country, so that neither poverty *per se* nor its association with limited opportunity is sufficient to account for the varying correlations. It is only when the full configuration is considered, poverty, limited opportunity and a commonly shared system of success symbols, that we can explain the higher association between poverty and crime in our society than in others where rigidified class structure is coupled with *differential class symbols of achievement.*

In societies such as our own, then, the pressure of prestige-bearing success tends to eliminate the effective social constraint over means employed to this end. "The-end-justifies-the-means" doctrine becomes a guiding tenet for action when the cultural structure unduly exalts the end and the social organization unduly limits possible recourse to approved means. Otherwise put, this notion and associated behavior reflect a lack of cultural coordination. In international relations, the effects of this lack of integration are notoriously apparent. An emphasis upon national power is not readily coordinated with an inept organization of legitimate, i.e., internationally defined and accepted, means for attaining this goal. The result is a tendency toward the abrogation of international law, treaties become scraps of paper, "undeclared warfare" serves as a technical evasion, the bombing of civilian populations is rationalized, just as the same societal situation induces the same sway of illegitimacy among individuals.

The social order we have described necessarily produces this "strain toward dissolution." The pressure of such an order is upon outdoing one's competitors. The choice of means within the ambit of institutional control will persist as long as

the sentiments supporting a competitive system, i.e., deriving from the possibility of outranking competitors and hence enjoying the favorable response of others, are distributed throughout the entire system of activities and are not confined merely to the final result. A stable social structure demands a balanced distribution of affect among its various segments. When there occurs a shift of emphasis from the satisfactions deriving from competition itself to almost exclusive concern with successful competition, the resultant stress leads to the breakdown of the regulatory structure. With the resulting attenuation of the institutional imperatives, there occurs an approximation of the situation erroneously held by utilitarians to be typical of society generally wherein calculations of advantage and fear of punishment are the sole regulating agencies. In such situations, as Hobbes observed, force and fraud come to constitute the sole virtues in view of their relative efficiency in attaining goals, which were for him, of course, not culturally derived.

It should be apparent that the foregoing discussion is not pitched on a moralistic plane. Whatever the sentiments of the writer or reader concerning the ethical desirability of coordinating the means-and-goals phases of the social structure, one must agree that lack of such coordination leads to anomie. Insofar as one of the most general functions of social organization is to provide a basis for calculability and regularity of behavior, it is increasingly limited in effectiveness as these elements of the structure become dissociated. At the extreme, predictability virtually disappears and what may be properly termed cultural chaos or anomie intervenes.

This statement, being brief, is also incomplete. It has not included an exhaustive treatment of the various structural elements which predispose toward one rather than another of the alternative responses open to individuals; it has neglected, but not denied the relevance of, the factors determining the specific incidence of these responses; it has not enumerated the various concrete responses which are constituted by combinations of specific values of the analytical variables; it has omitted, or included only by implication, any consideration of the social functions performed by illicit responses; it has not tested the full explanatory power of the analytical scheme by examining a large number of group variations in the frequency of deviate and conformist behavior; it has not adequately dealt with rebellious conduct which seeks to refashion the social framework radically; it has not examined the relevance of cultural conflict for an analysis of culture-goal and institutional-means malintegration. It is suggested that these and related problems may be profitably analyzed by this scheme.

DISCUSSION QUESTIONS

1. With respect to Merton's theory, what two elements of social and cultural structure are the most important?

2. Consider your own academic pursuits and the college or university that you attend. What "cultural goals" and "institutional means" exist there? Do you think that they are well-balanced?

3. Describe Merton's adaptations that people might implement when they cannot achieve the culturally prescribed goals.

4. Discuss how the extreme emphasis on wealth in this country relates to crime. Does it suggest that poverty, in and of itself, causes crime?

REFERENCE

Durkheim, E. (1933). *The division of labor in society.* New York: Macmillan. (Original work published 1895)

10

CRIME AND THE AMERICAN DREAM

STEVEN F. MESSNER AND RICHARD ROSENFELD

EDITOR'S INTRODUCTION—In their text *Crime and the American Dream*, Messner and Rosenfeld attempt to address an often neglected component of Merton's theory of "social structure and anomie," namely why the United States has such a high rate of crime. Messner and Rosenfeld present an "institutional anomie" theory, which addresses the issue of anomie at the societal level. Like Merton, Messner and Rosenfeld seek to explain the excessively high rate of crime in the United States. They accomplish this goal by pointing to the "American Dream." Messner and Rosenfeld draw heavily from Merton's anomie theory, asserting that the high rate of crime in the United States stems partly from the fact that our society encourages everyone to pursue the goal of monetary success but places little value on the legitimate means for achieving that success. In other words, the legitimate, culturally accepted norms are sacrificed for the goal itself, which becomes larger than life.

However, Messner and Rosenfeld also extend Merton's theory. Primarily, they maintain that the cultural emphasis on monetary success parallels the notion that the economy pervades and dominates every other institution in America, including the family, education, and polity. They argue that the dominance of the economy interferes with the proper functioning of these institutions to such a great extent that they can no longer effectively and adequately socialize individuals or even sanction deviant behavior. Messner and Rosenfeld argue that if other aspects of American life were emphasized over material success, the United States might not have such a high crime rate. They point to the mixed economies of Western Europe and Japan as examples of societies that ensure that a level of economic well-being is not completely dependent upon economic performance, as it is in the United States.

Although their "institutional anomie" theory is still undergoing empirical testing, their theory provides important consideration of societal differences in crime rates. Additionally, their approach forces Americans to answer some tough questions about the core values that underlie the American Dream. In other words, maybe we should ask whether this emphasis placed on monetary success (seemingly, by any means necessary) is something we really want for our society.

THE VIRTUES AND VICES OF THE AMERICAN DREAM

The thesis of this book is that the American Dream itself and the normal social conditions engendered by it are deeply implicated in the problem of crime. In our use of the term "the American Dream," we refer to a broad cultural ethos that entails a commitment to the goal of material success, to be pursued by everyone in society, under conditions of open, individual competition.

The American Dream has both an evaluative and a cognitive dimension associated with it. People are socialized to accept the desirability of pursuing the goal of material success, and they are encouraged to believe that the chances of realizing the Dream are sufficiently high to justify a continued commitment to this cultural goal. These beliefs and commitments in many respects define what it means to be an enculturated member of our society. The ethos refers quite literally to the *American* dream. . . .

THE VALUE FOUNDATIONS OF THE AMERICAN DREAM

What sets the United States apart from other modern industrial nations, according to Merton, is the cultural ethos of the American Dream. Merton himself does not provide a formal definition of the American Dream, but it is possible to formulate a reasonably concise characterization of this cultural orientation based on Merton's discussion of American culture in general, his scattered references to the American Dream, and the commentary of others on Merton's work.[1] Our definition . . . is as follows: The American Dream refers to a commitment to the goal of material success, to be pursued by everyone in society, under conditions of open, individual competition.

The American Dream is a powerful force in our society because it embodies the basic value commitments of the culture: its achievement orientation, individualism, universalism, and peculiar form of materialism that has been described as the "fetishism of money" (Taylor, Walton, and Young, 1973, p. 94). Each of these value

orientations contributes to the anomic character of the American Dream: its strong emphasis on the importance of realizing cultural goals in comparison with its relatively weak emphasis on the importance of using the legitimate means to do so.

Before examining the value complex underlying the American Dream, we caution against an overly simplistic interpretation of American culture. The United States is a complex and, in many respects, culturally pluralistic society. It neither contains a single, monolithic value system nor exhibits complete consensus surrounding specific value orientations. Historically, certain groups have been completely excluded from the American Dream. An obvious example is that of enslaved African-Americans in the antebellum South. In addition, cultural prescriptions and mandates are filtered through prevailing gender roles. Indeed, we argue later in this chapter that the interpretation of the American Dream differs to some extent for men and women. We nevertheless concur with Jennifer Hochschild's claim that the American Dream has been, and continues to be, a "defining characteristic of American culture," a cultural ethos "against which all competitors must contend" (Hochschild, 1995, p. xi). An adequate understanding of the crime problem in the United States, therefore, is impossible without reference to the cluster of values underlying the American Dream: achievement, individualism, universalism, and materialism.

Achievement

A defining feature of American culture is its strong achievement orientation. People are encouraged to make something of themselves, to set goals, and to strive to reach them. At the same time, personal worth tends to be evaluated on the basis of the outcome of these efforts. Success, in other words, is to a large extent the ultimate measure of a person's value. . . . Given such a value orientation, the failure to achieve is readily equated with a failure to make any meaningful contribution to society at all. The cultural pressures to achieve at any cost are thus very intense. In this way, a strong achievement orientation, at the level of basic cultural values, is highly conducive to the mentality that "it's not how you

Messner, S., & Rosenfeld, R. (2001). *Crime and the American Dream* (3rd ed.). Belmont, CA: Wadsworth.

play the game; it's whether you win or lose" (Orru, 1990, p. 234).

Individualism

A second basic value orientation at the core of American culture is individualism. Americans are deeply committed to individual rights and individual autonomy. . . . This obsession with the individual, when combined with the strong achievement orientation in American culture, exacerbates the tendency toward anomie. In the pursuit of success, people are encouraged to "make it" on their own. Fellow members of society thus become competitors and rivals in the struggle to achieve social rewards and, ultimately, to validate personal worth. . . .

Universalism

A third basic value orientation in American culture is universalism. Socialization into the cultural goals of American society has a decidedly democratic quality. With few exceptions, everyone is encouraged to aspire to social ascent, and everyone is susceptible to evaluation on the basis of individual achievements. An important corollary of this universal entitlement to dream about success is that the hazards of failure are also universal. . . .

The "Fetishism" of Money

Finally, in American culture, success is signified in a distinctive way: by the accumulation of monetary rewards. Money is awarded special priority in American culture. As Merton observes, "In some large measure, money has been consecrated as a value in itself, over and above its expenditure for articles of consumption or its use for the enhancement of power." The point to emphasize here is not that Americans are uniquely materialistic, for a strong interest in material well-being can be found in most societies. Rather, the distinctive feature of American culture is the preeminent role of money as the "metric" of success. . . . There is an important implication of the signification of achievement with reference to monetary rewards. Monetary success is inherently open-ended. It is always possible in principle to have more money. Hence, the American Dream offers "no final stopping

point." It requires "never-ending achievement" (Merton, 1968, p. 190; Passas, 1990, p. 159).

In sum, the dominant value patterns of American culture—specifically, its achievement orientation, its competitive individualism, its universalism in goal orientations and evaluative standards, when harnessed to the preeminent goal of monetary success—crystallize into the distinctive cultural ethos of the American Dream. . . .

Cultural forces thus play a prominent role in our explanation of the high levels of crime in American society. However, a complete sociological explanation of crime must extend beyond features of culture and incorporate social structural factors as well. Culture does not exist in isolation from social structure but rather is expressed in, reproduced by, and occasionally impeded by, social structure. Any comprehensive explanation that emphasizes "culture" as a cause of crime must therefore also consider the relevant range of structural conditions through which the cultural sources of crime are enacted. In our view, the most important of these structural conditions are the institutional arrangements of society.

The Nature and Functioning of Social Institutions

Social institutions are the building blocks of whole societies. As such, they constitute the basic subject matter of macrolevel analysis. . . . The functions of institutions in social systems have been compared with the functions of instincts in biological organisms: both channel behavior to meet basic system needs. . . . The basic social needs around which institutions develop include the need to (1) adapt to the environment, (2) mobilize and deploy resources for the achievement of collective goals, and (3) socialize members to accept the society's fundamental normative patterns (Downes & Rock, 1982; Parsons, 1951).

Adaptation to the environment is the primary responsibility of economic institutions. The *economy* consists of activities organized around the production and distribution of goods and services. It functions to satisfy the basic material requirements for human existence, such as the need for food, clothing, and shelter.

The political system, or *polity,* mobilizes and distributes power to attain collective goals. One collective purpose of special importance is the maintenance of public safety. Political institutions are responsible for "protecting members of society from invasions from without, controlling crime and disorder within, and providing channels for resolving conflicts of interest" (Bassis, Gelles, & Levine, 1991, p. 142). As part of the polity, agencies of the civil and criminal justice systems have major responsibility for crime control and the lawful resolution of conflicts.

The institution of the *family* has primary responsibility for the regulation of sexual activity and for the replacement of members of society. These tasks involve establishing and enforcing the limits of legitimate sexual relations among adults, the physical care and nurturing of children, and the socialization of children into the values, goals, and beliefs of the dominant culture. Families also bear much of the responsibility for the care of dependent persons in society more generally (for example, caring for the infirm and the elderly). In addition, a particularly important function of the family in modern societies is to provide emotional support for its members. To a significant degree, the family serves as a refuge from the tensions and stresses generated in other institutional domains. . . .

The institution of *education* shares many of the socialization functions of the family. Like the family, schools are given responsibility for transmitting basic cultural standards to new generations. In modern industrial societies, schools are also oriented toward the specific task of preparing youth for the demands of adult roles and, in particular, occupational roles. In addition, education is intended to enhance personal adjustment, facilitate the development of individual human potential, and advance the general knowledge base of the culture.

These four social institutions—the economy, the polity, the family, and education—are the central focus of our analysis of crime. They do not, of course, exhaust the institutional structure of modern societies, nor are they the only institutions with relevance to crime. Religion and mass communications, for example, have been the subjects of important criminological research (Stark, Kent, & Doyle, 1982; Surette, 1992). However, the economy, the polity, the family, and education are, in our view, central to what

may be called an "institutional understanding" of crime. . . . Any given society therefore will be characterized by a distinctive arrangement of social institutions that reflects a balancing of the sometimes competing claims and requisites of the different institutions, yielding a distinctive institutional balance of power. . . .

THE AMERICAN DREAM AND THE INSTITUTIONAL BALANCE OF POWER

The core elements of the American Dream—a strong achievement orientation, a commitment to competitive individualism, universalism, and, most important, the glorification of material success—have their institutional underpinnings in the economy. The most important feature of the economy of the United States is its capitalist nature. The defining characteristics of any capitalist economy are private ownership and control of property, and free-market mechanisms for the production and distribution of goods and services.

These structural arrangements are conducive to and presuppose certain cultural orientations. For the economy to operate efficiently, the private owners of property must be profit oriented and eager to invest, and workers must be willing to exchange their labor for wages. The motivational mechanism underlying these conditions is the promise of financial returns. The internal logic of a capitalist economy thus presumes that an attraction to monetary rewards as a result of achievement in the marketplace is widely diffused throughout the population (Passas, 1990, p. 159; Polanyi, [1944] 1957).

A capitalist economy is also highly competitive for all those involved, property owners and workers alike. Firms that are unable to adapt to shifting consumer demands or to fluctuations in the business cycle are likely to fail. Workers who cannot keep up with changing skill requirements or who are unproductive in comparison with others are likely to be fired. This intense competition discourages economic actors from becoming wedded to conventional ways of doing things and instead encourages them to substitute new techniques for traditional ones if these techniques offer advantages in meeting economic goals. Therefore, a capitalist economy naturally cultivates a competitive, innovative spirit.

What is distinctive about the United States, however, is the *exaggerated* emphasis on monetary success and the *unrestrained* receptivity to innovation. The goal of monetary success overwhelms other goals and becomes the principal measuring rod for achievements. The resulting proclivity and pressures to innovate resist any regulation that is not justified by purely technical considerations. The obvious question arises: Why have cultural orientations that express the inherent logic of capitalism evolved to a particularly extreme degree in American society? The answer, we submit, lies in the inability of other social institutions to tame economic imperatives. In short, the institutional balance of power is tilted toward the economy.

The historical evidence suggests that this distinctive institutional structure has always existed in the United States. In his analysis of American slavery, the historian Stanley Elkins observed that capitalism emerged "as the principle dynamic force in American society," free to develop according to its own institutional logic without interference from "prior traditional institutions, with competing claims of their own." Whereas capitalism developed in European societies (and later in Japan) within powerful preexisting institutional frameworks, the institutional structure of American society emerged simultaneously with, and was profoundly shaped by, the requirements of capitalist development. American capitalism thus took on a "purity of form" unknown in other capitalist societies (Elkins, 1968, p. 43). Moreover, other institutions were cast in distinctly subsidiary positions in relation to the economy. . . .

. . . . Robert Heilbroner writes that "*American* capitalism, not American *capitalism*" is responsible for the features of our society that distinguish it, for better or worse, from other capitalist societies (Heilbroner, 1991, pp. 539–540). . . . [S]erious crime rates in the United States are unusually high when compared with those in other modern capitalist societies. These differences, therefore, cannot be accounted for by capitalism alone. Variation in levels of crime and other aspects of these nations is rooted . . . in their contrasting institutional settings. . . . We accept the basic argument that capitalism developed in the United States without the institutional restraints found in other societies. As a consequence, the economy assumed an unusual

dominance in the institutional structure of society from the very beginning of the nation's history, and this distinctive institutional arrangement has continued to the present.

Our notion of economic dominance in the institutional balance of power is similar to Elliott Currie's concept of a "market society" as distinct from a "market economy." According to Currie, in a market society "the pursuit of private gain becomes the organizing principle of all areas of social life—not simply a mechanism that we may use to accomplish certain circumscribed ends" (Currie, 1991, p. 255). Economic dominance characteristic of the American market society is manifested, we argue, in three interrelated ways:

1. devaluation of noneconomic institutional functions and roles,

2. accommodation to economic requirements by other institutions, and

3. penetration of economic norms into other institutional domains.

Devaluation

Noneconomic goals, positions, and roles are devalued in American society relative to the ends and means of economic activity. An example is the relative devaluation of the distinctive functions of education and of the social roles that fulfill these functions. Education is regarded largely as a means to occupational attainment, which in turn is valued primarily insofar as it promises economic rewards. Neither the acquisition of knowledge nor learning for its own sake is highly valued. . . .

Similar processes are observed in the context of the family, although the tendency toward devaluation is perhaps not as pronounced as in other institutional arenas. There is a paradox here, because "family values" are typically extolled in public rhetoric. Nevertheless, family life has a tenuous position in American culture. It is the home*owner* rather than the home*maker* who is widely admired and envied—and whose image is reflected in the American Dream. . . .

The distinctive function of the polity, providing for the collective good, also tends to be devalued in comparison with economic functions. The general public has little regard for politics as an intrinsically valuable activity and confers little social honor on the role of the politician. Indeed, the label "politician" is commonly used in a disparaging way. . . . ,

Interestingly, one distinctive function of the polity does not appear to be generally devalued, namely, crime control. There is widespread agreement among the American public that government should undertake vigorous efforts to deal with the crime problem. If anything, Americans want government to do more to control crime. Fifty-four percent of Americans think the government spends too little on law enforcement; only 8 percent think the government spends too much.[2] Yet this apparent exception is compatible with the claim of economic dominance. Americans' obsession with crime is rooted in fears that crime threatens, according to political analyst Thomas Edsall [1992], "their security, their values, their rights, and their livelihoods and the competitive prospects of their children." . . . [B]ecause crime control bears directly on the pursuit of the American Dream, this particular function of the polity receives high priority.

Accommodation

A second way in which the dominance of the economy is manifested is in the *accommodations* that emerge in those situations where institutional claims are in competition. Economic conditions and requirements typically exert a much stronger influence on the operation of other institutions than vice versa. For example, family routines are dominated by the schedules, rewards, and penalties of the labor market. Whereas parents worry about "finding time" for their families, few workers must "find time" for their jobs. On the contrary, many feel fortunate that the economy has found time for them. Consider the resistance to parental leave in the United States. Most industrialized nations mandate paid maternity or parental leave by law to enable parents to care for infants at home without threat of job loss. . . .

Educational institutions are also more likely to accommodate to the demands of the economy than is the economy to respond to the requirements of education. The timing of schooling reflects occupational demands rather than intrinsic features of the learning process or personal interest in the pursuit of knowledge. People go to school largely to prepare for "good" jobs. And once they are in the labor market, there is little opportunity to pursue further education for its own sake. When workers do return to school, it is almost always to upgrade skills or credentials to keep pace with job demands, to seek higher-paying jobs, or to "retool" during spells of unemployment. . . .

The polity likewise is dependent on the economy for financial support. To run effective campaigns, politicians and political parties rely on private donations. Even if money does not guarantee the outcome of an election, any candidate who hopes to win must attract significant financial support from private sources. . . .

Penetration

A final way in which the dominance of the economy in the institutional balance of power is manifested is in the *penetration* of economic norms into other institutional areas. Learning takes place within the context of individualized competition for external rewards, and teaching becomes oriented toward testing. Schools rely on grading as a system of extrinsic rewards, like wages, to ensure compliance with goals. . . .

Education itself is increasingly viewed as a commodity, no different from other consumer goods. Economic terminology permeates the very language of education, as in the emphasis on the "customer-driven classroom . . . accountability" conceptualized in terms of the "value added" to students in the educational production process, and the emphasis on students themselves as "products."[3] . . . Within the polity, a "bottom-line" mentality develops. Effective politicians are those who deliver the goods. Moreover, the notion that the government would work better if it were run more like a business continues to be an article of faith among large segments of the American public. Many Americans in fact seem to prefer business leaders over public officials to perform key political functions. . . .

The family has probably been most resistant to the intrusion of economic norms. Yet even here, pressures toward penetration are apparent. Contributions to family life tend to be measured against the all-important breadwinner role, which has been extended to include women who work in the paid labor force. No corresponding movement of men into the role of homemaker has occurred. Here again, shifts in popular terminology are also instructive. Husbands and wives are "partners" who "manage" the household "division of labor" in accordance with the "marriage contract." We are aware of few comparable shifts in kin-based terminology, or primary group norms, from the family to the workplace.[4]

In sum, the social organization of the United States is characterized by a striking dominance of the economy in the institutional balance of power. As a result of this economic dominance, the inherent tendencies of a capitalist economy to orient the members of society toward an unrestrained pursuit of economic achievements are developed to an extreme degree. These tendencies are expressed at the cultural level in the preeminence of the competitive, individualistic pursuit of monetary success as the overriding goal—the American Dream—and in the relative deemphasis placed on the importance of using normative means to reach this goal—anomie. The anomic nature of the American Dream and the institutional structure of American society are thus mutually supportive and reinforcing. In the next section, we turn to the implications of this type of social organization for crime.

ANOMIE AND THE WEAKENING OF INSTITUTIONAL CONTROL

Both of the core features of the social organization of the United States—culture and institutional structure—are implicated in the genesis of high levels of crime. At the cultural level, the dominant ethos of the American Dream stimulates criminal motivations and at the same time promotes a weak normative environment (anomie). At the institutional level, the dominance of the economy in the institutional balance of power fosters weak social control. And, as just explained, both culture and institutional structure are themselves interdependent. These interconnections between culture, social structure, and crime are presented schematically in Figure 10.1.

The cultural stimulation of criminal motivations derives from the distinctive content of the American Dream. Given the strong, relentless pressure for everyone to succeed, understood in terms of an inherently elusive monetary goal, people formulate wants and desires that are difficult, if not impossible, to satisfy within the confines of legally permissible behavior. This feature of the American Dream helps explain criminal behavior with an instrumental character, behavior that

offers monetary rewards. This type of behavior includes white collar offenses, street crimes such as robbery and drug dealing, and other crimes that occur as a consequence of these activities.

At the same time, the American Dream does not contain within it strong injunctions against substituting more effective, illegitimate means for less effective, legitimate means in the pursuit of monetary success. To the contrary, the distinctive cultural message accompanying the monetary success goal in the American Dream is the devaluation of all but the most technically efficient means. This anomic orientation leads not simply to high levels of crime in general but to especially violent forms of economic crime, for which the United States is known throughout the industrial world, such as mugging, carjacking, and home invasion.

Of course, the American Dream does not completely subsume culture. Other elements of culture affirm the legitimacy of legal prohibitions and the desirability of lawful behavior. In principle, these other elements of culture could counterbalance the anomic pressures emanating from the American Dream. However, the very same institutional dynamics that contribute to the pressures to "innovate" in the pursuit of economic goals also make it less likely that the anomic pressures inherent in the American Dream will in fact be counterbalanced by other cultural forces. . . .

This generalized anomie ultimately explains, in our view, the unusually high levels of gun-related violence in the United States. In the final analysis, guns are very effective tools for enforcing compliance. The American penchant for owning guns and using them reflects, in other words, a more general anomic cultural orientation, a willingness to pursue goals by any means necessary. The basic social organization of the United States contributes to high levels of crime in another way. Institutions such as the family, schools, and the polity bear responsibility not only for socialization, and hence the normative control associated with culture, but also for the more external type of social control associated with social structure. External control is achieved through the active involvement of individuals in institutional roles and through the dispensation of rewards and punishments by institutions. . . .

[W]eak institutions invite challenge. Under conditions of extreme *competitive* individualism, *people* actively resist institutional control. Not

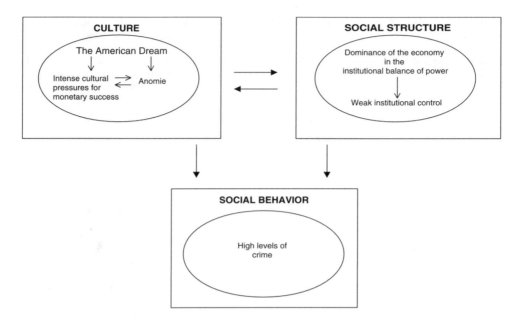

Figure 10.1   An Analytical Model of the Linkages Between Macrosocial Organization and Crime

only do they fall from the insecure grasp of powerless institutions, sometimes they deliberately, even proudly, push themselves away. The problem of external control by major social institutions, then, is inseparable from the problem of the internal regulatory force of social norms, or anomie. Anomic societies will inevitably find it difficult and costly to exert social control over the behavior of people who feel free to use whatever means prove most effective in reaching personal goals. Hence, the very sociocultural dynamics that make American institutions weak also enable and entitle Americans to defy institutional controls. If Americans are exceptionally resistant to social control—and therefore exceptionally vulnerable to criminal temptations—the resistance occurs because they *live in* a society that enshrines the unfettered pursuit of individual material success above all other values. In the United States, anomie is considered a virtue. . . .

DISCUSSION QUESTIONS

1. What are the core features of the American Dream? Messner and Rosenfeld maintain that

the American Dream, though appealing for many people, has a dark side. What is it?

2. Describe the value foundations of the American Dream. What role do they play in terms of influencing the American Dream?

3. How does the dominance of the American Dream disrupt the balance of power of various institutions in the United States? To what extent do you agree with Messner and Rosenfeld's position that noneconomic goals, positions, and roles—such as education for the sake of learning and parenting—are devalued in this country?

4. Do you think that the American Dream and the dominance of the economy also produce the types of strain described by Merton and Agnew, as discussed in this section? What crime control policies might Messner and Rosenfeld suggest in light of their theory?

NOTES

1 In our analysis of the value foundations of the American Dream, we rely heavily on Marco Orru's (1990) excellent exegesis of [M]erton's theory. Characterization[s] of this cultural ethos that are very

similar to ours can also be found in studies of the "success theme" in American literature. . . . See Hearn (1977) and Long (1985).

2 Authors' calculations from the 1998 GSS [General Social Survey].

3 For commentary on the notion of the "customer-driven classroom," see *The Teaching Professor* (1994). The references to "accountability" [and] "value-added" education are from Kozol (1992, p. 277). See also Kozol's (1991) discussion of the state of American public education, and Bellah et al.'s (1991, 170) critique of the idea of an "education industry."

4 For a particularly insightful discussion of the penetration of market-based norms and metaphors into noneconomic realms of social life, see Schwartz (1994a, 1994b). . . .

11

FOUNDATION FOR A GENERAL STRAIN THEORY OF CRIME AND DELINQUENCY

ROBERT AGNEW

EDITOR'S INTRODUCTION—Agnew's general strain theory builds on several principles present in earlier strain theories, but Agnew's approach offers a substantial revision of the earlier theoretical developments. According to these earlier strain theories, namely the ideas found in Merton, crime results from the inability to achieve monetary success or other culturally prescribed goals in a legitimate fashion. This blockage results in *strain*, or frustration, within the person who is unable to fulfill the goal, which in turn is likely to lead to crime as the only path to success. Several factors influence whether or not someone will respond to strain with crime. These factors typically include the level of social control present and whether the individual associates with delinquent peers. Empirical support for this theory has been mixed over the years, and it has therefore yielded some of its theoretical dominance to other, more empirically successful approaches.

In his reformulation, Agnew presents a broader version of strain theory that focuses primarily on negative relationships with others. He argues that these negative relationships produce negative emotions within a person, which later are expressed through crime. It is intended to be a general theory of crime, but Agnew uses it primarily to explain why adolescents engage in delinquency and drug use. In the first part of his article, he distinguishes strain theory from social control and differential association/social learning theories and argues that failure to achieve culturally prescribed goals may be only one of the many possible sources of strain or frustration. Secondly, Agnew lists three major sources of strain—strain as the failure to achieve positively valued goals, strain as the removal of positively valued stimuli that one possesses, and strain as the presentation of negative stimuli. Agnew describes the types of situations that may anger or frustrate certain individuals under certain conditions. In this section, Agnew is careful to recognize that only some individuals will respond to strain with crime; therefore, it becomes very important for Agnew to describe the very factors that contribute to strain. In the last part of the article, Agnew offers various ways in which individuals can adapt to, or cope with, strain when faced with certain circumstances. These factors frequently play an important role in terms of whether an individual will choose delinquency or not in a given situation.

Several recent tests of Agnew's theory have generated positive results, finding that negative relationships and stressful life events were associated with a broad range of delinquent behaviors. Additionally, Agnew's theory has received important attention from the biosocial perspective of behavior genetics, which combines the general strain theory of crime with other biosocial and genetic considerations in a theory about crime and deviance (see Walsh, Chapter 36, this volume).

S train theory . . . is distinguished by its focus on negative relationships with others and its insistence that such relationships lead to delinquency through the negative affect—especially anger—they sometimes engender. . . .

THE MAJOR TYPES OF STRAIN

Negative relationships with others are, quite simply, relationships in which others are not treating the individual as he or she would like to be treated. The classic strain theories of Merton (1938), A. Cohen (1955), and Cloward and Ohlin (1960) focus on only one type of negative relationship: relationships in which others prevent the individual from achieving positively valued goals. In particular, they focus on the goal blockage experienced by lower class individuals trying to achieve monetary success or middle-class status. More recent versions of strain theory have argued that adolescents are not only concerned about the future goals of monetary success/middle-class status, but are also concerned about the achievement of more immediate goals such as good grades, popularity with the opposite sex, and doing well in athletics (Agnew, 1984; Elliott & Voss, 1974; Elliott et al., 1985; Empey, 1982; Greenberg, 1977; Quicker, 1974). The focus, however, is still on the achievement of positively valued goals. Most recently, Agnew (1985a) has argued that strain may result not only from the failure to achieve positively valued goals, but also from the inability to escape legally from painful situations. If one draws on the above theories—as well as the stress, equity/justice, and aggression literatures—one can begin to develop a more complete classification of the types of strain.

Three major types of strain are described—each referring to a different type of negative relationship with others. Other individuals may (1) prevent one from achieving positively valued goals, (2) remove or threaten to remove positively valued stimuli that one possesses, or (3) present or threaten to present one with noxious or negatively valued stimuli. These categories of strain are presented as ideal types. There is no expectation, for example, that a factor analysis of strainful events will reproduce these categories. These categories, rather, are presented so as to ensure that the full range of strainful events are considered in empirical research.

Strain as the Failure to Achieve Positively Valued Goals

Strain as the Disjunction Between Aspirations and Expectations/Actual Achievements

The classic strain theories of Merton, A. Cohen, and Cloward and Ohlin argue that the cultural system encourages everyone to pursue the ideal goals of monetary success and/or middle-class status. Lower-class individuals, however, [are] often prevented from achieving such goals through legitimate channels. In line with such theories, adolescent strain is typically measured in terms of the disjunction between aspirations (or ideal goals) and expectations (or expected levels of goal achievement). These theories, however, have been criticized for several reasons (see Agnew, 1986, 1991b; Clinard, 1964; Hirschi, 1969; Kornhauser, 1978; Liska, 1987; also see Bernard, 1984; Farnworth & Leiber, 1989). Among other things, it has been charged that these theories (1) are unable to explain the extensive nature of middle-class delinquency, (2) neglect goals other than monetary success/middle-class status, (3) neglect barriers to goal achievement other than social class, and (4) do not fully specify why only some strained individuals turn to delinquency. The

Agnew, R. (1992). Foundation for a general strain theory of crime and delinquency. *Criminology, 30*, 47-87.

most damaging criticism, however, stems from the limited empirical support provided by studies focusing on the disjunction between aspirations and expectations (see Kornhauser, 1978, as well [as] the arguments of Bernard, 1984; Elliott et al., 1985; and Jensen, 1986).

As a consequence of these criticisms, several researchers have revised the above theories. The most popular revision argues that there is a youth subculture that emphasizes a variety of immediate goals. The achievement of these goals is further said to depend on a variety of factors besides social class: factors such as intelligence, physical attractiveness, personality, and athletic ability. As a result, many middle-class individuals find that they lack the traits or skills necessary to achieve their goals through legitimate channels. This version of strain theory, however, continues to argue that strain stems from the inability to achieve certain ideal goals emphasized by the (sub)cultural system. As a consequence, strain continues to be measured in terms of the disjunction between *aspirations* and *actual achievements* (since we are dealing with immediate rather than future goals, actual achievements rather than expected achievements may be examined). It should be noted that empirical support for this revised version of strain theory is also weak (see Agnew, 1991b, for a summary). . . .

Strain as the Disjunction Between Expectations and Actual Achievements

As indicated above, strain theories in criminology focus on the inability to achieve *ideal* goals derived from the cultural system. This approach stands in contrast to certain of the research on justice in social psychology. Here the focus is on the disjunction between *expectations* and *actual achievements* (rewards), and it is commonly argued that such expectations are existentially based. In particular, it has been argued that such expectations derive from the individual's past experience and/or from comparisons with referential (or generalized) others who are similar to the individual (see Berger et al., 1972, 1983; Blau, 1964; Homans, 1961; Jasso and Rossi, 1977; Mickelson, 1990; Ross et al., 1971; Thibaut & Kelley, 1959). Much of the research in this area has focused on income expectations, although the above theories apply to expectations regarding all

manner of positive stimuli. The justice literature argues that the failure to achieve such expectations may lead to such emotions as anger, resentment, rage, dissatisfaction, disappointment, and unhappiness—that is, all the emotions customarily associated with strain in criminology. Further, it is argued that individuals will be strongly motivated to reduce the gap between expectations and achievements—with deviance being commonly mentioned as one possible option. This literature has not devoted much empirical research to deviance, although limited data suggest that the expectations-achievement gap is related to anger/hostility (Ross et al., 1971).

This alternative conception of strain has been largely neglected in criminology. This is unfortunate because it has the potential to overcome certain of the problems of current strain theories. First, one would expect the disjunction between expectations and actual achievements to be more emotionally distressing than that between aspirations and achievements. Aspirations, by definition, are *ideal* goals. They have something of the utopian in them, and for that reason, the failure to achieve aspirations may not be taken seriously. The failure to achieve expected goals, however, is likely to be taken seriously since such goals are rooted in reality—the individual has previously experienced such goals or has seen similar others experience such goals. Second, this alternative conception of strain assigns a central role to the social comparison process. As A. Cohen (1965) argued in a follow-up to his strain theory, the neglect of social comparison is a major shortcoming of strain theory. The above theories describe one way in which social comparison is important: Social comparison plays a central role in the formation of individual goals (expectations in this case; also see Suls, 1977). Third, the assumption that goals are culturally based has sometimes proved problematic for strain theory (see Kornhauser, 1978). Among other things, it makes it difficult to integrate strain theory with social control and cultural deviance theory (see Hirschi, 1979). These latter theories assume that the individual is weakly tied to the cultural system or tied to alternative/oppositional subcultures. The argument that goals are existentially based, however, paves the way for integrations involving strain theory.

Strain as the Disjunction Between
Just/Fair Outcomes and Actual Outcomes

The above models of strain assume that individual goals focus on the achievement of specific outcomes. Individual goals, for example, focus on the achievement of a certain amount of money or a certain grade-point average. A third conception of strain, also derived from the justice/equity literature, makes a rather different argument. It claims that individuals do not necessarily enter interactions with specific outcomes in mind. Rather, they enter interactions expecting that certain distributive justice rules will be followed, rules specifying how resources should be allocated. The rule that has received the most attention in the literature is that of equity. An equitable relationship is one in which the outcome/input ratios of the actors involved in an exchange/allocation relationship are equivalent (see Adams, 1963, 1965; Cook & Hegtvedt, 1983; Walster et al., 1978). Outcomes encompass a broad range of positive and negative consequences, while inputs encompass the individual's positive and negative contributions to the exchange. Individuals in a relationship will compare the ratio of their outcomes and inputs to the ratio(s) of specific others in the relationship. If the ratios are equal to one another, they feel that the outcomes are fair or just. This is true, according to equity theorists, even if the outcomes are low. If outcome/input ratios are not equal, actors will feel that the outcomes are unjust and they will experience distress as a result. Such distress is especially likely when individuals feel they have been underrewarded rather than overrewarded (Hegtvedt, 1990).

The equity literature has described the possible reactions to this distress, some of which involve deviance (see Adams, 1963, 1965; Austin, 1977; Walster et al., 1973, 1978; see Stephenson & White, 1968, for an attempt to recast A. Cohen's strain theory in terms of equity theory). In particular, inequity may lead to delinquency for several reasons—all having to do with the restoration of equity. Individuals in inequitable relationships may engage in delinquency in order to (1) increase their outcomes (e.g., by theft); (2) lower their inputs (e.g., truancy from school); (3) lower the outcomes of others (e.g., vandalism, theft, assault); and/or (4) increase the inputs of others (e.g., by being incorrigible or disorderly). In highly inequitable situations, individuals may leave the field (e.g., run away from home) or force others to leave the field. There has not been any empirical research on the relationship between equity and delinquency, although much data suggest that inequity leads to anger and frustration. A few studies also suggest that insulting and vengeful behaviors may result from inequity (see Cook & Hegtvedt, 1991; Donnerstein & Hatfield, 1982; Hegtvedt, 1990; Mikula, 1986; Sprecher, 1986; Walster et al., 1973, 1978).

It is not difficult to measure equity. Walster et al. (1978, pp. 234-242) provide the most complete guide to measurement. Sprecher (1986) illustrates how equity may be measured in social surveys; respondents are asked who contributes more to a particular relationship and/or who "gets the best deal" out of a relationship. A still simpler strategy might be to ask respondents how fair or just their interactions with others, such as parents or teachers, are. One would then predict that those involved in unfair relations will be more likely to engage in current and future delinquency.

The literature on equity builds on the strain theory literature in criminology in several ways. First, all of the strain literature assumes that individuals are pursuing some specific outcome, such as a certain amount of money or prestige. The equity literature points out that individuals do not necessarily enter into interactions with specific outcomes in mind, but rather with the expectation that a particular distributive justice rule will be followed. Their goal is that the interaction conform to the justice principle. This perspective, then, points to a new source of strain not considered in the criminology literature. Second, the strain literature in criminology focuses largely on the individual's outcomes. Individuals are assumed to be pursuing a specific goal, and strain is judged in terms of the disjunction between the goal and the actual outcome. The equity literature suggests that this may be an oversimplified conception and that the individual's inputs may also have to be considered. In particular, an equity theorist would argue that inputs will condition the individual's evaluation of outcomes. That is, individuals who view their inputs as limited will be more likely to accept limited outcomes as fair. Third, the equity literature also highlights the importance of the social comparison process. In particular, the equity literature stresses that one's evaluation of outcomes is at least partly a function of the outcomes (and inputs) of those with whom one is involved in exchange/allocation relations. A given outcome, then, may be evaluated as fair or unfair depending on the outcomes (and inputs) of others in the exchange/allocation relation.

Summary: Strain as the Failure to Achieve Positively Valued Goals

Three types of strain in this category have been listed: strain as the disjunction between (1) aspirations and expectations/actual achievements, (2) expectations and actual achievements, and (3) just/fair outcomes and actual outcomes. Strain theory in criminology has focused on the first type of strain, arguing that it is most responsible for the delinquency in our society. Major research traditions in the justice/equity field, however, argue that anger and frustration derive primarily from the second two types of strain. To complicate matters further, one can list still additional types of strain in this category. Certain of the literature, for example, has talked of the disjunction between "satisfying outcomes" and reality, between "deserved" outcomes and reality, and between "tolerance levels" or minimally acceptable outcomes and reality. No study has examined all of these types of goals, but taken as a whole the data do suggest that there are often differences among aspirations (ideal outcomes), expectations (expected outcomes), "satisfying" outcomes, "deserved" outcomes, fair or just outcomes, and tolerance levels (Della Fave, 1974; Della Fave & Klobus, 1976; Martin, 1986; Martin & Murray, 1983; Messick & Sentis, 1983; Shepelak & Alwin, 1986). This paper has focused on the three types of strain listed above largely because they dominate the current literature.

Given these multiple sources of strain, one might ask which is the most relevant to the explanation of delinquency. This is a difficult question to answer given current research. The most fruitful strategy at the present time may be to assume that all of the above sources are relevant—that there are several sources of frustration. Alwin (1987), Austin (1977), Crosby & Gonzalez-Intal (1984), Hegtvedt (1991b), Messick & Sentis (1983), and Tornblum (1977) all argue or imply that people often employ a variety of standards to evaluate their situation.

Strain theorists, then, might be best advised to employ measures that tap all of the above types of strain. One might, for example, focus on a broad range of positively valued goals and, for each goal, ask adolescents whether they are achieving their ideal outcomes (aspirations), expected outcomes, and just/fair outcomes. One would expect strain to be greatest when several standards were not being met, with perhaps greatest weight being given to expectations and just/fair outcomes.

Strain as the Removal of Positively Valued Stimuli From the Individual

The psychological literature on aggression and the stress literature suggest that strain may involve more than the pursuit of positively valued goals. Certain of the aggression literature, in fact, has come to de-emphasize the pursuit of positively valued goals, pointing out that the blockage of goal-seeking behavior is a relatively weak predictor of aggression, particularly when the goal has never been experienced before (Bandura, 1973; Zillman, 1979). The stress literature has largely neglected the pursuit of positively valued goals as a source of stress. Rather, if one looks at the stressful life events examined in this literature, one finds a focus on (1) events involving the loss of positively valued stimuli and (2) events involving the presentation of noxious or negative stimuli (see Pearlin, 1983, for other typologies of stressful life events/ conditions). So, for example, one recent study of adolescent stress employs a life-events list that focuses on such items as the loss of a boyfriend/girlfriend, the death or serious illness of a friend, moving to a new school district, the divorce/separation of one's parents, suspension from school, and the presence of a variety of adverse conditions at work (see Williams and Uchiyama, 1989, for an overview of life-events scales for adolescents; see Compas, 1987, and Compas & Phares, 1991, for overviews of research on adolescent stress).

Drawing on the stress literature, then, one may state that a second type of strain or negative relationship involves the actual or anticipated removal (loss) of positively valued stimuli from the individual. As indicated above, numerous examples of such loss can be found in the inventories of stressful life events. The actual or anticipated loss of positively valued stimuli may lead to delinquency as the individual tries to prevent the loss of the positive stimuli, retrieve the lost stimuli or obtain substitute stimuli, seek revenge against those responsible for the loss, or manage the negative affect caused by the loss by taking illicit drugs. While there are no data bearing directly on this type of strain, experimental data indicate that aggression often occurs when positive reinforcement previously administered to an individual is withheld or reduced (Bandura, 1973; Van Houten, 1983). And as discussed below, inventories of stressful life events, which include the loss of positive stimuli, are related to delinquency.

Strain as the Presentation of Negative Stimuli

The literature on stress and the recent psychological literature on aggression also focus on the actual or anticipated presentation of negative or noxious stimuli. Except for the work of Agnew (1985a), however, this category of strain has been neglected in criminology. And even Agnew does not focus on the presentation of noxious stimuli per se, but on the inability of adolescents to escape legally from noxious stimuli. Much data, however, suggest that the presentation of noxious stimuli may lead to aggression and other negative outcomes in certain conditions, even when legal escape from such stimuli is possible (Bandura, 1973; Zillman, 1979). Noxious stimuli may lead to delinquency as the adolescent tries to (1) escape from or avoid the negative stimuli; (2) terminate or alleviate the negative stimuli; (3) seek revenge against the source of the negative stimuli or related targets, although the evidence on displaced aggression is somewhat mixed (see Berkowitz, 1982; Bernard, 1990; Van Houten, 1983; Zillman, 1979); and/or (4) manage the resultant negative affect by taking illicit drugs.

A wide range of noxious stimuli have been examined in the literature, and experimental, survey, and participant observation studies have linked such stimuli to both general and specific measures of delinquency—with the experimental studies focusing on aggression. Delinquency/aggression, in particular, has been linked to such noxious stimuli as child abuse and neglect (Rivera & Widom, 1990), criminal victimization (Lauritsen et al., 1991), physical punishment (Straus, 1991), negative relations with parents

(Healy & Bonner, 1969), negative relations with peers (Short & Strodtbeck, 1965), adverse or negative school experiences (Hawkins & Lishner, 1987), a wide range of stressful life events (Gersten et al., 1974; Kaplan et al., 1983; Linsky & Straus, 1986; Mawson, 1987; Novy & Donohue, 1985; Vaux & Ruggiero, 1983), verbal threats and insults, physical pain, unpleasant odors, disgusting scenes, noise, heat, air pollution, personal space violations, and high density (see Anderson and Anderson, 1984; Bandura, 1973, 1983; Berkowitz, 1982, 1986; Mueller, 1983). In one of the few studies in criminology to focus specifically on the presentation of negative stimuli, Agnew (1985a) found that delinquency was related to three scales measuring negative relations at home and school. The effect of the scales on delinquency was partially mediated through a measure of anger, and the effect held when measures of social control and deviant beliefs were controlled. And in a recent study employing longitudinal data, Agnew (1989) found evidence suggesting that the relationship between negative stimuli and delinquency was due to the causal effect of the negative stimuli on delinquency (rather than the effect of delinquency on the negative stimuli). Much evidence, then, suggests that the presentation of negative or noxious stimuli constitutes a third major source of strain.

Certain of the negative stimuli listed above, such as physical pain, heat, noise, and pollution, may be experienced as noxious largely for biological reasons (i.e., they may be unconditioned negative stimuli). Others may be conditioned negative stimuli, experienced as noxious largely because of their association with unconditioned negative stimuli (see Berkowitz, 1982). Whatever the case, it is assumed that such stimuli are experienced as noxious regardless of the goals that the individual is pursuing.

The Links Between Strain and Delinquency

Three sources of strain have been presented: strain as the actual or anticipated failure to achieve positively valued goals, strain as the actual or anticipated removal of positively valued stimuli, and strain as the actual or anticipated presentation of negative stimuli. While these types are theoretically distinct from one another, they may sometimes overlap in practice. So, for example, the insults of a teacher may be experienced as adverse because they (1) interfere with the adolescent's aspirations for academic success, (2) result in the violation of a distributive justice rule such as equity, and (3) are conditioned negative stimuli and so are experienced as noxious in and of themselves. Other examples of overlap can be given, and it may sometimes be difficult to disentangle the different types of strain in practice. Once again, however, these categories are ideal types and are presented only to ensure that all events with the potential for creating strain are considered in empirical research.

Each type of strain increases the likelihood that individuals will experience one or more of a range of negative emotions. Those emotions include disappointment, depression, and fear. Anger, however, is the most critical emotional reaction for the purposes of the general strain theory. Anger results when individuals blame their adversity on others, and anger is a key emotion because it increases the individual's level of felt injury, creates a desire for retaliation/revenge, energizes the individual for action, and lowers inhibitions, in part because individuals believe that others will feel their aggression justified (see Averill, 1982; Berkowitz, 1982; Kemper, 1978; Kluegel and Smith, 1986, Ch. 10; Zillman, 1979). Anger, then, affects the individual in several ways that are conducive to delinquency. Anger is distinct from many of the other types of negative affect in this respect, and this is the reason that anger occupies a special place in the general strain theory. It is important to note, however, that delinquency may still occur in response to other types of negative affect—such as despair, although delinquency is less likely in such cases. The experience of negative affect, especially anger, typically creates a desire to take corrective steps, with delinquency being one possible response. Delinquency may be a method for alleviating strain, that is, for achieving positively valued goals, for protecting or retrieving positive stimuli, or for eliminating or escaping from negative stimuli. Delinquency may be used to seek revenge; data suggest that vengeful behavior often occurs even when there is no possibility of eliminating the adversity that stimulated it (Berkowitz, 1982). And delinquency may occur as adolescents try to manage

their negative affect through illicit drug use (see Newcomb and Harlow, 1986). The general strain theory, then, has the potential to explain a broad range of delinquency, including theft, aggression, and drug use.

Each type of strain may create a *predisposition* for delinquency or function as *a situational event* that instigates a particular delinquent act. In the words of Hirschi and Gottfredson (1986), then, the strain theory presented in this paper is a theory of both "criminality" and "crime" (or to use the words of Clarke and Cornish [1985], it is a theory of both "criminal involvement" and "criminal events"). Strain creates a predisposition for delinquency in those cases in which it is chronic or repetitive. Examples include a continuing gap between expectations and achievements and a continuing pattern of ridicule and insults from teachers. Adolescents subject to such strain are predisposed to delinquency because (1) nondelinquent strategies for coping with strain are likely to be taxed; (2) the threshold for adversity may be lowered by chronic strains (see Averill, 1982, p. 289); (3) repeated or chronic strain may lead to a hostile attitude—a general dislike and suspicion of others and an associated tendency to respond in an aggressive manner (see Edmunds and Kendrick, 1980, p. 21); and (4) chronic strains increase the likelihood that individuals will be high in negative affect/arousal at any given time (see Bandura, 1983; Bernard, 1990). A particular instance of strain may also function as the situational event that ignites a delinquent act, especially among adolescents predisposed to delinquency. Qualitative and survey data, in particular, suggest that particular instances of delinquency are often instigated by one of the three types of strain listed above (see Agnew, 1990; also see Averill, 1982, for data on the instigations to anger).

MEASURING STRAIN

As indicated above, strain theory in criminology is dominated by a focus on strain as goal blockage. Further, only one type of goal blockage is typically examined in the literature—the failure to achieve *aspirations,* especially aspirations for monetary success or middle-class status. The general strain theory is much broader than current strain theories, and measuring strain under this theory would require at least three sets of measures: those focusing on the failure to achieve positively valued goals, those focusing on the loss of positive stimuli, and those focusing on the presentation of negative stimuli. It is not possible to list the precise measures that should be employed in these areas, although the citations above contain many examples of the types of measures that might be used. Further, certain general guidelines for the measurement of strain can be offered. The guidelines below will also highlight the limitations of current strain measures and shed further light on why those measures are typically unrelated to delinquency.

Developing a Comprehensive List of Negative Relations

Strain refers to negative or adverse relations with others. Such relations are ultimately defined from the perspective of the individual. That is, in the final analysis adverse relations are whatever individuals say they are (see Berkowitz, 1982). This does not mean, however, that one must employ an idiosyncratic definition of adverse relations—defining adverse relations anew for each person one examines. Such a strategy would create serious problems for (1) the empirical study of delinquency, (2) the prediction and control of delinquency, and (3) efforts to develop the macroimplications of the general strain theory. Rather, one can employ a strategy similar to that followed by stress researchers. . . .

First, one can draw on theory and research to specify those objective situations that might reasonably be expected to cause adversity among adolescents. This parallels stress research, which relies on inventories of stressful life events, and several standard inventories are in wide use. The items in such inventories are based, to varying degrees, on the perceptions and judgments of researchers, on previous theory and research, and on reports from samples of respondents (see Dohrenwend, 1974). In developing inventories of strainful events, criminologists must keep in mind the fact that there may be important group differences in the types of strain or negative relations most frequently encountered. A list of negative relations developed for one group, then, may overlook certain negative relations important for another group (see Dohrenwend, 1974). It may eventually be possible, however, to develop a comprehensive list of negative relations applicable to most samples of adolescents.

Second, criminologists must recognize that individuals and groups may experience the strainful events in such inventories differently (see Thoits, 1983). Limited data from the stress literature, for example, suggest that the impact of family stressors is greatest among young adolescents, peer stressors among middle adolescents, and academic stressors among old adolescents (Compas & Phares, 1991). Stress researchers have responded to such findings not by abandoning their inventories, but by investigating those factors that determine why one group or individual will experience a given event as stressful and another will not. And researchers have identified several sets of variables that influence the perception and experience of negative events (e.g., Compas & Phares, 1991; Pearlin, 1982; Pearlin & Schooler, 1978). Many of the variables are discussed in the next section, and they represent a major set of conditioning variables that criminologists should consider when examining the impact of strainful events on delinquency.

Examining the Cumulative Impact of Negative Relations

In most previous strain research in criminology, the impact of one type of negative relation on delinquency is examined with other negative relations ignored or held constant. So, for example, researchers will examine the impact of one type of goal blockage on delinquency, ignoring other types of goal blockage and other potential types of strain. This stands in sharp contrast to a central assumption in the stress literature, which is that stressful life events have a cumulative impact on the individual. Linsky and Straus (1986, p. 17), for example, speak of the "accumulation theory," which asserts that "it is not so much the unique quality of any single event but the cumulation of several stressful events within a relatively short time span" that is consequential. As a result, it is standard practice in the stressful life-events literature to measure stress with a composite scale: a scale that typically sums the number of stressful life events experienced by the individual.

The precise nature of the cumulative effect, however, is unclear. As Thoits (1983, p. 69) points out, stressful events may have an additive or interactive effect on outcome variables. The additive model assumes that each stressor has a fixed effect on delinquency, an effect independent of the level of the other stressors. Somewhat more plausible, perhaps, is the interactive model, which assumes that "a person who has experienced one event may react with even more distress to a second that follows soon after the first two or more events[; this] results in more distress than would be expected from the simple sum of their singular effects."

Whether the effect is additive or interactive, there is limited support for the idea that the level of stress/strain must pass a certain threshold before negative outcomes result (Linsky & Straus, 1986; Thoits, 1983). Below that level, stress/strain is unrelated to negative outcomes. Above that level, stress/strain has a positive effect on negative outcomes, perhaps an additive effect or perhaps an interactive effect.

Given these arguments, one should employ a composite index of strain in all analyses or examine the interactions between strain variables. Examining interactions can become very complex if there are more than a few indicators of strain, although it does allow one to examine the differential importance of various types of strain. If stressors have an interactive effect on delinquency, the interaction terms should be significant or the composite index should have a nonlinear effect on delinquency (see the discussion of interactions and non-linear effects in Aiken and West, 1991). If the effect is additive, the interaction terms should be insignificant or the composite index should have a linear effect on delinquency (after the threshold level is reached). These issues have received only limited attention in the stress literature (see the review by Thoits, 1983), and they should certainly be explored when constructing measures of strain for the purposes of explaining delinquency. At a minimum, however, as comprehensive a list of negative events/conditions as possible should be examined.

There is also the issue of whether positive events/experiences should be examined. If prior stressors can aggravate the negative effect of subsequent stressors, perhaps positive events can mitigate the impact of stressors. Limited evidence from the stress literature suggests that lists of negative events predict better than lists examining the balance of negative and positive events (usually negative events minus positive events) (see Thoits, 1983, pp. 58-59; Williams and Uchiyama, 1989, p. 101; see Gersten et al., 1974, for a possible exception). This topic, however, is certainly in need of more research. In addition to looking at the *difference* between desirable and undesirable events, researchers may also want to look at the ratio of undesirable to desirable events.

It should be noted that tests of strain theory in criminology typically examine the disjunction between aspirations and expectations for one or two goals and ignore all of the many other types of strain. The tests also typically assume that strain has a linear effect on delinquency, and they never examine positive as well as negative events. These facts may constitute additional reasons for the weak empirical support given to strain theory in criminology.

Examining the Magnitude, Recency, Duration, and Clustering of Adverse Events

Limited research from the stress and equity literatures suggest[s] that adverse events are more influential to the extent that they are (1) greater in magnitude or size, (2) recent, (3) of long duration, and (4) clustered in time.

Magnitude

The magnitude of an event has different meanings depending on the type of strain being examined. With respect to goal blockage, magnitude refers to the size of the gap between one's goals and reality. With respect to the loss of positive stimuli, magnitude refers to the amount that was lost. And with respect to the presentation of noxious stimuli, magnitude refers to the amount of pain or discomfort *inflicted*. In certain cases, magnitude may be measured in terms of a standard metric, such as dollars or volts delivered. In most cases, however, there is no standard metric available for measuring magnitude and one must rely on the perceptions of individuals (see Jasso, 1980, on quality versus quantity goods). To illustrate, researchers in the stress literature have asked judges to rate events according to the amount of readjustment they require or the threat they pose to the individual (see Thoits, 1983, for other weighting schemes). Such judgments are then averaged to form a magnitude score for each event. There is evidence, however, of subgroup differences in weights assigned (Thoits, 1983, pp. 53-55).

Magnitude ratings are then sometimes used to weight the events in composite scales. A common finding, however, is that lists of life events weighted by magnitude do *not* predict any better than unweigh[t]ed lists (e.g., Gersten et al., 1974). This is due to the fact that the correlation between lists of weighted and unweighted events is typically so high (above .90) that the lists can be considered virtually identical (Thoits, 1983). Williams and Uchiyama (1989, pp. 99-100) explain this high correlation by arguing that severe life events, which are heavily weighted, have a low base rate in the population and so do not have a significant impact on scale scores. Studies that consider major and minor events separately tend to find that major events are in fact more consequential than minor events (Thoits, 1983, p. 66).

It should be noted that the previous research on strain theory has paid only limited attention to the dimension of magnitude, even in those cases in which standard metrics for measuring magnitude were available. Samples, in fact, are often simply divided into strained and nonstrained groups, with little consideration of variations in the magnitude of strain.

Recency

Certain data suggest that recent events are more consequential than older events and that events older than three months have little effect (Avison & Turner, 1988). Those data focus on the impact of stress on depression, and so are not necessarily generalizable to the strain-delinquency relationship. Nevertheless, the data suggest that the recency of strain may be an important dimension to consider, and findings in this area might be of special use in designing longitudinal studies, in which the issue of the appropriate lag between cause and effect is central (although the subject of little research and theory).

Duration

Much theory and data from the equity and stress literatures suggest that events of long duration (chronic stressors) have a greater impact on a variety of negative psychological outcomes (Folger, 1986; Mark & Folger, 1984;

Pearlin, 1982; Pearlin and Lieberman, 1979; Utne & Kidd, 1980). Some evidence, in fact, suggests that discrete events may be unimportant except to the extent that they affect chronic events (Cummings & El-Sheikh, 1991; Gersten et al., 1977; Pearlin, 1983). Certain researchers in the equity/justice literature have suggested that the expected duration of the event into the future should also be considered (Folger, 1986; Mark & Folger, 1984; Utne & Kidd, 1980; see especially the "likelihood of amelioration" concept).

Clustering

Data from the stress literature also suggest that events closely clustered in time have a greater effect on negative outcomes (Thoits, 1983). Such events, according to Thoits (1983), are more likely to overwhelm coping resources than events spread more evenly over time. Certain data, in particular, trace negative outcomes such as suicide and depression to a series of negative events clustered in the previous few weeks (Thoits, 1983).

ADAPTATIONS TO (COPING STRATEGIES FOR) STRAIN

Constraints to Nondelinquent and Delinquent Coping

While there are many adaptations to objective strain, those adaptations are not equally available to everyone. Individuals are constrained in their choice of adaptation(s) by a variety of internal and external factors. The following is a partial list of such factors.

Initial Goals/Values/Identities of the Individual. If the objective strain affects goals/values/identities that are high in absolute and relative importance, and if the individual has few alternative goals/values/identities in which to seek refuge, it will be more difficult to relegate strain to an unimportant area of one's life (see Agnew, 1986; Thoits, 1991a). This is especially the case if the goals/values/identities receive strong social and cultural support (see below). As a result, strain will be more likely to lead to delinquency in such cases.

Individual Coping Resources. A wide range of traits can be listed in this area, including temperament, intelligence, creativity, problem-solving skills, interpersonal skills, self-efficacy, and self-esteem. These traits affect the selection of coping strategies by influencing the individual's sensitivity to objective strains and ability to engage in cognitive, emotional, and behavioral coping (Agnew, 1991a; Averill, 1982; Bernard, 1990; Compas, 1987; Edmunds & Kendrick, 1980; Slaby & Guerra, 1988; Tavris, 1984). Data, for example, suggest that individuals with high self-esteem are more resistant to stress (Averill, 1982; Compas, 1987; Kaplan, 1980; Pearlin & Schooler, 1978; Rosenberg, 1990; Thoits, 1983). Such individuals, therefore, should be less likely to respond to a given objective strain with delinquency. Individuals high in self-efficacy are more likely to feel that their strain can be alleviated by behavioral coping of a nondelinquent nature, and so they too should be less likely to respond to strain with delinquency (see Bandura, 1989, and Wang & Richarde, 1988, on self-efficacy; see Thoits, 1991b, on perceived control).

Conventional Social Support. Vaux (1988) provides an extended discussion of the different types of social support, their measurement, and their effect on outcome variables. Thoits (1984) argues that social support is important because it facilitates the major types of coping. The major types of social support, in fact, correspond to the major types of coping listed above. Thus, there is informational support, instrumental support, and emotional support (House, 1981). Adolescents with conventional social supports, then, should be better able to respond to objective strains in a nondelinquent manner.

Constraints to Delinquent Coping. The crime/delinquency literature has focused on certain variables that constrain delinquent coping. They include (1) the costs and benefits of engaging in delinquency in a particular situation (Clarke and Cornish, 1985), (2) the individual's level of social control (see Hirschi, 1969), and (3) the possession of those "illegitimate means" necessary for many delinquent acts (see Agnew, 1991a, for a full discussion).

Macro-Level Variables. The larger social environment may affect the probability of delinquent versus nondelinquent coping by affecting all of the above factors. First, the social environment may affect coping by influencing the importance attached to selected goals/values/identities. For

example, certain ethnographic accounts suggest that there is a strong social and cultural emphasis on the goals of money/status among certain segments of the urban poor. Many poor individuals, in particular, are in a situation in which (1) they face strong economic/status demands, (2) people around them stress the importance of money/status on a regular basis, and (3) few alternative goals are given cultural support (Anderson, 1978; MacLeod, 1987; Sullivan, 1989). As such, these individuals should face more difficulty in cognitively minimizing the importance of money and status.

Second, the larger social environment may affect the individual's sensitivity to particular strains by influencing the individual's beliefs regarding what is and is not adverse. The subculture of violence thesis, for example, is predicated on the assumption that young black males in urban slums are taught that a wide range of provocations and insults are highly adverse. Third, the social environment may influence the individual's ability to minimize cognitively the severity of objective strain. Individuals in some environments are regularly provided with external information about their accomplishments and failings (see Faunce, 1989), and their attempts at cognitively distorting such information are quickly challenged. Such a situation may exist among many adolescents and among those who inhabit the "street-corner world" of the urban poor. Adolescents and those on the street corner live in a very "public world"; one's accomplishments and failings typically occur before a large audience or they quickly become known to such an audience. Further, accounts suggest that this audience regularly reminds individuals of their accomplishments and failings and challenges attempts at cognitive distortion. Fourth, certain social environments may make it difficult to engage in behavioral coping of a nondelinquent nature. Agnew (1985a) has argued that adolescents often find it difficult to escape legally from negative stimuli, especially negative stimuli encountered in the school, family, and neighborhood. Also, adolescents often lack the resources to negotiate successfully with adults, such as parents and teachers (although see Agnew, 1991a). Similar arguments might be made for the urban underclass. They often lack the resources to negotiate successfully with many others, and they often find it difficult to escape legally from adverse environments—by, for example, quitting their job (if they have a job) or moving to another neighborhood. The larger social environment, then, may affect individual coping in a variety of ways. And certain groups, such as adolescents and the urban underclass, may face special constraints that make nondelinquent coping more difficult. This may explain the higher rate of deviance among these groups.

Factors Affecting the Disposition to Delinquency

The selection of delinquent versus nondelinquent coping strategies is not only dependent on the constraints to coping, but also on the adolescent's disposition to engage in delinquent versus nondelinquent coping. This disposition is a function of (1) certain temperamental variables (see Tonry et al., 1991), (2) the prior learning history of the adolescent, particularly the extent to which delinquency was reinforced in the past (Bandura, 1973; Berkowitz, 1982), (3) the adolescent's beliefs, particularly the rules defining the appropriate response to provocations (Bernard's, 1990, "regulative rules"), and (4) the adolescent's attributions regarding the causes of his or her adversity. Adolescents who attribute their adversity to others are much more likely to become angry, and as argued earlier, that anger creates a strong predisposition to delinquency. Data and theory from several areas, in fact, suggest that the experience of adversity is most likely to result in deviance when the adversity is blamed on another.

A key variable affecting several of the above factors is association with delinquent peers. It has been argued that adolescents who associate with delinquent peers are more likely to be exposed to delinquent models and beliefs and to receive reinforcement for delinquency (see especially, Akers, 1985). It may also be the case that delinquent peers increase the likelihood that adolescents will attribute their adversity to others.

The individual's disposition to delinquency, then, may condition the impact of adversity on delinquency. At the same time, it is important to note that continued experience with adversity may create a disposition for delinquency. This argument has been made by Bernard (1990), Cloward and Ohlin (1960), A. Cohen (1955), Elliott et al. (1979), and others. In particular, it has been argued that under certain conditions the experience of adversity may lead to beliefs favorable to delinquency, lead adolescents to join or form delinquent peer groups, and lead adolescents to blame others for their misfortune.

Virtually all empirical research on strain theory in criminology has neglected the constraints to coping and the adolescent's disposition to delinquency. Researchers, in particular, have failed to examine whether the effect of adversity on delinquency is conditioned by factors such as self-efficacy and association with delinquent peers. This is likely a major reason for the weak empirical support for strain theory. . . .

DISCUSSION QUESTIONS

1. How does Agnew distinguish strain theory from social control and social learning theories of crime?

2. What are the three major types of strain, according to Agnew? How might these types of strain be measured in an empirical test of the theory?

3. Now that you've read Agnew's discussion of the strain typology, what type of person would be most apt to respond to strain with delinquency?

4. What are some of the adaptations to strain Agnew offers? How might strain and these adaptations be taken into consideration in the development of crime control policies?

PART IV

Social Process Theories of Crime

Social process theories of crime encompass those sociological theories of crime that focus on the processes involved in becoming delinquent or criminal. In contrast to the social structural theories, which focus on environmental conditions, social norms and values, and the level of integration in a given society, these theories examine the different mechanisms and pathways that delinquents and criminals implement when they commit crime. This broad category includes the theories of differential association and social learning, neutralization and social control, and labeling. This section also provides a special focus on the ways in which certain crimes are *socially constructed,* meaning that certain segments of society establish the criteria by which certain behaviors are defined as criminal and how these crimes are to be sanctioned. This subsection of the reader focuses implicitly on the issue of white-collar crime and whether it should be treated theoretically as a distinct category of crime.

Differential Association and Social Learning Theories of Crime

Differential association and social learning theories of crime argue generally that individuals commit crime as a result of learning and socialization experiences within intimate relationships. Sutherland (1939/1947) originated this theory within criminology, asserting that criminals and conformists alike, including white-collar criminals, learn to engage in delinquent behavior just as they learn to engage in other types of conforming, nondelinquent behavior. Sutherland's theory contains two basic elements, which derive from Mead's (1934) theory of *symbolic interactionism.* The *content* of what is learned includes specific techniques for committing crimes; appropriate motives, drives, and attitudes; and more general "definitions favorable to law violation" (Vold, Bernard, & Snipes, 1998, p. 185). Because these elements consist of ideas rather than behaviors, they are considered cognitive in nature. Second, the process by which the learning takes place involves associations with others in intimate personal groups.

Additionally, Sutherland (1939/1947) specifies the general social conditions that underlie this differential association process. His earlier conception of this process, published in 1939, described these general social conditions in terms of culture conflict, whereby different groups in society have different notions about how people should behave. At that time, Sutherland used the term *social disorganization* to describe the existence of culture conflict in society. In his later, and final, reformulation of the theory, published in 1947, Sutherland rejected the term *social disorganization* in favor of *differential social organization.* In contrast with social disorganization, which suggests an underlying lack of organization, differential social organization suggests that there are a wide variety of divergent associations organized around different interests for different purposes. Sutherland highlights the inevitability of some groups' subscribing to and supporting criminal patterns of behavior, the neutrality of other groups, and the consciously law-abiding behavior of other members of society.

In light of some confusion over the term *culture conflict,* Donald Cressey eventually replaced this term with *normative conflict* following Sutherland's death (Vold et al., 1998). Normative conflict refers to the situation in which different social groups hold different views about the appropriate ways to behave in specific situations and circumstances. Cressey merely reinforced the central points behind Sutherland's argument: that in a situation of differential social organization and normative conflict, differences in behavior arise out of differential associations.

Recent analyses of Sutherland's differential association theory, such as Matsueda's (1988), suggest that, with some reformulations, Sutherland's theory can be tested, and a substantial amount of research supports this proposition.

Sutherland's differential association theory (Chapter 12, this volume) has influenced a wide range of criminological theories, including even the cultural and subcultural theories discussed in the previous section. Whereas cultural and subcultural theories follow Sutherland's arguments about normative conflict and emphasize the content of what is learned, other theories focus on the learning process that Sutherland described in his theory. Akers (Chapter 13, this volume) has made the most significant development and reformulation of Sutherland's theory. His social learning or "differential reinforcement" approach asserts that social interaction in the environment, mainly in subcultural groups, is a major source of behavioral reinforcement. In an original article with Burgess, Akers rewrote the major principles of differential association theory into operant conditioning terms (Burgess & Akers, 1966). This revision suggests that criminal behavior is learned both in nonsocial situations (i.e., the environment) that are reinforcing and through social interaction in which the behavior of other people influences one's involvement in criminal behavior. The inclusion of nonsocial situations recognizes the significance that the environment can play in terms of reinforcing criminality, in addition to and separate from the person's social interaction with others (Akers, 2001).

This reformulation of differential association theory assumes that individuals are rational responders to external stimuli and thereby will maximize pleasure and avoid pain. Therefore, it can be said that individuals will be considerably affected by the consequences of their actions, whether those consequences come in the form of rewards or punishments. In other words, this system of *differential reinforcement* suggests that individuals can be conditioned through the manipulation of the system of rewards and punishments, which tends to reward (or reinforce) conventional norms and punish deviant action.

In the text excerpt from Akers included in this volume (Chapter 13), Akers outlines the major premises of his most recent reformulation of social learning theory and its similarities to and differences from Sutherland's theory of differential association. In this excerpt, Akers discusses four major concepts of his theory, namely differential association, differential reinforcement, definitions, and imitation. Akers maintains that the social learning process explains the link between social structural conditions and the individual's behaviors. Akers's theory has enjoyed wide empirical support, probably the most of any of the current major criminological theories. Akers has found that his theory supports the typical sequence in which social learning operates, in which criminal behaviors are acquired through differential associations, definitions, imitation, and social reinforcements and are then maintained through and by nonsocial reinforcements (Akers, 2001, and Chapter 13 of this volume; Vold et al., 1998).

NEUTRALIZATION AND CONTROL THEORIES

In a variety of ways, neutralization theories of crime extend and strengthen one characteristic of social learning theory, the element of the theory that reintroduces the issue of free will. Although neutralization theory became fully developed by Sykes and Matza (Chapter 14, this volume), early formulations of the theory can be found in Cressey's (1953) research on embezzlers. Cressey demonstrated how embezzlers would consider their behaviors prior to action in light of how they would be able to justify their behaviors afterward, should they be questioned about them. Cressey's research focused on the words embezzler's used, such as *borrowing* money rather than *stealing* it, in order to justify their actions (Henry & Einstadter, 1998).

Techniques of Neutralization

Several years later, Sykes and Matza (Chapter 14, this volume) developed this theory more completely in their critique of the overly deterministic nature of subcultural theories. Neutralization theory assumes that most people are socialized into conventional behavior. It also assumes that what is learned in this process includes attitudes and techniques that effect individuals by temporarily freeing them from the confines of conventionality and enable them to commit crime without the burden of moral uncertainties about their behaviors. Thus, crime becomes a behavioral option for those individuals who, under typical circumstances, are not usually compelled to break the law; it becomes an option when their commitment to conventional norms and values is neutralized by justifications and excuses that cause them to feel morally free from conventional behavioral obligations.

Early Control Theories

Other types of theories that examine individuals' degree of attachment to conventional norms and their subsequent behaviors involve the various control theories that have been developed over the course of several decades. Many of the theories of crime examined up to this point assume that people naturally obey the law if left to their own devices and argue that special forces and circumstances, whether they be biologically, psychologically, or socially based, drive people to commit crime. Control theories take the opposite point of view and support the assumption that people would naturally engage in criminal behavior if left to their own devices. The critical question for control theorists, then, becomes why most people do *not* commit crime. To answer this question, control theorists focus on the "controlling forces" that hold people in check and restrain them from committing crime or acting out their "uncontrolled" behaviors. Under this theory, individuals are said to commit crime because of weakness in the forces that are supposed to be reining them in toward conventionality.

In an early version of control theory, referred to as *containment theory,* Reckless (1950) constructed the theory in terms of *inner containment* (what we internalize) and *outer containment* (external sources of sanctions and disapproval, including families and law enforcement). More specifically, he argued that the formation of positive or negative self-concepts in young people could affect their "inner controls" over their biopsychological "pushes" and universal environmental "pulls" toward law violation (Reckless, 1950). Likewise, Nye (1958) focused on the controlling force of the family. In another early contribution, Reiss (1951) found in his study of juvenile probationers that probation revocation was more likely to occur when juveniles did not regularly attend school and when they were described by school authorities as having behavior problems. Reiss argued that these were measures of the acceptance or the submission of juveniles to "social controls," such as the control by socially approved institutions such as juvenile probation (Reiss, 1951).

Social Bonding Theory

The leading statement in the field of criminology on social control can be found in Hirschi's (1969) version of control through social bonding with individuals and institutions that follow conventional norms, which he outlines in his seminal text, *The Causes of Delinquency.* According to Hirschi, it was not necessary to explain the motivation for delinquency, because he makes the assumption that most people are already disposed to nonconformity unless they receive proper protective socialization in the form of controls. Social control theory asserts that inadequate or ineffective external socialization can result in weak or absent internal controls over behavior (Hirschi, 1969). The theory centers on the ways in which relational ties, or bonds, between youth and adults result in some youths' developing respect for the values and norms of conventional adults while others do not.

Hirschi's (1969) version of social control theory, social bonding theory, proposes that individuals who are tightly bonded to social groups such as the family, the school, and peers will be less apt to engage in delinquent behavior. The most important element of the social bond is *attachment,* or affection for and sensitivity to others. Attachment forms the basic element necessary for the internalization of norms and behaviors. *Commitment,* the second element, is best described as having a "stake in conformity."

Involvement in conventional activities is the third element, and it is based on the idea that if youth are involved in traditional activities, they will be too busy to engage in delinquent behaviors. The final element, *belief,* suggests that the more a person believes he or she should obey the laws of society, the more likely he or she is to do so.

Integrated Control Theories: Power-Control and Control-Balance Theories

In the growing trend toward theoretical integration, power-control and control-balance theories offer unique approaches to the understanding of how control—on the larger social and institutional levels—regulates deviant behavior. Power-control theory (Hagan, Simpson, & Gillis, Chapter 15, this volume) combines control theory and conflict approaches to explain how social class affects delinquency. In the original formulation of this approach, the authors provided an explanation of how gender differences in delinquency vary by social class. The extension of the theory in the article included in this volume also considers husbands' and wives' positions of authority in the workplace as well as household structure in terms of whether this power structure affects levels of delinquency for girls and boys.

This variation of control theory is important not only because of the way in which it integrates control theory with elements from the conflict perspective but also because it addresses the fact that macro forces in society and micro forces in individuals' more immediate environment are important in determining criminality.

The article exchanges between Braithwaite and Tittle (Chapters 16 and 17, respectively, this volume) regarding Tittle's control balance theory provide another unique focus and dimension of this anthology on the level of integration of these theories. Control balance theory is important because it distinguishes between an individual's internally self-imposed self-controls and those controls that are imposed externally on an individual. Tittle argues that deviant behavior is most likely to occur when these levels of control, or control ratios (i.e., between control surpluses and deficits), become imbalanced. Tittle finds that people will likely conform to conventionally held values and norms when these control ratios are in equilibrium. Braithwaite's commentary provides a thorough overview of Tittle's theory and suggests that it could be made much simpler and clearer if the various types of deviance Tittle proposes were collapsed into one type. He also offers important insight into the possibility of a normative theory of political economy.

Labeling Theories and the Social Construction of Crime

Like learning theories, the roots of labeling or interactionist theory can be traced to Mead, who advanced the idea that the human self is a social construction created in interaction with others. According to Mead, individuals become who they are in interaction with others: We tend to define ourselves in terms of how others view or define us. Therefore, we do not live in a state of passivity; rather, we interact with others in terms of the meanings derived from certain symbols that emerge during this interactive process.

Additionally, symbolic interactionism asserts that human actions are best understood in terms of the meanings that those actions have for the actors, rather than in terms of preexisting biological, psychological, or social structural conditions (Vold et al., 1998). Meanings are generally created to a certain extent by the individual, but they are mainly derived from intimate personal interactions with others. In other words, people typically construct meaning in relation to circumstances in which they find themselves, and then they act toward those circumstances in the various ways that make sense within the context of their meanings. It is through these interactions that we become constituted as social actors, and what type of interactions we have with others and how we react to those interactions become very critical in this process. Not all interactions are significant, and we learn to determine which ones will have importance to us.

Interactionist theory found a place in the realm of criminology in terms of explaining the effect that defining an individual as a criminal has upon that individual's behavior, the meaning of crime to criminals, the processes by which certain categories of behavior are defined as crimes in the criminal law and by which specific people and events are defined as criminal by criminal justice agencies, and the meaning of crime in state power (Vold et al., 1998, p. 219). In terms of labeling theory, interactionist theory emerged most clearly in the work of Becker (1963) and his research on jazz musicians and marijuana smokers and in the analysis of different kinds of deviance by Lemert (1951). Becker argued that social deviants are created largely as a consequence of the negative reactions by agents of social control to certain people's violations of the law. Through social reaction, actors are "labeled" as deviant types based on certain characteristics of their behavior.

In its simplest formulation, the labeling/interactionist approach explains crime in terms of the negative reactions by agents of social control to a person's violations of the law, which subsequently induce a change in that person's identity. That person comes to view him- or herself as deviant or criminal. When conventional avenues and opportunities are not available to labeled persons, individuals adopt the negative reactions and definitions of themselves and become "outsiders" (Becker, 1963).

Under Lemert's (1951) conception of deviance, people become transformed from participating in minor forms of deviancy to having social identities committed to secondary deviance as a result of the negative reaction to their behavior and the label given to them. Secondary deviance occurs when the societal response to primary deviance is so pervasive that the individual so labeled can no longer function normally and resorts to deviance. Lemert argues that the situational contexts in which these transformations occur are just as important as the transformations themselves.

The work of Goffman (1963) proves to be quite informative in terms of pointing out not only the various contexts and strategies of interaction but also the damaging effects that deviant labels can have and the ways in which those so labeled learn to cope with the stigma of the label.

The text and article excerpts included in the labeling and social constructionist subsections effectively illustrate the negative, stigmatizing effects of a deviant label, but they also go further than that. For example, Curra's recent text (Chapter 18, this volume) addresses the dynamic nature of deviance and stresses that deviance is a dynamic force that fluctuates according to historical time and social and geographic place. He stresses that in order to get a full understanding of deviance, we need to consider the roots of how

deviance evolves in the first place. Therefore, he turns our attention to the socialization process and to how notions of ethnocentrism, symbols, and ideal culture are produced. He argues that these concepts shape people's outward perspective on certain behaviors and contribute greatly to the manner in which deviance, like many other concepts, is socially constructed.

Additionally, Margolin's article (Chapter 19, this volume) provides an interesting view of labeling theory—from the perspective of the labelers. She finds in her study of official caseworker reports of child abuse that other external institutional and bureaucratic concerns shape the manner in which social workers develop certain labels for these offenders. She concludes that bureaucratic goals and pressures often supercede the objective of arriving at the truth of the situation.

Finally, Hay's comment (Chapter 20, this volume) on and evaluation of Braithwaite's reintegrative shaming theory provides readers with insight into how Braithwaite's theory may be tested on the microlevel by examining family relations. Reintegrative shaming emphasizes the notion that an individual's likelihood of continued delinquency or crime will be minimized if that offender is brought back into the normative context of the community rather than being stigmatized, which can lead to further ostracism and deviance. The theory, a version of labeling theory, holds promise not only for further theoretical analysis and development within criminology but also for criminal justice agencies in terms of effective crime control strategies.

The separate section that considers the issue of the social construction of crime focuses mainly on white-collar crime and another aspect of control theory, namely Gottfredson and Hirschi's theory of low self-control (Chapter 22, this volume). Sutherland's important article on white-collar crime (Chapter 21, this volume) raises the issue of whether white-collar crime is really crime. This question clearly illustrates the central thrust of social constructionism. Sutherland contends that crimes committed by corporations, whether these be antitrust violations, false advertising, or fraud, are often considered and defined in a different light because the law does not typically recognize or accept the image of the "businessman" as a criminal. He raises these issues from a "sociology of law" standpoint and suggests that in order to understand how white-collar crime, or any type of crime, is defined, people need to recognize the importance of the role of the law in the defining process and the social context in which that law was enacted and subsequently implemented.

In Chapter 23, Reed and Yeager exemplify the importance of social context in interaction as well. In their critique of Gottfredson and Hirschi's general theory of crime, they focus on white-collar crime and show how, in the unique setting of the corporation, certain acts considered criminal in other contexts would not be defined and reacted to as criminal. Why not? Because this type of offending is socially constructed in a broad institutional context that calls attention to profits, and thus it is not seen within the general scope of criminality.

Additionally, Reed and Yeager assert that Gottfredson and Hirschi's focus on low self-control as a general explanatory variable for all crime falls short of the mark in terms of explaining white-collar or corporate crime for several reasons, one of which is that business environments are not structured in such a way that individuals who exhibit characteristics of low self-control, such as aggression and impulsivity, would be automatically weeded out. Additionally, unlike conventional street crime, business crimes do distinguish themselves in terms of the level of skill required to commit the crime and the manner in which offenders see themselves as business-persons rather than as criminals. Recall that Gottfredson and Hirschi contend that low self-control emerges out of inadequate socialization toward effective patterns of control. Despite the limitations of the general theory in terms of white-collar crime, the theory of low self-control does illustrate how low self-control may be manifested in other types of behaviors besides crime.

REFERENCES

Akers, R. (2001). *Criminological theories: Introduction, evaluation, and application* (3rd ed.). Los Angeles: Roxbury.

Becker, H. S. (1963). *Outsiders: Studies in the sociology of deviance*. New York: Free Press.

Burgess, R. L., & Akers, R. L. (1966). A differential association-reinforcement theory of criminal behavior. *Social Problems, 14,* 128-147.

Cressey, D. R. (1953). *Other people's money*. Glencoe, IL: Free Press.

Goffman, E. (1963). *Stigma: Notes on the management of spoiled identity*. Englewood Cliffs, NJ: Prentice Hall.

Henry, S., & Einstadter, W. (Eds.). (1998). *The criminology theory reader*. New York: New York University Press.

Hirschi, T. (1969). *Causes of delinquency*. Berkeley: University of California Press.

Lemert, E. (1951). *Social pathology: A systematic approach to the theory of sociopathic behavior*. New York: McGraw-Hill.

Matsueda, R. (1988). The current state of differential association theory. *Crime and Delinquency, 34,* 277–306.

Mead, G. H. (1934). *Mind, self, and society: From the standpoint of a social behaviorist*. Chicago, IL: University of Chicago Press.

Nye, F. I. (1958). *Family relationships and delinquent behavior*. New York: John Wiley.

Reckless, W. (1950). *The crime problem*. New York: Appleton-Century-Crofts.

Reiss, A., Jr. (1951). Delinquency as the failure of personal and social controls. *American Sociological Review, 16,* 196–207.

Sutherland, E. (1947). *Principles of criminology*. Philadelphia: J. B. Lippincott. (Original work published 1939)

Vold, G. B., Bernard, T. J., & Snipes, J. B. (1998). *Theoretical criminology* (4th ed.). Oxford, UK: Oxford University Press.

12

A Sociological Theory of Criminal Behavior

Edwin H. Sutherland

EDITOR'S INTRODUCTION—When Sutherland put forth his theory of differential association, it was largely an effort to correct what he viewed as problems with current theories of crime, namely social disorganization, that were being proposed by researchers in the Chicago School. Prior to the development of differential association theory, theorists explained crime in terms of multiple causal factors, such as social class, broken homes, race, age, area of residence (urban or rural), and mental abnormality. Sutherland developed his theory to explain why these factors contributed to crime. More specifically, he wanted to explain why only certain individuals, even those living in high-crime areas, actually became criminals. In this sense, differential association theory is best conceptualized as a *social process theory* of crime, because its main premises center on the process of becoming delinquent or criminal.

Sutherland explicates his theory in terms of nine propositions. He argues that criminal behavior is learned in intimate interaction with others. Criminals learn the techniques of committing crime and the definitions favorable to crime from these other individuals. Sutherland's sixth proposition forms the heart of differential association theory: "A person becomes delinquent because of an excess of definitions favorable to law violation over definitions unfavorable to violation of law" (p. 132, this volume). Sutherland adds that other factors such as those listed above influence crime because they affect the likelihood that individuals will associate with others who introduce definitions favorable to law breaking.

As readers will undoubtedly realize, Sutherland's theory has had a tremendous impact on crime research over the 20th century, and it still remains one of the dominant theories of crime causation today, though it has seen some modifications to its central premises. Many theories today, which are becoming more multidisciplinary in scope, typically include questions that measure the extent to which individuals are associating with delinquent or nondelinquent peers and how much of an influence this association has on subsequent behavior. Many of these studies, which focus primarily on Sutherland's theory, find that association with delinquent peers is one of the best predictors of delinquency.

GENETIC EXPLANATION OF CRIMINAL BEHAVIOR

The following statement refers to the process by which a particular person comes to engage in criminal behavior.

1. *Criminal behavior is learned.* Negatively, this means that criminal[ity] is not inherited, as such; also, the person who is not already trained in crime does not invent criminal behavior, just as a person does not make mechanical inventions unless he has had training in mechanics.

2. *Criminal behavior is learned in interaction with other persons in a process of communication.* This communication is verbal in many respects but includes also "the communication of gestures."

3. *The principal part of the learning of criminal behavior occurs within intimate personal groups.* Negatively, this means that the impersonal agencies of communication, such as movies and newspapers, play a relatively unimportant part in the genesis of criminal behavior.

4. *When criminal behavior is learned, the learning includes (a) techniques of committing the crime, which are sometimes very complicated, sometimes very simple; (b) the specific direction of motives, drives, rationalizations, and attitudes.*

5. *The specific direction of motives and drives is learned from definitions of the legal codes as favorable or unfavorable.* In some societies an individual is surrounded by persons who invariably define the legal codes as rules to be observed, while in others he is surrounded by persons whose definitions are favorable to the violation of the legal codes. In our American society these definitions are almost always mixed, with the consequences that we have culture conflict in relation to the legal codes.

6. *A person becomes delinquent because of an excess of definitions favorable to violation of law over definitions unfavorable to violation of law.* This is the principle of differential association. It refers to both criminal and anti-criminal associations and has to do with counteracting forces. When persons become criminal, they do so because of contacts with criminal patterns and also because of isolation from anti-criminal patterns. Any person inevitably assimilates the surrounding culture unless other patterns are in conflict; a Southerner does not pronounce 'Y' because other Southerners do not pronounce "r." Negatively, this proposition of differential association means that associations which are neutral so far as crime is concerned have little or no effect on the genesis of criminal behavior. Much of the experience of a person is neutral in this sense, e.g., learning to brush one's teeth. This behavior has no negative or positive effect on criminal behavior except as it may be related to associations which are concerned with the legal codes. This neutral behavior is important especially as an occupier of the time of a child so that he is not in contact with criminal behavior during the time he is so engaged in the neutral behavior.

7. *Differential associations may vary in frequency, duration, priority, and intensity.* This means that associations with criminal behavior and also associations with anti-criminal behavior vary in those respects. "Frequency" and "duration" as modalities of associations are obvious and need no explanation. "Priority" is assumed to be important in the sense that lawful behavior developed in early childhood may persist throughout life, and also that delinquent behavior developed in early childhood may persist throughout life. This tendency, however, has not been adequately demonstrated, and priority seems to be important principally through its selective influence. "Intensity" is not precisely defined but it has to do with such things as the prestige of the source of a criminal or anti-criminal pattern and with emotional reactions related to the associations. In a precise description of the criminal behavior of a person these modalities

Sutherland, E. H. (1955). A theory of crime: Differential association. In E. H. Sutherland & D. Cressey, *Principles of criminology* (5th ed.). Chicago: J. B. Lippincott.

would be stated in quantitative form and a mathematical ratio be reached. A formula in this sense has not been developed, and the development of such a formula would be extremely difficult.

8. *The process of learning criminal behavior by association with criminal and anti-criminal patterns involves all of the mechanisms that are involved in any other learning.* Negatively, this means that the learning of criminal behavior is not restricted to the process of imitation. A person who is seduced, for instance, learns criminal behavior by association, but this process would not ordinarily be described as imitation.

9. *While criminal behavior is an expression of general needs and values, it is not explained by those general needs and values since non-criminal behavior is an expression of the same needs and values.* Thieves generally steal in order to secure money, but likewise honest laborers work in order to secure money. The attempts by many scholars to explain criminal behavior by general drives and values, such as, the happiness principle, striving for social status, the money motive, or frustration, have been and must continue to be futile since they explain lawful behavior as completely as they explain criminal behavior. They are similar to respiration, which is necessary for any behavior but which does not differentiate criminal from non-criminal behavior.

It is not necessary, at this level of explanation, to explain why a person has the associations which he has; this certainly involves a complex of many things. In an area where the delinquency rate is high a boy who is sociable, gregarious, active, and athletic is very likely to come in contact with the other boys *in* the neighborhood, learn delinquent behavior from them, and become a gangster; in the same neighborhood the psychopathic boy who is isolated, introvert, and inert may remain at home, not become acquainted with the other boys in the neighborhood, and not become delinquent. In another situation, the sociable, athletic, aggressive boy may become a member of a scout troop and not become involved in delinquent behavior. The person's associations are determined in a general context of social organization. A child is ordinarily reared in a family; the place of residence of the family is determined largely by family income; and the delinquency rate is, in many respects, related to the rental value of the houses. Many other factors enter into this social organization, including many of the small personal group relationships.

The preceding explanation of criminal behavior is stated from the point of view of the person who engages in criminal behavior. As indicated earlier, it is possible, also, to state sociological theories of criminal behavior from the point of view of the community, nation, or other group. The problem, when thus stated, is generally concerned with crime rates and involves a comparison of the crime rates of various groups or the crime rates of a particular group at different times. The explanation of a crime rate must be consistent with the explanation of the criminal behavior of the person, since the crime rate is a summary statement of the number of persons in the group who commit crimes and the frequency with which they commit crimes. One of the best explanations of crime rates from this point of view is that a high crime rate is due to social disorganization. The term "social disorganization" is not entirely satisfactory and it seems preferable to substitute for it the term "differential social organization." The postulate on which this theory is based, regardless of the name, is that crime is rooted in the social organization and is an expression of that social organization. A group may be organized for criminal behavior or organized against criminal behavior. Most communities are organized both for criminal and anti-criminal behavior and in that sense the crime rate is an expression of the differential group organization. Differential group organization as an explanation of variations in crime rates is consistent with the differential association theory of the processes by which persons become criminals. . . .

DISCUSSION QUESTIONS

1. What are the nine propositions of differential association theory?

2. What does Sutherland mean by "definitions favorable to violation of law"?

3. How might Sutherland respond to the propositions of strain theorists, who contend that frustration plays a major role in delinquency, and to the new biosocial approaches, which argue that biological and psychological factors do play a role in crime causation?

4. How might differential association theory be used to explain the recent school shootings by male adolescents? What policies could Sutherland recommend for controlling crime in these environments?

13

A SOCIAL LEARNING
THEORY OF CRIME

RONALD L. AKERS

EDITOR'S INTRODUCTION—Akers's social learning involves a reformulation and extension of Sutherland's differential association theory. According to differential association theory, behavior is learned in intimate interaction with other people, but the theory fails to stipulate the *mechanisms* by which that behavior is learned. Akers draws on contributions from the psychological literature on learning and behavioral theory in order to describe more precisely how crime is learned.

Akers's theory is quite congruent with Sutherland's approach. As Akers maintains, "The basic assumption in social learning theory is that the same learning process, operating in a context of social structure, interaction, and situation, produces both conforming and deviant behavior" (p. 136, this volume). In other words, we learn to engage in crime through exposure to definitions favorable to crime. However, Akers goes on to more fully describe the nature of these definitions. Akers draws on Sykes and Matza's (Chapter 14, this volume) techniques of neutralization, but he contends that definitions favorable to crime involve more than merely rationalizing crime. Essentially, Akers's social learning theory can be stated simply in terms of four components that make up a testable hypothesis. A person is more likely to commit law violations when

1. He or she differentially associates with others who commit, model, and support violations of social and legal norms.

2. The violative behavior is differentially reinforced over behavior in conformity to the norm.

3. He or she is more exposed to and observes more deviant than conforming models.

4. His or her own learned definitions are favorable toward committing the deviant acts. (p. 136, this volume)

As readers will observe, Akers also extends Sutherland's differential association theory by arguing that crime is learned by imitation *and* through reinforcement. As Akers has suggested, his theory may be able to incorporate most other major sociological theories of crime into its main premises because of the various issues and factors that it takes into consideration. In fact, this theory has received the widest empirical support of all of the major theories of crime.

CONCISE STATEMENT OF THE THEORY

The basic assumption in social learning theory is that the same learning process, operating in a context of social structure, interaction, and situation, produces both conforming and deviant behavior. The difference lies in the direction of the process in which these mechanisms operate. In both, it is seldom an either-or, all-or-nothing process; what is involved, rather, is the balance of influences on behavior. That balance usually exhibits some stability over time, but it can become unstable and change with time or circumstances. Conforming and deviant behavior is learned by all of the mechanisms in this process, but the theory proposes that the principal mechanisms are in that part of the process in which differential reinforcement (instrumental learning through rewards and punishers) and imitation (observational learning) produce both overt behavior and cognitive definitions that function as discriminative (cue) stimuli for the behavior. Always implied, and sometimes made explicit when these concepts are called upon to account for deviant/conforming behavior, is the understanding that the behavioral processes in operant and classical conditioning are in operation (see below). However, social learning theory focuses on four major concepts—differential association, differential reinforcement, imitation, and definitions. The central proposition of the social learning theory of criminal and deviant behavior can be stated as a long sentence proposing that criminal and deviant behavior is more likely when, on balance, the combined effects of these four main sets of variables instigate and strengthen non-conforming over conforming acts:

> The probability that persons will engage in criminal and deviant behavior is increased and the probability of their conforming to the norm is decreased when they differentially associate with others who commit criminal behavior and espouse definitions favorable to it, are relatively more exposed in-person or symbolically to salient criminal/deviant models, define it as desirable or justified in a situation discriminative for the behavior, and have received in the past and anticipate in the current or future situation relatively greater reward than punishment for the behavior.

The probability of conforming behavior is increased and the probability of deviant behavior is decreased when the balance of these variables moves in the reverse direction.

Each of the four main components of this statement can be presented as a separate testable hypothesis. The individual is more likely to commit violations when:

1. He or she differentially associates with other[s] who commit, model, and support violations of social and legal norms.

2. The violative behavior is differentially reinforced over behavior in conformity to the norm.

3. He or she is more exposed to and observes more deviant than conforming models.

4. His or her own learned definitions are favorable toward committing the deviant acts.

GENERAL PRINCIPLES OF SOCIAL LEARNING THEORY

Since it is a general explanation of crime and deviance of all kinds, social learning is not simply a theory about how novel criminal behavior is learned or a theory only of the positive causes of that behavior. It embraces variables that operate to both motivate and control delinquent and criminal behavior, to both promote and undermine conformity. It answers the questions of why people do and do not violate norms. The probability of criminal or conforming behavior occurring is a function of the variables operating in the underlying social learning process. The main concepts/variables and their respective empirical indicators have been identified and measured, but they can be viewed as indicators of a general latent construct, for which additional indicators can be devised (Akers & La Greca, 1991; Akers & Lee, 1996).

Social learning accounts for the individual becoming prone to deviant or criminal behavior and for stability or change in that propensity. Therefore, the theory is capable of accounting for the development of stable individual differences, as well as changes in the individual's behavioral patterns or tendencies to commit

Akers, R. L. (1998). A social learning theory of crime. In R. L. Akers, *A social learning theory of crime* (pp. 50-59, 77-81). Boston: Northeastern University Press.

deviant and criminal acts, over time and in different situations. . . . The social learning process operates in each individual's learning history and in the immediate situation in which the opportunity for a crime occurs.

Deviant and criminal behavior is learned and modified (acquired, performed, repeated, maintained, and changed) through all of the same cognitive and behavioral mechanisms as conforming behavior. They differ in the direction, content, and outcome of the behavior learned. Therefore, it is inaccurate to state, for instance, that peer influence does not explain adolescent deviant behavior since conforming behavior is also peer influenced in adolescence. The theory expects peer influences to be implicated in both; it is the content and direction of the influence that is the key.

The primary learning mechanisms are differential reinforcement (instrumental conditioning), in which behavior is a function of the frequency, amount, and probability of experienced and perceived contingent rewards and punishments, and imitation, in which the behavior of others and its consequences are observed and modeled. The process of stimulus discrimination/generalization is another important mechanism; here, overt and covert stimuli, verbal and cognitive, act as cues or signals for behavior to occur. As I point out below, there are other behavioral mechanisms in the learning process, but these are not as important and are usually left implied rather than explicated in the theory.

The content of the learning achieved by these mechanisms includes the simple and complex behavioral sequences and the definitions (beliefs, attitudes, justifications, orientations) that in turn become discriminative for engaging in deviant and criminal behavior. The probability that conforming or norm-violative behavior is learned and performed, and the frequency with which it is committed, are a function of the past, present, and anticipated differential reinforcement for the behavior and the deviant or nondeviant direction of the learned definitions and other discriminative stimuli present in a given situation.

These learning mechanisms operate in a process of differential association—direct and indirect, verbal and nonverbal communication, interaction, and identification with others. The relative frequency, intensity, duration, and priority of associations affect the relative amount, frequency, and probability of reinforcement of conforming or deviant behavior and exposure of individuals to deviant or conforming norms and behavioral models. To the extent that the individual can control with whom she or he associates, the frequency, intensity, and duration of those associations are themselves affected by how rewarding or aversive they are. The principal learning is through differential association with those persons and groups (primary[,] secondary, reference, and symbolic) that comprise or control the individual's major sources of reinforcement, most salient behavioral models, and most effective definitions and other discriminative stimuli for committing and repeating behavior. The reinforcement and discriminative stimuli are mainly social (such as socially valued rewards and punishers contingent on the behavior), but they are also nonsocial (such as unconditioned physiological reactions to environmental stimuli and physical effects of ingested substances and the physical environment).

Sequence and Reciprocal Effects in the Social Learning Process

Behavioral feedback effects are built into the concept of differential reinforcement—actual or perceived changes in the environment produced by the behavior feed back on that behavior to affect its repetition or extinction, and both prior and anticipated rewards and punishments influence present behavior. Reciprocal effects between the individual's behavior and definitions or differential association are also reflected in the social learning process. This process is one in which the probability of both the initiation and the repetition of a deviant or criminal act (or the initiation and repetition of conforming acts) is a function of the learning history of the individual and the set of reinforcement contingencies and discriminative stimuli in a given situation. The typical process of initiation, continuation, progression, and desistance is hypothesized to be as follows:

1.   The balance of past and current associations, definitions, and imitation of deviant models, and the anticipated balance of reinforcement in particular situations, produces or inhibits the initial delinquent or deviant acts.

2.   The effects of these variables continue in the repetition of acts, although imitation becomes less important than it was in the first commission of the act.

3. After initiation, the actual social and nonsocial reinforcers and punishers affect the probability that the acts will be or will not be repeated and at what level of frequency.

4. Not only the overt behavior, but also the definitions favorable or unfavorable to it, are affected by the positive and negative consequences of the initial acts. To the extent that they are more rewarded than alternative behavior, the favorable definitions will be strengthened and the unfavorable definitions will be weakened, and it becomes more likely that the deviant behavior will be repeated under similar circumstances.

5. Progression into more frequent or sustained patterns, rather than cessation or reduction, of criminal and deviant behavior is promoted to the extent that reinforcement, exposure to deviant models, and norm-violating definitions are not offset by negative formal and informal sanctions and norm abiding definitions.

The theory does not hypothesize that definitions favorable to law violation always precede and are unaffected by the commission of criminal acts. Although the probability of a criminal act increases in the presence of favorable definitions, acts in violation of the law do occur (through imitation and reinforcement) in the absence of any thought given to whether the acts are right or wrong. Furthermore, the individual may apply neutralizing definitions retroactively to excuse or justify an act without having contemplated them beforehand. To the extent that such excuses become associated with successfully mitigating others' negative sanctions or one's self-punishment, however, they become cues for the repetition of deviant acts. Such definitions, therefore, precede committing the same acts again or committing similar acts in the future.

Differential association with conforming and nonconforming others typically precedes the individual's committing crimes and delinquent acts. This sequence of events is sometimes disputed in the literature because it is mistakenly believed to apply only to differential peer association in general or to participation in delinquent gangs in particular without reference to family and other group associations. It is true that the theory recognizes peer associations as very important in adolescent deviance and that differential association is most often measured in research by peer associations. But the theory also hypothesizes that the family is a very important primary group in the differential association process, and it plainly stipulates that other primary and secondary groups besides peers are involved (see Sutherland, 1947, pp. 164-65). Accordingly, it is a mistake to interpret differential association as referring only to peer associations. The theoretical stipulation that differential association is causally prior to the commission of delinquent and criminal acts is not confined to the balance of peer associations; rather, it is the balance (as determined by the modalities) of family, peer, and other associations. According to the priority principle, association, reinforcement, modeling, and exposure to conforming and deviant definitions occurring within the family during childhood, and such antisocial conduct as aggressiveness, lying, and cheating learned in early childhood, occur prior to and have both direct and selective effects on later delinquent and criminal behavior and associations. . . .

The socializing behavior of parents, guardians, or caretakers is certainly reciprocally influenced by the deviant and unacceptable behavior of the child. However, it can never be true that the onset of delinquency precedes and initiates interaction in a particular family (except in the unlikely case of the late-stage adoption of a child who is already delinquent or who is drawn to and chosen by deviant parents). Thus, interaction in the family or family surrogate always precedes delinquency.

But this is not true for adolescent peer associations. One may choose to associate with peers based on similarity in deviant behavior that already exists. Some major portion of this behavioral similarity results from previous association with other delinquent peers or from anticipatory socialization undertaken to make one's behavior match more closely that of the deviant associates to whom one is attracted. For some adolescents, gravitation toward delinquent peers occurs after and as a result of the individual's involvement in delinquent behavior. However, peer associations are most often formed initially around interests, friendships, and such circumstances as neighborhood proximity, family similarities, values, beliefs, age, school attended, grade in school, and mutually attractive behavioral patterns that have little to do directly with co-involvement or similarity in specifically law-violating or serious deviant behavior. Many of these factors in peer association are not under the adolescents' control, and some are simply happenstance. The theory does not, contrary to the Gluecks' distorted characterization, propose that "accidental differential association of non-delinquents with delinquents is the basic cause of crime" (Glueck & Glueck, 1950, p. 164). Interaction and socialization in the family precedes and affects choices of both conforming and deviant peer associations.

Those peer associations will affect the nature of models, definitions, and rewards/punishers to which the person is exposed. After the associations have been established, their reinforcing or punishing consequences as well as direct and vicarious consequences of the deviant behavior will affect both the continuation of old and the seeking of new associations (those over which one has any choice). One may choose further interaction with others based on whether they too are involved in deviant or criminal behavior; in such cases, the outcomes of that interaction are more rewarding than aversive and it is anticipated that the associates will more likely approve or be permissive toward one's own deviant behavior. Further interaction with delinquent peers, over which the individual has no choice, may also result from being apprehended and confined by the juvenile or criminal-justice system.

These reciprocal effects would predict that one's own deviant or conforming behavioral patterns can have effects on choice of friends; these are weaker in the earlier years, but should become stronger as one moves through adolescence and gains more control over friendship choices. The typical sequence outlined above would predict that deviant associations precede the onset of delinquent behavior more frequently than the sequence of events in which the delinquent associations begin only after the peers involved have already separately and individually established similar patterns of delinquent behavior. Further, these behavioral tendencies that develop prior to peer association will themselves be the result of previous associations, models, and reinforcement, primarily in the family. Regardless of the sequence in which onset occurs, and whatever the level of the individual's delinquent involvement, its frequency and seriousness will increase after the deviant associations have begun and decrease as the associations are reduced. That is, whatever the temporal ordering, differential association with deviant peers will have a causal effect on one's own delinquent behavior (just as his actions will have an effect on his peers).

Therefore, both "selection," or "flocking" (tendency for persons to choose interaction with others with behavioral similarities), and "socialization," or "feathering" (tendency for persons who interact to have mutual influence on one another's behavior), are part of the same overall social learning process and are explained by the same variables. A peer "socialization" process and a peer "selection" process in deviant behavior are not mutually exclusive, but are simply the social learning process operating at different times. Arguments that social learning posits only the latter, that any evidence of selective mechanisms in deviant interaction run counter to social learning theory (Strictland, 1982; Stafford & Ekland-Olson, 1982), or that social learning theory recognizes only a recursive, one-way causal effect of peers on delinquent behavior (Thornberry et al., 1994; Catalano et al., 1996) are wrong.

Behavioral and Cognitive Mechanisms in Social Learning

The first statement in Sutherland's theory was a simple declarative sentence maintaining that criminal behavior is learned, and the eighth statement declared that this involved all the mechanisms involved in any learning. What little Sutherland added in his (1947, p. 7) commentary downplayed imitation as a possible learning mechanism in criminal behavior. He mentioned "seduction" of a person into criminal behavior as something that is not covered by the concept of imitation. He defined neither imitation nor seduction and offered no further discussion of mechanisms of learning in any of his papers or publications. Recall that filling this major lacuna in Sutherland's theory was the principal goal of the 1966b Burgess-Akers reformulation. To this end we combined Sutherland's first and eighth statements into one: "Criminal behavior is learned according to the principles of operant conditioning." The phrase "principles of operant conditioning" was meant as a shorthand reference to all of the behavioral mechanisms of learning in operant theory that had been empirically validated.

Burgess and I delineated, as much as space allowed, what these specific learning mechanisms were: (1) operant conditioning, differential reinforcement of voluntary behavior through positive and negative reinforcement and punishment; (2) respondent (involuntary reflexes), or "classical," conditioning; (3) unconditioned (primary) and conditioned (secondary) reinforcers and punishers; (4) shaping and response differentiation; (5) stimulus discrimination and generalization, the environmental and internal stimuli that provide cues or signals indicating differences and similarities across situations that help elicit, but do not directly reinforce, behavior; (6) types of reinforcement schedules, the rate and ratio in which rewards and punishers follow behavior; (7) stimulus-response constellations; and (8) stimulus satiation and deprivation. We also reported research showing the applicability of these mechanisms of learning to both conforming and deviant behavior.

Burgess and I used the term "operant conditioning" to emphasize that differential reinforcement (the balance of reward and punishment contingent upon behavioral responses) is the basic mechanism around which the others revolve and by which learning most relevant to conformity or violation of social and legal norms is produced. This was reflected in other statements in the theory in which the only learning mechanisms listed were differential reinforcement and stimulus discrimination.

We also subsumed imitation, or modeling, under these principles and argued that imitation "may be analyzed quite parsimoniously with the principles of modern behavior theory," namely, that it is simply a sub-class of behavioral shaping through operant conditioning (Burgess and Akers, 1966b, p. 138). For this reason we made no specific mention of imitation in any of the seven statements. Later, I became persuaded that the operant principle of gradual shaping of responses through "successive approximations" only incompletely and awkwardly incorporated the processes of observational learning and vicarious reinforcement that Bandura and Walters (1963) had identified. Therefore, without dismissing successive approximation as a way in which some imitative behavior could be shaped, I

came to accept Bandura's conceptualization of imitation. That is, imitation is a separate learning mechanism characterized by modeling one's own actions on the observed behavior of others and on the consequences of that behavior (vicarious reinforcement) prior to performing the behavior and experiencing its consequences directly. Whether the observed acts will be performed and repeated depends less on the continuing presence of models and more on the actual or anticipated rewarding or aversive consequences of the behavior. I became satisfied that the principle of "observational learning" could account for the acquisition, and to some extent the performance, of behavior by a process that did not depend on operant conditioning or "instrumental learning." Therefore, in later discussions of the theory, while continuing to posit differential reinforcement as the core behavior-shaping mechanism, I included imitation as another primary mechanism in acquiring behavior. Where appropriate, discriminative stimuli were also specifically invoked as affecting behavior, while I made only general reference to other learning mechanisms.

Note that the term "operant conditioning" in the opening sentence of the Burgess-Akers revision reflected our great reliance on the orthodox behaviorism that assumed the empirical irrelevance of cognitive variables. Social behaviorism, on the other hand, recognizes "cognitive" as well as "behavioral" mechanisms (see Bandura, 1969; 1977a; 1977b; 1986a; 1989; Grusec, 1992; Staats, 1975; Baldwin & Baldwin, 1981). My social learning theory of criminal behavior retains a strong element of the symbolic interactionism found in Sutherland's theory (Akers, 1985, pp. 39-70). As a result, it is closer to cognitive learning theories, such as Albert Bandura's, than to the radical operant behaviorism of B. F. Skinner with which Burgess and I began. It is for this reason, and the reliance on such concepts as imitation, anticipated reinforcement, and self-reinforcement, that I have described social learning theory as "soft behaviorism" (Akers, 1985, p. 65).

The unmodified term "learning" implies to many that the theory only explains the acquisition of novel behavior by the individual, in contrast to behavior that is committed at a given time and place or the maintenance of behavior over time (Cornish and Clarke, 1986). It has also been interpreted to mean only "positive" learning of novel behavior, with no relevance for inhibition of behavior or of learning failures (Gottfredson and Hirschi, 1990). As I have made clear above, neither of these interpretations is accurate. The phrase that Burgess and I used, "effective and available reinforcers and the existing reinforcement contingencies," and the discussion of reinforcement occurring under given situations (Burgess & Akers, 1966b, pp. 141, 134) make it obvious that we were not proposing a theory only of past reinforcement in the acquisition of a behavioral repertoire with no regard for the reward/cost balance obtaining at a given time and place. There is nothing in the learning principles that restrict[s] them to prior socialization or past history of learning. Social learning encompasses both the acquisition and the performance of the behavior, both facilitation and inhibition of behavior, and both learning successes and learning failures. The learning mechanisms account not only for the initiation of behavior but also for repetition, maintenance and desistance of behavior. They rely not only on prior behavioral processes but also on those operating at a given time in a given situation. . . .

DEFINITIONS AND DISCRIMINATIVE STIMULI

[In] *The Concept of Definitions,* Sutherland asserted that learning criminal behavior includes "techniques of committing the crime which are sometimes very complicated, sometimes very simple" and the "specific direction of motives, drives, rationalizations and attitudes" (1947, p. 6). I have retained both definitions and techniques in social learning theory, with clarified and modified conceptual meanings and with hypothesized relationships to criminal behavior. The qualification that "techniques" may be simple or complex shows plainly that Sutherland did not mean to include only crime-specific skills learned in order to break the law successfully. Techniques also clearly include ordinary, everyday abilities. This same notion is retained in social learning theory.

By definition, a person must be capable of performing the necessary sequence of actions before he or she can carry out either criminal or conforming behavior—inability to perform the

behavior precludes committing the crime. Since many of the behavioral techniques for both conforming and criminal acts are the same, not only the simple but even some of the complex skills involved in carrying out crime are not novel to most or many of us. The required component parts of the complete skill are acquired in essentially conforming or neutral contexts to which we have been exposed—driving a car, shooting a gun, fighting with fists, signing checks, using a computer, and so on. In most white-collar crime, the same skills needed to carry out a job legitimately are put to illegitimate use. Other skills are specific to given deviant acts—safe cracking, counterfeiting, pocket picking, jimmying doors and picking locks, bringing off a con game, and so on. Without tutelage in these crime-specific techniques, most people would not be able to perform them, or at least would be initially very inept.

Sutherland took the concept of "definitions" in his theory from W. I. Thomas's "definition of the situation" (Thomas and Thomas, 1928) and generalized it to orienting attitudes toward different behavior. It is true that "Sutherland did not identify what constitutes a definition 'favorable to' or 'unfavorable to' the violation of law" (Cressey, 1960, p. 53). Nevertheless . . . there is little doubt that "rationalizations" and "attitudes" are subsumed under the general concept of definitions—normative attitudes or evaluative meanings attached to given behavior. Exposure to others' shared definitions is a key (but not the only) part of the process by which the individual acquires or internalizes his or her own definitions. They are orientations, rationalizations, definitions of the situation, and other attitudes that label the commission of an act as right or wrong, good or bad, desirable or undesirable, justified or unjustified.

In social learning theory, these definitions are both general and specific. General beliefs include religious, moral, and other conventional values and norms that are favorable to conforming behavior and unfavorable to committing any of a range of deviant or criminal acts. Specific definitions orient the person to particular acts or series of acts. Thus, there are people who believe that it is morally wrong to steal and that laws against theft should be obeyed, but at the same time see little wrong with smoking marijuana and rationalize that it is all right to violate laws against drug possession. The greater the extent to which one holds attitudes that disapprove of certain acts, the less likely one is to engage in them. Conventional beliefs are negative toward criminal behavior. The more strongly one has learned and personally believes in the ideals of honesty, integrity, civility, kindness, and other general standards of morality that condemn lying, cheating, stealing, and harming others, the less likely he or she is to commit acts that violate social and legal norms. Conversely, the more one's own attitudes approve of, or fail to condemn, a behavior, the greater the chances are that he or she will engage in it. For obvious reasons, the theory would predict that definitions in the form of general beliefs will have less effect than specific definitions on the commission of specific criminal acts.

Definitions that favor criminal or deviant behavior are basically positive or neutralizing. Positive definitions are beliefs or attitudes that make the behavior morally desirable or wholly permissible. They are most likely to be learned through positive reinforcement in a deviant group or subculture that carries values conflicting with those of conventional society. Some of these positive verbalizations may be part of a full-blown ideology of politically dissident, criminal, or deviant groups. Although such ideologies and groups can be identified, the theory does not rest only on this type of definition favorable to deviance; indeed, it proposes that such positive definitions occur less frequently than neutralizing ones.

Neutralizing definitions favor violating the law or other norms not because they take the acts to be positively desirable but because they justify or excuse them. Even those who commit deviant acts are aware that others condemn the behavior and may themselves define the behavior as bad. The neutralizing definitions view the act as something that is probably undesirable but, given the situation, is nonetheless justified, excusable, necessary, all right, or not really bad after all. The process of acquiring neutralizing definitions is more likely to involve negative reinforcement; that is, they are verbalizations that accompany escape or avoidance of negative consequences like disapproval by one's self or by society.

While these definitions may become part of a deviant or criminal subculture, acquiring them does not require participation in such subcultures. They are learned from carriers of conventional culture, including many of those in social control and treatment agencies. The notions of techniques of neutralization and subterranean values (Sykes and Matza, 1957; Matza and Sykes, 1961; Matza, 1964) come from the observation that for nearly every social norm there is a norm of evasion. That is, there are recognized exceptions or ways of getting around the moral imperatives in the norms and the reproach expected for violating them. Thus, the general prohibition "Thou shalt not kill" is accompanied by such implicit or explicit exceptions as "unless in time of war," "unless the victim is the enemy," "unless in self-defense," "unless in the line of duty," "unless to protect others"! The moral injunctions against physical violence are suspended if the victim can be defined as the initial aggressor or is guilty of some transgression and therefore deserves to be attacked.

The concept of neutralizing definitions in social learning theory incorporates not only notions of verbalizations and rationalizations (Cressey, 1953) and techniques of neutralization (Sykes & Matza, 1957) but also conceptually similar if not equivalent notions of "accounts" (Lyman & Scott, 1970), "disclaimers" (Hewitt & Stokes, 1975), and "moral disengagement" (Bandura, 1976, 1990). Neutralizing attitudes include such beliefs as "Everybody has a racket"; "I can't help myself, I was born this way"; "It's not my fault"; "I am not responsible"; "I was drunk and didn't know what I was doing"; "I just blew my top"; "They can afford it"; "He deserved it." Some neutralizations (e.g., nonresponsibility) can be generalized to a wide range of disapproved and criminal behavior. These and other excuses and justifications for committing deviant acts and victimizing others are definitions favorable to criminal and deviant behavior.

Exposure to these rationalizations and excuses may be through after-the-fact justifications for one's own or others' norm violations that help to deflect or lessen punishment that would be expected to follow. The individual then learns the excuses either directly or through imitation and uses them to lessen self-reproach and social disapproval. Therefore, the definitions are themselves behavior that can be imitated and reinforced and then in turn serve as discriminative stimuli accompanying reinforcement of overt behavior. Deviant and criminal acts do occur without being accompanied by positive or neutralizing definitions, but the acts are more likely to occur and recur in situations the same as or similar to those in which the definitions have already been learned and applied. The extent to which one adheres to or rejects the definitions favorable to crime is itself affected by the rewarding or punishing consequences that follow the act.

DISCUSSION QUESTIONS

1. According to Akers's social learning theory, why does associating with delinquent peers usually result in increased levels of delinquency?

2. What are the general principles of social learning theory?

3. Discuss the importance of behavioral feedback effects that are built into the concept of differential reinforcement. Why are reciprocal effects important?

4. Discuss the concept of "definitions" and provide an example of a definition favorable to crime. In what way does Akers draw on Sykes and Matza's theory (see Chapter 14, this volume) to explain criminality within his own approach?

14

TECHNIQUES OF NEUTRALIZATION

A Theory of Delinquency

GRESHAM M. SYKES AND DAVID MATZA

EDITOR'S INTRODUCTION—Following Sutherland, Sykes and Matza believe that all human behavior, including delinquency, is learned. They rearticulate the central components of Sutherland's differential association theory, which maintains that criminal or delinquent behavior involves learning techniques of committing crime and the motives, drives, rationalizations, and attitudes that favor law violation. Sykes and Matza's approach ran counter to the popular theories of crime. When they published their article in 1957, criminology was dominated by subcultural theories of crime, which asserted that delinquents held values that were opposite to middle-class values. In this vein, delinquents were thought to approve of behaviors such as theft, vandalism, and fighting.

In marked contrast to these approaches, Sykes and Matza spend the first half of their article explaining that delinquents do not generally approve of delinquency, despite the fact that they become involved with it. This paradox suggests that delinquents, like nondelinquents, do believe in the norms and values of their communities because of the manner in which they express shame or guilt over their actions, and these norms influence why they might select one path, or target, of delinquent action and not another. The latter half of the article centers on an alternative approach, which maintains that delinquents enable themselves to participate in delinquent behavior by applying certain "techniques of neutralization." Although delinquents generally feel that delinquency is wrong, they claim that their delinquent behavior can be justified on any number of grounds, such as "the victim deserved it" or "the person just got in the way." These justifications come before the delinquent act itself, and they enable the delinquent process by neutralizing the individual's belief that the acts he or she is about to commit are wrong.

Research suggests that these justifications, or neutralization techniques, will differ from individual to individual. People who accept more neutralizing techniques are probably more likely to engage in delinquent or criminal behavior, although the effect of neutralization is influenced by various factors. Exposure to delinquent peers may have a strong impact on neutralization. Neutralization is more likely to occur among individuals who associate with delinquent peers because these individuals are more likely to respond to certain problems with delinquency. In this sense, Sykes and Matza's theory of delinquency may be better conceived of as a critical part of Sutherland's differential association theory because of the way in which it provides a context for understanding how specific definitions become more favorable to violating the law.

In attempting to uncover the roots of juvenile delinquency, the social scientist has long since ceased to search for devils in the mind or stigma of the body. It is now largely agreed that delinquent behavior, like most social behavior, is learned and that it is learned in the process of social interaction. The classic statement of this position is found in Sutherland's theory of differential association, which asserts that criminal or delinquent behavior involves the learning of (a) techniques of committing crimes and (b) motives, drives, rationalizations, and attitudes favorable to the violation of law. Unfortunately, the specific content of what is learned—as opposed to the process by which it is learned—has received relatively little attention in either theory or research. Perhaps the single strongest school of thought on the nature of this content has centered on the idea of a delinquent subculture. The basic characteristic of the delinquent sub-culture, it is argued, is a system of values that represents an inversion of the values held by respectable, law-abiding society. The world of the delinquent is the world of the law-abiding turned upside down and its norms constitute a countervailing force directed against the conforming social order. Cohen sees the process of developing a delinquent sub-culture as a matter of building, maintaining, and reinforcing a code for behavior which exists by opposition, which stands in point by point contradiction to dominant values, particularly those of the middle class. Cohen's portrayal of delinquency is executed with a good deal of sophistication, and he carefully avoids overly simple explanations such as those based on the principle of "follow the leader" or easy generalizations about "emotional disturbances." Furthermore, he does not accept the delinquent sub-culture as something given, but instead systematically examines the function of delinquent values as a viable solution to the lower-class, male child's problems in the area of social status. Yet in spite of its virtues, this image of juvenile delinquency as a form of behavior based on competing or countervailing values and norms appears to suffer from a number of serious defects. It is the nature of these defects and a possible alternative or modified explanation for a large portion of juvenile delinquency with which this paper is concerned.

The difficulties in viewing delinquent behavior as springing from a set of deviant values and norms—as arising, that is to say, from a situation in which the delinquent defines his delinquency as "right"—are both empirical and theoretical. In the first place, if there existed in fact a delinquent subculture such that the delinquent viewed his illegal behavior as morally correct, we could reasonably suppose that he would exhibit no feelings of guilt or shame at detection or confinement. Instead, the major reaction would tend in the direction of indignation or a sense of martyrdom. It is true that some delinquents do react in the latter fashion, although the sense of martyrdom often seems to be based on the fact that others "get away with it" and indignation appears to be directed against the chance events or lack of skill that led to apprehension. More important, however, is the fact that there is a good deal of evidence suggesting that many delinquents do experience a sense of guilt or shame, and its outward expression is not to be dismissed as a purely manipulative gesture to appease those in authority. Much of this evidence is, to be sure, of a clinical nature or in the form of impressionistic judgments of those who must deal first hand with the youthful offender. Assigning a weight to such evidence calls for caution, but it cannot be ignored if we are to avoid the gross stereotype of the juvenile delinquent as a hardened gangster in miniature.

In the second place, observers have noted that the juvenile delinquent frequently accords admiration and respect to law-abiding persons. The "really honest" person is often revered, and if the delinquent is sometimes overly keen to detect hypocrisy in those who conform, unquestioned probity is likely to win his approval. A fierce attachment to a humble, pious mother or a forgiving, upright priest (the former, according to many observers, is often encountered in both juvenile delinquents and adult criminals) might be dismissed as rank sentimentality, but at least it is clear that the delinquent does not necessarily regard those who abide by the legal rules as immoral. In a similar vein, it can be noted that the juvenile delinquent may exhibit great resentment if illegal behavior is imputed to "significant others" in his immediate social environment or to heroes in the world of sport and entertainment. In

Sykes, G. M., & Matza, D. (1957). Techniques of neutralization: A theory of delinquency. *American Sociological Review, 22,* 664-670.

other words, if the delinquent does hold to a set of values and norms that stand in complete opposition to those of respectable society, his norm-holding is of a peculiar sort. While supposedly thoroughly committed to the deviant system of the delinquent sub-culture, he would appear to recognize the moral validity of the dominant normative system in many instances.

In the third place, there is much evidence that juvenile delinquents often draw a sharp line between those who can be victimized and those who cannot. Certain social groups are not to be viewed as "fair game" in the performance of supposedly approved delinquent acts while others warrant a variety of attacks. In general, the potentiality for victimization would seem to be a function of the social distance between the juvenile delinquent and others and thus we find implicit maxims in the world of the delinquent such as "don't steal from friends" or "don't commit vandalism against a church of your own faith." This is all rather obvious, but the implications have not received sufficient attention. The fact that supposedly valued behavior tends to be directed against disvalued social groups hints that the "wrongfulness" of such delinquent behavior is more widely recognized by delinquents than the literature has indicated. When the pool of victims is limited by considerations of kinship, friendship, ethnic group, social class, age, sex, etc., we have reason to suspect that the virtue of delinquency is far from unquestioned.

In the fourth place, it is doubtful if many juvenile delinquents are totally immune from the demands for conformity made by the dominant social order. There is a strong likelihood that the family of the delinquent will agree with respectable society that delinquency is wrong, even though the family may be engaged in a variety of illegal activities. That is, the parental posture conducive to delinquency is not apt to be a positive prodding. Whatever may be the influence of parental example, what might be called the "Fagin" pattern of socialization into delinquency is probably rare. Furthermore, as Redl has indicated, the idea that certain neighborhoods are completely delinquent, offering the child a model for delinquent behavior without reservations, is simply not supported by the data. The fact that a child is punished by parents, school officials, and agencies of the legal system for his delinquency may, as a number of observers have cynically noted, suggest to the child that he should be more careful not to get caught. There is an equal or greater probability, however, that the child will internalize the demands for conformity. This is not to say that demands for conformity cannot be counteracted. In fact, as we shall see shortly, an understanding of how internal and external demands for conformity are neutralized may be crucial for understanding delinquent behavior. But it is to say that a complete denial of the validity of demands for conformity and the substitution of a new normative system is improbable, in light of the child's or adolescent's dependency on adults and encirclement by adults inherent in his status in the social structure. No matter how deeply enmeshed in patterns of delinquency he may be and no matter how much this involvement may outweigh his associations with the law-abiding, he cannot escape the condemnation of his deviance. Somehow the demands for conformity must be met and answered; they cannot be ignored as part of an alien system of values and norms.

In short, the theoretical viewpoint that sees juvenile delinquency as a form of behavior based on the values and norms of a deviant sub-culture in precisely the same way as law-abiding behavior is based on the values and norms of the larger society is open to serious doubt. The fact that the world of the delinquent is embedded in the larger world of those who conform cannot be overlooked nor can the delinquent be equated with an adult thoroughly socialized into an alternative way of life. Instead, the juvenile delinquent would appear to be at least partially committed to the dominant social order in that he frequently exhibits guilt or shame when he violates its proscriptions, accords approval to certain conforming figures, and distinguishes between appropriate and inappropriate targets for his deviance. It is to an explanation for the apparently paradoxical fact of his delinquency that we now turn.

As Morris Cohen once said, one of the most fascinating problems about human behavior is why men violate the laws in which they believe. This is the problem that confronts us when we attempt to explain why delinquency occurs despite a greater or lesser commitment to the usages of conformity. A basic clue is offered by the fact that social rules or norms calling for valued behavior seldom if ever take the form of categorical imperatives. Rather, values or norms appear as *qualified* guides for action, limited in their applicability in terms of time, place, persons, and social circumstances. The moral injunction against killing, for example, does not apply to the enemy during combat in time of war, although a captured enemy comes once again under the prohibition. Similarly, the taking and distributing of scarce goods in a time of acute social need is felt by many to be right, although under other circumstances private property is held inviolable. The normative system of a society, then, is marked by what Williams has termed *flexibility*; it does not consist of a body of rules held to be binding under all conditions.

This flexibility is, in fact, an integral part of the criminal law in that measures for "defenses to crimes" are provided in pleas such as nonage, necessity, insanity, drunkenness, compulsion, self-defense, and so on. The individual can avoid moral culpability for his criminal action—and thus avoid the negative sanctions of society—if he can prove that criminal intent was lacking. *It is our argument that much delinquency is based on what is essentially an unrecognized extension of defenses to crimes, in the form of justifications for deviance that are seen as valid by the delinquent but not by the legal system or society at large.*

These justifications are commonly described as rationalizations. They are viewed as following deviant behavior and as protecting the individual from self-blame and the blame of others after the act. But there is also reason to believe that they precede deviant behavior and make deviant behavior possible. It is this possibility that Sutherland mentioned only in passing and that other writers have failed to exploit from the viewpoint of sociological theory. Disapproval flowing from internalized norms and conforming others in the social environment is neutralized, turned back, or deflected in advance. Social controls that serve to check or inhibit deviant motivational patterns are rendered inoperative, and the individual is freed to engage in delinquency without serious damage to his self image. In this sense, the delinquent both has his cake and eats it too, for he remains committed to the dominant normative system and yet so qualifies its imperatives that violations are "acceptable" if not "right." Thus the delinquent represents not a radical opposition to law-abiding society but something more like an apologetic failure, often more sinned against than sinning in his own eyes. We call these justifications of deviant behavior techniques of neutralization; and we believe these techniques make up a crucial component of Sutherland's "definitions favorable to the violation of law." It is by learning these techniques that the juvenile becomes delinquent, rather than by learning moral imperatives, values or attitudes standing in direct contradiction to those of the dominant society. In analyzing these techniques, we have found it convenient to divide them into five major types.

The Denial of Responsibility. In so far as the delinquent can define himself as lacking responsibility for his deviant actions, the disapproval of self or others is sharply reduced in effectiveness as a restraining influence. As Justice Holmes has said, even a dog distinguishes between being stumbled over and being kicked, and modern society is no less careful to draw a line between injuries that are unintentional, i.e., where responsibility is lacking, and those that are intentional. As a technique of neutralization, however, the denial of responsibility extends much further than the claim that deviant acts are an "accident" or some similar negation of personal accountability. It may also be asserted that delinquent acts are due to forces outside of the individual and beyond his control such as unloving parents, bad companions, or a slum neighborhood. In effect, the delinquent approaches a "billiard ball" conception of himself in which he sees himself as helplessly propelled into new situations. From a psychodynamic viewpoint, this orientation toward one's own actions may represent a profound alienation from self, but it is important to stress the fact that interpretations of responsibility are cultural constructs and not merely idiosyncratic beliefs. The similarity between this mode of justifying illegal behavior assumed by the delinquent and the implications of a "sociological" frame of reference or a "humane" jurisprudence is readily apparent. It is not the validity of this orientation that concerns us here, but its function of deflecting blame attached to violations of social norms and its relative independence of a particular personality structure. By learning to view himself as more acted upon than acting, the delinquent prepares the way for deviance from the dominant normative system without the necessity of a frontal assault on the norms themselves.

The Denial of Injury. A second major technique of neutralization centers on the injury or harm involved in the delinquent act. The criminal law has long made a distinction between crimes which are *mala in se* and *mala prohibita*—that is between acts that are wrong in themselves and acts that are illegal but not immoral—and the delinquent can make the same kind of distinction in evaluating the wrongfulness of his behavior. For the delinquent, however, wrongfulness may turn on the question of whether or not anyone has clearly been hurt by his deviance, and this matter is open to a variety of interpretations. Vandalism, for example, may be defined by the delinquent simply as "mischief"—after all, it may be claimed, the persons whose property has been destroyed can well afford it. Similarly, auto theft may be viewed as "borrowing," and gang fighting may be seen as a private quarrel, an agreed upon duel between two willing parties, and thus of no concern to the community at large. We are not suggesting that this technique of neutralization, labeled the denial of injury, involves an explicit dialectic. Rather, we are arguing that the delinquent frequently, and in a hazy fashion, feels that his behavior does not really cause any great harm despite the fact that it runs counter to law. Just as the link between the individual and his acts may be broken by the denial of responsibility, so may the link between acts and their consequences be broken by the denial of injury. Since society sometimes agrees with the delinquent, e.g., in matters such as truancy, "pranks," and so on, it merely reaffirms the idea that the delinquent's neutralization of social controls by means of qualifying the norms is an extension of common practice rather than a gesture of complete opposition.

The Denial of The Victim. Even if the delinquent accepts the responsibility for his deviant actions and is willing to admit that his deviant actions involve an injury or hurt, the moral indignation of self and others may be neutralized by an insistence that the injury is not wrong in light of the circumstances. The injury, it may be claimed, is not really an injury; rather, it is a form of rightful retaliation or punishment. By a subtle alchemy the delinquent moves himself into the position of an avenger and the victim is transformed into a wrong-doer. Assaults on homosexuals or suspected homosexuals, attacks on members of minority groups who are said to have gotten "out of place," vandalism as revenge on an unfair teacher or school official, thefts from a "crooked" store owner—all may be hurts inflicted on a transgressor, in the eyes of the delinquent. As Orwell has pointed out, the type of criminal admired by the general public has probably changed over the course of years and Raffles no longer serves as a hero; but Robin Hood, and his latter day derivatives such as the tough detective seeking justice outside the law, still capture the popular imagination, and the delinquent may view his acts as part of a similar role.

To deny the existence of the victim, then, by transforming him into a person deserving injury is an extreme form of a phenomenon we have mentioned before, namely, the delinquent's recognition of appropriate and inappropriate targets for his delinquent acts. In addition, however, the existence of the victim may be denied for the delinquent, in a somewhat different sense, by the circumstances of the delinquent act itself. Insofar as the victim is physically absent, unknown, or a vague abstraction (as is often the case in delinquent acts committed against property), the awareness of the victim's existence is weakened. Internalized norms and anticipations of the reactions of others must somehow be activated, if they are to serve as guides for behavior; and it is possible that a diminished awareness of the victim plays an important part in determining whether or not this process is set in motion.

The Condemnation of The Condemners. A fourth technique of neutralization would appear to involve a condemnation of the condemners. . . . The delinquent shifts the focus of attention from his own deviant acts to the motives and behavior of those who disapprove of his violations. His condemners, he may claim, are hypocrites, deviants in disguise, or impelled by personal spite. This orientation toward the conforming world may be of particular importance when it hardens into a bitter cynicism directed against those assigned the task of enforcing or expressing the norms of the dominant society. Police, it may be said, are corrupt, stupid, and brutal. Teachers always show favoritism and parents always "take it out" on their children. By a slight extension, the rewards of conformity—such as material success—become a matter of pull or luck, thus decreasing still further the stature of those who stand on the side of the law-abiding. The validity of this jaundiced viewpoint is not so important as its function in turning back or deflecting the negative sanctions attached to violations of the norms. The delinquent, in effect, has changed the subject of the conversation in the dialogue between his own deviant impulses and the reactions of others; and by attacking others, the wrongfulness of his own behavior is more easily repressed or lost to view.

The Appeal to Higher Loyalties. Fifth, and last, internal and external social controls may be neutralized by sacrificing the demands of the larger society for the demands of the smaller social groups to which the delinquent belongs such as the sibling pair, the gang, or the friendship clique. It is important to note that the delinquent does not necessarily repudiate the imperatives of the dominant normative system, despite his failure to follow them. Rather, the delinquent may see himself as caught up in a dilemma that must be resolved, unfortunately, at the cost of violating the law. One aspect of this situation has been studied by Stouffer and Toby in their research on the conflict between particularistic and universalistic demands, between the claims of friendship and general social obligations, and their results suggest that "it is possible to classify people according to a predisposition to select one or the other horn of a dilemma in role conflict." For our purposes, however, the most important point is that deviation from certain norms may occur not because the norms are rejected but because other norms, held to be more pressing or involving a higher loyalty, are accorded precedence. Indeed, it is the fact that both sets of norms are believed in that gives meaning to our concepts of dilemma and role conflict.

The conflict between the claims of friendship and the claims of law, or a similar dilemma, has of course long been recognized by the social scientist (and the novelist) as a common human problem. If the juvenile delinquent frequently resolves his dilemma by insisting that he must "always help a buddy" or "never squeal on a friend," even when it throws him into serious difficulties with the dominant social order, his choice remains familiar to the supposedly law-abiding. The delinquent is unusual, perhaps, in the extent to which he is able to see the fact that

he acts in behalf of the smaller social groups to which he belongs as a justification for violations of society's norms, but it is a matter of degree rather than of kind.

"I didn't mean it." "I didn't really hurt anybody." "They had it coming to them." "Everybody's picking on me." "I didn't do it for myself." These slogans or their variants, we hypothesize, prepare the juvenile for delinquent acts. These "definitions of the situation" represent tangential or glancing blows at the dominant normative system rather than the creation of an opposing ideology; and they are extensions of patterns of thought prevalent in society rather than something created *de novo*.

Techniques of neutralization may not be powerful enough to fully shield the individual from the force of his own internalized values and the reactions of conforming others, for as we have pointed out, juvenile delinquents often appear to suffer from feelings of guilt and shame when called into account for their deviant behavior. And some delinquents may be so isolated from the world of conformity that techniques of neutralization need not be called into play. Nonetheless, we would argue that techniques of neutralization are critical in lessening the effectiveness of social controls and that they lie behind a large share of delinquent behavior. Empirical research in this area is scattered and fragmentary at the present time, but the work of Redl, Cressy, and others has supplied a body of significant data that has done much to clarify the theoretical issues and enlarge the fund of supporting evidence. Two lines of investigation seem to be critical at this stage. First, there is need for more knowledge concerning the differential distribution of techniques of neutralization, as operative patterns of thought, by age, sex, social class, ethnic group, etc. On *a priori* grounds it might be assumed that these justifications for deviance will be more readily seized by segments of society for whom a discrepancy between common social ideals and social practice is most apparent. It is also possible however, that the habit of "bending" the dominant normative system—if not "breaking" it—cuts across our cruder social categories and is to be traced primarily to patterns of social interaction within the familial circle. Second, there is need for a greater understanding of the internal structure of techniques of neutralization, as a system of beliefs and attitudes, and its relationship to various types of delinquent behavior. Certain techniques of neutralization would appear to be better adapted to particular deviant acts than to others, as we have suggested, for example, in the case of offenses against property and the denial of the victim. But the issue remains far from clear and stands in need of more information.

In any case, techniques of neutralization appear to offer a promising line of research in enlarging and systematizing the theoretical grasp of juvenile delinquency. As more information is uncovered concerning techniques of neutralization, their origins, and their consequences, both juvenile delinquency in particular, and deviation from normative systems in general may be illuminated.

DISCUSSION QUESTIONS

1. In their article, Sykes and Matza highlight the paradoxical nature of delinquency: Juvenile delinquents violate laws in which they believe but about which they exhibit shame and guilt, and they distinguish between appropriate and inappropriate targets for crime. How can this paradoxical problem be resolved?

2. Copyright laws exist to protect various types of publications, including music and lyrics. Even though they know that it is wrong to download music from Internet sites and copy it onto writable CDs, many people do it anyway. What justifications might these people use to explain this behavior? What "neutralization" techniques do the justifications demonstrate?

3. According to Sykes and Matza, these techniques of neutralization are learned in interaction with others. What groups of individuals, do you think, would be most apt to use these various neutralization techniques? Why? Give an example of the circumstances in which they might be used.

15

CLASS IN THE HOUSEHOLD

A Power-Control Theory of Gender and Delinquency

JOHN HAGAN, JOHN SIMPSON, AND A. R. GILLIS

EDITOR'S INTRODUCTION—Although this article finds itself in the section with other social control theories of crime, it really demonstrates the importance of integrated approaches to the study of crime and criminality. At its most basic level, this article by Hagan, Simpson, and Gillis combines control theory and conflict theory to explain how social class and authority in the workplace affect delinquency. They extend a power-control theory of common delinquent behavior developed by Hagan, Gillis, and Simpson in 1985. The authors accomplish this theoretical task by bringing the class analysis of delinquency into the household, using a new model of class relations based on the relative positions of husbands and wives in the workplace. This selection also highlights the fact that both macro forces in society and micro forces in individuals' existing environments are important in determining both criminality and victimization.

The initial formulation of power-control theory centered on a class analysis of heads of households. However, it is clear that power in the family also derives from the positions in the workplace. Therefore, the extension of power-control theory begins with a single question: "What differences do the relative class positions of husbands *and* wives in the workplace make for gender variations in parental control and in delinquent behavior of adolescents?" (p. 152, this volume). From this question, the authors build a model of familial relations that is used to answer that question.

More specifically, the authors find that in patriarchal families, wives have little power relative to husbands, daughters have little freedom relative to sons, and daughters are less delinquent than sons. These differences are diminished in egalitarian families. Power-control theory explains this variation in terms of (a) gender divisions in domestic social control, and (b) the resulting attitudes toward risk taking. Power-control theory thereby accounts for class-specific declines in gender-delinquency relationships that previously required separate deprivation and liberation theories of gender and delinquency. The new theory calls for major changes in the study of class, gender, and delinquency, as well as for a new appreciation of the importance of gender and structures of patriarchy in many other social processes, namely the workplace.

The authors base their new model of family class relations on Dahrendorfian conceptions of power and authority and their use in the control of collective units. Following Dahrendorf (1959), these collective units make up all "imperatively coordinated associations," meaning that they include the family as well as the workplace. Dahrendorfian classes are distinguished on the basis of their relations to authority. Hagan, Simpson, and Gillis use the terms *command class* and *obey class* to distinguish these positions. In their analysis of delinquency, which is defined in terms of risk-taking behavior, the authors examine these relations of authority within the distinct family structures and then determine how this relationship affects delinquency among boys and girls.

The authors contend that a predominantly male pattern of delinquency results from the class structure of modern patriarchal families. In these families, an instrument-object relationship takes the form of fathers' and, mainly, mothers' controlling their daughters more than their sons. This relationship plays a central role in the reproduction of a gender division between family and work: Patriarchal families will prepare daughters for a "cult of domesticity" that makes their involvement in delinquency unlikely. Using the Dahrendorfian model of family class relationships, the authors contend that the instrument-object relationship between parents and daughters will be most acute in patriarchal families, whereas it will be least acute in more egalitarian family structures, which tend to have more balanced positions of authority. In egalitarian families, daughters gain a sense of freedom and increased openness to risk-taking behaviors.

This extension of power-control theory is very important to the understanding of how the changing class dynamics of gender and delinquency are really part of a much larger process of social change that involves the decline in the gender division between consumption, production, and, as I will add, reproduction spheres in our postindustrial society. Additionally, this article shows how both theoretical frameworks of social control and conflict can inform and influence each other in terms of arriving at a more comprehensive understanding of the dynamics involved in delinquent behavior.

A recently formulated power-control theory of common delinquent behavior (Hagan, Gillis, & Simpson, 1985) brings together a macro-level consideration of class in the workplace with a micro-level analysis of gender differences in the parental control and delinquent behavior of adolescents. This initial formulation of power-control theory was based on a class analysis of heads of households. However, it is increasingly evident that power in the family derives from the positions in the workplace held by husbands *and* wives (Coser & Coser, 1974). . . .

The question for power-control theory therefore is this: What differences do the relative class positions of husbands *and* wives in the workplace make for gender variations in parental control and in delinquent behavior of adolescents? This paper extends power-control theory by developing a model of familial class relations

that is then used to answer this question. In this model, power-control theory subsumes two earlier deprivation and liberation theories of gender and delinquency.

The ability of power-control theory to subsume earlier formulations is important because, as Homans points out, a good test of a theory is its ability to deduce a variety of empirical findings from a limited number of general propositions, "with the help of a variety of given conditions" (1967, p. 27). Below, we demonstrate that circumstances of deprivation and liberation constitute scope conditions within which power-control theory makes important, and perhaps surprisingly similar, predictions. However, specification of these scope conditions requires an analysis of the class dynamics of the family. The origins of this class analysis are in the deprivation and liberation theories of gender and delinquency.

Hagan, J., Simpson, J., & Gillis, A. R. (1987). Class in the household: A power-control theory of gender and delinquency. *American Journal of Sociology, 92,* 788-816.

FROM DEPRIVATION TO LIBERATION

It is well known that men markedly exceed women in criminality, and, until recently, it was believed that only economic deprivation might appreciably alter this relationship. For example, early in this century Bonger articulated the important effect deprivation may have on gender and crime, observing that "the criminality of men differs more from that of women in the well-to-do classes than in classes less privileged" (1916, p. 477). Bonger's point is that differences in the "manner of life" for the sexes decrease as we descend the social scale and that therefore only in the underclasses should the criminality of women be expected to approach that of men.

A modern version of this deprivation theory of gender and crime is offered by Giordano, Kerbel, and Dudley, who argue that contemporary increases in the criminality of women "reflect the fact that certain categories of women (e.g., young, single, minority) are now in an even more unfavorable position in the labor market at the same time that they are increasingly expected to function independently" (1981, p. 81). The Giordano et al. formulation focuses particular attention on female-headed households, which are of recurring concern in contemporary studies of delinquency and poverty (see McLanahan, 1985). These households are of special interest for our extension of power-control theory and our analysis of the class dynamics of the family. Because men are not an integral part of these households, these families constitute a unique comparison group that is useful in assessing the impact on children of power relations between husbands and wives in households with two active parents.

The "expectations of independence" noted by Giordano et al. bring us to the liberation theory of gender and crime. This theory is most provocatively formulated by Freda Adler (1975), who asserts that female criminal behavior has become widespread in recent years largely as a result of the women's movement. Adler argues that we are observing "a gradual but accelerating social revolution in which women are closing many of the gaps, social and criminal, that have separated them from men" (1979, pp. 93-94). This is clearly a different kind of formulation from that found in the writings about deprivation and gender discussed previously. However, both deprivation and liberation are assumed to decrease differences between men and women. "The closer they get," writes Adler, "the more alike they look and act. . . . Differences do exist . . . but it seems clear that those differences are not of prime importance in understanding female criminality" (1979, p. 94).

Perhaps the most interesting fact about the deprivation and liberation theories is that, although they both specify conditions under which men and women seem to become more alike, both socially and in terms of criminality, they do so by pointing to opposite ends of the class structure. While deprivation theory points to the lower end, and, increasingly, to female-headed households, liberation theory points to the upper end, where the liberation of women may be most likely to occur. Empirical tests of deprivation and liberation theories of gender and crime have produced equivocal results (for a recent review of this literature, see Box & Hale, 1984). We believe this is because the structural relationships that can result in gender equality and that are found at high and low positions in the class hierarchy have not yet been adequately conceptualized or operationalized.

POWER-CONTROL THEORY AND THE CLASS DYNAMICS OF THE FAMILY

Our extension of power-control theory begins with the observation of Weber (1947) that an important juncture in the development of modern capitalism was the separation of the workplace from the home. Two distinct spheres, which Weber regarded as crucial to the rationalization of an industrial capitalist economy, resulted from this separation: the first was populated by women and focused on domestic labor and consumption, and the second was populated by men and centered around labor power and direct production. The new family, and particularly its mothers, was responsible for socially reproducing (Vogel, 1983) the gender division of these separate spheres. This family was patriarchal in form and created a "cult of domesticity" around women (Welter, 1966).

Today, there is a declining division of the consumption and production spheres, which is reflected in the increased participation of women in the labor force (Coser, 1985). The studies mentioned above indicate that, as women joined the labor force, they gained new power in the family, particularly in the upper class. This results in a considerable variation in family structures in our model of family class relations. These structures can be thought of as varying between two extreme family class relations that form real-life counterparts to two ideal-type families.

The first of these ideal types is largely a residue from the earlier period, in which the consumption and production spheres were more strictly divided by gender. To reflect this legacy, we will call this the patriarchal family. Of the family class relations we identify below, the one that should most closely correspond to the ideal-type patriarchal family consists of a husband who is employed in an authority position and a wife who is not employed outside the home. It seems plausible that patriarchal families would tend to socially reproduce daughters who focus their futures around domestic labor and consumption, as contrasted with sons who are prepared for participation in direct production. We will say more about how this happens. Here we simply repeat that Weber regarded this process of social reproduction as crucial to the rationalization of industrial capitalism.

At the other extreme is an ideal type we call the egalitarian family, in which the consumption and production spheres are undivided by gender. Of the family class relations we identify below, the one that should most closely correspond to the ideal-type egalitarian family includes a mother and father who both are employed in authority positions outside the home. It seems plausible that egalitarian families will tend to socially reproduce daughters who are prepared along with sons to join the production sphere. Such families are therefore a part of an overlapping of the consumption and production spheres, which a postindustrial society no longer so clearly keeps apart; such families are a part as well as a product of changing economic relations.

So the patriarchal family perpetuates a gender division in the consumption and production spheres, whereas the egalitarian family facilitates an overlapping of these spheres. How does this happen and what are its consequences? Power-control theory answers these questions by joining a class analysis of the family with an analysis of domestic social control labor, the link between them being based on parents' social reproduction of their own power relationships through the control of their children. The key process involves an instrument-object relationship (Hagan, Simpson, & Gillis, 1979) that is at its extreme in the patriarchal family. Here fathers and especially mothers (i.e., as instruments of social control) are expected to control their daughters more than they do their sons (i.e., objects of social control). In regard to mothers, we should note that our point here is not that they are, in any ultimate causal sense, more important than fathers in the control of daughters but rather that mothers are assigned a key instrumental role that involves them more in the day-to-day control of their children, especially their daughters, in patriarchal families. This imbalanced instrument-object relationship is a product of a division in domestic social control labor and is a distinguishing feature of the control of daughters in patriarchal families. The instrument-object relationship is a key part of the way in which patriarchal families socially reproduce a gender division in the spheres of consumption and production.

Alternatively, it is through the diminution of this relationship that egalitarian families can generationally reproduce an overlap of the production and consumption spheres. This does not necessarily mean that fathers will become as involved as mothers are in the parental control of children; indeed, there is continuing evidence that this is not the case (e.g., Huber, 1976). What it does mean is that parents in egalitarian families will redistribute their control efforts so that daughters are subjected to controls more like those imposed on sons. In other words, in egalitarian families, as mothers gain power relative to husbands, daughters gain freedom relative to sons. In terms of social reproduction, the presence of the imbalanced instrument-object relationship helps perpetuate patriarchy and its absence facilitates equality.

Our next theoretical task is to link this discussion of ideal-type families and the instrument-object relationship with predicted gender differences in common delinquent behavior. This final intervening link involves attitudes toward risk taking. At one extreme, the patriarchal family and its acute instrument-object relationship between parents and daughters engenders a lower preference for risk taking among daughters. Risk taking is the antithesis of the passivity that distinguishes the "cult of domesticity." So, in patriarchal families, daughters are taught by their parents to avoid risk. Alternatively, in egalitarian families, daughters and sons alike are encouraged to be more open to risk taking. In part, this accommodation of risk is an anticipation of its role in the entrepreneurial and other activities associated with the production sphere, for which daughters and sons are similarly prepared in egalitarian families. Control theories have often regarded delinquency as a form of risk taking (Thrasher, 1937; Bordua, 1961; Hirschi, 1969), sometimes seeing it as an unanticipated consequence of a rewarded willingness to take risks (Veblen, 1934, p. 237; Sykes & Matza, 1961, p. 718). Bearing this in mind, we use power-control theory to predict that patriarchal families will be characterized by large gender differences in common delinquent behavior while egalitarian families will be characterized by smaller gender differences in delinquency. In egalitarian families, daughters become more like sons in their involvement in such forms of risk taking as delinquency.

Note that we have not yet said anything about either the female-headed households emphasized in deprivation theory or the various other kinds of households that we will be considering. We have formulated the theory in terms of households with both parents present and in terms of the polar ideal types of power relations (patriarchal and egalitarian) that can result. However, the theory does have important implications for female-headed households, as well as for other kinds of families. For example, because fathers are not an integral part of female-headed households, there should be no manifest power imbalance between parents, and therefore, here, too, daughters should gain in freedom relative to sons. These female-headed households provide a unique kind of comparison group; a special kind of egalitarian family that allows us to test our theory further. The expectation is that female-headed households should parallel other kinds of egalitarian households in many of the characteristics and consequences so far discussed. It is the common focus on freedom from male domination in these different kinds of households that allows our extension of power-control theory to subsume both deprivation and liberation theories of gender and delinquency. . . .

A DAHRENDORFIAN MODEL OF FAMILY CLASS RELATIONS

The extension of power-control theory tested here asserts that the gender-based relationships we have discussed are conditioned by the combined class positions of fathers and mothers (i.e., the class composition of the household). Parents of 463 students from a survey conducted in 1979 in the Toronto metropolitan area (see Hagan et al., 1985) were followed up by telephone to collect the information we now use to construct a new model of family class relations.

Our new model of family class relations is based on Dahrendorfian conceptions of power and authority and their use in the control of collective units. Following Dahrendorf (1959, p. 198), these collective units include all "imperatively coordinated associations"; that is, they include the family as well as the workplace. Because they occupy so central a place in most people's lives, authority relations in industrial production often overshadow and determine authority relations in other collective units, including the family (see Litwak, 1968). . . .

Dahrendorfian classes (see Dahrendorf, 1959, pp. 166-74) are distinguished on the basis of their relations to authority. We follow Lopreato (1968) and Robinson and Kelly (1979) in using the terms "command class" and "obey class" to distinguish Dahrendorfian class positions. Members of the command class exercise authority, regardless of whether they are subject to it themselves. In contrast, persons in the *obey* class are subject to the authority of others and exercise none themselves. Finally, a small classless group neither exercises authority nor is subject to it; its members work on their own. Robinson and Kelly (1979, p. 44) demonstrate that separating the latter classless group from the obey class adds nothing to the explained variance in their analysis of income and attitudes, so these classes are therefore collapsed in our analysis.

We use the above ideas in the following ways: We begin with households in which both parents are present and the father is employed (female-headed households are brought into our analysis below). In these households, fathers are categorized as exercising authority on the basis of affirmative responses to questions asking whether there are people who work for him or

Table 15.1   Dahrendorfian Model of Family Class Relations

	Husband's Authority in Workplace	
Wife's Authority in Workplace	Has Authority	Has No Authority
Has authority	Upper command class: husband and wife in command class (12.45% [57])[a]	Husband in obey class and wife in command class (6.77% [31])[b]
Has no authority	Husband in command class and wife in obey class (20.96% [96])[b]	Upper obey class: husband and wife in obey class (18.12% [83])[a]
Not employed	Husband in command class and wife not employed (16.38% [75])[b]	Lower obey class: husband in obey class and wife not employed (10.48% [48])[a]

Note: Family class relation not subsumable under table categories: female-headed household (14.85% [68]).
a. Balanced class relation.
b. Unbalanced class relation.

are supervised by him. Where these conditions are not met, fathers are categorized as not exercising authority. Mothers are divided into three categories, being considered (1) unemployed if they indicate, in response to an item asking about full- or part-time work, that they were "not employed during the past year," or, if they are or were employed part- or full-time during that period, as (2) exercising or (3) not exercising authority on the basis of responses to questions like those posed for fathers. The dichotomized measure of father's workplace authority is then cross-classified with our trichotomized measure of mother's workplace authority to generate the six family class relations indicated in Table 15.1. . . .[1]

. . . [Three of the] family class relations in Table 15.1 are . . . characterized by an unbalanced authority-subject relationship, in that one member of the household has authority in the workplace while the other does not. In two of these conditions, the father occupies a position of authority while the mother is either unemployed (16.38%) or employed in a position without authority (20.96%). These are the family class relations that come closest to matching the conditions of the ideal-type patriarchal family described above, with the first relation providing the clearest empirical match. The final and most unusual family class relation (6.77%) shows the father employed in a position without authority and the mother employed in one with authority. Because this kind of family is so atypical, in size as well as meaning, we do not consider it in subsequent analyses. The

power differential in the above families is indicated in Table 15.1 by their aggregate designation as "unbalanced class relations.". . .

Finally, a Marxian dimension can be added to the above model by including consideration of business ownership as a means of distinguishing, within the Dahrendorfian upper command class, between spouses in the "capitalist" or "employer class" and spouses in the "managerial class." This further distinction allows us to isolate a class that comes even closer to the social relations that should form the basis of the ideal-type egalitarian family (i.e., families in which the spouses are both managers) and a class that reintroduces the potential for patriarchy (i.e., a family class structure in which the husband is an employer while the wife is only a manager). However, this modification of our model involves the creation of very small class categories, and we will therefore defer their consideration.

Again, our basic premise is that authority in the workplace is translated into power in the household, with consequent effects on the relationship between gender and delinquency. More specifically, our refined power-control theory predicts that the relationship between gender and delinquency should be reduced in those family class structures in which the potential for the existence of more balanced, egalitarian family relations is greatest—that is, in the lower levels of the class structure (e.g., in the upper obey class and in female-headed households) and also in the higher levels of the class structure (e.g., in the upper command class).

Alternatively, the relationship between gender and delinquency should be most intense in the unbalanced family class relations that most closely approximate an ideal-type patriarchal family, that is, in those situations in which the father has authority in the workplace and the mother is either unemployed or employed in an obey-class position.

The intervening theoretical link in these predictions is that, in the class relations that characterize life in female-headed, upper-obey-class and upper-command-class families, mothers and fathers are less likely to reproduce, through the control of their daughters, the aversion to risk taking that produces large gender differences in delinquency. In these more balanced, egalitarian families, daughters and sons alike are prepared for life in the productive sphere. Alternatively, it is precisely this instrument-object relationship that our theory predicts will characterize the unbalanced class relations identified above, especially, for example, the family class relation that forms the most likely base for the ideal-type patriarchal family in our data—that is, that family class relation in which the husband occupies a command-class position and the spouse is either not employed or employed in a position without authority. It is here that we expect the instrument-object relationship between parents and daughters and the gender differences in risk preferences to be particularly apparent— and the gender-delinquency relationship to be consequently quite strong. These relationships, power-control theory argues, are part and parcel of patriarchy. They are the basis of the "cult of domesticity" and an accompanying gender division between the consumption and production spheres. . . .

MEASUREMENT OF INTERVENING AND DEPENDENT VARIABLES

Parental controls are the key intervening variables in our proposed power-control theory. Our additively scaled measures of maternal . . . and paternal . . . control ask, "Does your (father/mother) know (where you are/who you are with) when you are away from home?" We use these items to explore the instrument-object relationship emphasized between parents and daughters.

"Taste for risk" is a socially acquired attitude expected to mediate further the link between gender and delinquency. Taste for risk . . . is measured by adding Likert-scaled responses to two statements: "I like to take risks" and "The things I like to do best are dangerous." Power-control theory predicts that taste for risk is sexually stratified and that this attitude in turn stratifies perceived risks of getting caught in delinquent behavior, our last intervening link. Three "risk of getting caught" items from the work of Jensen, Erickson, and Gibbs (1978) form an additive scale. . . . They involve the following estimations: "Could you (break into a spot/steal from a store/write graffiti) and not get caught?"

We use an adapted version of Hirschi's (1969) self-report delinquency scale as our dependent variable. The six-item additive scale asked how often in the last year the respondents had taken little things (worth less than $2/between $2 and $50/more than $50) that did not belong to them; taken a [car] for a ride without the owner's permission; purposely banged up something that did not belong to them; and, not counting fights with a brother or sister, purposely beaten up on anyone or hurt anyone. . . .

DISCUSSION AND CONCLUSIONS

. . . . Our data are generally consistent with this extension of power-control theory. For example, in our most patriarchal families, in which fathers have authority in the workplace and mothers are not employed outside the home, the instrument-object relationship is most acute; daughters are discouraged from taking risks, and sons are more delinquent than daughters. In more egalitarian kinds of families—for example, those in which mothers and fathers both have authority in the workplace—the instrument-object relationship between parents and daughters is reduced, risk preferences of daughters are more like those of sons, and gender differences in delinquency decline, with average levels of delinquency among daughters increasing. Interestingly, these latter patterns also prevail in families from which fathers are largely absent (i.e., female-headed households). So, apparently, circumstances of both liberation and deprivation can produce the results we have described. Power-control theory asserts that what both these kinds of circumstances have in common is a freedom from male domination; that is, our analyses demonstrate that gender differences result from unbalanced and patriarchal as compared with more balanced and egalitarian kinds of family class structures and, in turn, confirm that these differences can be removed when variables associated with unbalanced, patriarchal class relations are taken into account. When daughters are freed from patriarchal family relations, they too become delinquent.

A Marxian consideration of business ownership provides an interesting kind of additional evidence for our theory. This refinement of our class analysis further specified power relations that increased and decreased gender-control and gender-delinquency relationships. More specifically, within the upper command class, we were able to show that extremely large gender differentials in maternal control and delinquency occur when the father is in the employer class and the mother is in the manager class and that these differentials are almost entirely absent when both spouses occupy managerial positions. The latter is the most egalitarian kind of family structure we were able to establish in our data, with the possible exception of female-headed households (from which fathers are largely absent). These are the two kinds of families in our data in which daughters are freest to be delinquent.

We should again emphasize that, by giving particular attention here to the instrument-object relationship between mothers and daughters, we have not meant to imply that mothers are, in any ultimate causal sense, more responsible than fathers for the control of daughters. Our point is that, in patriarchal settings, mothers in particular are assigned an instrumental role in imposing this selective control. Our theory actually implies that fathers and/or a patriarchal social structure are the sources of this role assignment. Exactly how, why, and with what consequences this role assignment occurs are important issues for further research. One purpose of power-control theory is to call attention to such issues.

By fully incorporating power relations between spouses into our class analysis, using a common set of concepts, and focusing on power relations at low and high ends of the class structure, we can use power-control theory to account for declines in gender-delinquency relationships that previously either went unexplained or required for their explanation separate theories of deprivation and liberation. We have here reduced those two theories to one power-control theory. . . .

DISCUSSION QUESTIONS

1. How does this article extend the authors' earlier conception of power-control theory? What is the importance of the deprivation and liberation theories of gender and delinquency to this new reformulation and extension?

2. How do the class dynamics of the family play out in terms of power-control theory? Specifically, discuss the different ideal family types and how they relate to social class, control, and power.

3. What role does risk taking, as delinquency, play in the relationship between family structure and the instrument-object relationships in that structure?

4. Discuss the Dahrendorfian model of family-class relations. How do the authors integrate it with their theories about family structure and delinquency? Which family structure and workplace authority is the best predictor of male and female delinquency?

NOTE

1 Our operational definition of a female-headed household is one in which the mother is not married and has affirmatively answered a question asking whether she is the sole or major source of family income. This operationalization excludes 11 cases in which the spouses are no longer married but the spouse is still the major source of income. These cases illustrate a more general point—that when fathers leave, they nonetheless often maintain some kind of presence in the family. That is why we include a paternal control variable in our analysis of female-headed families.

REFERENCE

Dahrendorf, R. (1959). *Class and class conflict in industrial society*. Palo Alto, CA: Stanford University Press.

16

Charles Tittle's Control Balance and Criminological Theory

John Braithwaite

EDITOR'S INTRODUCTION—Though it is considered a type of control theory, Charles Tittle's *control balance* theory of deviance is really an integrated approach that incorporates essential elements from differential association, Merton's anomie, Marxian conflict, social control, labeling, deterrence, and routine activities theories (Vold, Bernard, & Snipes, 1998). Tittle (1995) claims that these other approaches do not fully account for a broad range of deviant behaviors. Tittle's main premise is that "the amount of control to which an individual is subject, relative to the amount of control he or she can exercise, determines the probability of deviance occurring as well as the type of deviance likely to occur" (p. 135). The theory accepts the central thesis of control theories in that controls are seen as the predominant variables explaining conformity. However, the control balance theory contradicts other theories because it also maintains that control is the central motivating factor that explains deviance. In other words, the theory argues that people who are controlled by others (i.e., having a "control deficit") tend to engage in deviance to escape that control, whereas people who possess control (i.e., having a "control surplus") tend to engage in deviance in order to further it (Tittle, 1995). In this, conformity is defined in terms of "control balance" rather than as control itself: People will engage in conforming behavior when they perceive that the control they exert over others is equal to the control that others exert over them. Deviance is placed on the ends of two extremes: It is committed by those who have the least and those who have the most control (Tittle, 1995).

In his article, Braithwaite contends that although Tittle's control balance theory of deviance makes an important theoretical contribution to the theoretical literature, it should be simplified into a theory that possesses more explanatory power and greater parsimony. Important in Tittle's (1995) theory is his definition of deviance, which he defines as "any behavior that the majority of a given group regards as unacceptable or that typically evokes a collective response of a negative type" (p. 124). But rather than constructing deviance as a single construct, Tittle divides deviance into six types: predation, exploitation, defiance, plunder, decadence, and submission.

For Braithwaite, this is one source of the problem with Tittle's theory. Braithwaite maintains that Tittle's theory could be simplified by conceptualizing it as a "theory of predation" rather than a "theory of deviance." Braithwaite states that predatory deviance (i.e., directly taking things from others, directly inflicting violence on them, or directly forcing them to do things they do not want to do, such as rape) is lowest in societies where control ratios are more balanced, where small proportions of the population are in control deficit or control surplus. Control ratios refer to the degree of control one can exercise relative to the control that one experiences. Because power can corrupt in a number of different ways, predatory deviance increases consistently with increasing control surpluses. However, predatory deviance increases with widening control deficits only up to a certain point, at which people give up on resistance (e.g., women who have been battered for long periods of time may give up, which could lead to severe depression and possibly suicide). Past this point, predatory deviance falls and retreatist forms of deviance, such as drug abuse and suicide, increase. Braithwaite adds that the explanatory power of Tittle's theory comes from the fact that people with control imbalances find themselves exposed to greater provocation and opportunity for deviance. This aspect of the theory provides a good account of the patterning of deviance by gender, race, and age.

In addition to reformulating part of Tittle's theory, Braithwaite expands upon this approach by advancing four normative implications of the theory. They include a greater equality of control; republican virtue in the exercise of control; given these two implications, then greater acceptance of control; and, last, nurture of social bonds, social support, and community. The simplification proposed by Braithwaite allows for a more well-designed synthesis of explanatory and normative theory, but systematic empirical research will be needed to determine whether this reformulation or Tittle's original theory has more explanatory power.

I n *Control Balance: Toward a General Theory of Deviance*, Charles Tittle (1995) has given us one of the more important theoretical contributions to the sociology of deviance. Tittle advances in a bold way Jack Gibbs' (1989) idea that control should become the central organizing concept of the discipline of sociology. The objectives of this chapter are to show why the theory of control balance is a major advance, yet to show how it could and should be simplified into a theory that has at once more explanatory power and greater parsimony. . . .

THE IMPORTANCE OF TITTLE'S CONTRIBUTION

The variable to be explained in Tittle's theory is 'deviance' defined as 'any behavior that the majority of a given group regards as unacceptable or that typically evokes a collective response of a negative type' (Tittle, 1995, p. 124). The crucial independent variable is the 'control ratio.' The control ratio is the degree of control that one can exercise relative to that which one

experiences. If by virtue of the roles and statuses one occupies and the personal strengths one has, one has the potential to exert more control over others and their environment than others (and the environment) do in fact exert over oneself, then one has a control surplus. Obversely, a person who by virtue of lowly status has little potential to control but who actually experiences enormous control has a control deficit.

The interesting theoretical move Tittle makes is to suggest that either kind of control imbalance—surplus or deficit—conduces to deviance. To see why this is an important move, consider one of the most influential sentences in the history of criminology, first uttered by Edwin Sutherland in his 1939 Presidential address to the American Sociological Society: 'If it can be shown that white collar crimes are frequent, a general theory that crime is due to poverty and its related pathologies is shown to be invalid' (Sutherland, 1983, p. 7). In light of *Control Balance*, a riposte to Sutherland is: If it can be shown that both control surpluses and control deficits explain deviance, it may be that crime in the suites can be explained by control surplus,

Braithwaite, J. (1997). Charles Tittle's control balance and criminological theory. *Theoretical Criminology, 1*, 77-97.

crime in the streets by control deficit, so that control imbalance structured into a society becomes a common cause of both types of crime. Another of what Kathleen Daly (1995) describes as the central paradoxes of crime and justice that Tittle's theory enables us to tackle is why women and girls in all societies we know commit much less crime than men and boys, while it is the latter who enjoy the greater wealth and power. If both control surplus and control deficit are involved in the explanation of crime, then as we will see below, we might come to grips with this paradox as well. And a good many more which are compellingly documented in Tittle's monograph.

Another attractive feature of Tittle's theory is that it manages synthesis of explanation by rational choice, virtuous choice and sociology of the emotions mechanisms. Unlike almost all traditional criminological theories, Tittle's theory includes an account of why people are motivated to commit crime. For present purposes, the crucial part of that motivational story is that the pursuit of autonomy is more or less a learned human universal. This is true to the point where when people enjoy a control surplus, they are still motivated to extend it. When they suffer a control deficit, they are motivated to eliminate it. Deviance results when *motivation* is triggered by *provocation* and enabled by the presence of *opportunity* and absence of *constraint.* Building opportunity and constraint into the theory brings into play the explanatory power of rational choice. Provocation is built into the theory in a way that brings the sociology of the emotions in. A person highly motivated to deviate by virtue of a control deficit, who is exposed to an opportunity with low risk that constraint would be mobilized may be virtuous enough not to deviate until there is a provocation—a racial insult or some other discourtesy, challenge or display of vulnerability that elicits resentment or shame over a control deficit (or temptation to exploit in the case of a control surplus). Provocations are 'contextual features that cause people to become more keenly cognizant of their control ratios and the possibilities of altering them through deviant behavior' (Tittle, 1995, p. 163). *Virtue* (or 'moral commitment' as Tittle prefers in his more normatively neutral approach) is snuck into the theory here not as a causal mainspring (like motivation, provocation, opportunity and constraint)

but as a limiting contingency on the operation of those mainsprings of the theory (Tittle, 1995, pp. 208-9). At least it is there.

Tittle's core contention that control imbalance motivates and explains rates and types of deviance seems a powerful and testable explanation for a lot of things we know from the sociology of deviance. Equally, his claim that control imbalance affects patterns of provocation, opportunity and constraint, which in turn affect deviance, adds to the power of the theory, if not to its testability. Tittle suggests in various places (e.g. pp. 170, 177, 182, 276) that deviance is a result of a desire to rectify a control imbalance. This is odd because while those with a control deficit may do this, those with control surpluses pursue ever bigger surpluses. It is both simpler and more plausible to assert that most people want more control, however much they have, than that they seek to 'rectify the [control] imbalance' (p. 177). Elsewhere, Tittle is more careful on this matter, if more convoluted, where he speaks of 'motivation to correct a control imbalance or to extend a control surplus' (p. 182). . . .

But why do control surpluses stimulate deviance? Tittle has a kind of 'power corrupts' explanation here. One effect of having a control surplus is that other people recognize this and subordinate themselves to you; most people with a control surplus take advantage of this proffered subordination. Because it is harder to control someone with a control surplus (by definition), deviance carries lower risk for persons with control surpluses. Therefore, they can and do take advantage of the subordination preferred to them in deviant ways when this is gratifying. . . .

According to Tittle, the iterated subordination experienced by persons with control surpluses renders them ungrateful for the things subordinates are subordinate about. They come to presume subordination to the point where any resistance to it becomes an insult and a provocation to deviance.

EFFECTS OF REDISTRIBUTING CONTROL

Tittle's control ratio idea seems a more fruitful way of reconceptualizing my own work on why reducing inequality based on class, race, sex, age and political power (slavery, totalitarianism) might simultaneously reduce crimes of exploitation and crimes of the exploited, crimes of the powerful and crimes of the powerless (Braithwaite, 1979, 1991). A materialist and then a sociology of the emotions argument will be reformulated into Tittle's framework here. The first is an opportunity theory argument that: (1) crime is motivated in part by needs, often transient, episodic needs (Wright & Decker, 1994, pp. 36-48); (2) needs are more likely to be satisfied as control ratios increase; (3) policies to foster control balance will do more to increase the need satisfaction of those with control deficits than to decrease the need satisfaction of those with control surpluses. The latter is true because of a standard welfare economics point that marginal gains from satisfying needs decline as need satisfaction increases. . . . When people feel that few of their needs are met, they are more likely to perceive that they have little to lose through a criminal conviction, little stake in conformity. In contrast, a person with basic needs satisfied will suffer more from a prison sentence that deprives him of a comfortable home, a loving family life and a stimulating job.

Because people with large control surpluses are likely to be in a position where most of their needs are met, they are most unlikely to steal in order to increase need satisfaction. Their theft is more likely to be motivated by greed. The reformulated materialist argument becomes therefore that control imbalance increases.

People with control surpluses tend to steal to gratify greed; in Marxist terms, not to acquire goods for use, but acquisition of goods for exchange that are surplus to what is required for use. Control surpluses result in the accumulation of economic surpluses to control. Surplus can be disposed of in a variety of ways such as inheritance, charitable contributions and conspicuous consumption to signify status. The important application of surpluses from a criminological point of view, however, is through exchanges which constitute new illegitimate opportunities. The best way to rob a bank is to own it. But that in turn requires a large quantity of capital. . . .

. . . Extreme control surpluses foster extraordinarily lucrative minority strategies. People and organizations that control large surpluses can pursue criminal strategies that are novel and that excel because they cannot be contemplated by those without extreme surpluses. It follows from Cohen and Machalek's (1988) analysis that those with extreme control surpluses will rarely resort to the illegitimate means which are the deviant staples of those with control deficits, because they can secure much higher returns by pursuing strategies to which those with control deficits have no access. There will be little direct competition between the control deficit criminal and the control surplus criminal. Yet it would be a mistake to conclude that separate explanations are required simply because these worlds of deviance take such different forms. On the contrary, Tittle's theory shows how there can be a common explanation for the two patterns of deviance in the form of the extent of control balance or imbalance.

Just as greed fetishizes money for its value for exchange rather than use, so control itself can be fetishized. Control can be exchanged, invested to generate more control. Hence, the crimes of J. Edgar Hoover (Geis & Goff, 1990) might be understood in terms of an insatiable desire to accumulate more power for exchange. In this way, the purchase of the materialist analysis can be extended beyond property crime to many other forms of deviance. The most terrible crimes of our history, of Hitler against the Jews, Cortez and the Conquistadors, the genocides in Rwanda and Cambodia, are explained by the pursuit of power by actors whose lust to dominate was insatiable, who would never have been satisfied by a balance of control.

The second argument to be reconceptualized from Braithwaite (1991) is directly adopted by Tittle. This is a sociology of the emotions account about control ratios and humiliation. Tittle reads the criminal episodes analysed by Jack Katz (1988) rather as I do, and somewhat differently from the way Katz himself reads them, since Katz eschews general explanation. 'The latent argument' in Katz, according to Tittle (Tittle, 1995, p. 278), is that 'deviant behavior is attractive because it puts the person in control.' Indeed, the argument is not very latent when Katz characterizes the 'badass,' for example, as one who takes pride in defiance at being bad:

> The badass, with searing purposiveness, tries to scare humiliation off; as one ex-punk explained to

Crimes of poverty (control deficit)	*Crimes of wealth (control surplus)*
motivated by *need*	motivated by *greed*
for goods for *use*	for goods for *exchange* (that are surplus to those required for use)

me, after years of adolescent anxiety about the ugliness of his complexion and the stupidness of his every word, he found a wonderful calm in making 'them' anxious about *his* perceptions and understandings. (Katz, 1988, pp. 312-313)

Beyond Katz, Tittle quotes ethnographies of burglars, for example: 'As I rifled through those people's most private possessions, I felt a peculiar power over them, even though we'd never met' (Tittle, 1995, p. 193). Katz does see violence as 'livid with the awareness of humiliation' (Katz, 1988, p. 23). Rage transcends the offender's humiliation by taking him to dominance over a proximate person. Just as humiliation of the offender is implicated in the onset of his rage, so the need to humiliate the victim enables her humiliation. Similar conclusions have been reached by psychiatric scholars (Kohut, 1972; Lewis, 1971; Lansky, 1984, 1987) and other scholars working in the sociology of the emotions tradition (Scheff, 1987; Scheff and Retzinger, 1991).

. . . . Like the materialist argument, the sociology of the emotions argument applies with as much force to crimes of control surplus as to those of control deficit. Hitler, as I have already said, enjoyed a control surplus. His fascism was structurally humiliating. In *Mein Kampf* he explained how the German people had been humiliated at Versailles, tricked and betrayed by Jews for generations. His was an appeal to a humiliated people, an appeal to transcend it through the violent assertion of world domination, and along the way to assert a right to humiliate the Jews. The historical stupidity of the Allies at Versailles was to saddle the Germans with a control imbalance which was an emotional as well as a material burden they were bound to defy (Scheff, 1994). It was the emotional dynamics of that control imbalance that handed the world the holocaust. An enormous appeal of Tittle's theory is the sweep of its relevance—from the most fragmentary domestic altercation to explaining global conflicts.

CONTROL RATIOS AND TYPES OF DEVIANCE

The aspect of Tittle's theory I would want to abandon is his account of how different types of deviance are associated with different levels of control imbalance. Consider his account of the effect of different levels of control surplus. When individuals exercise slightly more control than that to which they are subject, *exploitation* is said to be the most common form of deviance, examples of which are price-fixing, shake-down schemes by gang leaders who sell protection to merchants, bribery and extortion. In the zone of medium control surplus, the modal type of deviance shifts from exploitation to *plunder*—

> selfish acts—forms of plunder—that include things like environmental pollution inflicted by imperialist countries whose leaders are in search of scarce resources in underdeveloped countries, programs of massive destruction of forests or rivers for the personal gain of corporate owners or executives, unrealistic taxes or work programs imposed by autocratic rulers, enslavement of natives by invading forces for the benefit of military commanders, pillage of communities by hoods doing the bidding of crime bosses, pogroms. . . . (Tittle, 1995, p. 191)

When control surpluses are very large, *decadence* becomes the characteristic form of deviance. . . . The distinctions between exploitation, plunder and decadence are not clearly defined. Nor do they seem distinctions worth making. Tittle gives no empirical evidence to suggest that there might be some correspondence between the three zones of control surplus and these three types of deviance. So why render the theory more complex in this way? Why not adopt the more parsimonious, and one might add more plausible, view that the larger the control surplus, the more likely exploitation, plunder and decadence all become?

On the control deficit side, there are some suggestive empirical grounds for taking Tittle's partition into zones of deficit more seriously. Here *predation is* said to be associated with marginal control deficits. The classic instances of predation involve directly taking things from others, directly inflicting violence on them or directly forcing them to do things they do not want to do (e.g. rape). In the moderate zone of control deficit, defiance is said to be the modal form of deviance. Defiance means deviant acts of protest [of people] against the control to which they are subjected such as mocking authority or sullen conformity. Withdrawn or escapist deviance, such as 'alcoholism, drug abuse, suicide, family desertion, mental illness, or countercultural involvement' (Tittle, 1995, p. 190), is also a possibility in this intermediate zone of control deficit, though it is not clear how or whether most of this is classified as defiance. In the extreme zone of control deficit, submissive deviance is said to be typical. Perhaps controversially, Tittle suggests that most people find slavish submission or grovelling compliance deviant. People in this zone are so dominated, according to Tittle, that they are too afraid of countercontrol to engage in either predation or defiance.

Again, the distinctions among predation and defiance are not especially clear, though they are sharply distinguished from submissive deviance. But then one wonders that many withdrawn forms of deviance such as mental illness or drug abuse might not be submissive. While the categorization across the zones of control deficit is not very compelling, Tittle is on to an underlying insight. This is that more predatory forms of deviance require a certain degree of autonomy; they require that one not be so dominated as to be afraid of standing up to others. When control deficits are extreme, people may be so terrified of countercontrol that they are beyond predation and even beyond sullen forms of defiance. This core insight is not only plausible; in contrast with the control surplus distinctions there is some empirical evidence which suggests that plausibility. Tittle points out that submission or defiance was more common than predation among black Americans during the period of slavery (Tittle, 1995, p. 250). With emancipation, predation became more possible because the countercontrol they feared reduced as their domination became less total. . . .

Another form of support for Tittle's key insight here comes from experimental psychological research organized under Brehm's (1966) theory of psychological reactance as revised by Wortman and Brehm (1975). The key idea of the theory is that a threat to a freedom motivates the individual to restore that freedom. . . . Empirical work derived from the 'learned helplessness' research program (Seligman, 1975) led to a modification of Brehm's (1966) original reactance theory to accommodate the finding that extended experience with uncontrollable outcomes leads to passivity. The learned helplessness and psychological reactance literatures do highlight a problem with Tittle's theory. When there is a control deficit, deviance for Tittle is a way that people restore some sort of control. Yet submission, the form of deviance associated with the most extreme deficits, is hardly a means of restoring control; on the contrary, it amounts to yielding to a downward spiral into helplessness. As with the effect of control surpluses, there is therefore a need on the deficit side to reformulate the theory of control balance. The reformulation proposed is that as control deficits increase, predatory deviance increases up to a point where people become so dominated that the fear of countercontrol eventually throws this trend into reverse. Domination increases predation until people become so dominated that they are afraid to reassert their own control through predation (or even less predatory forms of defiance). Resistance is reinterpreted as pointless in the face of utter domination. At extremes of control deficit, people submit undefiantly or they withdraw, giving up on the mainstream of life, retreating into drugs, depression or even suicide. In summary, as control deficits become larger, predatory deviance increases until a point is reached where predation declines in favour of retreatist forms of deviance. To this control deficit reformulation, we can add the simplified surplus reformulation: as control surpluses increase, exploitation, plunder and decadence all increase. . . .

The following simpler theory has attractions. Predatory deviance is least likely in societies where high proportions of citizens are in control balance and low proportions in control deficit or surplus. Predatory deviance increases monotonically with increasing control surpluses; predatory deviance increases with rising control deficits up to the point where people give up on resistance (see Figure 16.1). Beyond

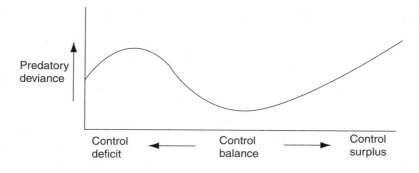

Figure 16.1 Hypothesized Simplification of the Relationship Between Control Imbalance and Predatory Deviance

this turning point, predatory deviance declines, submission increases, as does the deviance of disengagement—drug abuse, alcoholism, depressive disorders and suicide. The simplified theory is not meant to suggest that there is no difference between the predatory deviance on the surplus side compared with the deficit side of balance. While predatory deviance is enabled both by having nothing to lose (high deficit) and by having little likelihood of losing it (high surplus), the power dynamics of being in surplus enable forms of deviance which are impossible for those with little control, as we saw in the discussion of Cohen and Machalek (1988). In their choices of predation, the powerless must make the best of a bad job, while those with control surpluses can take advantage of a good job. Where there is competition between the two over the same predatory strategies, it is fragile. The small drug dealer can be crushed by a powerful organized criminal unless she finds a way of complementing him or picking up his crumbs.

There is no way of saying anything clear about the specific forms of deviance that will attract those with extreme control surpluses. According to the evolutionary ecological understanding of crime, as in nature, a strategy of predation is more likely to persist if it is different from that used by other predators. Predation flourishes on the basis of innovation to discover niches untouched by competitors. For this reason, criminologists do not even know about the most lucrative forms of crime among the powerful; they are lucrative precisely because so few have the knowledge and resources to exploit them. Similarly, as control is exerted to further narrow the predations available to the powerless, they innovate by trying new scams on people less powerful than themselves (either permanently or momentarily).

This simplified formulation salvages the really important aspects of the explanatory power of Tittle's theory. It explains why the retired elderly should engage in little predatory deviance—their control deficit is so high that they generally have given up on resistance to control. Similarly, the very young, those under 10, generally have yet to imagine that they might have the power for predatory deviance in response to the enormous control deficit they suffer. Yet it explains why by the time young people pass adolescence, they have rounded the turning point and are near the maximum risk of predatory deviance. It explains why women in circumstances of extreme family and workplace domination can be beyond feeling the power for predation, why the ratio of submissive and withdrawn deviance to predatory deviance is so high for them. It explains why 18th and 19th century African Americans might have been dominated beyond predation, while late 20th century African Americans can imagine predation as within their grasp. At the same time, the simplified version of the theory avoids some predictions that are unlikely to be sustained. For example, the fact that control ratios are higher for men than for women should imply under Tittle's original theory that both predation and defiance are more common for women than for men (see p. 173, this volume).

Control Ratios, Provocation and Opportunity

Part of Tittle's theory is that control imbalance explains deviance, not only because it increases motivation and emotional commitment to reclaim or extend control in ways such as those demonstrated by Katz (1988). The explanatory power of control imbalance also comes from the fact that people with control imbalances, according to Tittle, are exposed to greater provocation and opportunity for deviance. Hence, people who are dominated because of their race are also more likely to be *provoked* by racial insults and subtle forms of disrespect and as young people, they are exposed to the illegitimate *opportunities* constituted by stigmatized subcultures or criminal gangs that are organized in slums. Note the role of stigmatization in the constitution of criminal subcultures (Braithwaite, 1989, pp. 65-8, 127-33); put another way, criminal subculture formation maps the social structuring of provocation. Powerful men are provoked to predation and exploitation by the submission proffered by potential targets of their domination, by the way they experience power as unchecked, and by the opportunities (e.g. surplus capital for investment in scams) their control imbalance generates. On gender, the theory gives an interesting account of why men care more about loss or extension of control than women and how this engenders provocation (Tittle, 1995, p. 239).

Traditionally, and to some extent continuing into the present, the male role was defined by active subjugation of the forces of nature and protection of his domain. . . . These role distinctions made sense in primitive environments because they meshed with the superior physical strength of males and the relative confinement and dependency of females handicapped by child bearing and nursing. . . . Because of these role distinctions calling for dominance, males are more concerned about their relative control ratios. Consequently, they suffer much anxiety about whether they are living up to expectations, and uncertainty stimulates tests. Recurring challenges within male culture (Luckenbill, 1977, 1984) produce more potentially demeaning situational provocations than are faced by females. (Sanders, 1981; Short and Strodtbeck, 1974).

. . . . The extent to which people in different structural locations care about their domination is important because of the considerable experimental evidence that psychological reactance is greater when people care most about the freedoms under threat (Brehm & Brehm, 1981, pp. 58-63). Not only do crime-prone demographic groups such as adolescents, young adults and men care more about loss of control than others, those who select themselves into power-exerting vocations, such as politics, policing and the military, are likely to care more about debasement, humiliation and domination than those who have not been so socially selected. It is a recurrent tragedy of the human condition that those who are socially selected into the power-exerting vocations are so predisposed to predation and exploitation. This is one reason why throughout human history we have had so much rape in war, police violence, so much political corruption and war-mongering.

So the theory gives redundantly strong grounds for predicting some of the strongest correlates of predatory deviance we have—with age, gender, race and business and political elite status, plus a number of others that are discussed in the book itself.

Implications for Normative Political Theory

. . . . From the standpoint of republican political theory, what are the implications of the control balance explanatory theory? I will argue that they are:

1. greater equality of control;

2. republican virtue in the exercise of control;

3. given (1) and (2), greater acceptance of control;

4. nurture of social bonds, social support, community.

Greater Equality of Control

This is the only one of the four implications which Tittle himself explicitly draws. If the extent of control imbalance in a society predicts predatory deviance, then redistributing control from those with surpluses to those with deficits will simultaneously reduce the predations of the powerful and the predations of the powerless. An important qualification here is that redistribution will shift some people with large control deficits from submission and retreatist pathologies such as suicide and drug addiction to predation. From a republican perspective, this qualification is not a deeply troubling one, since submission, like predation, is a political state that is unattractive (see p. 172, this volume). . . .

. . . . Freedom as non-domination cannot be a practical accomplishment for someone who lives in abject poverty, for someone who has not been given the education accorded to those who are regarded as active citizens of the society under consideration. As in standard civic republican thinking (Sunstein, 1988), it follows that freedom and greater equality of control must be pursued through redistributing wealth from the rich to the poor.

Republican Virtue in the Exercise of Control

Of course, control cannot and should not be eliminated. Otherwise, individuals, families and societies could not get the things done that are needed for them to flourish. The republican normative dispensation is simply that control should be distributed in a more balanced way. But the other important element of the republican normative tradition is that it should be exercised in a more virtuous way. The key aspect of the virtuous exercise of control raised by Tittle's analysis is that it should be exercised without debasing, defiling or humiliating others, so that it does not become a provocation to predation. Republican control requires respect for persons, humility by the controllers. It rejects lording it over (to apply a feudal usage against which republicanism reacts), mastering (the reaction against slavery as the antithesis of citizenship), decreeing (the republican reaction against monarchy) or dictating (the republican reaction against totalitarianism) to the controlled. Commitment to an ideal of rule of law is one of the cultural preconditions for republican virtue in the exercise of control. The rule of law ideal means that no one feels they are above the law when they exercise control, not even the head of state. . . . The favoured republican way of exercising control virtuously is dialogue which leads to the voluntary assent of the controlled to their control (Sunstein, 1988). . . .

Greater Acceptance of Control

Tittle's work suggests that persons and types of persons (e.g. young men) who are less willing to accept control are more likely to respond to it with predatory reassertions of control. The psychological reactance literature shows that control is more likely to engender defiant reactions for freedoms over which we are more reluctant to accept control (Brehm & Brehm, 1981). It follows that if we can persuade people to be more accepting of control, there will be less predation. This is a worrying inference because if people are in slavery, republicans concerned about domination must want them to resist that domination rather than accept it, even if the effect is that their conduct becomes more predatory. At the same time, we know that control is necessary for most of the good things in life. . . .

We should support those controls that in their ultimate effects increase freedom as non-domination, resist controls that reduce republican freedom. In a society where the first two republican implications of control balance theory have been implemented—where equality of control is as great as is consistent with maximizing freedom as non-domination, where control is exercised with the virtue consistent with maximizing liberty—then we should want citizens to accept that control, enjoy its benefits.

Stronger Social Bonds, Social Support, Communities

. . . . Strong social bonds between individuals or strong communities at the macro level reduce predation and exploitation (Braithwaite, 1989). Where the social bond between an employer and employee is strong, the respect this breeds makes exploitation more difficult to sustain. Where social bonds in families are strong, predatory conduct is more vulnerable to shame because we care about the disapproval of those to whom we are strongly bonded (Braithwaite, 1989). Families are precisely the institution in modern society where we are most likely to learn the virtues of non-domination and respect for others because that is where social bonds tend to be strongest. In short, republican attraction to strong social bonds within strong communities arises from the fact that this creates the structural conditions where the first three republican normative implications of the control balance theory apply. . . .

DISCUSSION QUESTIONS

1. What roles do "deviance" and "control ratios" play in Tittle's theory? In what way(s) is a control imbalance—either a surplus or deficit—conducive to deviancy, according to Tittle's explication of his theory?

2. How does Braithwaite reformulate Tittle's theory by using a "materialist," or opportunity theory, argument and a "sociology of the emotions" argument? How do control surpluses and deficits influence motivation, provocation, opportunity, and constraint?

3. Braithwaite explains that the aspect of the theory that he wants to abandon is Tittle's account of how different types of deviance are associated with different levels of control imbalance. By abandoning this proposition, how does Braithwaite simplify Tittle's theory into a "theory of predation" rather than a "theory of deviance"?

4. According to Braithwaite, what are the normative implications of the control balance explanatory theory? In what ways does this approach provide a synthesis of normative theories and explanatory theories?

REFERENCES

Tittle, C. (1995). *Control balance: Toward a general theory of deviance.* Boulder, CO: Westview Press.

Vold, G. B., Bernard, T. J., & Snipes, J. B. (1998). *Theoretical criminology* (4th ed.). Oxford, UK: Oxford University Press.

17

THOUGHTS STIMULATED BY BRAITHWAITE'S ANALYSIS OF CONTROL BALANCE THEORY

CHARLES R. TITTLE

EDITOR'S INTRODUCTION—Tittle's reply to Braithwaite provides a unique point of analysis of the implications of *control balance* theory, as originally proposed by Tittle in his 1995 text *Control Balance: Toward a General Theory of Deviance*. Tittle attempted to accomplish two goals with his book. First, he wanted to set forth a paradigm for theory building, and second, he wanted to present an exemplar, or a prototype, to be used as a starting point for the application of that paradigm. A primary theme in the paradigm is that the theory must represent the collective efforts of a community of scholars. The paradigm also includes several technical suggestions for how to accomplish and structure the components of general theories. Tittle's exemplar, *control balance* theory, was then established. Braithwaite's article really represents a response to Tittle's invitation to scholars to consider the potential worth of control balance theory.

Although Tittle finds Braithwaite's suggestions and commentary to be informative and enlightening, he believes that Braithwaite may have misunderstood some of the central elements of control balance theory, mainly in terms of his suggestions of how the theory can be made more parsimonious. For example, Tittle states that he is "intrigued" by Braithwaite's suggested simplifications, which consist mainly of collapsing the categories of deviance and focusing on motivation for deviance as the prime causal force. According to Tittle, this simplification sacrifices the essence of the theory. Additionally, Tittle claims that Braithwaite may have misunderstood the implications of the theory for gender differences in the probabilities of predation and defiance.

These differences of opinion notwithstanding, Tittle does find common ground with Braithwaite on a couple of points. First, Tittle maintains that he is inclined to adopt Braithwaite's corollary of his parsimony suggestion, namely to abandon the effort to make qualitative distinctions among forms of deviance. According to Tittle, two other modifications suggested by Braithwaite—namely to characterize the unitary desire for autonomy now described as having two different thrusts as simply wanting more control and, second, to transform the theory into one of predation—might be acceptable, but adoption would be "premature" at this point. Finally, Tittle finds Braithwaite's suggestion that submission be regarded as a unique, nondeviant form of behavior appealing, and he fully endorses the idea and has begun to implement it in his work on this theory. But he does not think it would be wise to move ahead with the idea that some of the behaviors he considers "defiant" be reconceptualized as "submissive."

Generally speaking, both Braithwaite's and Tittle's works afford readers a more complete analysis of the control balance theory. In some ways, this format resembles the "author-meets-critic" panels, which are popular at professional conferences, though, of course, the dynamic, "live" interaction is missing here. Nonetheless, the exchange certainly provides fertile ground for further consideration, evaluation, and redevelopment of this approach to the problem of deviance.

My Reactions

I cannot really add anything to Braithwaite's discussion of the parallels between control balance theory and his work or to his application of control balancing ideas to philosophical questions about good societies, but it may be useful to address his proposed modifications of the theory. . . .

Modifications

Streamlining the Major Assumption

Instead of stating, as I do, that people with control deficits are predisposed to overcome them while people with control surpluses are predisposed to extend their surpluses, Braithwaite suggests that it would be better to say simply that people want more control, however much they have. . . .

However, distinctions between 'overcoming' a deficit and 'extending' a surplus were deliberately made for four specific reasons. One was to emphasize for the reader that the control balancing process applies to both ends of a continuum of relative control and is therefore capable of accounting for what has conventionally been called elite deviance as well as non-elite deviance. Second, since the activating mechanisms that transform predispositions into actual motivations for deviance—in one case sharply being reminded of one's subordination by confronting actual behavioral limitations and in the other . . . [case] acutely being prompted to recall one's dominance by encountering either prostrating responses from others or their resistance to being controlled—are somewhat different, it seems useful linguistically to recognize that something more than simply wanting more control is operative. Third, differentiating between

efforts to overcome deficits and efforts to extend surpluses calls attention to the non-linearity of the relationship between control ratios and the probability of deviance. As the theory is currently formulated, that relationship is U-shaped with the lowest probability of deviance in the center, or balanced, zone of the continuum, and increasing outward in both directions. To simplify as Braithwaite suggests, may mislead people who are accustomed to thinking in linear terms to assume that there is an increasing probability of deviance from one side of the control continuum to the other. If they study the theory carefully, they will not be misled, of course, but one of the strengths of the control balancing argument is its challenge to the linear model that has dominated theory and research about crime and deviance. I wanted that challenge to be clear, so it is enunciated linguistically by speaking of overcoming deficits and extending surpluses.

Finally, in trying to understand why there is a universal impulse for autonomy, I came to believe that the desire to overcome a control deficit is actually somewhat different from an urge to extend a control surplus, though they are both forms of autonomy seeking. Some speculations about their sources are offered in the book, although accounting for autonomy drives [is] in no way essential to the theory itself. I suggest that people develop a desire to escape control because they resent the dependence on and consequent subordination to adults inherent in their infancy and childhood. Simultaneously, they develop a desire to dominate because as infants and children they envy powerful adults and vicariously identify with those who exercise control. In my mind the two kinds of autonomy seeking are somewhat different, stem from different causes and, as noted above, are played out in the deviance-generating process somewhat differently. Hence, it seems worthwhile to

Tittle, C. R. (1997). Thoughts stimulated by Braithwaite's analysis of control balance theory. *Theoretical Criminology, 1*, 99-110.

maintain the distinction between overcoming a deficit and extending a surplus, and as long as that potential difference is not forgotten, it may be useful to simplify the language.

Collapse Categories of Autonomous Deviance

Braithwaite notes that the distinctions among types of deviance on both the repressive and autonomous sides of the control balance continuum are unclear. . . . I admit that the qualitative distinctions among the categories of deviance are imprecise. In fact, differentiating them qualitatively was a heuristic device, probably doomed to failure from the beginning. The theory is founded on the notion that deviance can be arrayed on a continuum of *seriousness* that reflects the likelihood of activating the potential countercontrol inherent in a control ratio. Some deviance is more likely to bring about counter-controlling responses than is other deviance. The more likely a form of deviance is to invoke countercontrol, the more of a control surplus one has to have in order to imagine realistically being able to experience its gratification without unbearable consequences. Trying to capture this quantitative dimension of seriousness in qualitative categories is not easy; and trying to reduce it to three such categories was probably a mistake. Yet, it seems quite contrary to the entire control balancing argument to imagine that the probabilities of all forms of autonomous deviance, regardless of their seriousness, or likelihood of stimulating countercontrol, are equal for a person with a specific control surplus. If decadence, or whatever one wants to call the most serious form of autonomous deviance, is . . . equally likely for a person with, say, a modest control surplus, as is exploitation, or whatever one wants to call the least serious form of autonomous deviance, then the theory of control *balancing* is useless.

I'm not sure Braithwaite realizes his proposed simplification in effect rejects, or reduces, the part played by constraint and thereby jeopardizes a central component of the theory; indeed, he seems to appreciate the effect of countercontrol when he describes the good society as one with balanced controls to restrain predation and when he analyses the effect of overwhelming constraint in producing submission. Yet, when this particular proposed modification is considered in conjunction with some of his other comments, it becomes clear that the part of control balance theory he finds appealing is that part portraying motivation for deviance as a reflection of a control imbalance. As I interpret the thrust of his remarks, he would like a control-oriented theory that explains deviance or crime mainly as a product of the strength of motivation—the greater the motivation for deviance, the greater the chances of any form of it occurring—with some accommodation for opportunity and moral elements. And he likes the idea that motivation stems from a control imbalance, so he would shift the focus of the causal process by which individuals come to commit deviance away from *balancing* different forces toward the expression of one force—motivation.

In my opinion, such a simplification would deny one of the main contributions of the theory. Moreover, it is regressive to propose a theory that puts so much stress on one causal force, no matter how potent that causal force might appear. One of the reasons for developing control balance theory, and for building in motivational, control, opportunity and contingent forces, was to improve the simple theories that have dominated the field with their foci on single cause systems. The main dynamic of control balance theory is provided by the tension between motivation and constraint, although the control balancing process is fed and modulated by other variables, conditions and processes. It just does not seem prudent to put all of the causal eggs in a motivation basket unless the evidence ultimately mandates it.

I do agree, however, that it would be useful to abandon the *qualitative* distinctions among types of deviance. The theory really should be understood to predict different types of deviance distinguished by their seriousness, or likelihood of stimulating countercontrolling responses. . . .

Transform the Formulation Into a Theory of Predation

. . . . A continuum of behaviors arrayed by the probability of countercontrolling reactions certainly reflects the extent to which various actions threaten others in direct material ways, so seriousness does to a large extent express predatory potential. However, countercontrol is not generated entirely by the direct material effects of deviant actions. Sometimes reactions are provoked by sentiment, or values. . . .

Similarly, many of the behaviors that I classify as defiance are not necessarily predatory, yet they carry the potential for countercontrol. Such things include disobedience to authority, sulking, refusal to participate in economic or other endeavors, or direct protest against social institutions. Since control balance theory is about behavior that is disapproved, and therefore likely to evoke controlling responses, it encompasses both predation and other behaviors.

To be sure, predation is an important phenomenon, and developing a theory to explain it is urgent. Moreover, it is a good thing to grasp the abstract quality of predation in a variety of behaviors that ostensibly appear different. Indeed, *Control Balance* urges abstraction as an important theoretical tool. But, in my opinion the theory already explains predation, and more. To reduce it to a strict theory of predation would not really achieve anything and it would sacrifice a lot.

Treat Submissiveness As a Unique Response

. . . . Regarding submission as a form of deviance is a problem with the theory, although there are good reasons to think submissive acts are regarded as unacceptable by most people in western societies. In fact, Braithwaite himself implies as much when he states in his discussion of a 'republican perspective' that 'submission, like predation, is a political state that is unattractive' (p. 167 in this volume). Casting submission as deviance, as I did in my presentation of the theory, is somewhat incongruent with the thrust of the overall formulation, which was intended as a theory of deviance, meant to apply to all societies and all individuals. That is because submissiveness may not be deviant in all societies, and because submission, unlike other forms of deviance, does not solve the problem of control; it marks the loss of the spirit of resistance. So, to the extent that deviance is characterized as a maneuver to alter a control imbalance, which is the mainspring of the control balancing argument, submission does not fit.

While I have known that all along, I was initially too wedded to the idea that a good theory ought to have symmetry to avoid the problem. By the time the book appeared in print, I had already begun, in public presentations, to describe the

theory differently, and when I saw an advance copy of Braithwaite's comments, I became even more convinced that control balance theory should now be described not as a theory of deviance but as a theory of conformity, deviance, and submission (or more simply as a theory of human behavior). The treatment of submission as unique rather than as a special sort of deviance, then, is one of Braithwaite's suggested modifications that I completely and fully accept.

This, however, does not overcome the underlying problem involved in classifying acts as indicative of submission rather than indicative of either defiance (my term) or of less serious predation (Braithwaite's implication). In my formulation, things such as alcohol and drug addiction, suicide and various forms of mental illness are treated as defiance—forms of protest against control or against the systems of norms enforced by control. In Braithwaite's modification, they are conceived as forms of submission—ways of expressing defeat and surrender of all effort to assert autonomy. In my formulation and in his modification, submission stems from confrontation of overwhelming potential countercontrol, and it represents a reversal of causal forces that up to that point stimulate deviant acts to overcome a control deficit. Thus, to explain some acts it is crucial to know if they are examples of defiance (predation, in his terminology) or of submission.

Solving this problem is not as easy as dealing with the comparable problem on the autonomous end of the continuum. One cannot simply abandon the qualitative distinctions on the repressive end of the control ratio continuum and restate the theory to say that the probability of repressive deviance varies inversely with the chances of activating countercontrol, which is directly related to the seriousness of the potential act. That is because the differences between submission and the other forms of repressively generated behavior are in fact qualitative. Though submission, when regarded as deviance, is no doubt the least serious form, it is not behavior that overcomes, or counters, a control deficit; it is a residual style of behavior adopted when one cannot visualize alternatives. In effect, since it is a way of giving up, it stands the causal process involved in other behaviors on its head.

But, if saying the theory is about deviance, conformity and submission does not solve the basic problem, neither does Braithwaite's suggestion to reclassify some things. If various forms of what has traditionally been called 'retreatist' behavior actually represent defiance, simply employing traditional thinking and declaring them to be acts of surrender will not work. Here, theory has to give way to research to establish the character of these problematic behaviors. My understanding of the literature is that many forms of 'retreatist' behavior, especially substance abuse and bizarre behaviors sometimes defined as mental illness, clearly start out as defiance by youth, only later coming to look like capitulation, as physiological processes of addiction or habit formation take over. Similarly, though the evidence is less clear-cut, suicide seems to me to be mainly an active rather than a passive maneuver. Rather than yield to the controls this life prescribes, those who take their own lives seem to be saying that they will not submit, that there is one last thing they can do. And at least some suicide, as suggested by decedents' notes, is undertaken to influence the behavior of others. Hence, suicide may be a grand statement of defiance, even if it is often accompanied by a depressive mood.

Maybe I'm wrong about this, and maybe further research will demonstrate unequivocally that substance abuse, mental illness and suicide involve capitulation to overwhelming control. If so, the theoretical issue will be moot. The advantage of theory, of course, is that it directs us toward important empirical concerns. Up to this point, since most students of pathological behaviors operated more or less from a Mertonian view, few seem to have imagined investigating the possibility that mental illness and suicide, except in a few dramatic instances, are acts of defiance.

Not only may 'pathological' behaviors be defiant rather than submissive, but some forms of behavior ostensibly appearing to be capitulations to overwhelming control may actually be examples of defiance. Submissive styles can sometimes enhance one's control. . . . If submissive persons realize that their dependency requires effort from those . . . to whom they submit—that capitulation actually controls those they dominate—and adopt the submissive style for that reason, then what seems on the surface to be submission would actually be defiance, as I have defined defiance in the theory. Thus, if Braithwaite is right that some of the things I regard as defiance are really instances of submission, it is also possible that some ostensibly submissive behaviors are actually instances of defiance.

A POSSIBLE MISUNDERSTANDING

Despite Braithwaite's admirable grasp of control balance theory, which is complicated and tedious in places, he seems to misunderstand some parts of it, or at least he seems to forget some important elements when applying it. I have already discussed one apparent lapse where he seems to have lost sight of the import of the magnitude of potential countercontrol. Another possible slippage concerns the implication of the theory for gender differences in the probabilities of predation and defiance. He states (on p. 165 in this volume): 'the fact that control ratios are higher for men than for women should imply under Tittle's original theory that both predation and defiance are more common for women than for men.' I do not believe the theory implies this; indeed, I discuss this very point at length (Tittle, 1995, pp. 231-232), concluding: 'Therefore, females should have far higher rates of submissive deviance and slightly higher or about equal rates of defiant deviance, but they should have lower relative rates of all other forms of deviance, including predation and the autonomous forms of deviance.'

I reach this conclusion by first noting that most females in all societies suffer control deficits, and that this imbalance of control is so great that the largest proportion of females is probably in the extreme repressive area of the continuum where submission is most likely. Successively smaller proportions of females are likely in each zone of the control ratio continuum as one moves toward the right. Correspondingly, males are portrayed as being most concentrated in the center of the continuum and to have successively smaller proportions in each zone as one moves outward in both directions. Superimposing these patterns shows that females predominate in the extreme and moderate repressive zones while males predominate in the rest of the zones of the entire continuum. . . . If these projections are accurate and one's control ratio were the only relevant variable, then we would expect more submissive deviance among females than males, and we would expect slightly more defiance among females, but we would expect more of all other forms of deviance among males and females—somewhat more predation, and considerably more exploitation, plunder and decadence. But other things are relevant, including greater chances that males encounter provoking circumstances that bring deviant predispositions into actual deviant motivations, greater risk involved in much female deviance, and more extensive opportunities for males to commit some sorts of deviance. Given all of these variables, contrary to Braithwaite's statement, there should be considerably less predation among females than males, and possibly about equal amounts of defiance. Perhaps this is not a slip but simply reflects Braithwaite's disagreement about the implications of the theory. . . .

Braithwaite does not comment on the theory's implications about historical trends in differences between male and female rates of various kinds of deviance, about likely future patterns, or about some of its unusual linkages. In particular, the argument hinges on some demographic patterns and on features of male and female roles and life patterns that are seldom taken seriously by students of deviance. His attenuated discussion of the gender and deviance question, however, again calls attention to the need for research. One point repeatedly made in my book is that we have limited information about deviant behavior, particularly as it is conceptualized in control balance theory, and its distribution among population categories. Most of our data concern only criminal deviance, and even those are skimpy and riddled with error. But of more import for assessing the implications of control balance theory, is the fact that there are no directly relevant measures of control ratios.

The necessity of reciprocal interplay between theory and research is obvious here. Though the theory needs to be evaluated on strictly theoretical grounds, and modified as needed—a process that Braithwaite has so effectively begun—there is an even greater need for systematic collection of relevant data, careful testing of derived hypotheses, especially where such hypotheses could reconcile differences between the original formulation and Braithwaite's, or others', proposed modifications, and feeding back the results of that research to correct and improve the theory.

DISCUSSION QUESTIONS

1. Why does Tittle distinguish between "overcoming" a deficit and "extending" a surplus?

2. Although Tittle does agree with Braithwaite that his qualitative distinctions among the categories of deviance are imprecise, he formulated them in that manner for a specific reason. What is that reason, and why does Tittle believe that Braithwaite's simplification, or collapse, of the six categories of deviance into one undermines the central thrust of the theory, that is, balance?

3. How does Tittle clarify Braithwaite's misunderstanding of the implications of the theory for gender differences in the probabilities of predation and defiance? Why does Tittle feel that, contrary to Braithwaite's interpretation of the theory, there should be considerably less predation among women than men (not more), and possibly about equal amounts of defiance (not more for women)?

REFERENCE

Tittle, C. (1995). *Control balance: Toward a general theory of deviance.* Boulder, CO: Westview Press.

18

THE DYNAMIC NATURE OF DEVIANCE

JOHN CURRA

EDITOR'S INTRODUCTION—Curra's recent analysis of deviance in his new text, *The Relativity of Deviance* (2000), will provide readers with a broad overview of the labeling perspective on deviance. In another part of the text from which this excerpt is taken, Curra addresses the dynamic nature of deviance and asserts that "what qualifies as deviance varies from place to place, time to time, and situation to situation" (Curra, 2000, p. viii). Curra notes that nothing can be deviant in a social vacuum, and the definitions and social reactions to such behaviors strongly affect the types of deviance that exist in societies.

Additionally, he makes an important point by adding that in order to understand deviance better, we need to be concerned initially with human diversity and, at a fundamental level, with why people in one setting are different from people in another setting. But Curra also states that our understanding of human nature and diversity must press further than that. He suggests that we also must understand that some people in society are responsible for constructing claims about what they find disturbing in other people. Drawing these social divisions makes some differences between groups of people seem larger than they really are, or than they need to be, and some similarities smaller than they actually are. It is these artificial social divisions that categorize and segregate people, telling others what to recognize and what to ignore in people. This point is critical to Curra's argument; he explains that "because we seek to understand deviance as a social relationship, we cannot only examine the diversity of human behavior; we must also examine the diversity of claims, labels, or definitions of it" (p. 177, this volume).

In the remainder of his excerpt, Curra explains how egocentricity and ethnocentricity contribute to the shaping of one's values and to the manner in which one comes to define particular behaviors as deviant or normative. He claims that these processes of "being centered" develop in our childhoods, but that socialization can alter the level of centeredness we all have to the rest of the world. He states that the assessment of what is abnormal, or deviant, always reflects the interests or preferences of some group in some particular society at some particular place in time. Changes in people, places, or times produce changes in definitions of normal and abnormal.

Moreover, Curra discusses how the symbolic organization of human experience and ideal culture shape how we view ourselves in relation to others and how we are able to formulate rules about proper and improper ways of behaving. However, "ideal culture" may play a larger role in that it is a system of standards to which members of a culture can refer in order to convince themselves that they should act in a certain socially and culturally approved way.

A central component of many theories regarding deviance concerns the notion that humans construct much of the reality in which they live. Because nothing can really be considered a "natural" state of existence for everyone, it is extremely difficult to identify one reality that might exist for all people. In terms of deviance, deviants are constructed in such a way that they do not pose a threat to the dominant "reality." According to Curra, the construction of deviant labels and their assignment to particular individuals serve to hide social conflicts and make those who label feel more self-assured that their way is not only the best way but also the only way.

In this excerpt, Curra provides a thorough discussion of the major theoretical developments regarding deviance. This discussion is important because it will provide readers with a general overview of the theoretical contributions from sociologists and anthropologists regarding deviance and the impact that a deviant label has on an individual so labeled. Curra also makes important points regarding the role of agents of social control in the labeling process and about the control of these individuals once they have been labeled as criminals. Therefore, as he points out, it is important to understand not only the effects that the deviant label has for a particular individual but also which actors are deciding that something is deviant, why they make that decision, and their level of success in convincing others that they really are the best persons to be making these decisions.

UNDERSTANDING SOCIAL DEVIANCE

Social deviance is a persistent and common feature of societies, communities, and groups. Whenever people get together, some of them seem to hurt, annoy, or unsettle others. This does not mean, however, that deviance is some personal imperfection. *People acting together* create social deviance by what they believe, feel, say, and do, and we will find deviance and deviants almost everywhere that we go. Nothing can be deviant in a social vacuum, and definitions and social reactions strongly affect the types of deviance that exist in societies (Schur, 1971, pp. 16-17). The study of social deviance is more than a study of a type of behavior or of an individual attribute; it is a study of social relationships and socially constructed *perspectives* on human behavior and human individuals (Goffman, 1961). Good and bad are mutually defined, and each of them has meaning only in terms of the other (Margolin, 1993, p. 511). We must always know what is made of an act or attribute socially.

Deviance changes from society to society, and it changes in any given society over time. At one time or place, for some people, drinking alcohol is perfectly proper, and at another time and place it is forbidden; at one time or place, smoking cigarettes may be a sign of maturity and sophistication, and at some other time or place, it is a sign of immaturity and irresponsibility. The deviancy of some action or attribute cannot be determined simply by examining it closely and objectively. No human act or attribute will be universally judged as improper by people in all societies—large and small, industrial and nonindustrial—at all times. Human beings are simply too inventive in assigning positive and negative labels to the many things that they do for us to believe that deviance is separable from nondeviance because of some inherent, intrinsic, or objective quality of acts or attributes. Social deviance exists because some groups judge and evaluate what other groups are doing (Matza, 1969, pp. 41-53).

Though we must be concerned with human diversity and come to some understanding of why people in one setting are different from people in another setting, this is not enough. We must also understand that some people are responsible for constructing claims or understandings about what they find troubling or upsetting in other people (Spector & Kitsuse, 1977). Drawing these social lines makes some differences between groups look bigger than they are and some similarities look smaller than they are. These social divisions, artificial as they are, categorize and segregate, so they tell beholders what to recognize and what to ignore (Zerubavel, 1991). We must examine the content of these conceptions of deviance and understand why some people created them in the first place. Because we seek to understand

Curra, J. (2000). The dynamic nature of deviance. In J. Curra, *The relativity of deviance* (pp. 1-19). Thousand Oaks, CA: Sage.

deviance as a social relationship, we cannot only examine the diversity of human behavior; we must also examine the diversity of claims, labels, or definitions of it.

BEING CENTERED: EGOCENTRICITY AND ETHNOCENTRICITY

As children, we were all *egocentric* (Piaget, 1948). We each lived in our own little world, and we were not yet aware of, or concerned with, the viewpoint of others. We could be aware of other people, but we had much more difficulty imagining how we appeared to them. This egocentricity colored everything that we did and everything that we believed and felt. . . . It was only through a great deal of interaction with others that we reached the point where we came to see ourselves through their eyes, and we wondered more and more about their thoughts and feelings.

The egocentricity of childhood colored our attitudes about right and wrong, good and bad, proper and improper, and correct and incorrect. When we were children, we decided what should or should not be done in a very selfish and direct way: If it brought us pleasure, it was "right," and if it brought us displeasure, it was "wrong." Others may not have liked what we did, and they took time to correct us, but in the initial period of social development, egocentricity was the rule. Most of us tried to maximize our own personal pleasure and minimize our own personal displeasure even if our selfishness was irritating or upsetting to others.

Socialization is a continuing process of acquiring the fundamentals necessary for group living and learning the heritage of a society. As individuals are socialized, they internalize the perspectives and expectations of others, and they become more conscious of, and potentially more sympathetic toward, others' outlooks and interests. Fully socialized individuals are able to take the roles of others, and they may refuse to do anything that would hurt others even if doing so would bring them some immediate advantage.

The internalization of a culture (or at least parts of it) is an important goal of socialization. Culture is a system of designs for living or shared understandings that members of a society use as they act together (Kluckhohn, 1949). These designs or understandings are created by people at some place and at some time, and they are then transmitted from group to group or generation to generation. People in a society (or a part of it) find that certain ways of acting, thinking, or feeling seem better than other ways, and these designs for living are then encouraged or even demanded. . . .

Socialization alters the egocentricity of childhood. As we become more aware of others, we are forced to start looking at our society and the people in it in new ways. We eventually come to think, feel, and act in *anticipation of* the impact we will have on others. This continual movement away from egocentricity makes it less likely that we will intentionally injure someone else, but it does not automatically guarantee it. Though the centeredness of childhood is modified by the socialization process, centeredness does not end. People will maintain some of their egocentricity throughout their lives (Kumbasar, Romney, & Batchelder, 1994, p. 499). . . .

The process of socialization itself creates another kind of centeredness called *ethnocentrism*. Socialization encourages people to believe that their society's values, standards, and customs are better than the values, standards, and customs of people in other societies. It is easy to see how ethnocentrism could lead to a vilification of members of some out-group. If Americans were to decide that they were better than, say, Martians because Americans played football better, this could easily be a reflection of ethnocentrism. . . . Egocentricity and ethnocentrism— individual- and group-based centeredness—have important consequences for what we do and how we view each other. Egocentricity and ethnocentrism make it easy for some people in some cultures to devalue ways of acting, feeling, and thinking different from their own. Egocentricity and ethnocentrism make it more likely that some people will define as inferior other people who are different from them or who do things differently from what they do. Difference is easily transformed into deviance, and deviance is easily transformed into abnormality.

THE SYMBOLIC ORGANIZATION OF HUMAN EXPERIENCE

A *symbol* stands for or represents a person, object, situation, or experience because of group agreement and learning. Symbols are very flexible and can be used to evoke images of the thing symbolized even if that thing is not physically present or is abstract and never had physical substance. Practically any sound or physical gesture could be a symbol if enough people understood what the symbol represented and agreed to use it. . . . Symbols are always learned, and they form the basis of language systems. The learning of symbols makes it possible for individuals to know how they are viewed from the standpoint of others. In time, most of us actually become objects of our own actions: We define and react to ourselves in some of the same ways that others have defined and reacted to us (Mead, 1934). We come to learn that we are sons or daughters, males or females, attractive or ugly, and overweight, skinny, or just right, and we treat ourselves accordingly. We view ourselves from the perspectives of others, and we take account of how they have treated us and develop a sense of what and who we are as a result.

IDEAL CULTURE

. . . . Most people in a society are familiar with its ideal culture; they may sometimes try to follow it themselves, and they may sometimes encourage others to follow it. People who do not follow the rules of ideal culture may be negatively sanctioned by others, or they may define themselves as less worthy because they have broken the rules and may experience guilt or embarrassment as a result (Scheff, 1990). Ideal culture gives the appearance of great uniformity and consistency within a culture; ideal culture may even give the false impression that only one proper way exists for all people to act, think, and feel. Ideal culture may become so important to individuals in a group that they condemn anybody who fails to live up to its standards.

It is possible for the ideal norms of one society or group to be drastically different from the ideal norms of another society or group. This means that even if people are acting properly with regard to one set of standards, from the standpoint of other people in different places (or from the standpoint of people who have different understandings), they are acting improperly. . . . Ideal culture, rather than being an important influence on human behavior, may simply be a system of standards to which members of a culture can refer in order to convince themselves that they regularly act in exemplary ways.

THE SOCIAL CONSTRUCTION OF REALITY

Humans construct so much of the reality within which they live that it is difficult to identify one reality that exists for all people (Berger & Luckmann, 1966, p. 86; Sarbin & Kitsuse, 1994, p. 8). Every social world is complex, and it changes all the time in uncontrollable and unpredictable ways (Gove, 1994, pp. 365-366); this fact means that every social world has a provisional quality (Troyer, 1992, p. 36). However, because social reality is so extensive and enveloping, it attains the status of a force of nature, and its conventional nature is easy enough to miss (Searle, 1995, p. 4). Because particular people with particular interests and resources come to imbue certain ways of doing things and certain preferences with great significance, certain social forms are justified as better than all others. It is usually impossible to know if this is true or if these claims are merely the ideological rumblings of some particular group.

Because most social encounters that people have are typical and ordinary, they do not call into question the taken-for-granted nature of human experience, and the apparent objectivity of social reality is continually reaffirmed in everyday interaction (Berger & Luckmann, 1966, p. 23). . . . Deviants are cast in such a way that their deviance really offers no serious threat to the dominant construction of reality. Deviance is branded as dysfunctional, unhealthy, evil, dangerous, or abnormal. The successful definition of alternate realities as inauthentic, pathological, or deviant reinforces the dominant view of reality and makes it appear more immutable and concrete than it actually is (Berger & Luckmann, 1966, pp. 112-115). The construction of deviant labels and their assignment to particular individuals serve to mask social conflicts and make the labelers more confident that their way is the only way (Parsons, 1951, p. 266).

THEORETICAL VIEWS: THE OLD AND THE NOT-SO-OLD

One of the earliest conceptions (which is still around) was founded on the belief that deviants could be separated from nondeviants and deviance from nondeviance on the basis of inherent or intrinsic characteristics (Gibbs, 1966).

Usually, some biological, psychological, or sociological factor such as body chemistry, intelligence, or social disorganization was identified and then blamed for the existence of the deviance (Vold, Bernard, & Snipes, 1998). Because the deviance was almost always viewed as unacceptable and unnecessary, the temptation to see defect, abnormality, or degeneracy in the biology, psychology, or social situation of deviants was too great to resist. Sometimes the acts themselves were classified as inherently or intrinsically deviant. Parsons (1951, p. 250) insisted that deviance could be identified by its potential to produce a disturbance in the equilibrium of interactive systems, and Schwendinger and Schwendinger (1975) argued that deviance is behavior that harms individuals.

But as more and more was learned about deviance, and as sociologists and anthropologists got more involved in its study and demonstrated the great variety of human customs and experiences, the meaning of deviance changed. New conceptions were developed that were not predicated on a belief in the existence of intrinsic characteristics of either deviance or deviants. Sumner's (1906) discussion of mores, folkways, and other social rules declared that they are inherited from the past and that they direct human behavior almost automatically (pp. 76-77). When they are followed, they facilitate the adjustment of individuals to life conditions and to the particular demands of the time and the place (p. 58). It was an easy leap to the view that deviance is a normative departure (Gibbs, 1966, p. 14). Sumner (1906, pp. 521-522) believed that social rules could make anything right and prevent the condemnation of anything. If this is true, norms could also make anything wrong. According to Becker (1963), groups create deviance by making rules whose violation qualifies as deviance, identifying rule breakers, and treating them as outsiders (p. 9).

We must see deviance, and the outsiders who personify the abstract conception, as a consequence of a process of interaction between people, some of whom in the service of their own interests make and enforce rules which catch others who, in the service of their own interests, have committed acts which are labeled deviant (p. 163). The creation and enforcement of rules is a moral enterprise that depends on the willingness of some individuals to go to the time and trouble to get their particular view of right and wrong adopted by others.

> A successful, and enforceable, social construction of a particular label of deviance depends on the ability of one, or more, groups to use (or generate) enough power so as to enforce *their* definition and version of morality on others.... Deviance ... always results from negotiations about morality and the configuration of power relationships. (Ben-Yehuda, 1990, pp. 6-7)

Some crusades may be very successful and have enduring effects; other crusades may be short-lived, dying quickly and with little fanfare (Becker, 1963, pp. 147-163).

The meaning of *norm* changed. No longer were norms necessarily viewed as reflective of a society wide consensus, as embodying a shared morality, or even as essential designs for living. C. Wright Mills (1943, p. 170) showed us that the prevailing norms almost always reflect some specific group's biased view of what is proper and what is improper; norms reflect the power, the interests, and the outlooks of the groups that create them. The greater the social conflict and cultural heterogeneity, the less likely it is that any normative system could even come close to reflecting a universal consensus or agreement on the proper and improper ways of acting, thinking, feeling, and being.

Once theoretical explanations of deviance evolved to the point where they were sensitive to the role played by the "other" in the construction of deviance, a whole new world of possibilities was opened up. It could be maintained with credibility and authority that social control itself has the ironic effect of actually creating deviance and channeling the direction that it takes (Lemert, 1972, p. ix). Tannenbaum (1938) insisted that social labels and other social reactions actually create deviance: "The process of making the criminal, therefore, is a process of tagging, defining, identifying, segregating, describing, emphasizing, making conscious and self-conscious; it becomes a way of stimulating, suggesting, emphasizing, and evoking the very traits that are complained of" (pp. 19-20). A new wrinkle had been added: The understanding of social deviance required an analysis of the processes by which persons came to be defined and treated as deviant by others. The definition of deviance changed to reflect this new understanding: "Deviance is not a property *inherent in* certain forms of behavior; it is a property *conferred upon* these forms by the audiences which directly or indirectly witness them" (Erikson, 1962, p. 308). Characterizations of behaviors and attributes became the principal target of study, not the behaviors and attributes themselves (Schur, 1975, p. 287).

The assertion that social control can create deviance can mean many things; however, two possibilities stand out. First, social control may identify something as deviant and separate it from other behaviors or attributes that are not considered deviant. Something so identified may be called "deviancy by definition."

> Deviance may be conceived as a process by which the members of a group, community, or society (1) interpret behavior as deviant, (2) define persons who so behave as a certain kind of deviant, and (3) accord them the treatment considered appropriate to such deviants. (Kitsuse, 1962, p. 248)

A second possibility is that the reactions of some people—what they say, do, or believe—can propel other people in the direction of greater involvement with deviant pursuits. Such involvement may be called "secondary deviance."

> [W]e start with the idea that persons and groups are differentiated in various ways, some of which result in social penalties, rejection and segregation. These penalties and segregative reactions of society or the community are dynamic factors which increase, decrease, and condition the form which the initial differentiation or deviation takes. (Lemert, 1951, p. 22)

According to the secondary deviance proposition, an individual's deviance can be channeled or even amplified by the reactions of others if the social dynamics are right, but this is not the same thing as constructing deviancy through naming, classifying, and judging some behaviors and attributes as proper and others as improper. The secondary deviance proposition is about the ironic nature of social control: Social censure can actually cause more deviance, not less. Deviancy by definition is about the arbitrary nature of social control. Social censure is the event that transforms human diversity into social deviance by altering how behaviors and attributes are defined and perceived (Sumner, 1994, p. 222).

Deviance came to be viewed as an inevitable and rather ordinary feature of life in a pluralistic society, and deviants came to be viewed as more sinned against than sinning. Empathizing with the deviant who had been labeled, stigmatized, and forced to associate with other deviants became a very legitimate enterprise in the sociology of deviance (Becker, 1967). In fact, siding with deviants became as defensible as siding with representatives of conventional society such as police, judges, or psychiatrists, and the deviant's right to be different and to be free from stigma and harassment was actively defended. Deviance came to be viewed in political terms, and power—the power to label and the power to legitimate one's own view of proper and improper in some hierarchy of credibility (Becker, 1967)—was identified as *the* critical resource that allowed some people to benefit themselves by transforming the actions and attributes of others into something strange or even despicable.

Whose side are we on? The emergence of a radical view of deviance meant that some theorists took the side of the deviants with a vengeance. Not only did these theorists defend the right of deviants to be different, but they condemned representatives of conventional society and branded them as the dangerous, odd, or misguided ones. Life in an unequal, competitive, insecure society, they believed, was brutalizing for some people, and brutal conditions generate brutal behaviors. Radicals viewed deviance as one of the choices that people consciously make as one possible solution to the difficulties posed for them by life in a contradictory society (Taylor, Walton, & Young, 1973, p. 271). Radicals insisted that the control of deviants and the suppression of deviance are both principal ways that threats to the economic and political systems are counteracted and that the status quo is preserved for the benefit of powerful groups (Quinney, 1974, p. 52). Quinney (1973, p. 60) went so far as to claim that the really bad people are those who make laws to protect their own interests and to legitimate the repressive social control of powerless groups.

Deviance is a construction of social actors, and social meanings of deviance are always problematic, just like the social world itself (Lyman & Scott, 1989, p. 7). We must always have a clear understanding of exactly which actors are deciding that something is deviant, why they are making the claims that they are (Spector & Kitsuse, 1977), and their level of success in convincing others that they are really authorities on the issue in question (Best, 1990, pp. 11-13). Each relationship contains rules, understandings, and background assumptions that might very well seem odd to people from different relationships (Denzin, 1970, pp. 131-132).

DISCUSSION QUESTIONS

1. What is meant by the following statements in Curra's excerpt: "Good and bad are mutually defined, and each of them has meaning only in terms of the other. . . . We must always know what is made of an act or attribute socially" (see p. 176 of this volume).

2. What roles do ethnocentricity, symbols, and ideal culture play in terms of deviance?

3. On what basis does Curra claim that because deviants are defined in a certain way, their deviance does not offer any serious threat to the dominant construction of reality?

4. According to some of the theorists Curra identifies in his text, what role do the lawmakers play with respect to deviance? Why is it that some "moral crusades" against deviance have great success and endure whereas others are short-lived and die quickly with little fanfare? Can you think of any contemporary examples that may fit these profiles?

REFERENCE

Curra, J. (2000). *The relativity of deviance*. Thousand Oaks, CA: Sage.

19

DEVIANCE ON THE RECORD

Techniques for Labeling Child Abusers in Official Documents

LESLIE MARGOLIN

EDITOR'S INTRODUCTION—Traditional labeling theory typically examines the impact of the deviant label from the perspective of the person being labeled. For example, classic works in this theoretical domain have described how communities create deviance and criminality through their very efforts to control it. When communities react to certain individuals as "deviants" or "law breakers," a continuing series of interactions is set in motion that eventually leads to a change in that person's identity. These individuals so labeled come to see themselves as criminals, which subsequently leads to a change in their behavior. This change typically manifests itself in continued criminality (see Lemert, 1951; Schur, 1971). In this example, the focus is on the individual labeled "deviant."

In contrast, Margolin focuses on the opposite side of the labeling coin by considering the perspective of the persons doing the labeling. In her article, she demonstrates how a criminal label is constructed by caseworkers and how the label "child abuser" comes to be attached to accused individuals. Margolin's analysis consists of 120 official records. Her primary objective aimed at showing how social workers "prove" that someone committed child abuse. She found that the denial of accusations by and the lack of interviews with more than half of the suspects was not perceived as a limitation, because suspects were routinely defined as "noncredible" witnesses. Margolin found, in the course of her study, that suspects' testimony was taken seriously only when they agreed with the allegations.

In contrast, caseworkers frequently viewed victims as "credible" witnesses, and their testimony was only rejected when they claimed that suspects were innocent. Margolin later found that social workers developed a variety of methods for simplifying the labeling process as it became reflected in official records. For example, hitting that resulted in an injury was always treated as if it indicated the intent to injure, and behavior commonly known as "sexual" was always treated as if it were the same as the intent to sexually injure someone.

Margolin's findings include bureaucrats' determination to translate sex and violence into "endlessly accumulated verbal detail," to "make do" with whatever information is available, to create proofs of child abuse based on the new "common sense" that children's testimony is more credible than that of adults, and to develop simple, successful ways of imputing intentionality on the part of the suspects that are unchanged by suspects' accounts. Margolin asserts that institutional and bureaucratic forces, such as a large caseload, frequently contribute to this significant problem. Additionally, the existence of bureaucracies with large budgets and many employees often depends upon the acceptance of a particular term of deviance. In other words, "bureaucratic industries" have a vested interest not only in the deviant label but in the labeling process as well.

Margolin's article is important not only for the focus she takes in her study, but for the larger implications her findings have on the behavior of institutions and bureaucracies and the weight of importance they give to a particular deviant label.

Some sociologists believe that wrong-doers have considerable capacity to defend and mollify attributions of deviance by offering excuses, apologies, and expressions of sorrow. For example, conceptual formulations such as Mills's (1940) "vocabularies of motive," Scott and Lyman's (1968) "accounts," Sykes and Matza's (1957) "techniques of neutralization," and Hewitt and Stokes' (1975) "disclaimers" reflect a belief in the almost limitless reparative potential of talk. In the parlance of these sociologists, deviant identities are negotiable because attributions of wrong-doing are seen to depend not only on an assessment of what the wrongdoer did but on an understanding of his or her mental state during and after the violation. As Douglas (1970, p. 12) observes, "an individual is considered responsible for his actions if and only if . . . he has intended to commit those actions and knows the rules relevant to them". . . .

Given these conditions, accused persons may argue that the violation in question was unanticipated, unplanned, and contrary to what they wished. Still, limited evidence exists that people win such arguments. Although account theorists (e.g., Scott & Lyman, 1968, pp. 46-47) claim that "the timbers of fractured sociations" can be repaired through talk, investigators addressing the ways social control agents process putative deviants have found few instances of people talking their way out of deviant labels (cf. Margolin, 1990). On the whole, social control agents tend to pigeon-hole clients fairly quickly. As Waegel (1981) has shown, the organizational demand to meet deadlines, process an expected number of cases, and turn out paperwork reduces the amount of time agents can give their clients. The

more bureaucrats are hurried, the greater their need to rely on shorthand methods for dealing with clients, and thus, the greater the necessity to interpret people and situations by means of stereotypes. In this regard, stereotypical or "normal" case conceptions guide responses to homicide defendants (Swigert & Farrell, 1977), juvenile delinquents (Piliavin & Briar, 1964), clients in a public defender's office (Sudnow, 1965), skid-row residents (Bittner, 1967), and shoplifters (Steffensmeier & Terry, 1973).

The paperwork demand has a second effect on the putative deviant's capacity to negotiate effectively. Because oral and written communication have different potentialities for conveying information and structuring argument, agencies emphasizing the creation of records place proportional pressure on bureaucrats to note the "recordable" features of their clients' situations. By implication, the contingencies of a case which best lend themselves to being described in written language are given the most prominence in records, and those contingencies most difficult to capture on paper (those aspects of a case best understood through face-to-face interaction) are minimized or neglected.

Studies examining the types of information bureaucrats leave out of written accounts have shown that clients' feelings are often omitted because the inner life of the individual is not only difficult to defend as objective evidence, but it is difficult to defend as evidence in writing (Kahn, 1953; Lemert, 1969). In face-to-face encounters, however, feelings and intentions are available through a series of gestures, tonal changes, and bodily movements which accompany the other's words (Schutz & Luckmann, 1973). There is

Margolin, L. (1992). Deviance on the record: Techniques for labeling child abusers in official documents. *Social Problems, 39*, 58-70.

continual exchange between words and gestures. Such reciprocity cannot be duplicated in written communication, particularly when the writing is part of an official document. This means that putative deviants' capacity to argue their cases is seriously reduced when cases must be made in writing.

While documents may be a poor medium for describing internal states, bureaucrats are also reluctant to designate deviance on something as indefinite as "feelings"—theirs or the client's. The primary risk of citing the client's mental state at the time of the violation as a criterion for labeling or not labeling is that it makes agents vulnerable to accusations of subjectivity and personal bias. Since records are permanently available to supervisory scrutiny, agents feel pressure to make written assessments defendable displays of bureaucratic competence (Meehan, 1986). For this reason, agents must use records to display not only "what happened" but that they performed their jobs rationally and objectively (Garfinkel, 1967; Zimmerman, 1969). These practical considerations oblige agents whose decision processes are recorded to place singular emphasis on the tangible aspects of the case— what the putative deviant's behavior was and what harm resulted—at the same time giving relatively little weight to clients' excuses, apologies, and expressions of sorrow.

Conceptualizing the deviant identity, then, as a mosaic assembled out of imputations of behavior and intention, this study examines how such a mosaic is pieced together in written documents. I explore how the "deviant's" point of view is documented and displayed, and how evidence is organized on paper to create the appearance that "deviance" has occurred. These dynamics are addressed through the examination of 120 case records designating child abuse.

Since the documentary reality of child abuse provides the vehicle and substantive focus of the analysis, what follows shows how child care providers are constituted as intentionally harmful to children. Like other "dividing practices" which categorize people as either healthy/sick, law abiding/criminal, or sane/insane, the separation of child abusers from normals is seen as an accomplishment of asymmetric power relations (cf. Foucault, 1965, 1973, 1977). This chapter focuses on the power imbalance between child abuse investigators and suspects and the means by which the former impose their version of reality on the latter. Since this imposition is an accomplishment of contemporary modes of discourse (cf. Foucault, 1978), I focus on investigators' vocabularies, the structure of their arguments, and the types of common sense reasoning they utilize.

METHODS

The idea for this research emerged while I was involved in a study of child abuse by babysitters. As part of that study, I had to read "official" case records documenting that child abuse had occurred. The more records I read, the more it appeared that the social workers devoted a rather large portion of their writing to describing children's injuries, as well as the violent and sexual interactions which often preceded and followed them. By contrast, the alleged perpetrator's intentions, feelings, and interpretations of what happened appeared to occupy a relatively small portion of the documents. This imbalance roused interest in view of the agency's formal regulations that social workers satisfy two criteria to establish that a caregiver committed child abuse: (1) They must establish that a caregiver performed acts which were damaging or exploitive to a child; (2) They must prove that the caregiver *intended* to damage or exploit the child—that the trauma was non-accidental. In the chapter, I examine how social workers managed to label child abusers in a manner consistent with these regulations without appearing to give much weight to subjective factors such as suspects' excuses and justifications.

The sample consisted of 60 case records documenting physical abuse and 60 records documenting sexual abuse. They were randomly selected from all case records of child abuse by babysitters substantiated by a state agency during a two year period (N = 537). A babysitter was defined as someone who took care of a child who was not a member of the child's family, was not a boyfriend or girlfriend of the child's parent, and was not employed in a registered or licensed group care facility.

I do not treat these records as ontologically valid accounts of "what happened"; rather, I treat them as a "documentary reality" (Smith, 1974), indicating the ways the social workers who constructed them want to be seen by their superiors. As such, the records provide evidence that the social workers utilized the unstated yet commonly known procedures which represent "good work." The following analysis attempts to make these procedures explicit and to show how the social workers who used them "prove" that child abuse took place by constructing good (bureaucratically sound) arguments supporting the view that a specific person intentionally damaged a child. I also explore the degree to which deviants' excuses, denials, and other accounts were incorporated into these decision processes. Finally, I look at how each type of information—descriptions of the injuries and accounts of what happened—was used as evidence that child abuse occurred and could have only been performed by the person who was labeled.

DISPLAYING VIOLENCE AND SEXUALITY

At the beginning of each record, the social worker described the physical injuries which were believed to have been inflicted on the child by the babysitter. These descriptions did not specify how the child's health or functioning were impaired but were presented as evidence that an act of transformative social import had occurred (cf. Denzin, 1989). To illustrate this reporting style, one three-year-old who was spanked by his babysitter was described by the physician as having "a contusion to the buttocks and small superficial lacerations." However, the social worker who used these injuries as evidence of child abuse described them as follows:

> The injuries gave the appearance of an ink blot, in that they were almost mirror images of each other, positioned in the center of each buttock. The bruising was approximately four inches long by about two and a half inches wide, and was dark red on the perimeter and had a white cast to the inside of the bruise. There was a long linear line running across the bottom of both buttocks extending almost the entire width of the child's buttock. There was lighter reddish bruising surrounding the two largest bruises on each buttock and faint bluish-red bruising extending up to the lower back. The bruising would be characterized as being red turning to a deeper reddish-purple than true bright red.

This unusually graphic style of presentation gave the bruises a special status. They were no longer simply bruises but were now defined as out of the ordinary, strange, and grotesque. By removing the bruises from everyday experience, the stage was set for redefining the babysitter who supposedly did this to the child. In this manner, a person whose social status had been taken for granted could now be seen as potentially suspicious, foreign, and malevolent (Garfinkel, 1956).

A parallel line of reportage was apparent in the sexual abuse cases. To the degree that the available information permitted, reports contained no obscurity in the descriptions of sexual interactions. No detail of what happened appeared too small to be pursued, named, and included in the records as evidence (cf. Foucault, 1978). This excerpt from a social worker's recorded interview with an eight-year-old girl illustrates:

S.W.: How did the bad touch happen? Can you think?

Child: I can't remember.

S.W.: Did you ever have to kiss?

Child: No.

S.W.: Anybody?

Child: Uh uh.

S.W.: Did you have to touch anybody?

Child: Yeah.

S.W.: Ah, you had to touch 'em. Where did you have to touch 'em?

Child: Down below.

S.W.: Oh, down below. Do you have a word for that body part?

Child: A thing-a-ma-jig.

S.W.: A thing-a-ma-jig. OK, let's look. . . . Is P [the suspect] a man?

Child: Yeah.

S.W.: OK, let's take a look at the man doll. Can you show me on the man doll what part you're talking about?

Child: This part.

S.W.: Oh, the part that sticks out in front. We have another word for that. Do you know the other word for that part?

Child: Dick.

S.W.: Yeah. Dick is another word for it. Another word is penis.

Child: Penis?

S.W.: Yeah.

Child: Oh.

S.W.: Can you tell me what—Did you see his body? Did you see his penis with your eyes?

Child: No.

S.W.: OK. Did he have his pants on or off?

Child: Unzipped.

S.W.: Unzipped. I see. How did his penis happen to come out of his pants?

Child: By the zipper.

S.W.: I see. Who took his penis out of his pants?

Child: He did.

S.W.: What did you have to touch his penis with?

Child: My fingers.

S.W.: I see. How did you know you had to do that?

Child: He told me to.

S.W.: What did he say?

Child: Itch it.

S.W.: Itch it. I see. Did he show you how to itch it? How did he have to itch it? One question at a time. Did he show you how to itch it?

Child: He said just go back.

S.W.: So you showed me that you're kind of scratching on it.

Child: Um hum.

S.W.: Did anything happen to his penis or his thing-a-ma-jig when you did that?

Child: No.

S.W.: OK. When he took his penis out of his pants, how did it look?

Child: Yucky.

S.W.: Yeah, I know you think it's yucky, but um, what does yucky mean? Can you tell me with some other words besides yucky?

Child: Slimy.

S.W.: Looked slimy. OK. Was it big?

Child: Yeah.

S.W.: Was it hard or soft?

Child: Soft and hard.

S.W.: OK. Explain how you mean that. . . .

I offer this dialogue not as evidence that sexual abuse did or did not occur, but rather, to display the means by which equivocal behavior is translated into the "fact" of sexual abuse. Whatever it is that "really happened" to this child, we see that her experience of it is not a concern when "documentation" is being gathered. She is an object of inquiry, not a participant (Cicourel, 1968; Smith, 1974). Whatever reasons compel social workers to bring her to their offices and ask these questions are their reasons not hers. And as the child learns, even features of the "event"— such as the size, hardness, and overall appearance of a penis—can assume critical importance within interviewers' frames of reference.

While social workers used these details of sexual interactions and injuries to set the stage for the attribution of deviance, I noted four cases in which the analysis of the injuries themselves played a conspicuously larger role in determining who was responsible. In these cases the injured children were too young to explain how their injuries were caused, the babysitters denied causing the injuries, and there were no witnesses. This meant that the only way the investigators were able to label the babysitters as abusive was to argue that the injuries occurred during the time the suspects were taking care of the children. The parents of the injured children testified that the children were sent to the babysitters in good health, without any marks, but returned from the babysitters with a noticeable injury. This allowed the social workers to determine responsibility through the following method: if a babysitter cannot produce any plausible alternative explanation for the child's injuries, the babysitter must be responsible for the injuries.

Since children who had allegedly been sexually abused did not have conspicuous or easily described injuries, attributing sexual abuse on the absence of any plausible alternative explanation for the injury was, of course, impossible.

This would appear to severely limit social workers' capacity to document that a babysitter committed sexual abuse when the babysitter denied the charges, when the child was too young to provide coherent testimony, and when there were no other witnesses. However, this was not always the case. Like the investigators described by Garfinkel (1967, p. 18) who were able to determine the cause of death among possible suicides with only "*this* much; *this* sight; *this* note; *this* collection of whatever is at hand," child abuse investigators showed the capacity to "make do" with whatever information was available. In one case of sexual abuse, for example, there were no witnesses, no admission from the suspect, no physical evidence, and no charge from the alleged victim; still, "evidence" was summoned to establish a babysitter's guilt. Here, the social worker cited a four-year-old girl's fears, nightmares, and other "behavior consistent with that of a child who was sexually traumatized by a close family friend." Additionally, the babysitter in question was portrayed as a "type" capable of doing such things:

> Having no physical evidence, and no consistent statement from the alleged victim, I am forced to make a conclusion based on the credibility of the child as opposed to that of the perpetrator. This conclusion is supported by similar allegations against him from an independent source. It is also supported by behavioral indications and what we know of his history.

Using Witnesses to Determine Who Did What to Whom

Since the children and alleged child abusers often had different versions of what happened (40 cases), social workers needed a decision-rule to settle the question of who had the correct story. The rule used for resolving disagreements was fairly simple: The child's version was considered the true one. The children were called "credible" witnesses when describing assaults which were done to them because it was assumed they had nothing to gain by falsely accusing the babysitter. The babysitters, on the other hand, were seen as "non-credible" (when they attempted to establish their innocence) because they had everything to gain by lying. Even children as young as two and

three years old were believed in preference to their adult babysitters. In fact, the main reason given for interpreting children as superior witnesses was precisely their youth, ignorance, and lack of sophistication. As one social worker observed, "It's my experience that a four-year-old would not be able to maintain such a consistent account of an incident if she was not telling the truth." Particularly in cases of sexual abuse, it was believed that the younger the witness, the more credible his or her testimony was. Social workers made the point that children who were providing details of sexual behavior would not know of such things unless they had been abused (cf. Eberle & Eberle, 1986).

The children's accounts were rejected in only three instances. In one of these cases, two teenage boys claimed they witnessed a babysitter abuse a child as they peered through a window. Both the babysitter and the child said this was not true. The social worker did not feel it was necessary to explain why the babysitter would deny the allegations, but the child's denial was seen as problematic. . . . A child's version of what happened (his denial of abuse) was rejected in a second case on the grounds that he was protecting a babysitter described as his "best friend." Finally, a 12-year-old female who repeatedly denied that anyone had touched her sexually was seen as non-credible because of her "modesty." As the social worker put it, "She did seem to have a very difficult time talking about it, and I feel she greatly minimized the incident due to her embarrassment about it."

In general, however, testimony from children was treated as the most credible source of evidence of what happened, since most social workers believe that children do not lie about the abuse done to them. By contrast, babysitters were presented as credible witnesses only when they agreed with the allegations made against them (56 cases). When they testified to the contrary, they were portrayed as biased. What does not happen, therefore, is the child implicating someone, the accused saying nothing happened, and the investigator siding with the accused. This suggests an underlying idealization that precedes and supports the ones operating on the surface of most cases: *the accused is guilty.* It goes without saying that this organizational stance runs roughly opposite to the Constitutional one of "innocent until proven guilty". . . .

While babysitters accused of child abuse may in theory be only "suspects," at the level of practice, they are "perpetrators." This discrepancy between "theory" and "practice" is more than an example of how the formal structures of organizations are accompanied by unintended and unprogrammed structures (Bittner, 1965). In this instance, child protection workers are formally enjoined to gather evidence about "perpetrators," not "suspects." Consider these guidelines from the agency's official handbook:

> Information collected from the person [witness] should include precise description of size, shape, color, type, and location of injury. [I]t may be possible to establish the credibility of the child, the responsible caretaker or the *perpetrator* as a source of this information. . . . The *perpetrator* and victim may be credible persons and need to be judged on the basis of the same factors as any other persons. (Italics added.)

The implicit message is that the goal of the child abuse investigation is not to determine an individual's guilt or innocence but to find evidence to be used in recording or "documenting" what is already taken for granted, that parties initially identified as the "perpetrator" and "victim" are in fact the "perpetrator" and "victim." Strictly speaking, then, the goal is not to determine "who did what to whom," since that information is assumed at the outset, but rather, to document that agency rules have been followed, and that the investigation was conducted in a rational, impersonal manner.

DETERMINING INTENTIONALITY

A decision-rule was also needed to determine the babysitter's intentions. While babysitters were portrayed in the allegations as malicious or exploitive, many babysitters offered a different version of their motivations. Among the babysitters accused of physical abuse, [some] acknowledged hitting the children but also claimed they intended no harm. Three said they were having a bad day, were under unusual stress, and simply "lost it." They attributed their violence to a spontaneous, non-instrumental, expression of frustration. For example, one male caregiver took a two-year-old to the potty several times but the child did not go. Later he noticed that the child's diaper was wet; so he hurried him to the potty.

However, just before being placed on the potty the child had a bowel movement. At that point the caregiver lost his temper and hit the child.

One woman who was labeled abusive claimed she was ill and never wanted to babysit in the first place. She only agreed to take care of a two-year-old girl because the girl's mother insisted. The mother had an unexpected schedule change at work and needed child care on an emergency basis. The abusive event occurred soon after the babysitter served lunch to the child. While the sitter rested on a couch in the living room, she observed the girl messing with her lunch. The sitter got up and tried to settle the child. When this did not work, she took away the girl's paper plate and threw it in the garbage. At that point the girl began to cry for her mother. The babysitter returned to the living room to lie down on the couch. But the girl followed her, wailing for her mother. When the girl reached the couch, the babysitter sat up and slapped her.

Other babysitters described their violence in instrumental terms: their goal was to discipline the children and not to hurt or injure them. They said that whatever injuries occurred were the accidental result of hitting (in one case, biting) the children harder than they meant to do. Some sitters indicated that the only reason children were injured during a disciplinary action was that the children moved just as they were being hit, exposing a sensitive part of the body to the blow. Others protested that the child's movements made it impossible to aim the blows accurately or to assess how hard they were hitting. . . .

To sift out the babysitters' "official" intentions from the versions offered by the sitters themselves, several social workers explicitly invoked the following reasoning: Physical damage to the child would be considered "intentional" if the acts which produced them were intentional. Thus, a social worker wrote:

> I am concluding that this injury to the child was non-accidental in that the babysitter did have a purpose in striking the child, that purpose being to discipline her in hopes of modifying her behavior.

While close examination of this logic reveals an absurdity (the injury was seen as "intentional" despite the fact that it was produced by an act aimed at an entirely different outcome, "modifying her behavior"), the practical consequence of such a formula was a simple method of determining a suspect's intentions: If a babysitter was known to intentionally hit a child, causing an injury, the social worker could conclude the babysitter intended to cause the injury. Through such a formula, the most common excuse utilized by babysitters to account for their actions, that the injury was the accidental result of a disciplinary action, was interpreted a confession of responsibility for physical abuse.

To give another example of how this formula provided a short-cut to determining intentionality, one social worker concluded her recording as follows:

> Physical abuse is founded in that the caretaker did hit the child on the face because she was throwing a temper tantrum and left a bruise approximately one inch long under the right eye. This constitutes a non-accidental injury. The bruise is still visible after five days.

In cases involving allegations of physical abuse, the problem of figuring out what the babysitter was really contemplating at the time of the violation never came up as a separate issue because the alleged perpetrator's motivation to injure the child was seen as the operational equivalent of two prior questions, "Does the child have an injury resulting from a blow?" and "Did the babysitter intentionally strike the child?" When each of these questions was answered affirmatively, intent to harm the child was inferred. Thus, it was possible for a social worker to observe, "It was this writer's opinion that the babysitter was surprised at the injury she left on the child by spanking the child," and later conclude, "the injury occurred as a result of a non-accidental incident". . . .

There were only two cases of sexual abuse in which the alleged abuser acknowledged touching the child in a manner consistent with the allegations, but at the same time denied sexual intent. In one of these cases, the alleged abuser said he only touched a 10-year-old boy's genitals in the process of giving him a bath. In the other case, the alleged abuser claimed he only touched the girl's body as part of an anatomy lesson, to show her where her crib and pelvic bones were located. Both of these accounts were dismissed as preposterous. The social workers expressed the opinion that sexual intent was the only possible reason any one would enact the types of behavior attributed to the accused in the allegations. . . .

To summarize, in cases of both physical and sexual abuse, the intent to commit these acts was seen as a necessary component of the specific behaviors used to accomplish them. Hitting which resulted in an injury was always treated as if it was a direct indicator of the motivation to injure. Similarly, behavior commonly known as "sexual" was always treated as if it was identical with the suspect's intent to sexually exploit. The fact that social workers sometimes described the suspects' surprise and horror at the physical damage their violence caused the child did not make the attribution of "intent to harm" more problematic because suspects' accounts were not organizationally defined as indicators of intent. Consistent with Mills (1940), motives for child abuse are not features of the perpetrator's psyche, but rather, of the bureaucracy and profession. That 50 of the babysitters labeled as abusive denied performing the actions imputed to them, and another 14 were not interviewed at all (either because they could not be located or refused to speak to the social worker) demonstrated that it was possible to "officially" determine babysitters' intentions without confirmatory statements from the babysitters themselves.

DISCUSSION

Sociologists have often questioned official records on the grounds of their accuracy, reliability, and representativeness. However, the methods through which and by which deviance is routinely displayed in records have rarely been investigated (cf. Cicourel & Kitsuse, 1963; Kitsuse & Cicourel, 1963). This study has treated as problematic the standardized arguments and evidence which social workers use in official documents to prove that child abuse has taken place. In this regard, child abuse is seen as an accomplishment of a bureaucratic system in which members agree to treat specific phenomena as if they were "child abuse." The proof of abuse was problematic since more than half of the suspects either denied the accusations or were not interviewed. Social workers "made do" without supportive testimony suspects by routinely defining them as "non-credible" witnesses. Also, social workers managed to conform to agency regulations requiring proof that suspects intended to harm or exploit children by agreeing to treat specific observables as if they represented the intent to harm or exploit.

Thus, the designation of child abuse was simplified. Testimony from the person most likely to disagree with this label, the accused, did not have to be considered. This is not to say that testimony from the accused might overcome the processes of institutional sense-making. It is to suggest, rather, that defining the accused as non-credible makes the designation of child abuse more "cut and dried," defendable, and recordable, since abuse that might otherwise be denied, excused, or justified, either in whole or in part, can then be fully attributed to suspects.

While it can be argued that simplifying the means by which suspects are labeled is desirable for a society concerned about keeping dangerous people away from children, the negative consequences should be acknowledged. As already shown, individuals who assign child abuse labels have more power than suspects, making it impossible for parties at risk of being labeled to "negotiate" on an equal footing with labelers. Indeed, any disjuncture between suspects' and investigators' versions of "what really happened" do not have to be resolved prior to the attribution of child abuse (cf. Pollner, 1987, pp. 77-81). Since investigators have the capacity to impose their versions of reality on suspects, the only "resolution" needed from the investigators' perspective entails finding ways to make their decisions defendable in writing.

As might also be expected, the personal, social, and legal stigma resulting from designating this label is enormous. Once the impression has been formed that a person is a child abuser, the expectation exists that he or she will continue to be abusive. Moreover, there is [nothing] a person can do to remove this label. It exists as part of a permanent record that can be [accessed] whenever a person's child care capacities or moral standing are questioned (cf. Rosenshan, 1973).

While most who write about child abuse are enmeshed in that system, either as practitioners or idealogues and so are strained to defend its existence, in recent years critics have [expressed] concern about the growing numbers of people labeled as child abusers (Besharov, 1986; Eberle & Eberle, 1986; Elshtain, 1985; Johnson, 1985; Pride, 1986; Wexler, 1985). Most trace this "overattribution" of child abuse to professional and lay people's "emotionally charged desire to 'do something' about child abuse, fanned by repeated and often sensational media coverage" (Besharov, 1986, p. 19). However, Conrad and Schneider (1980, p. 270) provide a more general explanation: "bureaucratic 'industries' with large budgets and many employees . . . depend for their existence on the acceptance of a particular deviance designation. They become 'vested interests' in every sense of the term." To take their analysis one step farther, "bureaucratic industries" have a vested interest not only in a label, but in a labeling process—specifically in finding ways of reducing complexity and making labeling accomplishable. . . .

To conclude, this study has shown some of the ways in which the construction of documents labels deviance. The main findings include bureaucrats' determination to translate sex and violence into endlessly accumulated verbal detail, to "make do" with whatever information is available, to fashion proofs of child abuse based on the new "common sense" that children's testimony is more credible than adults', and to develop simple, accomplishable ways of imputing intentionality that are unaffected by suspects' accounts.

DISCUSSION QUESTIONS

1. Bureaucracies use official records to document "what happened," as is the case in Margolin's study. But for what else do bureaucrats use these official records?

2. By referring to these suspects as "perpetrators" in the official reports, what is the underlying message that the agency is sending?

3. What methods did social workers develop and use in order to simplify the labeling process?

4. What did Margolin conclude about how social workers and bureaucracies in general officially document deviance?

REFERENCES

Lemert, E. M. (1951). *Social pathology: A systematic approach to the theory of sociopathic behavior.* New York: McGraw-Hill.

Schur, E. M. (1971). *Labeling deviant behavior: Its sociological implications.* New York: Harper & Row.

20

PARENTAL SANCTIONS AND DELINQUENT BEHAVIOR

Toward Clarification of Braithwaite's Theory of Reintegrative Shaming

CARTER HAY

EDITOR'S INTRODUCTION—This reading selection addresses a fascinating component of labeling theory, namely reintegrative shaming, an innovative theory put forth by John Braithwaite in his 1989 text *Crime, Shame, and Reintegration.* The theory evolved out of Braithwaite's observation that, when viewed separately, existing theories of crime causation make limited contributions to our understanding of crime. Braithwaite felt that an integrated approach was needed, one that would consider empirically verified propositions with current knowledge about crime. Therefore, in a variety of ways, this theory extends the basic premises of labeling theory by examining the reactions of offenders and agents of crime control on the macro- and microlevels.

In his theory of reintegrative shaming, Braithwaite finds the source of crime control in "reactions to deviance that simultaneously evoke remorse from offenders for the rules they have violated and reinforce the individual's membership in the community of law-abiding citizens" (p. 192, this volume). Braithwaite contrasts reintegrative shaming with stigmatization, or disintegrative shaming, in which little effort is made to forgive offenders or reconcile them with their families or communities. Braithwaite argues that stigmatization will lead to higher rates of crime and delinquency by increasing the likelihood of subcultural association and by insulating offenders from future attempts at shaming (p. 192, this volume).

Since its inception, reintegrative shaming theory has influenced both the field of criminal justice and academic criminology, but this interest has sparked few empirical tests of the theory. Hay contends that this lack of empirical testing stems largely from the lack of theoretical clarity in Braithwaite's statement of the theory. Hay finds that, in general, the theory provides for definitions of key concepts and measurement strategies only at a minimum level, and, at times, the theory omits seemingly necessary conditions for the analysis of such important factors as the likelihood of corrective reactions and the nature of corrective reactions.

In his article, Hay attempts to correct these errors and demonstrate how the microlevel portion of the theory—the level that considers family relations—can be tested. According to Hay, the theory embodies much potential as a valuable theory of crime causation, and he hopes that his analysis will eventually encourage empirical tests of this approach.

Almost a decade ago, John Braithwaite (1989) put forth an innovative theory of crime causation in *Crime, Shame and Reintegration.* The theory of reintegrative shaming was inspired in part by Braithwaite's observation that, when viewed separately, existing theories of crime causation make limited contribution to our understanding of crime. However, most of the prominent theories do contain at least some empirically verified propositions. Thus, there was need for some integrating framework that could subsume such propositions, while laying to rest those propositions less consistent with current knowledge. For Braithwaite, this framework is provided by the concept of reintegrative shaming.

Braithwaite locates the source of crime control in reactions to deviance that simultaneously evoke remorse from offenders for the rules they have violated and reinforce the individual's membership in the community of law-abiding citizens. Punishments of this sort are examples of reintegrative shaming and are argued to reduce crime by reinforcing basic moral norms of society and restoring the strength of social ties that may have been damaged by the rule violation.

Reintegrative shaming is contrasted with stigmatization, or disintegrative shaming, in which little effort is made to forgive offenders or reconcile them with their families or communities. Stigmatization is argued to increase crime and delinquency by increasing the likelihood of subcultural affiliation and insulating offenders against future attempts at shaming. In the period since its publication, the theory has influenced the fields of both criminal justice and academic criminology. In criminal justice, the theory has laid the foundation for the increasing use of pre-trial diversion to programs that require a meeting between the victim, offender, and other interested parties to discuss and repair the harm caused by the offense. This is seen most prominently in the USA with victim-offender mediation programs in the juvenile justice system (Umbreit & Coates, 1993), and in Australia and New Zealand with 'family group conferences' for juvenile offenders (Braithwaite & Mugford, 1994).

In academic criminology, on the other hand, much recent work has incorporated the logic of reintegrative shaming. As part of his defiance theory, Sherman (1993) has argued that sanctions based on reintegrative shaming are likely to promote deterrence, whereas stigmatizing sanctions are likely to promote defiance. Sampson and Laub (1993) also make reference to reintegrative shaming principles in their description of the type of family environment that is conducive to informal social control. Braithwaite's theory has also been used in the more general study of social control. Heimer and Staffen (1995) applied the theory to the decisions of medical care providers regarding the 'labeling' of parents with infants in a neonatal intensive care unit.

Thus, the theory seems to have generated some degree of interest. Interest in the theory has not, however, been translated into empirical tests of it. In fact, there is only one explicit test to date (which found basic support for the theory), and Braithwaite is one of its authors (Makkai & Braithwaite, 1994). But there is potentially much to be gained by testing this theory. The theory directly bears on two issues at the heart of criminological theorizing: the relationship between sanctions and criminal behavior and the role of child-rearing in preventing the onset of delinquency. Not only does the theory address these two important issues, but with the notion of reintegrative shaming, it presents a new and potentially powerful concept for doing so.

The question remains, why no empirical tests? The position of this chapter is that this scarcity of tests stems from the lack of theoretical clarity in Braithwaite's statement of the theory. In general, definitions of key concepts and strategies for their measurement are provided at a minimum level and at times the theory omits seemingly necessary considerations. The purpose of this chapter is to correct these errors and instill clarity into an otherwise impressive theory, with the hope of encouraging empirical tests of it in the future. Before this, however, it is necessary to provide a more elaborate description of the theory.

Hay, C. (1998). Parental sanctions and delinquent behavior: Toward clarification of Braithwaite's theory of reintegrative shaming. *Theoretical Criminology, 2,* 419-433.

THE THEORY OF REINTEGRATIVE SHAMING

The theory of reintegrative shaming is intended to explain, among both individuals and societies, rates of predatory offenses against persons and property. The reason for this slightly restricted definition of crime is that reintegrative shaming is thought to be relevant only for offenses in which there is normative consensus regarding their wrongfulness. For offenses in which consensus is lacking, shaming will be sporadic and inconsistent at best. Marijuana use in the USA is an example of such an offense.

The key explanatory variable in the theory is *shaming,* which is defined as 'all social processes of expressing disapproval which have the intention or effect of invoking remorse in the person being shamed and/or condemnation by others who become aware of the shaming' (Braithwaite, 1989, p. 100). Braithwaite distinguishes between two types of shaming. Shaming is *reintegrative* when it is followed by efforts to reintegrate the offender back into the community of law-abiding citizens. This may be achieved through words or gestures of forgiveness or ceremonies to decertify the offender as deviant (pp. 100-101). The use of reintegrative shaming is argued to reduce crime by two principal mechanisms, both of which operate at multiple units of analysis. First, it reinforces the basic moral norms underlying the rule that was violated, such that both shamed individuals and those that participate in or become aware of the shaming will be more likely to deem commission of the crime 'unthinkable' (1989, p. 81). Second, there is thought to be a deterrent effect, both specific and general. The shamed individual will wish to avoid the discomfort of feeling guilty and ashamed in the future. This effect is enhanced by the coupling of shame with reintegration, which serves to foster attachment between the individual and those who might shame future criminality, thereby increasing the perceived costs of future shaming. Also, in addition to specifically deterring the shamed offender, shame also generally deters those that become aware of or participate in the shaming (1989, p. 81).

Reintegrative shaming is contrasted with *stigmatization,* which is disintegrative shaming in which little or no effort is made to forgive offenders or affirm the basic goodness of their character, and thus, reconcile them with their community (1989, p. 101). The significance of stigmatization is that it breaks attachments to those who might shame future criminality, essentially rejecting offenders as outcasts. . . . Thus, stigmatization is argued to increase subsequent rates of crime and delinquency by increasing the likelihood of subcultural affiliation and insulating offenders against future attempts at shaming.

In addition to this treatment of the key explanatory variables, Braithwaite also discusses the structural factors that increase the likelihood that reintegrative shaming will be used. For individuals, social characteristics that contribute to *interdependency* predict the extent to which reintegrative shaming will be used in response to their criminal acts. Interdependency refers to the extent to which individuals are involved in networks in which they are dependent on others to achieve valued ends and others are dependent on them (pp. 99-100). Characteristics that predict interdependency are age (being under 15 and over 25), being married, female, employed, and having high educational and occupational aspirations.

At the community or societal level, factors that contribute to *communitarianism* are said to predict an area's overall use of reintegrative shaming. Communitarianism refers to a condition of communities or societies whereby individuals are densely enmeshed in interdependencies, which are characterized by mutual help and trust (p. 100). A territorial unit's levels of urbanization and residential mobility are identified as factors that affect the level of communitarianism.

It may be readily apparent from even this brief description that the novelty of Braithwaite's theory follows from the way Braithwaite cleverly fuses together the dominant theories of crime to develop a new theory that builds upon their strengths. For example, the notions of interdependency and reintegration follow from social control theory's emphasis on attachment to conventional others; stigmatization comes from labeling theory and its recognition that sanctions may have unintended effects; the role of criminal subcultures comes obviously from subcultural theories of gang and delinquent peer group involvement; and lastly, as Braithwaite (1989, p. 15) points out, the whole theory can be understood in terms of cognitive social learning theory—in short, this is a theory about how individuals and social groups learn to perceive the commission of crime as unthinkable.

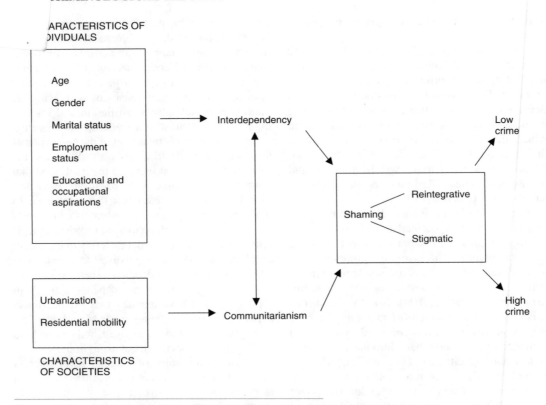

Figure 20.1   Braithwaite's Theory of Reintegrative Shaming

What is truly unique, however, is Braithwaite's emphasis on shaming. Though the notion of normative validation was introduced long ago by Durkheim, Braithwaite's emphasis on shaming goes well beyond this. Durkheim argued that the act of sanctioning deviance validates the norms that proscribe deviance in the first place. Braithwaite, on the other hand, insists that corrective reactions must be *explicitly directed* toward validating norms; from his perspective, they must *shame*. Mere 'punishment,' with the numerous forms it may take, does not guarantee the validation of norms.

EVALUATION AND CRITIQUE

Measuring Reintegrative Shaming

Perhaps the most important reason for the paucity of tests is that the theory deals with concepts that are difficult to measure and Braithwaite provides little direction in this regard. . . . [There are] substantial barriers to measuring reintegrative shaming at the societal level, and thus [to] fully testing the theory. At the individual level, however, there is more cause for optimism. As Braithwaite points out, survey research can be used to measure individuals' perceptions of having been exposed to reintegrative shaming or stigmatization. However, Braithwaite provides little direction as to how this might be done. The theory does not provide an explicit inventory of the necessary and/or sufficient conditions of reintegrative shaming and stigmatization, nor does it make suggestions for survey questions to measure these concepts. These tasks will be addressed in a later section of the chapter.

Formal Event Versus Informal Process

Another possible critique of Braithwaite's statement of the theory is that it does not systematically distinguish between reintegrative shaming as a formal event and reintegrative shaming as an informal process. When viewed as a formal event, reintegrative shaming can be described in the following way: a shaming ceremony occurs in which the offender, the victim, and other interested parties are all present. The victim and other members of the community openly express their abhorrence of the crime that has been committed, thereby evoking remorse from the offender and soliciting an apology and other gestures of repentance. The victim and other participants then forgive the offender and affirm that they still believe in the basic goodness of his or her character. The community's act of shaming, combined with the offender's repentance, bolsters commitment to the moral principle in question among all of those involved with or aware of the ritual.

When viewed as an informal process, however, reintegrative shaming takes a form that is less definite and tangible, but of a more serial nature. Transgressions can be responded to consistently with a frown, a disapproving glance, a brief verbal admonishment, or any one of many other possible reactions, all of which are intended to evoke remorse or shame and an apologetic reaction. To be reintegrative, these reactions would have to be delivered within the context of relationships that are overwhelmingly characterized by social approval (p. 68). Reintegrative shaming as an informal process is almost always going to be directed at offenders by primary agents of social control, most notably parents, teachers, and peers, and awareness of the shaming is generally going to be limited to the shamed individual and those in close physical or social proximity. Consideration of both of these manifestations of reintegrative shaming is critical to fully testing the theory, but Braithwaite makes virtually no explicit reference to the distinction, except in passing reference to the *general* and *specific* effects of reintegrative shaming. . . .

The Incomplete Conceptualization of Sanctions

An omission of an important consideration further hinders testing the theory. Braithwaite perceives sanctions in terms of a continuum with reintegrative shaming on one end and stigmatization on the other. He argues that reintegrative shaming decreases crime and that stigmatization increases crime, but he makes no mention of the

effect of *other* possible reactions to crime. One example of another possibility is *no reaction to crime.* . . .

A similar problem is the failure to consider situations in which there is a reaction to deviance, but it in no way involves shaming. Shaming involves evoking remorse from the offender for the rule that has been violated, and can be done either in a reintegrative or stigmatizing manner. But what about sanctions that make little or no effort to evoke remorse? For example, some reactions to deviance may be intended to evoke fear of future punishments instead. The modern criminal justice system is seemingly based on just such a premise. . . .

Toward Clarification of the Theory

The previous section addressed several issues that have made interpretation of Braithwaite's theory difficult, and in so doing, have precluded empirical tests of the theory. This section clarifies the micro-level portion of the theory, first, by making explicit the necessary conditions of reintegrative shaming, and second, by considering in detail the range of cases in which the necessary conditions are not met, thereby establishing a reference point for analyzing the effects of reintegrative shaming.

Limiting the Scope of the Theory

In previous sections, it was discussed that Braithwaite's theory is intended to explain crime at both macro- and micro-levels of analysis. Undoubtedly, this is a strength of the theory. However, given that it is in the initial stages of empirical verification, it will be more productive to concentrate on the micro-level portion of the theory. The reasons for doing so relate to feasibility and efficiency. First, as was demonstrated earlier, there are substantial barriers to testing the macro-level portion of the theory. A measurable definition of a society's level of reintegrative shaming does not yet exist, and conducting nationally representative surveys of individuals' perceived exposure to reintegrative shaming is not feasible. Thus, it is reasonable to begin with tests of its micro-level hypotheses, which are more testable. Specifically, the recommendations in this article will be most applicable to a research design that takes juveniles as the unit of analysis and focuses on the sanctions used by their parents. The strategy would seem acceptable to Braithwaite, who commented that 'the best place to see reintegrative shaming at work is in loving families' (p. 56).

It should be noted that limiting the focus to a micro-level analysis of the family not only affects *whose* behavior is measured but also *what* is measured. Recall that in a previous section, reintegrative shaming as a formal event was distinguished from reintegrative shaming as an informal process. An event involves a single occurrence, whereas a process involves a series of actions, changes, or functions. Though one could analyse reintegrative shaming events within a family, the focus of this discussion will be on the *process* of punishment within a family; specifically, the focus is on youths' perceptions of the general nature of their direct experience with parental sanctioning. This approach is logically more sensible, given that single punishment events may be trivial in comparison to the on-going, daily patterns that persist within a household. Additionally, this approach appears to be more consistent with Braithwaite's description of reintegrative shaming within families.

Necessary Conditions of Reintegrative Shaming

A first step toward explicitly defining and measuring reintegrative shaming involves specifying its necessary conditions. It is argued here that reintegrative shaming as a process exists within a household if all of the following conditions are met:

1. a high probability of detection of rule violations;

2. a high probability of corrective reaction upon detection;

3. shaming is used as a corrective reaction;

4. offenders are reintegrated.

Notice that these four conditions stem from two different considerations. The first two conditions deal with the likelihood that a rule violation will evoke a corrective reaction sanction, whereas the last two conditions deal with the nature of corrective reactions. These two considerations will be dealt with in some detail

later, but a brief discussion is appropriate here. The first two conditions refer to social controllers' levels of supervision and intolerance of rule-violations, respectively. Braithwaite includes neither of these two in his discussion of testing the theory, but a full test of the theory requires that they be considered. A comparison between the effects of reintegrative shaming and stigmatization is of little relevance if offenses are detected and reacted to only sporadically.

If an offense is both detected and reacted to, we then consider the nature of those reactions. The third condition refers to the extent to which shaming is used—the extent to which a sanctioning agent uses expressions of disapproval intended to elicit remorse from the offender. Shaming is intended to weigh on the conscience of the offender. In short, shaming involves some sort of communication that admonishes individuals about how guilty they should feel over their conduct. The last condition refers to the extent to which the offender is reintegrated. Braithwaite seems to identify four different components of reintegration (to be discussed later), all of which affirm the basic goodness in character of the person being shamed.

Taking these four necessary conditions, one can identify the different reactive outcomes relevant to a test of the theory of reintegrative shaming. This is done in the following sections, beginning with the outcomes associated with the likelihood of corrective reactions.

The Likelihood of Corrective Reactions

Evaluating the effects of different processes of corrective reaction assumes that a corrective reaction occurs in the first place. Since this assumption is questionable, a test of this theory requires some knowledge on subjects' likelihood of experiencing a corrective reaction. This probability can be seen as a function of two factors, the probability of detection and the probability of corrective reaction upon detection.

Table 20.1 illustrates the four possibilities that emerge when combinations of these two factors are considered. An analysis of the differential effects of different types of punishment should be most relevant for individuals for [whom] there is a high probability of both detection and corrective reaction upon detection, since these

Table 20.1   The Likelihood of Corrective Reactions

		Probability of Detection	
		High	Low
Probability of corrective reaction upon detection	High	Necessary conditions satisfied	Necessary conditions *not* satisfied
	Low	Necessary conditions *not* satisfied	Necessary conditions *not* satisfied

individuals are most subject to corrective responses. At the other extreme, reintegrative shaming can be of little significance for individuals whose violations are rarely detected and rarely reacted to even when detected.

For individuals in [whom] the two probabilities are mixed, neither both high nor both low, the relevance of reintegrative shaming should be limited as well. For example, if the probability of detection is high, but there is a low probability of corrective reaction upon detection, then sanctions are relatively absent, thus precluding an analysis of the nature of sanctions. Similarly, when detection is low, it can be expected that whether or not reintegrative shaming is used will be of only limited relevance because violations are only [seldom] punished. It should be noted, however, that this is an empirically testable question. It may be that the nature of punishment is significant, even if detection is low, so long as detection is virtually always accompanied by a corrective reaction.

The Nature of Corrective Reactions

If the likelihood of corrective reaction is high, or if at the very least, there is a high likelihood of corrective reaction in the event of detection, then one can consider the nature of those corrective reactions. From the perspective of this theory, the nature of corrective reactions is a function of two factors, shaming and reintegration. Table 20.2 shows the different possibilities that emerge when combinations of these two factors are considered. Most pertinent to the theory are reintegrative shaming and stigmatization, both of which involve the use of shaming. The theory hypothesizes that reintegrative shaming decreases offending and stigmatization increases it.

As Table 20.2 shows, however, these are not the only outcomes that emerge when the theory's two key variables, shaming and reintegration, are considered. Specifically, not all corrective reactions involve shaming. The likelihood of a corrective reaction may be high, but the use of shaming may be low. Thus, one must consider what these other reactions might involve. The most obvious possibility involves the use of fear. It is reasonable to expect that in many instances, reactions to deviance may be intended to evoke fear of future sanctions. This is certainly a part of the formal justice system and reactions of this sort in a household are easy to imagine as well. It is suggested, therefore, that corrective reactions not intended to shame are intended to *deter*. Similar to shaming, deterrence may be attempted in either a reintegrative or stigmatizing manner.

One may reasonably ask, what is the utility of considering non-shaming sanctions in a test of this theory? First, a consideration of other types of sanctioning does nothing to interfere with a test of Braithwaite's original assertions. The effect of reintegrative shaming may still be compared to that of stigmatic shaming. But a consideration of non-shaming reactions allows for a more informative evaluation of the theory. Notice that if shaming is not used as a corrective reaction, the theory is of little use—its *basic hypothesis cannot be tested*. This is unfortunate because Braithwaite's emphasis on reintegration may be of some significance. For example, one may ask if attempts at deterrence that are done reintegratively have a different effect than those that are done in a more stigmatizing manner? As currently stated, Braithwaite's theory does not allow for such a question, instead deeming reintegration important only as it interacts with shaming. The theory can make that argument, but whether or not it is true is an empirical question that should be considered.

Table 20.2   The Nature of Corrective Reactions

		Shaming	Shaming
		High	Low
Reintegration	High	Reintegrative shaming	Reintegrative deterrence?
	Low	Stigmatic shaming	Stigmatic deterrence?

MEASURING KEY VARIABLES IN THE THEORY

The previous section discussed the necessary conditions of reintegrative shaming. Furthermore, it was demonstrated that consideration of a broader range of sanctions allows for a more useful test of the theory's basic tenets. In this section, strategies for measuring the theory's key explanatory variables are put forth.

Introductory Comments

A few comments about the following discussion should be made in advance. First, this section focuses on indicators for survey research. This should not be construed as discouraging qualitative tests of this theory. Quite the opposite; it is hoped that these indicators can provide a useful guide for data collection and interpretation for qualitative and ethnographic tests of the theory.

Second, because the measurement of shaming and reintegration are the most obvious obstacles to testing the theory, the emphasis here is on the measurement of these explanatory variables. There will be no detailed treatment of the theory's other variables. . . .

Third, the survey questions are designed to ask children about their perceptions of parental sanctioning rather than parents about their perceptions of their own sanctioning practices. The rationale is that Braithwaite's theory emphasizes individuals' cognitive perceptions of sanctioning. Individuals are expected to react to sanctions according to their subjective perceptions of them, regardless of how accurate or inaccurate these perceptions are. Whether children's perceptions correlate with parents' perceptions is an interesting empirical issue, but not critical to a test of Braithwaite's theory. Nevertheless, it should be noted that the process of modifying the questions to inquire about parents' perceptions would be both simple and logically obvious.

Next, the questions are designed to pertain to two frames of reference regarding adolescents' experiences with parental sanctioning:

1. parents' typical reaction to the violation of some rule that they consider important; and

2. parents' reaction to the most *recent* violation of some rule that they consider important.

As noted previously, the reason for considering the former is that the focus here is on respondents' general impressions of their experiences with sanctioning. These general impressions, rather than impressions of one particular event, are expected to be the basis for how one responds to sanctioning. Nevertheless, it may also be important to inquire about respondents' most recent experiences. The reasoning is simply that the more specific question may be easier for respondents to answer, thus resulting in more accurate reports of past experiences (Sudman & Bradburn, 1991, p. 39). Furthermore, asking about the most recent sanctioning event will increase reporting of extreme events (since for some respondents, as a matter of chance, the most recent event will be an extreme event). When respondents are asked only about parents' typical reaction to rule violations, then extreme events are less likely to be reported. This is a liability to the extent that extreme sanctioning events influence behavior as much or more than the general experience of sanctioning.

Last, and most important, this section seeks in part to resolve an issue neglected in Braithwaite's statement of the theory; namely, in testing the micro-level portion of the theory, for which rule-violating behaviors should researchers evaluate the nature of corrective reactions? In most instances, Braithwaite discusses reintegrative shaming as a response to illegal offenses. On the other hand, his discussion of 'the family model' of reintegrative shaming (pp. 56-7) seems to emphasize the on-going, daily punishment processes in response to normal, expected rule violations that occur in all households. The significance of the issue is this: if reintegrative shaming is important only as it is used in response to law-violating behavior, then the micro-level portion of the theory is in no way a general theory of criminal behavior (contrary to what is suggested in the book's preface), but rather, a theory about recidivism or secondary deviance (that is, a theory about the effect of reactions to criminal behavior on subsequent rates of criminal behavior). . . .

The Measurement of Shaming and Deterrence

The first obstacle to testing this theory involves the measurement of shaming. In the one empirical test thus far, Makkai and Braithwaite (1994) operationalized shaming as simply the expression of disapproval. The use of shame was measured by pooling responses to two questions posed to health care regulators, regarding the extent to which they agreed that:

1. 'Standards monitoring teams should not hide their disapproval of poor practices in nursing homes'; and

2. 'It is important for standards monitoring teams to appear tolerant at all times, to rate nursing homes without openly expressing disapproval when the ratings are poor' (1994, p. 368).

In Braithwaite's original statement of the theory, however, shaming is defined more specifically as an expression of disapproval that is explicitly intended to evoke remorse in the person being shamed. In other words, punishment and threats of punishment may be considered expressions of disapproval, but they are not shaming. Because this distinction is critical to the theory, suggestions for measurement provided here will adhere to the more stringent view of shaming originally put forth. The following question can be used to ascertain the extent to which shaming is the reaction of parents to a respondent's rule violations:

> I want you to think of your parents' ([normal reaction to you when you have]/[reaction to you the last time you]) violated some rule that they consider important.

From your perspective, how important (is/was) it to your parents to make you feel guilty or ashamed for having broken the rule?

> a. very important;
> b. somewhat important;
> c. only slightly important;
> d. not important at all.

It is assumed here that the terms 'guilty' and 'ashamed' are sufficiently close in meaning that they present no problems related to 'double-barreled' questions (Sudman & Bradburn, 1991, p. 132), but instead, increase the chances of easy comprehension for respondents. Braithwaite (1989, p. 57) notes that: 'For our purposes, to induce guilt and to shame are inextricably part of the same set of social processes.'

Regarding deterrence, recall that in the previous section it was discussed that in the event that a respondent reports that shaming is not the normal corrective response, it would be of some theoretical importance to know what is the normal response. Specifically, it was suggested that reactions not intended to evoke shame may be intended to evoke fear of future punishment. In other words, there may be an attempt at deterrence. The following two questions could be used to measure this possibility:

> I want you to think of your parents' ([normal reaction to you when you have]/[reaction to you the last time you]) violated some rule that they consider important. In these situations:

> How important (is/was) it to them to punish you so severely that you will never consider doing this sort of thing again?

> a. very important;
> b. somewhat important;
> c. only slightly important;
> d. not important at all.

> How important (is/was) it to them to make you think that if you break the rule again, you will be punished even more severely?

> a. very important;
> b. somewhat important;
> c. only slightly important;
> d. not important at all.

Reintegration and Stigmatization

In both Braithwaite's original statement of the theory and Makkai and Braithwaite's (1994) test of it, stigmatization is discussed only in reference to reintegration: stigmatization is defined as the absence of reintegration. Thus, the best measurement strategy involves a single reintegration scale that includes each of the essential aspects of reintegration.

Braithwaite's discussion of reintegration seems to suggest four different, though not entirely distinct, components of a reintegrative corrective reaction. These are:

1. respectful;

2. directed at the evil of the act, not the person;

3. delivered in a context of general social approval; and

4. followed by gestures of forgiveness.

Each of these four components should be measured independently and their responses pooled in order to generate a reintegration scale. The following set of questions could be used to measure the four components of reintegration:

I want you to think of situations (the most recent situation) in which one or both of your parents have disciplined you for violating some rule that they consider important.

In (these situations/this situation), how respectful (are/were) your parents of your feelings and perspective?

a. very respectful;
b. somewhat respectful;
c. only slightly respectful;
d. not at all respectful.

Consider the following two statements:

(1) 'what you did was very wrong';

(2) 'only a bad kid such as yourself would do something like this.'

In your parents' reaction to what you did, which of these two statements were they more likely to have made?

a. statement (1);
b. statement (2);
c. both statement (1) and (2)
d. neither statement (1) [nor statement (2)]

To what extent do you agree or disagree with the following two statements?

Even when my parents ([are disciplining me for some rule that I have broken]/[were disciplining me]), I (know/knew) that they (see/saw) me as a good person:

a. strongly agree;
b. agree;
c. neither agree nor disagree;
d. disagree;
e. strongly disagree.

Their disciplining of me (is/was) followed by a clear communication of forgiveness.

a. strongly agree;
b. agree;
c. neither agree nor disagree;
d. disagree;
e. strongly disagree.

TESTING THE THEORY

If one is able to collect data for all the key variables of this theory, how should one go about testing its propositions? This section briefly addresses this question, taking into consideration the changes and clarifications that this chapter has proposed thus far.

Analysing the Likelihood of a Corrective Reaction

The first two variables to examine are the probability of detection and the probability of a corrective reaction upon detection. . . . An analysis of these two variables also allows one to assess how they interact to affect delinquency. . . . Therefore, two groups should be retained for the basic tests of the theory: those who perceive high probabilities of both detection and corrective reaction upon detection, and those who perceive a low probability of detection, but a high probability of corrective reaction upon detection.

Analysing the Correlates With Different Corrective Reactions

Recall that Braithwaite argues that individuals' involvement in interdependent relationships is associated with the type of corrective reaction (see Table 20.2) to which they are most likely to be exposed. Thus, one would need to look at how variables such as age, sex, attachment to parents, employment status, and educational and occupational aspirations are related to delinquency.

Analysing the Effects of Different Types of Corrective Reactions

Perhaps the most fruitful way to begin this examination is to evaluate bivariate relationships. For example, leaving aside the notion of reintegration, which is most strongly related to delinquency, the use of shame, deterrence, or an interaction between the two? Or, leaving aside the distinction between shame and deterrence, how is the use of reintegration related to delinquency? Note that Braithwaite makes no explicit mention of these comparisons; findings with respect to these questions do not bear on the theory's central hypothesis that the interaction between reintegration and shame is negatively related to delinquency. Nevertheless, the data requirements for testing the full theory provide the opportunity for such comparisons, many of which may provide useful knowledge regarding the effects of sanctions and the relationship between child-rearing practices and delinquency.

Next, we are interested in the theory's central hypothesis and a related hypothesis suggested by this article. First, the theory hypothesizes that a reintegration-shame interaction term should be negatively related to delinquency. Second, because not all corrective reactions will involve shaming, it will be useful to evaluate the relationship between a reintegration-deterrence interaction term and delinquency. In short, this allows us to test the generality of Braithwaite's concept of reintegration. Braithwaite discusses reintegration only as it relates to shaming practices, but its effect may be relevant for other types of corrective reactions as well.

DISCUSSION QUESTIONS

1. What are the key components of Braithwaite's theory of reintegrative shaming?

2. Although the theory has generated a fairly substantial amount of interest, why hasn't it been tested empirically? What problems with the theory does Hay suggest limit full consideration of reintegrative shaming?

3. In order to clarify the theory, Hay suggests that it must specify certain conditions under which shaming can occur. What are these conditions? Taking these conditions, how can you assess the likelihood and nature of corrective reactions?

4. What suggestions does Hay offer in terms of measuring key variables in the theory? Why is it important for Hay to focus on the testing of the "microlevel" component—the "family model"—of reintegrative shaming? What implications does that focus have for the entire theory?

REFERENCE

Braithwaite, J. (1989). *Crime, shame, and reintegration.* Cambridge, UK: Cambridge University Press.

21

Is "White Collar Crime" Crime?

Edwin H. Sutherland

EDITOR'S INTRODUCTION—In this 1945 article, Sutherland raises a timeless question for criminologists, legal scholars, and members of the corporate world: Is "white collar crime" crime? Sutherland stirs the semantic debate of whether the word *crime* can be applied to situations involving the violation of laws regarding antitrust, false advertising, and National Labor Relations and infringements of patent, copyright, and trademark laws. He then proceeds to ask why criminologists have not placed white-collar crime on the same level as other types of crime.

Sutherland provides readers with several examples of cases involving violations of various types of laws. He concludes that the legal decisions rendered in the decisions properly considered the violations to be criminal, namely on the grounds that the legal violations were injurious to certain parties and the law provided a penalty—a punishment, or sanction—for the criminal act.

But what is most striking about these cases, and perhaps other white collar crime cases as well, is the differential implementation of the criminal law to the cases and the subsequent elimination or minimization of the stigma that typically attaches to crime. Sutherland contends that the well-regarded status of the businessman, the trend away from punishment, and the relatively unorganized resentment of the public against white collar criminals explain this differential implementation of the criminal law.

Finally, Sutherland notes the importance of the relationship between law and the community within which it exists. Drawing a connection between public sentiment, morality, and white collar crime, Sutherland contends that although the same procedures are used in the enforcement of laws, which regulate all types of businesses and citizens, the laws regarding white collar crime tend to be less effective than other laws in the reinforcement of social mores. The fact that laws regulating white collar crime conceal the criminality of the behavior affects not only the public perception of the seriousness of these acts, but the very issue of whether the acts truly are "criminal."

The argument has been made that business and professional men commit crimes which should be brought within the scope of the theories of criminal behavior. In order to secure evidence as to the prevalence of such white collar crimes an analysis was made of the decisions by courts and commissions against the seventy largest industrial and mercantile corporations in the United States under four types of laws, namely, antitrust, false advertising, National Labor Relations, and infringement of patents, copyrights, and trademarks. This resulted in the finding that 547 such adverse decisions had been made, with an average of 7.8 decisions per corporation and with each corporation having at least 1. Although all of these were decisions that the behavior was unlawful, only 49 or 9 per cent of the total were made by criminal courts and were ipso facto decisions that the behavior was criminal. Since not all unlawful behavior is criminal behavior, these decisions can be used as a measure of criminal behavior only if the other 498 decisions can be shown to be decisions that the behavior of the corporations was criminal.

This is a problem in the legal definition of crime and involves two types of questions: May the word "crime" be applied to the behavior regarding which these decisions were made? If so, why is it not generally applied and why have not the criminologists regarded white collar crime as cognate with other crime? The first question involves semantics, the second interpretation or explanation.

A combination of two abstract criteria is generally regarded by legal scholars as necessary to define crime, namely: legal description of an act as socially injurious, and legal provision of a penalty for the act. When the criterion of legally defined social injury is applied to these 547 decisions the conclusion is reached that all of the classes of behaviors regarding which the decisions were made are legally defined as socially injurious. This can be readily determined by the words in the statutes—"crime" or "misdemeanor" in some, and "unfair," "discrimination," or "infringement" in all the others. The persons injured may be divided into two groups: first, a relatively small number of persons engaged in the same occupation as the offenders or in related occupations, and, second, the general public either as consumers or as constituents of the general social institutions which are affected by the violations of the laws.

The antitrust laws are designed to protect competitors and also to protect the institution of free competition as the regulator of the economic system and thereby to protect consumers against arbitrary prices, and to protect the institution of democracy against the dangers of great concentration of wealth in the hands of monopolies. Laws against false advertising are designed to protect competitors against unfair competition and also to protect consumers against fraud. The National Labor Relations Law is designed to protect employees against coercion by employers and also to protect the general public against interferences with commerce due to strikes and lockouts. The laws against infringements are designed to protect the owners of patents, copyrights, and trademarks against deprivation of their property and against unfair competition, and also to protect the institution of patents and copyrights which was established in order to "promote the progress of science and the useful arts." Violations of these laws are legally defined as injuries to the parties specified.

Each of these laws has a logical basis in the common law and is an adaptation of the common law to modern social organization. False advertising is related to common law fraud, and infringement to larceny. The National Labor Relations Law, as an attempt to prevent coercion, is related to the common law prohibition of restrictions on freedom in the form of assault, false imprisonment, and extortion. For at least two centuries prior to the enactment of the modern antitrust laws the common law was moving against restraint of trade, monopoly, and unfair competition.

Each of the four laws provides a penal sanction and thus meets the second criterion in the definition of crime, and each of the adverse decisions under these four laws, except certain decisions under the infringement laws to be discussed later, is a decision that a crime was committed. This conclusion will be made more specific by analysis of the penal sanctions provided in the . . . laws.

The Sherman antitrust law states explicitly that a violation of the law is a misdemeanor.

Sutherland, E. H. (1945). Is "white collar crime" crime? *American Sociological Review, 10,* 132-139.

Three methods of enforcement of this law are provided, each of them involving procedures regarding misdemeanors. First, it may be enforced by the usual criminal prosecution, resulting in the imposition of fine or imprisonment. Second, the attorney general of the United States and the several district attorneys are given the "duty" of "repressing and preventing" violations of the law by petitions for injunctions, and violations of the injunctions are punishable as contempt of court. This method of enforcing a criminal law was an invention and, as will be described later, is the key to the interpretation of the differential implementation of the criminal law as applied to white collar criminals. Third, parties who are injured by violations of the law are authorized to sue for damages, with a mandatory provision that the damages awarded be three times the damages suffered. These damages in excess of reparation are penalties for violation of the law. They are payable to the injured party in order to induce him to take the initiative in the enforcement of the criminal law and in this respect are similar to the earlier methods of private prosecutions under the criminal law. All three of these methods of enforcement are based on decisions that a criminal law was violated and therefore that a crime was committed; the decisions of a civil court or a court of equity as to these violations are as good evidence of criminal behavior as is the decision of a criminal court.

The Sherman antitrust law has been amended by the Federal Trade Commission Law, the Clayton Law, and several other laws. Some of these amendments define violations as crimes and provide the conventional penalties, but most of the amendments do not make the criminality explicit. A large proportion of the cases which are dealt with under these amendments could be dealt with, instead, under the original Sherman Law, which is explicitly a criminal law. In practice, the amendments are under the jurisdiction of the Federal Trade Commission, which has authority to make official decisions as to violations. The Commission has two principal sanctions under its control, namely: the stipulation and the cease and desist order. The Commission may, after the violation of the law has been proved, accept a stipulation from the corporation that it will not violate the law in the future. Such stipulations are customarily restricted to the minor or technical violations. If a stipulation is violated or if no stipulation is accepted, the Commission may issue a cease and desist order; this is equivalent to a court's injunction except that violation is not punishable as contempt. If the Commission's desist order is violated, the Commission may apply to the court for an injunction, the violation of which is punishable as contempt. By an amendment to the Federal Trade Commission Law in the Wheeler-Lea Act of 1938 an order of the Commission becomes "final" if not officially questioned within a specified time and thereafter its violation is punishable by a civil fine. Thus, although certain interim procedures may be used in the enforcement of the amendments to the antitrust law, fines or imprisonment for contempt are available if the interim procedures fail. In this respect the interim procedures are similar to probation in ordinary criminal cases. An unlawful act is not defined as criminal by the fact that it is punished, but by the fact that it is punishable. Larceny is as truly a crime when the thief is placed on probation as when he is committed to prison. The argument may be made that punishment for contempt of court is not punishment for violation of the original law and that, therefore, the original law does not contain a penal sanction. This reasoning is specious since the original law provides the injunction with its penalty as a part of the procedure for enforcement. Consequently all of the decisions made under the amendments to the antitrust law are decisions that the corporations committed crimes. . . .

. . . . In the preceding discussion the penalties which are definitive of crime have been limited to fine, imprisonment, and punitive damages. In addition, the stipulation, the desist order, and the injunction, without reference to punishment for contempt, have the attributes of punishment. This is evident both in that they result in some suffering on the part of the corporation against which they are issued and also in that they are designed by legislators and administrators to produce suffering. The suffering is in the form of public shame, as illustrated in more extreme form in the colonial penalty of sewing the letter "T" on the clothing of the thief. The design is shown in the sequence of sanctions used by the Federal Trade Commission. The stipulation involves the least publicity and the least discomfort, and it is used for minor and technical violations. The desist order is used if the stipulation is violated and also if the violation of the law is appraised by the Commission as willful and major. This involves more public shame; this shame is somewhat mitigated by the statements made by corporations, in exculpation, that such orders are merely the acts of bureaucrats. Still more shameful to the corporation is an injunction issued by a court. The shame resulting from this order is sometimes mitigated and the corporation's face saved by taking a consent decree. The corporation may insist that the consent decree is not an admission that it violated the law. For instance, the meat packers took a consent decree in an antitrust case in 1921, with the explanation that they had not knowingly violated any law and were consenting to the decree without attempting to defend themselves because they wished to co-operate with the government in every possible way. This patriotic motivation appeared questionable, however, after the packers fought during almost all of the next ten years for a modification of the decree. Although the sequence of stipulation, desist order, and injunction indicates that the variations in public shame are designed, these orders have other functions, as well, especially a remedial function and the clarification of the law in a particular complex situation.

The conclusion in this semantic portion of the discussion is that 473 of the 547 decisions are decisions that crimes were committed. This conclusion may be questioned on the ground that the rules of proof and evidence used in reaching these decisions are not the same as those used in decisions regarding other crimes, especially that some of the agencies which rendered the decisions did not require proof of criminal intent and did not presume the accused to be innocent. These rules of criminal intent and presumption of innocence, however, are not required in all prosecutions under the regular penal code and the number of exceptions is increasing. In many states a person may be committed to prison without protection of one or both of these rules on charges of statutory rape, bigamy, adultery, passing bad checks, selling mortgaged property, defrauding a hotel keeper, and other offenses. Consequently the criteria which have been used in defining white collar crimes are not categorically different from the criteria used in defining other crimes, for these rules are abrogated both in regard to white collar crimes and other crimes, including some felonies. The proportion of

decisions rendered against corporations without the protection of these rules is probably greater than the proportion rendered against other criminals, but a difference in proportions does not make the violations of law by corporations categorically different from the violations of laws by other criminals. Moreover, the difference in proportion, as the procedures actually operate is not great. On the one side, many of the defendants in usual criminal cases, being in relative poverty, do not get good defense and consequently secure little benefit from these rules; on the other hand, the Commissions come close to observing these rules of proof and evidence although they are not required to do so. This is illustrated by the procedure of the Federal Trade Commission in regard to advertisements. Each year it examines several hundred thousand advertisements and appraises about 50,000 of them as probably false. From the 50,000 it selects about 1,500 as patently false. For instance, an advertisement of gum-wood furniture as "mahogany" would seldom be an accidental error and would generally result from a state of mind which deviated from honesty by more than the natural tendency of human beings to feel proud of their handiwork.

The preceding discussion has shown that these seventy corporations committed crimes according to 473 adverse decisions, and also has shown that the criminality of their behavior was not made obvious by the conventional procedures of the criminal law but was blurred and concealed by special procedures. This differential implementation of the law as applied to the crimes of corporations eliminates or at least minimizes the stigma of crime. This differential implementation of the law began with the Sherman antitrust law of 1890. As previously described, this law is explicitly a criminal law and a violation of the law is a misdemeanor no matter what procedure is used. The customary policy would have been to rely entirely on criminal prosecution as the method of enforcement. But a clever invention was made in the provision of an injunction to enforce a criminal law; this was not only an invention but was a direct reversal of previous case law. Also, private parties were encouraged by treble damages to enforce a criminal law by suits in civil courts. In either case, the defendant did not appear in the criminal court and the fact that he had committed a crime did not appear in the face of the proceedings.

The Sherman antitrust law, in this respect, became the model in practically all the subsequent procedures authorized to deal with the crimes of corporations. When the Federal Trade Commission bill and the Clayton bill were introduced in Congress, they contained the conventional criminal procedures; these were eliminated in committee discussions, and other procedures which did not carry the external symbols of criminal process were substituted. The violations of these laws are crimes, as has been shown above, but they are treated as though they were not crimes, with the effect and probably the intention of eliminating the stigma of crime. . . .

If a civil fine were substituted for a criminal fine, a violation of the antitrust law would be as truly a crime as it is now. The thing which would be eliminated would be the stigma of crime. Consequently, the stigma of crime has become a penalty in itself, which may be imposed in connection with other penalties or withheld, just as it is possible to combine imprisonment with a fine or have a fine without imprisonment. A civil fine is a financial penalty without the additional penalty of stigma, while a criminal fine is a financial penalty with the additional penalty of stigma.

When the stigma of crime is imposed as a penalty it places the defendant in the category of criminals and he becomes a criminal according to the popular stereotype of "the criminal." In primitive society "the criminal" was substantially the same as "the stranger," while in modern society "the criminal" is a person of less esteemed cultural attainments. Seventy-five per cent of the persons committed to state prisons are probably not, aside from their unesteemed cultural attainments, "criminals in the usual sense of the word." It may be excellent policy to eliminate the stigma of crime in a large proportion of cases, but the question at hand is why the law has a different implementation for white collar criminals than for others.

Three factors assist in explaining this different implementation of the law, namely, the status of the business man, the trend away from punishment, and the relatively unorganized resentment of the public against white collar criminals. Each of these will be described.

First, the methods used in the enforcement of any law are an adaption to the characteristics of the prospective violators of the law, as appraised by the legislators and the judicial and administrative personnel. The appraisals regarding business men, who are the prospective violators of the four laws under consideration, include a combination of fear and admiration. Those who are responsible for the system of criminal justice are afraid to antagonize business men; among other consequences, such antagonism may result in a reduction in contributions to the campaign funds needed to win the next election. Probably much more important is the cultural homogeneity of legislators, judges, and administrators with business men. Legislators admire and respect business men and cannot conceive of them as criminals, that is, business men do not conform to the popular stereotype of "the criminal." The legislators are confident that these business men will conform as a result of very mild pressures. This interpretation meets with considerable opposition from persons who insist that this is an egalitarian society in which all men are equal in the eyes of the law. It is not possible to give a complete demonstration of the validity of this interpretation but four types of evidence are presented in the following paragraphs as partial demonstration.

The Department of [J]ustice is authorized to use both criminal prosecutions and petitions in equity to enforce the Sherman-antitrust law. The Department has selected the method of criminal prosecution in a larger proportion of cases against trade unions than of cases against corporations, although the law was enacted primarily because of fear of the corporations. From 1890 to 1929 the Department of [J]ustice initiated 438 actions under this law with decisions favorable to the United States. Of the actions against business firms and associations of business firms, 27 per cent were criminal prosecutions, while of the actions against trade unions 71 per cent were criminal prosecutions. This shows that the Department of Justice has been comparatively reluctant to use a method against business firms which carries with it the stigma of crime. The method of criminal prosecution in enforcement of the Sherman antitrust law has varied from one presidential administration to another. It has seldom been used in the administrations of the presidents who are popularly appraised as friendly toward business, namely, McKinley, Harding, Coolidge, and Hoover.

Business men suffered their greatest loss of prestige in the depression which began in 1929.

It was precisely in this period of low status of business men that the most strenuous efforts were made to enforce the old laws and enact new laws for the regulation of business men. The appropriations for this purpose were multiplied several times and persons were selected for their vigor in administration of the laws. Of the 547 decisions against the seventy corporations during their life careers, which have averaged about forty years, 63 per cent were rendered in the period 1935-43, that is, during the period of the low status of business men.

The Federal Trade Commission Law states that a violation of the antitrust laws by a corporation shall be deemed to be, also, a violation by the officers and directors of the corporation. However, business men are practically never convicted as persons and several cases have been reported, like the six percent case against the automobile manufacturers, in which the corporation was convicted and the persons who direct the corporation were all acquitted.

A second factor in the explanation of the differential implementation of the law as applied to white collar criminals is the trend away from reliance on penal methods. This trend advanced more rapidly in the area of white collar crimes than of other crimes because this area, due to the recency of the statutes, is least bound by precedents and also because of the status of business men. This trend is seen in the almost complete abandonment of the most extreme penalties of death and physical torture; in the supplanting of conventional penal methods by non-penal methods such as probation and the case work methods which accompany probation; and in the supplementing of penal methods by non-penal methods, as in the development of case work and educational policies in prisons. These decreases in penal methods are explained by a series of social changes: the increased power of the lower socio-economic class upon which previously most of the penalties were inflicted; the inclusion within the scope of the penal laws of a large part of the upper socio-economic class as illustrated by traffic regulations; the increased social interaction among the classes, which has resulted in increased understanding and sympathy; the failure of penal methods to make substantial reductions in crime rates; and the weakening hold on the legal profession and others of the individualistic and hedonistic psychology which had

placed great emphasis on pain in the control of behavior. To some extent overlapping those just mentioned is the fact that punishment, which was previously the chief reliance for control in the home, the school, and the church, has tended to disappear from those institutions, leaving the State without cultural support for its own penal methods.

White collar crime is similar to juvenile delinquency in respect to the differential implementation of the law. In both cases, the procedures of the criminal law are modified so that the stigma of crime will not attach to the offenders. The stigma of crime has been less completely eliminated from juvenile delinquents than from white collar criminals because the procedures for the former are a less complete departure from conventional criminal procedures, because most juvenile delinquents come from a class with low social status, and because the juveniles have not organized to protect their good names. Because the juveniles have not been successfully freed from the stigma of crime they have been generally held to be within the scope of the theories of criminology and in fact provide a large part of the data for criminology; because the external symbols have been more successfully eliminated from white collar crimes, white collar crimes have generally not been included within these theories.

A third factor in the differential implementation of the law is the difference in the relation between the law and the mores in the area of white collar crime. The laws under consideration are recent and do not have a firm foundation in public ethics or business ethics; in fact certain rules of business ethics, such as the contempt for the "price chiseler," are generally in conflict with the law. These crimes are not obvious, as is assault and battery, and can be appreciated readily only by persons who are expert in the occupations in which they occur. A corporation often violates a law for a decade or longer before the administrative agency becomes aware of the violation, and in the meantime the violation may have become accepted practice in the industry. The effects of a white collar crime upon the public are diffused over a long period of time and perhaps over millions of people, with no person suffering much at a particular time. The public agencies of communication do not express and organize the moral sentiments of the community as to white collar crimes in part because the crimes are complicated and not easily presented as news, but probably in greater part because these agencies of communication are owned or controlled by the business men who violate the laws and because these agencies are themselves frequently charged with violations of the same laws. Public opinion in regard to picking pockets would not be well organized if most of the information regarding this crime came to the public directly from the pick-pockets themselves.

This third factor, if properly limited, is a valid part of the explanation of the differential implementation of the law. It tends to be exaggerated and become the complete explanation in the form of a denial that white collar crimes involve any moral culpability whatever. On that account it is desirable to state a few reasons why this factor is not the complete explanation. The assertion is sometimes made that white collar crimes are merely technical violations and involve no moral culpability, i.e., violation of the mores, whatever. In fact, these white collar crimes, like other crimes, are distributed along a continuum in which the *mala in se* are at one extreme and the *mala prohibita* at the other. None of the white collar crimes is purely arbitrary, as is the regulation that one must drive on the right side of the street, which might equally well be that he must drive on the left side. The Sherman antitrust law, for instance, is regarded by many persons as an unwise law and it may well be that some other policy would be preferable. It is questioned principally by persons who believe in a more collectivistic economic system, namely, the communists and the leaders of big business, while its support comes largely from an emotional ideology in favor of free enterprise which is held by farmers, wage-earners, small business men, and professional men. Therefore, as appraised by the majority of the population it is necessary for the preservation of American institutions and its violation is a violation of strongly entrenched moral sentiments.

The sentimental reaction toward a particular white collar crime is certainly different from that toward some other crimes. This difference is often exaggerated, especially as the reaction occurs in urban society. The characteristic reaction of the average citizen in the modern city toward burglary is apathy unless he or his immediate friends are victims or unless the case is very spectacular. The average citizen, reading in his morning paper that the home of an unknown person has been burglarized by another unknown person, has no appreciable increase in blood pressure. Fear and resentment develop in modern society primarily as the result of the accumulation of crimes as depicted in crime rates or in general descriptions, and this develops both as to white collar crimes and other crimes.

Finally, although many laws have been enacted for the regulation of occupations other than business, such as agriculture or plumbing, the procedures used in the enforcement of those other laws are more nearly the same as the conventional criminal procedures, and law-violators in these other occupations are not so completely protected against the stigma of crime as are business men. The relation between the law and the mores tends to be circular. The mores are crystallized in the law and each act of enforcement of the laws tends to re-enforce the mores. The laws regarding white collar crime, which conceal the criminality of the behavior, have been less effective than other laws in re-enforcement of the mores.

DISCUSSION QUESTIONS

1. According to Sutherland, how do legal scholars define *crime,* and in what way are the antitrust violations discussed in the article "criminal"?

2. How does the differential implementation of the law, as it is applied to white collar criminals, eliminate or minimize the stigma of crime?

3. Discuss the roles of morality and social mores in relation to white collar crime. What influence, if any, do these societal factors have on the enforcement of laws and mores against white collar criminals?

22

THE NATURE OF CRIMINALITY

Low Self-Control

MICHAEL R. GOTTFREDSON AND TRAVIS HIRSCHI

EDITOR'S INTRODUCTION—The foundation of Gottfredson and Hirschi's theory of low self-control builds upon Hirschi's (1969) earlier conception of social control by asserting that crime, like other forms of deviance, results from an individual's inability to develop adequate self-control. In their theory, which is fully developed in their 1990 text *A General Theory of Crime*, Gottfredson and Hirschi turn the focus inward toward the family. They look at early childhood development as a critical determinant of patterns of criminal and deviant behavior later in life. This approach moves away from traditional sociological theories of crime, which tend to focus on the social experiences of youths outside the family. For Gottfredson and Hirschi, those youths who fail to develop good self-control when they are very young ordinarily do not develop it later in life. They assert that this lack of self-control is the cause of crime, in addition to other dysfunctional behaviors such as alcoholism, unstable work histories, and divorce.

Although Gottfredson and Hirschi derive some of their theoretical strength from Hirschi's social control theory, their theory differs from Hirschi's approach in an important way. Whereas Hirschi places a significant amount of emphasis on the importance of "indirect controls," such as attachment to parents, which manifests itself in a psychological presence when youths are not being watched, Gottfredson and Hirschi argue that "direct control" is critical to effective parenting. Unless parents closely monitor their children, self-control will not be imparted, and children will tend to be impulsive, insensitive, physical rather than mental, risk takers, short-sighted, and nonverbal (p. 210, this volume). This lack of self-control born and fostered in youth will continue through adulthood. In general, Gottfredson and Hirschi view crime as a consequence of low self-control within individuals who frequently come into contact with the numerous opportunities to commit crime. Because these opportunities are fairly constant, low self-control becomes the main determining factor for crime over the life course.

Although there has been steady theoretical support for Gottfredson and Hirschi's theoretical predictions, the theory does have some limitations. Primarily, in empirical tests, low self-control cannot explain the effects of other sociological factors on crime, especially those of differential association/social learning theory. Likewise, in terms of white-collar crime, the general theory of crime itself has received much criticism, mainly in terms of its assertion of generality to all forms of crime (see Reed & Yeager, Chapter 23, this volume).

The Elements of Self-Control

Criminal acts provide *immediate* gratification of desires. A major characteristic of people with low self-control is therefore a tendency to respond to tangible stimuli in the immediate environment, to have a concrete "here and now" orientation. People with high self-control, in contrast, tend to defer gratification. Criminal acts provide *easy or simple* gratification of desires. They provide money without work, sex without courtship, revenge without court delays. People lacking self-control also tend to lack diligence, tenacity, or persistence in a course of action. Criminal acts are *exciting, risky, or thrilling.* They involve stealth, danger, speed, agility, deception, or power. People lacking self-control therefore tend to be adventuresome, active, and physical. Those with high levels of self-control tend to be cautious, cognitive, and verbal.

Crimes provide *few or meager long-term benefits.* They are not equivalent to a job or a career. On the contrary, crimes interfere with long-term commitments to jobs, marriages, family, or friends. People with low self-control thus tend to have unstable marriages, friendships, and job profiles. They tend to be little interested in and unprepared for long-term occupational pursuits. Crimes require *little skill or planning.* The cognitive requirements for most crimes are minimal. It follows that people lacking self-control need not possess or value cognitive or academic skills. The manual skills required for most crimes are minimal. It follows that people lacking self-control need not possess manual skills that require training or apprenticeship. Crimes often result in *pain or discomfort for the victim.* Property is lost, bodies are injured, privacy is violated, trust is broken. It follows that people with low self-control tend to be self-centered, indifferent, or insensitive to the suffering and needs of others. It does not follow, however, that people with low self-control are routinely unkind or antisocial. On the contrary, they may discover the immediate and easy rewards of charm and generosity.

Recall that crime involves the pursuit of immediate pleasure. It follows that people lacking self-control will also tend to pursue immediate pleasures that are *not* criminal: they will tend to smoke, drink, use drugs, gamble, have children out of wedlock, and engage in illicit sex. Crimes require the interaction of an offender with people or their property. It does not follow that people lacking self-control will tend to be gregarious or social. However, it does follow that, other things being equal, gregarious or social people are more likely to be involved in criminal acts. The major benefit of many crimes is not pleasure but relief from momentary irritation. The irritation caused by a crying child is often the stimulus for physical abuse. That caused by a taunting stranger in a bar is often the stimulus for aggravated assault. It follows that people with low self-control tend to have minimal tolerance for frustration and little ability to respond to conflict through verbal rather than physical means.

Crimes involve the risk of violence and physical injury, of pain and suffering on the part of the offender. It does not follow that people with low self-control will tend to be tolerant of physical pain or to be indifferent to physical discomfort. It does follow that people tolerant of physical pain or indifferent to physical discomfort will be more likely to engage in criminal acts whatever their level of self-control. The risk of criminal penalty for any given criminal act is small, but this depends in part on the circumstances of the offense. Thus, for example, not all joyrides by teenagers are equally likely to result in arrest. A car stolen from a neighbor and returned unharmed before he notices its absence is less likely to result in official notice than is a car stolen from a shopping center parking lot and abandoned at the convenience of the offender. Drinking alcohol stolen from parents and consumed in the family garage is less likely to receive official notice than drinking in the parking lot outside a concert hall. It follows that offenses differ in their validity as measures of self-control: those offenses with large risk of public awareness are better measures than those with little risk.

In sum, people who lack self-control will tend to be impulsive, insensitive, physical (as opposed to mental), risk-taking, short-sighted, and nonverbal, and they will tend therefore to engage in

Gottfredson, M., & Hirschi, T. (1990). The nature of criminality: Low self-control. In M. Gottfredson & T. Hirschi, *A general theory of crime* (pp. 85-102). Palo Alto, CA: Stanford University Press.

criminal and analogous acts. Since these traits can be identified prior to the age of responsibility for crime, since there is considerable tendency for these traits to come together in the same people, and since the traits tend to persist through life, it seems reasonable to consider them as comprising a stable construct useful in the explanation of crime.

The Many Manifestations of Low Self-Control

Our image of the "offender" suggests that crime is not an automatic or necessary consequence of low self-control. It suggests that many noncriminal acts analogous to crime (such as accidents, smoking, and alcohol use) are also manifestations of low self-control. Our image therefore implies that no specific act, type of crime, or form of deviance is uniquely required by the absence of self-control. Because both crime and analogous behaviors stem from low self-control (that is, both are manifestations of low self-control), they will all be engaged in at a relatively high rate by people with low self-control. Within the domain of crime, then, there will be much versatility among offenders in the criminal acts in which they engage.

Research on the versatility of deviant acts supports these predictions in the strongest possible way. The variety of manifestations of low self-control is immense. In spite of years of tireless research motivated by a belief in specialization, no credible evidence of specialization has been reported. In fact, the evidence of offender versatility is overwhelming (Hirschi, 1969; Hindelang, 1971; Wolfgang, Figlio, & Sellin, 1972; Petersilia, 1980; Hindelang, Hirschi, & Weis, 1981; Rojek & Erickson, 1982; Klein, 1984).

By versatility we mean that offenders commit a wide variety of criminal acts, with no strong inclination to pursue a specific criminal act or a pattern of criminal acts to the exclusion of others. Most theories suggest that offenders tend to specialize, whereby such terms as robber, burglar, drug dealer, rapist, and murderer have predictive or descriptive import. In fact, some theories create offender specialization as part of their explanation of crime. For example, Cloward and Ohlin (1960) create distinctive subcultures of delinquency around particular forms of criminal behavior, identifying subcultures

specializing in theft, violence, or drugs. In a related way, books are written about white-collar crime as though it were a clearly distinct specialty requiring a unique explanation. Research projects are undertaken for the study of drug use, or vandalism, or teen pregnancy (as though every study of delinquency were not a study of drug use and vandalism and teenage sexual behavior). Entire schools of criminology emerge to pursue patterning, sequencing, progression, escalation, onset, persistence, and desistance in the career of offenses or offenders. These efforts survive largely because their proponents fail to consider or acknowledge the clear evidence to the contrary. Other reasons for survival of such ideas may be found in the interest of politicians and members of the law enforcement community who see policy potential in criminal careers or "career criminals" (see, e.g., Blumstein et al., 1986).

Occasional reports of specialization seem to contradict this point, as do everyday observations of repetitive misbehavior by particular offenders. Some offenders rob the same store repeatedly over a period of years, or an offender commits several rapes over a (brief) period of time. Such offenders may be called "robbers" or "rapists." However, it should be noted that such labels are retrospective rather than predictive and that they typically ignore a large amount of delinquent or criminal behavior by the same offenders that is inconsistent with their alleged specialty. Thus, for example, the "rapist" will tend also to use drugs, to commit robberies and burglaries (often in concert with the rape), and to have a record for violent offenses other than rape. There is a perhaps natural tendency on the part of observers (and in official accounts) to focus on the most serious crimes in a series of events, but this tendency should not be confused with a tendency on the part of the offender to specialize in one kind of crime.

Recall that one of the defining features of crime is that it is simple and easy. Some apparent specialization will therefore occur because obvious opportunities for an easy score will tend to repeat themselves. An offender who lives next to a shopping area that is approached by pedestrians will have repeat opportunities for purse snatching, and this may show in his arrest record. But even here the specific "criminal career" will tend to quickly run its course and to be followed by offenses whose content and character is likewise determined by convenience and opportunity (which is the reason why some form of theft is always the best bet about what a person is likely to do next).

The evidence that offenders are likely to engage in noncriminal acts psychologically or theoretically equivalent to crime is, because of the relatively high rates of these "noncriminal" acts, even easier to document. Thieves are likely to smoke, drink, and skip school at considerably higher rates than nonthieves. Offenders are considerably more likely than nonoffenders to be involved in most types of accidents, including household fires, auto crashes, and unwanted pregnancies. They are also considerably more likely to die at an early age (see, e.g., Robins, 1966; Eysenck, 1977; Gottfredson, 1984).

Good research on drug use and abuse routinely reveals that the correlates of delinquency and drug use are the same. As Akers (1984) has noted, "compared to the abstaining teenager, the drinking, smoking, and drug-taking teen is much more likely to be getting into fights, stealing, hurting other people, and committing other delinquencies." Akers goes on to say, "but the variation in the order in which they take up these things leaves little basis for proposing the causation of one by the other." In our view, the relation between drug use and delinquency is not a causal question. The correlates are the same because drug use and delinquency are both manifestations of an underlying tendency to pursue short-term, immediate pleasure. This underlying tendency (i.e., lack of self-control) has many manifestations, as listed by Harrison Gough (1948):

> unconcern over the rights and privileges of others when recognizing them would interfere with personal satisfaction in any way; impulsive behavior, or apparent incongruity between the strength of the stimulus and the magnitude of the behavioral response; inability to form deep or persistent attachments to other persons or to identify in interpersonal relationships; poor judgment and planning in attaining defined goals; apparent lack of anxiety and distress over social maladjustment and unwillingness or inability to consider maladjustment qua maladjustment; a tendency to project blame onto others and to take no responsibility for failures; meaningless prevarication, often about trivial matters in situations where detection is inevitable; almost complete lack of dependability . . . and willingness to assume responsibility; and, finally, emotional poverty. [p. 362]

This combination of characteristics has been revealed in the life histories of the subjects in the famous studies by Lee Robins. Robins is one of the few researchers to focus on the varieties of deviance and the way they tend to go together in the lives of those she designates as having "antisocial personalities." In her words: "We refer to someone who fails to maintain close personal relationships with anyone else, [who] performs poorly on the job, who is involved in illegal behaviors (whether or not apprehended), who fails to support himself and his dependents without .outside aid, and who is given to sudden changes of plan and loss of temper in response to what appear to others as minor frustrations" (1978, p. 255).

For 30 years Robins traced 524 children referred to a guidance clinic in St. Louis, Missouri, and she compared them to a control group matched on IQ, age, sex, and area of the city. She discovered that, in comparison to the control group, those people referred at an early age were more likely to be arrested as adults (for a wide variety of offenses), were less likely to get married, were more likely to be divorced, were more likely to marry a spouse with a behavior problem, were less likely to have children (but if they had children were likely to have more children), were more likely to have children with behavior problems, were more likely to be unemployed, had considerably more frequent job changes, were more likely to be on welfare, had fewer contacts with relatives, had fewer friends, were substantially less likely to attend church, were less likely to serve in the armed forces and more likely to be dishonorably discharged if they did serve, were more likely to exhibit physical evidence of excessive alcohol use, and were more likely to be hospitalized for psychiatric problems (1966, pp. 42-73).

Note that these outcomes are consistent with four general elements of our notion of low self-control: basic stability of individual differences over a long period of time; great variability in the kinds of criminal acts engaged in; conceptual or causal equivalence of criminal and noncriminal acts; and inability to predict the specific forms of deviance engaged in, whether criminal or noncriminal. In our view, the idea of an antisocial personality defined by certain behavioral consequences is too positivistic or deterministic, suggesting that the offender must do certain things given his antisocial personality. Thus we would say only that the subjects in question are *more likely* to commit criminal acts (as the data indicate they are). We do not make commission of criminal acts part of the definition of the individual with low self-control.

Be this as it may, Robins's retrospective research shows that predictions derived from a concept of antisocial personality are highly consistent with the results of prospective longitudinal and cross-sectional research: offenders do not specialize; they tend to be involved in accidents, illness, and death at higher rates than the general population; they tend to have difficulty persisting in a job regardless of the particular characteristics of the job (no job will turn out to be a good job); they have difficulty acquiring and retaining friends; and they have difficulty meeting the demands of long-term financial commitments (such as mortgages or car payments) and the demands of parenting.

Seen in this light, the "costs" of low self-control for the individual may far exceed the costs of his criminal acts. In fact, it appears that crime is often among the least serious consequences of a lack of self-control in terms of the quality of life of those lacking it.

THE CAUSES OF SELF-CONTROL

We know better what deficiencies in self-control lead to than where they come from. One thing is, however, clear: low self-control is not produced by training, tutelage, or socialization. As a matter of fact, all of the characteristics associated with low self-control tend to show themselves in the absence of nurturance, discipline, or training. Given the classical appreciation of the causes of human behavior, the implications of this fact are straightforward: the causes of low self-control are negative rather than positive; self-control is unlikely in the absence of effort, intended or unintended, to create it. (This assumption separates the present theory from most modern theories of crime, where the offender is automatically seen as a product of positive forces, a creature of learning, particular pressures, or specific defect. We will return to this comparison once our theory has been fully explicated.)

At this point it would be easy to construct a theory of crime causation, according to which

characteristics of potential offenders lead them ineluctably to the commission of criminal acts. Our task at this point would simply be to identify the likely sources of impulsiveness, intelligence, risk-taking, and the like. But to do so would be to follow the path that has proven so unproductive in the past, the path according to which criminals commit crimes irrespective of the characteristics of the setting or situation.

We can avoid this pitfall by recalling the elements inherent in the decision to commit a criminal act. The object of the offense is clearly pleasurable, and universally so. Engaging in the act, however, entails some risk of social, legal, and/or natural sanctions. Whereas the pleasure attained by the act is direct, obvious, and immediate, the pains risked by it are not obvious, or direct, and are in any event at greater remove from it. It follows that, though there will be little variability among people in their ability to see the pleasures of crime, there will be considerable variability in their ability to calculate potential pains.

But the problem goes further than this: whereas the pleasures of crime are reasonably equally distributed over the population, this is not true for the pains. Everyone appreciates money; not everyone dreads parental anger or disappointment upon learning that the money was stolen. So, the dimensions of self-control are, in our view, factors affecting calculation of the consequences of one's acts. The impulsive or short sighted person fails to consider the negative or painful consequences of his acts; the insensitive person has fewer negative consequences to consider; the less intelligent person also has fewer negative consequences to consider (has less to lose).

No known social group, whether criminal or noncriminal, actively or purposefully attempts to reduce the self-control of its members. Social life is not enhanced by low self-control and its consequences. On the contrary, the exhibition of these tendencies undermines harmonious group relations and the ability to achieve collective ends. These facts explicitly deny that a tendency to crime is a product of socialization, culture, or positive learning of any sort.

The traits composing low self-control are also not conducive to the achievement of long-term individual goals. On the contrary, they impede educational and occupational achievement, destroy interpersonal relations, and undermine physical health and economic well being. Such facts explicitly deny the notion that criminality is an alternative route to the goals otherwise obtainable through legitimate avenues. It follows that people who care about the interpersonal skill, educational and occupational achievement, and physical and economic well-being of those in their care will seek to rid them of these traits.

Two general sources of variation are immediately apparent in this scheme. The first is the variation among children in the degree to which they manifest such traits to begin with. The second is the variation among caretakers in the degree to which they recognize low self-control and its consequences and the degree to which they are willing and able to correct it. Obviously, therefore, even at this threshold level the sources of low self-control are complex.

There is good evidence that some of the traits predicting subsequent involvement in crime appear as early as they can be reliably measured, including low intelligence, high activity level, physical strength, and adventuresomeness (Glueck & Glueck, 1950; West & Farrington, 1973). The evidence suggests that the connection between these traits and commission of criminal acts ranges from weak to moderate. Obviously, we do not suggest that people are born criminals, inherit a gene for criminality, or anything of the sort. In fact, we explicitly deny such notions. . . . What we do suggest is that individual differences may have an impact on the prospects for effective socialization (or adequate control). Effective socialization is, however, always possible whatever the configuration of individual traits.

Other traits affecting crime appear later and seem to be largely products of ineffective or incomplete socialization. For example, differences in impulsivity and insensitivity become noticeable later in childhood when they are no longer common to all children. The ability and willingness to delay immediate gratification for some larger purpose may therefore be assumed to be a consequence of training. Much parental action is in fact geared toward suppression of impulsive behavior, toward making the child consider the long-range consequences of acts. Consistent sensitivity to the needs and feelings of others may also be assumed to be a consequence of training. Indeed, much parental behavior is directed toward teaching the child about the rights and feelings of others, and of how these rights and feelings ought to constrain the child's behavior. All of these points focus our attention on child-rearing.

CHILD-REARING AND SELF-CONTROL: THE FAMILY

The major cause of low self-control thus appears to be ineffective child-rearing. Put in positive terms, several conditions appear to produce a socialized child. Perhaps the place to begin looking for these conditions is the research literature on the relation between family conditions and delinquency. This research (e.g., Glueck & Glueck, 1950; McCord & McCord, 1959) has examined the connection between many family factors and delinquency. It reports that discipline, supervision, and affection tend to be missing in the homes of delinquents, that the behavior of the parents is often "poor" (e.g., excessive drinking and poor supervision (Glueck & Glueck 1950, pp. 10-11); and that the parents of delinquents are unusually likely to have criminal records themselves. Indeed, according to Michael Rutter and Henri Giller, "of the parental characteristics associated with delinquency, criminality is the most striking and most consistent" (1984, p. 182).

Such information undermines the many explanations of crime that ignore the family, but in this form it does not represent much of an advance over the belief of the general public (and those who deal with offenders in the criminal justice system) that defective upbringing, or "neglect" in the home is the primary cause of crime.

To put these standard research findings in perspective, we think it necessary to define the conditions necessary for adequate child-rearing to occur. The minimum conditions seem to be these: in order to teach the child self-control, someone must (1) monitor the child's behavior; (2) recognize deviant behavior when it occurs; and (3) punish such behavior. This seems simple and obvious enough. All that is required to activate the system is affection for or investment in the child. The person who care[s] for the child will watch his behavior, see him doing things he should not do, and correct him. The result may be a child more capable of delaying gratification, more sensitive to the interests and desires of others, more independent, more willing to accept restraints on his activity, and more unlikely to use force or violence to attain his ends.

When we seek the causes of low self-control, we ask where this system can go wrong. Obviously, parents do not prefer their children to be unsocialized in the terms described. We can therefore rule out in advance the possibility of positive socialization to unsocialized behavior (as cultural or subcultural deviance theories suggest). Still, the system can go wrong at any one of four places. First, the parents may not care for the child (in which case none of the other conditions would be met); second, the parents, even if they care, may not have the time or energy to monitor the child's behavior; third, the parents, even if they care *and* monitor, may not see anything wrong with the child's behavior; finally, even if everything else is in place, the parents may not have the inclination or the means to punish the child.

So, what may appear at first glance to be nonproblematic turns out to be problematic indeed. Many things can go wrong. According to much research in crime and delinquency, in the homes of problem children many things have gone wrong: "Parents of stealers do not track ([they] do not interpret stealing . . . as 'deviant'); they do not punish; and they do not care" (Patterson, 1980, pp. 88-89; see also Glueck & Glueck, 1950; McCord & McCord, 1959; West & Farrington, 1977). Let us apply this scheme to some of the facts about the connection between child socialization and crime, beginning with the elements of the child-rearing model.

The Attachment of the Parent to the Child

Our model states that parental concern for the welfare or behavior of the child is a necessary condition for successful childrearing. Because it is too often assumed that all parents are alike in their love for their children, the evidence directly on this point is not as good or extensive as it could be. However, what exists is clearly consistent with the model. Glueck and Glueck (1950, pp. 125-28) report that, compared to the fathers of delinquents, fathers of nondelinquents were twice as likely to be warmly disposed toward their sons and one-fifth as likely to be hostile

towards them. In the same sample, 28 percent of the mothers of 'delinquents' were characterized as "indifferent or hostile" toward the child as compared to 4 percent of the mothers of nondelinquents. The evidence suggests that stepparents are especially unlikely to have feelings of affection toward their stepchildren (Burgess, 1980), [since it is thought that these] children will be "reared" by people who do not especially care for them.

Parental Supervision

The connection between social control and self-control could not be more direct than in the case of parental supervision of the child. Such supervision presumably prevents criminal or analogous acts and at the same time trains the child to avoid them on his own. Consistent with this assumption, supervision tends to be a major predictor of delinquency, however supervision or delinquency is measured (Glueck & Glueck, 1950; Hirschi, 1969; West & Farrington, 1977; Riley & Shaw, 1985).

Our general theory in principle provides a method of separating supervision as external control from supervision as internal control. For one thing, offenses differ in the degree to which they can be prevented through monitoring; children at one age are monitored much more closely than children at other ages; girls are supervised more closely than boys. In some situations monitoring for some offenses is virtually absent. In the present context, however, the concern is with the connection between supervision and self-control, a connection established by the stronger tendency of those poorly supervised when young to commit crimes as adults (McCord, 1979).

Recognition of Deviant Behavior

In order for supervision to have an impact on self-control, the supervisor must perceive deviant behavior when it occurs. Remarkably, not all parents are adept at recognizing lack of self-control. Some parents allow the child to do pretty much as he pleases without interference. Extensive television-viewing is one modern example, as is the failure to require completion of homework, to prohibit smoking, to curtail the use of physical force, or to see to it that the child actually attends school. . . .

DISCUSSION QUESTIONS

1. How do Gottfredson and Hirschi define *low self-control*? What are the elements of low self-control?

2. What acts are "analogous" to crime, and how can Gottfredson and Hirschi's theory explain these behaviors?

3. What is the main reason why people have low self-control? Do the authors indicate that crime is an automatic or necessary result of low self-control?

4. Where do Gottfredson and Hirschi locate the primary source of low self-control? What implications does this theory have for crime control and other policies aimed at controlling dysfunctional behaviors?

REFERENCE

Hirschi, T. (1969). *Causes of delinquency*. Berkeley: University of California Press.

23

ORGANIZATIONAL OFFENDING AND NEOCLASSICAL CRIMINOLOGY

Challenging the Reach of a General Theory of Crime

GARY E. REED AND PETER CLEARY YEAGER

EDITOR'S INTRODUCTION—Reed and Yeager's article completes a trio of articles that have attempted, on some level, to explain the manner in which certain types of crime—namely white-collar crimes, in this case—are socially constructed. The social construction emerges through the manner in which the crimes themselves are defined and how agents of social control sanction, or frequently fail to sanction, them. In this article, Reed and Yeager critically examine Gottfredson and Hirschi's general theory of crime (1990; also see Chapter 22 in this volume), focusing particularly on its applicability to organizational offending. Recall that this theory maintains that "human behavior is premised on individual calculations of relative costs and benefits of action" (Reed & Yeager, 1996, p. 358). According to this argument, criminal and noncriminal behavior results from the pursuit of self-interest. Reed and Yeager question whether Gottfredson and Hirschi's theory is sufficiently "general" and whether specific typologies of crime are therefore unnecessary for criminological theory.[1]

Gottfredson and Hirschi have used white-collar crime to support their arguments, but, as Reed and Yeager point out, they limited the scope of the theory to white-collar offenses that most closely resemble conventional crimes. Gottfredson and Hirschi argue that white-collar crime exhibits the same demographic distribution as ordinary crime. Second, they assert that white-collar crime is relatively uncommon, implying that the business culture routinely selects out traits such as impulsiveness and aggression that would contribute to criminality. Last, they generalize to the white-collar offender their argument that offenders do not specialize in types of crime.

Reed and Yeager point out the problems inherent in these claims about white-collar offending. They assert that when organizational offending is included in white-collar crime, empirical and theoretical limitations of the general theory emerge. These limitations include the matters of defining and counting the phenomena of interest, the nature of the interest that commonly underlies them, and the role of opportunity in them. Reed and Yeager conclude by stipulating that organizational offending has unique characteristics that require specific explanation. Moreover, as the authors suggest, perhaps some of these characteristics that are common to corporate law breaking may also be found in other arenas such as government, health care, and higher education.

In this chapter, we examine and critique the application of Gottfredson and Hirschi's (1990; Hirschi & Gottfredson, 1987, 1994) general theory of crime to organizational crime and deviancy, focusing specifically on the context of corporate misdeeds. Gottfredson and Hirschi use white-collar crime to argue the generality of their theory and for the consequent proposition that typologies of crime are unnecessary. From Sutherland (1949) onward criminologists have used white-collar crime to demonstrate the inadequacy of theories based on causal factors like poverty, the disintegration of basic institutions, or personal pathologies. Sutherland and others (e.g., Clinard & Quinney, 1973; Clinard & Yeager, 1980; Coleman, 1987; Stone, 1975; Vaughan, 1983) have used the example of white-collar crime to forward their own general theories or to develop specific theoretical arguments about this sort of offending as a unique type.

While we are sympathetic with the quest for criminological theorizing of the widest possible scope, we do not believe that Gottfredson and Hirschi have delivered a general theory of crime. We argue that organizational wrongdoing has unique characteristics that require specific explanation. It is likely that many, perhaps most, of these characteristics are common to corporate lawbreaking and offending in other bureaucracies, such as those in government, health care, and higher education.

In the sections that follow, we . . . summarize and assess their application of the theory to white-collar offending. We question their characterization of this type of lawbreaking, and we argue that a more complex specification of motivation and opportunity is required for theorizing about its organizational variant. . . .

THE GENERAL THEORY
AND WHITE-COLLAR CRIME

In applying their arguments to white-collar crime, Gottfredson and Hirschi stay with their definition of crime as the use of force or fraud in the perpetrator's self-interest. It is noteworthy that like many white-collar crime analysts (e.g., Clinard & Yeager, 1980; Sutherland, 1949), they are less interested in technical legal distinctions than in the nature and causes of harmful conduct. More important is their operational definition of white-collar crime. They adopt the crimes of embezzlement, fraud, and forgery, which enables them to compare distributions in offending using Uniform Crime Report (UCR) data (Gottfredson & Hirschi, 1990, pp. 180-201; Hirschi & Gottfredson, 1987, pp. 961-967). From these data, they draw several key conclusions in support of the argument that their general theory readily accounts for white-collar offending.

First, they assert that white-collar crime exhibits the same demographic distribution (e.g., race and age) as does ordinary crime. Moreover, they find that white-collar crimes bear the defining characteristics of all crime: "They provide relatively quick and relatively certain benefit with minimal effort. They *require no motivation or pressure that is not present in any other form of human behavior*" (Gottfredson and Hirschi, 1990, p. 190; italics added). Second, the authors argue that white-collar crime is relatively uncommon (e.g., Gottfredson & Hirschi, 1990, 1991). They offer the explanation that business culture is hostile to white-collar crime because it selects out such traits of criminality as impulsiveness and aggression in favor of such traits as the ability to defer gratification and willingness to defer to the interests (and, by implication, the authority) of others, keys to conventional careers and bureaucratic functioning. Thus, their theory "explicitly predicts lack of social support for most white-collar crimes since (1) they are contrary to general social norms and (2) are against the interests of the organization itself" (Hirschi & Gottfredson, 1987, p. 970).

Third, Gottfredson and Hirschi (1990, p. 190) generalize to the white-collar lawbreaker their argument that offenders do not specialize in types of crime. Like her "blue collar" counterpart, she will act out her criminal impulses

Reed, G. E., & Yeager, P. C. (1996). Organizational offending and neoclassical criminology: Challenging the reach of a general theory of crime. *Criminology, 34,* 357-382.

when favorable opportunities arise for easy and immediate benefit. Finally, these authors make two claims about the concept of corporate—or organizational—crime (as a subtype of white-collar crime): that it has not yet produced data that require it for their explanation, and that researchers who say the unit of study is the organization—rather than the individual—do not actually apply it in their interpretive efforts:

> It seems to us that [these researchers] take the corporation as a setting in which crimes may or may not occur, but they do not treat the corporation as the criminal actor (Gottfredson & Hirschi, 1990, p. 188).

Below we inspect each of these premises and conclusions in light of the accumulating research on organizational offending.

ORGANIZATIONAL OFFENDING: RETYING THE GORDIAN KNOT

There are three principal types of weakness in Gottfredson and Hirschi's argument as applied to lawbreaking by business organizations. These weaknesses involve defining and counting the phenomena of interest, the nature of the interest that commonly underlies them, and the role of opportunity in them. A satisfactory theory of organizational offending requires an adequate account of all of these matters and will look substantially different from Gottfredson and Hirschi's theory of crime.

Defining and Counting: The Role of Screens

In operationalizing their definition of crime in terms of embezzlement, fraud, and forgery, Gottfredson and Hirschi have incorporated conceptual and methodological screens that too narrowly constrain the phenomena of interest. Their definition identifies data whose demographic distributions most resemble those for at least some conventional crimes and best fit their thesis. As Steffensmeier (1989) has pointed out, for example, the UCR data on embezzlement include many such offenses as teenaged cashiers taking money from registers. Similarly, fraud and forgery are commonly committed by poor individuals acting alone or in small groups.

As Gottfredson and Hirschi suggest, these "white-collar" crimes are typically uncomplicated, requiring little skill or special motivation. Such acts lend themselves well to an account emphasizing the undersocialized pursuit of short-term self-interest. So defined, however, they appear to have much less in common with many of the offenses included in standard notions of white-collar crime, especially those falling under the rubric of organizational offending. As we argue below, this type of lawbreaking suggests the importance of such factors as organizational (sub)cultures and structures and the social construction of opportunities, matters left untheorized by Gottfredson and Hirschi.

The offenses we have in mind are not logically excluded by the definition of crime as the use of force or fraud for self-interested reasons. Indeed, most such violations involve either force, fraud, or both, whether perpetrated against customers, employees, citizens, competitors, or government. For example, the knowing marketing of unsafe products or maintenance of unsafe workplaces combines elements of fraud and force in victimizing consumers and workers, respectively. Victims are defrauded when they are not made aware of the unreasonable physical risks they face, and [they are] too commonly harmed, while employees may be effectively coerced into exposure to illegal workplace hazards by fear of job loss or other retribution. Price-fixing conspiracies, military contract fraud, tax fraud, securities fraud, and bank fraud clearly fit this conceptual definition of crime. So, too, do many environmental violations. Here, costs and risks are knowingly imposed upon the environment and citizens, fraudulent transfers that also often impose real physical harms.

Researchers have documented significant rates of such corporate offending, the high monetary and physical costs they collectively impose on victims, the forces that underlie them, and legal efforts at social control. Clearly, Gottfredson and Hirschi's arguments must be examined against this evidence, most of which escapes the UCR data they have utilized. That such offenses are numerous and quite costly is now a commonplace in criminological research. Sutherland (1949) reported that his sample of 70 major American corporations had an average of 14 legal decisions against them for illegal acts, roughly 1 for every three years of their average corporate lifetime. The offenses ranged from restraint of trade and false advertising to patent and trademark infringement and unfair labor practices. He also found significant levels of recidivism. The 41 companies that had been criminally convicted of offenses averaged four convictions each. . . .

. . . . The accumulated research on business lawbreaking demonstrates that lawbreaking by even powerful corporations occurs sufficiently frequently to be of substantial concern and that much of this offending readily fits the definition of crime as the use of force and fraud. Moreover, it is important to note that this research includes only those offenders that the government has officially labeled. While such legal processes always disproportionately select the simpler offenses because of their greater ease of detection and legal proof, this screening process operates with more force for organizational offenses than for the types of violations Gottfredson and Hirschi have targeted in their assessment of white-collar crime. And it does so for reasons entailed in the causal nexus of such offenses, as we shall demonstrate. The result is that organizational violations of law are both underrepresented and "undertheorized" in *A General Theory of Crime.*

Many studies report that the offenses of business firms are often highly complex in technical detail, and especially difficult to detect and burdensome to prove in terms of specific responsibilities and *mens rea* (cf., Clinard & Yeager, 1980; Cullen et al., 1987; Shapiro, 1984; Stone, 1975). In his close study of the white-collar crime defense bar, Mann (1985) shows how many complex white-collar offenses are screened out of the criminal justice system prior to the decision to charge (or arrest). Because of the great complexity of many tax and securities transactions, for example, and the ambiguity of relevant legal concepts (e.g., of fraud), defense counsel are often able to convince prosecutors to drop potential cases, commonly on the grounds that proving specific offenses is not feasible (see also McBarnet, 1991; Reichman, 1992). While some of these cases may indeed not have involved violations, a key implication to be drawn from Mann's work is that many of them are dropped because facts and/or the law are rendered more complex in negotiations (prior to charging) between specialized defense counsel and government regulators.

These negotiations provide advantages to such white-collar crime defendants that more conventional criminal defendants do not enjoy. Moreover, the sort of high-priced expertise required to make technical legal and factual arguments favors screening out of enforcement the larger, resource-rich businesses. . . .

. . . . In sum, not only is organizational offending substantially more diverse and widespread than Gottfredson and Hirschi suppose, but official criminal justice data on such offenses significantly distort the profile of offenses and offenders. The available research shows that organizational offending does not mirror the demographic distribution of conventional offending. This research does not squarely address the question of whether organizational offenders are generalists in crime, as Gottfredson and Hirschi argue, but there is little to suggest that these lawbreakers commonly engage in offenses like embezzlement, drug use, assault, or general theft. . . .

Finally, as against Gottfredson and Hirschi's account of embezzlement, check forgery, and the like, research has produced data that require specific white-collar crime concepts for their explanation, concepts lodged at the organizational and institutional levels of analysis. If this sort of white-collar crime is ordinary, it is ordinary only in the way of neatly fitting into the routines of business management, thus appearing to be unremarkable.

The Structure and Culture of Motivation

Gottfredson and Hirschi's account de-emphasizes motivation, arguing instead that crime is simply a product of the low self-control of self-interest in the face of opportunities. They place great weight on the assumptions that self-interest is an unproblematic concept and that self-control is an evident and stable property of personalities. Neither assumption adequately bears the weight, perhaps especially on the evidence of organizational lawbreaking. An important weakness of the authors' neoclassical emphasis on the calculation of interests is its nonfalsifiable character. Gottfredson and Hirschi argue that if a person's calculations and subsequent actions produce an outcome that contradicts her self-interest, this cannot be taken as evidence that she was not pursuing her self-interest. Rather, unfavorable outcomes may simply be taken as evidence that the person is either not very good at calculating her own interest or not adept at connecting means to ends.

Taylor et al. (1973) highlighted a related weakness in classical criminological theorizing. The classical argument implies that theorists have special access to the criteria by which to judge an act's rationality. Similarly, Gottfredson and Hirschi (1990, p. 184) imply that they have access to criteria by which to judge a person's self-interest and how it is best pursued, even if the individual is unable to apply these criteria or disagrees with them. Classical theorizing further begs the question of whether individuals have a singular self-interest or competing self-interests that need to be reconciled. Particularly in the context of large bureaucratic organizations, with their highly specialized divisions of labor and complexly differentiated responsibilities, individuals are likely to develop conflicting views of their own self-interests, as when business requirements contradict the conventions of ordinary morality learned early in one's socialization (e.g., in decisions to break laws to secure profits and jobs [Yeager, 1995]). In short, rather than being evident or given in the "human condition," interests are perceptions that are socially constructed and evolve in the patterns of interaction in which people find themselves and are socialized.

Relatedly, Gottfredson and Hirschi's emphasis on crime as involving the pursuit of short-term gains at the expense of long-term gains is problematic. The most obvious difficulty with the distinction is that its vagueness renders it virtually impossible to measure. It is not clear what counts as "short-term." In addition, it is not clear who sets the standard for distinguishing short-term from long-term. Does the analyst or the subject set the standard? If these perceptions differ, who arbitrates the dispute? And must an act, a choice, be directed at one or the other of these time frames rather than both?

Even if one treats the measurement of short-term and long-term as unproblematic, it does not necessarily help distinguish between organizational offending and standard business practices. Gottfredson and Hirschi imply that organizational lawbreaking is occasioned by short-term interests, whereas standard business practice is premised upon a longer, strategic view. An important point here is that while organizations sometimes commit offenses in the pursuit of interests such as quick profits, they also violate laws in order to realize financial health several years in the future (e.g., price-fixing conspiracies, contract fraud). In either case, the offenses are commonly motivated by the rational pursuit of legitimate goals rather than by the undersocialized, impulsive pursuit of immediate self-gratification.

Gottfredson and Hirschi's concept of self-control is similarly troubled. Along with the stability thesis, they assert that business organizations select managers and executives on self-control, screening out impulsive, under-controlled personalities likely to commit acts of force or fraud. Given the evidence of these acts in organizations, they subsequently suggested that self-control is a continuous variable across individuals (Hirschi & Gottfredson, 1993, p. 53, fn.1; 1994, p. 12). Thus, organizational offenders commit fewer offenses (and offense types) because they have more self-control than other criminals, but less self-control than their business peers.

There are two difficulties here. First, this specific argument enlarges the problem of tautology since, given the organizational screen for self-control and the purported infrequency of crimes and analogous acts, the offense may be the only measure of self-control. A second problem inheres in the position-specific nature of many organizational offenses. Because of the highly refined division of labor in complex organizations, these offenses can be committed only by specific role incumbents, whose acts and reasons cannot simply be compared with those of incumbents in other roles. Gottfredson and Hirschi therefore must argue either that a less self-controlled person found his or her way through substantial screens and into the relevant role "by accident" or that "unusual" processes selected him or her into the role. In the first case, theory stands silent in the face of "unexplained" variance; in the second case, theory must specify the apparently extraordinary selection mechanisms.

To theorize such offenses fully, therefore, requires that one attend to such factors as the structures of roles in organizations, role requirements, and selection and socialization into them, factors that may shape aspects of motivation (i.e., perception of self-interest) and (perceived) opportunity.

Organizational Managers

Views from—and of—the inside of corporations consistently suggest the routine nature of much offending and of the forces in organization and culture that occasion it. Indeed, surveys of corporate officials indicate that unethical and illegal practices are common. For example, studies find that substantial majorities of executives agree that criminal antitrust violations and other unethical acts are rather common in business (Baumhart, 1961; Nader & Green, 1972; Silk & Vogel, 1976). This body of research also finds that managers see superiors as pressuring them toward ethical and legal offenses. For example, in a Harvard *Business Review* survey on corporate ethics, half the sampled managers thought that their superiors frequently did not wish to know how results were obtained so long as the desired outcomes were achieved. Moreover, "Respondents frequently complained of superiors' pressure to support incorrect viewpoints, sign false documents, overlook superiors' wrongdoing, and do business with superiors' friends" (Brenner & Molander, 1977, p. 60). Relatedly, Clinard's (1983) interviewees, retired middle managers, reported that unethical and illegal acts were connected to the culture established by top management. Intriguingly, these managers further suggested that the nature of the ethical climate depended in part on the professional backgrounds of corporate leaders and their mode of recruitment. Respondents saw leaders with engineering backgrounds, and those recruited from among long-standing employees, as being more likely to establish positive ethical climates than financial specialists and recruits from outside the firm, who focused more on bottom-line results (Clinard, 1983, pp. 136-137).

At first blush, these suggestive data would appear to comport with Gottfredson and Hirschi's arguments connecting of their theory for organizational offending. Rather than describing undersocialized "bad apples" who occasionally defeat institutional and organizational selection mechanisms and rise to positions of authority within firms, Clinard's respondents point to highly structured patterns of socialization and selection that are embedded in fundamental processes of corporate capitalism. Combined with findings that tendencies toward unethical and illegal acts are common in corporations, these data indicate a necessary place for both socialization in the professions and processes of selection into organizational roles in theorizing such offenses.

Moreover, a substantial body of research indicates that corporate bureaucracies shape members' views in ways that affect the moral quality of their decision making (e.g., Jackall, 1988; Kram et al., 1989; Stone, 1975; Yeager, 1995). . . . [B]ureaucracy [also has the] tendency to convert moral issues into pragmatic ones as managers are routinely socialized to "a world where the etiquette of authority relationships and the necessity of protecting and covering for one's boss, one's network, and oneself supersede all other considerations and where nonaccountability for action is the norm" (Jackall, 1988, p. 111). This tendency is founded upon the segmentation of roles, duties, and knowledge that characterizes bureaucratic structures (Jackall, 1988; Stone, 1975; Yeager, 1995). Indeed, the very strengths of rational hierarchy—efficient pursuit of goals through specialization in a complex division of labor, impartiality, and universalism—virtually assure conflicts between the obligations of managers and at least some requirements of conventional morality, often including those of law. In corporate hierarchies, authority and goal setting are established in the upper ranks while responsibility for achieving goals is delegated downward and subdivided among functions, divisions, and departments. Combined with a "conspiracy of ignorance," in which top managers do not wish to hear of problems and lower level managers do not wish to tell them (for fear of being labeled incompetent) (Jackall, 1988, pp. 20-21, 89-90, 122-123; Stone, 1975), decisions are routinely reached in a context of secrecy and plausible deniability in which everyone evades a sense of moral responsibility for wrongdoing (Clinard & Yeager, 1980; Yeager, 1995). The evasion, of course, only reinforces the potential for misdeeds when managers face obstacles to the achievement of corporate purposes.

Our own fieldwork research in large companies underscores the *ordinariness* of corporate offending (Kram et al., 1989; Yeager, 1995). Legal and moral violations are "built into" the goal orientations, structures, and processes of complex business organizations. Moreover, the findings clearly indicate the intricate structuring of moral interests in managerial behavior. They suggest that when corporate officials break the law, they commonly do not do so on the basis of naked self-interest or antipathy for legal and moral requirements. Instead, our interview data portray highly trained, properly ambitious, and conventionally socialized individuals who strain to manage ethical and legal dilemmas they regularly face and to find moral justification for delicts.

A particularly rich case involves a middle manager who manipulated accounts and inventory data to inflate corporate profits in a manner that clearly violated standard accounting principles and federal law. Under pressure from superiors to improve annual profits during a bleak financial period, he falsified the profit statement despite his clear recognition that the action violated accounting controls and the law. This manager had originally strongly resisted the pressure from above, but ultimately carried out the act. His behavior gave him pause:

> What we [had been] doing was right and was in compliance with accounting regulations and the [law], and what [I was asked to do] was wrong. . . . [I thought it was] unethical, if you will. I had to compromise my *financial ethics* (emphasis added).

Later, in assessing the role of the superior who had pressured him to commit the offense despite his principled resistance, he said:

> What he did was not unethical. . . . What he did was he made the best of a bad situation without having to sacrifice the company's progress. If we wouldn't have gotten the [profits increased this way] . . . we might have had to cut back on some things we didn't want to sacrifice, like our marketing budget, or on people. You know, I mean the alternatives to [the decision] were probably a lot uglier.

It was clear not only that he had originally resisted the pressure to violate the law, but also that he was engaged in a complex process of distancing himself from full moral responsibility for the offense. For example, while clearly seeing the action as wrong in isolation, he was able to contextualize the event in two ways. First, he interpreted his struggle with the act in terms of a violation of professional [financial] norms rather than as a more fundamental matter of personal or ordinary morality, that is, of lying to or cheating shareholders and potential investors. Second, he asserted that his superior's pressure served

"higher" organizational purposes in the context of real market pressures. In this moral calculus, therefore, the manager interpreted his role as standing between two competing sets of ethical requirements—those of the organization's needs and those of his profession—while bracketing any sense that his personal morality was at stake. In one view, this amounts to little more than rationalization by someone who should have shown more moral courage. In Gottfredson and Hirschi's account, perhaps this individual is doing nothing more than maximizing his self-interest in the short term with little regard for others; he is less self-controlled than his peers in this large company and in comparable firms.

But as criminological or deviancy theory, such an argument fails to capture adequately the realm of meaning that underlies this form of human action. We agree with Gottfredson and Hirschi that human behavior is generally intentional; we also agree that self-interest underlies most behavior. But in stark contrast to the predatory, conscience-free criminality their theory depicts, corporate lawbreaking commonly springs from normative requirements of the organization itself, as they are interpreted against business exigencies and compellingly communicated in authority relationships. Rather than simply rationalizing after the fact of impulsive behavior, corporate executives and managers often construct and negotiate justifications as they contemplate and take wayward action, justifications lodged in the normative orientations of legitimate business and its various constituencies, including shareholders and employees among others (cf., Benson, 1985). . . .

Other evidence also illustrates the normative status of lawbreaking in some companies and even industries. This status is commonly indicated in the taken-for-granted orientation personnel exhibit toward the offending, and it is often communicated through reward and promotion systems. . . . Socialization into the illegal practices was part of the normal process of induction into the managerial role. For example, one executive said that, "[e]ach was introduced to price-fixing practices by his superiors . . . when he [achieved] price-fixing responsibility" (Clinard & Yeager, 1980, pp. 64-65). Finally, analysis of this case in the Harvard *Business Review* indicates that this criminal behavior was not only routine within and between these leading manufacturers, but also that it was importantly motivated by the companies' standard practices for rewarding managers. Clearly, such practices represent and communicate a firm's normative priorities. . . .

Taken together, these case study and fieldwork data highlight the importance of normative constructions and socialization in managers' decisions to violate laws. As in virtually all human action, self-interest is at work here, as managers and executives seek success and/or to avoid failure (cf., Coleman, 1987; Wheeler, 1992). But commonly these offenses appear not to be the product of undersocialized, relatively less restrained individuals looking only to their own near-term interests. Instead, they are the behaviors of men and women well socialized to standard corporate practices and expectations, who often exhibit strong loyalties to their firms and their specific work units, and who as a result find their own self-interest firmly married to corporate purposes and goals. To theorize such offenses adequately . . . one must understand the socially constructed intentions that underlie action; one must fully understand motivation.

The Construction of Opportunity

The other factor in the basic crime equation is opportunity. In their general theory Gottfredson and Hirschi construe the role of opportunity narrowly, essentially limiting it to its influence on the distribution of illegalities. In this conception opportunities either exist in one's environment, or they do not. What this objectivist notion misses is the intersubjective *construction* of opportunities and its relationship with motivation. . . .

Importantly, it is not merely an intrapersonal process that renders opportunities psychologically available. Opportunity is socially constructed in persons' relationships with other group members experiencing—while creating—shared contexts. The structural and cultural features of social settings shape motivation and opportunity in distinctive ways and must therefore be specifically accounted for in theorizing crime.

One such unique feature in the lawbreaking of corporations involves the role of law. In this context, unlike for most conventional offending, the relation between legal regulation and the regulated is highly dynamic. Not only may

perceptions of law increase (or decrease) the psychological availability of illegal acts, but the regulated parties may be actively involved in shaping both law and the regard with which it is viewed. As such processes occur, motivation and opportunity will be dynamically produced and reproduced.

As we earlier noted, the implementation and enforcement of law regulating business commonly give way to complex deliberations between corporate and government experts regarding the costs and benefits of various degrees of control and even the nature and degree of compliance. In environmental law, for example, industry's technical input on technologies and feasibility takes precedence over citizens' and public interest concerns with the broader ethical bases of regulation (e.g., environmental values) because of inequalities in political, monetary and technical resources (Yeager, 1991, 1993, 1995; cf., Hawkins, 1983, 1984; Lynxwiler et al., 1983; Shover et al., 1986). Thus, there is a shift in moral emphasis—from the often passionately held values that motivated the original legislation to a "demoralized" focus on technical problems and solutions. Part of the historical rationalization of social relations, this is Weber's "disenchantment" of law, the displacement from legal process of substantive (or moral) criteria and their replacement by "rational" calculations of means and ends (cf., Ewing, 1987).

The key consequence is that this process reinforces business managers' perception that much regulatory law itself is (at best) morally neutral or ambivalent, which in turn strengthens the limited, utilitarian moral calculus that emphasizes the imperative of financial success over other social considerations. At stake, then, is negotiation over the essential legitimacy of law and, therefore, over the moral weight of lawbreaking. When regulatory compliance costs compete with the fundamental profit-making aims of industry in a corporate context in which law has been morally neutralized, the "moral opportunities" for lawbreaking expand as law's moral salience declines, and they expand in close connection with systems of motivation.

It is in this sense, then, that opportunities are socially constructed rather than "naturally" given, as in the simple availability of goods to steal or gullible citizens to fleece.

CONCLUSIONS

In sum, the explanation for corporate lawbreaking goes well beyond the concept of self-interest and necessarily outstrips the idea that criminality simply lies in its undersocialized pursuit. To the contrary, one must understand how political, economic, and bureaucratic systems of action create notions of self-interest and merge them with the legitimate goals of those systems. And one must assess the conditions under which such socially constructed interests lead to socially harmful outcomes, including law breaking. Whatever one ultimately determines about these conditions, it is already clear that an argument centered on the naked pursuit of short-term self-interest explains too little and ignores too much.

DISCUSSION QUESTIONS

1. Recall Gottfredson and Hirschi's general theory of crime in the previous chapter. How do the authors apply their theory to white-collar offending?

2. Why do Reed and Yeager disagree with this application of the general theory to white-collar crime? What are the three primary weaknesses in the theory?

3. What is so unique about white-collar offenders that exempts them from the wide net of the general theory of crime?

4. Why does Gottfredson and Hirschi's concept of self-control, and perhaps self-interest, fail to adequately explain the underlying dimensions of causality of white-collar crime?

NOTE

1 I questioned this very issue myself. The issue weighed heavily on my mind as I tried to determine whether to include a separate section on white-collar crime in this reader. The original compilation of readings did have a separate white-collar crime section, which was met with mixed responses. I feel that this present section adequately addresses the central theoretical issues without compromising my original intentions.

REFERENCES

Gottfredson, M., & Hirschi, T. (1990). *A general theory of crime*. Palo Alto, CA: Stanford University Press.

Reed, G. E., & Yeager, P. C. (1996). Organizational offending and neoclassical criminology: Challenging the reach of a general theory of crime. *Criminology, 34,* 357-382.

PART V

CRITICAL PERSPECTIVES IN CRIME AND CRIMINOLOGY

The article and text excerpts contained in this section comprise both new and somewhat older perspectives of social philosophical thought in terms of the criminological enterprise. These perspectives offer criminology a rich and revitalizing way to examine crime and criminality. Taken separately, the readings address the theoretical frameworks of Marxist criminology, conflict theory, constitutive criminology, postmodern and radical criminology, the new penology and the McDonaldization of punishment, and feminist criminology. Despite these differences, these readings all focus on the wider societal processes that are rooted in social conflict. In addition, all of these perspectives tend to dismiss traditional, individualistic explanations of crime for failing to consider how the offenders themselves are oppressed by societal inequities. Additionally, critical theorists indicate that there seems to be a selective focus on individual forms of harming that are conceived as operating outside of one's social context and to the exclusion of institutional and organizational activity, which can also exhibit criminality. In one way or another, critical theories of crime consider inequalities in the social structure as important contributions to the causal equation. They argue that crime rates will decrease only if there are fundamental changes in the social and political organization of society itself.

In sum, the essential features of critical theories of crime can be narrowed down to several central propositions:

1. An understanding of crime and crime control requires recognition of the central role played by inequality and power.

2. "Crime" does not exist as a value-free concept. Instead, it is imbued with political overtones. Critical criminologists assert that what is defined as criminal and as conforming behavior reflects the larger power structure in society.

3. Capitalism is viewed as being the root cause of crime.

4. The criminal justice system defends the interests of the capitalist class, because the capitalist class represents the defenders of the dominant political and social order.

5. Crime solutions can be found in a more equitable society with more equal distribution of power through various social structures (see Arrigo and Bernard, Chapter 26, this volume; Chambliss & Seidman, 1982; Greenberg, 1993; Quinney, 1974, 1980; Taylor, Walton, & Young, Chapter 24, this volume; Turk, 1966).

CONFLICT THEORY AND STATE-ORGANIZED CRIME

According to Vold, Bernard, and Snipes (1998), conflict theory finds its roots in the sociological theories of Weber and Simmel and assumes that greater levels of conflict than consensus characterize societies. Additionally, certain segments of society gain power by forming strategic alliances among certain members of a particular group. In the consensus view, society is based on a consensus of values among its members, and the state is organized to promote and protect societal interests. This view formed the basis of many of the early sociological theories, which viewed the various parts of society as contributing to, or performing a function for, the greater whole. The conflict view also has a long history and argues that societies are composed of groups with conflicting values and interests (Vold et al., 1998).

Power is based on a number of different dimensions, not solely money and wealth. It may include political power, social power, and the prestige that comes from occupying a particular social position. Conflict sociologists demonstrated that a consequence of the asymmetry of power is the fact that some groups are more influential than other groups. For example, Dahrendorf (1959) introduced the notion of conflict as a central dynamic force of social systems. Recall the important role that Dahrendorf's classifications of workplace authority contributed to the theoretical enhancement of Hagan, Simpson, and Gillis's (Chapter 15, this volume) extension of power-control theory. The groups with the most power use it to influence and maintain their position at the expense of those less powerful. Other important contributions from conflict criminologists include those of Vold (1958) and Turk (1969), who applied the ideas of conflict theory to the concepts of law and crime. They examined the process by which laws are passed in society and found that, because of their dominance, powerful groups are able to exercise that power and shape the very law-making process that determines who and what will be defined as criminal (Turk, 1969; Vold, 1958). As Vold points out, a consequence of this process is that members of a group that opposed the passage of a particular law are more apt to violate it, because the law's interests and purposes are in direct conflict with their own.

MARXIST THEORY AND ITS INFLUENCE ON RADICAL CRIMINOLOGY

Some critical theorists looked to the writings of Karl Marx in their analysis of society. Later known as radical criminologists, these theorists viewed power as based primarily on the control of economic resources. Marx and Friedrich Engels developed a theory of economic determinism that asserted that all aspects of social life and all of its institutions were influenced by the dominant economic structure of that society, mainly in terms of who owned the wealth (i.e., the means of production) and who owned only their labor, which they sold to capitalists for wages. Bonger (1916) was among the first of this group of theorists to apply these principles to the study of crime. Bonger found capitalist societies to be highly criminogenic because they promoted selfishness and greed to the exclusion of the welfare of others. Taylor, Walton, and Young (Chapter 24, this volume) examined Bonger's assertions and concluded that an adequate social theory needs to place crime within the context of a capitalist political economy. In a way, they extended previous claims made by conflict theorists by claiming that the state operates to promote the interests of the *economically* powerful to protect their interests.

Some theorists have criticized this instrumentalist view of crime and criminal justice for being too narrow. Instead, critics have offered a structural view of crime, which many argue is more consistent with Marx's theory. From a structural-Marxist perspective, the primary function of the state is not to serve the short-term interests of capitalists directly, but instead to make sure that the social relations of capitalism endure for the long haul. This process requires that a variety of competing interests be served at different times in order to prevent the rise of conditions that would bring down the capitalist structure (Vold et al., 1998).

POSTMODERN APPROACHES TO CRIME

Most recently, critical criminologists have turned their attention toward postmodern approaches to the study of crime, criminality, and crime control. Proponents of this perspective contend that if its premises are fulfilled, postmodern thought on criminology could have a very powerful, transforming effect on the discipline itself. Postmodernist theory separates itself from modernist approaches in several ways. First, modernism is associated with the "naturalistic" approach to the world, meaning that science is viewed as an objective process aimed at predicting and controlling the world (Vold et al., 1998). Most of criminology is "modernist" or "naturalistic" by this definition. Postmodernism stands in marked contrast to modernist assumptions. Generally speaking, postmodernist theory challenges all traditional assumptions in social science broadly speaking and in criminology in particular. Postmodernism argues that all thinking and all knowledge are mediated by language and that language itself never emerges within a neutral space. Whether people are conscious of it or not, language always privileges certain points of view to the disparagement of others (Vold et al., 1998).

Consequently, for postmodernists, there are no eternal truths, because all truth claims fall subject to challenge and deconstruction. For postmodernists, the important emphasis rests on alternative discourse and on uncovering underlying meanings that shape and are shaped by language. Because meaning itself is consequently evolving and changing in an eternal state of fluidity, no certainties exist within a postmodernist framework. Everything is in a constant state of flux; people and objects are constantly being defined and redefined within the varying contexts in which they find themselves.

In an extreme view, with no one explanation better than another, some people may conclude, "What's the point?" thereby adopting a nihilistic view of the entire discipline itself! However, criminologists who identify with this approach certainly have not traveled this theoretical or philosophical route. Criminologists writing in this framework have come to accept the need to challenge traditional theoretical constructs of causality and methodological purity by engaging in the practice of deconstruction. In contrast to some deconstructionists, criminologists who identify themselves as constitutive criminologists wish not only to deconstruct the dominant crime and crime control discourse but also to reconstruct or reconstitute it in terms of better reflecting the human condition, but as a condition that is always subject to change. They view this task as being accomplished through a new "replacement discourse," which is really a way of talking about crime, harm, social justice, and, to a certain extent, criminal justice that shifts the focus away from negative discourse that supports oppressive structures in society (Henry & Milovanovic, Chapter 25, this volume).

Constitutive criminology is examined in the article by Henry and Milovanovic, who attempt to "constitute" a new direction for criminology.

In general, they argue that crime can be abated by changing the way that people think and talk about it. The authors acknowledge that this will not be an easy goal to accomplish, but they do encourage all criminologists to stop advancing the construction of oppressive structures and redirect their energies into a replacement discourse that encourages the construction of less harmful, less oppressive institutions.

Moreover, readers will appreciate the inclusion of Arrigo and Bernard's (Chapter 26) comprehensive and comparative analysis of conflict, radical, and postmodern criminology, all of which have developed over the past decade. This article provides a clear overview and explanation of the major themes within each theory and points out similarities and differences with respect to one another.

NEW PENOLOGY AND McDONALDIZATION OF PUNISHMENT

The constitutive perspective is illustrated in this volume by the article by Shichor (Chapter 27), which uses the frameworks of the new penology and the concept of *McDonaldization* to examine the scope and problems associated with California's three-strikes law. The inclusion of this article in this section is significant for both theoretical and criminal justice policy concerns. In terms of theoretical concerns, the new penology illustrates how penal policy emerges and is transformed through discursive construction. More specifically, the framework of the new penology, developed by Feeley and Simon (1992), shows how during the 1980s and 1990s, the United States shifted its corrective and sentencing policies toward more punitive approaches, and how this shift was driven by a discourse of risk. Feeley and Simon focused their concerns on the emergence of new strategies being used in correctional ideology. They maintain that three central areas reflect this change: a greater emphasis on risk, the correctional system's shift from rehabilitation to control (i.e., incapacitation), and the employment of surveillance technologies to target offenders and treat them as aggregates of risk rather than as individuals.

Shichor (Chapter 27) provides readers with a thorough overview of Feeley and Simon's (1992) theory and then discuss how the three-strikes law illustrates the core elements of the new penology, especially in terms of the law's focus on dangerous groups of offenders, the attempt to manage this dangerous group by removing them from the larger population for a long time (i.e., the maximum potential of a third-strike conviction), and the use of a variety of surveillance techniques to regulate the behavior of these offenders.

Additionally, Shichor (Chapter 27) applies Ritzer's (1993) theory of McDonaldization to the three-strikes law. This theory, which emerges from the sociological literature, argues that certain processes in American institutions mirror the principles inherent in the fast-food industry, namely efficiency, calculability, prediction, and control. Shichor asserts that although the three-strikes law attempted to achieve these goals, it fell short of the mark, namely in terms of the inefficiency of the judicial system (i.e., backlogged court dockets), failure to adequately calculate and predict the (extremely high) costs and the number of offenders brought into the system under this law because of the wide use of prosecutorial discretion, and last, the ineffective use of security and control over offenders.

FEMINIST CRIMINOLOGY

Feminist theory challenges existing theories of crime in a holistic manner. Feminist theory attacks criminological theories at their fundamental core, because feminists view them as being based on taken-for-granted patriarchal assumptions of the world and of human behavior that ignore women's voices in the construction and shaping of reality and that draw on masculine-based conclusions about how the world works. Knowledge, like our values, attitudes, and beliefs, is derived from experiences conditioned by gender, as well as by one's race, ethnicity, and class. Consequently, as a field dominated by white males, criminology, according to feminists, is problematic, because the questions and answers as well as the theoretical and methodological frameworks are developed by white, economically privileged men (Daly & Chesney-Lind, Chapter 28, this volume). As Daly and Chesney-Lind point out, feminists, "although tutored in 'male-stream' theory and methods . . . work within these structures of knowledge to ask new questions, to put old problems in a fresh light, and to challenge the cherished wisdom

of their disciplines" (p. 268, this volume). Therefore, feminist theory aims to generate a new framework for understanding both gender relations in our society and how the relations affect and shape crime and criminal justice.

Although feminist writings appeared in the field of criminology prior to Daly and Chesney-Lind's article (Chapter 28), it was their seminal piece on feminism and criminology that provided some coherence and understanding of the mission of what feminist criminology should be. This article persuaded feminists to adopt a global perspective that is traditionally not presented in mainstream criminological theories. From this perspective, feminism challenges assumptions and beliefs about the origins and consequences of the gendered structure and organization of society and provides direction for social change. This broader view of feminism has enabled many feminist criminologists to see and understand crime as part of the larger pattern of social structure and relations, including perspectives and analyses from both men and women.

In order to understand the point to which feminist theory has evolved in criminology, some consideration should be given to the initial, important literature as well as to the major themes in feminist criminology.

Overview of Criticisms and the Development of the Feminist Framework Within Criminology

Initial writings in feminist theory as it applied to crime, criminology in general, and criminology centered on critiques that argued that a variety of topics related to female offenders had largely been ignored or profoundly distorted within feminist criminology. These criticisms can be summarized into several points:

1. Traditional criminology failed to explain female criminality fully or accurately. Most of these theories offered simplistic, stereotypical views of women who violated the law.

2. The gender-neutral framework of traditional criminological theories failed to explain the differences between women and men in their participation in crime. When differences were addressed, they focused on characteristics that suggested women's inferiority and that often reinforced their subordination to men in society.

3. Traditional criminological theories also failed to address the different manner in which women were treated by the criminal justice system. A double standard was thought to have existed within those traditional theories: Women who violated the law were often treated more harshly than men because it was thought that they had violated their traditional gender role as well. Differences in treatment led to differences in official crime rates, which then led to different theoretical interpretations of male and female crime.

4. Traditional criminological theories ignored women's new roles in society. For example, mainstream theories failed to consider the impact of "women's liberation" on crime and how women's new roles may affect their participation in criminality (Vold et al., 1998).

Two of the most prominent feminist criminologists, Freda Adler and Rita Simon, provided a foundation on which later perspectives in feminist criminology could build and transform. These authors pointed out the critiques summarized above in two critical texts that were published in 1975. Freda Adler's (1975) contribution, *Sisters in Crime: The Rise of the New Female Criminal,* argued that women were becoming more aggressive and competitive as they freed themselves from traditional gender roles of domesticity and moved into the male-dominated world of the marketplace. She argued that this new assumption of "masculine" traits and attitudes in the workplace paralleled an increase in arrest rates and crime among women, a behavior characteristically associated with men. She concluded that the women's movement contributed to the decreasing differences between male and female crime rates. In other words, equal opportunity knew no boundaries in terms of both legitimate and illegitimate pursuits; women were now thought of as being just as capable as men of using violence and aggression in the commission of a crime (Adler, 1975).

Rita Simon (1975) offered a similar theory to that of Adler in her text *Women and Crime.* Simon also recognized recent changes in the types and volume of crime committed by women, but she asserted that these changes did not result from an adoption by women of masculine behavioral traits and characteristics. Instead, Simon focused on the changes in women's status in labor force participation, education, income, and a variety of professions, and she argued that as women moved out of traditional domestic roles, they encountered more opportunities to commit crime. Simon showed that property crime for women increased, leading to higher arrest and incarceration rates, but that violent crimes committed by women remained the same. Simon proposed that white-collar crimes, as they related to the workplace, would increase among women.

Adler's (1975) and Simon's (1975) research and propositions formulated the basis for the "liberation hypothesis," which argued that women's liberation from traditional domestic roles would result in increases in female criminality. The central difference between the two theorists involved the *type* of crime each thought that women would commit. Adler thought women would assume more masculine traits and characteristics and become more violent, whereas Simon argued that women's new opportunities in the workforce would give them access to white-collar crime opportunities (i.e., embezzlement, check forgery, and fraud). Future research found more support for Simon's thesis; however, both theories subsequently failed to predict the rise of the "new female criminal." In fact, more recent feminist criminologists argued that Adler's and Simon's theories should not be considered a part of feminist criminology because they both failed to consider the structural and cultural forces that shape women's lives and experiences. In other words, these early theories ignored the gender relations that constitute and are constituted by the society in which we all live.

Major Themes in Feminist Criminology

Although these early attempts at explaining female criminality were later rejected, they did form the basis upon which more complex and comprehensive approaches could evolve. Generally speaking, there is no single feminist theory directed at one particular aspect of crime, criminality, and crime control. For example, some feminist theories attempt to explain the differences in male and female crime and have demonstrated that these differences have not been considered with any theoretical consistency. Other feminist theorists have focused on the absence of gender from criminological theories.

Likewise, feminist theory itself assumes many forms and perspectives. Four major approaches, or themes, have been identified as liberal, radical, socialist, and Marxist. These branches of feminism and feminist criminology disagree about the meaning of particular terms and even about how feminists should approach the study of crime and criminality. *Liberal feminism* centers on gender discrimination as an issue of equal rights between men and women. Many of the early feminist writings, which were considered to be a part of traditional criminology, fell into this category largely because they failed to take a critical position on gender issues. Liberal feminism operated within the existing social structure, focusing on women's issues, equal rights, and the transformation of women's roles in society (Daly & Chesney-Lind, Chapter 28, this volume; Vold et al., 1998).

Radical feminism emerged as another branch of critical theories, and it directly challenged the social structures within which liberal feminism worked to effect change. Radical feminism viewed the problem of gender inequality and the subordination of women to men as a systemic problem of "patriarchy." Rooted in male aggression and male domination, patriarchy seeks to control women in both the public and private spheres and to control women's sexuality while indulging that of men. Patriarchy is thought to be the most pervasive and fundamental form of domination in all societies. Societies establish patriarchy through sex role socialization and the development of gendered identities through which men and women come to believe that men are superior to women in many different ways. As a result of these gender identities and sex role expectations, men tend to dominate women in personal interactions, such as in the family or in intimate relationships, thereby politicizing the personal (Vold et al., 1998).

Marxist feminists, like radical feminists, recognize the patriarchal structure and gender relations within that structure, but they see these relations as rooted in class relations of production. In other words, the root of the problem of male dominance stems from the fact that men own and control the means of economic production. As a result, women in economically weak positions find themselves, like minorities, frequently exploited (Henry & Einstadter, 1998, p. 384). From a Marxist feminist perspective,

then, patriarchy is directly tied to the capitalist economy. Therefore, crime is viewed as an offense not only against the law but also against the capitalist economic structure and patriarchy itself. For example, typical actions by women considered criminal include property crime—which usually comes in the form of embezzlement, check forgery, or fraud—and sexual crimes. Both types of crime threaten male dominance, either economically or sexually. Like Marxist criminologists, some Marxist feminists take an instrumentalist view of the law, where the law is thought to be a direct weapon of male oppression, whereas other Marxist feminists follow a structural view of the law, which looks at the various structural patterns in society that maintain patriarchy over a long period of time (Hagan, 1989; Vold et al., 1998).

Socialist feminists shifted their emphasis away from the firm Marxist framework, though they still stress the importance of examining social roles and their relationship to economic production. The socialist feminist framework combines elements from radical and Marxist feminism to center on women's oppression that is found in the capitalist economy. Socialist feminists argue that class relations and the technology of production as well as the construction of gender roles in the home, workplace, and with respect to childbearing and child care need to be recognized (Henry & Einstadter, 1998).

More particularly, socialist feminists focus on the issue of the natural reproductive differences between men and women, which underlie male-female relationships in our society. In the past, women were much more dependent on men, both physically and economically, especially in terms of pregnancy, childbirth, and nursing. Women's biological role enabled them to become the primary child care providers in the family unit and subsequently contributed to the "sexual division of labor," in which men work outside the home and women spend their days "working" in the home. This dichotomy forms the basis for the subordination of women to men: Women's role and the tasks she performs in the home are not really considered "work" and are not valued as much as the work men do as active participants in the capitalist economy. Socialist feminists contend that one way in which egalitarian societies can succeed is for women not only to take ownership of the means of economic production, but also to take control of their bodies and their own reproductive systems as well. Once women can make their own decisions about what happens to their bodies, a greater sense of equality and agency can be achieved.

Some theorists have argued that many of the gender differences that exist in both the home and even the workplace are based not so much in the socialization patterns of girls and boys, but on the "essential" characteristics of men and women (Daly & Chesney-Lind, Chapter 28, this volume). For example, men are not socialized into violent behavior patterns; rather, it is their aggressive nature that eventually becomes transformed into expressions of violence. Essentialism argues that the fundamental biological differences between men and women form the heart of patriarchy. Therefore, essentialism led to the celebration and championing of women and everything that was "essentially female" and the condemnation of everything associated with men. Some criminologists have rejected the essentialist framework and have argued that the social structure within which one is raised plays a much stronger role in terms of socializing men toward violence and aggression than does biology (Messerschmidt, 1993).

Other Dimensions of Feminist Thought Within Feminist Criminology

The four feminist themes described above—liberal, radical, Marxist, and socialist—have all been identified in the literature as separate aspects of feminist thought. *Postmodern feminism* is another aspect of feminism that has been receiving more attention in feminist criminology. As you will recall from the previous section, which focused on the critical theories in criminology, *postmodernism* refers to a way of thinking that threatens to overturn the essential premises of modern thought within which the natural and physical sciences have emerged and upon which sociology and other social sciences have been founded (Smart, 1995). More specifically, postmodern feminism rejects the one reality that arises from the universalizing perspective of those in power (i.e., men). Postmodern feminism does not wish to impose a different unitary reality. Rather, it refers to subjugated knowledges, which tell different stories and have different specificities (Smart, 1995).

Briefly, the rise of modernity in the 19th century marks the placing of "man" at the center of all knowledge, "man" who is author and creator of his own knowledge and actions and who simultaneously becomes the object of human scientific inquiry (Smart, 1995). In addition to positioning the human subject at the center of scientific knowledge and inquiry, modernism also fosters the notion that knowledge must be generated for the purpose of progress and advancement, hence the emphasis of modernity on the applicability of knowledge to visible problems.

Consequently, at the end of the 20th century and the beginning of the 21st, modernity has been seen as synonymous with racism; sexism; heterosexism; Eurocentric thought; and the attempt to reduce social, cultural, racial, and sexual differences to one dominant set of values and beliefs. In contrast, postmodernism argues that no set of unitary values exists, and this view also includes feminism. As Smart (1995) argues, the

> aim of feminism ceases to be the establishment of the feminist truth and becomes the aim of deconstructing Truth and analysing the power effects that claims to truth entail. So, there is a shift away from treating knowledge as ultimately objective, or at least the final standard, and hence able to reveal the concealed truth, towards recognizing that knowledge is part of that power and that power is ubiquitous. Feminist knowledge therefore becomes part of a multiplicity of resistances. (pp. 44-45)

Postmodern feminism, for example, focuses on how discourse is used to set particular women apart from the rest as criminals. Postmodern feminism has also tackled the issue of rape and how traditional feminists fail to consider how men's and women's bodies have been constructed and constituted (socially). In other words, "Instead of sidestepping the problem of sex's relation to power by divorcing one from the other in our minds, we need to analyze the social mechanisms, including language and conceptual structures, that bind the two together in our culture" (Woodhull, 1988, as quoted in Smart, 1995, p. 46). Other feminists reject postmodernism, asserting that feminism should be seen as a modernist project that follows the standards of scientific objectivity.

The Selected Readings in Feminist Criminology

The reading selections in this anthology highlight many of the problems with mainstream criminology and its failure to focus attention on these issues. Daly and Chesney-Lind's article (Chapter 28) provides an exceptionally thorough overview of feminism and its application to criminology and offers suggestions about how some of the problems previously identified here can be overcome. The article in this section by Daly (Chapter 29) offers different ways of conceptualizing sex and gender in feminist theory and suggests how that reconceptualization may affect criminology. Daly's article stresses the importance of giving voices to those often ignored in feminist theory, including not only the relations of class-race-gender, but also age, sexuality, and physical ability. Daly pushes readers to think of all of these variables not as separate aspects of inequality that have an additive and discrete quality to them, but as interlocking and contingent. In sum, she offers new ways of looking at the interrelationships among these variables and what they hold for criminologists, especially in terms of empirical research.

REFERENCES

Adler, F. (1975). *Sisters in crime: The rise of the new female criminal*. New York: McGraw-Hill.

Bonger, W. (1916). *Criminality and economic conditions*. Boston: Little, Brown.

Chambliss, W., & Seidman, R. (1982). *Law, order, and power* (2nd ed.). Reading, MA: Addison-Wesley.

Dahrendorf, R. (1959). *Class and class conflict in an industrial society*. London: Routledge & Kegan Paul.

Feeley, M., & Simon, J. (1992). The new penology: Notes on the emerging strategy of corrections and its implications. *Criminology, 30,* 449-474.

Greenberg, D. (1993). *Crime and capitalism: Readings in Marxist criminology*. Philadelphia: Temple University Press.

Hagan, J. (1989). *Structural criminology*. New Brunswick, NJ: Rutgers University Press.

Henry, S., & Einstadter, W. (Eds.). (1998). *The criminology theory reader*. New York: New York University Press.

Messerschmidt, J. (1993). *Masculinities and crime: Critique and reconceptualization and theory*. Totowa, NJ: Rowan & Littlefield.

Quinney, R. (1974). *Critique of legal order: Crime control in capitalist society*. Boston: Little, Brown.

Quinney, R. (1980). *Class, state, and crime*. New York: Longman.

Ritzer, G. (1993). *The McDonaldization of society*. Newbury Park, CA: Pine Forge.

Simon, R. (1975). *Women and crime*. Lexington, MA: D. C. Heath.

Smart, C. (1995). *Law, crime and sexuality: Essays in feminism*. Thousand Oaks, CA: Sage.

Turk, A. (1966). Conflict and criminality. *American Sociological Review, 31,* 143-172.

Turk, A. (1969). *Criminality and the legal order*. Chicago: Rand McNally.

Vold, G. B. (1958). *Theoretical criminology*. New York: Oxford University Press.

Vold, G. B., Bernard, T. J., & Snipes, J. B. (1998). *Theoretical criminology* (4th ed.). Oxford, UK: Oxford University Press.

24

MARX, ENGELS, AND BONGER
ON CRIME AND SOCIAL CONTROL

IAN TAYLOR, PAUL WALTON, AND JOCK YOUNG

EDITOR'S INTRODUCTION—In the conclusion of their important text, *The New Criminology: For a Social Theory of Deviance*, Taylor, Walton, and Young argue "for a political economy of criminal action and of the reaction it excites, and for a politically-informed social psychology of these ongoing social dynamics. We have . . . laid claim to have constructed the formal elements of a theory that would be adequate to move criminology out of its own imprisonment in artificially segregated specifics" (Taylor et al., 1973, p. 279). Taylor, Walton, and Young's call for a new approach in criminology reflects the views of a number of radical theorists at the time who argued for a theory of crime that would place crime in the context of a capitalist political economy. These theorists suggested that not only is crime determined largely by the behavior of those in power (i.e., what is criminalized threatens their position), but that the state operates on behalf of the economically powerful to protect their interests.

In the text excerpts selected for this anthology, Taylor, Walton, and Young provide readers with the historical background of Marxist theory through the work of Willem Bonger (1916) as well as a brief overview of the more contemporary contributions of conflict theorists. Marxist theory forms the basis of many of the later conflict and radical theories of crime. These theorists, sometimes lumped together in the category of *critical theorists*, view power as primarily based on the control of economic resources. Marx and Engels argued that all other dimensions such as honor and prestige were ultimately shaped by whether people were owners of wealth or whether they owned their labor, which they sold to capitalists for wages.

Bonger (1916) was the first person to apply these views to crime. Bonger viewed capitalism as criminogenic. The capitalist system promoted egoism, competition, and selfishness at the expense of altruism, sharing, and cooperation. From this perspective, Bonger felt that egoism contributed to crime because it disconnected people from one another, encouraging them to be greedy and selfish and to pursue their own interests without regard for their fellow citizens. Bonger asserted that crime would be eliminated within a socialist society because socialism promotes concern for the welfare of the entire state and because it would remove any legal biases that favor the wealthy.

In part, Marxism stands or falls on the basis of certain assumptions it makes about the nature of man. Where other social theories operate with implicit assumptions about man's nature, Marx made his starting-point a quite explicit philosophical anthropology of man. In *The Economic and Philosophical Manuscripts of 1844,* Marx is concerned to show that man is distinct in a crucial and precise way from the members of the animal world:

> Man is a *species-being* not only in the sense that he makes the community (his own as well as those of other things) his object both practically and theoretically, but also (and this is simply another expression of the same thing) in the sense that he treats himself as the present living species, as a *universal* and consequently free being.

The bulk of Marx's later work is concerned with the demonstration of the ways in which man's social nature and consciousness have been distorted, imprisoned or diverted by the social arrangements developed over time. These social arrangements are the product of man's struggle to master the conditions of scarcity and material underdevelopment. These social arrangements, developed as a response to man's domination by poverty, imprison man tightly in social relationships of an exploitative nature and alienate men from men, and thus from the objects of their labour. Man is struggling to be free, but cannot realize freedom (or himself as a fully-conscious, 'sensuous' species-being) until such time as he is free of the exploitative relationships which are outmoded and unnecessary.

The continuing debates over Marxism in sociology and philosophy, (as well as within socialist movements) in the twentieth century, therefore, have had to do with problems of consciousness, contradictions and social change. That is, the image of society offered out by classical Marxism is one of competing social groups, each with a distinct set of interests and cultural world views, caught within a network of essentially temporary (or historically-specific) social arrangements, which in their turn are more or less likely to be revolutionized in periods of crisis. Capitalism, as a set of social relationships, is conceptualized as the most highly-developed form of social exploitation, within which are sown the seeds of man's leap to a liberating consciousness. Capitalism 'contains the seeds of its own destruction' not only in the sense that it creates the technology whereby physical and material need may be satisfied but also because it prevents a more sophisticated set of social relationships developing alongside such productive forces.

A full-blown Marxist theory of deviance, or at least a theory of deviance deriving from a Marxism so described, would be concerned to develop explanations of the ways in which particular historical periods, characterized by particular sets of social relationships and means of production, give rise to attempts by the economically and politically powerful to order society in particular ways. It would ask with greater emphasis the question that Howard Becker poses (and does not face), namely, who makes the rules, and why? A Marxist theory would attempt, that is, to locate the defining agencies, not only in some general market structure, but quite specifically in their relationship to the overweening structure of material production and the division of labour. Moreover, to be a satisfactory explanation, a Marxist theory would proceed with a notion of man which would distinguish it quite clearly from classical, positivist, or interactionist 'images' of man. It would assume, that is, a degree of consciousness, bound up with men's location in a social structure of production, exchange and domination, which of itself would influence the ways in which men defined as criminal or deviant would attempt to live with their outsider's status. That is, men's reaction to labeling by the powerful would not be seen to be simply a cultural problem—a problem of reacting to a legal status or a social stigma: it would necessarily be seen to be bound up with men's degree of consciousness of domination and subordination in a wider structure of power relationships operating in particular types of economic context. One consequence of such an approach—which, it must be stated, has been conspicuous for its absence in deviancy theory—would be the possibility of building links between the insights of interactionist theory, and other approaches sensitive to men's subjective world, and the theories of social structure implicit

Taylor, I., Walton, P., & Young, J. (1973). Marx, Engels, and Bonger on crime and social control. In Taylor, I., Walton, P., & Young, J., *The new criminology: For a social theory of deviance* (pp. 219-221, 222-235). London: Routledge & Kegan Paul.

in orthodox Marxism. More crucially, such a linkage would enable us to escape from the strait-jacket of an economic determinism and the relativism of some subjectivist approaches to a theory of contradiction in a social structure which recognizes in 'deviance' the acts of men in the process of actively making, rather than passively taking, the external world. It might enable us to sustain what has until now been a polemical assertion, made (in the main) by anarchists and deviants themselves, that much deviance is in itself a political act, and that, in this sense, deviance is a property of the act rather than a spurious label applied to the amoral or the careless by agencies of political and social control.

WILLEM BONGER AND FORMAL MARXISM

In the study of crime and deviance, the work of Willem Bonger (1876-1940) . . . has assumed the mantle of the Marxist orthodoxy—if only because (with the exception of untranslated writers inside the Soviet bloc) no other self-proclaimed Marxist has devoted time to a full-scale study of the area. Bonger's criminology is an attempt to utilize some of the formal concepts of Marxism in the understanding of the crime-rates of European capitalism in the late nineteenth and early twentieth centuries. Importantly, however, Bonger's efforts appear, for us, not so much the application of a fully-fledged Marxist theory as they are a recitation of a 'Marxist catechism' in an area which Marx had left largely untouched—a recitation prompted by the growth not of the theory itself, but by the growth of a sociological pragmatism. Bonger must, therefore, be evaluated in his own terms, in terms of the competence of his extension of the formal concepts of Marxism to the subject-matter, rather than in terms of any claim that might be made for him as *the* Marxist criminologist.

In at least two respects, Bonger's analysis of crime differs in substance from that of Marx. On the one hand, Bonger is clearly very much more seriously concerned than Marx with the causal chain linking crime with the precipitating economic and social conditions. On the other, he does not confine his explanations to working-class crime, extending his discussions to the criminal activity of the industrial bourgeoisie as defined by the criminal laws of his time. Whilst differing from Marx in these respects, however,

Bonger is at one with his mentor in attributing the activity itself to demoralized individuals, products of a dominant capitalism.

Indeed, in both Marx and Bonger, one is aware of a curious contradiction between the 'image of man' advanced as the anthropological underpinning of 'orthodox' Marxism and the questions asked about men who deviate. . . . The criminal thought, which runs through the bulk of Bonger's analysis of crime, is seen as the product of the tendency in industrial capitalism to create 'egoism' rather than 'altruism' in the structure of social life. It is apparent that the notion performs two different notions for Bonger, in that he is able to argue, at different points, that, first, 'the criminal thought' is engendered by the conditions of misery forced on sections of the working class under capitalism and that, second, it is also the product of the greed encouraged when capitalism thrives. In other words, as an intermediary notion, it enabled Bonger to circumvent the knotty problem of the relationship between general economic conditions and the propensity to economic crime.

Now, whilst the ambiguity in the notion may help Bonger's analysis, it does not stem directly from his awareness of dual problems. For Bonger, it does appear as an autonomous psychic and behavioural quality which is to be deplored and feared; 'the criminal thought,' and its associated 'egoism,' are products of the brutishness of capitalism, but at the same time they do appear to 'take over' individuals and independently direct their actions.

The Marxist perspective, of course, has always emphasized the impact that the dominant mode of production has had on social relationships in the wider society, and, in particular, has spelt out the ways in which a capitalist means of production will tend to 'individuate' the nature of social life. But to understand that 'egoism' and 'individuation' are products of particular sets of social arrangements is to understand that egoism and individuation have no force or influence independently of their social context. For Bonger, the 'criminal thought'—albeit a product of the egoistic structure of capitalism—assumes an independent status as an intrinsic and behavioural quality of certain (criminal) individuals. It is enormously paradoxical that a writer who lays claim to be writing as a sociologist and a Marxist should begin his analysis with an assumed individual quality (which he deplores) and proceed only later to the social conditions and relationships sustaining and obstructing the acting-out quality.

In the first place, the emphasis in Bonger on 'the criminal thought' as an independent factor for analysis is equivalent to the biological, physiological, and sociological (or environmental) factors accorded an independent and causative place in the writings of the positivist theorists of crime. The limitations of this approach have been pointed out, amongst others, by Austin T. Turk:

> students of crime have been preoccupied with the search for an explanation of distinguishing characteristics of criminality, almost universally assuming that the implied task is to develop scientific explanations of the behaviour of persons who deviate from 'legal norms.' The quest has not been very successful . . . the cumulative impact of efforts to specify and explain differences between 'criminal' and 'non-criminal' cultural and behaviour patterns is to force serious consideration of the possibility that there may be *no* significant differences between the overwhelming majority of legally identified criminals and the *relevant* general population, *i.e.* that population whose concerns and expectations impinge directly and routinely upon the individuals so identified.

More succinctly: 'the working assumption has been that *crime* and *non-crime* are classes of behaviour instead of simply labels associated with the processes by which individuals come to occupy ascribed . . . *statuses* of criminal and non-criminal.'

It is a comment on the nature of Bonger's Marxism that the actor is accorded such an idealistic independence; when to have started with a model of a society within which there are conflicting interests and a differential distribution of power would have revealed the utility of the criminal law and the 'criminal' label (with a legitimating ideology derived from academia) to the powerful elites of capitalist society. In fact, of course, a criminology which proceeds in recognition of competing social interests has two interrelated tasks of explanation. Certainly it has the task of explaining the causes for an individual's involvement in 'criminal' behaviour, but, prior to that, it has the task of explaining the derivation of the 'criminal' label (whose content, function and applicability we have argued will vary across time, across cultures, and internally within a social structure).

One cannot entirely avoid the conclusion that Bonger's analysis, irrespective of the extent to which it is guided by a reading and acceptance of Marxist [precepts], is motivated (and confused) by a fear of those with 'criminal thoughts.' For Bonger 'criminal thought' is by and large a product of the lack of moral training in the population. Moral training has been denied the proletariat, in particular, because it is not the essential training for work in an industrializing society. The spread of 'moral training' is the antidote to 'criminal thoughts,' but, since such an education is unlikely under the brutish capitalism of the imperialist period, capitalism—or more precisely, the economic conditions (of inequality and accumulation)—are indeed a cause of crime.

In so far as Bonger displays any concern for the determinant nature of social relationships of production, he does so in order to illustrate the tendencies of different social arrangements to encourage . . . 'criminal thoughts' in the population at large. As against ameliorarist school, which saw an inevitable advance of man from conditions of primitive and brutish living to societies in which altruistic relationships would predominate, Bonger, in fundamental agreement with the value placed on altruism and liberalism, identified the advent of capitalism with the break in the process of civilizing social relationships. . . . Bonger comments: 'The fact that the duty of altruism is so much insisted upon is the most convincing proof that it is not generally practised.'

The demise of egoism, and the creation of social conditions favourable to the 'criminal thought' parallels, for Bonger, the development of social arrangements of production as described by Marx. . . . Under capitalism, the transformation of work from its value for use to its value for exchange (as fully described by Marx) is responsible for the 'cupidity and ambition,' the lack of sensitivity between men, and the declining influence of men's ambitions on the actions of their fellows. . . . Capitalism, in short, 'has developed egoism at the expense of altruism.'

'Egoism' constitutes a favourable climate for the commission of criminal acts, and this, for Bonger, is an indication that an environment in which men's social instincts are encouraged has been replaced by one which confers legitimacy on asocial or 'immoral' acts of deviance. The commission of these acts, as Bonger explicitly states in *Introduction to Criminology,* has a demoralizing effect on the whole of the body politic.

Bonger's substantive analysis of types of crime, covering a range of 'economic crimes,' 'sexual crimes,' 'crimes from vengeance and other motives,' 'political crimes' and 'pathological crimes,' is taken up with a demonstration of the ways in which these crimes are causatively linked with an environment encouraging egoistic action. Even involvement of persons born with 'psychic defects' in criminal activity can be explained in terms of these enabling conditions:

> These persons adapt themselves to their environment only with difficulty . . . [and] have a smaller chance than others to succeed in our present society, where the fundamental principle is the warfare of all against all. Hence they are more likely to seek for means that others do not employ (prostitution, for example).

The whole of Bonger's analysis, however much it is altered or qualified at particular points in his discussion, rests on the environmental determinism of his 'general considerations.' In a social structure encouraging of egoism, the obstacles and deterrents to the emergence of the presumably ever-present 'criminal thought' are weakened and/or removed; whereas, for example, under primitive communism, the communality was constructed around, and dependent upon, an interpersonal altruism. Capitalism is responsible for the free play granted to the pathological will, the 'criminal thought' possessed by certain individuals.

The bulk of Bonger's work, indeed, so far from being an example of dialectical procedure, is a kind of positivism in itself, or at least an eclecticism reminiscent of 'inter-disciplinary' positivism. Where the general theory appears not to encompass all the facts (facts produced by positivist endeavor), mediations of various kinds are introduced. In Bonger, it is possible to find examples of the elements of anomie theory, differential opportunity theory and, at times, the frameworks of structural-functionalism (much of it well in advance of its time). In his discussion of economic crime, for example, Bonger approached a Mertonian stance on larceny:

> Modern industry manufactures enormous quantities of goods without the outlet for them being

known. The desire to buy must, then, be excited in the public. Beautiful displays, dazzling illuminations, and many other means are used to attain the desired end. The perfection of this system is reached in the great modern retail store, where persons may enter freely, and see and handle everything—where, in short, the public is drawn as a moth to a flame. The result of these tactics is that the cupidity of the crowd is highly excited.

And Bonger is not unaware of the general, or the more limited, theories of criminality and deviance produced by the classical thinkers of his time and earlier. Where appropriate, Bonger attempts to incorporate elements of these competing theorists, though always in a way which subordinates their positions to his own 'general considerations.' On Gabriel Tarde's 'law of imitation,' for example, which purports to explain criminality as a function of association with 'criminal types,' Bonger writes:

> In our present society, with its pronounced egoistic tendencies, imitation strengthens these, as it would strengthen the altruistic tendencies produced by another form of society. . . . It is only as a consequence of the predominance of egoism in our present society that the error is made of supposing the effect of imitation to be necessarily evil.

Our concern here is not to dispute particular arguments in Bonger for their own sakes, but rather to point to the way in which a single-factor environmentalism is given predominance, with secondary considerations derived from the body of existing literature being introduced eclectically. That is, Bonger's method, though resting on an environmentalism explicitly derived from Marx, appears in the final analysis as a method reminiscent of the eclecticism practised by positivist sociologists operating with formal concepts lacking a grounding in history and structure.

This eclectic approach is accompanied by a crudely statistical technique of verification and elaboration. We are presented, amongst other things, with statistical demonstrations of the relationship between levels of educational attainment and violent crime, declines in business and 'bourgeois' crime (fraud, etc.), degrees of poverty and involvement in sexual crime (especially prostitution), crimes of 'vengeance' and the season of the year and many more.

Consistently, the objective is to demonstrate the underlying motivation as being bound up with an egoism induced and sustained by the environment of capitalism. . . . And, lest we should think that egoism is directly a product of poverty and subordination, as opposed to being a central element of a general moral climate, Bonger is able to offer explanations of crime among the bourgeoisie. These crimes he sees to be motivated by need, in cases of business decline and collapse, or by cupidity. In the latter case, 'what [men] get by honest business is not enough for them, they wish to become richer.' In either case, Bonger's case is contingent on the moral climate engendered by the economic system:

> It is only under special circumstances that this desire for wealth arises, and . . . it is unknown under others. It will be necessary only to point out that although cupidity is a strong motive with all classes of our present society, it is especially so among the bourgeoisie, as a consequence of their position in the economic life.

Now, Bonger's formal Marxism does enable him to make an insightful series of comments about the nature of the deprivations experienced under capitalism. Judged in Bonger's own terms—that is, in terms of the social positivism of his time—his work surpasses much that was, and is, available. Notably, Bonger's discussion[s] of the effects of the subordination of women (and its contribution to the aetiology of female criminality) and of 'militarism' (in sustaining an egoistic and competitive moral climate) seem far ahead of their time.

Writing of the criminality of women, for example, Bonger asserts that:

> The great power of a man over his wife, as a consequence of his economic preponderance, may equally be a demoralizing cause. It is certain that there will always be abuse of power on the part of a number of those whom social circumstances have clothed with a certain authority. How many women there are now who have to endure the coarseness and bad treatment of their husbands, but would not hesitate to leave them if their economic dependence and the law did not prevent. . . .

The contemporary ring of these comments is paralleled in Bonger's comments, made, it should be remembered, at the time when the 'Marxist' parties of Europe found their members rushing to the 'national defence' in the 'Great War.'. . . Thus, whilst much of Bonger's formal Marxism appears as a form of abstracted and eclectic positivism when viewed across its canvas, he still derives a considerable benefit and understanding from the Marxist perspective in his sensitivity to the demoralizing and destructive consequences of the forms of domination characteristic of a capitalist society. Paradoxically, however, this sensitivity does not extend to an understanding of the nature of domination and social control in defining and delineating the field of interest itself, namely what passes for crime and deviance in societies where 'law' is the law determined by powerful interests and classes in the population at large. . . .

Bonger asserts that 'there are instances where an action stamped as criminal is not felt to be immoral by anybody.' But these statements, and others like them, are made in passing and do not constitute the basis for the thoroughgoing analysis of the structure of laws and interests. And Bonger is ambivalent throughout on the role of social control in the creation of crime. He seems aware only in certain cases, of 'societal reaction' in determining degrees of apprehension. So, for example: 'the offences of which women are most often guilty are also those which it is most difficult to discover, namely those committed without violence. Then, those who have been injured are less likely to bring a complaint against a woman than against a man.'

But later, in dealing with sexual crimes in general, Bonger uncritically accepts the official statistics of apprehension as an indication of 'the class of the population that commits these crimes.' In fact, Bonger's position is that the law (and its enforcement) whilst certainly the creation of a dominant class—is a genuine reflexion of some universal social and moral sentiment. . . . The manifest explanation for the inclusion within the criminal law of sanctions controlling behaviour which is not directly harmful to the class interests of the powerful is that the working classes themselves are not without power. That is, one supposes, it is in the interests of the powerful to operate a system of general social control in the interests of order (within which individual and corporate enterprise can proceed unimpeded). However, there is more than a suspicion that Bonger's equation of social control with a universal moral sentiment is based on a belief he shares with the bourgeoisie in order for its own sake. Socialism is preferable to capitalism because it is more orderly. . . .

Bonger's formal Marxism, therefore, tells us that the solution to the problems of criminality is not so much to challenge the labels and the processing of capitalist law as it is to wage a responsible and orderly political battle for the reform of a divisive social structure. Even in the case of political opposition, a crucial distinction is to be drawn between responsible activity (the acts of a noble man) and the irresponsible and pathological activity—especially that of the anarchist movement (characterized, argues Bonger, by 'extreme individualism,' 'great vanity,' 'pronounced altruistic tendencies' 'coupled with a lack of intellectual development'). . . .

. . . . For us, the outstanding feature of Bonger's essentially correctional perspective is that, quite aside from the premises on which it operates (the contingency of criminality on an egoistic moral climate), it does not reveal a consistent social psychology, or, by the same token, a systematic social theory. At one moment, the actor under consideration is seen to be inextricably caught up in a determined and identifiable set of circumstances (or, more properly, a set of economic relationships); at another, he appears as the victim of an assumed personal quality (the 'criminal thought') sustained and (often) apparently developed by the moral-climate of industrial capitalism.

In so far as a social theory reveals itself in Bonger, the central assumptions on which it is built appear to be Durkheimian in nature rather than to derive from the avowedly Marxist theory of its author. Criminal man is consistently depicted not so much as a man produced by a matrix of unequal social relationships, nor indeed as a man attempting to resolve those inequalities of wealth, power and life-chances; rather, criminal man is viewed as being in need of social control. 'Socialism,' in this perspective, is an alternative and desirable set of social institutions, which carry with them a set of Durkheimian norms and controls. 'Socialism' thus expressed is the resort of an idealist, wishing for the substitution of a competitive and egoistic moral climate by a context in which the co-operativeness of men is encouraged. Socialism is preferable to capitalism, most of all, because it will control the baser instincts of man. Bonger does not assert that the 'egoistic' man will 'wither away' under socialism: it is only that the social relationships of socialism will not reward the endeavours of an egoist. . . .

DISCUSSION QUESTIONS

1. What is Bonger's central thesis regarding crime? How does his approach differ from that of Marx?

2. In what way does Bonger's approach reflect the reflect the positivism practiced by sociologists?

3. Why is altruism so antithetical to capitalism and egoism so central? Why does Bonger favor socialism and feel that it may lead to a decline in crime rates?

REFERENCES

Bonger, W. (1916). *Criminality and economic conditions.* Boston: Little, Brown.

Taylor, I., Walton, P., & Young, J. (1973). Marx, Engels, and Bonger on crime and social control. In Taylor, I., Walton, P., & Young, J., *The new criminology: For a social theory of deviance.* London: Routledge & Kegan Paul.

25

CONSTITUTIVE CRIMINOLOGY

The Maturation of Critical Theory

STUART HENRY AND DRAGAN MILOVANOVIC

EDITOR'S INTRODUCTION—Stuart Henry and Dragan Milovanovic's work contributes to a growing body of literature within criminology that undertakes a critical approach to the study of crime, criminality, and the control of offenders. Their approach, *constitutive criminology, draws* on developments in the areas of social constructionism, left realism, socialist feminism, and poststructuralism. Additionally, they borrow strands of thought from social and critical theory, constitutive thinking, and discourse analysis to develop a perspective that aims "to examine reflexively the paradigmatic umbrella under which these saplings of critical growth can gain strength" (p. 243, this volume).

Constitutive criminology consists of a number of important themes: "(1) the codetermination of crime and human subjects through crime control ideology and how this ideology has the capacity to reproduce and to transform; (2) discursive practices as the medium for the structuring of crime and its control institutions; (3) symbolic violence as the hidden ideological dimension of legal domination; and (4) the use, by control agencies, of sense data to construct meaning that claims space and displaces the intersubjective construction of meaning" (p. 243, this volume).

In their explication of these themes, the authors reject criminological theories that reduce crime to an outcome of microcauses and macrocontexts. By following this "reductionist" vision, criminologists fail to see how crime is both *in* and *of* society: Crime is constituted as a part of society by those who attempt to control it (i.e., the criminal justice system) and by those who attempt to research, philosophize about, and explain it.

Criminologists need to "write a new script": Traditional theories and ways of talking, researching, and writing about crime need to be "replaced" by a new discourse that entertains the notion that "human agents are inextricably social beings whose total script is the medium of birth to our differences and whose differences continuously, but cumulatively, shape our total script" (p. 249, this volume).

Critical criminology has recently seen the delineation of several new and competing perspectives (Schwartz, 1989; Thomas & O'Maochatha, 1989). These include left realist criminology, socialist-feminist criminology, peace making criminology, and post-structuralist criminology. Each of these perspectives is undergoing internal critique, while variously engaging each of the other perspectives. Such developments might raise the specter of a Kuhnian paradigm crisis, with fragmentation taken as indicative of a failure of the existing critical criminological paradigm to resolve the mounting anomalies with which it is confronted (Greenberg, 1981; Klockars, 1980). Indeed, a not dissimilar crisis has been identified in critical legal studies (Boyle, 1985; Coombe, 1989; Friedrichs, 1986, 1989; Hunt, 1987; Milovanovic, 1988c).

An alternative interpretation of these transformations might be that the current divergence of perspectives is the foundation of a new critical paradigm, whose character will depend on one of the emerging positions becoming victorious. The problem here is that such divisions might also lead to the all-too-familiar radical factionalism in which internecine wars among critical thinkers sap new life from each other's potential growth. Put simply, the recent developments are subject to the dialectic of enlightenment and constraint. In constructing distinctions between different theoretical positions, criminologists must be cautious not to overlook the connections that exist between them. Thus, rather than address these issues through criticism, we sketch an approach that draws on developments in social construction, left realism, socialist feminism, and post-structuralism. We also borrow heavily from social and critical legal theory, from the rich intellectual history of constitutive thinking, and from discourse analysis.

Our aim here is not to add another shot to the paradigmatic cross fire, but to examine reflexively the paradigmatic umbrella under which these saplings of critical growth can gain strength. It is this umbrella that we term *constitutive criminology* (Henry, 1989a). In the following sections, we address core themes that will lead to the establishment of the necessary and logically ordered elements of a constitutive criminology. These themes are (1) the codetermination of crime and human subjects through crime control ideology and how this ideology has the capacity to reproduce and to transform; (2) discursive practices as the medium for the structuring of crime and its control institutions; (3) symbolic violence as the hidden ideological dimension of legal domination; and (4) the use, by control agencies, of sense data to construct meaning that claims space and displaces the intersubjective construction of meaning, and through this process sustains control institutions as relatively autonomous structures. The core theme of constitutive criminology is its rejection of reductionism.

THE CODETERMINATION OF CRIME AS IDEOLOGY

A core theme of constitutive criminology is its rejection of reductionism. Advocates decline the seduction that either human agents through choice or predisposition, or structural arrangements at institutional and societal levels, have priority in shaping crime, victims, and control. Rather, following Giddens (1984), they see social structure and its constituent control institutions as the emerging outcome of human interaction that both constrains and enables criminal action and [they] recognize that those structures are simultaneously shaped by the crime and crime control talk that is part of their reproduction. Constitutive criminology is not an exercise in polemics, in which human agency is separated from the structures that it makes. . . .

The Making of Human Subjects: Transpraxis

Constitutive criminology, then, is concerned with identifying the ways in which the interrelationships among human agents constitute crime, victims, and control as realities. Simultaneously, it is concerned with how these emergent realities themselves constitute human agents. It follows from this that the current notion of praxis needs to be replaced. If praxis is taken to be purposive social activity born of human agents' consciousness of their world, mediated through the social

Henry, S., & Milovanovic, D. (1991). Constitutive criminology: The maturation of critical theory. *Criminology, 29,* 293-315.

groups to which they belong, then this must be supplanted by the richer notion of transpraxis. Transpraxis assumes that critical opposition must be aware of the reconstitutive effects—the reproductions of relations of production—in the very attempts to neutralize or challenge them. The dialectic of control is such that praxis assumes dualistic forms negation/affirmation, denial/expression. In the process of negation, relations of production are often reconstituted along with the human subjects that are their supports. But often neglected is that with affirmation, relations of production are also deconstructed, along with those same human subjects. Thus, its very dynamic reveals [the] nature of the ideological structure on which it is based. Critical theorists have been particularly myopic . . . to the potential for change afforded by this insight.

Labeling theory tried to cover some of this ground, particularly in its notions of role engulfment and deviancy amplification. But labeling separated meaning from the agents generating it. It posited a dualism between agency and structure rather than a duality (Giddens, 1984). Ignored was any sense of an interconnected whole. Although early symbolic interactionism elaborated the ways that the human actor became that which the audience constructed, it said little about the way audiences—their imageries, symbolic repertoire, and *verstehen*—are constructed, constituted, and undermined by historically situated human agents in the context of a historically specific political economy. The construction process tacitly acknowledged and uncritically accepted that the power relationship flowed one way, monolithically and asymmetrically. While those who were officially designated deviant actively participated in their own identity transformation, little construction was done of the control agents, by themselves. Actors designated as deviant or criminal ultimately became passive acceptors of audiences' degradation and fulfillers of their prophecies. Audiences made victims. But little was said of the making of audiences during their attempt to construct labels for others; absent was the dialectic of control. . . .

Constitutive criminology, then, recognizes human agents' power to undermine the structures that confront them and asserts that agents both use and are used in the generation of knowledge and truth about what they do. Agents' ability to

undermine and invert structures of control, to episodically render them edifices of subordination, is one of the major missing dimensions of conventional and critical criminology. . . . Occasional glimpses of the dual nature of this process are exposed in examples of prisoners' power over prison guards through trade in contraband, of police committing or facilitating the commission of property crime, and of police provocation of the very riots they are supposed to prevent (Jefferson, 1990). The notion of "confinement by consent" found in the accounts by Milovanovic (1988a) and Milovanovic and Thomas (1989) of the inmate, turned jailhouse lawyer, who inadvertently maintains legitimation and conventional understandings of capitalist legality, is as constitutive of the hegemony of overarching capitalist relations as is the workplace trade unionist defending employee disciplinary cases in settings of private justice (Henry, 1983). But both are also undermining . . . that which had previously been constructed. . . .

Two Sides of Transpraxis

These contradictions are not temporary aberrations of the structure of control but fundamental pillars of its constitution. In Bourdieu's (1977) terms, they are instances of the way in which the discourse of control in society is in harmony, even when in apparent opposition. This dialectic of control must be addressed. That criminologists and practitioners ignore it is part of the constitutive silence that sustains crime and control as object-like entities. A transpraxis must envision oppositional practices themselves as inadvertently reaffirming instruments of hierarchy and control.

Transpraxis should not, however, ignore the reverse side of this dialectic of control. The affirmative reproduction of social control by human purposeful action also undermines that which is being constituted. For example, it has been shown (Henry, 1988a) that when state agencies seek to control economic relations that fall outside national tax accounting, they attach derogatory labels to such activity and attribute to it motives carrying negative connotations. Terms such as the "black . . . hidden . . . underground," "shadow," "secret," "subterranean," "submerged" economy are used to suggest that the economic relations of those working "off-the-books" are perpetrated by nefarious creatures of the night who are interested unilaterally in pecuniary rewards incommensurate with effort, who are dishonest, and who cannot be trusted. Although such attempts at control may initially dissuade some from participation, they also show many of those who participate, and others who subsequently do so, that these accounts are inaccurate descriptions of the meaning of their relations. . . .

Thus, the more state agencies elaborate their control talk, and the more people experience the different reality of relations subject to control, the more contempt accrues to the controllers and their control institutions. As a result, people begin to question other distinctions, such as those between theft and the legitimate acquisition of property, between honesty and dishonesty, between street crime and white-collar crime, and between hard and soft drugs. Such questioning, stemming from the attempts of control institutions to control, actually undermines that which the controls were designed to protect: the existing relations of production and the moral and social order. We now turn to three additional foci (discursive practices, symbolic violence, and sense data and meaning construction) that are integral to the process of codetermination, as seen by constitutive criminology.

Discursive Practices as the Medium of Codetermination

A central issue in constitutive criminology is the role of human agents' discursive practices. The use of particular ways of talking, as in Cohen's (1985) "control talk," Manning's (1988) "organizational talk," or Milovanovic's (1986, 1988a, in press) and Thomas's (1988) "law talk," both reflects and constitutes narratives that provide the continuity to reproduce social structures of crime and its control, in time and space. As Knorr-Cetina and Cicourel (1981) have argued, human agents transform events that they see or experience as micro-events into summary representations, or mind patterns, by relying on routine practices through which they convince themselves of having achieved the appropriate representation of these events; these are then objectified in coherent narrative constructions. The well-documented media synthesis of harmful incidents into crime waves is allied with

Fitzpatrick's notion of the "synoptic process," whereby disparate patterns of regulation are synthesized into formalized law (Fitzpatrick, 1988). But no clearer example exists than the very categorization of the diversity of human conflicts and transgressions into crime, or of the multitude of variously motivated acts of personal injury into violent crime or types of violent crime, such as when various disputes between family members are termed "domestic violence" or "spouse abuse."

In the constitutive criminological vision, social structures are the categories used to classify the events that they allegedly represent. As such, they are strengthened by routine construction in everyday life and by activity organized in relation to them, as though they were concrete entities. The principal means through which social structures are constituted is language and discursive practices that make conceptual distinctions through the play of differences (Derrida, 1973, 1981; Lacan, 1977).

At the organizational level of analysis, the complexity of the human condition is given a static, decontextualized meaning to enable controllers to better negotiate routine cases (Cicourel, 1968; Manning, 1988; Sudnow, 1965; Thomas, 1988). Discourse, indeed, is the "disciplinary mechanism" by which "docile bodies" are created and "bodies of utility" stabilized (Foucault, 1977). At the societal level of analysis, capital logic and the integrally related described under the unifying processes of rationalization are constitutive of categories that capture essential relations, be it often in fetishistic forms. Not the least are rhetorical structures, figurative expressions, and verbal mannerisms that are used as primary signifiers of meaning. Consider, for example, those signifiers used to give material form to capital logic (e.g., commodities, market forces, producers and consumers, the juridic subject), to technological imageries (e.g., "she's a dynamo," "coiled for action"), and to the phallocentric order itself in which male signifiers occupy a privileged position (e.g., the power "to penetrate," as opposed to the weakness of "seduction"). Hence, at the levels of intersubjective communication, organizational processing, and capital logic, discursive practices are given anchorings, a "pinning down" (Lacan, 1977; Manning, 1988; Milovanovic, in press). In other words, discursive practices produce texts (narrative constructions), imaginary constructions, that anchor signifiers to particular signifieds, producing a particular image claiming to be the reality. These texts become the semiotic coordinates of action, which agents recursively use and [which], in so doing, provide a reconstruction of the original form.

Once social structures are constituted as summary representations, their ongoing existence depends on their continued and often unwitting reconstruction in everyday discourse, a discourse replete with tacit understandings whose basis lies outside the realm of intrinsic intersubjective communication and intersubjectively established meaning. Core meanings are typically preconstructed elsewhere as part of a common "stock of knowledge" (Schutz, 1967; see also, Manning, 1988). Agents in organizational settings tend to reduce feedback that represents contaminating and disruptive "noise." The fluidity of organizational processing in criminal justice contexts demands a high degree of rationality and formalism, which is both the product and the effect of crime control practices. In part, this is due to the increasing complexity in the social formation, which demands more abstract categorization encompassing more and more variants—a "surplus of possibilities" (Luhmann, 1985), but which produces, in the process, symbolizations that are steps removed from the "real" (e.g., concrete reality). For example, process justice is held to require equality of treatment, [which] is claimed to be enabled by general rules of procedure that reduce people to like individuals, decontextualized of their different cosmologies of meaning, and substituted by a universal individual intent tied to units of material reward. In order to sustain abstractly constructed distinctions, these representations are made applicable to events, despite the contradictory evidence that comes from renewed micro-interaction. Contradictory evidence and potential disruptions are engendered by the internal transfer of messages, a basis of instability that is best negotiated by framing it into already understood narrative constructs (Goffman, 1974, 1981; Manning, 1988; Thomas, 1988).

It is often not enough, however, simply to repeat distinctions in order that such representations be sustained as apparent realities. Part of the reality constituting process involves routinely investing faith and interest in them; fighting over them, manipulating them, and above all defending them (Knorr-Cetina & Cicourel, 1981). These morality plays often take place in symbolic form in publicized trials, political and business scandals, "moral panics," and other boundary-policing structures. In more subtle forms, they take place by the use of prevailing discursive practices, even in the use of the oppositional form. As Foucault (1977) and others (e.g., Morrissey, 1985) have reminded us, oppositional discourse is as constitutive of existing reality as is supportive discourse, since each addresses and thereby reproduces the prevailing distinctions while disputing their content rather than deconstructing them or discrediting them through the construction of a new, replacement discourse. . . .

Organizing action to defend representations—framed and objectified in narrative texts—is one of the principal means of defending and conferring object-like reality on them, providing life, form, energy, sustenance, and a high degree of permanence. The institutions of capitalist legality (involving formal police, courts, and prisons) represent the visible manifestation of human agents organized to defend the overarching social form of capitalist society from internal deconstruction. Capital logic is a ubiquitous rationalizing form; the more investment that is made in it, the more difficult it is to sustain that which it is not. This is not to imply conspiracy but to specify formal function, for while defending the wider totality, agents and agencies also compete to defend their own integrity within the framework of capital logic. . . . Consider, also, Daly and Chesney-Lind's (1988) insightful analysis advocating a socialist-feminist perspective and critiquing "first-wave feminism," which often advertently or inadvertently (1) situated itself in legal discourse with its reliance on notions of formal "justice" and "equality" and hence celebrated the fetishistic notion of the juridic subject, (2) used male standards as the criteria of correctness and an ideal end, (3) laid the groundwork for greater and more pervasive forms of state and informal control in women's lives, and (4) grasped too quickly the get-tough approach, thereby rejuvenating deterrence and retributivist theory.

From the perspective of constitutive criminology, then, control institutions are the relations among human agents acting to police the conceptual distinctions among discursively constructed social structures. Those relations are mediated by the availability, through intersubjective relations, of a sedimented, differentiated symbolic system, a repository of value-laden signs that are politically anchored. Once constituted, those relations, expressed in symbolic form, themselves become structures, and, as agencies and institutions, appear to have relative autonomy from both wider structure and human agency. In turn, they too are policed by further "private" or internal relations of control. Thus, signifying chains, narrative constructions, and objectified bits and pieces of everyday actively float within specific discourses, within which distinctive, discursive subject-positions exist that structure what can be framed, thought, and said. Tacit understanding is rooted in these subterranean semiotic systems that continuously receive support through their use (Manning, 1988).

SYMBOLIC VIOLENCE AS IDEOLOGICAL DOMINATION

According to Bourdieu (1977, p. 192) "symbolic violence" is a form of domination that is exerted through the very medium in which it is disguised, wherein it is the "gentle, invisible form of violence, which is never recognized as such, and is not so much undergone as chosen, the violence of credit, confidence, obligation, personal loyalty, hospitality, gifts, gratitude, piety. . . ." But criminologists have forgotten this dimension of domination. . . . The omission of informal, nonstate social control from consideration as part of criminal justice is how "criminal justice" is constituted. Buying into dominant definitions of what counts as law, crime policing, and justice by excluding rules, deviance, informal social control, and private justice is part of the way these concepts, as entities, are made and remade as realities. Take as an example again, a constitutive view of law (Fitzpatrick, 1984; Harrington and Merry, 1988; Hunt, 1987; Klare, 1979). Rather than treating law as an autonomous field of inquiry linked only by external relations to the rest of society, or investigating the way law and society, as concrete entities, influence or affect each other, as is typically done in nonconstitutive approaches, constitutive criminology takes law

as its subject of inquiry, but as Hunt (1987) and Harrington and Yngvesson (1990) have argued, constitutive theory pursues the study of law by exploring the interrelations between legal relations and other social relations. . . .

From the constitutive perspective, the notion of the "juridic subject" (i.e., the reasonable man/woman in law), for example, can only be understood in its inherent dualistic relation of being both a constitutive element and a recursive outcome of capital logic. As Henry (1983) argues, with such an approach one begins to see the possibility of transcending the view that law is either a product of structure or the outcome of interaction. One begins to see how informal social control is not so much an alternative form of law but a necessary part of the ideological process whereby the crystallized, formalized, object like qualities of law are created and sustained in an ongoing manner, be it within a different arena. Thus, constitutive criminology directs attention to the way law, crime, and criminal justice are conceptualized and implied as objective realities having real consequences, consequences attributed to their claim. . . .

SENSE DATA AND MEANING CONSTRUCTION

All this leads to recognizing the high premium on collecting, filtering, categorizing, and disseminating increasingly complex information framed in coherent narrative constructions (Jackson, 1988; Manning, 1988; Thomas, 1988). The process of constructing meaning intersubjectively is increasingly being both abdicated and usurped by agents of organizations who use these constructions as the criteria by which to survey, control, and act on subjects, particularly those in predicted high-risk categories in the existing social arrangements. Simultaneously, these constructions are inadvertently given ideological support through oppositional attacks on the autonomization of social control instruments. Oppositional attacks by some critical theorists and reformers take as a given many of the concepts, presuppositions, or working hypothes[e]s of these same agents of control, thereby in the end, reproducing the self-perpetuating machine. We are reminded of how escape from reproduction is constrained, even in the most radical perspectives, by the actions of others who read criticism as simply more of the same. . . .

. . . . Social control agents both produce and sustain deviant categories, and they tacitly frame coherent narratives of "what happened," hence objectifying primordial sense data. These objectifications become increasingly the anchoring points for everyday constructions by those in the social formation, which in turn, sustain the organizationally framed narrative. Routine investment of time and energy make this constitutive process recursive and self-referential, cyclically generating a more refined and purified version of the substance of their actions as object. To refer to control institutions as relatively autonomous, then, is not to say they are separate from the wider social structure since they are part of its constitution. It is to say, rather, that recursivity reinforces conventional notions by giving permanence and stability to them. Nor do control institutions support the wider structure simply because that is their assigned social function. Such a vision is rabidly reifying because it ignores the integral role of human agency in this process. Rather, as Fitzpatrick (1984) reminds us, control institutions support the relations of reproduction within the totality of society because they are some of those relations of reproduction. Therefore as we have argued elsewhere (Henry, 1985, 1987; Milovanovic, in press), these social relations do not exist independently of human agents who repeatedly bring them into being.

Likewise the "internal" relations that monitor control institutions are some of the relations of the control institutions that they police. A police agency would not be what it is without the relations that police it, informal or otherwise, and those relations would not be what they are without the action of human agents. As a result, any examination of control institutions that analyzes them outside of the structural context that they police, that ignores the internal relations that police them, or that ignores human agents' recursive action, produces a partial account that itself becomes part of the constitutive discourse that sustains their reproduction. Concomitantly, any challenging practices used by agents not sensitive to the reconstituting effects of their very practices, further reproduce, elaborate, and stabilize the existent structural arrangements. Thus, although relations of control are most visible in their institutional form, that should not lead one to neglect their pervasive presence in informal and alternative modes of control or even in Foucault's sense of a dispersed disciplinary technology pervasive throughout our society. Neither should it lead one to gloss over the human agent's renditions and intersubjective creative work that daily make these relations into organizations and structures. So what is to be done? As implied in our preceding argument, there are a number of ways that a constitutive approach to criminology can be transformative. In the concluding section we suggest a direction that this might take, but a more elaborated treatment must await further analysis.

CONCLUSION

In short then, constitutive criminology, in the tradition of dialectical theory, is the framework for reconnecting crime and its control with the society from which it is conceptually and institutionally constructed by human agents. Through it criminologists are able to recognize, as a fundamental assumption, that crime is both in and of society. Our position calls for an abandoning of the futile search for causes of crime because that simply elaborates the distinctions that maintain crime as a separate reality while failing to address how it is that crime is constituted as a part of society. We are concerned, instead, with the ways in which human agents actively coproduce that which they take to be crime. As a signifier, this perspective directs attention to the way that crime is constituted as an expansive and permeating mode of discourse, a continuously growing script—a text, narrative—whose writers are human agents, obsessed with that which we produce, amazed that it is produced, denying that it is created by us, claiming that it grows independently before us, but yet worshipping the very alienating, hierarchical creations that are our own. A direct consequence of such an approach is that any "rehabilitation" from crime requires that criminologists and practitioners alike deconstruct crime as a separate entity, cease recording it, stop dramatizing it, withdraw energy from it, deny its status as an independent entity. Through this vision, we are suggesting that criminologists write a new script, a replacement discourse that connects human agents and our product back to the whole of which we are a part. "Control talk" (Cohen, 1985), "organizational talk" (Manning, 1988), and "law talk" (Milovanovic, 1986, 1988a; Thomas, 1988) must be replaced by a reflexive discourse that allows for change, chance, being, becoming, multiplicity, and irony, and that reflects a sensitivity to the nuances of being human. Criminologists must explore "alternative logics" in criminology, as Nelken calls them. We must cease to invest in the myth that human agents are either individuals with free choices driven by a utilitarian calculus or biologically and psychologically programmed, when all that is known shows that human agents are inextricably social beings whose total script is the medium of birth to our differences and whose differences continuously, but cumulatively, shape our total script. . . . Constitutive criminology, then, is a step in the deconstitution of crime, a peacemaking movement (Pepinsky & Quinney, 1991) toward an alternative vision of what is and what might be. Transpraxis must be the guide for those challenging hierarchical structures of domination. . . .

DISCUSSION QUESTIONS

1. What are the core elements of constitutive criminology?

2. Human agency is a frequent theme within a number of theories addressed in this reader. In this chapter, what role does human agency play for constitutive criminologists? In terms of transpraxis, how does human agency stand in contrast to the reductionist principles articulated by more traditional criminological theories?

3. What is symbolic violence, and how is it a form of domination? What are some examples of symbolic violence raised in this chapter?

4. In what ways does constitutive criminology contribute to the body of theoretical work in criminology? How is it considered a "peaceful" approach to the problem of crime, and what implications may this approach have for crime prevention and control?

26

POSTMODERN CRIMINOLOGY IN RELATION TO RADICAL AND CONFLICT CRIMINOLOGY

BRUCE A. ARRIGO AND THOMAS J. BERNARD

EDITOR'S INTRODUCTION—This article by Arrigo and Bernard provides an important point of clarification of postmodern criminology, which has emerged over the past decade, in relation to radical and conflict criminology. Readers who have perhaps struggled with some of the postmodern literature, as well as the literature addressing radical and conflict approaches, will find this article a welcome contribution to this important and critically necessary perspective on crime, criminality, and crime control.

Their review of the literature on postmodern criminology has revealed a relationship between that theory and radical criminology. This relationship stems in part from the fact that both theoretical perspectives are related to conflict theory. However, the authors find that conceptual analyses of these perspectives have not fully explicated the essential differences among them. Their essay attempts to clarify these approaches and their relationship to one another by identifying six core theoretical assertions in conflict criminology and comparing them to parallel assertions in radical and postmodern criminology. These theoretical concerns include the focus of the theory, the goal of conflict, control of crime definitions, nature of crime, explanation of crime, and policy implications of the theory under consideration.

Arrigo and Bernard find that postmodern criminology is consistent with conflict theory on two of the six issues under review. Both agree that violations of human rights and definitions of crime are not absolute and that, in terms of policy implications, the aim of individual and group conflict is to produce a more inclusive, less crime-ridden society. The equalization of power is fundamental to both perspectives. However, postmodern criminology is inconsistent with conflict theory, especially in terms of their respective positions on core criminological principles. The authors conclude that conflict theory only marginally helps to advance the understanding of postmodern criminology.

The authors also consider whether radical or postmodern criminology is more or less compatible with conflict theory. They find that radical criminology is consistent with conflict theory in only two categories: the focus of the theory (conflict oriented) and the goal of conflict. In terms of consistency, the authors find that postmodern and radical criminology are equally conflict oriented. In terms of the relationship between radical and postmodern criminologies, the authors find that there are no points of convergence between them. Therefore, they conclude that radical criminology does not fundamentally advance the overall understanding of postmodern criminology.

The authors' analysis of postmodern criminology suggests that it is best not to conceptualize the theory as a type of conflict theory or as a variation of radical thought. Although there is still some confusion regarding where best to place postmodern criminology in relation to both conflict and radical models, the authors think that it would be best to think of postmodern criminology as an independent orientation and method of analysis.

In general, conflict theories in criminology assert that there is an inverse relationship between political and economic power and the distribution of official crime rates (Vold & Bernard, 1986, p. 269). In contrast, radical theories in criminology generally explain crime in terms of the demoralizing effects of the capitalist economic system, with particular emphasis on the political economy of late capitalism (Keller, 1976, p. 283; Lynch & Groves, 1989, pp. 51-71). Radical theories apparently are a type of conflict theory (see, Bernard, 1981; Olim, 1982), but the two are not identical and the similarities and differences between them are not entirely clear (Bernard, 1981, pp. 370-379; Bohm, 1982, pp. 566-569; Lynch & Groves, 1989, pp. 45-50).

More recently, postmodern criminology has appeared. It ostensibly embraces an even more critical agenda than radical criminology. The term 'postmodern' refers to an approach in which reality is no longer understood as being dominated by foundational truths, cause-effect relationships, linear thought processes, syllogistic reasoning, global assumptions, objective analyses, and other conventions of modern science. Postmodernism rejects these notions because of the intervening variable of language, which conditions, shapes, modifies, and defines all social relationships, all institutional practices, and all methods of knowing. Essentially, postmodernism argues that language structures thought—i.e., the words and phrases people use are not neutral but rather support *dominant* views of the world, whether they know it or not (Milovanovic, 1994, pp. 143-145, 155-184; Arrigo, 1993a, pp. 27-75).

Postmodern criminologists have examined the marginalizing, alienating, and oppressive effects of language on those involved in various aspects of the criminal justice process. These include jailhouse lawyers (Milovanovic, 1988), psychiatric patients petitioning for institutional release (Arrigo, 1996a), police officers responding to 911 calls (Manning, 1988), and female attorneys seeking gendered justice in courtrooms (Arrigo, 1992). In each instance, postmodern criminologists argue that the language expressing one view of reality (e.g., the views of prisoners, the mentally challenged, patrol officers, and women) is replaced by the language expressing a different view (e.g., the views of the legal, medical, and correctional systems). This replacement of languages eclipses reality as lived and spoken by others and thereby affirms and re-legitimizes the status quo as expressed by the latter groups.

The relationship between postmodern and radical criminology is unclear. Some commentators suggest that postmodern criminology is a variation of radical thought best positioned at its extreme outer edge (Schwartz & Friedrichs, 1994, pp. 221-222). Others suggest that all radical criminologies are differing expressions of postmodern discontent (Henry & Milovanovic, 1993, p. 1; Einstadter & Henry, 1995, pp. 402-405). There also is a question about the relationship of postmodern criminology to conflict theory (Arrigo, 1995, p. 452). Postmodern thought describes a 'conflict' between prevailing and oppressed modes of speech encountered in everyday interaction but does not focus on political and economic power. In conflict theory, language could be described as an instrument of political and economic power, but that argument has not been explicitly made.

In sum, it appears that postmodern criminology is related to both radical and conflict criminology but the specifics of the relationships remain largely undefined. This lack of specificity contributes to the isolation that postmodern crimi- nology experiences within the academy today (cf., Handler, 1992, pp. 697-731). This essay clarifies the association between conflict, radical, and

Arrigo, B. A., & Bernard, T. J. (1997). Postmodern criminology in relation to radical and conflict criminology. *Critical Criminology, 8,* 39-60.

postmodern criminology by concisely presenting their positions on six basic theoretical issues.

CONFLICT, RADICAL, AND POSTMODERN CRIMINOLOGY: A THEORETICAL ASSESSMENT

Focus of the Theory

Conflict criminology focuses on social structure. Conflict criminology proposes a 'structural' theory because its major assertions concern the characteristics of entire societies rather than the characteristics of individuals or groups within those societies. Specifically, conflict criminology asserts that there is an inverse relationship between the distribution of political and economic power and the distribution of official crime rates in every society. The explanation of this ahistorical and cross-cultural relationship is as follows.

Conflict criminology broadly argues that people tend to behave in ways that are consistent with their moral values and economic interests, that their moral values tend to be shaped by their economic interests, and that their economic interests tend to be shaped by their social structural location. All of these result in a general assertion that individual behaviors tend to be consistent with socially-structured interests. This is said to be a basic tendency consistent enough to produce patterns at the aggregate level, but not a prediction about the behavior of any particular individual or individuals.

Conflict criminology also argues that people attempt to promote and defend their values and interests by influencing the official enactment and enforcement of criminal laws. This necessarily involves a conflict and compromise process with other people who are attempting to promote and defend different or opposing values and interests. The outcome of this conflict and compromise process is difficult to predict in individual cases but, at the aggregate level, conflict theory asserts, the existence of a broad pattern: the criminal law tends to protect and defend values and interests in direct proportion to the political and economic power of those who hold those values and interests. As a result, people with more political and economic power find that fewer of their actions are officially defined and processed as criminal, while people with less political and economic power find that more of their actions are officially defined and processed

as criminal. Thus, the distribution of official crime rates at the aggregate level is an inverse function of the distribution of political and economic power in the society.

Radical criminology also focuses on social structure. Radical criminology focuses on social class and class structure to ultimately account for and explain crime (cf., Bernard, 1981, p. 372; Lynch & Groves, 1989, pp. 32-39, 51-71). The term 'social class' refers to an individual's position in relation to the means of production, while the term 'class structure' refers to the extent to which the distribution of interests (e.g., economic and political power) are disproportionately concentrated in the hands of a few thereby producing structural inequalities and a stratified social system. The variables of social class and class structure represent key determinants by and through which radicals draw inferential and causal relationships between the prevailing economy and its influence on routine social life (cf., Lynch, 1988; Reiman, 1995).

Radical criminology may be considered a form of conflict criminology because it makes an argument which is consistent with it but which is much more specific. Conflict criminology speaks generally of economic and political power but contains no assertions about how that power is acquired or retained. Radical theory asserts that political and economic power ultimately is based on ownership of the means of production. Conflict criminology implicitly assumes that power can be unequally distributed even in societies with common ownership of the means of production. Radical theory assumes that common ownership of the means of production equalizes the distribution of power.

Postmodern criminology focuses on the human subject. Postmodern [c]riminology is not a structural theory. It is a theory of the human subject or person. Postmodern criminology examines the relationship between human agency and language in the creation of meaning, identity, truth, justice, power, and knowledge (Henry & Milovanovic, 1996, pp. 8-11, 26-44). This relationship is studied through the process of discourse analysis, which is a method of investigating how meaning and sense are constructed. Discourse analysis focuses on the values and assumptions implied in the language used by the author of speech or of a text (e.g., Lacan, 1977;

Foucault, 1970, 1972). It does not analyze the sociological roles or statuses people occupy but rather considers the 'discursive subject positions' that inform the way people speak and think. For example, lawyering, counseling, policing, and offending are discursive subject positions. These structures are historically mediated and, thus, experience changing definitions over time (Goodrich, 1984). Subjects who assume these [p]ositions speak, think, act, feel, and know through that language embodied in these structures (Arrigo, 1995, pp. 453-455). To that extent, these subjects can be described as 'decentered,' (Lacan, 1977; see also Kristeva, 1980; Moi, 1985)—i.e., as not entirely in control of their own thoughts. . . . Subjects . . . are described as 'decentered' because their speech does not represent who they really are and instead tends to represent what the language system in use demands or expects (Henry & Milovanovic, 1996, p. 27). . . .

What Is at Stake in Societal Conflict?

Conflict criminology generally suggests that money, status, and power are goals that individuals and groups seek in their conflict with other individuals and groups in societies. Conflict theorists argue that there are many valued and scarce commodities over which different individuals and groups may conflict. In general, money, status, and power are said to be the major goals or 'prizes' at stake in societal conflicts. However, the specific goals may vary at different times and places. Conflicts in capitalist societies tend to be over the goal of money, and individuals and groups may pursue it without regard for whether it produces other valued commodities such as status and power. In this case, the conflict occurs primarily in the economic arena. In some societies, conflict over money is the dominant conflict, so that those who acquire money also acquire high social status and great political power. . . .

Radical criminology identifies the conflict over which individuals and groups of society struggle to be about the acquisition and accumulation of economic power. According to radical criminologists, the interests at stake in the conspicuous consumerism of late capitalism are wealth and income (Lynch & Groves, 1989,

pp. 52-53; Taylor, Walton, & Young, 1973, pp. 270-271). These interests must be understood in relation to the larger political economy (macro-level analysis) and its capacity to condition more local and immediate events (micro-level analysis). Social status and political power are important to radical criminology, but they are regarded as indirect effects of the acquisition and accumulation of capital. This view is consistent with Marx's argument that the cultural and political 'superstructures' of a society tend to be built on its economic 'base.' To that extent, radical theorists view conflict as ultimately occurring in the economic arena, over economic goals, and the competition for status and power are secondary. Again, this argument is consistent with, but much more specific than, the conflict argument about the goals of conflict.

Postmodern criminology identifies the conflict over which various segments of society struggle to be about languaging reality/existence through multiple voices and ways of knowing. Postmodern criminology offers an entirely different conception on the nature of the conflict. What is at stake is neither money, status, nor power. Instead, postmodern criminology identifies the conflict to be waged over how a person's very existence is defined and lived through language and prevailing discourses. In that sense, the goal of the conflict is control of 'reality.'

The interests at stake in postmodern society address the inclusion of various ways of expressing (i.e., languaging) and living reality, as illustrated in all institutional aspects of social life. One facet of social life is crime. Postmodern criminologists maintain that there is a conflict that underscores our understanding of crime, law, order, justice, victimization, etc. In short, only certain definitions are used to convey society's meaning for these constructs. . . . Postmodern criminologists, therefore, ask whose grammar and way of communicating is reflected in theories and policies on gang delinquency and youth violence, white-collar and corporate crime, serial killing and mass murder, sexual assault and domestic abuse, drug use and distribution, and every classification upon which definitions of crime are articulated and enacted as law (Arrigo & Young, 1998). . . .

Who Controls Official and Prevailing Definitions of Crime?

In conflict criminology, control over official definitions of crime is a continuous variable in which some individuals and groups in society have more influence while others have less. Conflict is a social process essential and central to the routine functioning of society (Vold & Bernard, 1986, p. 272; Coser, 1967, pp. 37-51). . . . One arena in which this conflict is played out is in the official enactment and enforcement of criminal laws. Influence over the official enactment and enforcement of criminal laws is proportional to the political and economic power an individual or group possesses. In most societies, power is a continuous variable where some individuals and groups have more power while others have less, rather than a dichotomous variable in which some individuals and groups have all power and others have none. Influence over the enactment and enforcement of criminal laws is directly proportional to the extent of power. . . .

In radical criminology, those who own the means of economic production ultimately control the prevailing and official definitions of law and crime. Radical criminologists agree with the basic conflict argument about the relationship between power and the ability to influence official definitions of crime. In advanced economic systems, however, radicals make an additional argument about private ownership of the means of economic production ([cf.] Frank & Lynch, 1992; Friedrichs, 1995). [R]adicals would argue that, regardless of whose other values and interests are served in the official enactment and enforcement of criminal laws, the economic interests of the owners of the means of economic production must be served, or the entire society will tend to be impoverished. To that extent, the owners of the means of production can be described as a 'ruling class,' and the control of the official definitions of crime is a dichotomous rather than continuous variable.

In postmodern criminology, those who control the means of linguistic production also control the prevailing and official definitions of crime. Postmodern criminologists identify the ownership of the means of linguistic production as pivotal to current definitions of law and crime. Language is a commodity; that is, words and phrases, whether written or spoken, possess both a use- and an exchange-value. The use-value of language is the ability to express, to convey meaning. This expression and conveyance of meaning is unique; that is, the language used has intrinsic significance for the one writing or speaking it. When interacting with others, our language takes on exchange-value. The exchange-value of language is its shared, common, or equivalent meanings created among the marketplace of speakers or writers. These meanings are more universal, more abstract. Potentially lost in our communication with others, however, are the subtleties and shadings of significance informing our understanding of what we say or what we write.

According to postmodernists, not only is language a commodity but so, too, is it fetishized. Where Marx and radical criminologists identify money as the universal form, postmodernists identify speech as the universal form. Marxists argue that we create money as an abstraction to establish an artificial ratio of exchange. Postmodernists maintain that we do the same with language. Just as Marxists (and radicals) claim we reduce everything to a money value, postmodernists claim we reduce everything to a language value. The inherent use-value[s] (significance) of words or phrases disappear or are masked through a more universal, more abstract, linguistic form. . . .

Is There an 'Absolute' Definition of Criminal Behavior?

Conflict criminology neither asserts nor denies that certain actions are socially harmful and violate fundamental human rights. However, the theory focuses solely on the processes by which actions are officially defined and processed as criminal. All individuals and groups define crime in ways that are consistent with their moral values and economic interests. In differentiated and complex societies, different people will at least, to some extent, have different values and interests. Conflict theory argues that those possessing the most money, status, and power will have the most influence over which definitions of crime will prevail in the official enactment and enforcement of criminal law.

Radical criminology asserts that violations of human rights and social acts of wrongdoing are absolute. Radicals assert that there is an objective basis to harm or behaviors defined as harmful (Bernard, 1981, p. 369; Lynch & Groves, 1989, p. 48). Reiman (1995, pp. 43-47), for example, claims that 'crimes should be crimes because their consequences are dangerous and undesirable.' The radical position finds support in its use of impartial criteria that operationalize definitions of crime. Such criteria have been the basis for several empirical and related studies (cf., Lynch, 1987; Chambliss, 1988; Friedrichs, 1995). Consistent with the radical position, behaviors that would otherwise be considered violations of human rights or social acts of wrongdoing are not defined as crimes by the official criminal justice system if committed by capitalists (Bernard, 1981, p. 370). Again, this is because these people have the economic power to protect themselves from most forms of criminal sanction.

Postmodern criminology asserts that violations of human rights and social acts of wrongdoing are not absolute. Postmodernists question the existence of *any* foundational, certifiable truths (Arrigo, 1995, pp. 452-454, 458-460), including explanations of social harm. Such skepticism stems from the conviction that language structures thought in ways that are consistent with dominant views of the world. These principal perspectives (e.g., law, medicine, science) do not demonstrate that such ways of knowing and experiencing are, in and of themselves, the 'correct' way of knowing and experiencing for all citizens. Postmodernists accept that there are violations of human rights and socially harmful behaviors. However, they fundamentally examine the language that is used to define such phenomena. Postmodernist criminologists ask: whose languaged (and therefore social) interests are valued and de-valued in prevailing (or alternative) definitions of crime (ibid.: 466)? They contend that the explanations and meanings excluded from definitions of crime represent the voice of various disempowered collectives.

The Explanation of Crime

Conflict criminology explains crime in terms of a natural tendency to pursue economic self-interests, together with the social structural distribution of those interests. This explanation is in the form of a probability statement. Conflict criminology asserts that people behave in ways that are consistent with their moral values and economic interests. It also argues that moral values tend to be shaped by economic interests, and that economic interests are shaped by social structural location. The result is that human behavior tends to be shaped by socially structured economic interests. In conflict criminology, the tendency to pursue economic interests is said to lie in human nature, while the specific behaviors in which people engage are determined by how their interests are distributed in the social structure. The explanation of human behavior generally, and criminal behavior in particular, therefore is found in the interaction between human nature and social structure.

Radical criminology explains crime by focusing on the influence of capitalist economic systems. The radical explanation of crime focuses on the social structure of capitalism and the inequitable distribution of economic interests (Quinney & Wildeman, 1991; for the development of this concept, see also Engels, 1845; Marx, 1868; Bonger, 1916). It is similar to the conflict explanation described above in that it assumes people have a tendency to pursue their socially structured interests. However, it holds that this tendency is rooted in the social structure of capitalism rather than in human nature. Thus, changes in that social structure will result in changes in the tendency to pursue self interests, leading to a more consensual society. In general, the radical model argues that in capitalist societies, class is based on the private ownership of property where a few citizens (the bourgeoisie) own a large percentage of the interests and many citizens (the prolet[a]riat) own only their labor (Marx 1868, 1964, 1975). Thus crime is a rational response to class divided systems featuring the disproportionate acquisition and/or accumulation of capital (Lynch and Groves, 1989, p. 64). Explanations for law and crime take on meaning through and are an expression of such class-based inequalities.

Postmodern criminology identifies the essential problem of crime to be linguistic domination as prevalent in various situations or encounters. Ultimately, this is seen as the source of criminal behavior itself. Postmodern criminology identifies the official power and authority of dominant grammars as the source of definitions of law and crime. The linguistic hegemony perpetrated through prevailing discourses is that process in which agents of the dominant language in use transform, channel, or re-present the speech of non-agents to be consistent with the language system in effect (Milovanovic, 1994, pp. 145-150).

One effect of linguistic domination is to insist that certain ways of communicating be observed. It is this insistence which creates a dilemma resulting, at times, in crime. Depending on the specific situation, individuals routinely confront a choice of how to speak, of how to convey meaning. On the one hand, a person can adopt the preferred method of communicating. On the other hand, an individual can resist and invoke his/her own way of speaking. Depending on the (criminal justice) context, problems arise when one opposes the dominant discourse. . . .

Policy Implications

In conflict criminology, the sources of economically self-interested behavior lie in human nature, so there is no full 'solution' to the problem of crime. Conflict criminology does not seek to replace one hierarchical distribution of power and crime rates with another. Instead, it seeks to equalize the distribution of power, thereby equalizing the distribution of crime rates. In general, if power were more evenly distributed, the presently high-power (and low official crime rate) groups would find that their official crime rates would increase because they would be less able to promote and defend their values and interests in the official criminal law enactment and enforcement process. Simultaneously, presently low-power (and high official crime rate) groups would find that they could pursue and defend their values and interests more effectively in the official processes, and that they could then be officially criminalized less. . . .

In radical criminology, because class-based inequality ultimately is rooted in the capitalist economic system, the problem of crime can only be solved by overthrowing capitalism. Radical criminology seeks an end to the capitalist economic system because, as it is ingrained within the socio-political structure of society, a series of

class-based inequalities are routinely reproduced (Bernard, 1981, pp. 375-76). As previously stated, these class inequalities create greater disparities in the acquisition and accumulation of segment interests, and, thus, those quasi-groups receiving fewer economic rewards will increasingly experience marginality and will, consequently, be more likely to engage in criminal behavior. Radicals contend that the only meaningful response to the problem of crime generated by capitalist social and economic structures is the transition to socialism (Lynch and Groves, 1989, p. 127). . . .

Because the problem is rooted in linguistic realities, the problem of crime can be solved by developing replacement discourses. Postmodern criminology seeks to neutralize the power of privileged grammars that regulate, normalize, and discipline the lives of alienated collectives. This neutralization process entails the cultivation of replacement discourses. Replacement discourses are ways of communicating that embody both one's meaning and one's desire at the same time (Henry & Milovanovic, 1991, pp. 305-307; Henry & Milovanovic, 1996, pp. 185-213). Replacement discourses substitute methods of control with languages of possibility (Henry & Milovanovic 1996, pp. 214-243). . . .

Postmodern criminologists maintain that the goal of replacement discourses and multiple ways of knowing is greater inclusivity, diverse communication, and a pluralistic culture. To achieve these ends, postmodernists listen carefully and incorporate the otherwise excluded points of view in the constitution of crime definitions and acts of social harm. . . .

CONFLICT, RADICAL, AND POSTMODERN CRIMINOLOGY: A COMPARATIVE SUMMARY

Contributions of Conflict and Radical Criminology to Understanding Postmodern Criminology

. . . . From our analysis of postmodern criminology and its relationship to conflict and radical theory, it is best to not conceptualize postmodern criminology as a type of conflict theory nor a variation of radical thought. As we described

Table 26.1   Analysis of Conflict, Radical and Postmodern Criminology in Relation to Core
Criminological Principles

Issue Under Review	Conflict Criminology	Radical Criminology	Postmodern Criminology
1 Focus of Theory	Social Structure	Social Structure	Human Subject
2 Goal of Conflict	Money, status, power	Money	'Existence' or 'reality'
3 Control of Crime definitions	Continuous: distribution of power	Dichotomous: own means of economic production	Continuous: control of linguistic production
4 Nature of Crime	Not Absolute	Absolute	Not Absolute
5 Explanation of Crime	Human Nature: Socially Structured Interests	Capitalist Economic System	Hegemony of Dominant Discourse(s)
6 Policy Implication	Equalize Power	Common Ownership of Means of Production	Replacement Discourses

in our introduction, there is some confusion regarding where best to position postmodern criminology in relation to both the radical and conflict models. Our investigation indicates that it is wise to think of postmodern criminology as an independent orientation and method of analysis. While there are certainly some points of convergence between it and conflict theory, postmodern criminology is a very different perspective from which to engage in social scientific research. The same is true about postmodern criminology's association with radical thought. While there are some approximate areas of agreement, the two orientations are mostly different. Thus they, too, should be viewed as conceptually distinct in all future criminological endeavors addressing matters of import for theory, method, and practice. . . .

DISCUSSION QUESTIONS

1. What is meant by the term *postmodern*? What do postmodern criminologists examine?

2. What are the six core theoretical assertions in conflict theory with which postmodern and radical criminologies are compared and analyzed? Is postmodern criminology consistent with conflict theory? With which assertions does it find consistency?

3. Discuss the policy implications for each theoretical orientation. Are there any consistencies among these theories?

4. How does postmodern criminology enhance our understanding of crime, how criminals are controlled, and how crime is defined?

27

"THREE STRIKES" AS PUBLIC POLICY

The Convergence of the New Penology and the McDonaldization of Punishment

DAVID SHICHOR

EDITOR'S INTRODUCTION—David Shichor's piece, which analyzes the theoretical principles of the three-strikes law in California, provides a unique example of the nexus between criminological theory and criminal justice. More important, the chapter demonstrates how criminological theory can provide a context for and explain not only crime and criminality among offenders but also crime control policies. Shichor employs two theoretical frameworks in his critique of the three-strikes law. In terms of a paradigmatic framework, Shichor couches his analysis within the new penology, which shifts the crime control focus away from the individual offender and toward the control of aggregates (Feeley & Simon, 1992). Second, Shichor applies the principles of McDonaldization to demonstrate the goals and principles that the law was intended not only to represent but also to fulfill in its full implementation. _McDonaldization,_ a term developed by Ritzer (1993), maintains that the principles of the fast-food chain dominate many aspects of American society and culture. These principles include efficiency, calculability, predictability, and control mainly by nonhuman technology.

Shichor contends that the three-strikes law, enacted in 1994 in reaction to a high-profile case in California, embraces principles of the new penology because it was designed to remove the "worst of the worst" of offenders from society by locking them up for a very long time, perhaps even for life if offenders are convicted on a third strike. The law stipulates that "felons found guilty of a third serious crime be locked up for 25 years to life" (p. 259, this volume). The goal of this law is not rehabilitation or even deterrence; rather, it is containment and control.

Shichor argues that the three-strikes law promotes penal policies in accordance with the principles of McDonaldization. In the context of the law, proponents claim that the law is _efficient_ because it maximizes the optimum punishment (incapacitation) for the most dangerous offenders. Second, the law makes punishment easily _calculable_ because the release date is calculable at the time of sentencing, and the sentence is based on the seriousness of the offense and the offender's prior record. Additionally, the three-strikes law is assumed to provide a high degree of _predictability_ because the penal sanctions are known and discretion is limited. Last, *control* is maximized under the three-strikes law because of mandatory sentencing policies and the increased use of nonhuman surveillance technology as security within prisons.

Theoretically, the three-strikes law presents a plausible and rational argument for controlling society's highly dangerous offenders. However, Shichor points out that although the law was largely supported by public initiative in California, it has been attacked by numerous criticisms, many of which highlight the shortsightedness of policymakers. These criticisms range from the bloated net in the formal justice system (i.e., prison overcrowding, the growing elderly prison population, and the inclusion of offenders who would be better off being handled informally or diverted into correction programs); excessive costs; and the misuse of prosecutorial discretion, even with mandatory sentencing policies in effect.

Shichor indicates that the laws were enacted in reaction to a moral panic that originated in the 1970s with the "get-tough"/law-and-order movement and that reached its apex in the 1990s. Some would argue that punitive policy making in America has not crested, though that argument is not appropriate in this context. Shichor's contribution raises important issues about the rationality and overall implementation of legislation like the three-strikes law. More important for purposes of this reader, it illustrates the importance of using criminological and social theories to inform criminal justice policies.

. . . . In spite of the chronic problems of overcrowding and the bulging correctional costs and budget shortages, the pursuit of penal policies of deterrence incapacitation continues unabated (Shichor, 1987). In 1994, as an incremental step toward increasingly punitive crime policies (Saint-Germain & Calamia, 1996), the Violent Crime Control and Law Enforcement Act, also known as the Federal Crime Bill, was enacted by Congress. Among other things, this law "mandates life in prison for criminals convicted of three violent felonies or drug offenses if the third conviction is a federal crime" (Lewis, 1994, p. 6). It became labeled, using the popular baseball lingo, as the "three strikes and you're out" law. Several states followed suit and enacted similar measures. One of those mentioned most often was the California mandatory sentencing law, which came into effect in March 1994 and prescribes that "felons found guilty of a third serious crime be locked up for 25 years to life." It stipulates the following:

> Although the first two "strikes" accrue for serious felonies, the crime that triggers the life sentence can be for any felony. Furthermore, the law doubles sentences for a second strike, requires that these extended sentences be served in prison (rather than in jail or on probation), and limits "good time" earned during prison to 20 percent of the sentence given (rather than 50 percent, as under the previous law). (Greenwood, Rydell, Abrahamse, Caulkins, Chiesa, Model, & Klein, 1994, p. xi)

It is not clear yet how the further implementation of the California law will be affected by the recent state supreme court ruling that judges have the discretion to overlook prior convictions in three-strikes cases (Dolan & Perry, 1996).

. . . . Although there are differences in some of the details among the various three-strikes laws, their main aims and principles are similar. Several scholars maintain that recent penal thinking and the ensuing policies have gone through a major paradigm change. According to them, a "new penology" has emerged shifting the traditional penological concern that focused on the individual offender to an actuarial model focusing on the management of aggregates. Feeley and Simon (1992) argued that this change "facilitates development of a vision or a model of a new type of criminal that embraces increased reliance on imprisonment . . . that shifts away from concern with punishing individuals to managing aggregates of dangerous groups" (p. 449).

The analysis to follow examines three-strikes laws in relation to the new penology and in relation to their connections to a more general sociocultural orientation, identified by Ritzer (1993) as the "McDonaldization" of society, based on the rationalization process suggested by Max Weber (one of the pioneers of sociological thought), that is embodied in the model of fast-food restaurants (Weber, 1968). Although these two models have many similar and mutually supportive characteristics that define current

Shichor, D. (1997). "Three strikes" as public policy: The convergence of the new penology and the McDonaldization of punishment. *Crime & Delinquency, 43,* 470-492.

criminal justice policies, they diverge in some of the details.

THREE STRIKES AND THE NEW PENOLOGY

In a widely cited article, Feeley and Simon (1992) claimed that the conservative turn in the social and penal ideology of the 1970s and 1980s led to a new trend in penology that involves changes in three major aspects:

1. The emergence of new discourses: In particular, the language of probability and risk increasingly replaces earlier discourses of clinical diagnosis and retributive judgment.

2. The formation of new objectives: [T]he increasing primacy [is] given to the efficient control of internal system processes in place of the traditional objectives of rehabilitation and crime control.

3. The deployment of new techniques: These techniques target offenders as an aggregate in place of traditional techniques for individualizing or creating equity. (p. 450)

Three-strikes measures are one manifestation of these changes. Their language employs terms such as "high-risk offenders" or "strikeable offenses," and their objectives center around efficient control of the operation of the criminal justice system.

Feeley and Simon (1992) contrasted the new trend with what they called the "old penology" based on American law focusing on individuals and in which penal sanctioning "has been aimed at individual-based theories of punishment." By contrast, the new penology is "concerned with techniques to identify, classify, and manage groupings sorted by dangerousness" (pp. 451-52). This approach is more concerned with responses to social harm "based on aggregations and statistical averages" than with the punishment and treatment tailored to individual perpetrators (Alschuler, 1990, pp. 15-16). Accordingly, certain subpopulations, which are identified by officials as "high-rate offenders," "career criminals," or "habitual offenders" and by social scientists as the "underclass" or the "truly disadvantaged," are to be singled out for special surveillance, aggregate management, and selective incapacitation (Hagan, 1995). This view has centered on criminal justice policies that are in accord with an orientation of penal administrators that is focused on managerial goals (Garland, 1990). As a consequence, "Sanctioning rates are determined by the ways in which official actors use strategic discretion to manage their domains of action and only indirectly by reform or socioeconomic imperatives" (Sutton, 1987, p. 613). Henry and Milovanovic (1996) described this new penology as a "discourse based on utilitarian considerations rather than on moral ones" (p. 114).

In an earlier work, Cohen (1985) reviewed some of the results of this move toward "containment and coercion" (p. 108). Among other things, he foresaw "increasing rates of imprisonment," "increasing severity of punishment," "a widening net of criminalization," and "greater publicity given to street crimes." He pointed out that the new direction that abandoned rehabilitation as an objective in favor of the management of controlled groups has created a bifurcation of penal policies. The "hard" side of the control system became harsher, resulting in more incarceration, longer prison stays, and determinate and mandatory sentences for "hard core," "career," and "dangerous" offenders, whereas the less serious offenders (Cohen referred to them as "deviants") were to be handled by the "soft end" of the system, mostly in community settings under various surveillance practices often referred to as "intermediate sanctions." These measures are more severe than traditional probation but less restrictive than incarceration; they include home arrest and intensive probation often monitored by electronic surveillance systems, boot camps, and drug rehabilitation programs (Morris & Tonry, 1990). These policies have led to "net widening" because the extended use of intermediate sanctions has brought people who otherwise would have been handled informally under some type of supervision or into formal correctional programs.

The change from penal policies aimed at punishment and rehabilitation of individuals to the management and control of certain categories of people has followed the pessimism expressed about the criminal justice system's ability to change offenders, making them into law-abiding citizens (Gottfredson & Hirschi, 1990; Martinson, 1974). In this vein, Bottoms (1980) noted that "the abandonment of the rehabilitative ethic has led to a widespread abandonment of hope" (p. 20) because the idea of rehabilitation was an expression of optimism about human nature and about the ability of social organizations to bring out the positive in people. The new penology takes for granted that a high level of criminal behavior will continue to occur, and its concern is how to manage the criminal justice system efficiently rather than to effect major changes in crime rates or to bring about rehabilitation of a significant number of offenders.

The new penology has rekindled the historical notion of "dangerous classes" that traditionally has been linked to the urban poor. Feeley and Simon (1992) claimed that the new penology is oriented toward the management of a "permanently dangerous population" (p. 463). Their description of this population parallels Wilson's (1987) depiction of the "underclass," which, because of the social realities of capitalist industrial societies in which production is based on a high level of technology and a reduction of manual labor, became a marginal population, unemployable, lacking in adequate education and marketable skills, and without any real prospects or hope to change its situation. This approach bears a similarity to the Marxist concept of the "lumpenproletariat," an exploited and potentially dangerous class whose members lack class consciousness and, instead of fighting the ruling class to change their inferior social and economic conditions, prey mainly on their poor working-class compatriots (Bonger, [1916] 1969).

The new penal approach, focusing on the control and management of specific aggregates, has made increasing use of actuarial methods that rely heavily on statistical decision theory, operations research techniques, and system analysis to devise and implement penal policies (Simon, 1988). These reflect the positivist orientation in criminology that concentrates on "methods, techniques, or rules of procedure" rather than on "substantive theory or perspectives" (Gottfredson and Hirschi, 1987, p. 10). . . .

Three-strikes laws have historical roots in American penology (Feeley & Kamin, 1996; Zeigler & Del Carmen, 1996; Turner, Sundt, Applegate, & Cullen, 1995). They are based on the penal principle of incapacitation. The rationale behind this principle is that "some crimes are produced exclusively by exceptional people, as some commodities are. If some of these people are incapacitated, production is reduced" (Van den Haag, 1975, p. 53). In theory, three-strikes laws were meant to target repeating violent and dangerous felons, similar to "selective incapacitation" strategies that "target a small group of convicted offenders, those who are predicted to commit serious crimes at high rates, for incarceration" (Visher, 1987, p. 513). Implicitly, three-strikes laws also involve the probability and risk assessment of certain aggregates and the "management" (through long prison sentences) of those high-risk groups that are considered to be the most harmful to society.

In one respect, however, three-strikes laws do not seem to be in tune with the new penology, which, according to Feeley and Simon (1992), in addition to focusing on the management and control of "a permanently dangerous population," is concerned with "maintaining the system at a minimum cost" (p. 463). Three-strikes legislation does not put a major emphasis on dealing with the material consequences of its implementation. In this regard, Simon and Feeley (1994) criticized the three-strikes measures, stating, "This spate of three-strikes laws as well as other types of mandatory sentences can easily be characterized as mindless 'spending sprees' or 'throwing money at a problem' without likelihood of benefit" (p. 13). However, advocates may claim that indirectly, through the reduction of serious crimes that is expected as a result of the implementation of these measures and the ensuing "bifurcation" according to which intermediate punishments, therapies, fines, or even release are applied to categories of offenders classified as less serious criminals (including many white-collar crime offenders), certain concern with correctional cost is implied.

The new penology's approach of controlling "permanently dangerous people," depicted as potentially habitual criminals often connected with the drug scene, is related to a sociocultural atmosphere in which phenomena similar to moral panics may easily emerge (Cohen, 1973). There is a pervasive public perception, reinforced by the mass media, that these dangerous offenders "pose a threat to the society and to the moral order. . . . Therefore, 'something should be done' about them and their behavior" (Goode & Ben-Yehuda, 1994, p. 31). This "something" usually is the increased severity of punishment. One major reflection of this trend is the legislation of three-strikes laws. But in addition, the contention of this article is that these measures also are related to, and are characteristic of, the social control policies that may be derived from the McDonaldization model of society.

THE MCDONALDIZATION OF PUNISHMENT

In a recent book, Ritzer (1993) used the analogy of fast-food establishments to characterize and analyze the social and cultural ethos of modern technological societies, particularly that of the United States. He defined McDonaldization as "the process by which the principles of the fast-food restaurant are coming to dominate more and more sectors of American society as well as the rest of the world" (p. 1). This process also has a major impact on the social control policies of these societies. The theoretical underpinnings of the three-strikes measures, their definitions of strikeable offenses, and the wide-scale public support of these types of legislation are closely related to, and are influenced by, McDonaldization.

In this model, which is based on the Weberian concept of "formal rationality" (Weber, 1968), there are four basic dimensions of the fast-food industry: efficiency, calculability, predictability, and control. Efficiency refers to the tendency to choose the optimum means to a given end, calculability is identified as the tendency to quantify and calculate every product and to use quantity as a measure of quality, predictability has to do with the preference to know what to expect in all situations at all times, and control involves the replacement of human technology with nonhuman technology in a way that goods, services, products, and workers are better controlled. Ritzer (1993) suggested that there are various degrees of McDonaldization and that some phenomena are more McDonaldized than others. As mentioned previously, the contention of this article is that three-strikes laws are promoting punishment policies in accordance with this model.

Efficiency and Penal Policy

Efficiency in the context of three strikes can be defined as the achievement of the maximum possible incapacitation effect for dangerous offenders. Incapacitation can be seen as an indicator of efficiency because offenders are prevented during their prison sentences from causing harm in their outside communities. . . . Three-strikes laws make incapacitation mandatory and long lasting; therefore, many consider them as a major step in the "search for a far better means to an end than would be employed under ordinary circumstances" (Ritzer, 1993, p. 35), a hallmark of efficiency.

One of this policy's major attractions is that, like the new penology, it focuses on a specific discredited group, the "dangerous" violent criminals who are mainly from lower class backgrounds. Therefore, by incapacitating these offenders who are responsible for a disproportionately high percentage of violent crimes, this measure is seen as potentially very efficient. An additional expectation is that three-strikes laws will have an increased deterrent effect (both specific and general) as a result of the increase in the severity of punishment. Theoretically, the deterrence factor coupled with incapacitation should enhance preventive efficiency; thus, this measure carries the promise that a substantial reduction of crime rates can be achieved. . . . But a major question remains: At what price will this decline be achieved, if at all?

Calculability

According to commonsense thinking, three-strikes laws make punishment easily calculable. In a three-strikes sentence, as in other mandatory and determinate sentences, the release date is calculable at the time of the sentencing because only a limited good time range is stipulated in the law. The calculation of the sentence is based on the seriousness of the offense and the prior record of the offender. . . .

Calculability also implies that quantity becomes the indicator of quality. In terms of punishment, the fact that three-strikes laws increase substantially the length of punishment for "dangerous" criminals is an indicator for many politicians, officials, and citizens that the "quality" of justice is improved. Also, the severe reduction of prisoners' good time included in these measures (e.g., for a second strike, offenders in California have to serve at least 80% of their sentences instead of 50% as before) increases the calculability of punishment by lessening the disparities of time served among inmates. . . .

Predictability

Prediction is one of the aims of science. The method of scientific inquiry, based on the principle of rationality that provides predictive ability, is highly valued in modern societies. In them, government authorities try to base public policies on rational foundations to be able to predict and control what is going to happen in the future. Thus, McDonaldization follows a highly rational model:

> Rationalization involves the increasing effort to ensure predictability from one time or place to another. In a rational society, people prefer to know what to expect in all settings and at all times. . . . In order to ensure predictability over time and place, a rational society emphasizes such things as discipline, order, systematization, formalization, routine, consistency, and methodical operation. (Ritzer, 1993, p. 83)

Three-strikes laws are assumed to provide a high level of predictability regarding the nature and extent of penal sanctions because, by curtailing judicial discretion, the punishment is known and, consequently, the variations in sentences among jurisdictions and among individual judges are reduced or eliminated. Thus, theoretically, these measures are in line with the retributive ideal of uniformity of punishment.

Control

McDonaldization involves the increased control over production and products, especially through the substitution of nonhuman for human technology (Ritzer, 1993). Three-strikes laws increase substantially the control over sentencing. . . . The fact that upon conviction the sentence is mandatory and determined is supposed to give a great deal of control over the punishment into the hands of legislators and prosecutors and, as seen, is supposed to limit considerably the courts' discretion. This development is a major shift in the power structure of the criminal justice system. . . .

Mechanical control and nonhuman technology are applied not only to the determination of sentences but also to the location and conditions of punishment (e.g., the security level of prisons, the type of intermediate sentences). This is a part of the growing trend toward the application of nonhuman technology such as electronic surveillance, urinalysis, computerbased offender-tracking systems, or electronic monitoring as well as the use of other technical devices such as hydraulic doors or other automated security systems in prisons in penal practice. . . .

THE IRRATIONAL CONSEQUENCES OF MCDONALDIZATION IN PENOLOGY

Three-strikes laws and McDonaldization are phenomena of modernization that put a high value on rationality. However, although McDonaldization represents rationalism (i.e., scientific approach, positivism, modernity), it also leads to irrational consequences. Borrowing from Weber's (1968) concept of the "iron cage of rationality," Ritzer (1993) referred to these consequences as the "irrationality of rationality" (p. 12). In the case of McDonaldization, irrationalities may result in inefficiency, incalculability, unpredictability, and lack of control, which may have serious effects on penal policies and practices.

Inefficiency

One of the inefficiencies of fast-food sites is that although they are meant to be "fast," often long lines of people have to wait to be served (Ritzer, 1993). In the criminal justice system, three-strikes laws contribute to the clogging up of courts and the overcrowding of confinement facilities. . . .

Although the three-strikes law is presented as a rational measure to curb serious crime and to punish serious habitual offenders, it may be a very expensive or even wasteful policy (O'Connell, 1995), a suggestion that certainly merits a careful cost-benefit analysis. Ritzer (1993, p. 123) cited the columnist Richard Cohen, who observed that rational systems are not less expensive than other systems; indeed, they may cost more. According to all indications, the three-strikes law will increase considerably the cost of criminal justice operations because (a) more people will be detained in jails, (b) the increase in the number of trials will necessitate the building of more courts and the hiring of more judges and other court personnel, (c) the number of long-term prisoners will grow and so more prisons will have to be built, (d) the growing number of elderly prisoners will need additional (and more expensive) health care than prisons usually provide (Merianos, Marquart, Damphouse, & Herbert, 1997), and (e) welfare agencies will have to support a larger number of dependents of incarcerated felons for longer periods of time than ever before. It is a major concern that rapidly increasing correctional expenditures will have detrimental effects on other public services. . . .

Incalculability

The outcomes of three-strikes cases, which were supposedly easily calculable, often are not so. Concerning mandatory laws, Blumstein, Cohen, Martin, and Tonry (1983) observed that they are "vulnerable to circumvention because they are inflexible and require imposition of penalties that judges and prosecutors may believe to be inappropriate in individual cases" (p. 179).

This observation seems to be valid regarding three-strikes laws as well. One reason is that they are not being applied uniformly by prosecutors in the different jurisdictions. Cushman (1996) and Feeley and Kamin (1996) documented differences among California counties in the extent of use of this measure. Also, there have been many instances in which the incalculability of punishment has been demonstrated in jurisdictions where the three-strikes law was widely applied. For example, because of overcrowding of jails by detainees who were reluctant to plea bargain, many minor offenders have been released early from jail, and a large number of misdemeanants have not even been prosecuted. Thus, the calculability of punishment for minor offenders has been neglected and even sacrificed for that of three-strikes offenders. In other instances, some arrests that could have been qualified as three-strikes cases have been processed as parole violations rather than new offenses and, thus, were not considered as felonies (Spiegel, 1994). In other cases, prosecutors and judges have ignored some previous felonies or redefined them as nonstrike offenses (Colvin & Rohrlich, 1994).

As noted, the quantity of punishment delivered (i.e., the length of incarceration) has been touted as a major virtue of three-strikes measures, whereas its effects on other aspects of social life and culture have not been considered to be important. For example, little concern has been paid to the concept of justice that requires a balance between the seriousness of the crime and the severity of punishment. In 1994, a California offender was sentenced to prison for 25 years to life for grabbing a slice of pepperoni pizza from a youngster (this sentence was reduced in January 1997, and he will be released by 1999). Another offender received 30 years to life for stealing a video recorder and a coin collection. . . . These and similar cases pose serious questions concerning the proportionality of punishment even though the offenders had prior felony convictions. . . .

Similarly, another aspect of justice, equal treatment, is being neglected because three-strikes measures focus almost exclusively on street crimes that usually are committed by poor offenders. Meanwhile, crimes of the middle and upper classes either are not affected or will be handled even more leniently than before because the criminal justice system that is overoccupied by predatory street crimes will have diminishing resources to deal with them. . . . Another factor that adds to the incalculability of this measure is that it is not applied uniformly. Data pertaining to the first six months of implementation compiled by the Los Angeles Public Defender's Office indicate that minorities with criminal histories comparable to those of White offenders were being charged under the three-strikes law at 17 times the rate of Whites (Donziger, 1996).

Although many citizens see the long sentences meted out under the three-strikes law as indicators of "high-quality" justice, there are others who will raise questions concerning justice, just desert, and injustice in American society. Some will consider this measure as an expression of the "triumph of vengeance over retribution" (Haas, 1994, p. 127) when vengeance becomes institutionalized as a public policy (Shichor & Sechrest, 1996).

Unpredictability

Several of the issues concerning predictability resemble those that emerged in relation to efficiency and calculability. For various reasons, the outcomes of three-strikes cases are not as clearly predictable as they were intended to be, based on this law's mandatory and determinate nature. For example, in some instances victims refuse to testify when the convictions would carry sentences of long-term incarceration under the three-strikes law ("California Judge Refuses" 1994). In other cases, juries may fail to convict for the same reason. . . . Moreover, as has been seen, the outcome of a case under this law may be entirely different from what was foreseen because juries may refuse to convict, authorities may refuse to press a felony charge, or the courts may not count previous felonies. . . . Thus, it seems that in many instances, including three-strike laws, instead of increasing the predictability of punishment as they were meant to do, determinate and mandatory sentences may contribute to unpredictability.

Similarly, by placing the emphasis on the predictability of "aggregate control and system management rather than individual success and failure" (Feeley & Simon, 1992, p. 455), three-strikes laws cannot predict, and are not interested in predicting, the effects of the punishment on individual convicts, and they may waste a great deal of money, time, and effort on false positives by keeping those who would not cause further harm to society incarcerated for long periods of time. Finally, because the application of three-strikes laws may vary from one jurisdiction to another, the extent and accuracy of predictability also may vary among jurisdictions, as was the case concerning the calculability of punishment. In short, like the case with many other public policies, the implementation of three-strikes laws is likely to lead to many unintended consequences that may defeat some of the very same purposes that the laws were supposed to fulfill.

Lack of Control

Rational systems often can spin out of the control of those who devise and use them (Ritzer, 1993). Sentencing based on an almost automatic decision making system drastically reduces the court's authority to consider particular circumstances of offenses and individual differences among offenders. However, there are experts who maintain that to render a high quality of justice, a certain degree of judicial discretion is essential.

There also is the issue of "hidden discretion"; that is, whereas the court's decision-making power in the imposition of punishment is severely curtailed, the discretion of law enforcement, and especially that of the prosecution, increases greatly. The charges brought against a suspect will be determined by these agencies. The major discretionary decision in many instances will be whether a case should be filed as a misdemeanor or a felony, which bears directly on the application of three-strikes laws. The changes in the locus of discretion in the criminal justice process mean that decision making will become less visible than before because courts are an open forum, and their decisions, even in plea bargaining cases, can be scrutinized and monitored much more easily than the ones made by law enforcement and the prosecution behind closed doors. In sum, the promise of a high level of control over punishment, which was one of the major aims of mandatory and determinate sentencing including three-strikes laws (the other was the increase in the severity of punishment), can spin out of control and result in unintended and unforeseen consequences. . . .

DISCUSSION QUESTIONS

1. Discuss the social and legal context within which the three-strikes laws were enacted. Why is that context important, and how does it feed the McDonaldization of punishment in the United States today?

2. What are the core elements of the new penology and McDonaldization? How are they exemplified by the three-strikes law?

3. How does Shichor characterize the "irrationality" of the three-strikes law?

4. What are the potential consequences for the criminal justice system and for the United States of laws like the three-strikes laws?

REFERENCES

Feeley, M., & Simon, J. (1992). The new penology: Notes on the emerging strategy of corrections and its implications. *Criminology, 30,* 449-474.

Ritzer, G. (1993). *The McDonaldization of society.* Newbury Park, CA: Pine Forge.

28

FEMINISM AND CRIMINOLOGY

KATHLEEN DALY AND MEDA CHESNEY-LIND

EDITOR'S INTRODUCTION—Two prominent feminist criminologists today, Kathleen Daly and Meda Chesney-Lind, undertake the task of providing an overview of feminist thought and explaining what relevance it might have for criminology. This contribution provided a foundation for a number of later works in the arena of feminist criminology, namely Simpson (1989), Chesney-Lind and Shelden (1992), and Simpson and Elis (1995), as well as another work in this section of the book, Daly (Chapter 29).

Daly and Chesney-Lind note that a feminist perspective requires that theorists and researchers move beyond traditional frameworks in criminology. Defining feminism has been difficult at best, with little consensus on a "one-size-fits-all" meaning. Nonetheless, Daly and Chesney-Lind have identified a number of central principles that run through feminist analyses. They stipulate that gender is not rooted in biological sex difference but instead is the product of social, historical, and cultural complexities. Additionally, they claim that gender relations and constructs of masculinity and femininity are based on an "organizing principle of men's superiority and social and political-economic dominance over women" (p. 268, this volume). Because systems of knowledge tend to be male centered, reflecting mainly men's views of the world, the production of knowledge is said to be gendered (p. 268, this volume). Placing women at the center of intellectual inquiry, rather than on the periphery as a male "appendage," is one way to rectify the problem.

How is feminist thought relevant to criminology? Daly and Chesney-Lind note that when explaining the relationship of gender to criminality, most criminological inquiries have focused on the "generalizability of the problem," which questions whether "theories of men's crime apply to women," and the "gender ratio problem," which asks why women are "less likely than men to be involved in crime" and why "are men more crime-prone than women" (p. 270, this volume)? Although factors suggested by traditional approaches may be generalizable to female criminality, Daly and Chesney-Lind contend that these approaches do not sufficiently address the importance of gender in crime causation.

In other words, as Simpson and Elis (1995) point out in their work, traditional approaches to female criminality ignore the place, or context, within which gender relations are shaped. Both Daly and Chesney-Lind and Simpson and Elis want to elevate gender to a higher level and point out that crime itself is a source for gender to "play itself out," hence the gendered nature of crime.

Daly and Chesney-Lind go on to add that even if the male-centered theories were empirically relevant to female criminality, they do not consider all that might be known about female offending. The authors call for research that moves beyond the quantitative analyses of the generalizability and gender ratio problems and ask criminologists to "get [their] hands dirty" and unveil the detailed social context that molds the lives of female offenders.

In the final section of their work, Daly and Chesney-Lind point out the significant role that feminist criminology has played in studying the victimization of women by men. More specifically, they note that feminist scholars have made important contributions in the criminal justice arena in terms of the role of the state in controlling pornography, prostitution, rape, and domestic violence.

DEFINING FEMINISM

Distinguishing Feminist From Nonfeminist Analyses

. . . . Neither a scholar's gender nor the focus of scholarship—whether women, gender difference, or anything else—can be used to distinguish feminist, nonfeminist, or even antifeminist works. Scholars' theoretical and methodological points of view are defined by the way in which they frame questions and interpret results, not by the social phenomenon alone. Thus to Morris's (1987, p. 15) question—"Does feminist criminology include criminologists who are feminist, female criminologists, or criminologists who study women"—we reply that research on women or on gender difference, whether conducted by a male or a female criminologist, does not in itself qualify it as feminist. Conversely, feminist inquiry is not limited to topics on or about women; it focuses on men as well. For criminology, because most offenders and criminal justice officials are men, this point is especially relevant; allied social institutions such as the military have not escaped feminist scrutiny (Enloe, 1983, 1987). When feminist, nonfeminist, or not-really-feminist distinctions are drawn, the main source of variation is how inclusively scholars (or activists) define a continuum of feminist thought. . . .

Although some scholars (typically, liberal and Marxist feminists who do not accord primacy to gender or to patriarchal relations) assume that previous theory can be corrected by including women, others reject this view, arguing that a reconceptualization of analytic categories is necessary. Working toward a reinvention of theory is a major task for feminists today. Although tutored in "male-stream" theory and methods, they work within and against these structures of knowledge to ask new questions, to put old problems in a fresh light, and to challenge the cherished wisdom of their disciplines.

Such rethinking comes in many varieties, but these five elements of feminist thought distinguish it from other types of social and political thought:

- Gender is not a natural fact but a complex social, historical, and cultural product; it is related to, but not simply derived from, biological sex difference and reproductive capacities.
- Gender and gender relations order social life and social institutions in fundamental ways.
- Gender relations and constructs of masculinity and femininity are not symmetrical but are based on an organizing principle of men's superiority and social and political-economic dominance over women.
- Systems of knowledge reflect men's views of the natural and social world; the production of knowledge is gendered.
- Women should be at the center of intellectual inquiry, not peripheral, invisible, or appendages to men.

These elements take different spins, depending on how a scholar conceptualizes gender, the causes of gender inequality, and the means of social change. Generally, however, a feminist analysis draws from feminist theories or research, problematizes gender, and considers the implications of findings for empowering women or for change in gender relations. Finally, we note that scholars may think of themselves as feminists in their personal lives, but they may not draw on feminist theory or regard themselves as feminist scholars. For personal or professional reasons (or both), they may shy away from being marked as a particular kind of scholar.

THE RELEVANCE OF FEMINIST THOUGHT TO CRIMINOLOGY

Can There Be a Feminist Criminology?

Morris (1987, p. 17) asserts that "a feminist criminology cannot exist" because neither

Daly, K., & Chesney-Lind, M. (1988). Feminism and criminology. *Justice Quarterly, 5,* 497-539.

feminism nor criminology is a "unified set of principles and practices." We agree. Feminists engaged in theory and research in criminology may work within one of the feminist perspectives; thus, like feminist thought generally, feminist criminology cannot be a monolithic enterprise. We also agree with Morris's observation that "the writings of Adler and Simon do not constitute a feminist criminology" (p. 16). Yet we think it important to identify Simon's and Adler's arguments as liberal feminist, to assess them on those terms, and to compare them with analyses adopting other feminist perspectives. Similarly, in the debates between radical and socialist feminists about controlling men's violence toward women, one can evaluate their different assumptions of gender and sexuality. A single feminist analysis across many crime and justice issues is not possible, but that fact does not preclude a criminologist who uses feminist theory or research from calling herself (or himself) a feminist criminologist. It's a convenient rubric, but only as long as criminologists appreciate its multiple meanings.

Feminist theories and research should be part of any criminologist's approach to the problems of crime and justice. They demonstrate that a focus on gender can be far more than a focus on women or sexism in extant theories. They offer an opportunity to study still-unexplored features of men's crime and forms of justice, as well as modes of theory construction and verification. In tracing the impact of feminist thought on studies of crime and justice, we find that the promise of feminist inquiry barely has been realized.

TRACING DEVELOPMENTS: THE AWAKENING TO THE 1980s

The Awakening

In the late 1960s, Bertrand (1969) and Heidensohn (1968), respectively a Canadian and a British female criminologist, drew attention to the omission of women from general theories of crime. Although they were not the first to do so, their work signaled androcentric slumber. Several years earlier Walter Reckless had observed in the third edition of *The Crime Problem* (1961, p. 78),

if the criminologist, before propounding or accepting any theory of crime or delinquency, would

pause to ask whether that theory applied to women, he would probably discard it because of its inapplicability to women.

Then, as today, the problem identified by Bertrand, Heidensohn, and Reckless has two dimensions. First, it is uncertain whether general theories of crime can be applied to women's (or girls') wrongdoing. Second, the class-, race-, and age-based structure of crime forms the core of criminological theory, but the gender-based structure is ignored. Although related, these dimensions pose different questions for criminology. The first is whether theories generated to describe men's (or boys') offending can apply to women or girls (the *generalizability problem*). The second is why females commit less crime than males (the *gender ratio problem*). Both questions now occupy a central role in research on gender and crime. . . .

ISSUES AND DEBATES IN THE 1980s: APPROACHES TO BUILDING THEORIES OF GENDER AND CRIME

Theories of gender and crime can be built in several ways, and we see criminologists taking three tacks. Some are focusing on what we have called the generalizability problem, while others are interested in what we have termed the gender ratio problem. Still others want to bracket both problems, regarding each as premature for an accurate understanding of gender and crime.

The Generalizability Problem

Do theories of men's crime apply to women? Can the logic of such theories be modified to include women? In addressing the generalizability problem, scholars have tested theories derived from all-male samples to see if they apply to girls or women (e.g., Cernkovich & Giordano, 1979; Datesman & Scarpitti, 1975; Figueira-McDonough & Selo, 1980; Giordano, 1978; Warren, 1982; Zietz, 1981). Others have borrowed elements from existing theories (e.g., Moyer, 1985 on conflict theory) or have recast the logic of a theory altogether (e.g., Schur, 1984 on labeling). According to Smith and Paternoster's (1987) review of the large body of studies taking this approach, the available evidence is limited, mixed, and inconclusive. More studies likely will confirm a consistent, logical answer to the question "Do theories of men's crime apply to women?" The answer is "yes and no": the truth lies in this equivocation.

The Gender Ratio Problem

The gender ratio problem poses the following questions: Why are women less likely than men to be involved in crime? Conversely, why are men more crime-prone than women? What explains gender differences in rates of arrest and in variable types of criminal activity? In contrast to the gender composition of generalizability scholars, almost all gender ratio scholars seem to be men. Their approach is to develop new theoretical formulations by drawing primarily from statistical evidence, secondary sources, elements of existing theory (e.g., social control, conflict, Marxist), and at times from feminist theory. Box (1983), Gove (1985), Hagan, Simpson and Gillis (1987), Harris (1977), Messerschmidt (1986), Steffensmeier (1983), and Wilson and Herrnstein (1985) have offered ideas on this issue. Heidensohn (1985) is one of few female criminologists to take this route.

Juxtaposing the Generalizability and Gender Ratio Problems

Much of the confusion and debate that surround the building of gender and crime can be resolved when scholars realize that they are on different tracks in addressing the generalizability and gender ratio problems. Members of each camp seem to be unaware of the other's aims or assumptions; but when the two are juxtaposed, their logic and their limitations are revealed. Analogous developments have taken place in building theories of gender and the labor market; thus we sketch some of that literature to clarify problems in developing theories of gender and crime.

A model of occupational status attainment outlined by Blau and Duncan (1967) and using an all-male sample, was applied subsequently to samples of women. This research suggested that the same variables predicted occupational status for men and for women (see Sokoloff's 1980 review); the implication was that the processes of intergenerational occupational mobility were the same for men and women. Those taking a more structural approach to the labor market soon raised this question, however: how was it that the "same" processes produced such distinctive distributions of men and women in the paid occupational structure (job segregation) and caused such marked differences in men's and women's wages? That query inspired a rethinking of the structural and *organizational contexts* of men's and women's work (paid and unpaid), which now commands the attention of many sociologists and economists.

The gender and labor market literature today is several steps ahead of that for gender and crime, but similarities at different stages are clear. Generalizability scholars are not concerned with gender differences in rates of arrest or in arrests for particular crimes (or in rates and types of delinquent acts). Instead they want to know whether the same processes (or variables) describe intragender variability in crime and delinquency. Setting aside the mixed research findings, they (like status attainment theorists) confront a vexing question. Even if (for the sake of argument) the same processes or variables explain intragender variability in crime and delinquency or in its detection, why do such similar processes produce a distinctive gender-based structure to crime or delinquency? Moreover, what does it mean to develop a gender neutral theory of crime, as some scholars now advocate, when neither the social order nor the structure of crime is gender neutral?

Smith and Paternoster (1987) propose developing a gender-neutral theory of crime because gender-specific theories of the past (meaning theories of *female* criminality) held sexist and stereotypic assumptions of female behavior. (Note that theories of male crime are assumed to be universal and are not construed as gender-specific.) When Smith and Paternoster then consider the gender ratio problem, they suggest that the volume of criminal deviance may reflect "*differential exposure* to factors that precipitate deviant behavior among both males and females" (1987, p. 156). Their surmise begs the question of how gender relations structure "differential exposure" and "factors," and seemingly denies the existence of gender relations.

Like structural analysts of gender and the labor market, gender ratio criminologists take the position that patterns of men's and women's crime are sufficiently different to warrant new theoretical formulations. Focusing on intergender variability in rates of arrest or in arrests for particular crimes, several theorists offer these starting points: the power relations both between and among men and women, the control and commodification of female sexuality, sources of informal social control, and the greater enforcement of conformity in girls' and women's lives. In contrast to generalizability scholars, gender ratio scholars assume that different (or gender-specific) variables predict intergender variability in crime or delinquency.

In the wake of arguments developed by gender ratio scholars, those who pursue the generalizability problem may begin to rethink concepts or variables, or they may abandon their enterprise as too limiting. That change may require some time, however, because the contributions of the gender ratio scholars are also limited and provisional. Although they acknowledge that crime (like the occupational order) is gendered, many display only a primitive understanding of what this fact means, and all face problems of slim evidence (save statistical distributions) from which to develop sound propositions about female crime or gender differences in crime.

Bracketing the Two Problems

Many feminist criminologists tend for the present to bracket the generalizability of the gender ratio problems. They are skeptical of previous representations of girls' or women's lives and want a better understanding of their social worlds. Moreover, they are unimpressed with theoretical arguments derived from questionable evidence and having little sensitivity to women's (or men's) realities. Like criminologists of the past (from the 1930s to the 1960s), they seek to understand crime at close range, whether through biographical case studies, autobiographical accounts, participant observation, or interviews (e.g., Alder, 1986; Bell, 1987; Campbell, 1984; Carlen, 1983, 1985; Carlen & Worrall, 1987; Chesney-Lind & Rodriguez, 1983; Delacoste & Alexander, 1987; Miller, 1986; Rosenbaum, 1981). For this group of scholars, the quality and the depth of evidence are insufficient to address the generalizability or gender ratio problems. Perhaps more important, the ways in which questions are framed and results are interpreted by

many (though not all) of those pursuing the generalizability or gender ratio problems remain tied to masculinist perspectives, ignoring the insights from feminist scholarship.

Observations

Because the building of theories of gender and crime is recent, and because a focus on women or on gender differences is viewed as a marginal problem for the field, we think it imprudent to judge some efforts more harshly than others. We may find, for example, that different explanations for intra- and intergender variability are necessary, or that a more careful examination of patterns of girls' or women's crime may improve our understanding of boys' or men's criminal deviance, among other possibilities. At this stage of theory building, all approaches must be explored fully. In advocating this position we are aware that some varieties of theory building and some methodological approaches are thought to be more elegant (or, as our male colleagues like to say, more powerful). Specifically, global or grand theoretical arguments and high-tech statistical analyses are valued more highly by the profession. Thus we examine the approaches taken by criminologists in this intellectual context. Our concern is that scholars begin to see that the dimensions of a major criminological problem—the place of men and of women in theories of crime—cannot be separated from a problem for the sociology of knowledge—the place of men and of women in constructing theory and conducting research. Harris (1977, p. 15) alluded to this problem when he said:

> Dominant typifications about what kinds of actors "do" criminal behavior—typifications which have served dominant male interests and have been held by both sexes have played a crucial dual role in . . . keeping sociologists from seeing the sex variable in criminal deviance and . . . keeping men in crime and women out of it.

If the words "criminal behavior," "criminal deviance," and "crime" are replaced with "criminology" in this statement, we can extend Harris's insight with the following observations.

Preferable modes of theory building are gender-linked. Male scholars, for example, have moved rather boldly into theoretical work on the gender ratio problem in both juvenile (e.g., Hagan et al., 1987) and adult arenas (e.g., Messerschmidt, 1986). Meanwhile female scholars have displayed more tentativeness and a discomfort with making global claims. In a related vein, it is clear that preferred modes of data collection are also gender-linked. Although both male and female criminologists are required to display their statistical talents, the women's empirical approaches in understanding crime today are more likely than the men's to involve observations and interviews. They are more interested in providing texture, social context, and case histories, in short, in presenting accurate portraits of how adolescent and adult women become involved in crime. This gender difference is not related to "math anxiety" but rather to a felt need to comprehend women's crime on its own terms, just as criminologists of the past did for men's crime.

As increasing numbers of women (and feminists) enter criminology, they face dilemmas if they wish to understand men's, women's, or gender differences in crime or delinquency. A safe course of action—intellectually and professionally—is to focus on the generalizability problem and to use a domesticated feminism to modify previous theory. Something may be learned by taking this tack (i.e., intragender variability), but there remains an issue, not yet pursued vigorously: whether theoretical concepts are inscribed so deeply by masculinist experiences that this approach will prove too restrictive, or at least misleading.

Our final observation is more speculative. It is inspired by Heidensohn's (1985) remarks on studies of adolescent boys' gangs, both the classics and more recent efforts. She suggests that the men conducting these studies were "college boys . . . fascinated with the corner boys" (1985, p. 141). These researchers "vicariously identified" with the boys, romanticizing their delinquency in heroic terms. We think that this sense of affinity has eluded female criminologists thus far in their analyses of girls' or women's crime. An example will illustrate this point.

Miller (1986, p. 189) reports at the close of her book on street hustlers that the "details of these women's lives would run together in my mind and make me angry, generally upset, and depressed." Angered at the lives these women had led as children and at the daily brutality in their current lives, she saw little hope for the women's or their children's futures. As empathetic as Miller was in describing women's illicit work, her story contains few heroines; the initial excitement of criminal activity turns into self-destruction and pain. How strongly her impressions differ from men's ethnographies of juvenile males, who are described as "cool cats" or as "rogue males [engaging in] untrammeled masculinity" (Heidensohn, 1985, pp. 125-44). Heidensohn terms this genre the "delinquent machismo tradition in criminology" (1985, p. 141), in which the boys' deviance, and to some degree their violence, are viewed as normal and admirable. By contrast, it is far more difficult for female criminologists to find much to celebrate in girls' or women's crime.

As suggested earlier, all three approaches to reformulating theories of gender and crime have merit. Nevertheless we think that the most pressing need today is to bracket the generalizability and the gender ratio problems, to get our hands dirty, and to plunge more deeply into the social worlds of girls and women. The same holds true for boys and men, whose patterns of crime have changed since the 1950s and 1960s, when ethnographies of delinquency flourished in criminology. Recent changes in youth gangs highlight the need for this work (Hagedorn, 1988; Huff, 1988; Moore, 1978). Our concern is that explicitly feminist approaches to women's crime or to the gender patterns of crime will not be noticed, will be trivialized merely as case studies, or will be written off as not theoretical enough. That sort of dismissal would be unfortunate but perhaps not surprising, in view of the professional norms governing the discipline and their masculinist bias.

CONTROLLING MEN'S VIOLENCE TOWARD WOMEN

The victimization (and survivorship) of women is a large and growing part of criminology and is of central interest to feminists in and outside criminology. The relatively high feminist visibility in this area may lead criminologists to regard it as the only relevant site for feminist inquiry in criminology. Not so; the more one reads the literature on victimization—the physical and sexual abuse of children, women, and men—the more difficult it becomes to separate victimization from offending, especially in the case of women (Browne, 1987; Chesney-Lind, forthcoming; Chesney-Lind & Rodriguez, 1983; McCormack, Janus, & Burgess, 1986; Silbert & Pines, 1981).

In research on physical abuse and sexual I violence by men against women, these major themes and findings are seen:

- Rape and violence—especially between intimates—are far more prevalent than imagined previously.
- Police, court officials, juries, and members of the general public do not take victims of rape or violence seriously, especially when victim-offender relations involve intimates or acquaintances.
- Myths about rape and intimate violence are prevalent. They appear in the work of criminologists, in criminal justice practices, and in the minds of members of the general public.
- Whereas female victims feel stigma and shame, male offenders often do not view their behavior as wrong.
- Strategies for change include empowering women via speakouts, marches, shelters and centers, and legal advocacy, and changing men's behavior via counseling, presumptive arrest for domestic violence, and more active prosecution and tougher sanctions for rape.

Although feminists of all types agree that men's rape and battery of women require urgent attention, scholars and activists have different views on the causes and the malleability of men's sexual and physical aggression. Pornography (and its links to men's sexual violence) and prostitution (and its links to pornography) are prominent in the dissensus. We turn to these debates and their implications for criminal justice policy.

Causes of Men's Violence Toward Women

Radical feminists tend to construct men's nature as rapacious, violent, and oriented toward the control of women (see, e.g., Brownmiller, 1975; Dworkin, 1987; MacKinnon, 1982, 1983, 1987; Rich, 1980). Both rape and intimate violence are the result and the linchpin of patriarchal systems, in which women's bodies and minds are subject to men's dominion. Marxist and socialist feminists (e.g., Hooks, 1984; Klein, 1982; Messerschmidt, 1986; Schwendinger &

Schwendinger, 1983) differ from radical feminists on one key point: they believe that men's nature cannot be described in universalistic (or biologically based) terms but is a product of history and culture, and is related to other systems of domination such as classism, racism, and imperialism. In contrast, liberal feminists offer no theory of causes, but like Marxist and socialist feminists they envision the possibility that men's socially structured violent nature can change. What role, then, should the state play in controlling men's violence and protecting women from such violence? Feminist responses are contradictory and the dilemmas are profound.

Questioning the Role of the State

Pornography. Differences among feminists over the causes of men's violence and the state's role in controlling it are nowhere so clear as in the pornography issue. Part of the debate concerns the effect of pornography on increasing or causing men's sexual violence toward women. Research ethics preclude an answer, but clinical evidence to date shows that pornography with violent content increases aggression, whereas pornography without violent content diminishes aggression (see Baron and Straus, 1987, p. 468). Such evidence hardly settles the matter either for antipornography or anticensorship feminists. At issue are different views of men's sexuality and the causes of men's violence, with radical feminists initiating the antipornography movement. Also at issue is whether state officials can be trusted to render the judgments that antipornography activists seek via the proposed civil remedy (Waring, 1986). Finally, anticensorship feminists see greater harm for women and sexual minorities in efforts to suppress the many forms of commercialized pornography.

Prostitution. Debates among and between feminists and sex-trade workers (Bell, 1987; Delacoste and Alexander, 1987) reveal differences in how women view sexuality and sexual power, as well as problems in relying on a male-dominated state to protect women. These differences are often submerged in a coalition of civil liberties groups, women's groups, and sex-trade workers' organizations who reject state regulation or criminalization of prostitution. In advocating the decriminalization of prostitution and a range of issues associated with prostitutes' right to work, the concerned groups achieve a short-term solution: women can make a living and are not singled out as criminals in a commercial activity that men control, use, and profit from. Nevertheless, the institution of prostitution remains intact, and with it this feminist dilemma: will support for some women's right to work perpetuate an institution that ultimately objectifies women and exploits them sexually, may foster violence against women, and may harm female prostitutes? Today, however, as in the past, the state's stance on vigorous enforcement of prostitution and other related ordinances depends on how prostitution harms men via sexually transmitted diseases, rather than on the institution's impact on women (Alexander, 1987; Bland, 1985; Daly, 1988; Walkowitz, 1980).

In juxtaposing prostitution and pornography, one sees the contradictions and dilemmas for feminists who campaign for redress against men's violence toward women (often by seeking an expanded role for the state in protecting women) while simultaneously advocating women's economic and sexual freedom. Similar dilemmas arise in controlling intimate violence.

Intimate violence and rape. State criminal laws for the arrest and prosecution of spouse (or intimate) abuse and rape have changed significantly in a short period of time (see reviews by Bienen, 1980; Lerman, 1980). Civil remedies such as the temporary restraining order to protect battered women are more readily available than in the past. These legal changes are a symbolic victory for many feminists, who see in them the state's accommodation to their demands for protection against men's violence. Yet the effect of new laws and programs on changing police and court practices seems far less impressive. Officials' resistance and organizational inertia are common themes; program success can be short-lived (Berk, Loseke, Berk, & Rauma, 1980; Berk, Rauma, Loseke, & Berk, 1982; Crites, 1987; Grau, Fagan, & Wexler, 1984; Quarm & Schwartz, 1984; Spencer, 1987). Some scholars think legal reforms may serve a deterrent and educative function over the long term, and thus that it may be unreasonable to expect immediate change in men's violence or in the state's response (Osborne, 1984).

GENDER EQUALITY IN THE CRIMINAL JUSTICE SYSTEM

In the early days of second-wave feminism, calls for legal equality with men were apparent everywhere, and the early feminist critics of criminal law and justice practices reflected this ethos. Today feminist legal scholars are more skeptical of a legal equality model because the very structure of law continues to assume that men's lives are the norm, such that women's legal claims are construed as "special treatment." Alternatives to thinking about equality and difference have been proposed in view of women's social and economic subordinate status and gender differences in paid employment, sexuality, and parenthood; see, e.g., *International Journal of the Sociology of Law*, 1986; MacKinnon, 1987; Rhode, 1987; Vogel, forthcoming; *Wisconsin Women's Law Journal*, 1987. Feminist dissensus over what should be done partly reflects different perspectives on gender, but increasingly one finds that strategies for change reflect lessons learned from engaging in the legal process. As feminists have moved to change the law, so too has the law changed feminism.

Questioning Equality Doctrine and the Equal Treatment Model

Feminist analyses of criminal justice practices reflect a similar shift by moving away from a liberal feminist conceptualization of gender discrimination as a problem of equal treatment. This recent change is more pronounced in British than in American criminology (related, no doubt, to the preponderance of statistical approaches in the United States). It is seen in studies and literature reviews by Allen (1987), Chesney-Lind (1986, 1987), Daly (1987a, 1987b, forthcoming), Eaton (1983, 1985, 1986, 1987), Heidensohn (1986, 1987), Smart (1985), and Worrall (1987). Unlike previous statistical studies of gender-based disparities in court outcomes (for reviews see Nagel and Hagan, 1983; Parisi, 1982), more recent qualitative studies of legal processes analyze the interplay of gender, sexual and familial ideology, and social control in courtroom discourse and decision making at both the juvenile and the adult levels. This work addresses how gender relations structure decisions in the legal process, rather than when men and women are treated "the same" in a statistical sense. Eaton (1986, p. 15) sums up the limitations of analyzing sentencing as an equal treatment problem in this way: "The [discrimination] debate is conducted within the terms of legal rhetoric—'justice' and 'equality' mean 'equal treatment,' existing inequalities are to be ignored or discounted." Thus, just as feminist legal scholars are critiquing equality doctrine, feminist criminologists now are questioning how research on discrimination in the courts is conducted. . . .

The limitations of current equality doctrine are also apparent for changing the prison (or jail) conditions of incarcerated women. Litigation based on equal protection arguments can improve conditions for women to some degree (e.g., training, educational, or work release programs), but such legal arguments are poorly suited to the specific health needs of women and to their relationships with children (Leonard, 1983; Resnik & Shaw, 1980). Indirectly they may also make it easier to build new facilities for female offenders than to consider alternatives to incarceration. Historical studies of the emergence of women's prisons in the United States suggest that separate spheres notions, which were applied to penal philosophy, may have offered somewhat better conditions of confinement for women (notably white, not black women; see Rafter, 1985) than an equality-with-men model (Freedman, 1981; SchWeber, 1982). Therefore equality defined as equal treatment of men and women, especially when men's experiences and behavior are taken as the norm, forestalls more fundamental change and in some instances may worsen women's circumstances.

Conclusion

. . . . We are encouraged by the burst of research attention that has been given to women and to gender differences in crime, to the response to delinquency and crime in the juvenile and criminal justice systems, and to women's victimization. Yet with the possible exception of women's victimization, criminology has not felt the full impact of feminism except in its most rudimentary liberal feminist form. In this vein we underscore a point made several times in the essay: feminist inquiry is relevant and should be applied to *all* facets of crime, deviance, and social control, [not just a] focus on what some scholars term "women's issues" in a narrow sense. It is and should be a far more encompassing enterprise, raising questions about how gender organizes the discipline of criminology, the social institutions that fall within its scope, and the behavior of men and women.

We are surprised by those who continue to say that a focus on gender is unimportant for theories of crime because there are "so few women criminals." We have also been told that discussions of women's crime are "entertaining," meaning that they are a trivial footnote to more general and important problems. Still the fact remains: of whatever age, race, or class and of whatever nation, men are more likely to be involved in crime, and in its most serious forms. Without resorting to essentialist arguments about women's nature, we see in this pattern some cause for hope. A large price is paid for structures of male domination and for the very qualities that drive men to be successful, to control others, and to wield uncompromising power. Most theories of crime suggest the "normalcy" of crime in the light of social processes and structures, but have barely examined the significance of *patriarchal* structures for relations among men and for the forms and expressions of masculinity. Gender differences in crime suggest that crime may not be so normal after all. Such differences challenge us to see that in the lives of women, men have a great deal more to learn.

Discussion Questions

1. What does it mean to take a "feminist" approach to a social problem? How does a feminist approach, or feminist theory, differ from other explanations of human behavior, including criminality?

2. According to Daly and Chesney-Lind, what are the generalizability and gender-ratio problems? Why do the authors feel that they fail to explain properly and fully female criminality?

3. Wearing your "feminist criminologist hat," how would you explain the victimization of women by men?

4. Feminist criminologists contend that if patriarchy were eliminated from society, the crime rate might go down. Why? What is the relationship of patriarchy to crime?

REFERENCES

Chesney-Lind, M., & Shelden, R. G. (1998). *Girls, delinquency, and juvenile justice* (2nd ed.). Belmont, CA: Wadsworth.

Simpson, S. S. (1989). Feminist theory, crime, and justice. *Criminology, 27,* 605-631.

Simpson, S. S., & Elis, L. (1995). Doing gender: Sorting out the caste and crime conundrum. *Criminology, 33,* 47-81.

29

Different Ways of Conceptualizing Sex/Gender in Feminist Theory and Their Implications for Criminology

Kathleen Daly

EDITOR'S INTRODUCTION—Kathleen Daly, known for her extensive and important work in and contributions to feminist criminology, provides readers with another lens through which sex and gender can be conceptualized in feminist theory. Although the scope of the article focuses on the major challenges feminist theory has faced over the past 25 years and three modes of feminist inquiry that responded to these challenges, her essay has important implications for feminist criminologists and criminology, generally.

In the first part of her article, Daly points out that feminist theory faced numerous challenges in the 1980s by women of color and by postmodern/poststructuralist theorists. Highlighting various criticisms leveled at feminist theory, Daly finds that the main criticism centered on the manner in which *difference* had been conceptualized. Much of feminist theory focused on differences between men and women but excluded a wide number of voices (e.g., self-identified radical women of color and black feminists). Other criticisms concerned the manner in which *power* was defined in the production of feminist knowledge. Daly identified problems resulting from a dominance of the humanities in feminist scholarship: "theoretical imperialism, insufficient attention to and a misreading of social science enquiry, and analyzing women's 'differences' solely in linguistic or discursive terms" (p. 280, this volume). Daly stresses that today, social science research plays an important role in feminist knowledge.

The second part of the article offers reconceptualizations of sex and gender in feminist inquiry— "class-race-gender" and "doing gender"—that have been developed by feminists in the social sciences, especially those in sociology. She also considers the notion of "sexed bodies," which has been fostered by feminists in philosophy in the tradition of Foucault.

"Class-race-gender" conceptualizes inequalities "not as additive and discrete, but as interacting, interlocking, and contingent" (p. 281, this volume). In other words, this body of work stresses the importance of viewing multiple relations of inequality in a particular context or structure. In terms of criminology, the class-race-gender configuration strongly suggests—even insists—that "everyone is located in a matrix of multiple social relations." By emphasizing contingency, researchers can study the varied positions of "'black women'—as offenders, victims and mothers and wives of offenders and victims—to 'white justice'" (p. 282, this volume).

The construct "doing gender" essentially means to describe gender as a "situated accomplishment." In other words, one's gender is no longer a peripheral factor in a particular context or situation. It simultaneously defines and is defined by that context; it is *within* and of that context. Researchers have recently made strides to link "doing gender" with concepts of gender relations of power and structures of power that exist in social contexts.

Last, the notion of "sexed bodies" refers to the manner in which sex and gender are related yet distinct constructs and how power in society produces gender and sexual differences among men and women. In terms of criminology, Daly points out that various studies in criminology and law have analyzed the implications of gender-neutral policies, how the sensual aspects of crime are experienced differently for men and women, and how sexed bodies are produced in certain legal contexts such as family law and criminal law (i.e., rape and sexual assault).

Like the previous articles in this section, Daly's contribution highlights the importance of the intersection of class, race, and gender and the manner in which these constructs have been molded and changed over time and in certain contexts.

CHALLENGES TO FEMINIST THEORY

Engaging academic feminism in the 1960s and 1970s was how and whether sex, gender and 'women' could be linked or 'added on' to liberal and Marxist theories. A burgeoning literature developed that compared liberal, radical, Marxist and socialist feminist perspectives (see, for example, Jaggar, 1983; Sargeant, 1981). In 'Feminism and Criminology,' Meda Chesney-Lind and I appended an overview of these perspectives on the 'causes' of inequality and strategies for social change (Daly & Chesney-Lind, 1988, pp. 536-538). We did so reluctantly: while we wished to show that a range of feminist positions was possible, we worried the typology would become fixed precisely when it was unravelling. It became apparent by the mid-1980s that the task for feminist theory was no longer how 'to remove "biases" [from Marxism and liberalism] but to see this "bias" as intrinsic to the structure of the theories in question' (Gatens, 1996, p. 60).

Shifting Ground in the 1980s

... Feminists who drew from postmodern thought also challenged the term *woman,* though for the reason that it lacked a stable and unified referent. But, like the early critiques from women marginalized by feminist thought, which raised questions about whose knowledge or 'experience' was legitimate, feminists working with postmodern texts raised questions about power in the production of knowledge. Several major feminist literary theorists—Jane Gallop, Marianne Hirsch and Nancy Miller—discussed the role of feminist critique and their fears of being criticized by other scholars. As Gallop admitted, "I realize that the set of feelings that I used to have about French men I now have about African-American women. Those are the people I feel inadequate in relation to and try to please in my writing" (Gallop et al., 1990, pp. 363-364).

Gallop's comment suggests that her feminist literary analysis was first affected by French men and *then* by black women. I suspect this chronology was common for US feminist literary scholars. Certainly, it was more so for this group than for US feminists in sociology, who responded first to the charge of racism in feminist thought and who were relatively more resistant to postmodern influences. These different histories of coming to terms with 'French men and black women' have important consequences for how we think through the problem of 'difference' (both among and between men and women) and the degree to which postmodern/poststructuralist theoretical terms are embraced. For feminists in sociology, the problem of difference is commonly understood to mean mapping variation in women's (and men's) lives, of documenting power and resistance in interaction, and of assuming that one's engagement in social structures (and especially, class, race-ethnicity,

Daly, K. (1997) Different ways of conceptualizing sex/gender in feminist theory and their implications for criminology. *Theoretical Criminology, 1,* 25-51.

gender, sexuality and age) matter in shaping one's consciousness, patterns of speech, behavior and capacity to affect social structures. In sociological empirical terms, difference is hardly novel; it is another way to theorize variability and power in social life. For literary scholars, the problem of difference is more often understood primarily as a discursive construction, its elements being binary oppositions in language, the construction of the 'masculine' and 'feminine' as constitutive of hierarchical sexual difference, and for some, an interest in the unconscious psyche. . . .

. . . .[T]he problem of difference was framed by many feminist theorists solely as a problem for theory. Whereas [she] locates this tendency as stemming from 'white women's theorizing,' I see it stemming from a disciplinary-based theoreticism, especially evident in philosophy, but which may also [has] a class and racial nexus. In comparison to philosophy, there was a larger group of feminists in sociology who called for 'incorporating' class-race-gender into the curriculum and research (see Andersen & Collins, 1992). That incorporation is not without problems (see Platt, 1993), but it remains a major theoretical point of entry, especially for feminists of color, and a strategy for coalitional knowledge-building across groups.

Contrary to the claims of radical feminism of the early 1970s, Moira Gatens (1996, p. 62) suggests that it would be naive to think that feminists can produce 'pure or non-patriarchal theory.' This issue is central to the knowledge problem for feminism: it invites a rethinking of how we adjudicate among competing claims about 'women' or 'women's experiences.' Are some better than others, and how do we decide?

Empiricist-Standpoint-Postmodern Feminisms

In the mid-1980s, Sandra Harding made an important contribution when she compared different epistemologies in producing feminist knowledge: empiricist, standpoint and postmodern (Harding, 1986, 1987). She noted the paradox (Harding, 1986, p. 24) that feminism was a political movement for social change and yet feminist researchers were producing knowledge in the natural and social sciences that was more 'likely to be confirmed by evidence' than previous scientific claims. Harding wondered, 'How can such politicized research be increasing the

objectivity of inquiry? On what grounds should these feminist claims be justified?' She suggested that there were two 'solutions' (empiricism and standpointism) and one 'agenda for a solution' (postmodernism).

By *feminist empiricism,* Harding referred to improvements in knowledge by removing sexist and androcentric biases. This meant to 'correct' but not to transform the methodological norms of science. Such a stance was dominant in 1970s feminist social science work, including criminology, and it remains strong in the 1990s. An unfortunate legacy in Harding's analysis is the choice of the term empiricism in light of its connotations in social research. In the social sciences, empiricist or empiricism are distinguished from empirical. The former terms refer to nontheorized empirical enquiry: that which exhibits the 'imperialism of the technique' or that which assumes a firm foundation of knowledge through observation (Wagner, 1992). However, one can do empirical work without being empiricist or without assuming an epistemology of empiricism. It seems crucial, then, that the term empirical not be tied to a particular epistemology. It is as large as 'text,' and both can stand in a constructive tension in the practice of social research.

By *feminist standpoint,* Harding (1986, p. 26) referred to how 'women's subjugated position provides the possibility of more complete and less perverse understandings' than the dominant position of men. This 'standpoint' is informed by women's experiences as understood from the perspective of feminism; thus, it can be taken by both men and women. Several problems are immediately evident. Can there be just one feminist standpoint if subjugated experiences vary by class or race, etc.? And, 'Is it too firmly rooted in a problematic politics of essentialized identities?' (Harding, 1986, p. 27). . . .

By *feminist postmodernism,* Harding referred to a heterogeneous set of critiques of Enlightenment thought with its associated hierarchical dualisms (mind over body and reason over emotion, among others), disembodied claims of truth 'innocent of power,' and assumptions of a stable, coherent self (see Flax, 1990, pp. 41-42). During the 1980s, US feminist engagement with postmodern texts and theorists was emergent; more developed analyses and debates soon followed (e.g. Butler and Scott, 1992; Nicholson, 1990). . . .

Discourse and 'A Real World Out There'

. . . How has research in criminology been affected by these shifts in feminist thought? In the 1970s and 1980s feminist research on Real Women challenged the androcentrism of the field, as scholars filled knowledge gaps about women law-breakers, victims and criminal justice workers. By the 1990s, several scholars signaled a shift in interest from Real Women to The Woman of criminological or legal discourse (see Smart, 1990a, 1992). This reflected a move toward postmodern thinking on crime, courts and prisons, which is evident in the works of Bertrand (1994), Howe (1990, 1994), Smart (1995), Worrall (1990), and A. Young (1990, 1996). While sympathetic to postmodern texts, others have not wanted to abandon Real Women; they include Cain (1989), Carlen (1985, 1988), Carrington (1990), Daly (1992), Joe and Chesney-Lind (1995), and Maher and Daly (1996). Those studying violence against women may be especially resistant to letting go of Real Women because their voices and experiences have only recently been 'named' (compare Marcus, 1992 and Hawkesworth, 1989; see Radford et al., 1996). I am, of course, simplifying here, but I do so to highlight where feminist debate remains keen, both within and outside criminology, on the politics of knowledge. By retaining Real Women, feminists may take 'the ground of specifically *moral* claims against domination—the avenging of strength through moral critique' (Brown, 1991, p. 75). Real Women can be mobilized as 'our subject that harbors truth, and our truth that opposes power' (p. 77). But for others, Real Women, their moral grounds and 'truths,' must be set aside (Smart, 1990b, as discussed below). Concurring with Smart, Brown asks, '[w]hat is it about feminism that fears the replacement of truth with politics . . . privileged knowledge with a cacophony of unequal voices clamoring for position?' (Brown, 1991, p. 73).

A good deal, many reply (e.g. di Leonardo, 1991; di Stefano, 1990; Harding, 1987). And that is why the knowledge problem continues to be contentious for feminist theory and politics. One response has been sketched by Smart (1995, pp. 230-232), who now admits that while we 'need to address this Woman of legal [or criminological] discourse, . . . this kind of analysis alone gives me cause for concern.' She suggests that discourse analysis of, for example, 'the raped woman is of little value unless we are also talking to women who have been raped' (p. 231). To Smart, this is not the same as asserting some truth about Real Women, but rather to be cognizant that 'women discursively construct themselves' (p. 231).

Let me summarize and reflect on my argument in this first section. I identified problems resulting from a dominance of the humanities in feminist work: theoretical imperialism, insufficient attention to and a misreading of social science enquiry, and analyzing women's 'differences' solely in linguistic or discursive terms. I would not wish to claim superiority of 'the empirical' or of social science enquiry. Such a position does not reflect what I have learned from feminist work in philosophy, literature and media studies. Nor does it reflect my interests to develop interdisciplinary 'hybrid knowledges' that break down disciplinary boundaries (Seidman, 1994, p. 2). It is to say that social science research has a key role to play in feminist knowledge and that empirical enquiry can be as radical and subversive as deconstruction.

THREE MODES OF FEMINIST ENQUIRY

The challenges to feminist theory in the 1980s, both by women marginalized by its terms and by postmodern texts, were not isolated. They were part of a general mood to unsettle social theory and to re-engage a critique of positivist social science (Seidman, 1994). Thus, we would expect to see reworkings of old concepts and the emergence of new ones. Two ways of reconceptualizing sex/gender in feminist enquiry— 'class-race-gender' and 'doing gender'—have been developed by feminists in the social sciences, especially those in sociology. 'Sexed bodies' has been developed by feminists in philosophy, and more generally, by re-readings of Foucault.

Class-Race-Gender

My work has been most influenced by class-race-gender or what I have come to term *multiple inequalities* (Daly, 1993, 1995a). In the 1980s, it was not French men but black women whose critique of feminist thought had the greater influence on my thinking. Class-race-gender need not be interpreted literally to mean a sole focus on these three relations; its meaning can be stretched to include others, e.g. age, sexuality and physical ability. For many scholars, the term retains an allegiance, though not complete fealty, to notions of determining structures of inequality. For example, Pat Carlen (1994, pp. 139-40) suggests the need to theorize inequalities [in a way] that 'both recognizes and denies structuralism.'

Class-race-gender conceptualizes inequalities, not as additive and discrete, but as intersecting, interlocking and contingent. In the US, class-race-gender emerged from the struggles of black women in the Civil Rights Movement; it came into academic institutions (and especially sociology) in the late 1970s through articles and books by women of color. This early body of work not only critiqued ethnocentrism in feminist theory, but also established a rhetorical ground for women of color (see, e.g. Baca Zinn et al., 1986; Combahee River Collective, 1979; Dill, 1983).

Conceptualizing multiple relations of inequality has only just begun (for a recent effort in criminology, see Schwartz & Milovanovic, 1995). It will not take the same form as previous efforts to theorize 'systems of inequality' (as in relationships of capitalism and patriarchy). And while its proponents often claim its 'greater inclusiveness,' we should expect that like other ideas, it is 'condemned to be haunted by a voice from the margins . . . awakening us to what has been excluded, effaced, damaged' (Bordo, 1990, p. 138). Like others (e.g. Anthias & Yuval-Davis, 1992; Collins, 1993) I see the project as mapping the salience and contingency of gender, class, race-ethnicity, and the like, both separately and together. . . .

Bordo (1990, p. 145) observes that the 'analytics of class and race . . . do not seem to be undergoing the same deconstruction' as gender and women. I would agree: relatively less intellectual discussion has been devoted to showing the lack of a unified referent for racial and class categories compared to those for gender. One reason is an under-theorization of race [and] ethnicity and its links to other social relations, e.g. the 'gendering' of race or the 'racializing' of gender. This is one of several building blocks in developing a class-race-gender analysis in criminology,

but as yet, movement has been slow. Discomfort levels are high, not coincidentally because criminologists are so 'white' and advantaged, while the subjects of their crime theories more often are not (despite some attention to organizational crime). Moreover, scholars of color in criminology have only recently been in a position to challenge the white-centered assumptions of the field and to develop anti-racist theoretical and research agendas (see Russell, 1992; Walker & Brown, 1995; Young & Greene, 1995).

There are many ways to work with the idea of multiple inequalities. One is to use it to transform research and writing practices in the social sciences (see Daly, 1993, 1994). For example, to show how racial discrimination 'works,' one could use Richard Delgado's (1989) method of presenting multiple accounts of the 'same event.' In this case, Delgado describes what happened when a black man was interviewed for a job at a law school. The multiple perspectives of the participants, as orchestrated by Delgado, bring the white reader into the story in such a way that racial discrimination toward the black man becomes visible to the white reader as part of his/her routine interpretations and practices. Delgado offers a nuanced picture of how race relations routinely work to disadvantage black job applicants through the organizational frame of 'neutral' job criteria.

To date, class-race-gender has been most vividly revealed through literary and storytelling forms (see, for example, Bell, 1987; Delgado, 1989; Jordan, 1985; Lubiano, 1992; Pratt, 1984; Williams, 1991). Unlike a good deal of traditional social science, these works reveal (1) the shifting salience of race, class, gender, nation and sexuality, and the like as one moves through space and time, and (2) the different world-views or lenses that participants bring to social encounters. A major question is whether one can bring these literary or storytelling forms into research practices in sociology and criminology. It may be possible, if researchers use narrative modes of reasoning (see Richardson, 1990; Stivers, 1993; Ewick & Silbey, 1998).

The contribution of class-race-gender to criminology is an insistence that everyone is located in a matrix of multiple social relations, i.e. that race and gender are just as relevant to an analysis of white men as they are to black women. With an emphasis on contingency, one can explore the varied positions of 'black women'—as offenders, victims, and mothers and wives of offenders and victims—to 'white justice' (Daly, 1998b). And as Lisa Maher (1995, Ch. 9) demonstrates in her ethnographic research on women drug-users in New York City, one can reveal varied angles of vision for African- and European-American women and Latinas in neighborhood drug markets. Class-race-gender can also be used to politicize and problematize knowledge in collaboration with others. In this regard, Collins (1993) is right to emphasize the piecing together of work by different scholars as bits in a wider mosaic; the quest to theorize the 'totality' of multiple inequalities is ill-founded. One set of theoretical problems, discussed by Anthias and Yuval-Davis (1992, p. 17), is how to relate the 'different ontological spheres' of class, race and gender divisions, while simultaneously showing the ways they intermesh in concrete situations. Another challenge is to identify new vocabularies to discuss multiple, intersecting or interlocking inequalities. Otherwise, we may easily slip into additive, mechanical analyses of power, oppression and the heaping of disadvantage and advantage.

Doing Gender

Candace West and Donald Zimmerman (1987) coined the construct 'doing gender' to describe gender as a 'situated accomplishment':

> [Gender is not the] property of individuals . . . [but rather] an emergent feature of social situations: . . . an outcome of and a rationale for . . . social arrangements . . . a means of legitimating [a] fundamental division . . . of society. [Gender is] a routine, methodical, and recurring accomplishment (p. 126) . . . not a set of traits, nor a variable, nor a role [but] itself constituted through interaction. (p. 129)

R.W. Connell (1987, 1998) and James Messerschmidt (1993) have developed linkages between 'doing gender' (more precisely, 'doing masculinity') and gender relations of power. Susan Martin and Nancy Jurik (1996) have also utilized 'doing gender' in their analysis of women and gender in justice system occupations. All four authors have elements of 'class-race-gender' in their work. They view structure as ordering interaction, and interaction as producing structure, drawing on Anthony Giddens' (1984) efforts to transcend the sociological dualism of interaction and social structure. . . .

Some feminist skepticism toward 'doing gender' lies in a desire to retain 'structures of power' that both precede and are produced by gender or race, etc. as 'accomplishments.' Whether sex and gender are understood to be produced in interaction or in discourse, feminist critiques (specifically, by sociologists) are based on retaining some semblance of social structure or materialism. As we shall see, some feminists using 'sexed bodies' also wish to include a form of materialism ('materiality'), but its constituents are the body and sexual difference.

Messerschmidt (1993, p. 85) applied 'doing gender' in his analysis of crime as 'a resource for doing masculinity in specific social settings. . .':

> Crime . . . may be invoked as a practice through which masculinities (and men and women) are differentiated from one another. . . . [It] is a resource that may be summoned when men lack other resources to accomplish gender. (p. 85)

Whereas West and Zimmerman (1987, p. 137) had focused on how the doing of gender 'creat[es] differences between . . . women and men' that materialize as 'essential sexual natures' (p. 138), Messerschmidt suggested that the doing of gender also produces multiple forms of masculinity and crime.

One problem Messerschmidt encounters is how to conceptualize crime as a gendered line of social action without once again establishing boys and men as the norm, differentiating themselves from all that is 'feminine.' Although masculine subjectivity and lines of action may be described with these terms (see Jefferson, 1994), it is disputable that feminine subjectivity and lines of action could be. Specifically, would the claim that crime is a 'resource for doing femininity'—for women and girls 'to create differences from men and boys or to separate from all that is masculine'—have any cultural resonance? Probably not. But nor should theories necessarily have to employ symmetrical sex/gender terms. That is to say, arguments that crime is a resource or situation where masculinities are produced may be useful: they normalize crime but problematize men and masculinity.

In applying 'doing gender' to criminological research, scholars will have to let go of thinking about gender or race etc. as attributes of persons and examine how situations and social practices produce qualities and identities associated with membership in particular social categories. Despite the creative efforts of some to employ doing gender in quantitative analyses of self-reported delinquency (e.g. Simpson and Elis, 1995), it is better suited to analyses of social interaction. Researchers will need to be mindful that categories taken from theorizing masculinity may be inappropriately applied to femininity. Gender categories are not neutral, and the terms used to describe men and women 'doing gender' are not likely to be interchangeable. These are major points for those using the 'sexed bodies' construct.

Sexed Bodies

Gatens (1996, p. 67) observes that 'there is probably no simple explanation for the recent proliferation of writings concerning the body.' She credits Foucault's work on the (male) body as a site of disciplinary practices, coupled with that of feminist social scientists, who showed that even the most privileged women have not attained equality with men in the 'public sphere.' Perhaps feminists would need to face, yet again but in different ways, 'questions of corporeal specificity' (p. 68). The trick, Gatens suggests, is to acknowledge 'historical realities essentialism' (p. 69). . . .

Feminists have been analyzing a large philosophical literature on 'the body' and its connection with 'the mind' (see, for example, Butler, 1993; Gatens, 1996; Grosz, 1994, 1995). Sexed bodies is theorized in several ways: some emphasize the discursive construction of 'sex,' including cultural inscription on bodies, whereas others work at the edges of the materiality of 'sex' and 'culture.' For the moment, I will focus on the latter in reviewing three interrelated themes: the sex/gender distinction, power as productive of gender and sexual difference, and dualisms in western philosophy.

Sex/Gender. In 1983 Gatens challenged the familiar distinction between sex (the biological categories of 'male' and 'female') and gender (the social categories of 'masculinity' and 'femininity' that are linked to sex) (reprinted in Gatens, 1996, Ch. 1). She was critical of the assumption that 'the mind of either sex is initially a neutral, passive entity, a blank slate on which are inscribed various social "lessons."' The 'alleged *neutrality* of the body, the postulated *arbitrary* connection between femininity and the female body, masculinity and the male body' troubled Gatens because it 'encourage[s] . . . a neutralization of sexual difference and sexual politics . . . and the naive solution of resocialization' (p. 4, Gatens's emphasis). Moreover, by denying sex-specific corporeality, key differences are overlooked 'between feminine behavior or experience that is lived out by a female subject and feminine behavior or experience that is lived out by a male subject (and vice versa with masculine behavior)' (p. 9).

Power. Drawing on but moving beyond Foucault's account of 'the manner in which the micropolitical operations of power produce socially appropriate bodies,' Gatens (1996, p. 70) proposes that we view gender as not the effect of ideology or cultural values but as the way in which power takes hold of and constructs bodies in particular ways. . . . The sexed body can no longer be conceived as the unproblematic biological and factual base upon which gender is inscribed, but must itself be recognized as constructed by discourses and practices that take the body both as their target and as their *vehicle of expression.* . . .

Dualisms. Elizabeth Grosz (1994) argues that current understandings of 'the body' reflect dualisms in western thinking, and by rethinking 'the body,' subjectivity can be reconceptualized. She rejects the view of the body as 'natural' or having a 'presocial' existence and, simultaneously, she rejects the view of the body as '*purely* a social, cultural, and signifying effect lacking its own weighty materiality' (p. 21, Grosz's emphasis). (As such, she takes issue with feminist approaches she terms egalitarian and social constructionist.) She wants to . . . deny that there is the 'real' material body on the one hand and its various cultural and historical representations on the other. . . . These representations and cultural inscriptions quite literally constitute bodies and help to produce them as such (p. x). . . . Grosz and colleagues' work on sexed bodies is one way the construct can be used. Another emphasizes cultural inscription on the body (see review in Howe, 1994, pp. 194-205). The work I shall consider is Carol Smart's (1990b) on the production of sexed bodies in legal discourse.

Smart is interested in how 'law constructs and reconstructs masculinity and femininity, and maleness and femaleness' that produce a 'commonsense perception of difference' (p. 201). One sees affinity between Smart's claim that legal discourse produces gender and that of West and Zimmerman for whom situations produce gender; but there are key differences. Smart wants to consider how 'law constructs sexed (and not simply gendered) subjectivities' (p. 202), that is, 'the sexed body' (p. 203). She does so by examining rape and rape trials. Smart's (1990b) article was published at around the same time that analyses of the 'matter' or 'materiality of sex' were emerging; this may explain why she does not engage with authors like Grosz who viewed 'sexed bodies' neither as natural nor as signifying effects of culture. Instead, Smart analyzes the sexed body as produced both by legal and feminist discourse: the 'natural' sexed woman, who during a rape trial becomes a victimized sexed body. In feminist discourse this is the body of the eternal victim, whereas in legal discourse, it is the deserving victim (pp. 207-208). Smart cautions that it will be difficult for feminists to 'construct rape differently' because the effort to 'deconstruct the biological/sexed woman is silenced by the apparition of law's sexed woman to whose survival it is unwillingly tied' (p. 208). In other words, feminist efforts to challenge rape law will be thwarted by law's discursive power.

'Sexed bodies' can contribute to criminology in several ways. We can see that gender categories 'neuter' sexual difference, both in research and in policy. For research, we might explore how the 'sensual attractions' of crime (Katz, 1988) are differently available to and 'experienced' by male/female bodies and masculine/feminine subjectivities. We could analyze the variable production of sexed (and racialized, etc.) bodies across many types of harms (not just rape) or for other sites of legal regulation such as family law. We could take Howe's (1994) theoretical lead by investigating women's bodies as the object of penality. For policy, 'sexed bodies' is useful for showing that reputedly gender-neutral policies are tied to specific male bodies. Sexed bodies may worry some feminists because the construct seems to revisit the spectre of biologism and body types that has long haunted criminology. This need not be the case. Sexed bodies calls attention to how we 'experience' sexual difference and its relationship to gender. It also calls attention to dualisms in western philosophy and how dualisms such as reason/emotion, mind/body and male/female are constituted in and through law, science and criminology.

A problem with sexed bodies is the strong temptation to see social life primarily through a lens of sexual difference. It is not just that feminist analyses may unwittingly collude with say, legal discourse in 'reifying these differences' (Gatens, 1996, p. 69), as Smart's (1990b) analysis reveals so well. Nor that for those who take 'phallocentric culture' as the start point, the recommended strategy of 'thinking outside the confining concept of the natural/sexed woman' (Smart, 1990b, p. 208) may be foreclosed by its own terms. From an empirical point of view, the problem is that claims such as 'the utterances of judges constantly reaffirm [the natural/sexed woman]' and 'almost every rape trial tells the same story' (Smart, 1990b, pp. 205-206) are theoretical claims. While they may help us see a pattern of discursive power, they should be seen as open to empirical enquiry not asserted as ahistorical discursive 'fact' (see Carrington, 1994 on this point). A second problem is that variation and particularity in sexed bodies (e.g. by race or age, etc.) is posited by theorists but not explored with care. As a consequence, sex and gender are foregrounded whereas other socially relevant divisions are accorded secondary status. . . .

DISCUSSION QUESTIONS

1. What challenges have been made to feminist theory? In what way will these challenges enhance the scope and importance of feminist theory to various disciplines, namely criminology?

2. Discuss the three different epistemologies in producing feminist knowledge: empiricist, standpoint, and postmodern.

3. What are the three modes of feminist inquiry?

4. In what ways will the challenges and changes presented in Daly's article influence criminological thought and research?

PART VI

INTEGRATED THEORIES
AND UNIQUE APPROACHES

T his final section of the anthology contains readings that address primarilgfy newly developing perspectives in criminology, including the increasingly popular integrated approaches. Although several of these approaches, such as rational choice theory and developmental theories, have been around for a while,[1] they are getting renewed attention in the context of criminology. These perspectives provide other evolving theoretical frameworks within which criminologists and others can consider crime and criminality. Readers should keep in mind the common ground that these reading selections share with some of the other readings presented in other sections.

RATIONAL CHOICE AND ECOLOGY OF CRIME/ROUTINE ACTIVITIES APPROACHES

Rational Choice Theory

The emergence of rational choice theory within criminology paralleled the expansion of the concept of deterrence in the 1980s. Rational choice theory follows the principle of *expected utility,* which maintains that people will make rational decisions based on the extent to which they expect their choice to maximize their benefits (profits) or minimize the costs (losses) (Akers, 2001). These ideas stem back to classical criminology. The nexus between deterrence and rational choice theories finds its origins in 18th-century utilitarian philosophy, in which principles of deterrence were typically applied to

criminal law and principles of rational choice were applied to the economy. Despite rational choice theory's long history, it has only developed within criminology fairly recently.

Although some criminologists had focused on rational choice theory in their work on deterrence in the 1980s, rational choice theorists argued that rational choice theory involved more than merely an extension of deterrence theory. Rational choice theory purports to be a holistic theory in the sense that it seeks to explain the decisions both to commit and to desist from a career in crime. However, the theory examines criminality from a "situational" perspective or uses "situational analysis" in order to understand the connections between certain situational contexts and the behaviors that occur. Recent research that uses this theoretical approach focuses on various situational contexts to explain not only the likelihood of criminal activity but also who will likely be victimized.

The text excerpt in this section by Cornish and Clarke (Chapter 30, this volume) provides readers with an effective overview of modern rational choice theory that centers on situational contexts of offending. The underlying assumption of rational choice theory in this context suggests that rational, selfish, and pleasure-seeking individuals make personal choices and decisions about their future behavior by weighing both the consequences of punishment, should they get caught, and the costs in particular situations of criminal opportunity. In other words, these theorists assume that there will always be people who will commit crime if given the opportunity, so they do not explain the motivations underlying the crime. Thus, rational choice theorists propose that by manipulating a variety of environmental factors, it becomes possible to "harden targets" and reduce victimization.

This theory has been criticized mainly by positivists, who feel that if potential criminals operate independently of any fundamental motivation, then target hardening and environmental manipulation will only displace crime, not eradicate it. Cornish and Clarke's text excerpt (Chapter 30, this volume) counters this contention with evidence that suggests that switching crimes or locations does not typically occur over a short period of time. The true test of an impact on criminal motivation will be to look at these environmental changes and hardening of targets with respect to long-term solutions.

Routine Activities Theory

Routine activities theory, a closely related theory, also relies on rational choice assumptions in its explanations of criminal behavior. This theory suggests that the routine activities of some groups and individuals expose them to higher risks of victimization than others.[2] Cohen and Felson (1979), the most prolific theorists in this area, argue that certain changes and conditions in the modern world have furnished motivated offenders with an increased range of opportunities to commit crime. They contend that because most violent and property crimes involve direct contact between the offender and the "target," which can be either the victim or the victim's property, crimes necessitate three conditions: a convergence of time and space of a motivated offender, a suitable target, and an absence of a guardian capable of preventing the crime (i.e., police) (Cohen & Felson, 1979). Most criminologists who follow the positivist tradition assume that fluctuations in crime rates reflect changes in either the number of motivated offenders or their degree of motivation. However, routine activities theory suggests that crime rates may be explained in terms of changes in the availability of targets and a lack of capable guardians. For example, the article by Felson (Chapter 31, this volume) uses the routine activities perspective to show how city planners and managers can aim the flow of

opportunistic offenders away from crime by manipulating the environment. LaGrange's (1999) recent article also uses the routine activities approach to predict the distribution of minor property crimes in a medium-sized Canadian city during a one-year period. LaGrange extends the scope of routine activities theory with respect to her analysis of minor property damage and vandalism, which, she notes, occur much more frequently in urban areas than the more widely studied index crimes. Most of the work of Chicago School sociologists focused on index crimes such as homicide, robbery, rape, and burglary (LaGrange, 1999).

Cohen and Felson (1979) maintain that the modern world itself has contributed to an increase in the number of suitable and available targets and to a lack of capable guardians primarily because of the number of changes in routine activities among individuals. For example, they argue that because most people work outside the home, there are fewer capable guardians who can watch over property in the home. Likewise, the quantity and portable nature of goods provide thieves with a variety of opportunities to commit crime. Therefore, this approach provides an interesting point of theoretical contrast, especially in terms of earlier ecological theories of crime. For example, under Durkheim's anomie theory, crime occurs as a result of economic change. More specifically, it results from rapid social change, in terms of increased modernization and industrialization. Durkheim explains these changes in terms of a breakdown in traditional values and beliefs. In contrast, routine activities theory excludes values and beliefs from its framework, focusing instead on reducing crime by making changes in opportunities to commit crime (i.e., an increase in capable guardians and target hardening, which would lower crime rates), rather than advocating economic development or social change.

The rational choice and routine activities approaches have numerous similarities with the other ecology theories of crime, mainly social disorganization theory. Although more research will need to be done with respect to these recent approaches, they do suggest that the social context within which crime occurs is very critical in terms of understanding how victims become susceptible to risks of crime and what factors motivate offenders to commit crime.

DEVELOPMENTAL CRIMINOLOGY

Recently, "developmental" or "life-course" perspectives have made significant theoretical strides and have become more prominent in criminology. Developmental theories seek to understand more thoroughly the stability and changes in criminality and deviance through time and at particular stages of a person's life. Most criminological theories ignore the age factor in their analyses of crime. In other words, most criminological theories rest on the assumption that the relationships between biological, psychological, or sociological factors and criminal or deviant behavior have the same effect on offenders without regard for their age. Conversely, developmental theories assume that different factors may affect offenders differently at different stages of their lives. These theories explain crime in the context of the life course of an individual offender. For example, developmental theories may propose that factors that motivate children to engage in deviant behavior will likely be different from those that motivate adolescents or young adults. Likewise, the offender who enters criminality at age 50 will likely have different motivating factors than the chronic adolescent offender. The article by Loeber and Stouthamer-Loeber in this section (Chapter 33, this volume) provides readers with a general overview of the goals of developmental criminology and the factors that are considered in a developmental analysis.

Some debate exists as to whether developmental theories contribute anything new to the theoretical landscape in criminology or whether they represent new ways of integrating theoretical concepts and propositions from existing theories. Some of the theoretical frameworks from which developmental criminologists draw include social learning theory, developmental psychology, biological approaches, and social bonding. In this sense, it appears that this strand of criminological thought appears to be a serious attempt at theoretical integration, and that is the primary reason for the inclusion of this subsection within the larger section of integrated theories and unique approaches. I view developmental criminology as both and will leave it at that.[3]

The age-crime debate actually sparked renewed interest in a developmental criminology. Developmental criminologists have drawn significantly from research on criminal careers. For example, Rolf Loeber and Marc Le Blanc's (1990) thorough review of the developmental literature and call for a developmental criminology refers to the importance of concepts such as *activation, aggravation,* and *desistance,* which form the core of the criminal career literature. *Activation* refers to the continuity, frequency, and diversity of criminal activities. *Aggravation* involves an increase of seriousness in behavior over time, and *desistance* refers to a decrease in the frequency and specialization of offending as well as a reduction in seriousness of offending (Loeber & Le Blanc, 1990).

As mentioned earlier, developmental criminology draws from a number of other disciplinary and theoretical frameworks. For example, Moffitt's theory (Chapter 32 in this volume) derives from concepts in neuropsychology and developmental psychology. In her article, she argues that those who have behavioral problems as children and engage in delinquent behavior at an early age, whom she calls "life-course-persistent delinquents," differ in a number of important ways from those who begin delinquency in adolescence, whom she calls "adolescence-limited delinquents." Moffitt finds that peer influences play a stronger role in the lives of adolescence-limited delinquents, because these offenders are not likely to continue their delinquent behavior into adulthood. In contrast, the life-course-persistent offenders suffer from antisocial behavioral problems rooted in childhood. These behaviors include low verbal ability, hyperactivity, and impulsive personality.

Generally speaking, there is no uniform model of offending within developmental criminology, or within all of criminology for that matter. Criminologists and others employing this theoretical framework may look at a variety of factors in order to explain crime over the life course, mainly because those factors that influence criminal behavior depend on what stage of the life course a person is in. As the article by Moffitt (Chapter 32, this volume) will demonstrate to readers, there is much overlap in how variables from personality, bonding, learning, and other theories are used in these models. Therefore, the issue that developmental criminology poses for all criminologists is threefold. When analyzing crime and criminality, criminologists should either use several theories in their explanatory model(s) or incorporate these developmental characteristics into any analysis of crime. The third option involves integrating a number of theories into a more powerful explanatory framework.

INTEGRATED APPROACHES

Many criminologists have decried the weaknesses in the current theoretical frameworks. A number of options have been proposed. For example, Bernard, author of Chapter 1 in the first section of this anthology, argued that the way to reduce the number of existing theories and to make scientific progress within the discipline is to falsify the existing theories. If you'll recall, according to this perspective, different theories make different propositions about crime and criminality. These propositions can be tested against one another, leading to determinations about which predictions are consistent with the data and which are not. Theories with inconsistent predictions are said to be falsified and can be discarded. Bernard argued that most criminologists have failed to become engaged with theoretical falsification. Rather, most criminologists continue to focus on the explanatory power of certain frameworks. However, most of the attempts to falsify theories have been unsuccessful.

As a result, a number of criminologists have turned to theoretical integration as a way of limiting the number of theories. If one looks at the disciplinary development of criminology, evidence abounds regarding the oscillation between theoretical polarization and integration. Many of the current theories involve theoretical integration on some level; mainly, this integration involves drawing a few elements from older theoretical models and frameworks in order to develop new approaches or to reconceptualize earlier approaches in a new light. However, of late, new, bolder attempts have been made to integrate a multitude of theoretical approaches under a large theoretical umbrella.

Theoretical integration may seem very attractive because these approaches consider a wide number of different factors from a variety of perspectives. However, there are several problems with theoretical integration, the most significant being that these theories never stand on their own as distinct perspectives. Many theories, including the integrated approaches employed in the articles in this subsection, combine a range of concepts and propositions that span historical periods and other theories outside of the integrated framework. Therefore, all theories are only minimally integrated. Furthermore, theories do not stand alone as mutually exclusive approaches, nor do they work in terms of linear causality. All theories must consider a variety of intervening variables, which form the causal sequence of variables under consideration. For example, a variable such as delinquency can be the dependent variable in one theoretical context and the independent variable in another.

Debates regarding theoretical integration will continue as criminologists consider which approach will provide them with the most explanatory power. In the meantime, the articles in this subsection should provide readers with a taste of earlier attempts at theoretical integration and more contemporary approaches. Two of the articles in this subsection, Thornberry's (Chapter 35) interactional theory, which some consider to be a developmental theory of crime (see Vold, Bernard, & Snipes, 1998), and Elliott, Ageton, and Canter's (Chapter 34, this volume) integrated approach involving strain, control, and social learning perspectives, offer important initial steps toward theoretical development. Walsh's (Chapter 36, this volume) behavior genetics approach provides readers with a glimpse into the most recent theoretical integration in criminology.

NOTES

1 Rational choice theories of the 20th century derive their theoretical base from classical theory of the 18th century. Based on economic principles of costs and benefits, classical theory views individuals as autonomous agents who freely make their own decisions with respect to criminal and noncriminal behavior. Their behavior is controlled by costs, or sanctions, that have been built into the criminal justice system in the form of punishments. These costs are based on the principle of proportionality, whereby the punishment corresponds to the harm caused by the offender in the crime committed. The thrust behind rational choice theory concerns the notion of deterrence. Individuals will be deterred from committing crime (i.e., invoking the free-thinking rational thought process) if they think that the costs (i.e., punishment) outweigh the benefits of committing the crime.

Likewise, developmental theories were originally rooted in the psychological literature. Though developmental criminology seeks to establish itself as a specific theoretical approach within criminology, it draws on some ideas from the developmental psychology literature, namely factors such as antisocial behavior.

2 Hindelang, Gottfredson, and Garofalo (1978) argued that the differences in risk of victimization are related to differences in "lifestyles," which they define in terms of "routine daily activities" consisting of work-related, educational, household, and leisure activities (p. 241). The "lifestyle" approach has numerous similarities to routine activities theory.

3 A major debate regarding the importance of age and the life course in terms of explaining criminality ensued in the mid-1980s, with age and crime at the center of the argument. The debate also involved arguments about *criminal careers,* which refers to the development and continuance of offending over time. Readers who are interested in learning more about this debate and the research that was generated to support either side should turn to Vold et al. (1998) for a general, yet thorough, overview of it.

REFERENCES

Akers, R. (2001). *Criminological theories: Introduction, evaluation, and application* (3rd ed.). Los Angeles: Roxbury.

Cohen, L., & Felson, M. (1979). Social change and crime rate trends: A routine activity approach. *American Sociological Review, 44,* 588-608.

Hindelang, M. J., Gottfredson, M. R., & Garofalo, J. (1978). *Victims of personal crime.* Cambridge, MA: Ballinger.

LaGrange, T. (1999). The impact of neighborhoods, schools, and malls on the spatial distribution of property damage. *Journal of Research in Crime and Delinquency, 36,* 393-422.

Loeber, R., & Le Blanc, M. (1990). *Toward a developmental criminology.* In M. Tonry & N. Morris (Eds.), *Crime and justice: A review of research* (Vol. 12, pp. 375-473). Chicago: University of Chicago Press.

Vold, G. B., Bernard, T. J., & Snipes, J. B. (1998). *Theoretical criminology* (4th ed.). Oxford, UK: Oxford University Press.

30

CRIME AS A RATIONAL CHOICE

DEREK B. CORNISH AND RONALD V. CLARKE

EDITOR'S INTRODUCTION—The rational choice perspective outlined by Cornish and Clarke in their 1986 text, *The Reasoning Criminal: Rational Choice Perspectives on Offending*, synthesizes a variety of criminological theoretical perspectives, namely classical and economic theories of crime, and asserts that "crimes are the result of broadly rationalized choices based on analyses of anticipated costs and benefits" (Cornish & Clarke, 1986, p. vi). Rather than focusing on what makes criminals uniquely different, the theory centers on the similarities between criminals and noncriminals and locates its central focus on the criminal event itself and the situational factors that influence its commission.

The starting point for an analysis of crime from a rational choice perspective are the assumptions that offenders seek to benefit themselves by their criminal behavior; that this process involves the making of decisions and choices, however elementary they may be; and that these processes exhibit a measure of rationality, though the processes may be constrained by limits of time and ability and by the availability of relevant information. From this starting point, Cornish and Clarke argue that the choice process occurs in two major stages.

First, offenders must decide whether they are willing to become involved in crime to satisfy their needs. This factor is explained by the authors' "initial involvement model." Individuals may consider a wide variety of ways of satisfying their needs, and whether they decide to become involved in crime is influenced mainly by their previous learning experiences, including any experiences with crime, contact with law enforcement, moral attitudes, self-perception, and the degree to which they can plan ahead. These learning factors are shaped by various background factors, which include psychological, socialization, and social and demographic aspects of their lives.

Second, once individuals decide whether they will become involved in crime, they need to adopt a crime-specific focus. In other words, they need to decide what offense they will likely commit. This decision is heavily influenced by the individual's current situation. For example, the individual may have a severely pressing need for money and may be out with friends who suggest that they commit a crime. The individual then must select a target for the offenses, such as a residence, and weigh out the costs and benefits (i.e., is someone home or away?). The factors influencing an offender's decision differ dramatically from one situation to another, which is why rational choice theorists argue that a crime-specific model needs to be used.

The third aspect of the rational choice process requires a distinction between criminal involvement and criminal events. Criminal involvement refers to the processes through which individuals initially choose to become involved in particular forms of crime, to continue on this path, and then, later, to desist from crime. Conversely, event decisions are frequently shorter processes, using more limited information relating mainly to the immediate circumstances and situations.

As Cornish and Clarke contend, many of the leading theories of crime have largely ignored those factors that influence a person's decision to commit a particular offense under certain circumstances. In other words, most theories of crime are oriented toward criminal involvement, not event involvement. Therefore, this theory makes an important contribution not only in terms of understanding why certain individuals commit crime under certain circumstances, but also in terms of crime control policies.

The synthesis we suggested, a rational choice perspective on criminal behavior, was intended to locate criminological findings within a framework particularly suitable for thinking about policy relevant research. Its starting point was an assumption that offenders seek to benefit themselves by their criminal behavior; that this involves the making of decisions and of choices, however rudimentary on occasion these processes might be; and that these processes exhibit a measure of rationality, albeit constrained by limits of time and ability and the availability of relevant information. It was recognized that this conception of crime seemed to fit some forms of offending better than others. However, even in the case of offenses that seemed to be pathologically motivated or impulsively executed, it was felt that rational components were also often present and that the identification and description of these might have lessons for crime-control policy.

Second, a crime-specific focus was adopted, not only because different crimes may meet different needs, but also because the situational context of decision making and the information being handled will vary greatly among offenses. To ignore these differences might well be to reduce significantly one's ability to identify fruitful points for intervention (similar arguments have been applied to other forms of "deviant" behavior, such as gambling: cf. Cornish, 1978). A crime-specific focus is likely to involve rather finer distinctions than those commonly made in criminology. For example, it may not be sufficient to divide burglary simply into its residential and commercial forms. It may also be necessary to distinguish between burglaries committed in middle-class suburbs, in public housing, and in wealthy residential enclaves. Empirical studies suggest that the kinds of

individuals involved in these different forms of residential burglary, their motivations, and their methods all vary considerably (cf. Clarke and Hope, 1984, for a review). Similar cases could be made for distinguishing between different forms of robbery, rape, shoplifting, and car theft, to take some obvious cases. (In lay thinking, of course, such distinctions are also often made, as between mugging and other forms of robbery, for example.) A corollary of this requirement is that the explanatory focus of the theory is on crimes, rather than on offenders. Such a focus, we believe, provides a counter weight to theoretical and policy preoccupations with the offender.

Third, it was argued that a decision-making approach to crime requires that a fundamental distinction be made between criminal involvement and criminal events. Criminal involvement refers to the processes through which individuals choose to become initially involved in particular forms of crime, to continue, and to desist. The decision processes in these different stages of involvement will be influenced in each case by a different set of factors and will need to be separately modeled. In the same way, the decision processes involved in the commission of a specific crime (i.e., the criminal event) will utilize their own special categories of information. Involvement decisions are characteristically multistage, extend over substantial periods of time, and will draw upon a large range of information, not all of which will be directly related to the crimes themselves. Event decisions, on the other hand, are frequently shorter processes, utilizing more circumscribed information largely relating to immediate circumstances and situations.

The above points can be illustrated by consideration of some flow diagrams that the editors previously developed (Clarke and Cornish, 1985) to model one specific form of

Cornish, D. B., & Clarke, R. V. (1986). Introduction: Crime as a rational choice. In D. B. Cornish & R. V. Clarke, *The reasoning criminal: Rational choice perspectives on offending*. New York: Springer-Verlag.

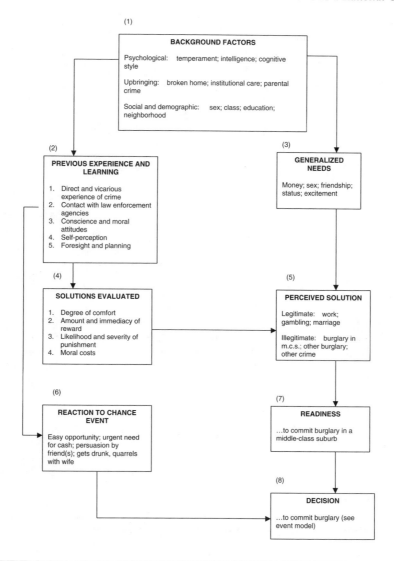

Figure 30.1   Initial Involvement Model (Example: Burglary in a Middle-Class Suburb).
SOURCE: From Clarke, R. V., & Cornish, D. B. (1985). Modeling offenders' decisions:
A framework for research policy. In M. Tonry & N. Morris (Eds.), *Crime and Justice, Vol. 6.*
Chicago, IL: University of Chicago Press. Used with permission.

crime, namely, burglary in a middle-class residential suburb. Figure 30.1, which represents the processes of initial involvement in this form of crime, has two decision points. The first (Box 7) is the individual's recognition of his or her "readiness" to commit the specific offense in order to satisfy certain needs for money, goods, or excitement. The preceding boxes indicate the wide range of factors that bring the individual to this condition. Box 1, in particular, encompasses

the various historical (and contemporaneous) background factors with which traditional criminology has been preoccupied; these have been seen to determine the values, attitudes, and personality traits that dispose the individual to crime. In a rational choice context, however, these factors are reinterpreted as influencing the decisions and judgments that lead to involvement. The second decision (Box 8) actually to commit this form of burglary is the outcome of

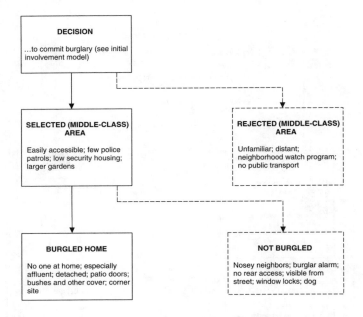

Figure 30.2 Continuing Involvement Model (Example: Burglary in a Middle-Class Suburb).
SOURCE: From Clarke, R. V., & Cornish, D. B. (1985). Modeling offenders' decisions:
A framework for research policy. In M. Tonry & N. Morris (Eds.), *Crime and Justice, Vol. 6.*
Chicago, IL: University of Chicago Press. Used with permission.

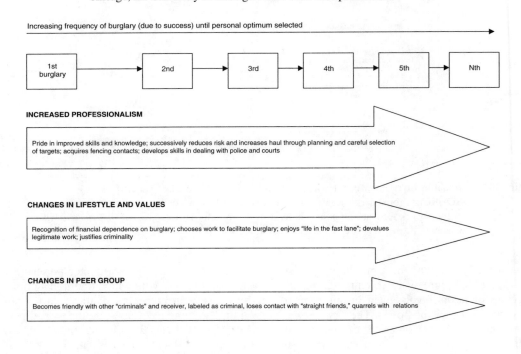

Figure 30.3 Event Model (Example: Burglary in a Middle-Class Suburb).
SOURCE: From Clarke, R. V., & Cornish, D. B. (1985). Modeling offenders' decisions:
A framework for research policy. In M. Tonry & N. Morris (Eds.), *Crime and Justice, Vol. 6.*
Chicago, IL: University of Chicago Press. Used with permission.

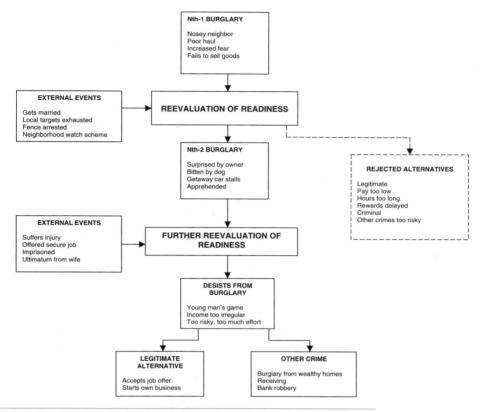

Figure 30.4   Desistance Model (Example: Burglary in a Middle-Class Suburb).
SOURCE: From Clarke, R. V., & Cornish, D. B. (1985). Modeling offenders' decisions:
A framework for research policy. In M. Tonry & N. Morris (Eds.), *Crime and Justice, Vol. 6.*
Chicago, IL: University of Chicago Press. Used with permission.

some chance event, such as an urgent need for cash, which demands action.

Figure 30.2, which is much simpler, depicts the further sequence of decision making that leads to the burglar selecting a particular house. The range of variables influencing this decision sequence is much narrower and reflects the influence of situational factors related to opportunity, effort, and proximal risks. In most cases this decision sequence takes place quite quickly.

Figure 30.3 sketches the classes of variables, relating to changes in the individual's degree of professionalism, peer group, life-style, and values, that influence the constantly reevaluated decision to continue with this form of burglary.

Figure 30.4 illustrates, with hypothetical data, similar reevaluations that may lead to desistance.

In this case, two classes of variables are seen to have a cumulative effect: life-events (such as marriage), and those more directly related to the criminal events themselves.

These, then, are the main features of the framework that was developed out of our review of recent work in a variety of disciplines that have an interest in crime. It differs from most existing formal theories of criminal behavior, however, in a number of respects. It is true that, like many other criminological theories, the rational choice perspective is intended to provide a framework for understanding all forms of crime. Unlike other approaches, however, which attempt to impose a conceptual unity upon divergent criminal behaviors (by subsuming them under more general concepts such as delinquency, deviance, rule breaking, short-run hedonism, criminality, etc.), our rational choice formulation sees these differences as crucial to the tasks of explanation and control. Unlike existing theories, which tend to concentrate on factors disposing individuals to criminal behavior (the initial involvement model), the rational choice approach, in addition, emphasizes subsequent decisions in the offender's career. Again, whereas most existing theories tend to accord little influence to situational variables, the rational choice approach explicitly recognizes their importance in relation to the criminal event and, furthermore, incorporates similar influences on decisions relating to involvement in crime. In consequence, this perspective also recognizes, as do economic and behaviorist theories, the importance of incentives—that is, of rewards and punishments—and hence the role of learning in the criminal career. Finally, the leitmotif encapsulated in the notion of a reasoning offender implies the essentially nonpathological and commonplace nature of much criminal activity.

DISCUSSION QUESTIONS

1. According to the rational choice model, do all offenders employ rational decisions and plan their crimes carefully and thoroughly?

2. Based on the initial involvement model, which factors tend to influence whether an individual will become involved in crime, continue in crime, and then desist from crime?

3. Discuss the importance of Cornish and Clarke's assertion that we need to use a "crime-specific focus" when attempting to describe the costs and benefits of crimes. Select several different crimes and discuss the various costs and benefits the offenders might consider when committing the crimes.

REFERENCE

Cornish, D. B., & Clarke, R. V. (1986). *The reasoning criminal: Rational choice perspectives on offending*. New York: Springer-Verlag.

31

ROUTINE ACTIVITIES AND CRIME PREVENTION IN THE DEVELOPING METROPOLIS

MARCUS FELSON

EDITOR'S INTRODUCTION—This article marks another advance in theoretical integration, but this time, the integrated focus is on ecology and rational choice theories of crime. Here, Marcus Felson, one of the founders of this perspective, outlines the development of the "routine activity theory," which argues that the victim plays an important role in the circumstances surrounding the criminal act. A primary goal of the theory is to identify the environmental triggers that facilitate crime. Specifically, the theory specifies three essential elements that must be present in order for crime to occur successfully: a likely offender, a suitable target, and the absence of a capable guardian against crime. Additionally, the theory considers how everyday life assembles these three elements in a particular geographic place and moment in time. Finally, the theory may help explain why the increased production of lightweight durable goods and the various activities that shifted people away from the family and the home may have led to higher crime rates in the 1960s and 1970s.

As Felson notes, modern societies invite high crime rates by offering to potential offenders numerous illegal opportunities. In the article, Felson demonstrates how city planners and managers can divert the flow of opportunistic offenders away from crime targets by manipulating the environment. He bases his arguments on a number of important points. First, Felson suggests that routine activity analysis and human ecology offer a "science of surprise." This concept leads to the principle of "systematic accident," which maintains that many surprises are structured and systematic through the physical world. Therefore, in terms of crime prevention, Felson argues that by engineering bodily convergences (i.e., manipulating the physical environment so as to minimize the number of bodies at a certain place at a certain time), crime rates could effectively decline.

Implementation of this principle requires knowledge of the urban landscape. Here, Felson reminds readers of the important contributions of the ecology school, which found that high rates of delinquency tended to cluster around urban centers. However, with modernization and the development and increased use of the automobile, the boundaries of physical entities such as communities seem to have become less clear. Felson provides an informative discussion of the evolution of the city street and the manner in which city streets are used in terms of people's access to various activities. He finds that city streets provide communities with arterial substance in terms of getting people to their jobs, homes, and consumer centers, but city streets are the offenders' pathways to crime as well.

Recognizing the form that this new urban landscape was taking, urban planners began to build their urban centers, facilities, and corporations in unique manners. Felson suggests that managers and city planners can implement a variety of strategies in order to prevent crime. Some of these strategies include increased surveillance (informal supervision); limiting pedestrian access to certain streets; separating commercial from residential uses; blocking access from open land; arranging apartment doors and windows to increase safety; favoring pedestrian overpasses, not subways; keeping schools visible from buildings serving adults; and encouraging resident caretakers in schools.

Routine activities approaches have much promise for the study of all types of crime in all types of urban, suburban, and rural areas. The theory provides important insight to the issue of crime prevention and should be a viable source of information for city planners as well as criminal justice officials and policymakers.

Pan was the humble Greco-Roman god of the woods, fields, and flocks. Originally a local deity who wandered the earth making love to the Dryads, Pan became the personification of nature and god of earthy realities. Following "Pan's criterion," criminologists can pay close attention to tangible terrestrial processes.

The "routine activity approach to crime rate analysis" (Cohen & Felson, 1979) does just that. (1) It specifies three earthy elements of crime: a likely offender, a suitable target, and the absence of a capable guardian against crime. (2) It considers how everyday life assembles these three elements in space and time. (3) It shows that a proliferation of lightweight durable goods and a dispersion of activities away from family and household could account quite well for the crime wave in the United States in the 1960s and 1970s, without fancier explanations. Indeed, modern society invites high crime rates by offering a multitude of illegal opportunities.

Despite recent declines in the proportion of the population in prime-crime ages (due to the aging of the baby boom), and despite increasing strictness of the criminal justice system, official crime rates have gone back up recently in the United States. These increments have a suspicious correspondence to the widespread marketing of light and valuable video cassette recorders. Moreover, evidence continues to indicate that, at least for recent decades, an improved economy tends to increase crime rates by providing more things to steal and more activities exposing person and property to illegal attack (Felson and Cohen, 1981). The routine activity approach offers the best explanation for the otherwise unforeseen upsurge, giving criminologists reason to keep tabs on metropolitan change. This paper discusses some important metropolitan trends which offer new opportunities to prevent crime. . . .

CRIME TYPES AND REQUIREMENTS

Crime has been classified in many ways, but seldom in terms of the earthy tasks and specific interdependence it requires. From this viewpoint, there are at least four types of crime (Felson, 1983): (1) The exploitative (or predatory) offense requires that at least one person wrongly take or damage the person or property of another. (2) The mutualistic offense (such as gambling or prostitution) links two or more illegal parties acting in complementary roles. (3) Competitive violations (such as fights) involve two illegal parties acting in the same role, usually a physical struggle against one another. (4) An individualistic offense is a lonely illegal act (such as solo drug use or suicide).

Although the original routine activity approach applied only to exploitative offenses, its reasoning can be extended to all four types of lawbreaking. Each type usually requires that certain minimal elements converge in space and time. Prostitute must meet john away from police and spouse. Fighters must fight without peacemakers. Suicides must avoid meddlers. Predatory violations require the offender, target, and absent guardian.

A fourth element applies to exploitative violations, also playing a role in the other types of

Felson, M. (1987). Routine activities and crime prevention in the developing metropolis. *Criminology, 25,* 911-931.

crime: the absence of an "intimate handler" (Felson, 1986). Although some offenders may have no social bonds (hence are not subject to informal social control), other offenders are "handled," having a social bond to a parent or some other "intimate handler" who is able to "seize the handle" and impose informal social control. Unfortunately for crime victims, handled offenders can evade their intimate handlers, thus avoiding informal social control for many hours each day. This evasion links routine activities to informal social control. As Hirschi (1969) noted, social bonds prevent delinquent behavior; yet, such prevention is difficult to accomplish by remote control. Indeed, informal social control is often carried out when youths (handled potential offenders) are within sight of their parents (intimate handlers). Felson and Gottfredson (1984) offer evidence of a major dispersion of adolescent activities away from parents and other adults, including strong declines in the probability of having family meals together, with dramatic increases in the tendency to stay out late with other teenagers.

In general, a potential offender must first shake loose from parent or handler, then find a target for crime unmonitored by a guardian. The next section examines offender routines relevant to seizing criminal opportunities.

OFFENDER ROUTINES

If offenders were well informed, forward looking, and unrelenting, crime prevention would be very tough indeed. The current paper assumes the contrary. This section considers the earthy rules of offender activity.

We begin with Zipf's (1950) "Principle of Least Effort," which states that people tend to find the shortest route, spend the least time, and seek the easiest means to accomplish something. Least effort means not wasting calories or time, not travelling forever to get someplace. Based on this principle, geographers and others can predict a good deal of human physical behavior from proximity and available routes. If offenders travel minimal distances and often carry out illegal activities while en route to other ones, then their routines will set the stage for the illegal opportunities which come their way. If the criminal seizes the most convenient and obvious target, using lazy reasoning and taking easy

action, this leaves no dramatic challenge for Mr. Sherlock Holmes. Although crime victims normally expend no effort *aiming* to be victimized, their exposures to risk are also subject to calculation.

The Principle of Least Effort leads to the Principle of the Most Obvious. According to this second principle, people (including offenders) rely on ready information, including sense data. Thus, the imperfect shopper picks the best buy right under his nose, missing a better buy in small print in another aisle. She picks the best store on the main street but misses a still better store on a side street. The reasoning criminal (Cornish & Clarke, 1986) finds an interesting target on the route home from school, neglecting better targets not far from that route. The thief picks the flashiest car; the corner house; the shiniest bicycle. Even pains avoided are those most obvious and proximate: a slap in the face, a punch in the nose, a dirty look from a passerby who might summon the police. (We can expect the offender to weigh flashy car against nosy neighbor, but is he really likely to consider threats by distant courts or legislatures?)

This second principle leads to the quick risk corollary, namely, that the offender tends to expose himself to risk for very little time over very little space. This makes the risk seem small because it is over in a flash. The child who drops a cookie on the floor picks it up immediately so that it still seems safe to eat. The driver who cuts in front of your car risks your life and his for but a moment. The trespasser takes a few short steps onto dangerous turf. One man steals one pass at another man's wife. Each forbidden pleasure tempts a quick dart, puff, snort, or grab, a short detour from a safe route. Even a long visit to an illegal house can be covered with fast entry through the back door.

SYSTEMATIC ACCIDENT

. . . . Routine activity analysis and human ecology in general offer such a science of surprise, since events which shock the victim can be collected and analyzed statistically by an outside observer and explained in terms of other activities. This leads to the principle of *systematic accident,* which states that many surprises are structured via the physical world. Systematic accident applies both to the crime victim's shock and the offender's windfall.

How can sporadic events be systematic? . . . . Just as lions look for deer near their watering hole, criminal offenders disproportionately find victims in certain settings or high-risk occupations (Block, Felson, & Block, 1985). Similarly, a professional sports event sets the stage for nearby traffic jams and car breakins. A convergence of picnickers helps feed neighboring insects. A convention supplies visitors to local art museums and massage parlors. Indeed, some of the principles of systematic accident are so general that they apply as well to volcanic eruptions as to criminal events (Felson, 1980, 1981). This is why criminology is partly a physical science, explaining how bodies move, how they mix, and how their mixtures produce reactions, even explosions not possible when they were separate.

By engineering bodily convergences, crime prevention can be effected. One of the most important principles for understanding such sociophysical processes is urbanization.

URBAN PHYSICAL STRUCTURES

For traditional urban ecologists, the local urban community was the basic unit of daily interaction, except for the important daily trip to the place of employment. The latter was contained in either the industrial zone or the Central Business District (CBD). People walked and used public transit, relying upon convenient community institutions. Neighborhoods covered far less area than what we call a community today, and neighborhood schools and shops were much smaller and nearer. Delinquency clustered near the industrial zone. Although sometimes rampant, crime was usually contained.

In the past three decades, the automobile and truck greatly dispersed metropolitan residence, work, schooling, shopping, and leisure. The dissipation of the CBD and the traditional industrial zone complicates urban ecology. Cars cross traditional community boundaries in a flash. The traditional notion of a city as a collection of communities is greatly strained when people can live here, work there, and shop yonder. Friends can visit one another after a short drive, not needing to rely upon a local community for daily sustenance. Commuters no longer head toward the urban core, as industry and shopping, too, disperse to suburbs and beyond. Years after males

gained automobility, females often remained housewives, keeping localism alive for a few extra decades. Subsequent increases in female employment and automobility freed women from their own communities, which were no longer the unit of daily sustenance save for children. Even the young are increasingly schooled and transported elsewhere. In light of these facts, a new ecology of crime is required for an age of automobility. Yet, urban ecologists cling to the old urban image, partly from nostalgia, partly for want of new ideas, and partly because traditional communities never seem to die completely. Meanwhile, new suburbs adopt old communal names and facades for marketing purposes, easily fooling those who are too young to remember what a real pedestrian community was like.

How can one describe a new physical entity which seems to have no boundaries? Many geographers have put mathematics to good use for describing metropolitan spatial behavior. Yet, one still needs to know what replaced the "community." Does some other bounded entity mediate between the individual and the modern metropolis? To answer this question, one can turn to Jacobs's (1961) classic work, *The Death and Life of Great American Cities*. Jacobs hated the suburbanized metropolis, which widened streets for autos and narrowed sidewalks. By killing pedestrian traffic, American cities undermined community life. Jacobs anticipated the crime wave which followed.

On the positive side (to depart from Jacobs), automobiles and roadways give people more choice, more nonlocal access, hence reducing the tyranny of the neighborhood. For better or worse, the modern metropolis provides new access to households, businesses, industries, schools, and places of leisure. People circulate over greater distances, gaining their sustenance in a new way. In effect, the city as a collection of neighborhoods gives way to the metropolis as a collection of buildings linked by automotive streets into a vast sociocirculatory system.

City streets are not new, but their function has changed. The world of pedestrians was a world of shortcuts, where a straight line offered the shortest route between two points. . . . The street is the core of the sociocirculatory system linking various buildings; people, equipment and supplies move via streets from one building to another, often several miles away. Although we are accustomed to think of streets as "outside," they might as well be inside; flanked by curbs and buildings, they impair the freedom of the great outdoors. One's home or business is an appendage to the street. If one's home burns down, this will probably affect one's neighbors only while the street is blocked by fire trucks. Because this sociocirculatory system leads so far so quickly, internal community interaction declines, although net movement increases. One cannot rely upon the "natural" community areas, on immediate proximity, as the basis for symbiosis. Families, friendships, and businesses may still thrive, but they use streets and automobiles in so doing, as people, equipment, and supplies circulate quickly. The Principle of Least Effort has new consequences when the only effort needed is stepping on the gas pedal. . . .

Streets not only provide the means for drawing sustenance from an urban environment, but also constitute its organ of growth. In a world of pedestrians, homes may precede streets; but in a world of cars, streets precede or accompany the construction of homes, businesses, and even parks. Few North Americans will buy a home or business without adequate parking and street access at the outset. Few will patronize a business or a forest preserve lacking automotive convenience. Even backpackers drive their cars to the foot of the trail. Indeed, modern North American growth is connective growth, with streets extending outwards from existing cities, allowing new units to append themselves. Sometimes large streets are constructed first, followed by small; sometimes small streets spread first, later widened into or supplemented by large ones. In either case, each new unit must connect to the larger sociocirculatory system before it can come to life.

This pattern of sustenance and growth can be dubbed the Great Metropolitan Reef. Each home and business clings to this metroreef like coral, gaining sustenance from the street-flows of people, equipment, and supplies. The metroreef proliferates, organizing and sustaining daily life for a vast array of human activities. Young delinquents flow rather freely about the metroreef, drawing illegal sustenance readily from its rich stores and routine activities. Will the reef simply continue to grow or will the metropolis evolve into a new phase?

METROREEF TO METROQUILT: THE ROLE OF FACILITIES

An important new urban form has emerged in recent decades. Business developers have begun to take care of sewers, sidewalks, streets, and security for a fee (Stenning & Shearing, 1980). An early example of this phenomenon was the shopping center, whose developers provided member businesses a package of many services: parking, security, utilities, and (they hoped) a crowd of big spenders. If all went well, the developer made a profit and the member businesses were satisfied with services rendered. A good word for such a setup is *facility*. Its Latin root is *facil* (meaning easy); the facility makes it easy for shoppers to shop and merchants to sell; for offices to get work done; for owners to have time to tend their own business; for people to park and feel safe.

The shopping center has been followed by other important types of facilities which, at least in southern California, are changing the urban landscape. Each development links several independent businesses or departments into a single territorial complex, offering facility management services. The condominium unites several owned apartments, providing maintenance, parking, and security for common rooms or yards, with moderate levels of privacy. The "smart" office building or office condominium provides financial and computer services, telecommunications, energy-efficient utilities, and security. The "mini-mall" assembles five to ten retailers with a parking lot in front, subject to routine informal security protection from onlookers. The industrial park unites several industrial facilities, perhaps offering food service, parking, utilities, communication, and a few trees and sculptures. The mobile home park offers hookups, landscaping, and pathways. The college or hospital campus joins several organizational functions, providing parking, security, and landscaping. The Los Angeles school district campus unites elementary, junior high, senior high, and adult school on a single site. The private recreation facility provides pool, weightroom, lockers, and parking. The public recreation facility offers baseball, basketball, parking, and picnicking. In general, these facilities attempt to draw all the benefits they can from the metroreef while trying to limit litter, crime, and extraneous traffic by privatizing internal traffic. Recent facilities developers are combining two or more activities, such as office space, hotels, homes, and apartments. Some include child care services. Although the apartment facility and feudal manor go back many centuries, today's facility serves without necessarily providing a community. This noncommunal symbiosis is an innovative way to provide services and protection in a dispersed metropolis, representing an important shift in the organization of routine activities. . . .

Why are modern developers so inclined to take over so many municipal functions at their own expense? Sometimes, they are compelled to do so by local authorities. Sometimes, unprofitable services draw profitable customers. Sometimes, customers pay extra for special services. Perhaps they are dissatisfied with government services. Perhaps their fear of crime is greater than before. Parking is tight. Land is more scarce, and that available has to be carved up more carefully. Those tired of time spent on the freeway may sacrifice privacy for convenience or seek to give up lawn care. A single provider may improve telecommunications and other services. In any case, one sees a growth of facilities in Los Angeles and some other parts of North America.

By taking on some new forms and increasing its share of the ecosystem, the facility can break the continuous extension of the metroreef. To be sure, today's metropolis mixes community, street, and facility. A majority of urban units continue to have their own direct hookup to the metroreef, while those facilities which exist merely attach to the much larger metroreef. Yet, urban specialists should begin to ponder whether the metropolis will become a collection of facilities rather than of communities!

How can facilities squeeze out the existing stand-alone units to transform the metroreef into something new? (1) Sometimes a university or hospital campus swallows up nearby housing like an amoeba digesting a food particle. They may bulldoze and rebuild, or simply convert the acquired property to their own uses, but the point is that facilities can spread. (2) Although facilities may begin at the edge of town, where land is vacant, the outward movement of industry and business may place them increasingly at the core

rather than the periphery of daily productive activity. (3) Cities can quickly revitalize an old area by using their rights of eminent domain to clear the space, then inviting facilities to reclaim and rebuild. (4) Sometimes stand-alone units band together to form a facility. . . .

Thus, one imagines a new metropolitan form: the Great Metropolitan Quilt, a patchwork of coterminous facilities intervening between homes, businesses, and the larger society. This metroquilt would divide urban space among a large set of corporations, whose facilities managers would be responsible for organizing everyday movements, including security.

This metroquilt would have a special sociocirculatory system, including two types of trips: those within facilities and those between facilities via boulevards and freeways. Within facilities, people would walk, drive, take elevators, escalators, and moving sidewalks. Between facilities, they would drive from the parking structure of the origin facility to that of the destination facility. All parking and walking would occur within a facility, unless a car breaks down. Public arteries would remain in the interstices, the last vestige of local government management responsibility. The evolution from metroreef to metroquilt would vastly alter the role of the police, as well as the ecological basis of lawbreaking. . . .

A New Role for Facilities

A facility has a distinct crime prevention advantage over the average street: it can limit access and direct flows of people. Facilities can remove many routine activities from the public domain, giving a business or corporation a chance to make a profit selling safety to the public or enhancing security for its own employees or property. Victims of street crime cannot ordinarily sue their city for negligence. However, victims of crime within private facilities are tempted to bring such lawsuits, compelling facility managers and their insurers to consider crime prevention.

If the metroreef gives way to the metroquilt, the facility would become the main organizational tool for crime prevention. That formal organizations take responsibility for large swaths of urban turf is encouraging for those interested in crime reduction. When the parking, paths, and trees are managed by a specific suable entity, the incentive for serious crime prevention emerges. Indeed, the shift from community to street to facility as the main unit of ecological organization implies a shift in crime prevention. When community is dominant, largely unaided informal social control reigns. When streets are dominant, crime control is largely charged to hit-or-miss public policing, diluted by suburban sprawl. When facilities become dominant, architects, security planners, and facilities managers become the central actors in the crime prevention process, for better or for worse.[1]

Private organizations cannot guarantee protection for their own property, much less anybody else's, simply by hiring guards. Large-scale organizations have difficulty monitoring their own employees, who can easily be tempted by "inside jobs." For this reason, those organizing crime prevention efforts need to think in terms of physical design and kinetic management. Facilities designers should attempt to divert flows of likely offenders away from likely targets, or else contain these flows within limited areas which are easily monitored. Facilities designers should also consider natural informal controls, working indirectly and inadvertently to control the flows of offenders and targets. Besides, what manager wants to pay wages when surveillance can be engineered almost for free?

Such criminokinetic analysis must be more sophisticated than posting rules and demanding compliance. As an example, consider a note placed on a car by authorities in a local public park: "Please do not angle park. Park vertically." Since the white lines were clearly drawn for angle parking, the authorities in effect designed a violation, then appealed to thousands of patrons one-by-one not to carry it out. Had they drawn the lines vertically in the first place, there would have been no need to struggle with the public about their new regulation. Similarly, if one designs products which seem to say "take me," yards which invite trespassing, and unsupervised areas which welcome intrusions, should one be surprised about what follows?

If the routines and routings of young people keep them systematically under informal supervision and away from interesting crime targets,

youths will be less likely to commit crimes. Thus, crime control must take into account the natural flows of people and things and try to guide them so that offenders and targets seldom converge in the absence of handlers and guardians, respectively. Crime control efforts must bear in mind that offenders seek quick risks and follow obvious routes. Similarly, potential victims of crime can be guided and channeled in their daily movements so as to minimize their risk. Just as unseen traffic engineers do us all a good deed by designing streets and intersections to minimize citizen danger, so can architects, planners, and facilities managers quietly and unobtrusively help prevent crime victimization. Alternatively, poor planning and management delivers crime right to the doorstep and offers ready temptation to youths.

A number of important ideas about flow management are assembled by Poyner (1983): privatizing residential streets; limiting pedestrian access; separating residential from commercial uses; limiting access to the rear of houses; blocking access from open land; arranging apartment doors and windows carefully; allocating residential child density; dispersing market facilities; favoring pedestrian overpasses, not subways; keeping schools visible from buildings serving adults; keeping school buildings compact; encouraging resident caretakers in schools. Brantingham and Brantingham (1987) report several ideas and experiences in crime prevention planning: segregating schools from self-service stores; channeling a youth hangout within view of an all-night taxistand; letting the recreation center caretaker live on the premises; building crime-impact planning into early design stages; in a high-rise building for the elderly, placing the recreation room on the first floor with direct view of the doors; regulating flows of adolescents by placement of fast food establishments and electronic arcades. Wise (1987) adds other ideas: minimizing obstructions and using bright pastel paints to protect flows through parking structures; carefully positioning bank tellers, doors, and flows of customers to discourage robberies; localizing taverns to create informal social control; providing specific crime prevention training for facilities managers.

Other ideas include designing public parks and parking lots in long strips to maximize visibility from those passing by, doing away with open-campus designs, and using telecommunications and computers to reduce the size of offices and to develop "scattered site" business practices. Facilities incorporating many young males will have special problems, but even these can be reduced in size and designed for maximal inadvertent adult surveillance. The United States pattern of several thousand students per secondary school is especially suspect. Facilities planning and management surely deserve consideration as a tool of future crime reduction. As the metroquilt grows, it may become the only tool available.

DISCUSSION QUESTIONS

1. What does a "routine activity approach to crime rate analysis" specify? How might it help city planners and managers battle the rise of crime in their communities and places of business?

2. What does Felson mean by the terms *systematic accident, metroreef,* and *metroquilt*? What role do they play in affecting crime rates through physical manipulation of the environment?

3. Discuss Felson's new role for facilities. Give some examples of the things facilities can do to prevent crime.

4. Has your college campus taken a routine activity approach to crime rate analysis and reduction on campus? Specifically, what things have college officials done to manipulate the campus environment to lessen crime rates?

NOTE

1 The growth of facilities has special significance for the inequality of security. Today's metroreef probably enhances crime risk for everyone, but especially for those who live within range of many offenders. On the other hand, the modern sociocirculatory system makes it difficult to purchase true security, since some offenders can easily find their way to wealthy victims and have an incentive to do so. Nice neighborhoods are not necessarily very secure. On the other hand, a walled facility with a 24-hour doorkeeper can protect those able to pay for it. The growth of facilities may render security more a matter of supply and demand in the future than it is today (Birkbeck, 1985; Cook, 1987).

Some facilities will undoubtedly protect themselves, not clients. For example, shopping centers sometimes patrol inside to protect their merchants, while neglecting the parking lot vulnerabilities after the customer has paid for the goods and left. Security vendors are often more interested in selling hardware than more intricate and comprehensive crime prevention. Facilities may offer what Waller (1979) calls a "security illusion," namely conspicuous locks and alarms. Some facilities (such as schools and housing for the poor) may tolerate high crime rates rather than admitting that they have a problem. However, knowledge of environmental crime control is growing (compare Clarke, 1983; Brantingham & Brantingham, 1984; Poyner, 1983). This subjects administrators charged with negligence to the embarrassing testimony of expert crime-prevention witnesses in courts of law. It can also provide course materials for training the next generation of crime prevention officers.

32

ADOLESCENCE-LIMITED AND LIFE-COURSE-PERSISTENT ANTISOCIAL BEHAVIOR

A Developmental Taxonomy

TERRIE E. MOFFITT

EDITOR'S INTRODUCTION—In her article, Terrie E. Moffitt asserts that there are two major types of antisocial persons: a small group of individuals who consistently engage in a high rate of antisocial behaviors, whom she calls "life-course-persistent" offenders, and a much larger group who confine their antisocial behavior to the adolescent years (or "adolescent-limited" offenders). She then proceeds to explicate her theory of antisocial behavior for each group of offenders. Although this article could be categorized within the biological and psychological perspectives, the theoretical premises of the article best represent an approach in the criminological literature that has received increasingly more attention over the past decade, *developmental criminology*. Additionally, this article represents a very thorough analysis and integration of biological, psychological, and sociological variables in the criminological literature.

The main premise of Moffitt's theory is her proposition that persistent antisocial behavior among adolescents results from the interaction between individual "neuropsychological vulnerabilities" and "criminogenic environments." Moffitt begins her analysis with a description of the various traits that predispose some adolescents to persistent delinquent behavior, and she argues that these traits are linked to biological factors and the childhood familial environment. She then goes on to explain the manner in which these individual traits and environmental factors influence one another. In certain situations, the persistent delinquent behavior escalates over time. A negative family environment will sometimes exacerbate existing negative traits, and, reciprocally, these negative traits often increase the likelihood of being exposed to negative environments. By adolescence, these traits and behaviors become so ingrained that any change in behavior is arduous at best. According to Moffitt, at this stage of development, a pattern of persistent antisocial behavior has been firmly incorporated into that adolescent's life.

Moffitt's research on the larger group of offenders, the "adolescent-limited" offenders, suggests that this type of antisocial behavior is not generated by individual traits. Rather, it is motivated by the gap between biological maturity and social maturity; it is learned from antisocial models who are easily mimicked; and it is sustained according to the reinforcement principles of learning theory. Therefore, this behavior typically disappears in early adulthood.

Moffitt's theory represents an emerging theoretical trend in criminology that describes the various ways in which individual traits and the environment may interact with one another to produce persistent antisocial behavior. Furthermore, Moffitt's approach provides important insight into the patterns of antisocial behavior that persist over the life course. Her work has subsequently contributed greatly to the recent work on behavior genetics by Walsh (Chapter 36 in this volume). Other developmental and integrated approaches in this volume include the articles by Loeber and Stouthamer-Loeber (Chapter 33, this volume) and Thornberry (Chapter 35, this volume). As Moffitt indicates, most criminological theories tend to emphasize crime causality, or explanation, rather than patterns of offending over the life course. As the other works in this volume demonstrate, her findings regarding persistent antisocial behavior have received wide empirical support and continue to do so.

There are marked individual differences in the stability of antisocial behavior. Many people behave antisocially, but their antisocial behavior is temporary and situational. In contrast, the antisocial behavior of some people is very stable and persistent. Temporary, situational antisocial behavior is quite common in the population, especially among adolescents. Persistent, stable antisocial behavior is found among a relatively small number of males whose behavior problems are also quite extreme. The central tenet of this paper is that temporary versus persistent antisocial persons constitute two qualitatively distinct types of persons. In particular, I suggest that juvenile delinquency conceals two qualitatively distinct categories of individuals, each in need of its own distinct theoretical explanation. . . .

For delinquents whose criminal activity is confined to the adolescent years, the causal factors may be proximal, specific to the period of adolescent development, and theory must account for the *dis*continuity in their lives. In contrast, for persons whose adolescent delinquency is merely one inflection in a continuous lifelong antisocial course, a theory of antisocial behavior must locate its causal factors early in their childhoods and must explain the continuity in their troubled lives.

AGE AND ANTISOCIAL BEHAVIOR

. . . . But whence the increase in the prevalence of offenders? One possibility is that some phenomenon unique to adolescent development causes throngs of new adolescent offenders to temporarily join the few stable antisocial individuals in their delinquent ways. Figure 32.1 depicts the typological thesis to be argued here. A small group of persons is shown engaging in antisocial behavior of one sort or another at every stage of life. I have labeled these persons *life-course-persistent* to reflect the continuous course of their antisocial behavior. A larger group of persons fills out the age-crime curve with crime careers of shorter duration. I have labeled these persons *adolescence-limited* to reflect their more temporary involvement in antisocial behavior. Thus, timing and duration of the course of antisocial involvement are the defining features in the natural histories of the two proposed types of offenders. . . .

I [argue] that juvenile delinquency conceals two categories of people. A very large group participates in antisocial behavior during adolescence. A much smaller group, who continues serious antisocial behavior throughout adulthood, is the same group whose antisocial behavior was stable across the years from early childhood. The categories remain hypothetical types, because no longitudinal study has yet repeatedly measured antisocial behavior in a representative sample of the same individuals from preschool to midlife. I describe in the next sections the two hypothetical types of antisocial youth: life-course-persistent and adolescence-limited. I argue that the two groups differ in etiology, developmental course, prognosis, and, importantly, classification of their behavior as either pathological or normative. The goal of this chapter is to proffer a description of the two types in the form of a set of testable predictions.

Moffitt, T. E. (1993). Adolescent-limited and life-course-persistent antisocial behavior: A developmental taxonomy. *Psychological Review, 100,* 674-701.

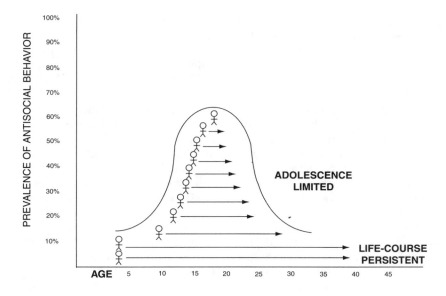

Figure 32.1 Hypothetical Illustration of the Changing Prevalence of Participation in Antisocial Behavior Across the Life Course. (The solid line represents the known curve of crime over age. The arrows represent the duration of participation in antisocial behavior by individuals.)

LIFE-COURSE-PERSISTENT ANTISOCIAL BEHAVIOR

Continuity of Antisocial Behavior Defined

As implied by the label, continuity is the hallmark of the small group of life-course-persistent antisocial persons. Across the life course, these individuals exhibit changing manifestations of antisocial behavior: biting and hitting at age 4, shoplifting and truancy at age 10, selling drugs and stealing cars at age 16, robbery and rape at age 22, and fraud and child abuse at age 30; the underlying disposition remains the same, but its expression changes form as new social opportunities arise at different points in development. This pattern of continuity across age is matched also by cross-situational consistency: Life-course-persistent antisocial persons lie at home, steal from shops, cheat at school, fight in bars, and embezzle at work (Farrington, 1991; Loeber, 1982; Loeber & Baicker-McKee, 1989; Robins, 1966, 1978; White et al., 1990). . . .

Although reports of the continuity of antisocial styles from childhood to young adulthood abound, the outcomes of antisocial individuals during midlife have seldom been examined. The pattern of official crime over age (see Figure 32.1)

. . . implies that criminal offending all but disappears by midlife, but there is no reason to expect that life-course-persistents miraculously assume prosocial tendencies after an antisocial tenure of several decades. Indeed, criminal psychopaths decrease their number of arrestable offenses at about age 40, but the constellation of antisocial personality traits described by Cleckley (1976) persists in male samples at least until age 69 (Harpur & Hare, 1991). . . .

Beginnings: Neuropsychological Risk for Difficult Temperament and Behavioral Problems

If some individuals' antisocial behavior is stable from pre-school to adulthood as the data imply, then investigators are compelled to look for its roots early in life, in factors that are present before or soon after birth. It is possible that the etiological chain begins with some factor capable of producing individual differences in the neuropsychological functions of the infant nervous system. Factors that influence infant neural development are myriad, and many of them have been empirically linked to antisocial outcomes.

One possible source of neuropsychological variation that is linked to problem behavior is disruption in the ontogenesis of the fetal brain. . . . There is good evidence that children who ultimately become persistently antisocial do suffer from deficits in neuropsychological abilities. I have elsewhere reviewed the available empirical and theoretical literatures; the link between neuropsychological impairment and antisocial outcomes is one of the most robust effects in the study of antisocial behavior (Moffitt, 1990b; Moffitt & Henry, 1991; see also Hirschi & Hindelang, 1977). Two sorts of neuropsychological deficits are empirically associated with antisocial behavior: verbal and "executive" functions. The verbal deficits of antisocial children are pervasive, affecting receptive listening and reading, problem solving, expressive speech and writing, and memory. In addition, executive deficits produce what is sometimes referred to as a comportmental learning disability (Price, Daffner, Stowe, & Mesulam, 1990), including symptoms such as inattention and impulsivity. . . . The evidence is strong that neuropsychological deficits are linked to the kind of antisocial behavior that begins in childhood and is sustained for lengthy periods. In a series of articles (Moffitt, 1990a; Moffitt & Henry, 1989; Moffitt & Silva, 1988b), I have shown that poor verbal and executive functions are associated with antisocial behavior, if it is extreme and persistent. . . . [L]ongitudinal studies suggest that neuropsychological dysfunctions that manifest themselves as poor scores on tests of language and self-control—and as the inattentive, overactive, and impulsive symptoms of ADHD—are linked with the early childhood emergence of aggressive antisocial behavior and with its subsequent persistence.

Neuropsychological Variation and the "Difficult" Infant.

Before describing how neuropsychological variation might constitute risk for antisocial behavior, it is useful to define what is meant here by neuropsychological. By combining *neuro* with *psychological,* I refer broadly to the extent to which anatomical structures and physiological processes within the nervous system influence psychological characteristics such as temperament, behavioral development, cognitive abilities, or all three. For example, individual variation in brain function may engender differences between children in activity level, emotional reactivity, or self-regulation (temperament);

speech, motor coordination, or impulse control (behavioral development); and attention, language, learning, memory, or reasoning (cognitive abilities).

Children with neurological difficulties severe enough to constitute autism, severe physical handicap, or profound mental retardation are usually identified and specially treated by parents and professionals. However, other infants have subclinical levels of problems that affect the difficulty of rearing them, variously referred to as difficult temperament, language or motor delays, or mild cognitive deficits. Compromised neuropsychological functions are associated with a variety of consequences for infants' cognitive and motor development as well as for their personality development (Rothbart & Derryberry, 1981). Toddlers with subtle neuropsychological deficits may be clumsy and awkward, overactive, inattentive, irritable, impulsive, hard to keep on schedule, delayed in reaching developmental mile stones, poor at verbal comprehension, deficient at expressing themselves, or slow at learning new things (Rutter, 1977, 1983; Thomas & Chess, 1977; Wender, 1971). . . .

Child-Environment Covariation in Nature: A Source of Interactional Continuity.

Up to this point, I have emphasized in this chapter the characteristics of the developing child as if environments were held constant. Unfortunately, children with cognitive and temperamental disadvantages are not generally born into supportive environments, nor do they even get a fair chance of being randomly assigned to good or bad environments. [M]ost low-birth weight infants are not born into intact, middle-class families. Vulnerable infants are disproportionately found in environments that will not be ameliorative because many sources of neural maldevelopment co-occur with family disadvantage or deviance.

Indeed, because some characteristics of parents and children tend to be correlated, parents of children who are at risk for antisocial behavior often inadvertently provide their children with criminogenic environments (Sameroff & Chandler, 1975). The intergenerational transmission of severe antisocial behavior has been carefully documented in a study of three generations (Huesmann et al., 1984). . . . [Studies have shown that] parents of children who are difficult to manage often lack the necessary psychological and physical resources to cope constructively with a difficult child (Scarr & McCartney, 1983; Snyder & Patterson, 1987). For example, temperamental traits such as activity level and irritability are known to be partly heritable (Plomin, Chipuer, & Loehlin, 1990). This suggests that children whose hyperactivity and angry outbursts might be curbed by firm discipline will tend to have parents who are inconsistent disciplinarians; the parents tend to be impatient and irritable too. The converse is also true: Empirical evidence has been found for a relationship between variations in parents' warmth and infants' easiness (Plomin, Chipuer, & Loehlin, 1990).

Parents and children also resemble each other on cognitive ability. The known heritability of measured intelligence (Plomin, 1990; Loehlin, 1989) implies that children who are most in need of remedial cognitive stimulation will have parents who may be least able to provide it. Moreover, parents' cognitive abilities set limits on their own educational and occupational attainment (Barrett & Depinet, 1991). As one consequence, families whose members have below-average cognitive capacities will often be least able financially to obtain professional interventions or optimal remedial schooling for their at-risk children. Even the social and structural aspects of the environment may be stacked against children who enter the world at risk. Plomin and Bergeman (1990) have shown that there are genetic components to measures that are commonly used by developmental psychologists to assess socialization environments. . . .

Importantly, although examples from behavior genetics research have been cited . . . , the perverse compounding of children's vulnerabilities with their families' imperfections does not require that the child's neuropsychological risk arise from any genetic disposition. In fact, for my purposes, it is immaterial whether parent-child similarities arise from shared genes or shared homes. A home environment wherein prenatal care is haphazard, drugs are used during pregnancy, and infants' nutritional needs are neglected is a setting where sources of children's neuropsychological dysfunction that are clearly environmental coexist with a criminogenic social environment.

Problem Child–Problem Parent Interactions and the Emergence of Antisocial Behaviors. I believe

that the juxtaposition of a vulnerable and difficult infant with an adverse rearing context initiates risk for the life-course-persistent pattern of antisocial behavior. The ensuing process is a transactional one in which the challenge of coping with a difficult child evokes a chain of failed parent-child encounters (Sameroff & Chandler, 1975). The assertion that children exert important effects on their social environments is useful in understanding this hypothetical process (Bell & Chapman, 1986). It is now widely acknowledged that personality and behavior are shaped in large measure by interactions between the person and the environment (cf. Buss, 1987; Plomin, DeFries, & Loehlin, 1977; Scarr & McCartney, 1983). One form of interaction may play a particularly important role both in promoting an antisocial style and in maintaining its continuity across the life course: *Evocative* interaction occurs when a child's behavior evokes distinctive responses from others (Caspi et al., 1987).

Children with neuropsychological problems evoke a challenge to even the most resourceful, loving, and patient families. For example, Tinsley and Parke (1983) have reviewed literature showing that low-birth-weight, premature infants negatively influence the behavior of their caretakers; they arrive before parents are prepared, their crying patterns are rated as more disturbing and irritating, and parents report that they are less satisfying to feed, less pleasant to hold, and more demanding to care for than healthy babies. . . . Numerous studies have shown that a toddler's problem behaviors may affect the parents' disciplinary strategies as well as subsequent interactions with adults and peers (Bell & Chapman, 1986; Chess & Thomas, 1987). . . . It may well be that early behavioral difficulties contribute to the development of persistent antisocial behavior by evoking responses from the interpersonal social environment, responses that exacerbate the child's tendencies (Goldsmith, Bradshaw, & Rieser-Danner, 1986; Lytton, 1990). "The child acts; the environment reacts; and the child reacts back in mutually interlocking evocative interaction" (Caspi et al., 1987, p. 308).

Such a sequence of interactions would be most likely to produce lasting antisocial behavior problems if caretaker reactions were more likely to exacerbate than to ameliorate children's problem behavior. . . . If the child who "steps off on the wrong foot" remains on an ill-starred path, subsequent stepping-stone experiences may culminate in life-course-persistent antisocial behavior. For life course-persistent antisocial individuals, deviant behavior patterns later in life may thus reflect early individual differences that are perpetuated or exacerbated by interactions with the social environment: first at home, and later at school. . . .

Maintenance and Elaboration Over the Life Course: Cumulative Continuity, Contemporary Continuity, and Narrowing Options for Change

In the previous section, the concept of evocative person-environment interaction was called on to describe how children's difficult behaviors might affect encounters with their parents. Two additional types of interaction may help to explain how the life-course-persistent individual's problem behavior, once initiated, might promote its own continuity and pervasiveness. *Reactive* interaction occurs when different youngsters exposed to the same environment experience it, interpret it, and react to it in accordance with their particular style. For example, in interpersonal situations where cues are ambiguous, aggressive children are likely to mistakenly attribute harmful intent to others and then act accordingly (Dodge & Frame, 1982). *Proactive* interaction occurs when people select or create environments that support their styles. For example, antisocial individuals appear to be likely to affiliate selectively with antisocial others, even when selecting a mate. Some evidence points to nonrandom mating along personality traits related to antisocial behavior (Buss, 1984), and there are significant spouse correlations on conviction for crimes (e.g., Baker, Mack, Moffitt, & Mednick, 1989).

The three types of person-environment interactions can produce two kinds of consequences in the life course: *cumulative consequences* and *contemporary consequences* (Caspi & Bem, 1990). Early individual differences may set in motion a downhill snowball of cumulative continuities. In addition, individual differences may themselves persist from infancy to adulthood, continuing to influence adolescent and adult behavior in a proximal contemporary fashion. Contemporary continuity arises if the life-course-persistent person continues to carry into adulthood the same underlying constellation of traits that got him into trouble as a child, such as high activity level, irritability, poor self-control, and low cognitive ability. . . .

Cumulative consequences were implied by the effect of childhood temper on occupational status at midlife: Tantrums predicted lower educational attainment, and educational attainment, in turn, predicted lower occupational status. Contemporary consequences were implied by the strong direct link between ill-temperedness and occupational stability. [For example], [m]en with childhood tantrums continued to be hot-tempered in adulthood, where it got them into trouble in the world of work. They had more erratic work lives, changing jobs more frequently and experiencing more unemployment between ages 18 and 40. Ill-temperedness also had a contemporary effect on marital stability. . . .

Elsewhere, I describe in detail some of the patterns of interaction between persons and their social environments that may promote antisocial continuity across time and across life domains (Caspi & Moffitt, in press-b). Two sources of continuity deserve emphasis here because they narrow the options for change. These processes are (a) failing to learn conventional prosocial alternatives to antisocial behavior and (b) becoming ensnared in a deviant life-style by crime's consequences. These concepts have special implications for the questions of why life-course-persistent individuals fail to desist from delinquency as young adults and why they are so impervious to intervention.

A Restricted Behavioral Repertoire. This theory of life-course-persistent antisocial behavior asserts that the causal sequence begins very early and the formative years are dominated by chains of cumulative and contemporary continuity. As a consequence, little opportunity is afforded for the life-course-persistent antisocial individual to learn a behavioral repertoire of prosocial alternatives. Thus, one overlooked and pernicious source of continuity in antisocial behavior is simply a lack of recourse to any other options. In keeping with this prediction, Vitaro, Gagnon, and Tremblay (1990) have shown that aggressive children whose behavioral repertoires consist almost solely of antisocial behaviors are less likely to change over years than are aggressive children whose repertoires comprise some prosocial behaviors as well.

Life-course-persistent persons miss out on opportunities to acquire and practice prosocial alternatives at each stage of development. Children with poor self-control and aggressive behavior are often rejected by peers and adults (Coie, Belding, & Underwood, 1988; Dodge, Coie, & Brakke, 1982; Vitaro et al., 1990). In turn, children who have learned to expect rejection are likely in later settings to withdraw or strike out preemptively, precluding opportunities to affiliate with prosocial peers (Dodge & Newman, 1981; Dodge & Frame, 1982; LaFrenier & Sroufe, 1985; Nasby, Hayden, & DePaulo, 1980). Such children are robbed of chances to practice conventional social skills. . . . Simply put, if social and academic skills are not mastered in childhood, it is very difficult to later recover lost opportunities.

Becoming Ensnared by Consequences of Antisocial behavior. Personal characteristics such as poor self-control, impulsivity, and inability to delay gratification increase the risk that antisocial youngsters will make irrevocable decisions that close the doors of opportunity. Teenaged parenthood, addiction to drugs or alcohol, school dropout, disabling or disfiguring injuries, patchy work histories, and time spent incarcerated are *snares* that diminish the probabilities of later success by eliminating opportunities for breaking the chain of cumulative continuity (Cairns & Cairns, 1991; J. Q. Wilson & Herrnstein, 1985). Similarly, labels accrued early in life can foreclose later opportunities; an early arrest record or a "bad" reputation may rule out lucrative jobs, higher education, or an advantageous marriage (Farrington, 1977; Klein, 1986; West, 1982). In short, the behavior of life-course-persistent antisocial persons is increasingly maintained and supported by narrowing options for conventional behavior.

Interventions with life-course-persistent persons have met with dismal results (Lipton, Martinson, & Wilks, 1975; Palmer, 1984; Sechrest, White, & Brown, 1979). This is not surprising, considering that most interventions are begun relatively late in the chain of cumulative continuity. The forces of continuity are formidable foes (Caspi & Moffitt, in press-a). After a protracted deficient learning history, and after options for change have been eliminated, efforts to suppress antisocial behavior will not automatically bring prosocial behavior to the surface in its place. Now-classic research on learning shows conclusively that efforts to extinguish undesirable behavior will fail unless alternative behaviors are available that will attract reinforcement (Azrin & Holz, 1966). My analysis of increasingly restricted behavioral options suggests the hypothesis that opportunities for change will often be actively transformed by life-course-persistents into opportunities for continuity. Residential treatment programs provide a chance to learn from criminal peers, a new job furnishes the chance to steal, and new romance provides a partner for abuse. This analysis of life-course-persistent antisocial behavior anticipates disappointing outcomes when such antisocial persons are thrust into new situations that purportedly offer the chance "to turn over a new leaf."

The Reason for Persistence: Traits, Environments, and Developmental Processes

According to some accounts of behavioral continuity, an ever present underlying trait generates antisocial outcomes at every point in the life span (e.g., Gottfredson & Hirschi, 1990). By other accounts, antisocial behavior is sustained by environmental barriers to change (e.g., Bandura, 1979, pp. 217-224). In this theory of life-course-persistent antisocial behavior, neither traits nor environments account for continuity. True, the theory begins with a trait: variation between individuals in neuropsychological health. The trait is truly underlying in that it seldom comes to anyone's attention unless an infant is challenged by formal examinations; it is manifested behaviorally as variability in infant temperament, developmental milestones, and cognitive abilities.

Next, the theory brings environments into play. Parents and other people respond to children's difficult temperaments and developmental deficits. In nurturing environments, toddlers' problems are often corrected. However, in disadvantaged homes, schools, and neighborhoods, the responses are more likely to exacerbate than amend. Under such detrimental circumstances, difficult behavior is gradually elaborated into conduct problems and a dearth of prosocial skills. Thus, over the years, an antisocial personality is slowly and insidiously constructed. Likewise, deficits in language and reasoning are incrementally elaborated into academic failure and a dearth of job skills. Over time, accumulating consequences of the youngster's personality problems and academic problems prune away the options for change.

This theory of life-course-persistent antisocial behavior emphasizes the constant process of reciprocal interaction between personal traits and environmental reactions to them. The original attribute is thus elaborated on during development, to become a syndrome that remains conceptually consistent, but that gains new behavioral components (Caspi & Bem, 1990). Through that process, relatively subtle childhood variations in neuropsychological health can be transformed into an antisocial style that pervades all domains of adolescent and adult behavior. It is this infiltration of the antisocial disposition into the multiple domains of a life that diminishes the likelihood of change. When in the life course does the potential for change dwindle to nil? How many person-environment interactions must accumulate before the life-course-persistent pattern becomes set? I have argued that a person-environment interaction process is needed to predict emerging antisocial behavior, but after some age will the "person" main effect predict adult outcomes alone? An answer to these questions is critical for prevention efforts. The well-documented resistance of antisocial personality disorder to treatments of all kinds seems to suggest that the life course-persistent style is fixed sometime before age 18 (Suedfeld & Landon, 1978). Studies of crime careers reveal that it is very unusual for males to first initiate crime after adolescence, suggesting that if an adult is going to be antisocial, the pattern must be established by late adolescence (Elliott, Huizinga, & Menard, 1989). At the same time, efforts to predict antisocial outcomes from childhood conduct problems yield many errors (e.g., White et al., 1990). These errors seem to suggest that antisocial styles become set sometime after childhood. . . .

ADOLESCENCE-LIMITED ANTISOCIAL BEHAVIOR

Discontinuity: The Most Common Course of Antisocial Behavior

As implied by the proffered label, discontinuity is the hallmark of teenaged delinquents who have no notable history of antisocial behavior in childhood and little future for such behavior in adulthood. However, the brief tenure of their delinquency should not obscure their prevalence in the population or the gravity of their crimes. In contrast with the rare life-course persistent type, adolescence-limited delinquency is ubiquitous. Several studies have shown that about one third of males are arrested during their lifetime for a serious criminal offense, whereas fully four fifths of males have police contact for some minor infringement (Farrington, Ohlin, & Wilson, 1986). Most of these police contacts are made during the adolescent years. Indeed, numerous rigorous self-report studies have now documented that it is statistically aberrant to refrain from crime during adolescence (Elliott et al., 1983; Hirschi, 1969; Moffitt & Silva, 1988c).

Compared with the life-course-persistent type, adolescence-limited delinquents show relatively little continuity in their antisocial behavior. Across age, change in delinquent involvement is often abrupt, especially during the periods of onset and desist[a]nce. . . . Adolescence-limited delinquents may also have sporadic, crime-free periods in the midst of their brief crime "careers." Also, in contrast with the life-course-persistent type, they lack consistency in their antisocial behavior across situations. For example, they may shoplift in stores and use drugs with friends but continue to obey the rules at school. Because of the chimeric nature of their delinquency, different reporters (such as self, parent, and teacher) are less likely to agree about their behavior problems when asked to complete rating scales or clinical interviews (Loeber, Green, Lahey, & Stouthamer-Loeber, 1990; Loeber & Schmaling, 1985).

These observations about temporal instability and cross-situational inconsistency are more than merely descriptive. They have implications for a theory of the etiology of adolescence-limited delinquency. Indeed, the flexibility of most delinquents' behavior suggests that their engagement in deviant life-styles may be under the control of reinforcement and punishment contingencies. Unlike their life-course-persistent peers, whose behavior was described as inflexible and refractory to changing circumstances, adolescence-limited delinquents are likely to engage in antisocial behavior in situations where such responses seem profitable to them, but they are also able to abandon antisocial behavior when prosocial styles are more rewarding. They maintain control over their antisocial responses and use antisocial behavior only in situations where it may serve an instrumental function. Thus, principles of learning theory will be important for this theory of the cause of adolescence-limited delinquency.

A theory of adolescence-limited delinquency must account for several empirical observations: modal onset in early adolescence, recovery by young adulthood, widespread prevalence, and lack of continuity. Why do youngsters with no history of behavior problems in childhood suddenly become antisocial in adolescence? Why do they develop antisocial problems rather than other difficulties? Why is delinquency so common among teens? How are they able to spontaneously recover from an antisocial life-style within a few short years? Just as the childhood onset of life-course-persistent persons compelled me to look for causal factors early in their lives, the coincidence of puberty with the rise in the prevalence of delinquent behavior compels me to look for clues in adolescent development. Critical features of this developmental period are variability in biological age, the increasing importance of peer relationships, and the budding of teenagers' self-conscious values, attitudes, and aspirations. These developmental tasks form the building blocks for a theory of adolescence-limited delinquency.

Beginnings: Motivation, Mimicry, and Reinforcement

Why do adolescence-limited delinquents begin delinquency? The answer advanced here is that their delinquency is "social mimicry" of the antisocial style of life-course-persistent youths. The concept of social mimicry is borrowed from ethology. Social mimicry occurs when two animal species share a single niche and one of the species has cornered the market on a resource that is needed to promote fitness (Moynihan, 1968). In such circumstances, the "mimic" species adopts the social behavior of the more successful species to obtain access to the valuable resource....

If social mimicry is to explain why adolescence-limited delinquents begin to mimic the antisocial behavior of their life-course-persistent peers, then, logically, delinquency must be a social behavior that allows access to some desirable resource. I suggest that the resource is mature status, with its consequent power and privilege. Before modernization, biological maturity came at a later age, social adult status arrived at an earlier age, and rites of passage more clearly delineated the point at which youths assumed new roles and responsibilities.... [S]ecular changes in health and work have lengthened the duration of adolescence. The ensuing gap leaves modern teenagers in a 5- to 10-year role vacuum (Erikson, 1960). They are biologically capable and compelled to be sexual beings, yet they are asked to delay most of the positive aspects of adult life (see Buchanan, Eccles, & Becker, 1992, for a review of studies of the compelling influence of pubertal hormones on teens' behavior and personality).... [Teens] remain financially and socially dependent on their families of origin and are allowed few decisions of any real import. Yet they want desperately to establish intimate bonds with the opposite sex, to accrue material belongings, to make their own decisions, and to be regarded as consequential by adults (Csikszentmihalyi & Larson, 1984). Contemporary adolescents are thus trapped in a *maturity gap*, chronological hostages of a time warp between biological age and social age.

This emergent phenomenology begins to color the world for most teens in the first years of adolescence.... At the time of biological maturity, salient pubertal changes make the remoteness of ascribed social maturity painfully apparent to teens. This new awareness coincides with their promotion into a high school society that is numerically dominated by older youth. Thus, just as teens begin to feel the discomfort of the maturity gap, they enter a social reference group that has endured the 3 to 4 years and has already perfected some delinquent ways of coping with it....

Life-course-persistent youngsters are the vanguard of this transition. Healthy adolescents are capable of noticing that the few life-course-persistent youths in their midst do not seem to suffer much from the maturity gap. (At a prevalence rate of about 5%, one or two such experienced delinquents in every classroom might be expected.) Already adept at deviance, life-course-persistent youths are able to obtain possessions by theft or vice that are otherwise inaccessible to teens who have no independent incomes (e.g., cars, clothes, drugs, or entry into adults-only leisure settings). Life-course-persistent boys are more sexually experienced and have already initiated relationships with the opposite sex. Life-course-persistent boys appear relatively free of their families of origin; they seem to go their own way, making their own rules. As evidence that they make their own decisions, they take risks and do dangerous things that parents could not possibly endorse. As evidence that they have social consequence in the adult world, they have personal attorneys, social workers, and probation officers; they operate small businesses in the underground economy; and they have fathered children (Weiher, Huizinga, Lizotte, & Van Kammen, 1991). Viewed from within contemporary adolescent culture, the antisocial precocity of life-course-persistent youths becomes a coveted social asset (cf. Finnegan, 1990a, 1990b; Jessor & Jessor, 1977; Silbereisen & Noack, 1988). [A]ntisocial behavior becomes a valuable technique that is demonstrated by life-course-persistents and imitated carefully by adolescence-limiteds. The effect of peer delinquency on the onset of delinquency is among the most robust facts in criminology research (Elliott & Menard, in press; Jessor & Jessor, 1977; Reiss, 1986; Sarnecki, 1986). However, is there evidence consistent with a social mimicry interpretation? I describe the evidence in the next section.

Social Mimicry and the Relationships Between Life-Course-Persistent and Adolescence-Limited Delinquents. One hypothesized by-product of the maturity gap is a shift during early adolescence by persistent antisocial youth from peripheral to more influential positions in the peer social structure. This shift should occur as aspects of the antisocial style become more interesting to other teens. In terms of its epidemiology, delinquent participation shifts from being primarily an individual psychopathology in childhood to a normative group social behavior during adolescence and then back to psychopathology in adulthood. Consider that the behavior problems of the few pioneering antisocial children in an age cohort must develop on an individual basis; such early childhood pioneers lack the influence of delinquent peers (excepting family members). However, near adolescence, a few boys join the life-course-persistent ones, then a few more, until a critical mass is reached when almost all adolescents are involved in some delinquency with age peers. . . .

The word *friends* . . . seems to imply a personal relationship between life-course-persistents and adolescence-limiteds that is implausible. Much evidence suggests that, before adolescence, life-course-persistent antisocial children are ignored and rejected by other children because of their unpredictable, aggressive behavior (Coie et al., 1988; Dodge et al., 1982). After adolescence has passed, life-course-persistent adults are often described as lacking the capacity for loyalty or friendship (Cleckley, 1976; Robins, 1985). At first, these observations may seem contrary to my assertion that life-course-persistents assume social influence over youths who admire and emulate their style during adolescence. However, it is important to recall that social mimicry required no exchange of affection between the successful birds and their monkey mimics. In this theory, adolescents who wish to prove their maturity need only notice that the style of life-course-persistents resembles adulthood more than it resembles childhood. Then they need only observe antisocial behavior closely enough and long enough to imitate it successfully. What is contended is that adolescence limited youths should regard life-course-persistent youths as models, and life-course-persistent teens should regard themselves as magnets for other teens. Neither perception need involve reciprocal liking between individuals. A modeling role would imply that measures of exposure to delinquent peers (e.g., knowledge of their delinquent behavior or time spent in proximity to them) should be better predictors of self-delinquency than measures of relationship quality (e.g., shared attitudes or attachment to delinquent peers) (see Agnew, 1991, and Warr & Stafford, 1991). . . . A magnet role would imply that children who were rejected and ignored by others should experience newfound "popularity" as teens, relative to their former rejected status. That is, life course-persistent youth should encounter more contacts with peers during adolescence when other adolescents draw near so as to imitate their life-style. . . .

Life-course-persistents serve as core members of revolving networks, by virtue of being role models or trainers for new recruits (Reiss, 1986). They exploit peers as drug customers, as fences, as lookouts, or as sexual partners. Such interactions among life-course-persistent and adolescence-limited delinquents may represent a symbiosis of mutual exploitation. Alternatively, life-course-persistent offenders need not even be aware of all of the adolescence-limited youngsters who imitate their style. Unlike adolescence-limited offenders, who appear to need peer support for crime, life-course-persistent offenders are willing to offend alone (Knight & West, 1975). The point is that the phenomena of "delinquent peer networks" and "co-offending" during the adolescent period do not necessarily connote supportive friendships that are based on intimacy, trust, and loyalty, as is sometimes assumed. Social mimicry of delinquency can take place if experienced offenders actively educate new recruits. However, it can also take place if motivated learners merely observe antisocial models from afar.

Reinforcement of Delinquency by Its "Negative" Consequences. For teens who become adolescence-limited delinquents, antisocial behavior is an effective means of knifing-off childhood apron strings and of proving that they can act independently to conquer new challenges (Erikson, 1960). Hypothetical reinforcers for delinquency include damaging the quality of intimacy and communication with parents, provoking responses from adults in positions of authority, finding ways to look older (such as by smoking cigarettes, being tattooed, playing the big spender with ill-gotten gains), and tempting fate (risking pregnancy, driving while intoxicated, or shoplifting under the noses of clerks). . . .

Ethnographic interviews with delinquents reveal that proving maturity and autonomy are strong personal motives for offending (e.g., Goldstein, 1990). Such hypothetical reinforcing properties have not been systematically tested for most types of delinquent acts. However, epidemiological studies have confirmed that adolescent initiation of tobacco, alcohol, and drug abuse are reinforced because they symbolize independence and maturity to youth (D. Kandel, 1980; Mausner & Platt, 1971). . . .

Why Doesn't Every Teenager Become Delinquent?

. . . . Some youths who refrain from antisocial behavior may, for some reason, not sense the maturity gap and therefore lack the hypothesized motivation for experimenting with crime. Perhaps such teens experience very late puberty so that the gap between biological and social

adulthood is not signaled to them early in adolescence. . . . Some nondelinquent teens may lack structural opportunities for modeling antisocial peers. Adolescent crime rates are generally lower in rural areas than in inner-city areas (Skogan, 1979, 1990). Teens in urban areas are surrounded by a greater density of age peers (and have readier unsupervised access to them through public transportation and meeting venues such as parks and shopping malls) than are teens in relatively isolated rural areas. . . . Youths may also be excluded from opportunities to mimic antisocial peers because of some personal characteristics that make them unattractive to other teens or that leave them reluctant to seek entry to newly popular delinquent groups. . . .

In summary, this theory of adolescence-limited delinquency suggests that adolescents who commit no antisocial behavior at all have either (a) delayed puberty, (b) access to roles that are respected by adults, (c) environments that limit opportunities for learning about delinquency, (d) personal characteristics that exclude them from antisocial peer networks, or (e) all four. Research is needed to determine whether or not abstaining from delinquency is necessarily a sign of good adolescent adjustment.

Desist[a]nce From Crime: Adolescence-Limiteds Are Responsive to Shifting Reinforcement Contingencies

By definition, adolescence-limited delinquents generally do not maintain their delinquent behavior into adulthood. The account of life-course-persistent persons I made earlier in this chapter required an analysis of maintenance factors. In contrast, this account of adolescence-limited delinquents demands an analysis of desist[a]nce: Why do adolescence-limited delinquents desist from delinquency? This theory's answer: Healthy youths respond adaptively to changing contingencies. If motivational and learning mechanisms initiate and maintain their delinquency, then, likewise, changing contingencies can extinguish it. . . .

Waning Motivation and Shifting Contingencies. In contrast with amplifying theories, the present maturity-gap theory does anticipate desist[a]nce. With the inevitable progression of chronological age, more legitimate and tangible adult roles become available to teens. Adolescence-limited delinquents gradually experience a loss of motivation for delinquency as they exit the maturity gap. Moreover, when aging delinquents attain some of the privileges they coveted as teens, the consequences of illegal behavior shift from rewarding to punishing, *in their perception.* An adult arrest record will limit their job opportunities, drug abuse keeps them from getting to work on time, drunk driving is costly, and bar fights lead to accusations of unfit parenthood.

Adolescence-limited delinquents have something to lose by persisting in their antisocial behavior beyond the teen years. There is some evidence that many young adult offenders weigh the relative rewards from illegal and conventional activities when they contemplate future offending. In a study of three samples, the effect of age on criminal participation was mediated by young men's expectations about whether illegal earnings would exceed earnings from a straight job (Piliavin, Thornton, Gartner, & Matsueda, 1986). Important for this theory, research shows that "commitment costs" are among the factors weighed by young adults when they decide to discontinue offending. In the criminological subfield of perceptual deterrence research, commitment costs are defined as a person's judgment that past accomplishments will be jeopardized or that future goals will be foreclosed (Williams & Hawkins, 1986).

Criminal behavior incurs commitment costs if it risks informal sanctions (disapproval by family, community, or employer) as well as formal sanctions (arrest or conviction penalty). Given that very few delinquent acts culminate in formal sanctions, perceptual deterrence theories consider informal sanctions as keys to deterrence. . . .

Options for Change. The issue left unaddressed by theory is why are some delinquents able to desist when others are not? What enables adolescence-limited delinquents to make these (often abrupt) transitions away from crime? Why do adolescence-limited delinquents come to realize that they have something to lose, whereas life-course-persistent delinquents remain undeterred? Here, two positions are advanced: Unlike their life-course-persistent counterparts, adolescence-limited delinquents are relatively exempt from the forces of (a) cumulative and (b) contemporary continuity. First, without a lifelong history of antisocial behavior, the forces of cumulative continuity have had fewer years in

which to gather the momentum of a downhill snowball. Before taking up delinquency, adolescence-limited offenders had ample years to develop an accomplished repertoire of prosocial behaviors and basic academic skills. These social skills and academic achievements make them eligible for postsecondary education, good marriages, and desirable jobs.

The availability of alternatives to crime may explain why some adolescence-limited delinquents desist later than others. . . . Although the forces of cumulative continuity build up less momentum over the course of their relatively short crime careers, many adolescence-limited youths will fall prey to many of the same snares that maintain continuity among life-course-persistent persons. Those whose teen forays into delinquency inadvertently attracted damaging consequences may have more difficulty desisting. A drug habit, an incarceration, interrupted education, or a teen pregnancy are snares that require extra effort and time from which to escape. Thus, this theory predicts that variability in age at desistance from crime should be accounted for by the cumulative number and type of ensnaring life events that entangle persons in a deviant life-style.

Second, in stark contrast with the earlier account of life-course-persistent offenders, personality disorder and cognitive deficits play no part in the delinquency of adolescence-limited offenders. As a result, they are exempt from the sources of contemporary continuity that plague their life-course-persistent counterparts. In general, these young adults have adequate social skills. They have a record of average or better academic achievement, their mental health is sturdy, they still possess the capacity to forge close attachment relationships, and they retain the good intelligence they had when they entered adolescence. . . .

At the crossroads of young adulthood, adolescence-limited and life-course-persistent delinquents go different ways. This happens because the developmental histories and personal traits of adolescence-limiteds allow them the option of exploring new life pathways. The histories and traits of life-course-persistents have foreclosed their options, entrenching them in the antisocial path. To test this hypothesis, research must examine conditional effects of individual histories on opportunities for desistance from crime. . . .

DISCUSSION QUESTIONS

1. What are some of the different ways in which individual traits and the environment influence persistent antisocial behavior?

2. According to Moffitt, what types of individual traits and environmental conditions encourage antisocial behavior among children and adolescents?

3. Discuss Moffitt's theory of adolescent-limited antisocial behavior. What is it about these individuals that enables them to discontinue involvement in antisocial, or even delinquent, behavior, while individuals who are "life-course-persistent" do not or cannot?

4. In terms of public policies, how might developmental approaches such as Moffitt's contribute to the prevention of antisocial or delinquent behavior in an environment such as school?

33

THE DEVELOPMENT OF OFFENDING

ROLF LOEBER AND MAGDA STOUTHAMER-LOEBER

EDITOR'S INTRODUCTION—In this article, Rolf Loeber and Magda Stouthamer-Loeber briefly review some historical approaches to the development of offending over time and stress the conceptualization of developmental criminology. In contrast to traditional cross-sectional approaches to the study of delinquency, the authors emphasize the study of within-individual changes in offending over time and the study of causal factors that may explain onset, escalation, de-escalation, and desistance in individuals' offending. An analysis of delinquency over a longer period of time rather than cross-sectionally provides researchers with a better understanding of individual differences in criminal careers. This understanding can help to explain why some youths become involved in delinquency only marginally and others more deeply, and which groups of individuals start to desist in crime at which part of the life cycle.

Developmental criminology has three main objectives. First, it encourages the description of temporal, within-individual changes in offending, which allows comparisons between individuals' offending at one time and at other times. With this approach, individuals serve as their own controls. Second, developmental criminology focuses on the identification of causal factors, which predate behavioral development and have an impact on its course. With this approach, the clarification of possible causes of onset, escalation, de-escalation, and desistance in offending and the identification of individual differences among offenders with respect to age of onset, variety, seriousness, and duration of delinquent acts become possible. A final objective of developmental criminology centers on the study of important transitions in the life cycle and covariates as they may affect offending. Transitions may include the shift in children's relationships from parents to peers and from same-sex to opposite-sex peers, and the transition from school to work. Instances of covariates include the stabilization of personality traits with age and physical maturation.

In the first part of their article, Loeber and Stouthamer-Loeber discuss the origins of developmental criminology and the various studies that have provided empirical support and that have offered unique theoretical contributions to the conceptualization of the perspective. The authors also point out that this approach has not been received without challenges. In particular, they note the criticisms from Gottfredson and Hirschi (1987), who argued that the developmental approach to the study of offending was unnecessary and not even pertinent to the study of crime, adding that cross-sectional analyses were sufficient. The authors countered these challenges with a number of points, the most significant being that only a developmental approach to offending can inform us about how individuals differ in their development of offending, especially over time.

The authors close their article with implications for the formulation of developmental theories and suggestions on how developmental criminology can contribute to and enhance practice in the criminal justice field. They maintain that developmental criminology is relevant for applied criminal justice for several reasons: (a) the formulation of developmental theories, (b) the study of individuals rather than of variables, and (c) decisions about which behaviors to target for intervention and when to intervene. Like the work of Moffitt (Chapter 32 in this volume), Walsh (Chapter 36), and Thornberry (Chapter 35), Loeber and Stouthamer-Loeber's article makes an important contribution to the study of persistent offending over the life course. By studying the interaction between individual traits and the environment, criminologists and criminal justice practitioners alike can become better informed not only about *why* these particular offenders fail to desist in their antisocial pursuits but *how* this negative behavior can be mitigated if not entirely prevented.

It is generally agreed that patterns of delinquency are not the same for young offenders, compared to older offenders, and that delinquency results from a variety of causes rather than from a single cause (Wilson & Herrnstein, 1985). There is less agreement about the nature of pathways from early to late offending, and there is a scarcity of evidence about to what extent causes affecting the onset of offending (irrespective of age) are similar to causes affecting the escalation in seriousness of offending. Even less is known about the causes of deescalation and desistance in offending.

We argue here that when behaviors and patterns of causes tend to change over time, conventional cross-sectional approaches to the study of delinquency are no longer sufficient. Instead, we need to think of a developmental approach to the study of offending. The term developmental criminology has been coined (Loeber & Le Blanc, 1990), with three main aims. First, it encourages the description of temporal, within-individual changes in offending, which allows comparisons between individuals' offending at one time and at other times. Characteristic of this approach is that individuals serve as their own controls. The second focus of developmental criminology is the identification of explicative or causal factors, which predate behavioral development and have an impact on its course. These two loci make it possible to clarify the possible causes of onset, escalation, deescalation, and desistance in offending and to clarify individual differences among offenders in the age at onset, variety, seriousness, and duration of their delinquent acts.

A third aim of developmental criminology is to study important transitions in the life cycle and covariates as they may affect offending. Examples of such transitions are the shift in youngsters' relationships from parents to peers and from same-sex to opposite-sex peers, and the transition from school to work. Instances of covariates are the stabilization of personality traits with age and physical maturation.

A HISTORICAL PERSPECTIVE

It can be argued that developmental criminology is not very new in the study of offending. As early as 1849, Worsley described a sequence "from petty delinquencies to greater and more heinous crimes" (cited by Morris & Giller, 1987, p. 12). In more recent decades, some examples are Lemert's (1951) theory of the temporal ordering of primary and secondary deviance and Sutherland and Cressey's (1960) differential association theory, with its emphasis on how criminal behavior is learned over time. Likewise, strain and cultural deviance theories underline some temporal aspects of offending. Control theory (Hirschi, 1969), although not intended as a developmental theory, has attachment and commitment as its pivotal constructs, both of which are formed progressively through interaction with others and society.

In recent years, work has been done that has accelerated the developmental study of offending. Empirical analysis of the course of offending dates to the pioneering work of Wolfgang, Figlio, and Sellin (1972). Another prime

Loeber, R., & Stouthamer-Loeber, M. (1996). The development of offending. *Criminal Justice and Behavior, 23,* 12-24.

development was the panel report of the National Academy of Sciences, *Criminal Careers and "Career Criminals"* (Blumstein, Cohen, Roth & Visher, 1986), which established a firm empirical framework for the study of developmental aspects of offending. Subsequent to the panel report, Loeber and Le Blanc (1990) described the key conceptual and methodological advantages of a developmental approach to criminology. This document was sharpened further by Le Blanc and Loeber (1993). Much of the inspiration for Loeber and his colleagues' conceptualizations and empirical work was derived from Farrington's numerous developmentally oriented papers (e.g., Farrington, 1986a, 1986b). Collaboration with him (Loeber & Farrington, 1994), among others, led to further specification of how longitudinal data can best contribute to the aims of developmental criminology.

Alongside these scholarly endeavors, Hawkins and his colleagues formulated the developmental aspects of control theory in a social development model of offending and substance use (Hawkins, Lishner, Catalano, & Howard, 1986). This model, which includes aspects of strain theory, social learning, and differential association, seeks to explain the origins of bonding through several social and opportunistic variables. It explicitly refers to distinct developmental phases in children's lives, aiming to connect certain influences and behaviors characteristic of one phase to those of another phase. In some ways, this model harks back to the work of Patterson and his colleagues (Dishion, French, & Patterson, in press; Patterson, 1982), which stressed a social learning model for antisocial behavior, with a particular emphasis on coercive interchanges in the family home and between children and their siblings and peers. Also in recent years, Sampson and Laub (1993), in their reanalysis of the Glueck data, formulated a theoretical model in which stability and change in offending over the life course was linked to shifts in structural background factors and social processes.

However, the study of the development of offending has not been without controversy. Particularly, Gottfredson and Hirschi (1987) argued that the developmental approach to the study of offending is unnecessary and not even pertinent to the study of crime and that, instead, cross-sectional studies are sufficient. They defended their position by two types of arguments, (a) high-stability coefficients between measures of delinquency, and (b) studies showing that early antisocial behavior predicts antisocial behavior in adulthood.

These arguments can be challenged on several grounds. First, stability coefficients rarely reach parity, even when measurement error is taken into account (e.g., Loeber & Dishion, 1983; Loeber & Stouthamer-Loeber, 1987; Olweus, 1979). Second, predictions over time are far from accurate. Individuals may continue to offend from the juvenile to the adult years, but this does not mean that their offense pattern is stable, because the frequency, seriousness, and variety often change during the interval. Third, and most important, only a developmental approach to offending can inform us about how individuals differ in their development of offending. Specifically, we need to know: (a) Which youth are likely to become chronic offenders? (b) Which youth are likely to offend for some time and then desist (late desisters)? (c) Which youth are likely to experience the onset of offending but to desist soon afterwards (experimenters)?

For all three groups, we need to know the defining parameters of their delinquent career. At what age did they start their offending, and when did their nondelinquent conduct problems first become apparent? What type(s) of criminal activities were characteristic of their delinquent careers? And, for the chronics and late desisters, how did the patterns of their offending (frequency, variety, seriousness) change over time?

The description of individual differences in criminal careers is a condition sine qua non for the better understanding of factors that can help to explain why some youth become involved in delinquency only marginally and others more deeply. This is contrary to the assumption by Hirschi and Gottfredson (1983, 1987) that causes are invariant with the age of the offender and that similar causes or constellations of causes operate at each developmental stage in offending. This assumption is contrary to evidence that, when youngsters grow older, they are exposed to considerable shifts in the presence of known risk factors, such as parental influences, peer influences, and academic failure (Farrington, 1986b; La Grange & White, 1985; Le Blanc, 1984). The assumption also implies that the ranking of the explanatory power of causal variables is the same whether offending is studied cross-sectionally or longitudinally; in other words, causal factors and their interrelationships operate at equal strength at any given point along the developmental timeline. The developmental approach to delinquency does not make assumptions of invariance but, instead, tests to what extent risk and protective factors that affect the onset of offending are similar or not to those that apply to escalation, deescalation, or desistance and to what extent there are shifts in the magnitude of risk and protective factors.

IMPLICATIONS OF DEVELOPMENTAL CRIMINOLOGY FOR THEORY AND PRACTICE

The Formulation of Developmental Theories

We want to stress here four pivotal aspects of theories: improvements in the conceptualization of the dependent variable, developmental shifts in risk factors, the impact of protective factors, and the issue of reciprocity. First, delinquency as a dependent variable needs more attention for the following reasons. In the past, it has been common practice among scholars to quantify delinquency in terms of participation rate (percentage of youth displaying delinquency) and in terms of the rate of offending (Blumstein et al., 1986). Although both are legitimate outcome measures, a better understanding of delinquency careers can be achieved by also quantifying the age of onset, as well as the severity and the variety of offending. Few studies accomplish all these parameters. Later in this article, we demonstrate how a better conceptualization of delinquency as a dependent variable can be achieved by an integration of such outcomes that can help to classify offenders according to the life course of their predelinquent problem behaviors and delinquent acts.

Another aspect where the formulation of theories can be improved is by extending their scope of risk factors. Although, as mentioned above, several criminological theories emphasize developmental phenomena, most of these theories have incorporated relatively few of the known risk factors. As a consequence, these theories, although strong in some domains, are weak in several other areas. The study of an expanded array of risk factors is also likely to demonstrate key shifts in the influence of risk factors as youth

grow older. Farrington (1986b) has already demonstrated this in his analyses of the London data for the Cambridge Study in Delinquent Development, showing that certain risk factors persist over time, whereas others emerge and disappear. Here the complexity, but also the sensitivity, of the results to developmental phenomena have not yet found a counterpart in theory formation. Similar analyses on the dynamic aspects of the potential causes of offending by males have been done by Le Blanc (1994).

Also in our work, risk factors have been emphasized in the explanation of delinquency to the neglect of protective factors. However, as Hirschi (1969) stressed years ago, we need to explain not only why some individuals become delinquent, but also why others do not. We would add that we also need to know why other individuals, after a bout of delinquent involvement, turn around and become more law-abiding. Most of the studies on protective factors have been outside the realm of criminology (e.g., Garmezy & Rutter, 1983), and many of these studies have concentrated on identifying those. . . . factors that buffer the impact of risk factors (e.g., which factors can help to explain why some youth from high-crime neighborhoods do not become delinquent). Although it is worth pursuing such interaction effects, we would argue that we first need to know more about the main effects of protective factors, particularly whether protective effects differentially affect the various aspects of delinquency processes: onset, escalation, deescalation, and desistance. Our recent work illustrates this (Loeber & Stouthamer-Loeber, 1994; Stouthamer-Loeber et al., 1993). One of the first questions we address in the study of protective factors in our longitudinal data of the Pittsburgh Youth Study is whether a potential protective factor affects delinquency in one or more of the following ways: (a) suppresses onset, (b) suppresses escalation, (c) promotes deescalation, and (d) promotes desistance.

We assume that the most powerful protective factors are those that affect all four processes in the direction described. We believe that once we have such information, we can more suitably advance to the testing of models in which the interaction between observed main effects of protective factors against the observed main effects of risk factors are incorporated.

All of this still can lead to an oversimplification of causal processes. As Thornberry and his colleagues (Thornberry, 1987; Thornberry, Lizotte, Krohn, Farnworth, & Jang, 1994) have shown, future theories of offending should also take more into account the limitations of developmental approaches to offending, particularly where temporal priority between phenomena cannot be established and where reciprocity of influences prevails instead. The challenge is to better incorporate such reciprocal influences in statistical models of causation and to represent them in theoretical models, distinguishing them from unidirectional influences.

The Potential Yield of Developmental Findings for Practice

We would argue that survey studies in the field of criminology have produced only a scattering of findings that are relevant for practice, either for the administration of juvenile justice or for intervention efforts to prevent or reduce delinquency. There are several reasons for this, of which we list a few.

Variable or individual? The essential goal of criminal justice interventions is to bring about change in individuals. However, most survey studies concentrate on the study of variables explaining between-group differences or change in group averages over time rather than on factors explaining within-subject change. Similarly, most theories and explanatory models concern relationships between sets of independent variables on the one hand and, usually, one dependent variable on the other. These relationships often are expressed in terms of correlations. We would argue that a practitioner's most central concern is, What should I do with this particular individual? Correlations are of little use here because they hide, rather than reveal, individual characteristics. In particular, correlations do not indicate which youth are likely to initiate offending, which are likely to become worse over time, and which are likely to desist. These distinctions are crucial for day-to-day decision making in juvenile justice and for the implementation of many interventions.

The variable approach does have a place in research. However, for research findings to be practical, analyses of variables should serve to inform analyses of individuals. For example, we have been interested in the study of developmental pathways toward serious delinquent outcomes (Loeber, 1988, 1991; Loeber, Keenan, & Zhang, 1994; Loeber et al., 1993). The definition of a pathway is a group of individuals who share a behavioral development that is distinct from the behavioral development of another group of individuals. Our work on pathways started with examining the factor structure of ratings of problem behaviors and delinquent acts. Meta-analyses of parent and teacher ratings (Frick et al., 1993; Loeber & Schmaling, 1985) showed that one major dimension of disruptive behavior places overt problem behavior (e.g., temper tantrums, attacks people) on one pole and covert problem behavior (e.g., theft, setting fires) on the other, with disobedience situated in the middle of this dimension. The distinction between overt and covert problem behaviors harks back to the much-used distinction in criminology between violent and property-related forms of delinquency.

The next step in our analyses was to examine the age of onset curves of problem behaviors and to determine which sets of behaviors had an earlier age of onset than other behaviors. These analyses then led to a third set of analyses, but now focusing on individuals. Given that we understood better the basic structure and ages of onset of problem behaviors, could we formulate one or more pathways to capture an individual's progression through these behaviors over time? We found that, for boys, the most optimal solution involved three sets of pathways:

1. An authority conflict pathway before the age of 12, consisting of a developmental sequence with stubborn behavior as a first step, defiance as a second step, and authority avoidance (staying out late at night, truancy, running away from home) as a third step.

2. A covert pathway, consisting of a developmental sequence starting with minor covert behaviors (frequent lying, shoplifting) as a first step, followed by property damage (fire setting, vandalism) as a second step, and moderate to serious forms of delinquency (burglary, fraud, car theft) as a third step.

3. An overt pathway, consisting of a developmental sequence with minor aggression (annoying others, bullying) as a first step, fighting

(physical fighting and gang fighting) as a second step, and violence (attacking someone, rape) as a third step.

One of the main validity tests of these pathway models was whether most boys with problem behavior fitted into one or more of the pathways, which was indeed the case (Loeber et al., 1993, 1994).

Even if we are able to conceptualize different pathways, we still may be in a quandary when we try to apply the information to individual cases when we are not certain whether the youth's misbehavior is temporary or not. After all, childhood and adolescence are periods in which youth learn right from wrong. This learning process is far from smooth, resulting in various forms of delinquency in a large number of boys, of whom only a proportion are truly at risk to persist in offending. Therefore, we need to differentiate between experimenters and persisters at an early phase of their delinquent careers (Loeber et al., 1994). This distinction is based on whether the problem behavior is incidental or repeated over time, and it can only be established by means of one or more reassessments. Thus, the decision concerning with whom to intervene is based partly on whether the youth is an experimenter or not and partly on whether he or she already has progressed into one or more of the pathways (given that our findings indicate that boys in the earliest step of a pathway are at less serious risk than those at later steps).

Thus, we would argue that knowledge of an individual's position with respect to developmental pathways provides answers to three crucial questions: Is this youth a persister? Has this youth progressed beyond the first step in a pathway? If so, what is the problem behavior that we can expect him to manifest in this particular pathway, judging from developmental progressions in other boys? The latter piece of information is crucial in order for practitioners to better judge what to prevent. In this fashion, the individual approach of pathways incorporates the important aspects of offending (i.e., onset, frequency, variety, and seriousness), while also allowing measurement of the speed by which individuals advance through a pathway.

The Decision of What to Change and When. One of the crucial decisions in interventions is what to treat, at what age, and for whom. The issue of what to treat requires answers to several questions. Which behaviors appear to be keystone behaviors for the development of other behaviors (given that in the absence of the keystone behavior, there is a sharply reduced likelihood of the emergence of other behaviors)? If there are several candidates for keystone behaviors, which should be targeted first? At what age or developmental level is such intervention most optimal? In other words, we should know at what ages or developmental stages certain potential targets for intervention become more stable and less malleable. Obviously, with such knowledge, interventions should be timed for periods in which malleability is still high.

These are but a few of the issues that we as criminologists may want to focus on if our work is to be of optimal use to criminal justice, school, mental health, and child protection personnel who are trying to help youngsters. Developmentally and individually oriented information may eventually have the greatest use for these professionals.

DISCUSSION QUESTIONS

1. What are the main objectives of developmental criminology?

2. Contrast developmental criminology with the argument offered by Gottfredson and Hirschi (1987) that conventional cross-sectional approaches to the study of delinquency are adequate. According to Loeber and Stouthamer-Loeber, what are the inherent problems with Gottfredson and Hirschi's challenges to developmental criminology?

3. How can developmental criminology inform criminal justice practice?

REFERENCE

Gottfredson, M., & Hirschi, T. (1987). The methodological adequacy of longitudinal research on crime. *Scientology, 25,* 581-614.

34

An Integrated Theoretical Perspective on Delinquent Behavior

Delbert S. Elliott, Suzanne S. Ageton, and Rachelle J. Canter

EDITOR'S INTRODUCTION—This article by Elliott, Ageton, and Canter presents an integrated theoretical model of the etiology of delinquent behavior. The proposed model makes an important theoretical contribution to criminology for the way in which it synthesizes dominant theories of crime: strain, social control, and social learning perspectives. More specifically, this model integrates these theoretical frameworks into a single explanatory paradigm that considers multiple causal pathways to sustained patterns of delinquent behavior. The theoretical model of Elliott et al. revises the classical strain theories proposed by Merton (1938), Cohen (1955), and Cloward and Ohlin (1960).

The authors contend that adolescents may pursue a variety of goals and that achievement of these goals is not necessarily a function of social class. Therefore, the revisions of strain theory allow the authors to explain middle-class and lower-class delinquency. Their integrated theoretical paradigm begins with the assumption that different adolescents have different socialization experiences, which can result in varying degrees of commitment to and integration into conventional social groups. The effect of failure to achieve conventional social goals on subsequent delinquent variables is related to the strength of one's initial social bonds. Elliott et al. argue that limited opportunities to achieve conventional goals constitute a source of strain and provide an incentive for delinquency but only if an individual is committed to these particular goals. Conversely, limited opportunities to achieve such goals should have little or no impact on individuals with weak ties and commitment to the conventional social order.

To elaborate on the integrated model, Elliott et al. propose two primary pathways for delinquent behavior. In the first, individuals with low social control (i.e., weak ties and commitment to the conventional social order) become involved with delinquent peers, which increases their likelihood of engaging in a pattern of delinquency that is sustained over time. The second pathway represents an integration of traditional strain and social learning perspectives, and it suggests that individuals with high social control (i.e., strong bonds and commitment to the conventional social order) have certain experiences that may weaken their level of control, such as the failure to achieve conventional goals. These individuals may then become involved with delinquency. Exposing and committing oneself to delinquent peer groups forms the primary variable of the integrated theory, although Elliott et al. do contend that strain and low social control may have small direct effects on delinquency.

The authors assert that their integrated model of strain, social control, and social learning theories has several advantages over other conceptualizations that treat each theory as separate and independent. First, their model provides a more comprehensive view of the causal pathways to delinquency. Second, the authors believe that the integrated paradigm is consistent with previous empirical findings and offers insight into contradictory findings. Last, the integrated paradigm also offers an explanation for the contradictory findings on aspirations and delinquency.

. . . Our concern here is to return to the consideration of the etiology of delinquent and criminal behavior and propose a new integrated theoretical formulation as a guide to research and understanding. The focus is on the offender and those social processes and features of social contexts which both generate and maintain delinquent patterns of behavior. More specifically, our objective is to provide a conceptual framework in which traditional strain, social-learning, and social control perspectives are integrated into a single explanatory paradigm which avoids the class bias inherent in traditional perspectives and which accounts for multiple etiologies of (multiple causal paths to) sustained patterns of delinquent behavior.

PREVIOUS THEORIES: STRAIN AND CONTROL

Anomie/Strain Perspective

. . . Strain theory has become the most influential and widely used contemporary formulation in the sociology of delinquent behavior. A specific application of strain theory to delinquency has been proposed by Cloward and Ohlin (1960) and, more recently, by Elliott and Voss (1974). Cloward and Ohlin's work is of particular interest to us because their formulation, like that proposed here, represents an attempt to integrate and extend current theoretical positions. Although their theory has been viewed primarily as an extension of the earlier work of Durkheim and Merton, it is equally an extension of the differential association perspective and the prior work of Sutherland (1947). Indeed, much of its significance lies in the fact that it successfully integrated these two traditional perspectives on the etiology of delinquent behavior. Cloward and Ohlin maintain that limited opportunity for achieving conventional goals is the motivational stimulus for delinquent behavior. The specific form and pattern of delinquent behavior are acquired through normal learning processes within delinquent groups. Experiences of limited or blocked opportunities (a result of structural limitations on success) thus lead to alienation (perceived anomie) and an active seeking out of alternative groups and settings in which particular patterns of delinquent behavior are acquired and reinforced (social learning).

Merton, Cloward and Ohlin have conceptualized the condition leading to anomie in terms of differential opportunities for achieving socially valued goals. Differential access to opportunity creates strain; this is postulated to occur primarily among disadvantaged, low-SES [socioeconomic status] youths, resulting in the concentration of delinquent subcultures in low-SES neighborhoods. It is important to note, however, that Cloward and Ohlin have changed the level of explanation from the macrosociological level which characterized Durkheim's work to an individual level. It is the *perception* of limited access to conventional goals that motivates the *individual* to explore deviant means. This change in level of explanation was essential for the integration of strain and learning perspectives.

Elliott and Voss's more recent work (1974) has attempted to deal with the class-bound assumptions inherent in strain theory. Their formulation extends Cloward and Ohlin's classic statement in the following three ways: (1) The focus on limited opportunities was extended to a wider range of conventional goals. (2) The goal-means disjunction was modified to be logically independent of social class. (3) The role of social learning in the development of delinquent behavior was further emphasized. Elliott and Voss have

Elliott, D. S., Ageton, S. S., & Canter, R. J. (1979). An integrated theoretical perspective on delinquent behavior. *Journal of Research in Crime and Delinquency, 16*, 3-27.

proposed a sequential, or developmental, model of delinquency: (1) Limited opportunities or failure to achieve conventional goals serves to (2) attenuate one's initial commitment to the normative order and (3) results in a particular form of alienation (normlessness), which serves as a "permitter" for delinquency, and (4) exposure to delinquent groups, which provide learning and rewards for delinquent behavior for those whose bonds have undergone the attenuation process.

From this perspective, aspiration-opportunity disjunctions provide motivation for delinquent behavior. As compared with Merton and Cloward and Ohlin, Elliott and Voss view *both* goals and opportunities as variables. They postulate that middle-class youths are just as likely to aspire beyond their means as are low-SES youths. While the absolute levels of aspirations and opportunities may vary by class, the discrepancies between personal goals and opportunities for realizing these goals need not vary systematically by class. Given Durkheim's (1897/1951, p. 254) view that poverty restrains aspirations, Elliott and Voss have postulated that aspiration-opportunity disjunctions would be at least as great, if not greater, among middle-class youths. In any case, the motivational stimulus for delinquent behavior in the form of aspiration-opportunity discrepancies or goal failure is viewed as logically independent of social class.

Normlessness, the expectation that one must employ illegitimate means to achieve socially valued goals (Seeman, 1959), is postulated to result from perceived aspiration-opportunity disjunctions. When a person cannot reach his or her goals by conventional means, deviant or illegitimate means become rational and functional alternatives. When the source of failure or blockage is perceived as external—resulting from institutional practices and policies—the individual has some justification for withdrawing his or her moral commitment to these conventional norms. In this manner, a sense of injustice mitigates ties to conventional norms and generates normlessness.

Once at this point in the developmental sequence, the relative presence or absence of specific delinquent learning and performance structures accounts for the likelihood of one's behavior. The time-ordering of the exposure to delinquency variable is not explicit. It may predate failure or it may be the result of seeking a social context in which one can achieve some success. While the exposure may result in the acquisition of delinquent behavior patterns, actual delinquent behavior (performance) will not result until one's attachment to the social order is neutralized through real or anticipated failure, and the delinquent behavior has been reinforced. The results of research relative to this set of propositions have been generally encouraging. . . .

While considerable empirical support for an integrated strain-learning approach to delinquency has been amassed, most of the variance in delinquency remains unexplained. If the power of this theoretical formulation is to be improved, some basic modification is required. One avenue is suggested by the weak predictive power of the aspiration-opportunity discrepancy variables. . . . [In some studies], limited academic success at school and failure in one's relationship with parents were predictive, but only weakly. To some extent, the low strength of these predictors might be anticipated, since they are the initial variables in the causal sequence and are tied to delinquency only through a set of other conditional variables. On the other hand, the strong emphasis placed on these specific variables in strain theories seems questionable, given the available data. It might be argued that the difficulty lies in the operationalization or measurement of the relevant goal-opportunity disjunctions. However, we are inclined to reject this position because previous findings as to this postulated relationship have been generally weak and inconclusive (Spergel, 1967; Short, 1964, 1965; Elliott, 1962; Short, Rivera, and Tennyson, 1965; Jessor et al., 1968; Hirschi, 1969; Liska, 1971; and Brennan, 1974). Furthermore, there is substantial evidence in the above-mentioned studies that many adolescents engaging in significant amounts of delinquent behavior experience no discrepancies between aspirations and perceived opportunities. The lack of consistent support for this relationship suggests that failure or anticipated failure constitutes only one possible path to an involvement in delinquency.

The Control Perspective

The different assumptions of strain and control theories are significant. Strain formulations assume a positively socialized individual who violates conventional norms only when his or her attachment and commitment are attenuated. Norm violation occurs only after the individual perceives that opportunities for socially valued goals are blocked. Strain theory focuses on this attenuation process. Control theories, on the other hand, treat the socialization process and commitment to conventional norms and values as problematic. Persons differ with respect to their commitment to and integration into the conventional social order. . . .

From a control perspective, delinquency is viewed as a consequence of (1) lack of internalized normative controls, (2) breakdown in previously established controls, and/or (3) conflict or inconsistency in rules or social controls. Strain formulations of delinquency appear to be focusing on those variables and processes which account for the second condition identified by Reiss (1951): attenuation or breakdown in previously established controls. On the other hand, most control theorists direct their attention to the first and third conditions, exploring such variables as inadequate socialization (failure to internalize conventional norms) and integration into conventional groups or institutions which provide strong external or social controls on behavior. From our perspective, these need not be viewed as contradictory explanations. On the contrary, they may be viewed as alternative processes, depending on the outcome of one's early socialization experience.

For example, Hirschi (1969) has argued that high aspirations involve a commitment to conventional lines of action that functions as a positive control or bond to the social order. Strain theories, on the other hand, view high aspirations (in the face of limited opportunities) as a source of attenuation of attachment to the conventional order. Recognizing this difference, Hirschi suggested that the examination of this relationship would constitute a crucial test of the two theories. Empirically, the evidence is inconsistent and far from conclusive. One possible interpretation is that both hypotheses are correct and are part of different etiological sequences leading to delinquent behavior.

Empirical studies using the control perspective have focused almost exclusively on the static relation of weak internal and external controls to delinquency without considering the longer developmental processes. These processes may involve an initially strong commitment to and integration into society which becomes attenuated over time, with the attenuation eventually resulting in delinquency. The source of this difficulty may lie in the infrequent use of longitudinal designs. Without a repeated-measure design, youths with strong bonds which subsequently become attenuated may be indistinguishable from those who never developed strong bonds.

AN INTEGRATED STRAIN-CONTROL PERSPECTIVE

Our proposed integrated theoretical paradigm begins with the assumption that different youths have different early socialization experiences, which result in variable degrees of commitment to and integration into conventional social groups. The effect of failure to achieve conventional goals on subsequent delinquency is related to the strength of one's initial bonds. Limited opportunities to achieve conventional goals constitute a source of strain and thus a motivational stimulus for delinquency only if one is committed to these goals. In contrast, limited opportunities to achieve such goals should have little or no impact on those with weak ties and commitments to the conventional social order.

Limited opportunities to achieve conventional goals are not the only experiences which weaken or break initially strong ties to the social order. Labeling theorists have argued that the experience of being apprehended and publicly labeled delinquent initiates social processes which limit one's access to conventional social roles and statuses, isolating one from participation in these activities and relationships and forcing one to assume a delinquent role (Becker, 1963; Schur, 1971, 1973; Kitsuse, 1962; Rubington & Weinberg, 1968; Ageton & Elliott, 1974; and Goldman, 1963). It has also been argued that the effects of social disorganization or crisis in the home (divorce, parental strife and discord, death of a parent) and/or community (high rates of mobility, economic depression, unemployment) attenuate or break one's ties to society (Thomas & Znaniecki, 1927; Shaw, 1931; Savitz, 1970; Monahan, 1957; Toby, 1957; Glueck & Glueck, 1970; Andry, 1962; and Rosen, 1970).

In sum, we postulate that limited opportunities, failure to achieve valued goals, negative labeling experiences, and social disorganization at home and in the community are all experiences which may attenuate one's ties to the conventional social order and may thus be causal factors in the developmental sequence leading to delinquent behavior for those whose early socialization experiences produced strong bonds to society. For those whose attachments to the conventional social order are already weak, such factors may further weaken ties to society but are not necessary factors in the etiological sequence leading to delinquency.

Our basic conceptual framework comes from control theory, with a slightly different emphasis placed on participation in and commitment to delinquent groups. Further, it identifies a set of attenuating/bonding experiences which weaken or strengthen ties to the conventional social order over time. Our focus is on experiences and social contexts which are relevant to adolescents. A diagram of our proposed theoretical scheme is shown in Figure 34.1. The rows in Figure 34.1 indicate the direction and sequence of the hypothesized relationships. While the time order designated in Figure 34.1 is unidirectional, the actual relationships between initial socialization, bonding/attenuation processes, normative orientations of groups, and behavior are often reciprocal and reinforcing. We have also presented the variables in dichotomized form to simplify the model and the discussion of its major elements.

Bonds

Control theorists disagree about sources of control, but they all accept the central proposition that delinquent behavior is a direct result of weak ties to the conventional normative order. In operationalizing control theory, major emphasis has been placed on the bond(s) which tie a person to society. Hirschi (1969) conceptualized four elements of this bond. First, attachment implies a moral link to other people and encompasses such concepts as conscience, superego, and internalization of norms. Commitment, the second factor, is the rational element in the bond. Hirschi views commitment to conformity as an investment in conventional lines of action, such as an educational or occupational career. Other theorists have tied the concept of commitment to such notions as "stake in conformity" (Goode, 1960) and "side bets" (Becker, 1960).

Involvement is the time and energy dimension of the bond for Hirschi. Given the limits of time and energy, involvement in conventional activities acts as a social constraint on delinquent behavior. The final bond, *belief*, refers to one's acceptance of the moral validity of social rules and norms. According to Hirschi, this psychological element of the bond is effective as long as a person accepts the validity of the rules. If one denies or depreciates the validity of the rules, one source of control is neutralized.

Other control theorists, such as Reiss (1951), Nye (1958), and Reckless (1967) use a more general classification of bonds as internal (personal) and external (social) controls. Hirschi's dimensions are not easily placed into these two general categories, although Hirschi identifies attachment as an internal and involvement as an external element of the bond (1969, p. 19). We believe that distinguishing internal controls, whose locus is within the person (beliefs, commitment, attitudes, perceptions), from external controls, whose locus is in the surrounding social and physical milieu, poses fewer difficulties and produces greater conceptual clarity than is found in Hirschi's four concepts.

The external, or social, bond we have defined as *integration*. By this, we refer to involvement in and attachment to conventional groups and institutions, such as the family, school, peer networks, and so on. Those persons who occupy and are actively involved in conventional social roles are, by this definition, highly integrated. Group controls exist in the form of sanctioning networks (the formal and informal rules and regulations by which the behavior of social role occupants or group members is regulated). This conceptualization of integration is akin to Hirschi's concepts of involvement and commitment.

The internal, or personal, bond is defined as *commitment*. Commitment involves personal attachment to conventional roles, groups, and institutions. At another level, it reflects the extent to which one feels morally bound by the social norms and rules and the degree to which one internalizes or adopts those norms as directives for action. Our notion of commitment is akin to Hirschi's concepts of attachment and belief. Integration and commitment together constitute the bonds which tie an individual to the prevailing social order. High levels of integration and

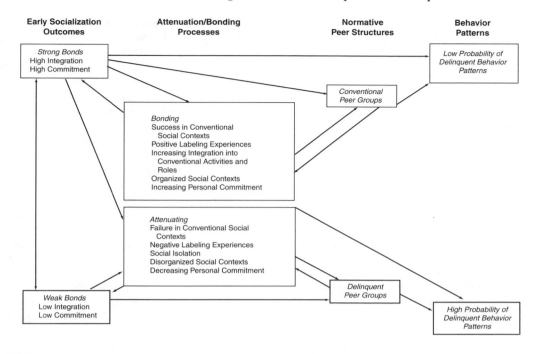

Figure 34.1 Integrated Strain-Control Paradigm

commitment imply strong bonds and general insulation from delinquent behavior. Conversely, low social integration and commitment presuppose weak bonds and a susceptibility to delinquent behavior. All gradations of integration and commitment are possible.

Building Social Control:
The Bonding/Attenuation Processes

The inclusion of the bonding/attenuation process in the model suggests that, throughout adolescence, youths are involved in experiences and processes which attenuate or reinforce their childhood bonds to the conventional social order. Adolescence is a critical life period, both psychologically and socially. As youths make the transition from childhood to adulthood, the level of involvement in the immediate family declines and they move into new and more complex social settings at school and in the community. For one who developed strong childhood bonds, such factors as (1) success experiences at school and in the larger community, (2) positive labeling in these new settings, and (3) a continuous, stable,

harmonious home life constitute positive reinforcements of initially strong bonds and continuing insulation from delinquency. For some, the transition is not as smooth, and failure, negative labeling, isolation, and rejection occur in these new social settings; these, in turn, may create difficulties in the youth's relationship with his family. The net effect of these new experiences may be a weakening of one's integration into . . . these social groups and institutions and an increasing likelihood of involvement in delinquent behavior. Finally, for those who never developed strong bonds during childhood, bonding/attenuation experiences will either strengthen the weak bonds, thus reducing the likelihood of delinquency, or further attenuate them, thus maintaining or increasing the probability of delinquent behavior.

We do not propose that this specific set of variables exhausts the possible experiences or conditions which might attenuate or reinforce one's bonds to society during adolescence. Rather, we have purposely selected those conditions and experiences which prior theory and research have suggested as critical variables to illustrate the major dimensions of the paradigm.

Delinquent Learning and Performance Structures

A major criticism of control theory has been that weak bonds and the implied absence of restraints cannot alone account for the specific form or content of the behavior which results. They may account for a state of "drift," as described by Matza (1964), but they do not explain why some youths in this state turn to delinquency, drug use, and various unconventional subcultures, while others maintain an essentially conforming pattern of behavior; nor can they account for emerging patterns of delinquency which may be unique to particular ages or birth cohorts. We therefore postulate that access to and involvement in delinquent learning and performance structures is a necessary (but not sufficient) variable in the etiology of delinquent behavior. Following Sutherland (1947), we maintain that delinquent behavior, like conforming behavior, presupposes a pattern of social relationships through which motives, rationalizations, techniques, and rewards can be learned and maintained (Burgess & Akers, 1966; Akers, 1977; Bandura, 1969, 1973; and Mischel, 1968). Delinquent behavior is thus viewed as behavior which has social meaning and must be supported and rewarded by social groups if it is to persist.

By the time children enter adolescence, virtually all have been sufficiently exposed to criminal forms of behavior to have "learned" or acquired some potential for such acts. The more critical issue for any theory of delinquency is why and how this universal potential is transformed into delinquent acts for some youths and not others. For most learning theorists, a distinction is made between learning and performance and the latter is directly tied to reinforcements (Rotter, 1954; Bandura & Walters, 1963; Mischel, 1968; and Bandura, 1969). . . .

According to the present social learning formulation, learning or acquisition of novel responses is regulated by sensory and cognitive processes; learning may be facilitated by reinforcement but does not depend on it (e.g., Bandura & Walters, 1963; Hebb, 1966). Direct and vicarious reinforcement are, however, important determinants of response selection in performance.

The delinquent peer group thus provides a positive social setting that is essential for the performance and maintenance of delinquent patterns of behavior over time. Those committed to conventional goals, although they may have been exposed to and learned some delinquent behaviors, should not establish patterns of such behavior unless (1) their ties to the conventional social order are neutralized through some attenuating experiences and (2) they are participating in a social context in which delinquent behavior is rewarded. In social learning terms, they may have acquired or learned delinquent behavior patterns, but the actual performance and maintenance of such behavior are contingent on attenuation of their commitment to conventional norms and their participation in a social context supportive of delinquent acts. Alternatively, for those with weak ties and commitments to the conventional social order, there is no reason for a delay between acquisition and performance of delinquent acts.

In the causal sequence described by strain theory, the individual holds conventional goals but is unable to attain them by conventional means. If attachment to the goals is strong enough, it may support delinquent behavior without participation in delinquent groups, for attaining these goals may provide sufficient reinforcement to maintain the behavior. Therefore, our model shows one direct route to delinquent behavior from attenuating experiences, without mediating group support for delinquency. We view this as the atypical case, however, and postulate that it is difficult to sustain this causal sequence for extended periods of time.

Involvement in a delinquent group is a necessary condition for sustained patterns of delinquency among persons who do not subscribe to conventional goals (the weakly socialized person described by control theory). Individual patterns of delinquency (without group support) are more viable for those committed to conventional goals because there are generally shared expectations and social supports for achievement of those goals. For youths with weak bonds, involvement in a delinquent peer group serves this support function. Cohen (1966) has observed that delinquency often involves a desire for recognition and social acceptance, and, therefore, requires group visibility and support. Maintenance of delinquent behavior patterns should require some exposure to and participation in groups supporting delinquent activities. Though not a necessary condition for delinquent behavior among those with initially strong bonds, contact with delinquent groups should, nevertheless, increase the likelihood of sustained delinquent behavior.

Delineation of the delinquent peer group as a necessary condition for maintenance of delinquent behavior patterns represents an extension of previous statements of control theory. . . . It is one thing to be a social isolate with weak bonds to conventional peer groups and another to be highly committed to and integrated into a delinquent peer group. Both persons may be characterized as having weak bonds to the social order, with few conventional restraints on their behavior; but those committed to and participating in delinquent peer groups have some incentive and social support for specifically delinquent forms of behavior. We agree with Hirschi's (1969) and Hepburn's (1976) argument that those with a large stake in conformity (strong bonds) are relatively immune to delinquent peer group influence. However, we postulate that, in addition to weak bonding and an absence of restraints, some positive motivation is necessary for sustained involvement in delinquent behavior. In the absence of positive motivation, we would not predict significant involvement in delinquency across time even for those with weak bonds, for there is no apparent mechanism for maintaining such behavior (Brennan, Huizinga, & Elliott, 1978). It may be that some exploratory, "primary" forms of delinquency (Lemert, 1951) may occur without group support, or that this constitutes a pathological path to delinquency, but the maintenance of delinquent behavior patterns usually requires some exposure to and participation in groups supporting delinquent activity.

In sum, we postulate that bonding to conventional groups and institutions insulates one from involvement in delinquent patterns of behavior and that bonding to deviant groups or subcultures facilitates and sustains delinquent behavior. When examining the influence of social bonds, it is critical that the normative orientation of particular groups be taken into account. This focus on the normative orientations of groups is the central theme in subcultural theories of delinquency (Cohen, 1955; Cloward and Ohlin, 1960; and Miller, 1958) and constitutes an important qualification to a simple interpretation

of the relationship between social bonds and delinquency. This position has an empirical as well as a theoretical base. . . .

Delinquent Behavior

Delinquent behavior is viewed as a special subclass of deviant behavior. While deviance includes all violations of all prevailing norms, delinquent behavior includes only violations of statutory proscriptive norms, or, as they are usually called, laws. Thus, delinquent behavior takes on special meaning because (1) there is generally broad community consensus for these norms, (2) virtually all persons are aware that these specific proscriptions are enforced by official sanctions, and (3) the risk of detection and punishment influences the performance of delinquent acts.

We are not concerned here with the isolated delinquent act. Our focus is on sustained patterns of delinquent behavior, whether the person involved is socially or self-defined as a delinquent or nondelinquent person. Although our definition of delinquency subsumes one characteristic of a delinquent role (sustained patterns of delinquent behavior), it is our view that continuing involvement in delinquency may not necessarily involve the enactment of a delinquent role (Becker, 1963). There is empirical evidence that many embezzlers, auto thieves, check forgers, shoplifters, and persons involved in violent assaults against persons (including rape) do not view themselves as criminal or delinquent (Cressey, 1971; Gibbons, 1977; Lemert, 1951, 1953; Cameron, 1964; Robin, 1974; Gauthier, 1959; and Gebhard et al., 1965). Furthermore, many adolescents involved in sustained patterns of delinquent behavior are never apprehended and publicly labeled as delinquent persons, and have neither a public nor a self-definition as a delinquent or criminal person (Sykes and Matza, 1957; Reiss, 1962; Cameron, 1964; Hirschi, 1969; Kelly, 1977; and Jensen, 1972). Thus, our conceptualization of delinquency focuses on sustained patterns of illegal behavior and is logically independent of the concept of delinquent role.

Etiological Paths to Delinquency

There are two dominant etiological paths to delinquency in the paradigm shown in Figure 34.1. The first involves an integration of traditional control theory and social-learning theory. Weak integration into and commitment to the social order, absence of conventional restraints on behavior, and high vulnerability to the influence of delinquent peer groups during adolescence characterize the socialization experiences related to the first path. Depending on the presence and accessibility of conventional and delinquent peer groups, some weakly bonded youths turn to delinquency while others maintain an essentially conforming pattern of behavior or a legal, but unconventional, lifestyle. The crucial element in this path is the delinquent peer group. Weakly bonded youths may not hold conventional aspirations (as for academic success), but they do share in more general aspirations for friendship and acceptance, as well as status and material rewards, which may be offered through participation in a group. Given an absence of conventional restraints and access to delinquent groups, the reasons for involvement are not unlike those for involvement in more conventional peer groups during adolescence.

The second path represents an integration of traditional strain and social-learning perspectives. Youths who follow this path develop strong bonds to the conventional social order through their socialization experiences. The crucial element in this sequence is the attenuation, or weakening, of these bonds. Attenuating experiences during adolescence involve personal failure to achieve conventional goals and/or threats to the stability and cohesion of one's conventional social groups. Once one's bonds are effectively weakened, like those who never developed strong bonds, one is free to explore alternative means for goal achievement and to participate in delinquent or unconventional groups.

In most instances, this path also involves participation in peer groups which tolerate or encourage delinquent forms of behavior. It is our view that truly individual adaptations to this situation are unlikely to survive long enough to generate detectable patterns of delinquent behavior. However, two possible subtypes deserve mention. The diagram of this integrated paradigm shows a direct causal path from initially strong bonds and subsequent attenuation experiences to delinquent behavior patterns. Under some circumstances, participation in groups providing reinforcements for delinquent acts is unnecessary. Attenuating experiences are sufficient to motivate repeated acts of delinquency, which are attempts to regain conventional rewards through unconventional means. This pattern involves the classic strain model, in which the person retains a strong commitment to conventional goals and values and uses illegal means as a temporary expedient. The attenuation process is only partial, and these youths retain some commitment to and integration into conventional groups. We anticipate such patterns to be of relatively short duration and to involve highly instrumental forms of delinquent behavior. Patterns of theft may characterize this etiological path.

A second subtype corresponds to that described generally by Simon and Gagnon (1976) in their article on the anomie of affluence. This path involves those whose commitments to conventional goals are attenuated by a decreasing gratification derived from goal achievement. Unlike the previously described subtype, which involved failure to achieve conventional success goals because of limited means or abilities, this type has ability and a ready access to legitimate means and is successful by conventional standards. The failure to derive personal gratification from "success" results in an attenuation of the commitment to these success goals and sets in motion a search for alternative goals whose attainment will provide a greater measure of personal gratification. This path to delinquency clearly requires participation in social groups in which delinquent behavior patterns can be learned and reinforced. This pattern of delinquency is characterized by a search for new experiences, which frequently involves illegal forms of behavior, such as illicit drug use and sex-related offenses.

At a more tentative level, we postulate that the two major paths (1) typically involve different forms of personal alienation and (2) result in different self-images and social labels. Conceptually, alienation plays a slightly different role within strain and control perspectives. From a control perspective, alienation, in the form of powerlessness, societal estrangement, and social isolation, directly reflects a weak personal commitment to conventional groups and norms. For strain theory, however, alienation represents a crucial intervening variable linking failure to delinquency. It is evidence of the attenuation of one's commitment bond or, in Hirschi's (1969) terms, the neutralization of "moral obstacles" to delinquency. In the form of alienation described by Cloward and Ohlin (1960), the neutralization is achieved through a blaming process in which failure is attributed to others or to general societal injustice. These same elements are present in Sykes and Matza's (1957) techniques of neutralization. Cartwright et al. (1966) and Cartwright (1971) identify four types of alienation which provide this direct encouragement, justification, or permission for delinquency: normlessness, futility, lack of trust, and perceived indifference. If we assume some relationship between the two causal paths and social class, there is some indirect empirical support for the hypothesis that the form of alienation is tied to the strength of one's initial commitment bond. . . .

We also hypothesize that those with initially strong bonds are less likely to view themselves as delinquent, even when they are involved in sustained patterns of delinquent behavior. Such persons are more likely to come from advantaged backgrounds and to have prosocial self-images. Consequently, they are likely to view their delinquent acts as temporary expedients, retaining at least a partial commitment to conventional goals. The probability of apprehension and public labeling by the police and courts is also much lower for such youths. In contrast, those who never developed strong bonds to the social order are more vulnerable to labeling processes and thus more likely to be viewed as delinquents by themselves and by others (Jensen, 1972). This may account, in part, for the persistent view among law enforcement officials and the general public that most delinquents are poor and/or nonwhite, in spite of the compelling evidence that the incidence of delinquent behavior is unrelated to these variables.

SUMMARY AND DISCUSSION

. . . . We believe the synthesis of traditional strain, social control, and social-learning perspectives into a single paradigm has several advantages over a conceptualization which treats each theory as separate and independent. First, the provision for multiple etiological paths to delinquency in a single paradigm presents a more comprehensive view. The integration of strain and control perspectives assumes that these two paths are independent and additive and that their integration will account for more variance in sustained patterns of delinquent behavior than

either can explain independently. Independent tests of these traditional perspectives in the past have often failed to include the variables necessary to test alternative explanations, and even when such variables were available, the alternative explanations were assumed to be competitive and were thus evaluated with respect to the relative strengths of the two competing hypotheses (Hirschi, 1969; and Eve, 1977). Such an approach misses the possibility that both hypotheses are correct and are accounting for different portions of the variance in delinquency. We have also suggested that different patterns of delinquency may be tied to alternative etiological paths; for example, we postulated that one of the strain paths (limited means/goal failure) should produce forms of delinquency which are considered very instrumental by conventional values. The alternative strain path (attenuated commitment to conventional goals) should result in less instrumental forms of delinquency, since it characteristically involves a search for new experiences (e.g., drug use) rather than attempts to achieve conventional goals.

Second, we believe that our integrated paradigm is consistent with previous empirical findings and offers some insight into contradictory findings. Previous research using the social control perspective has established a relationship between the strength of one's bonds and social class, with low-SES and minority youths characterized by weaker bonds (Nye, 1958; Gold, 1963; McKinley, 1964; and Hirschi, 1969). In contrast, the attenuated commitment strain path has been associated with affluence, and the limited means-strain path seems most relevant to working-class youths. The combined effect seems consistent with the observed class distribution of self-reported delinquent behavior. Our assumption that weakly bonded youths run the greatest risk of official processing (because of greater surveillance in their neighborhoods, more traditional forms of delinquent behavior, and limited resources with which to avoid processing in the justice system) would account for the observed class distribution of official measures of delinquency. . . .

DISCUSSION QUESTIONS

1. What elements from previous conceptualizations of strain theory do Elliott et al. share, and

in what ways do they differ from these earlier approaches?

2. What are the theoretical assumptions of the authors' integrated model? Why is the delinquent peer group the most critical variable in their theoretical model?

3. What are some of the major criticisms of the integrated model? Do you feel that the goal of theoretical integration is important enough to violate certain theoretical assumptions?

4. Why is it that certain individuals with strong social bonds may find those bonds weakening under certain circumstances? What reasons do Elliott et al. provide?

REFERENCES

Cloward, R. A., & Ohlin, L. E. (1960). *Delinquency and opportunity—A theory of delinquent gangs*. New York: Free Press.

Cohen, A. K. (1955). *Delinquent boys: The culture of the gang*. Glencoe, IL: Free Press.

Merton, R. K. (1938). Social structure and anomie. *American Sociological Review, 3*, 672-682.

35

TOWARD AN INTERACTIONAL THEORY OF DELINQUENCY

TERENCE P. THORNBERRY

EDITOR'S INTRODUCTION—Thornberry's interactional theory of delinquency provides an effective example of an integrated approach to the social process of delinquent behavior. In a variety of ways, this theory shares certain similarities with Elliott, Ageton, and Canter's integrated theory discussed in the previous reading selection (Chapter 34, this volume). More specifically, Thornberry argues that low social control, or weak social bonds, contributes to delinquency by increasing the likelihood of association with delinquent peers. In the model of Elliott et al., this path also leads primarily to delinquency. But unlike these authors, Thornberry draws on Hirschi's (1969) formation of the elements of the social bond. He defines them broadly, however, and leaves out elements of strain theory, which had not been receiving much empirical support at the time when Thornberry developed his integrated approach.

The main contribution of Thornberry's interactional theory lies in its incorporation of reciprocal effects and the developmental process. At the time of this article's publication, he argues, theories of delinquency were seen as limited: Unidirectional causal models represented delinquency as a static rather than a dynamic activity and failed to link processual concepts to the person's position in the social structure. Thornberry's interactional theory addresses both of these issues by viewing delinquency as resulting from the freedom afforded by the weakening of the person's bonds to conventional society and from an interactional setting in which delinquent behavior is learned and reinforced.

Moreover, the reciprocal effects emerge through the fact that delinquency variables are viewed as interrelated and mutually affecting one another over the person's entire life. This point is important because it suggests that although association with delinquent peers increases the likelihood of associating with delinquent peers, it also suggests that delinquency increases the likelihood of association with delinquent peers. Reciprocal effects are important because they suggest that many youths get involved in an "amplifying causal structure" that contributes to greater involvement in delinquency over time.

Thornberry also contends that the causes for delinquency change over the course of a person's life. For example, he notes that the importance of parental attachment becomes less significant in an adolescent's life when new variables, such as commitment to other conventional activities, begin to emerge (i.e., peers, college, employment). Thornberry's model also makes an important contribution in terms of his developmental component. Whereas most theories of delinquency center on adolescent delinquent behavior, his model allows for a fuller explanation of patterns of delinquency over the life course, such as the notion that most adolescents tend to desist from delinquency as they get older. A final important point centers on Thornberry's consideration of structural variables such as social class and gender, which can affect the primary level of social control and exposure to delinquent peers, values, and behaviors.

A variety of sociological theories have been developed to explain the onset and maintenance of delinquent behavior. Currently, three are of primary importance: social control theory (Hirschi, 1969), social learning theory (Akers, 1977), and integrated models that combine them into a broader body of explanatory principals (Elliott, Ageton, & Canter, 1979; Elliott, Huizinga, & Ageton, 1985). Control theory argues that delinquency emerges whenever the social and cultural constraints over human conduct are substantially attenuated. As Hirschi states in his classic presentation (1969), control theory assumes that we would all be deviant if only we dared. Learning theory, on the other hand, posits that there is no natural impulse toward delinquency. Indeed, delinquent behavior must be learned through the same processes and mechanisms as conforming behavior. Because of these different starting points, control and learning models give causal priority to somewhat different concepts, and integrated models capitalize on these complementary approaches. Muting the assumptive differences, integrated theories meld together propositions from these (and sometimes other theories—for example, strain) to explain delinquent behavior.

Although these approaches have substantially informed our understanding of the causes of delinquency, they and other contemporary theories suffer from three fundamental limitations. First, they rely on unidirectional rather than reciprocal causal structures. By and large, current theories ignore reciprocal effects in which delinquent behavior is viewed as part of a more general social nexus, affected by, but also affecting, other social factors. Second, current theories tend to be nondevelopmental, specifying causal models for only a narrow age range, usually mid-adolescence. As a result, they fail to capitalize on developmental patterns to explain the initiation, maintenance, and desistance of delinquency.

Finally, contemporary theories tend to assume uniform causal effects throughout the social structure. By ignoring the person's structural position, they fail to provide an understanding of the sources of initial variation in both delinquency and its presumed causes. In combination, these three limitations have led to theories that are narrowly conceived and which provide incomplete and, at times, misleading models of the causes of delinquency.

The present paper develops an interactional theory of delinquency that addresses and attempts to respond to each of these limitations. The model proposed here pays particular attention to the first issue, recursive versus reciprocal causal structures, since the development of dynamic models is seen as essential to represent accurately the interactional settings in which delinquency develops.

ORIGINS AND ASSUMPTIONS

The basic premise of the model proposed here is that human behavior occurs in social interaction and can therefore best be explained by models that focus on interactive processes. Rather than viewing adolescents as propelled along a unidirectional pathway to one or another outcome— that is, delinquency or conformity—it argues that adolescents interact with other people and institutions and that behavioral outcomes are formed by that interactive process. For example, the delinquent behavior of an adolescent is formed in part by how he and his parents *interact* over time, not simply by the child's perceived, and presumably invariant, *level* of attachment to parents. Moreover, since it is an interactive system, the behaviors of others—for example, parents and school officials—are influenced both by each other and by the adolescent, including his or her delinquent behavior.

Thornberry, T. P. (1987). Toward an interactional theory of delinquency. *Criminology, 25,* 863-891.

If this view is correct, then interactional effects have to be modeled explicitly if we are to understand the social and psychological processes involved with initiation into delinquency, the maintenance of such behavior, and its eventual reduction.

Interactional theory develops from the same intellectual tradition as the theories mentioned above, especially the Durkheimian tradition of social control. It asserts that the fundamental cause of delinquency lies in the weakening of social constraints over the conduct of the individual. Unlike classical control theory, however, it does not assume that the attenuation of controls leads directly to delinquency. The weakening of controls simply allows for a much wider array of behavior, including continued conventional action, failure as indicated by school dropout and sporadic employment histories, alcoholism, mental illness, delinquent and criminal careers, or some combination of these outcomes. For the freedom resulting from weakened bonds to be channeled into delinquency, especially serious prolonged delinquency, requires an interactive setting in which delinquency is learned, performed, and reinforced. This view is similar to Cullen's structuring perspective which draws attention to the [indeterminacy] of deviant behavior. "It can thus be argued that there is an *indeterminate* and not a determinate or etiologically specific relationship between motivational variables on the one hand and any particular form of deviant behavior on the other hand" (Cullen, 1984, p. 5).

Although heavily influenced by control and learning theories, and to a lesser extent by strain and culture conflict theories, this is not an effort at theoretical integration as that term is usually used (Elliott, 1985). Rather, this paper is guided by what we have elsewhere called theoretical elaboration (Thornberry, 1987). In this instance, a basic control theory is extended, or elaborated upon, using available theoretical perspectives and empirical findings to provide a more accurate model of the causes of delinquency. In the process of elaboration, there is no requirement to resolve disputes among other theories—for example, their different assumptions about the origins of deviance (Thornberry, 1987, pp. 15-18); all that is required is that the propositions of the model developed here be consistent with one another and with the assumptions about deviance stated above.

ORGANIZATION

The presentation of the interactional model begins by identifying the central concepts to be included in the model. Next, the underlying theoretical structure of the proposed model is examined and the rationale for moving from unidirectional to reciprocal causal models is developed. The reciprocal model is then extended to include a developmental perspective, examining the theoretical saliency of different variables at different developmental stages. Finally, the influence of the person's position in the social structure is explored. Although in some senses the last issue is logically prior to the others, since it is concerned with sources of initial variation in the causal variables, it is discussed last so that the reciprocal relationships among the concepts—the heart of an interactional perspective—can be more fully developed.

THEORETICAL CONCEPTS

Given these basic premises, an interactional model must respond to two overriding issues. First, how are traditional social constraints over behavior weakened and, second, once weakened, how is the resulting freedom channelled into delinquent patterns? To address these issues, the present paper presents an initial version of an interactional model, focusing on the interrelationships among six concepts: attachment to parents, commitment to school, belief in conventional values, associations with delinquent peers, adopting delinquent values, and engaging in delinquent behavior. These concepts form the core of the theoretical model since they are central to social psychological theories of delinquency and since they have been shown in numerous studies to be strongly related to subsequent delinquent behavior (see Elliott et al., 1985, Chs. 1-3, for an excellent review of this literature).

The first three derive from Hirschi's version of control theory (1969) and represent the primary mechanisms by which adolescents are bonded to conventional middle-class society. When those elements of the bond are weakened, behavioral freedom increases considerably. For that freedom to lead to delinquent behavior, however, interactive settings that reinforce delinquency are required. In the model, those settings are represented by two concepts: associations with delinquent peers and the formation of delinquent values which derive primarily from social learning theory. For the purpose of explicating the overall theoretical perspective, each of these concepts is defined quite broadly. Attachment to parents includes the affective relationship between parent and child, communication patterns, parenting skills such as monitoring and discipline, parent-child conflict, and the like. Commitment to school refers to the stake in conformity the adolescent has developed and includes such factors as success in school, perceived importance of education, attachment to teachers, and involvement in school activities. Belief in conventional values represents the granting of legitimacy to such middle-class values as education, personal industry, financial success, deferral of gratification, and the like.

Three delinquency variables are included in the model. Association with delinquent peers includes the level of attachment to peers, the delinquent behavior and values of peers, and their reinforcing reactions to the adolescent's own delinquent or conforming behavior. It is a continuous measure that can vary from groups that are heavily delinquent to those that are almost entirely nondelinquent. Delinquent values refer to the granting of legitimacy to delinquent activities as acceptable modes of behavior as well as a general willingness to violate the law to achieve other ends. Delinquent behavior, the primary outcome variable, refers to acts that place the youth at risk for adjudication; it ranges from status offenses to serious violent activities. Since the present model is an interactional one, interested not only in explaining delinquency but in explaining the effects of delinquency on other variables, particular attention is paid to prolonged involvement in serious delinquency. . . .

MODEL SPECIFICATION

A causal model allowing for reciprocal relationships among the six concepts of interest—attachment to parents, commitment to school, belief in conventional values, association with delinquent peers, delinquent values, and delinquent behavior—is presented in Figure 35.1. This model refers to the period of early adolescence, from about ages 11 to 13, when

delinquent careers are beginning, but prior to the period at which delinquency reaches its apex in terms of seriousness and frequency. In the following sections the model is extended to later ages.

The specification of causal effects begins by examining the three concepts that form the heart of social learning theories of delinquency—delinquent peers, delinquent values, and delinquent behavior. For now we focus on the reciprocal nature of the relationships, ignoring until later variations in the strength of the relationships. Traditional social learning theory specifies a causal order among these variables in which delinquent associations affect delinquent values and, in turn, both produce delinquent behavior (Akers, Krohn, Lanza-Kaduce, & Radosevich, 1979; Matsueda, 1982). Yet, for each of the dyadic relationships involving these variables, other theoretical perspectives and much empirical evidence suggest the appropriateness of reversing this causal order. For example, social learning theory proposes that associating with delinquents, or more precisely, people who hold and reinforce delinquent values, increases the chances of delinquent behavior (Akers, 1977). Yet, as far back as the work of the Gluecks (1950) this specification has been challenged. Arguing that "birds of a feather flock together," the Gluecks propose that youths who are delinquent seek out and associate with others who share those tendencies. From this perspective, rather than being a cause of delinquency, associations are the result of delinquents seeking out and associating with like-minded peers.

An attempt to resolve the somewhat tedious argument over the temporal priority of associations and behavior is less productive theoretically than capitalizing on the interactive nature of human behavior and treating the relationship as it probably is: a reciprocal one. People often take on the behavioral repertoire of their associates but, at the same time, they often seek out associates who share their behavioral interests. Individuals clearly behave this way in conventional settings, and there is no reason to assume that deviant activities, such as delinquency, are substantially different in this regard.

Similar arguments can be made for the other two relationships among the delinquency variables. Most recent theories of delinquency, following the lead of social learning theory, posit that delinquent associations lead to the formation

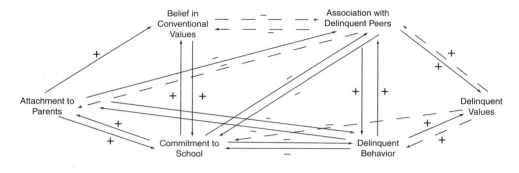

Figure 35.1   A Reciprocal Model of Delinquent Involvement at Early Adolescence

of delinquent values. Subcultural theories, however, especially those that derive from a cultural deviance perspective (Miller, 1958) suggest that values precede the formation of peer groups. Indeed, it is the socialization of adolescents into the "lower-class culture" and its particular value system that leads them to associate with delinquent peers in the first place. This specification can also be derived from a social control perspective as demonstrated in Weis and Sederstrom's social development model (1981) and Burkett and Warren's social selection model (1987).

Finally, the link between delinquent values and delinquent behavior restates, in many ways, the basic social psychological question of the relationship between attitudes and behavior. Do attitudes form behavior patterns or does behavior lead to attitude formation? Social psychological research, especially in cognitive psychology and balance models (for example, Festinger, 1957; Brehm and Cohen, 1962) points to the reciprocal nature of this relationship. It suggests that people indeed behave in a manner consistent with their attitudes, but also that behavior is one of the most persuasive forces in the formation and maintenance of attitudes.

Such a view of the relationship between delinquent values and behavior is consistent with Hindelang's findings: this general pattern of results indicates that one can "predict" a respondent's self approval [of illegal behaviors] from knowledge of that respondent's involvement/non-involvement [in delinquency] with fewer errors than vice-versa (1974, p. 382). It is also consistent with recent deterrence research which demonstrates that the "experiential effect," in

which behavior affects attitudes, is much stronger than the deterrent effect, in which attitudes affect behavior (Paternoster, Saltzman, Waldo, & Chiricos, 1982; Paternoster, Saltzman, Chiricos, & Waldo, 1983).

Although each of these relationships appears to be reciprocal, the predicted strengths of the associations are not of equal strength during the early adolescent period (see Figure 35.1). Beliefs that delinquent conduct is acceptable [and] positively valued may be emerging, but such beliefs are not fully articulated for 11- to 13-year-olds. Because of their emerging quality, they are viewed more effect than cause, produced by delinquent behavior and associations with delinquent peers. As these values emerge, however, they have feedback effects, albeit relatively weak ones at these ages, on behavior and associations. That is, as the values become more fully articulated and delinquency becomes positively valued, it increases the likelihood of such behavior and further reinforces associations with like-minded peers.

Summary. When attention is focused on the interrelationships among associations with delinquent peers, delinquent values, and delinquent behavior, it appears that they are, in fact, reciprocally related. The world of human behavior is far more complex than a simple recursive one in which a temporal order can be imposed on interactional variables of this nature. Interactional theory sees these three concepts as embedded in a causal loop, each reinforcing the others over time. Regardless of where the individual enters the loop the following obtains: delinquency increases associations with delinquent peers and delinquent values; delinquent values increase delinquent behavior and associations with delinquent peers; and associations with delinquent peers increases delinquent behavior and delinquent values. The question now concerns the identification of factors that lead some youth, but not others into this spiral of increasing delinquency.

SOCIAL CONTROL EFFECTS

As indicated at the outset of this essay, the promise of interactional theory is that the fundamental cause of delinquency is the attenuation of social controls over the person's conduct. Whenever bonds to the conventional world are substantially weakened, the individual is freed from moral constraints and is at risk for a wide array of deviant activities, including delinquency. The primary mechanisms that bind adolescents to the conventional world are attachment to parents, commitment to school, and belief in conventional values, and their role in the model can now be examined.

During the early adolescent years, the family is the most salient arena for social interaction and involvement and, because of this, attachment to parents has a stronger influence on other aspects of the youth's life at this stage than it does at later stages of development. With this in mind, attachment to parents is predicted to affect four other variables. Since youths who are attached to their parents are sensitive to their wishes (Hirschi, 1969, pp. 16-19), and, since parents are almost universally supportive of the conventional world, these children are likely to be strongly committed to school and to espouse conventional values. In addition, youths who are attached to their parents, again because of their sensitivity to parental wishes, are unlikely to associate with delinquent peers or to engage in delinquent behavior.

In brief, parental influence is seen as central to controlling the behavior of youths at these relatively early ages. Parents who have a strong affective bond with their children, who communicate with them, who exercise appropriate parenting skills, and so forth, are likely to lead their children towards conventional actions and beliefs and away from delinquent friends and actions.

On the other hand, attachment to parents is not seen as an immutable trait, impervious to the effects of other variables. Indeed, associating with delinquent peers, not being committed to school, and engaging in delinquent behavior are so contradictory to parental expectations that they tend to diminish the level of attachment between parent and child. Adolescents who fail at school, who associate with delinquent peers, and who engage in delinquent conduct are, as a consequence, likely to jeopardize their affective bond with their parents, precisely because these behaviors suggest that the "person does not care about the wishes and expectations of other people . . ." (Hirschi, 1969, p. 18), in this instance, his or her parents.

Turning next to belief in conventional values, this concept is involved in two different causal loops. First, it strongly affects commitment to school and in turn is affected by commitment to school. In essence, this loop posits a behavioral and attitudinal consistency in the conventional realm. Second, a weaker loop is posited between belief in conventional values and associations with delinquent peers. Youths who do not grant legitimacy to conventional values are more apt to associate with delinquent friends who share those views, and those friendships are likely to attenuate further their beliefs in conventional values. This reciprocal specification is supported by Burkett and Warren's findings concerning religious beliefs and peer associations (1987). Finally, youths who believe in conventional values are seen as somewhat less likely to engage in delinquent behavior.

Although belief in conventional values plays some role in the genesis of delinquency, its impact is not particularly strong. For example, it is not affected by delinquent behavior, nor is it related to delinquent values. This is primarily because belief in conventional values appears to be quite invariant; regardless of class of origin or delinquency status, for example, most people strongly assert conventional values (Short & Strodtbeck, 1965, Ch. 3). Nevertheless, these beliefs do exert some influence in the model, especially with respect to reinforcing commitment to school.

Finally, the impact of commitment to school is considered. This variable is involved in reciprocal loops with both of the other bonding variables. Youngsters who are attached to their parents are likely to be committed to and succeed in school, and that success is likely to reinforce the close ties to their parents. Similarly, youths who believe in conventional values are likely to be committed to school, the primary arena in which they can act in accordance with those values, and, in turn, success in that arena is likely to reinforce the beliefs.

In addition to its relationships with the other control variables, commitment to school also has direct effects on two of the delinquency variables. Students who are committed to succeeding in school are unlikely to associate with delinquents or to engage in substantial amounts of serious, repetitive delinquent behavior. These youths have built up a stake in conformity and should be unwilling to jeopardize that investment by either engaging in delinquent behavior or by associating with those who do. Low commitment to school is not seen as leading directly to the formation of delinquent values, however. Its primary effect on delinquent values is indirect, via associations with delinquent peers and delinquent behavior (Conger, 1980, p. 137). While school failure may lead to a reduced commitment to conventional values, it does not follow that it directly increases the acceptance of values that support delinquency.

Commitment to school, on the other hand, is affected by each of the delinquency variables in the model. Youths who accept values that are consistent with delinquent behavior, who associate with other delinquents, and who engage in delinquent behavior are simply unlikely candidates to maintain an active commitment to school and the conventional world that school symbolizes.

Summary. Attachment to parents, commitment to school, and belief in conventional values reduce delinquency by cementing the person to conventional institutions and people. When these elements of the bond to conventional society are strong, delinquency is unlikely, but when they are weak the individual is placed at much greater risk for delinquency. When viewed from an interactional perspective, two additional qualities of these concepts become increasingly evident.

First, attachment to parents, commitment to school, and belief in conventional values are not static attributes of the person, invariant over time. These concepts interact with one another during the developmental process. For some

youths the levels of attachment, commitment, and belief increase as these elements reinforce one another, while for other youths the interlocking nature of these relationships suggests a greater and greater attenuation of the bond will develop over time.

Second, the bonding variables appear to be reciprocally linked to delinquency, exerting a causal impact on associations with delinquent peers and delinquent behavior; they also are causally [a]ffected by these variables. As the youth engages in more and more delinquent conduct and increasingly associates with delinquent peers, the level of his bond to the conventional world is further weakened. Thus, while the weakening of the bond to conventional society may be an initial cause of delinquency, delinquency eventually becomes its own indirect cause precisely because of its ability to weaken further the person's bonds to family, school, and conventional beliefs. The implications of this amplifying causal structure [are] examined below. First, however, the available support for reciprocal models is reviewed and the basic model is extended to later developmental stages. . . .

DEVELOPMENTAL EXTENSIONS

The previous section developed a strategy for addressing one of the three major limitations of delinquency theories mentioned in the introduction, namely, their unidirectional causal structure. A second limitation is the non-developmental posture of most theories which tend to provide a cross sectional picture of the factors associated with delinquency at one age, but which do not provide a rationale for understanding how delinquent behavior develops over time. The present section offers a developmental extension of the basic model.

Middle Adolescence

First, a model for middle adolescence, when the youths are approximately 15 or 16 years of age is presented (Figure 35.2). This period represents the highest rates of involvement in delinquency and is the reference period, either implicitly or explicitly, for most theories of delinquent involvement. Since the models for the early and middle adolescent periods have essentially the same structure and causal relationships

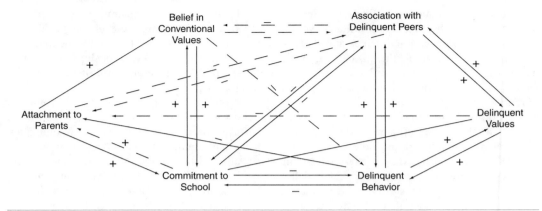

Figure 35.2   A Reciprocal Model of Delinquent Involvement at Middle Adolescence

(Figures 35.1 and 35.2), discussion focuses on the differences between them and does not repeat the rationale for individual causal effects.

Perhaps the most important difference concerns attachment to parents which is involved in relatively few strong relationships. By this point in the life cycle, the most salient variables involved in the production of delinquency are likely to be external to the home, associated with the youth's activities in school and peer networks. This specification is consistent with empirical results for subjects in this age range (Johnson, 1979, p. 105; and Schoenberg, 1975, quoted in Johnson). Indeed, Johnson concludes that "an adolescent's public life has as much or more to do with his or her deviance or conformity than do 'under-the-roof' experiences" (1979, p. 116).

This is not to say that attachment to parents is irrelevant; such attachments are involved in enhancing commitment to school and belief in conventional values, and in preventing associations with delinquent peers. It is just that the overall strength of parental effects [is] weaker than at earlier ages when the salience of the family as a locus of interaction and control was greater. The second major change concerns the increased importance of delinquent values as a causal factor. It is still embedded in the causal loop with the other two delinquency variables, but now it is as much cause as effect. Recall that at the younger ages delinquent values were seen as emerging, produced by associations with delinquent peers and delinquent behavior. Given their emergent nature, they were not seen as primary

causes of other variables. At mid-adolescence, however, when delinquency is at its apex, these values are more fully articulated and have stronger effects on other variables. First, delinquent values are seen as major reinforcers of both delinquent associations and delinquent behavior. In general, espousing values supportive of delinquency tends to increase the potency of this causal loop. Second, since delinquent values are antithetical to the conventional settings of school and family, youths who espouse them are less likely to be committed to school and attached to parents. Consistent with the reduced saliency of family at these ages, the feedback effect to school is seen as stronger than the feedback effect to parents.

By and large, the other concepts in the model play the same role at these ages as they do at the earlier ones. Thus, the major change from early to middle adolescence concerns the changing saliency of some of the theoretical concepts. The family declines in relative importance while the adolescent's own world of school and peers takes on increasing significance. While these changes occur, the overall structure of the theory remains constant. These interactive variables are still seen as mutually reinforcing over time.

Later Adolescence

Finally, the causes of delinquency during the transition from adolescence to adulthood, about ages 18 to 20, can be examined (Figure 35.3). At these ages one should more properly speak of crime than delinquency, but for consistency we

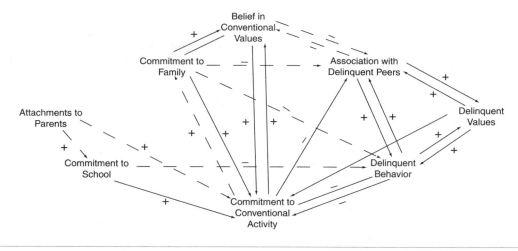

Figure 35.3   A Reciprocal Model of Delinquent Involvement at Later Adolescence

will continue to use the term delinquency in the causal diagrams and employ the terms delinquency and crime interchangeably in the text.

Two new variables are added to the model to reflect the changing life circumstances at this stage of development. The more important of these is commitment to conventional activities which includes employment, attending college, and military service. Along with the transition to the world of work, there is a parallel transition from the family of origin to one's own family. Although this transition does not peak until the early 20s, for many people its influence is beginning at this stage. Included in this concept are marriage, plans for marriage, and plans for child-rearing. These new variables largely replace attachment to parents and commitment to school in the theoretical scheme; they represent the major sources of bonds to conventional society for young adults. Both attachment to parents and commitment to school remain in the model but take on the cast of exogenous variables. Attachment to parents has only a minor effect on commitment to school, and commitment to school is proposed to affect only commitment to conventional activities and, more weakly, delinquent behavior.

The other three variables considered in the previous models—association with delinquent peers, delinquent values, and delinquent behavior—are still hypothesized to be embedded in an amplifying causal loop. As indicated above, this loop is most likely to occur among adolescents who, at earlier ages, were freed from the controlling influence of parents and school. Moreover, via the feedback paths delinquent peers, delinquent values, and delinquent behavior further alienate the youth from parents and diminish commitment to school. Once this spiral begins, the probability of sustained delinquency increases.

This situation, if it continued uninterrupted, would yield higher and higher rates of crime as the subjects matured. Such an outcome is inconsistent with the desistance that has been observed during this age period (Wolfgang, Thornberry, and Figlio, 1987). Rates of delinquency and crime begin to subside by the late teenage years, a phenomenon often attributed to "maturational reform." Such an explanation, however, is tautological since it claims that crime stops when adolescents get older, because they get older. It is also uninformative since the concept of maturational reform is theoretically undefined. A developmental approach, however, offers an explanation for desistance. As the developmental process unfolds, life circumstances change, developmental milestones are met (or, for some, missed), new social roles are created, and new networks of attachments and commitments emerge. The effects of these changes enter the processual model to explain new and often dramatically different behavioral patterns. In the present model, these changes are represented by commitment to conventional activity and commitment to family.

Commitment to conventional activity is influenced by a number of variables, including earlier attachment to parents, commitment to school, and belief in conventional values. And once the transition to the world of work is made, tremendous opportunities are afforded for new and different effects in the delinquency model. Becoming committed to conventional activities, work, college, military service, and so on— reduces the likelihood of delinquent behavior and associations with delinquent peers because it builds up a stake in conformity that is antithetical to delinquency. Moreover, since the delinquency variables are still embedded in a causal loop, the effect of commitment to conventional activities tends to resonate throughout the system. But, because of the increased saliency of a new variable, commitment to conventional activities, the reinforcing loop is now set in motion to *reduce* rather than increase delinquent and criminal involvement. The variable of commitment to family has similar, albeit weaker, effects since the transition to the family is only beginning at these ages. Nevertheless, commitment to family is proposed to reduce both delinquent associations and delinquent values and to increase commitment to conventional activity. In general, as the individual takes on the responsibilities of family, the bond to conventional society increases, placing additional constraints on behavior and precluding further delinquency.

These changes do not occur in all cases, however, nor should they be expected to since many delinquents continue on to careers in adult crime. In the Philadelphia cohort of 1945, 51% of the juvenile delinquents were also adult offenders, and the more serious and prolonged the delinquent careers were, the greater the odds of an adult career (Wolfgang et al., 1987, Ch. 4). The continuation of criminal careers can also be explained by the nature of the reciprocal effects included in this model. In general, extensive involvement in delinquency at earlier ages feeds back upon and weakens attachment to parents and commitment to school (see Figures 35.1 and 35.2). These variables, as well as involvement in delinquency itself, weaken later commitment to family and to conventional activities (Figure 35.3). Thus, these new variables, commitment to conventional activities and to family, are affected by the person's situation at earlier stages and do not "automatically" alter the probability of

continued criminal involvement. If the initial bonds are extremely weak, the chances of new bonding variables being established to break the cycle towards criminal careers are low and it is likely that criminal behavior will continue. . . .

STRUCTURAL EFFECTS

Structural variables, including race, class, sex, and community of residence, refer to the person's location in the structure of social roles and statuses. The manner in which they are incorporated in the interactional model is illustrated here by examining only one of them, social class of origin. Although social class is often measured continuously, a categorical approach is more consistent with the present model and with most theories of delinquency that incorporate class as a major explanatory variable—for example, strain and social disorganization theories. For our purposes, the most important categories are the lower class, the working lower class, and the middle class.

The lower class is composed of those who are chronically or sporadically unemployed, receive welfare, and subsist at or below the poverty level. They are similar to Johnson's "underclass" (1979). The working lower class is composed of those with more stable work patterns, training for semiskilled jobs, and incomes that allow for some economic stability. For these families, however, the hold on even a marginal level of occupational and economic security is always tenuous. Finally, the middle class refers to all families above these lower levels. Middle-class families have achieved some degree of economic success and stability and can reasonably expect to remain at that level or improve their standing over time.

The manner in which the social class of origin affects the interactional variables and the behavioral trajectories can be demonstrated by comparing the life expectancies of children from lower- and middle-class families. As compared to children from a middle-class background, children from a lower class background are more apt to have (1) disrupted family processes and environments (Conger, McCarty, Wang, Lahey, & Kroop, 1984; Wahler, 1980); (2) poorer preparation for school (Cloward and Ohlin, 1960); (3) belief structures influenced by the traditions of the

American lower class (Miller, 1958; Anderson, 1976); and (4) greater exposure to neighborhoods with high rates of crime (Shaw & McKay, 1942; Braithwaite, 1981). The direction of all these effects is such that we would expect children from lower-class families to be initially less bonded to conventional society and more exposed to delinquent values, friends, and behaviors.

As one moves towards the working lower class, both the likelihood and the potency of the factors just listed decrease. As a result, the initial values of the interactional variables improve but, because of the tenuous nature of economic and social stability for these families, both the bonding variables and the delinquency variables are still apt to lead to considerable amounts of delinquent conduct. Finally, youths from middle-class families, given their greater stability and economic security, are likely to start with a stronger family structure, greater stakes in conformity, and higher chances of success, and all of these factors are likely to reduce the likelihood of initial delinquent involvement.

In brief, the initial values of the interactional variables are systematically related to the social class of origin. Moreover, since these variables are reciprocally related, it follows logically that social class is systematically related to the behavioral trajectories described above. Youngsters from the lowest classes have the highest probability of moving forward on a trajectory of increasing delinquency. Starting from a position of low bonding to conventional institutions and a high delinquency environment, the reciprocal nature of the interrelationships leads inexorably towards extremely high rates of delinquent and criminal involvement. Such a view is consistent with prevalence data which show that by age 18, 50%, and by age 30, 70% of low SES minority males have an official police record (Wolfgang et al., 1987).

On the other hand, the expected trajectory of middle-class youths suggests that they will move toward an essentially conforming life-style, in which their stakes in conformity increase and more and more preclude serious and prolonged involvement in delinquency. Finally, because the initial values of the interactional variables are mixed and indecisive for children from lower working-class homes, their behavioral trajectories are much more volatile and the outcome much less certain.

Summary. Interactional theory asserts that both the initial values of the process variables and their development over time are systematically related to the social class of origin. Moreover, parallel arguments can be made for other structural variables, especially those associated with class, such as race, ethnicity, and the social disorganization of the neighborhood. Like class of origin, these variables are systematically related to variables such as commitment to school and involvement in delinquent behavior, and therefore, as a group, these structural variables set the stage on which the reciprocal effects develop across the life cycle. . . .

DISCUSSION QUESTIONS

1. Give examples of the reciprocal causal effects of Thornberry's model. As adolescents get older, what new variables enter the picture, and which ones gain or lose importance in terms of their effects on delinquency?

2. Recall some of the points raised in Moffitt's article (Chapter 32 in this volume) about adolescence-limited offenders. According to Thornberry, why are some adolescents able to desist from delinquency in early adulthood whereas others persist in criminal behavior? Are there any similarities or differences between Moffitt's and Thornberry's explanations?

3. What role do social structural variables play in Thornberry's model? Why does he believe that lower-class youth are most likely to find themselves on a path of increasing delinquency?

REFERENCE

Hirschi, T. (1969). *Causes of delinquency*. Berkeley: University of California Press.

36

BEHAVIOR GENETICS AND ANOMIE/STRAIN THEORY

ANTHONY WALSH

EDITOR'S INTRODUCTION—Biological approaches to crime and criminality have not received a warm welcome in the social sciences. Despite the increase in overviews of biological, psychological, and, more recently, biosocial theories that have been published in the last 10 years, few criminologists will take even a small step toward acknowledging that genes, or genetic factors, play an important role in criminality.

This chapter by Walsh represents the author's wake-up call to criminologists, and perhaps all social scientists, to "pull back [their] blinders and peek at what behavior genetics has to offer" (p. 347, this volume). So, what is behavior genetics? It might be prudent to first describe what it is not. Walsh maintains that behavior genetics is *not* a "biological" perspective of human behavior, hence its placement among integrated approaches and not biological and psychological approaches to crime. Rather, behavior genetics is a biosocial perspective that seriously considers the "proposition that all human traits, abilities, and behaviors are the result of the interplay of genetics and environments" (Walsh, 2000, p. 1097). *Biosocial* suggests that the perspective takes into account both biological and sociological factors.

Walsh adds that his is the only perspective that has the appropriate research tools to untangle the complicated effects of biology, genetics, and the environment. Behavioral genetics studies typically reveal that the environment accounts for more variance—or has a stronger impact—than genetics in most human traits, abilities, and behaviors. Therefore, this "biologically-friendly environmental discipline" (p. 347, this volume), may tell us more about environmental effects than about genetic effects.

Walsh's approach makes an important contribution to past and current criminological literature. Although it may not be strongly supported by "mainstream" criminologists, it brings us a little bit closer to the reality that, as researchers, theorists, and professionals, we cannot continue to "reject insights from behavior genetics if the discipline is to remain scientifically viable" (Walsh, 2000, p. 1097). Recall the general overtones of Bernard's chapter on the state of criminological theory (Chapter 1, this volume). Scientific advances sometimes do require recognition of a "theoretical crisis" and the need for a paradigm shift. Walsh's contribution brings us one step closer to that place.

In this chapter, I explore how behavior genetics can complement and expand traditional social science understanding of criminal behavior in the context of anomie/strain theory, a respected and long-lived criminological theory that focuses on cultural and structural causes of crime. I do not challenge these alleged causes in this paper; rather, I seek to show you how they can be better understood with the help of behavior genetic concepts.

The decade of the 1990s saw numerous reports of crisis within sociology in general (Crippen, 1994; Ellis, 1996a; Udry, 1995a; Walsh, 1995) as well as in criminology in particular (Bernard, 1990; Fishbein, 1998; Rock & Holdaway, 1998). The substance of most of these reports is that the discipline is moribund and desperately needs something to breathe fresh life into it. The reason most often given for this state of affairs is sociology's dogged refusal to entertain the possibility that biological factors may play an important role in helping us to understand phenomena of concern to us. Perhaps a major reason for this refusal can be found in what is probably the most cited passage in all of sociology: "The determining cause of a social fact should be sought among antecedent social facts and not among the states of the individual consciousness" (Durkheim, 1982, p. 134). This dictum has become a sociological mantra used to assert and defend the ontological autonomy of the discipline. According to Udry (1995a, p. 1267), however, although Durkheim clearly meant this statement to be a boundary axiom defining sociology's purview, sociologists came to think of it as "a true statement about the nature of the world instead of a set of deliberate blinders to help them focus their attention". . . .

There are signs that certain criminological theories are becoming more psychologically and biologically informed, and there have been a number of recent encapsulations of biosocial approaches in the criminology literature (e.g., Fishbein, 1990, 1992; Lykken, 1995; Raine, 1993). Authors of such overviews, however, tend not to be mainstream criminologists, but psychologists, psychiatrists, and biologists, and none of them has tried to show the relevance of biosocial variables to mainstream criminological theories. Perhaps biologically informed theories will continue to have minimal impact on mainstream criminology until it can be shown that they are not antithetical to current environmental theories of crime. My primary purpose in this paper is to demonstrate that at least one biologically informed discipline—behavior genetics—is not antithetical to at least one environmental theory—anomie/strain theory. . . .

BEHAVIOR GENETICS

I suggest that it is time for mainstream criminology to at least pull back its blinders and peek at what behavior genetics has to offer. Very few criminologists have taken biology beyond an introductory class, and even fewer believe that genetic factors are important in explaining criminal behavior, despite the overviews of biosocial theories that have been published in the past decade (Walsh & Ellis, 1999). The lack of human genetic knowledge is probably not as important as ideology in keeping our blinders on. To acknowledge that genes may play a role in criminality has been virtually taboo for decades (Wright & Miller, 1998), and many criminologists still suffer from "biophobia," to use Ellis's (1996a) expression. . . .

Behavior genetics, a branch of quantitative genetics, is not so much a "biological" discipline as it is a biologically-friendly environmental discipline. Although the discipline's main focus is to understand genetic influences on human behavior, traits, and abilities, behavior geneticists are aware that this cannot be accomplished without understanding the complementary role of the environment (Goldsmith, 1993). Behavioral genetic studies have typically found that the environment accounts for more variance than does genetics in . . . most human traits, behaviors, and abilities (McGue, 1994). Thus, an often unappreciated aspect of behavior genetics is that it tells us as much, or sometimes more, about environmental effects as it does about genetic effects (Plomin, 1995).

Behavior genetics research designs can also address and rectify a major problem with what has been called the standard social science

Walsh, A. (2000). Behavior genetics and anomie/strain theory. *Criminology, 38,* 1075-1108.

model (SSSM) of socialization (Tooby & Cosmides, 1992). The problem is that the SSSM can never determine if any observed effects are primarily genetically or environmentally driven, i.e., whether parent/child or sibling/sibling similarities are caused primarily by shared genes or shared environments. This has led some socialization researchers to dismiss the entire SSSM of socialization as essentially useless (Harris, 1995, 1998; Maccoby and Martin, 1983; Rowe, 1994).

It is axiomatic that we can only disentangle genetic from environmental effects if we can hold one or the other constant. Behavior genetics does this using twin and adoption studies. The twin method compares pairs of individuals reared together (e.g., monozygotic twins) with a known degree of genetic relatedness with other pairs of reared-together individuals with a different degree of genetic relatedness (e.g., dizygotic twins), which holds environments constant and allows genes to vary. The adoption method examines genetically related individuals reared in different homes (or genetically unrelated individuals reared in the same home), which holds genes constant and allows environments to vary. In other words, the effects of shared environment can be determined by studying genetically unrelated individuals raised in the same environment, and the effects of heredity can be gauged by the phenotypical similarities of genetically related individuals reared apart (Plomin & Bergeman, 1991).

Until molecular genetics is able to identify specific genes underlying specific traits, genetic effects must be inferred rather than directly demonstrated. Genetic effects are inferred by calculating a trait's heritability (h^2). Heritability coefficients range between 0 and 1, and estimate the extent to which variance in a trait in a population is attributable to genes. Heritability is based on the assumption that if genes affect a trait, the more genetically related two individuals are, the more similar they will be on that trait. If genes do not affect a trait, it would be logically and empirically impossible to calculate a heritability coefficient for that trait significantly greater than zero.

Heritability estimates fluctuate among different populations and within the same population as they experience different environments. Knowing what percentage of variance in a trait is attributable to genetic factors does not set limits on creating other environments that may influence the trait. A large heritability coefficient

informs us that the present environment [at] the present time has minimal effect (accounts for little variance) on the trait; it does not tell us what other environments may have appreciably greater effects on the trait (Bronfenbrenner & Ceci, 1993). To put it another way, heritability tells us what is affecting trait variance; it does no[t] tell us what can affect it. Moreover, the heritability of a trait informs us only about how much of the variance in a trait is attributable to genes, not how much the trait is attributable to genetic influences. Even a relatively high heritability coefficient may be calculated without the trait being strongly influenced by genes.

A related misunderstanding about heritability is the assumption that it carves nature neatly at the joint because it apportions traits into "genetic" and "environmental" components (e.g., 60% genetic, therefore, 40% environmental). Although heritability estimates statistically transform genes and environments into components, they are not separable ingredients in the real world. Genes and environments have the same relationship to phenotypic attributes as hydrogen and oxygen have to water and length and width have to area. It takes twice as many hydrogen atoms as oxygen atoms to make a molecule of water and an area's length may be twice its width, but in terms of the wholes they describe, the quantitative differences are meaningless. Without their complements, there would be no water or area, only a gas and a straight line. Likewise, genes and environments in isolation make no sense in terms of the phenotypic wholes they describe. There is no nature versus nurture, there is only nature via nurture.

In addition to apportioning variance into genetic and environmental components, the methods of behavior genetics yield a further benefit to social science in that they allow researchers to break down environmental variance into shared and nonshared components. Shared environments are environments of rearing that serve to make siblings alike (e.g., parental SES [socioeconomic status], religion, neighborhood, intactness of home), and nonshared environments are those microenvironments unique to each sibling (birth order, differential treatment, different peers, etc.) that serve to make them different. A cascade of behavior genetic research has shown unequivocally that although shared rearing effects are real, albeit modest, during childhood and adolescence, they almost completely disappear in adulthood (McGue et al., 1993; Rowe, 1994).

AGENCY AND GENE/ENVIRONMENT CORRELATION

Social scientists are increasingly acknowledging that people's choices are not passive responses to social and cultural situations, and that these choices are to some degree autonomous. Many social scientists have gravitated toward the concept of agency in response to the "oversocialized" conception of human nature that has for so long dominated the social sciences. Agency simply means that as individuals strive for autonomy, they affect their environments just as surely as they are affected by them. Genes account for substantial variance in the trait and . . . they have substantial influence on the trait (Bouchard & McGue, 1981). It should be mentioned that the correlations are not squared because the correlations express the proportion of total variance shared within pairs. We are not predicting one twin's score from the other's; rather, we are determining the extent to which the observed variance is because of covariance among the pairs (Plomin & Daniels, 1987).

Transformations of self and environment are achieved by the actions and interactions of human subjects propelled by the subjective meanings that different people assign to similar situations (Sztompka, 1994). This concept of agency, which has much to do with our wishes, goals, and desires, is highly congenial to behavior genetics, which has always emphasized that people make their environments (Scarr & McCartney, 1983). That is, people's unique genotypes will largely determine what aspects of the social environment will be salient to them. This is a position considerably more respectful of human dignity (and more scientifically defensible) than is the image of human development that views it as little more than a process of class-, race-, age-, or gender-based adjustment to structural and cultural demands made on us. The concept of agency pulls us away from thinking of socialization as a mechanistic parent-to-child process and provides us with the skeleton of reciprocal effects thinking. Behavior genetics goes a step further to put the flesh on the bones of this thinking.

The concept of gene/environment (G/E) correlation is philosophically related to the concept of agency, but goes beyond it to provide an understanding of the underlying mechanisms that constitute the basis for the subjective meanings agency theorists articulate. G/E correlation essentially means that genotypes and the environments they encounter are not random with respect to one another, and that individuals are active shapers of their lives (Plomin, 1995; Scarr & McCartney, 1983). The concept enables us to conceptualize the indirect way that genes exert their influence to help to determine the effective environment of the developing individual. Behavior geneticists differentiate between passive, reactive, and active G/E correlation (Plomin, 1995; Scarr, 1992).

Children raised by their biological parents experience passive G/E correlation by virtue of being provided with genes that underlie certain traits and a home environment favorable for their expression. A child born to highly intelligent parents, for example, typically receives genes conducive to high intelligence and a home in which intellectual activity is modeled and reinforced. The synergistic effects of correlated genes and environment will make for the unfolding of the child's intellectual abilities almost independently (passively) of what the child does. This means that the child has simply been exposed to the environment and has not been instrumental in forming it, not that the child does not actively engage it. On downside, children born to low IQ, impulsive, or bad-tempered parents receive both genes and an environment developmentally biasing them in the same direction. The influence of passive G/E correlation declines dramatically from infancy to adolescence as the scope of environmental interaction widens and the person is confronted with and engages a wider variety of other people and behavioral options (Plomin, 1995; Rowe, 1992; Scaff & McCartney, 1983).

Reactive G/E correlation picks up the developmental trajectory as children grow older and are exposed to an increasing number of people and situations in their environments and begin to respond more actively to them. Children bring their developing phenotypical characteristics and abilities with them to the interpersonal situations they encounter that increase or decrease the probability of evoking certain kinds of responses from others. A bad-tempered child will evoke less solicitude than will a good-natured child, and a hyperactive, moody, and mischievous child will evoke less benign responses from others than will one who is pleasant and well behaved. Likewise, a child who shows enthusiasm and ability for school work evokes better treatment from teachers and will be afforded greater opportunities for advancement than will a child who shows little enthusiasm and ability for school work.

The important lesson of reactive G/E correlation is that the behavior of others toward the child is as much a function of the child's evocative behavior as it is of the interaction style of those who respond to it. Socialization is not something that others simply do to children; it is a reciprocal process that children and their caretakers engage in together. Some children may be difficult to control for even the most patient and loving parents. Some parents may abuse difficult children in their efforts to make them conform, and other parents may just give up trying to socialize their children (Lykken, 1995). Both abusive and permissive responses to difficult children are likely to exacerbate their antisocial tendencies and drive them to seek others more accepting of their tendencies, presumably because the others toward whom they gravitate harbor such tendencies. Groups of individuals with similar tendencies provide positive reinforcement for each other and provide ample opportunities to exercise these tendencies. It is in this way that the feedback nature of *reactive* G/E correlation amplifies differences among phenotypes (Moffitt, 1993).

The seeking out of environments in which one feels accepted and psychologically comfortable is referred to as active G/E correlation, or "niche-picking" (Scarr & McCartney, 1983, p. 427). Large-scale twin studies provide striking evidence that genes play a very important role in "niche-picking." A number of studies have reported that the similarity in intelligence, personalities, attitudes, interests, and constructed environments of monozygotic (MZ) twins is essentially unaffected by whether they were reared together or apart (Bouchard et al., 1990; Rowe, 1994). That is, MZ twins reared apart construct their environments and order their lives about as similarly as they would have had they been raised together, and this similarity is considerably greater than is the similarity between dizygotic (DZ) twins reared together.

Although such findings are robust, they appear counterintuitive to those who believe that the rearing environment mostly determines life outcomes. However, they make perfect sense to behavior geneticists, for whom it would be counterintuitive for people to either accept or to seek out environments incompatible with their genetic dispositions. Because MZ twins share 100% of their genes and DZ twins share, on average, only 50%, it makes sense that MZ twins would order their lives more similarly than would DZ twins. People with genes facilitative of different temperaments, traits, and abilities will seek out environments that mesh well with them (genes and environments will covary positively). It is no surprise to behavior geneticists that within the range of cultural possibilities and constraints, our genes set us on a developmental trajectory that will largely determine what features of the social world will be meaningful and rewarding to us, and what features will not.

BEHAVIOR GENETICS AND ANTISOCIAL BEHAVIOR

I must strongly emphasize that there is absolutely nothing in the concept of G/E correlation that can in any way be construed as supporting the notion of congenital criminality. Genes are self-replicating slices of DNA that code for proteins, which code for hormonal and enzymatic processes. There is no mysterious cryptography by which genes code for certain kinds of brains, which in turn code for different kinds of behaviors. Genes do not code for feelings or emotions either; what they do is make us differentially sensitive to environmental cues and modulate our responses to them. Genes always exert whatever influence they have on behavior in an environmental context. Although there can be no gene(s) "for" crime, there are genes that, via a number of neuro-hormonal routes, lead to the development of different traits and characteristics that may increase the probability of criminal behavior in some environments and in some situations.

A recent behavior genetic study illustrates the role of G/E correlation for antisocial behavior in late childhood/early adolescence (O'Connor et al., 1998). A number of adopted children were classified as either being or not being at genetic risk for antisocial behavior on the basis of their biological mothers' self-reported antisocial behavior collected prior to the birth of their children. It was found that from ages 7 to 12, children at genetic risk for antisocial behavior consistently received more negative parenting from their adoptive parents than did children not at genetic risk. This effect was interpreted as reactive G/E correlation in that children's poor behavior was seen as evoking negative parenting. O'Connor et al. (1998) did, however, find an environmentally mediated parental effect not attributable to reactive G/E correlation.

Another adoption study of antisocial behavior focused on G/E interaction (the differential effects of similar environments on different genotypes). Cadoret et al. (1995) examined the antisocial history of adopted children separated at birth from biological mothers with verified antisocial histories, compared with other adoptees with biological mothers with no known history of antisocial behavior. It was found that adverse adoptive home environments (divorce/separation, substance abuse, neglect/abuse, marital discord) led to significant increases in antisocial behavior for adoptees at genetic risk, but not for adoptees without genetic risk. Thus, both genes and environments operating in tandem (interacting) were required to produce significant antisocial behavior, whereas neither seemed powerful enough in this study to produce such effects independent of the other.

Antisocial behaviors, especially adolescent antisocial behaviors, are an interesting exception to the modest shared environmental influences typically discovered for most human characteristics. Shared group influences reflect the socializing influences of peer groups, although such influences cannot be considered apart from the tendency of similar people to befriend one another (DiLalla & Gottesman, 1989; Rowe & Gulley, 1992). The shifting pattern of genetic and environmental effects is readily seen in studies of juvenile and adult offending. . . . Genetic factors do not have similar explanatory power across all environments and across all developmental periods. Few things point to the vital importance of the environment to gene expression more than the fact that heritability coefficients are always higher in advantaged than in disadvantaged environments. Just as a rose will express its fullest genetic potential planted in an English garden and wither when planted in the Nevada desert, human beings will realize their genetic potential to the fullest when reared in positive environments and fall short of doing so when reared in negative environments. High overall heritabilities for positive traits index how well a society is doing in equalizing environmental opportunities (Lykken, 1995). . . .

Differential genetic effects also apply to delinquent and criminal behaviors. In environments where resistance to crime is low, very little variance in criminal behavior will be attributable to genes; in environments where resistance to crime is high, the genetic contribution will be high. Venables (1987), for example, found that (low) tonic heart rate was a significant predictor of antisocial behavior among high SES children, but not among low SES children. Similarly, Walsh (1992) found that cognitive imbalance (as measured by verbal/performance IQ discrepancy scores) significantly predicted violent delinquency in advantaged environments, but not in disadvantaged environments. This does not mean these studies found that low tonic heart rate or cognitive imbalance was more prevalent in advantaged environments. On the contrary, what it means is that environmental causes tend to overwhelm putative genetic causes in disadvantaged environments (Gottesman & Goldsmith, 1994). . . . The environmental complexities illustrated by studies cited in this section make criminal/antisocial behavior especially appealing for behavior genetic analysis of environmental influence. . . .

TRAITS LINKED TO MIDDLE-CLASS SUCCESS

In the following section, I briefly review the literature on the two major individual-level factors (temperament and intelligence) stressed by Agnew (1992, 1997) as they relate to achieving middle-class success. Agnew (1997) remarks on a number of occasions that temperament and intelligence bear a strong relationship to problem-solving skills, and that the lower classes feel strain most acutely (1997, pp. 111-114). He never tries to make the connection between SES and these correlates of problem solving, although he is more than willing to state that such traits are a function of both biological and social factors (1997, p. 105). After the discussion of temperament and intelligence, I will attempt to show how other biosocial variables can be usefully integrated with Agnew's (1997) recently formulated developmental version of GST [General Strain Theory].

Temperament

Temperament refers to an individual's habitual mode of emotionally responding to stimuli. Temperamental style is identifiable very early in life, and it tends to be stable across the life course (Chess & Thomas, 1996). Variance in temperamental measures [is] largely a function of heritable variation in central and autonomic nervous system arousal (Kochanska, 1991; Rothbart & Ahadi, 1994). Heritability coefficients for the various components of temperament range from about .40 to .80, which also indicates a substantial (20% to 60%) contribution of the environment (Gottesman & Goldsmith, 1994).

Temperamental differences are largely responsible for making children differentially responsive to socialization. The unresponsiveness of a bad tempered (sour, unresponsive, quick to anger) child is exacerbated by the fact that temperaments of children and their parents are typically positively correlated. Parents of children with difficult temperaments tend to be inconsistent disciplinarians, irritable, impatient, and unstable, which makes them unable or unwilling to cope constructively with their children. Their children are thus burdened with both a genetic and an environmental liability (Lykken, 1995; Moffitt, 1996). A cascade of evidence shows that children with difficult temperaments evoke negative responses from parents, teachers, and peers, and that these children find acceptance only in association with peers with similar dispositions (Ellis, 1996b; Moffitt, 1996; Raine, 1993).

Various physiological measures confirm that disinhibited temperament is associated with central nervous system (CNS) and peripheral nervous system (PNS) underarousal (suboptimal levels of arousal under normal environmental conditions). Individuals differ in the level of environmental stimulation they find optimal because of variation in the CNS's reticular activating system (a finger-size cluster of cells extending from the spinal cord that monitors incoming stimuli for processing by the cerebral cortex), and the PNS's autonomic nervous system. What is optimal for most of us will be stressful for some and boring for others. Suboptimally aroused people are easily bored and continually seek to boost stimuli to more comfortable levels (Raine, 1993; Zuckerman, 1990). This search for amplified pleasure and excitement often leads the underaroused person into conflict with the law. A number of studies have shown that relative to the general population, criminals, especially those with the most serious criminal records, are chronically underaroused as determined by EEG brain wave patterns, resting heart rate and skin conductance, and histories of hyperactivity and attention deficit disorders (Ellis, 1996b). Individuals who are chronically bored and continually seeking intense stimulation are not likely to apply themselves to school or endear themselves to employers. . . .

Temperament provides the foundations for personality, which emerges from its interaction with the environment. Conscientiousness, one of the "big five" factors of personality, is a trait that is particularly important to success in the work force (Brand, 1995; Lykken, 1995; Lynn, 1996) and is thus important to anomie/strain theory. Conscientiousness is a continuous trait ranging from well organized, disciplined, reliable, responsible, and scrupulous at one end of the continuum, to disorganized, careless, unreliable, irresponsible, and unscrupulous at the other. As we might expect, variance in conscientiousness is heritable. . . . In short, individuals with temperaments biasing them in the direction of being lacking in conscientiousness typically do not possess the personal qualities needed to apply themselves to the often long and arduous task of achieving legitimate occupational success. They will become "innovators" or "retreatists," not because a reified social structure has denied them access to the race, but because, as Cohen (1955) and Cloward and Ohlin (1960) intimated, they find the race intolerably boring and busy themselves with more "exciting" pursuits instead.

Intelligence

Intelligence, as operationalized by IQ tests, is another obvious determinant of both occupational success and coping strategy, but also one that is conspicuously absent in sociological discussions of social status. . . . [Researchers are] aware of the inflammatory effects of linking SES with IQ, but . . . the link is in desperate need of dispassionate consideration. Few scientists who study intelligence seriously doubt the importance of genes as well as the environment to explaining IQ variation. Twin studies (e.g., Bouchard & McGue, 1981), adoption studies (e.g., Capron & Duyme, 1989), positron electron tomography and magnetic resonance image scan studies (e.g., Matarazzo, 1992), and even molecular genetic studies (e.g., Plomin et al., 1994) all point to substantial genetic effects on intelligence. Contrary to the claims of many social scientists, the National Academy of Sciences (Seligman, 1992), most of the 1,020 Ph.D.-level experts surveyed by Snyderman & Rothman (1988), and the American Psychological Association's Task Force on Intelligence (Neisser et al., 1995) have all concluded that there is no empirical evidence to indicate that IQ tests are biased against any racial/ethnic group or social class.

The litmus test for any assessment tool is its criterion-related validity, that is, its ability to predict outcomes. An examination of 11 meta-analyses of the relationship between IQ and occupational success found that IQ predicted success better than did any other variable in most occupations, particularly in higher status occupations, and that it predicted equally well for all races/ethnic groups (Gottfredson, 1986). Intelligence is particularly important in open and technologically advanced societies. As Bouchard and Segal (1985, p. 408) put it, "in open societies with high degrees of occupational mobility, individuals with high IQs migrate, relative to their parents, to occupations of higher SES, and individuals with lower IQs migrate to occupations of lower SES."

Although there is no such thing as a totally open society, unlike the rigid caste-like societies of the past, modern "class attainments do not represent environments imposed on adults by natural events beyond their control" (Rowe, 1994, p. 136). In the rigid and aristocratic caste societies of the past, genes played almost no role in determining social class. They play an increasingly important role in more modern and egalitarian societies, however. Genes, and the individual differences they underlie, become important in determining SES in roughly direct proportion

to equalization of environments. Although this may seem paradoxical at first blush, it is a basic principle of genetics: The more homogeneous (or equal) the environment, the greater the heritability of a trait; the more heterogeneous (unequal) the environment, the lower the heritability of a trait (Plomin et al., 1997). High heritability coefficients for socially important traits tell us that the society is doing a good job of equalizing the environment.

The degree of occupational mobility in the U.S. labor force can be gauged by a major study's finding that 48% of sons of upper white-collar status fathers had lower status occupations than did their fathers, with 17% falling all the way to "lower manual" status, and that 51% of sons of lower manual status fathers achieved higher status, with 22.5% achieving "upper white-collar" status (Hurst, 1995, p. 270). Given this degree of upward/downward social mobility, and given the degree to which IQ predicts it equally for all races and social classes, it is difficult to maintain that any group is systematically denied access to legitimate opportunities to attain middle-class status.[1]

Social scientists are more prone to attribute IQ level to SES level rather than the other way around. A large number of studies have found the correlation between parental SES and children's IQ to be within the .30 to .40 range (which is predictable from polygenetic transmission models). However, the correlation between individuals' IQ and their attained adult SES is in the .50 to .70 range (Jensen, 1998). . . . Offspring IQ thus accounts for about three times the variance in offspring SES than does parental SES.

If differential IQ predicts differential adult SES, and if the lack of success leads to a mode of adaptation that includes criminal activity, IQ must be a predictor of criminal behavior. When evaluating the relatively small (eight IQ points) difference said to separate criminals and non-criminals (Wilson & Herrnstein, 1985) we must remember that researchers do not typically separate what Moffitt (1993) calls adolescent-limited (AL) from what she calls "life-course-persistent" (LCP) offenders. As statistically normal individuals responding to the contingencies of their environments, we would not expect AL offenders to be significantly different from nonoffenders on IQ, and they are not. Moffitt (1996) reports a one-point mean IQ deficit between AL offenders and nonoffenders, but a 17-point deficit between LCP offenders and nonoffenders, and Stattin and Klackenberg-Larsson (1993) found a mean deficit of 4 points between nonoffenders and "sporadic" offenders and a 10-point difference between nonoffenders and "frequent" offenders. Aggregating temporary and persistent offenders creates the erroneous perception that IQ has minimal impact on antisocial behavior.

Although these studies separated temporary and persistent offenders, they did not separate IQ subtest scores. This also leads to an underestimation of the effects of IQ by pooling verbal IQ (VIQ), which uniformly shows a significant difference between offenders and nonoffenders, and performance IQ (PIQ), which typically does not (Herrnstein, 1989). The most serious and persistent criminal offenders tend to have a PIQ score exceeding their VIQ score by about 12 points (Miller, 1987; Walsh, 1991). Low verbal IQ (about one standard deviation below the mean) indexes poor abstract reasoning, poor judgment, poor school performance, impulsiveness, low empathy, and present orientedness. None of these traits is conducive to occupational success, but [they are] conducive to antisocial behavior, especially if combined with a disinhibited temperament (Farrington, 1996).

AGNEW'S DEVELOPMENTAL GST AND OTHER BIOSOCIAL PROCESSES

As we have seen, behavior genetic studies of juvenile delinquency typically find very little genetic influence. The high base rate for delinquency (it is claimed that the adolescent male who is not delinquent in some way is statistically abnormal [Moffitt, 1993]) [which] minimizes differences in MZ/DZ concordance rates, yielding only small heritability coefficients, is part of the problem (DiLalla and Gottesman, 1989). This suggests that we must go beyond behavior genetics, which is interested in differences between people, to examine the biosocial events surrounding adolescence that are relatively common to all adolescents.

Agnew's (1997) developmental strain theory attempts to explain why antisocial behavior peaks during adolescence, focusing on increases in negative relationships with others during this period and the tendency to cope with the resulting strain through delinquency. Thus, a number of situations experienced as aversive are hypothesized to account for the age effect on crime and delinquency. As other theorists (Gottfredson & Hirschi, 1990; Wilson & Herrnstein, 1985) have pointed out, however, the age effect tends to remain robust, controlling for a number of demographic and situational variables, indicating that none of the various social correlates of age predict crime as well as age. . . . For instance, Udry's (1990) sociological model found that age remained the strongest predictor of "problem behavior," controlling for a number of other independent variables. However, in his biosocial model that included measures of testosterone (T) and sex hormone binding globulin (SHBG), age dropped out of the equation, prompting him to suggest that age is a proxy for the hormonal changes of puberty. . . .

Recent MRI studies of brain development (Giedd et al., 1999; Sowell et al., 1999) confirm that the prefrontal cortex (PFC) is the last part of the human brain to fully mature. The PFC is the part of the brain that serves various executive functions, such as modulating emotions from the more primitive limbic system and making reasoned judgments. The PFC undergoes an intense prepubescent period of synaptogenesis and a period of pruning of excess synapses during adolescence (Giedd et al., 1999; Sowell et al., 1999). This process of synaptic elimination may be part of the reason many young persons find it difficult to accurately gauge the meanings and intentions of others and to experience more stimuli as aversive.

In addition to the synaptic pruning process, the adolescent's PFC is less completely myelinated than is the adult PFC (Sowell et al., 1999). Myelination is important to the speed and conductive efficiency of neurotransmission (Goldman-Racik et al., 1997). The fact that many syndromes associated with delinquency, such as oppositional disorder and conduct disorder/socialized type, first appear during this period (Benes, 1997) may reflect a brain that is sometimes developmentally not up to the task of dealing rationally with the strains of adolescence. . . . The increase in behavior-activating hormones coupled with an immature brain reflect two biological processes temporarily on conflicting trajectories that may both generate and exacerbate the strains of adolescence. This conjecture is supported by studies indicating that boys entering puberty early throw significantly more temper tantrums than do later maturing boys (Buchanan et al., 1992), and that early-maturing girls engage in significantly more problem behaviors than do later-maturing girls (Caspi et al., 1993). Also consistent with this is the finding that T levels predict future problem behavior only for early-pubertal-onset boys (Drigotas & Udry, 1993), again implying that the immature adolescent brain may facilitate a tendency to assign faulty attributions superimposed on an unfamiliar and diffuse state of physiological arousal.

Many other neurohormonal processes have the potential to assist anomie/strain theorists to understand strain across the life span, particularly during the teenage years. These include the shifting ratios of behavior facilitating dopamine and the behavior-moderating serotonin during adolescence. Both of these important neurotransmitters have fairly high heritabilities (Benes, 1997; Depue & Collins, 1999; Hur & Bouchard, 1997). . . . It has long been known that humans and other animals in a low serotonin state are prone to violence, impulsiveness, and risk taking (Clear & Bond, 1997; Moffitt et al., 1998), especially if combined with high T (Bernhardt, 1997). However, none of this means that teenagers are at the mercy of their biology, or that the environment has little impact. Serotonin levels, like T-levels, largely reflect environmental influences, and the lower average levels of serotonin during adolescence are as likely to be the effect of the increased strains of this period as they are to be the cause (Bernhardt, 1997). The stresses of adolescence outlined in Agnew's (1997) theory prompt the release of corticosteroids, which in turn suppress serotonin receptors (Sapolsky, 1992). Thus, the vicissitudes of biology and social situations during this period of life combine in synergistic fashion to become both the producers and the products of strain. Further exploration of these interesting processes is beyond the scope of this paper. . . .

DISCUSSION QUESTIONS

1. What is "behavior genetics," and why is it appropriate not to place it with other biological and psychological theories of crime?

2. What role does human agency play in terms of the gene/environment (G/E) correlation?

3. Recall Agnew's General Strain Theory (GST). How does behavior genetics expand on Agnew's theory?

4. Walsh states that the notion of linking IQ with socioeconomic status generates controversy. Why? How might behavior genetics contribute to or shape this relationship and provide a better understanding of it?

NOTE

1 Coincidentally, Merton's 1938 American Sociological Review article that introduced anomie/strain theory was followed by an article by Clark and Gist (1938) that examined IQ and occupational choice. They found that IQ was highly correlated with occupational level and that IQ served to funnel people into their various occupations, not "social structure." Clark and Gist were not arguing that IQ is the only cause of SES, but they did conclude that it was perhaps the most important cause.

REFERENCE

Walsh, A. (2000). Behavior genetics and anomie/strain theory. *Criminology, 38,* 1075-1108.

SELECTED REFERENCES

Abrams, K. (1991). Hearing the call of stories. *California Law Review, 79,* 971-1052.

Adams, J. S. (1963). Toward an understanding of inequity. *Journal of Abnormal and Social Psychology, 67,* 422-436.

Adams, J. S. (1965). Inequity in social exchange. In L. Berkowitz (Ed.), *Advances in experimental social psychology.* New York: Academic Press.

Adler, F. (1975). *Sisters in crime.* New York: McGraw-Hill.

Adler, F. (1979). Changing patterns. In F. Adler & R. Simon (Eds.), *The criminology of deviant women* (pp. 91-94). Boston: Houghton Mifflin.

Ageton, S., & Elliott, D. S. (1974). The effects of legal processing on delinquent orientations. *Social Problems, 22,* 87-100.

Agnew, R. (1983). Social class and success goals: An examination of relative and absolute aspirations. *Sociological Quarterly, 24,* 435-452.

Agnew, R. (1984). Goal achievement and delinquency. *Sociology and Social Research, 68,* 435-451.

Agnew, R. (1985a). Neutralizing the impact of crime. *Criminal Justice and Behavior, 12,* 221-239.

Agnew, R. (1985b). A revised strain theory of delinquency. *Social Forces, 64,* 151-167.

Agnew, R. (1985c). Social control theory and delinquency. *Criminology, 23,* 47-61.

Agnew, R. (1986). *Challenging strain theory: An examination of goals and goal-blockage.* Paper presented at the annual meeting of the American Society of Criminology, Atlanta, GA.

Agnew, R. (1987). On testing structural strain theories. *Journal of Research in Crime and Delinquency, 24,* 281-286.

Agnew, R. (1989). A longitudinal test of the revised strain theory. *Journal of Quantitative Criminology, 5,* 373-387.

Agnew, R. (1990). The origins of delinquent events: An examination of offender accounts. *Journal of Research in Crime and Delinquency, 27,* 267-294.

Agnew, R. (1991a). Adolescent resources and delinquency. *Criminology, 28,* 535-566.

Agnew, R. (1991b). The interactive effect of peer variables on delinquency. *Criminology, 29,* 4-72.

Agnew, R. (1991c). Strain and subcultural crime theory. In J. Sheley (Ed.), *Criminology: A contemporary handbook.* Belmont, CA: Wadsworth.

Agnew, R. (1992). Foundations for a general strain theory of crime and delinquency. *Criminology, 30,* 47-87.

Agnew, R. (1997). Stability and change in crime over the lifecourse: A strain theory explanation. In T. Thornberry (Ed.), *Developmental theories of crime and delinquency.* New Brunswick, NJ: Transaction.

Agnew, R., & Jones, D. (1988). Adapting to deprivation: An examination of inflated educational expectations. *Sociological Quarterly, 29,* 315-337.

Aiken, L. S., & West, S. G. (1991). *Multiple regression: Testing and interpreting interactions.* Newbury Park, CA: Sage.

Akers, R. (1977). *Deviant behavior: A social learning perspective.* Belmont, CA: Wadsworth.

Akers, R. L. (1984). Delinquent behavior, drugs, and alcohol: What is the relationship? *Today's Delinquent, 3,* 19-47.

Akers, R. L. (1985). *Deviant behavior: A social learning approach.* Belmont, CA: Wadsworth.

Akers, R. L., Krohn, M. D., Lanza-Kaduce, L., & Radosevich, M. (1979). Social learning theory and deviant behavior. *American Sociological Review, 44,* 635-655.

Akers, R. L., & La Greca, A. J. (1991). Alcohol use among the elderly: Social learning, community context, and life events. In D. J. Pittman & H. R. White (Eds.), *Society, culture, and drinking patterns re-examined* (pp. 242-262). New Brunswick, NJ: Rutgers Center of Alcohol Studies.

References are listed as "in press" here based on their designation as such in the original publications. Such references may have been published already.

Akers, R. L., & Lee, G. (1996). A longitudinal test of social learning theory: Adolescent smoking. *Journal of Drug Issues, 26,* 317-343.

Albini, J. L. (1971). *The American Mafia: Genesis of a legend.* New York: Irvington.

Alder, C. (1986). "Unemployed women have got it heaps worse": Exploring the implications of female youth unemployment. *Australian and New Zealand Journal of Criminology, 19,* 210-225.

Alexander, F. (1941). The psychiatric aspects of war and peace. *American Journal of Sociology, 46,* 504-520.

Alexander, P. (1987). Prostitutes are being scapegoated for heterosexual AIDS. In F. Délacoste & P. Alexander (Eds.), *Sex work: Writings by women in the sex industry* (pp. 248-263). San Francisco: Cleis.

Allen, H. (1987). Rendering them harmless: The professional portrayal of women charged with serious violent crimes. In P. Carlen & A. Worrall (Eds.), *Gender, crime and justice* (pp. 81-94). Philadelphia: Open University Press.

Alves, W. M., & Rossi, P. H. (1978). Who should get what? Fairness judgments of the distribution of earnings. *American Journal of Sociology, 84,* 541-564.

Alwin, D. F. (1987). Distributive justice and satisfaction with material well-being. *American Sociological Review, 52,* 83-95.

Ancona, L., & Bertini, M. (1963). Effect de fixation de l'aggressivité provoqué par des films à contenu émotif élevé. *IKON, 15,* 33-44.

Ancona, L., & Fontanesi, M. (1965). La dinamica dell'aggressività in un gruppo d criminali. *Quaderni di Criminologia Clinica, 7,* 3-30.

Andenaes, J. (1966). The general preventive effects of punishment. *University of Pennsylvania Law Review, 114,* 949-983.

Andenaes, J. (1968). Does punishment deter crime? *Criminal Law Quarterly, 11,* 76-93.

Andersen, M. L., & Collins, P. H. (Eds.). (1992). *Race, class, and gender: An anthology.* Belmont, CA: Wadsworth.

Anderson, C. A., & Anderson, D. C. (1984). Ambient temperature and violent crime: Tests of the linear and curvilinear hypotheses. *Journal of Personality and Social Psychology, 46,* 91-97.

Anderson, E. (1978). *A place on the corner.* Chicago: University of Chicago Press.

Andry, R. G. (1962). Parental affection and delinquency. In M. E. Wolfgang, L. Savitz, & N. Johnston (Eds.), *The sociology of crime and delinquency* (pp. 342-352). New York: Wiley.

Ansbacher, H. L. (1956). Anomie, the sociologist's conception of lack of social interest. *Indiana Psychology Newsletter, 5*(11-12), 3-5.

Anthias, F., & Yuval-Davis, N. (1992). *Racialized boundaries: Race, nation, gender, colour and class and the anti-racist struggle.* New York: Routledge.

Application of role and learning theories to the study of the development of aggression in children. (1961). *Psychological Reports, 9,* 292-334.

Archer, D., & Gartner, R. (1984). *Violence and crime in cross-national perspective.* New Haven, CT: Yale University Press.

Athens, L. (1980). *Violent criminal acts and actors: A symbolic interactionist study.* London: Routledge & Kegan Paul.

Austin, R. (1992). The black community, its lawbreakers, and a politics of identification. *Southern California Law Review, 65,* 1769-1817.

Austin, W. (1977). Equity theory and social comparison processes. In J. M. Suls & R. L. Miller (Eds.), *Social comparison processes.* New York: Hemisphere.

Averill, J. R. (1982). *Anger and aggression.* New York: Springer-Verlag.

Avison, W. R., & Turner, R. J. (1988). Stressful life events and depressive symptoms: Disaggregating the effects of acute stressors and chronic strains. *Journal of Health and Social Behavior, 29,* 253-264.

Azrin, N. H., & Holz, W. C. (1966). Punishment. In W. K. Honig (Ed.), *Operant behavior: Areas of research and application* (pp. 390-477). New York: Appleton-Century-Crofts.

Baca Zinn, M., Cannon, L. W., Higginbotham, E., & Dill, B. T. (1986). The costs of exclusionary practices in women's studies. *Signs: Journal of Women in Culture and Society, 11,* 290-303.

Bachman, J. G., Green, S., & Wirtanen, I. D. (1970). *Youth in transition.* Ann Arbor: University of Michigan, Institute for Social Research.

Bachman, J. G., O'Malley, P. M., & Johnston, J. (1978). *Youth in transition: Adolescence to adulthood—Change and stability in the lives of young men.* Ann Arbor: University of Michigan, Institute for Social Research.

Baker, L. A., Mack, W., Moffitt, T. E., & Mednick, S. A. (1989). Etiology of sex differences in criminal convictions in a Danish adoption cohort. *Behavior Genetics, 19,* 355-370.

Bakhtin, M. (1981). *The dialogical imagination.* Austin: University of Texas Press.

Bandura, A. (1961a). Psychotherapy as a learning process. *Psychological Bulletin, 58,* 143-195.

Bandura, A. (1961b). Social learning through imitation. In *Nebraska Symposium on Motivation.* Lincoln: University of Nebraska.

Bandura, A. (1963). Behavior theory and identificatory learning. *American Journal of Orthopsychiatry, 33,* 591-601.

Bandura, A. (1969). *Principles of behavior modification.* New York: Holt, Rinehart & Winston.

Bandura, A. (1973). *Aggression: A social learning analysis.* Englewood Cliffs, NJ: Prentice Hall.

Bandura, A. (1976). *Analysis of delinquency and aggression.* New York: Lawrence Erlbaum.

Bandura, A. (1977a). Self-efficacy: Toward a unifying theory of behavioral change. *Psychological Review, 84,* 191-215.

Bandura, A. (1977b). *Social learning theory.* Englewood Cliffs, NJ: Prentice Hall.

Bandura, A. (1979). The social learning perspective: Mechanisms of aggression. In H. Toch (Ed.), *Psychology of crime and criminal justice* (pp. 193-236). Prospect Heights, IL: Waveland Press.

Bandura, A. (1982). The psychology of chance encounters and life paths. *American Psychologist, 37,* 747-755.

Bandura, A. (1983). Psychological mechanisms of aggression. In R. G. Green & E. Donnerstein (Eds.), *Aggression: Theoretical and empirical reviews* (pp. 1-40). New York: Academic Press.

Bandura, A. (1986). *Social foundations of thought and action: A social cognitive theory.* Englewood Cliffs, NJ: Prentice Hall.

Bandura, A. (1989a). Human agency and social cognitive theory. *American Psychologist, 44,* 1175-1184.

Bandura, A. (1989b). Regulation of cognitive processes through perceived self-efficacy. *Developmental Psychology, 25,* 729-735.

Bandura, A. (1990). Selective activation and disengagement of moral control. *Journal of Social Issues, 46,* 27-46.

Bandura, A., & Huston, A. C. (1961). Identification as a process of incidental learning. *Journal of Abnormal and Social Psychology, 63,* 311-318.

Bandura, A., Ross, D., & Ross, S. A. (1961). Transmission of aggression through imitation of aggressive models. *Journal of Abnormal and Social Psychology, 63,* 575-582.

Bandura, A., Ross, D., & Ross, S. A. (1963). Imitation of film-mediated aggressive models. *Journal of Abnormal and Social Psychology, 66,* 3-11.

Bandura, A., & Walters, R. H. (1959). *Adolescent aggression.* New York: Ronald Press.

Bandura, A., & Walters, R. H. (1963). *Social learning and personality development.* New York: Holt, Rinehart & Winston.

Bannister, S., & Milovanovic, D. (1990). The necessity defense, substantive justice and oppositional linguistic praxis. *International Journal of the Sociology of Law, 18,* 179-198.

Barak, G. (1988). Newsmaking criminology: Reflections on the media, intellectuals, and crime. *Justice Quarterly, 5,* 565-587.

Barak, G. (1991). Homelessness and the case for community-based initiatives: The emergence of a model shelter as a short term response to the deepening crisis in housing. In H. Pepinsky & R. Quinney (Eds.), *Criminology as peacemaking.* Bloomington: Indiana University Press.

Barak, G., & Bohm, B. (1989). The crimes of the homeless or the crime of homelessness. *Contemporary Crisis, 13,* 275-288.

Barnes, B. (1985). *About science.* New York: Blackwell.

Baron, L., & Straus, M. A. (1987). Four theories of rape: A macrosociological analysis. *Social Forces, 34,* 467-488.

Barrett, G. V., & Depinet, R. L. (1991). A reconsideration of testing for competence rather than for intelligence. *American Psychologist, 46,* 1012-1024.

Barrett, M. (1992). Words and things: Materialism and method in contemporary feminist analysis. In M. Barrett & A. Phillips (Eds.), *Destabilizing theory* (pp. 201-219). Stanford, CA: Stanford University Press.

Bartholomew, A. A. (1959). Extraversion-introversion and neuroticism in first offenders and recidivists. *British Journal of Delinquency, 10,* 120-129.

Bassis, M. S., Gelles, R. J., & Levine, A. (1991). *Sociology: An introduction* (4th ed.). New York: McGraw-Hill.

Baudrillard, J. (1981). *For a critique of the political economy of the sign.* St. Louis, MO: Telos Press.

Beavon, D. J. (1985). *Crime and the environmental opportunity structures: The influence of street networks on the patterning of property offenses.* Paper presented at the annual meetings of the American Society of Criminology.

Becker, G. S. (1968). Crime and punishment: An economic approach. *Journal of Political Economy, 76,* 169-217.

Becker, H. S. (1960). Notes on the concept of commitment. *American Journal of Sociology, 66,* 32-40.

Becker, H. S. (1963). *Outsiders.* New York: Free Press.

Beirne, P. (1993). *Inventing criminology.* Albany: State University of New York Press.

Beirne, P., & Messerschmidt, J. W. (1995). *Criminology* (2nd ed.). San Diego, CA: Harcourt Brace Jovanovich.

Belkhir, J., Griffith, S., Sleeter, C., & Allsup, C. (1994). Race, sex, class & multicultural education: Women's angle of vision. *Race, Sex & Class, 1*(2), 7-22.

Bell, D. (1953). Crime as an American way of life. *The Antioch Review, 13,* 131-154.

Bell, D. (1987). *And we are not saved.* New York: Basic Books.

Bell, D. (1991). The Hegelian secret: Civil society and American exceptionalism. In B. E. Shafter (Ed.), *Is America different? A new look at American exceptionalism* (pp. 46-70). Oxford, UK: Clarendon Press.

Bell, L. (Ed.). (1987). *Good girls/bad girls: Feminists and sex trade workers face to face.* Seattle, WA: Seal.

Bell, R. Q., & Chapman, M. (1986). Child effects in studies using experimental or brief longitudinal approaches to socialization. *Developmental Psychology, 22,* 595-603.

Bellah, R. N., Madsen, R., Sullivan, W. M., Swidler, A., & Tipton, S. M. (1991). *The good society.* New York: Knopf.

Benes, F. (1997). Corticolimbic circuitry and the development of psychopathology during childhood and adolescence. In N. Krasnegor, G. R. Lyon, & P. Goldman-Racik (Eds.), *The development of the prefontal cortex: Evolution, neurobiology, and behavior.* Baltimore: Paul Brooks.

Bennett, T., & Wright, R. (1984). *Burglars on burglary.* Aldershot, Hants, UK: Gower.

Benveniste, E. (1971). *Problems in general linguistics.* Coral Gables, FL: University of Miami Press.

Berg, P. S. D., & Toch, H. H. (1946). Impulsive and neurotic inmates: A study in personality and perception. *Journal of Criminal Law, Criminology and Police Science, 55,* 230-234.

Berge, W. (1940). Remedies available to the government under the Sherman Act. *Law and Contemporary Problems, 7,* 111.

Berger, J., Fisck, M. H., Norman, R. Z., & Wagner, D. G. (1983). The formation of reward expectations in status situations. In D. M. Messick & K. S. Cook (Eds.), *Equity theory: Psychological and sociological perspectives.* New York: Praeger.

Berger, J., Zelditch, M., Jr., Anderson, B., & Cohen, B. (1972). Structural aspects of distributive justice: A status-value formulation. In J. Berger, M. Zelditch, Jr., & B. Anderson (Eds.), *Sociological theories in progress.* New York: Houghton Mifflin.

Bergler, E. A. (1962). A basic oversight in the discussion of violence on TV. *Diseases of Nervous System, 23,* 267-269.

Berk, R. A., Loseke, D. R., Berk, S. F., & Rauma, D. (1980). Bringing the cops back in: A study of efforts to make the criminal justice system more responsive to incidents of family violence. *Social Science Research, 9,* 193-215.

Berk, R. A., Rauma, D., Loseke, D. R., & Berk, S. F. (1982). Throwing the cops back out: The decline of a local program to make the criminal justice system more responsive to incidents of family violence. *Social Science Research, 11,* 145-179.

Berkowitz, L. (1958). The expression and reduction of hostility. *Psychological Bulletin, 55,* 257-271.

Berkowitz, L. (1962). *Aggression.* New York: McGraw-Hill.

Berkowitz, L. (1964). The effect of observing violence. *Scientific American, 210,* 35-41.

Berkowitz, L. (1978). Whatever happened to the frustration-aggression hypothesis? *American Behavioral Scientist, 21,* 691-708.

Berkowitz, L. (1982). Aversive conditions as stimuli to aggression. In L. Berkowitz (Ed.), *Advances in experimental social psychology* (Vol. 15). New York: Academic Press.

Berkowitz, L. (1986). *A survey of social psychology.* New York: Holt, Rinehart & Winston.

Berkowitz, L., Green, J. A., & Macaulay, J. R. (1962). Hostility catharsis as the reduction of emotional tension. *Psychiatry, 25,* 23-31.

Berkowitz, L., & Rawlings, E. (1963). Effects of film violence on inhibitions against subsequent aggression. *Journal of Abnormal and Social Psychology, 66,* 405-412.

Bernard, T. J. (1983). *The consensus-conflict debate.* New York: Columbia.

Bernard, T. J. (1984). Control criticisms of strain theories: An assessment of theoretical and empirical adequacy. *Journal of Research in Crime and Delinquency, 21,* 353-372.

Bernard, T. J. (1985). A response to Paternoster. *Journal of Criminal Law and Criminology, 76,* 519-525.

Bernard, T. J. (1987a). Structure and control. *Justice Quarterly, 4,* 409-424.

Bernard, T. J. (1987b). Testing structural strain theories. *Journal of Research in Crime and Delinquency, 24,* 262-280.

Bernard, T. J. (1989). A theoretical approach to integration. In S. F. Messner, M. D. Krohn, & A. E. Liska (Eds.), *Theoretical integration in the study of deviance and crime* (pp. 137-159). Albany: State University of New York Press.

Bernard, T. J. (1990a). Angry aggression among the truly disadvantaged. *Criminology, 28,* 73-96.

Bernard, T. J. (1990b). Twenty years of testing theories: What have we learned and why? *Journal of Research in Crime and Delinquency, 27,* 325-347.

Bernard, T. J., & Engel, R. S. (2001). Conceptualizing criminal justice theory. *Justice Quarterly, 18,* 1-30.

Bernard, T. J., & Ritti, R. R. (1990). The role of theory in scientific research. In K. Kempf (Ed.), *Measurement issues in criminology* (pp. 1-20). New York: Springer-Verlag.

Bernard, T. J., & Snipes, J. B. (1996). Theoretical integration in criminology. In M. Tonry (Ed.), *Crime and justice: A review of research* (pp. 301-348). Chicago: University of Chicago Press.

Bernhardt, P. (1997). Influences of serotonin and testosterone in aggression and dominance: Convergence with social psychology. *Current Directions in Psychological Science, 6,* 44-48.

Bernstein, I. N., Kelly, W. R., & Doyle, P. A. (1977). *Labeling and sanctioning: The differential processing of criminal defendants.* Paper presented at the meeting of the American Sociological Association, Chicago, IL.

Bertrand, M. A. (1969). Self-image and delinquency: A contribution to the study of female criminality and women's image. *Acta Criminologia: Études sur la Conduite Antisociale, 2,* 71-144.

Bertrand, M. A. (1994). 1893-1993, from la donna delinquente to a postmodern deconstruction of the woman question in social control theory. *The Journal of Human Justice, 5*(2), 43-57.

Besharov, D. J. (1986). Unfounded allegations—A new child abuse problem. *The Public Interest, 83,* 18-33.

Best, J. (1990). *Threatened children: Rhetoric and concern about child-victims*. Chicago: University of Chicago Press.

Bianchi, H., Simondi, M., & Taylor, I. (Eds.). (1975). *Deviance and control in Europe*. London: John Wiley.

Bianchi, H., & van Swaaningen, R. (Eds.). (1986). *Abolitionism: Towards a non-repressive approach to crime*. Amsterdam: Free Press.

Bienen, L. (1980). Rape III—Rape reform legislation. *Women's Rights Law Reporter, 6*, 170-213.

Birkbeck, C. (1985). *The concept of opportunities for crime: Its definition and theoretical consequences*. Unpublished manuscript, Universidad de Los Andes, Centro de Investigaciones Penales y Criminologicas, Merida, Venezuela.

Bittner, E. (1965). The concept of organization. *Social Research, 32*, 239-255.

Bittner, E. (1967). The police on skid row: A study of peace keeping. *American Sociological Review, 32*, 699-715.

Black, D. J. (1976). *The behavior of law*. New York: Academic Press.

Black, D. J. (1989). *Sociological justice*. New York: Oxford University Press.

Blackburn, R. (1988). On moral judgements and personality disorders: The myth of psychopathic personality revisited. *British Journal of Psychiatry, 153*, 505-512.

Blalock, H. M. (1984). *Basic dilemmas in the social sciences*. Beverly Hills, CA: Sage.

Bland, L. (1985). In the name of protection: The policing of women in the First World War. In J. Brophy & C. Smart (Eds.), *Women in law: Explorations in law, family, and sexuality* (pp. 23-49). Boston: Routledge & Kegan Paul.

Blau, P. (1964). Exchange and power in social life. New York: John Wiley.

Blau, P., & Duncan, O. D. (1967). *The American occupational structure*. New York: Wiley.

Blazicek, D. L. (1985, August). *Patterns of victim selection among robbers: A theoretical and descriptive analysis*. Paper presented at the Fifth International Symposium on Victimology, Zagreb, Yugoslavia.

Block, R., Felson, M., & Block, C. R. (1985). Crime victimization rates for incumbents of 246 occupations. *Sociology and Social Research, 69*, 442-451.

Blok, A. A., & Chambliss, W. J. (1981). *Organizing crime*. New York: Elsevier North Holland.

Blood, R., & Wolfe, D. (1960). *Husbands and wives: The dynamics of married living*. New York: Free Press.

Blumstein, A., Cohen, J., & Farrington, D. P. (1988a). Criminal career research. *Criminology, 26*, 1-36.

Blumstein, A., Cohen, J., & Farrington, D. P. (1988b). Longitudinal and criminal career research. *Criminology, 26*, 57-74.

Blumstein, A., Cohen, J., Roth, J. A., & Visher, C. (1986). *Criminal careers and career criminals*. Washington, DC: National Academy Press.

Blumstein, A., & Wallman, J. (2000). *The crime drop in America*. New York: Cambridge University Press.

Bonger, W. (1916). *Crime and economic conditions* (Vol. 2). Boston: Little, Brown.

Bordo, S. (1990). Feminism, postmodernism, and gender-scepticism. In L. J. Nicholson (Ed.), *Feminism/postmodernism* (pp. 133-156). New York: Routledge.

Bordo, S. (1993). *Unbearable weight: Feminism, western culture, and the body*. Berkeley: University of California Press.

Bordua, D. (1961). Delinquent subcultures: Sociological interpretations of gang delinquency. *Annals of the American Academy of Political and Social Science, 338*, 119-136.

Bossard, J. H. S. (1948). *The sociology of child development*. New York: Harper and Brothers.

Bouchard, T., Lykken, D., McGue, M., Segal, N., & Tellegen, A. (1981). Sources of human psychological differences: The Minnesota study of twins reared apart. *Science, 250*, 223-228.

Bouchard, T., & McGue, M. (1981). Familial studies of intelligence: A review. *Science, 250*, 1055-1059.

Bouchard, T., & Segal, N. (1985). Environment and IQ. In B. Wolman (Ed.), *Handbook of intelligence: Theories, measurements, and applications*. New York: Wiley.

Bourdieu, P. (1977). *Outline of a theory of practice*. New York: Cambridge University Press.

Bourdieu, P. (1989). Social space and symbolic power. *Social Theory, 7*, 14-25.

Box, S. (1983). *Power, crime, and mystification*. New York: Tavistock.

Box, S., & Hale, C. (1984). Liberation/emancipation, economic marginalization or less chivalry: The relevance of three theoretical arguments to female crime patterns in England and Wales, 1951-1980. *Criminology, 22*, 473-497.

Boyle, J. (1985). The politics of reason: Critical legal theory and local social thought. *University of Pennsylvania Law Review, 133*, 685-780.

Braithwaite, J. (1981). The myth of social class and criminality reconsidered. *American Sociological Review, 46*, 36-58.

Braithwaite, J. (1989). *Crime, shame and reintegration*. Cambridge, UK: Cambridge University Press.

Braithwaite, J., & Mugford, S. (1994). Conditions of successful reintegration ceremonies. *British Journal of Criminology, 34*, 139-171.

Bramel, D. (1962). A dissonance theory approach to defensive projection. *Journal of Abnormal and Social Psychology, 64*, 121-129.

Brand, C. (1995). How many dimensions of personality? The big 5, the gigantic 3, or the comprehensive 6? *Psychologica Belgica, 34*, 257-275.

Brantingham, P. J., & Brantingham, P. L. (1981). *Environmental criminology*. Beverly Hills, CA: Sage.

Brantingham, P. J., & Brantingham, P. L. (1982). Mobility, notoriety and crime: A study in crime patterns of urban nodal points. *Journal of Environmental Systems, 11,* 89-99.

Brantingham, P. J., & Brantingham, P. L. (1984). *Patterns of crime.* New York: Macmillan.

Braswell, M. (1990). Peacemaking: A missing link in criminology. *The Criminologist, 15,* 3-5.

Brehm, J. W., & Cohen, A. R. (1962). *Explorations in cognitive dissonance.* New York: Wiley.

Brennan, T. (1974). *Evaluation and validation regarding the National Strategy for Youth Development: A review of findings* (Report submitted to the Office of Youth Development). Boulder, CO: Behavioral Research and Evaluation Corporation.

Brennan, T., & Huizinga, D. (1975). *Theory validation and aggregate national data* (Integration Report of the Office of Youth Opportunity Research FY 1975). Boulder, CO: Behavioral Research Institute.

Brennan, T., Huizinga, D., & Elliott, D. S. (1978). *The social psychology of runaways.* Lexington, MA: D. C. Heath.

Brewin, C. R. (1988). Explanation and adaptation in adversity. In S. Fisher & J. Reason (Eds.), *Handbook of life stress, cognition and health.* Chichester, UK: John Wiley.

Brickman, P., & Bulman, R. J. (1977). Pleasure and pain in social comparison. In J. M. Suls & R. L. Miller (Eds.), *Social comparison processes.* New York: Hemisphere.

Brigham, J. (1987). Right, rage and remedy: Forms of law in political discourse. *Studies in American Political Development, 2,* 303-316.

Brigham, J., & Harrington, C. (1989). Realism and its consequences: An inquiry into contemporary sociolegal research. *International Journal of the Sociology of Law, 17,* 41-62.

Brizer, D. A., & Crowner, M. (1989). *Current approaches to the prediction of violence.* Washington, DC: American Psychiatric Press.

Bronfenbrenner, U., & Ceci, S. (1993). Heredity, environment, and the question how—A first approximation. In R. Plomin & G. McClearn (Eds.), *Nature, nurture, and psychology.* Washington, DC: American Psychological Association.

Brook, J. S., Gordon, S., & Whiteman, M. (1985). Stability of personality during adolescence and its relationship to stage of drug use. *Genetic, Social and General Psychology Monographs, 111,* 317-330.

Brown, R. M. (1991). *No duty to retreat: Violence and values in American history and society.* New York: Oxford University Press.

Brown, W. (1991). Feminist hesitations, postmodern exposures. *differences: A Journal of Feminist Cultural Studies, 3,* 63-84.

Browne, A. (1987). *When battered women kill.* New York: Free Press.

Brownmiller, S. (1975). *Against our will: Men, women, and rape.* New York: Simon & Schuster.

Buchanan, C. M., Eccles, J. S., & Becker, J. B. (1992). Are adolescents the victims of raging hormones: Evidence for activational effects of hormones on moods and behavior at adolescence. *Psychological Bulletin, 111,* 62-107.

Burgess, R. L. (1980). Family violence: Implications from evolutionary biology. In T. Hirschi & M. Gottfredson (Eds.), *Understanding crime* (pp. 91-101). Beverly Hills, CA: Sage.

Burgess, R. L., & Akers, R. L. (1966a). Are operant principles tautological? *Psychological Record, 16,* 305-312.

Burgess, R. L., & Akers, R. L. (1966b). A different association-reinforcement theory of criminal behavior. *Social Problems, 14,* 128-147.

Burkett, S. R., & Warren, B. O. (1987). Religiosity, peer influence, and adolescent marijuana use: A panel study of underlying causal structures. *Criminology, 25,* 109-131.

Burnstein, E., & Worchel, P. (1962). Arbitrariness of frustration and its consequences for aggression in a social situation. *Journal of Personality, 30,* 528-540.

Bursik, R. J., & Grasmick, H. G. (1995). Neighborhood-based networks and the control of crime and delinquency. In H. D. Barlow (Ed.), *Crime and public policy: Putting theory to work* (pp. 107-130). Boulder, CO: Westview.

Buss, A. H. (1961). *The psychology of aggression.* New York: Wiley.

Buss, A. H., & Brock, T. C. (1963). Repression and guilt in relation to aggression. *Journal of Abnormal and Social Psychology, 66,* 345-350.

Buss, D. M. (1984). Toward a psychology of person-environment correspondence: The role of spouse selection. *Journal of Personality and Social Psychology, 47,* 361-377.

Buss, D. M. (1987). Selection, evocation, and manipulation. *Journal of Personality and Social Psychology, 53,* 1214-1221.

Butler, J. (1990). *Gender trouble: Feminism and the subversion of identity.* New York: Routledge.

Butler, J. (1993). *Bodies that matter: On the discursive limits of sex.* New York: Routledge.

Butler, J., & Scott, J. W. (Eds.). (1992). *Feminists theorize the political.* New York: Routledge.

Butterfield, F. (1995). *All God's children, the Bosket family and the American tradition of violence.* New York: Knopf.

Cadoret, R., Yates, W., Troughton, E., Woodworth, G., & Stewart, M. (1995). Genetic-environmental interaction in the genesis of aggressivity and conduct disorders. *Archives of General Psychiatry, 52,* 916-924.

Cain, M. (1986). Realism, feminism, methodology, and law. *International Journal of the Sociology of Law, 14,* 255-267.

Cain, M. (1989). *Growing up good: Policing behaviour of girls in Europe.* London: Sage.

Cain, M. (1990). Realist philosophy and standpoint epistemologies or feminist criminology as a successor science. In L. Gelsthorpe & A. Morris (Eds.), *Feminist perspectives in criminology* (pp. 124-140). Philadelphia: Open University Press.

Cain, M. (1993). Foucault, feminism and feeling: What Foucault can and cannot contribute to feminist epistemology. In C. Ramazanoglu (Ed.), *Up against Foucault* (pp. 73-96). New York: Routledge.

Cain, M. (1995). Horatio's mistake: Notes on some spaces in an old text. *Journal of Law and Society, 22,* 68-77.

Cairns, R. B., & Cairns, B. D. (1991). *Adolescence in our time: Lifelines and risks.* Unpublished manuscript.

Cameron, M. O. (1964). *The booster and the snitch.* New York: Free Press.

Campbell, A. (1984). *The girls in the gang: A report from New York City.* New York: Blackwell.

Canestrari, R., & Battacchi, M. W. (1963). *Strutture e dinamiche della personalità minorile.* Bologna, Italy: Edizioni Malipiero.

Capron, C., & Duyme, M. (1989). Assessment of effects of socioeconomic status on IQ in a cross-fostering study. *Nature, 340,* 552-554.

Carlen, P. (1983). *Women's imprisonment: A study in social control.* Boston: Routledge & Kegan Paul.

Carlen, P. (Ed.). (1985). *Criminal women: Autobiographical accounts.* Cambridge, UK: Polity Press.

Carlen, P. (1988). *Women, crime and poverty.* Philadelphia: Open University Press.

Carlen, P. (1994). Gender, class, racism, and criminal justice: Against global and gender-centric theories, for poststructuralist perspectives. In G. S. Bridges & M. A. Myers (Eds.), *Inequality and social control* (pp. 134-144). Boulder, CO: Westview Press.

Carlen, P., & Worrall, A. (Eds.). (1987). *Gender, crime and justice.* Philadelphia: Open University Press.

Carrington, K. (1990). Aboriginal girls and juvenile justice: What justice? What justice. *Journal for Social Justice Studies, 3,* 1-18.

Carrington, K. (1994). Postmodern and feminist criminologies: Disconnecting discourses? *International Journal of the Sociology of Law, 22,* 261-277.

Carroll, B. J., & Steiner, M. (1987). The psychobiology of premenstrual dysphoria: The role of prolactin. *Psychoneuroendocrinology, 3,* 171-180.

Cartwright, D. S. (1971). *Summary of conceptual issues in the National Strategy for Delinquency Prevention* (Document No. 34 in Center for Action Research). Boulder, CO: University of Colorado, Bureau of Sociological Research.

Cartwright, D. S., Reuterman, N. A., & Vandiver, R. I. (1966). *Multiple-factor approach to delinquency.* Boulder: Department of Psychology, University of Colorado.

Caspi, A., & Bem, D. J. (1990). Personality continuity and change across the life course. In L. Pervin (Ed.), *Handbook of personality theory and research* (pp. 549-575). New York: Guilford Press.

Caspi, A., Elder, G. H., & Bem, D. J. (1987). Moving against the world: Life-course patterns of explosive children. *Developmental Psychology, 23,* 308-313.

Caspi, A., Lynam, D., Moffitt, T., & Silva, P. (1993). Unraveling girls delinquency: Biological, dispositional, and contextual contributions to adolescent misbehavior. *Developmental Psychology, 29,* 19-30.

Caspi, A., & Moffitt, T. E. (in press-a). Continuity amidst change: A paradoxical theory of personality coherence. *Psychological Inquiry.*

Caspi, A., & Moffitt, T. E. (in press-b). The continuity of maladaptive behavior: From description to understanding in the study of antisocial behavior. In D. Cicchetti & D. Cohen (Eds.), *Manual of developmental psychopathology.* New York: Wiley.

Catalano, R. F., Kosterman, R., Hawkins, J. D., Newcomb, M. D., & Abbott, R. D. (1996). Modeling the etiology of adolescent substance use: A test of the social development model. *Journal of Drug Issues, 26,* 429-455.

Ceaser, J. W. (1997). *Reconstructing America: The symbol of America in modern thought.* New Haven, CT: Yale University Press.

Cernkovich, S. A. (1977). *Evaluating two models of delinquency causation: Structural theory and control theory.* Paper presented at the meeting of the American Society of Criminology, Atlanta, GA.

Cernkovich, S. A., & Giordano, P. C. (1979). Delinquency, opportunity and gender. *Journal of Criminal Law and Criminology, 70,* 145-151.

Chesney-Lind, M. (1986). Women and crime: The female offender. *Signs: Journal of Women in Culture and Society, 12,* 78-96.

Chesney-Lind, M. (1987). Female offenders: Paternalism reexamined. In L. L. Crites & W. L. Hepperle (Eds.), *Women, the courts, and equality* (pp. 114-139). Newbury Park, CA: Sage.

Chesney-Lind, M. (in press). Girls crime and women's place: Towards a feminist model of female delinquency. *Crime and Delinquency.*

Chesney-Lind, M., & Rodriguez, N. (1983). Women under lock and key. *The Prison Journal, 63,* 47-65.

Chess, S., & Thomas, A. (1987). *Origins and evolution of behavior disorders: From infancy to early adult life.* Cambridge, MA: Harvard University Press.

Chess, S., & Thomas, A. (1996). *Temperament: Theory and practice.* New York: Brunner/Mazel.

Christie, N. (1981). *Limits to pain.* Oxford, UK: Martin Robertson.

Cicourel, A. (1968). *The social organization of juvenile justice.* New York: John Wiley.

Cicourel, A. V., & Kitsuse, J. I. (1963). *The educational decision-makers.* New York: Bobbs-Merrill.

Clare, A. W. (1985). Hormones, behaviour and the menstrual cycle. *Journal of Psychosomatic Research, 29,* 225-233.

Clark, J. P., & Haurek, E. W. (1966). Age and sex roles of adolescents and their involvement in misconduct: A reappraisal. *Sociology and Social Research, 50,* 495-508.

Clarke, R., & Mayhew, P. (Eds.). (1980). *Designing out crime.* London: HMSO.

Clarke, R. V. (1983). Situational crime prevention: Its theoretical basis and practical scope. In *Crime and justice: An annual review of research* (Vol. 4). Chicago: University of Chicago Press.

Clarke, R. V., & Cornish, D. B. (1985). Modeling offenders decisions: A framework for research and policy. In M. Tonry & N. Morris (Eds.), *Crime and justice: An annual review of research* (Vol. 6, pp. 147-185). Chicago: University of Chicago Press.

Clarke, R. V., & Hope, T. (1983). *Coping with burglary: Research perspectives on policy.* Boston: Kluwer-Nijhoff.

Clear, A., & Bond, A. (1997). Does central serotonergic function correlate inversely with aggression? A study using D-fenfluramine in healthy subjects. *Psychiatry Research, 69,* 89-95.

Clear, T. (1991). [Review of the book *Crime, shame and reintegration*]. *Social Science Quarterly, 72,* 397-398.

Cleckley, H. (1976). *The mask of sanity* (5th ed.). St. Louis, MO: Mosby.

Clinard, M. B. (1946). Criminological theories of violations of wartime regulations. *American Sociological Review, 11,* 258-270.

Clinard, M. B. (1951). Sociologists and American criminology. *Journal of Criminal Law and Criminology, 41,* 549-577.

Clinard, M. B. (1964). *Anomie and deviant behavior.* New York: Free Press.

Cloward, R. A., & Ohlin, L. E. (1960). *Delinquency and opportunity.* New York: Free Press.

Cocozza, J. J., & Steadman, H. J. (1974). Some refinements in the measurement and prediction of dangerous behavior. *American Journal of Psychiatry, 131,* 1012-1014.

Coe, C. L., & Levine, S. (1983). Biology of aggression. *Bulletin of the American Academy of Psychiatry Law, 11,* 131-148.

Cohen, A. (1955). *Delinquent boys.* New York: Free Press.

Cohen, A. (1966). *Deviance and control.* Englewood Cliffs, NJ: Prentice Hall.

Cohen, A. K. (1965). The sociology of the deviant act: Anomie theory and beyond. *American Sociological Review, 30,* 5-14.

Cohen, A. R. (1955). Social norms, arbitrariness of frustration and status of the agent of frustration in the frustration-aggression hypothesis. *Journal of Abnormal and Social Psychology, 51,* 222-226.

Cohen, L. E., & Felson, M. (1979). Social change and crime rate trends: A routine activity approach. *American Sociological Review, 4,* 588-608.

Cohen, L. E., & Machalek, R. (1988). A general theory of expropriative crime. *American Journal of Sociology, 94,* 465-501.

Cohen, R. L. (1982). Perceiving justice: An attributional perspective. In J. Greenberg & R. L. Cohen (Eds.), *Equity and justice in social behavior.* New York: Academic Press.

Cohen, S. (1985). *Visions of social control.* Oxford, UK: Polity Press.

Cohen, S. (1988). *Against criminology.* New Brunswick, NJ: Transaction Books.

Coie, J. D., Belding, M., & Underwood, M. (1988). Aggression and peer rejection in childhood. In B. Lahey & A. Kazdin (Eds.), *Advances in clinical child psychology* (Vol. 2, pp. 125-158). New York: Plenum Press.

Cole, J. B. (Ed.). (1986). *All American women: Lines that divide, ties that bind.* New York: Free Press.

Cole, S. (1975). The growth of scientific knowledge: Theories of deviance as a case study. In L. A. Coser (Ed.), *The idea of social structure: Papers in honor of Robert K. Merton.* New York: Harcourt Brace.

Coleman, J. W. (1989). *The criminal elite: The sociology of white-collar crime* (3rd ed.). New York: St. Martin's.

Collins, P. H. (1986). Learning from the outsider within: The sociological significance of black feminist thought. *Social Problems, 33*(6), 14-32.

Collins, P. H. (1990). *Black feminist thought: Knowledge, consciousness, and the politics of empowerment.* London: Unwin Hyman.

Collins, P. H. (1993). Toward a new vision: Race, class, and gender as categories of analysis and connection. *Race, Sex, and Class, 1,* 25-45.

Collins, P. H., Maldonado, L. A., Takagi, D. Y., Thorne, B., Weber, L., & Winant, H. (1995). Symposium: On West and Fenstermaker's "Doing Difference." *Gender & Society, 9,* 491-506.

Combahee River Collective. (1979). The Combahee River Collective statement. In Z. Eisenstein (Ed.), *Capitalist patriarchy and the case for socialist feminism* (pp. 362-372). New York: Monthly Review Press.

Compas, B. E. (1987). Coping with stress during childhood and adolescence. *Psychological Bulletin, 101,* 393-403.

Compas, B. E., Malcarne, V. L., & Fondacaro, K. M. (1988). Coping with stressful events in older children and young adolescents. *Journal of Consulting and Clinical Psychology, 56,* 405-411.

Compas, B. E., & Phares, V. (1991). Stress during childhood and adolescence: Sources of risk and vulnerability. In E. M. Cummings, A. L. Greene, & K. H. Karraker (Eds.), *Life-span developmental psychology: Perspectives on stress and coping.* Hillsdale, NJ: Lawrence Erlbaum.

Conger, R. (1976). Social control and social learning models of delinquent behavior: A synthesis. *Criminology, 14,* 17-40.

Conger, R. D. (1980). Juvenile delinquency: Behavior restraint or behavior facilitation? In T. Hirschi & M. Gottfredson (Eds.), *Understanding crime.* Beverly Hills, CA: Sage.

Conger, R. D., McCarty, J. A., Wang, R. K., Lahey, B. B., & Kroop, J. P. (1984). Perception of child, child-rearing values, and emotional distress as mediating links between environmental stressors and observed maternal behavior. *Child Development, 55,* 2234-2247.

Connell, R. W. (1987). *Gender and power.* Stanford, CA: Stanford University Press.

Connell, R. W. (1995). *Masculinities.* St. Leonards, New South Wales, Australia: Allen and Unwin.

Conrad, P., & Schneider, J. W. (1980). *Deviance and medicalization.* St. Louis, MO: C. V. Mosby.

Cook, K. S., & Hegtvedt, K. A. (1983). Distributive justice, equity, and equality. *Annual Review of Sociology, 9,* 217-241.

Cook, K. S., & Hegtvedt, K. A. (1991). Empirical evidence of the sense of justice. In M. Gruter, R. D. Masters, & M. T. McGuire (Eds.), *The sense of justice: An inquiry into the biological foundations of law.* New York: Greenwood Press.

Cook, K. S., & Messick, D. (1983). Psychological and sociological perspectives on distributive justice: Convergent, divergent, and parallel lines. In D. M. Messick & K. S. Cook (Eds.), *Equity theory: Psychological and sociological perspectives.* New York: Praeger.

Cook, K. S., & Yamagishi, T. (1983). Social determinants of equity judgments: The problem of multidimensional input. In D. M. Messick & K. S. Cook (Eds.), *Equity theory: Psychological and sociological perspectives.* New York: Praeger.

Cook, P. J. (1980). Research in criminal deterrence: Laying the groundwork for the second decade. In N. Morris & M. Tonry (Eds.), *Crime and justice: An annual review of research* (Vol. 2, pp. 211-268). Chicago: University of Chicago Press.

Cooke, P. J. (1987). The demand and supply of criminal opportunities. In N. Morris & M. Tonry (Eds.), *Crime and justice: An annual review of research* (Vol. 7). Chicago: University of Chicago Press.

Coombe, R. J. (1989). Room for manoeuver: Toward a theory of practice in critical legal studies. *Law and Social Inquiry, 14,* 69-121.

Cornish, D. B. (1978). *Gambling: A review of the literature and its implications for policy and research* (Home Office Research Studies No. 42). London: HMSO.

Cornish, D. B., & Clarke, R. V. (1986). *The reasoning criminal: Rational choice perspectives on offending.* New York: Springer-Verlag.

Cornish, D. B., & Clarke, R. V. (in press). Situational prevention, displacement of crime and rational choice theory. In K. Heal & G. Laycock (Eds.), *Situational crime prevention: From theory into practice.* London: HMSO.

Coser, R. (1985). *Power lost and status gained: The American middle-class husband.* Paper presented at the meetings of the American Sociological Association, Washington, DC.

Coser, R., & Coser, L. A. (1974). The housewife and her greedy family. In L. A. Coser (Ed.), *Greedy institutions* (pp. 89-100). New York: Free Press.

Coutu, W. (1949). *Emergent human nature.* New York: Knopf.

Cressey, D. R. (1952). Application and verification of the differential association theory. *Journal of Criminal Law, Criminology, and Police Science, 43,* 43-52.

Cressey, D. R. (1953). *Other people's money.* Glencoe, IL: Free Press.

Cressey, D. (1960). Epidemiology and individual conduct. *Pacific Sociological Review, 3,* 47-58.

Crippen, T. (1994). Neo-Darwinian approaches in the social sciences: Unwarranted concerns and misconception. *Sociological Perspectives, 37,* 391-401.

Crites, L. L. (1987). Wife abuse: The judicial record. In L. L. Crites & W. L. Hepperle (Eds.), *Women, the courts, and equality* (pp. 38-53). Newbury Park, CA: Sage.

Crittenden, K. S. (1983). Sociological aspects of attribution. *Annual Review of Sociology, 9,* 425-446.

Crittenden, K. S. (1989). Causal attribution in sociocultural context: Toward a self-presentational theory of attribution processes. *Sociological Quarterly, 30,* 1-14.

Crosby, F., & Gonzales-Intal, A. M. (1984). Relative deprivation and equity theories: Felt injustice and the undeserved benefits of others. In R. Folger (Ed.), *The sense of injustice: Social psychological perspectives.* New York: Plenum.

Crozier, M. (1984). *The trouble with America.* Berkeley: University of California Press.

Csikszentmihalyi, M., & Larson, R. (1984). *Being adolescent: Conflict and growth in the teenage years.* New York: Basic Books.

Cullen, F. T. (1984). *Rethinking crime and deviance theory: The emergence of a structuring tradition.* Totowa, NJ: Rowman and Allanheld.

Cummings, E. M., & El-Sheikh, M. (1991). Children's coping with angry environments: A process-oriented approach. In E. M. Cummings, A. L. Greene, & K. H. Karraker (Eds.), *Life-span developmental psychology: Perspectives on stress and coping.* Hillsdale, NJ: Lawrence Erlbaum.

Currie, D. (1986). Female criminality: A crisis in feminist theory. In B. MacLean (Ed.), *The political economy of crime.* Scarborough, Ontario, Canada: Prentice Hall.

Currie, D. (1989). Women and the state: A statement on feminist theory. *The Critical Criminologist, 1*(Spring), 4-5.

Currie, D. (1990). Battered women and the state: From the failure of theory to a theory of failure. *Journal of Human Justice, 1,* 77-96.

Currie, D., MacLean, B., & Milovanovic, D. (in press). Three traditions of critical justice inquiry: Class gender and discourse. In D. Currie & B. MacLean (Eds.), *Struggle for equality: Re-thinking the administration of justice.* Toronto, Ontario, Canada: Garamound Press.

Currie, E. (1991). Crime in the market society: From bad to worse in the nineties. *Dissent* (Spring), 254-259.

Currie, E. (1999). Radical criminology—or just criminology—then, and now. *Social Justice, 26*(2), 16-18.

Curtis, G. C. (1963). Violence breeds violence: Perhaps? *American Journal of Psychiatry, 120,* 386-389.

Curtis, R. (1986). Household and family in theory on inequality. *American Sociological Review, 51,* 168-183.

Cusson, M. (1983). *Why delinquency?* Toronto, Ontario, Canada: University of Toronto Press.

Dahrendorf, R. (1958). Toward a theory of social conflict. *Journal of Conflict Resolution, 2,* 170-183.

Dahrendorf, R. (1959). *Class and class conflict in industrial society.* Stanford, CA: Stanford University Press.

Daly, K. (1987a). Discrimination in the criminal courts: Family, gender, and the problem of equal treatment. *Social Forces, 66,* 152-175.

Daly, K. (1987b). Structure and practice of familial-based justice in a criminal court. *Law and Society Review, 21,* 267-290.

Daly, K. (1988). The social control of sexuality: A case study of the criminalization of prostitution in the progressive era. In S. Spitzer & A. T. Scull (Eds.), *Research in law, deviance, and social control* (Vol. 9, pp. 171-206). Greenwich, CT: JAI.

Daly, K. (1992). Women's pathways to felony court: Feminist theories of lawbreaking and problems of representation. *Southern California Review of Law and Women's Studies, 2,* 11-52.

Daly, K. (1993). Class-race-gender: Sloganeering in search of meaning. *Social Justice, 20*(1-2), 56-71.

Daly, K. (1994). Criminal law and justice system practices as racist, white, and racialized. *Washington & Lee Law Review, 51,* 431-464.

Daly, K. (1995a, June). *Black women, white justice.* Paper presented to the Law and Society Summer Institute, Niagara-on-the-Lake, Ontario, Canada.

Daly, K. (1995b, July). *Where feminists fear to tread? Working in the research trenches of class-race-gender.* Paper presented at the annual meeting of the British Criminology Conference, Loughborough, UK.

Daly, K. (in press). Paternalism re-examined: Gender, work-family relations, and sentencing. *Gender and Society.*

Daly, K., & Chesney-Lind, M. (1988). Feminism and criminology. *Justice Quarterly, 5,* 497-538.

Daly, K., & Stephens, D. (1995). The dark figure of criminology: Toward a black and multi-ethnic feminist agenda for theory and research. In N. H. Rafter & F. Heidensohn (Eds.), *International feminist perspectives in criminology* (pp. 189-215). Philadelphia: Open University Press.

Danner, M. J. E. (1989). Socialist feminism: A brief introduction. *Critical Criminologist, 1*(Summer), 1-2.

Datesman, S. K., & Scarpitti, F. R. (1975). Female delinquency and broken homes: A reassessment. *Criminology, 13,* 33-55.

Davis, A. (1981). *Women, race, and class.* New York: Vintage.

Davis, A., & Havighurst, R. J. (1946). Racial class and color difference in child rearing. *American Sociological Review, 2,* 698-710.

Davol, S. H., & Reimanis, G. (1959). The role of anomie as a psychological concept. *Journal of Individual Psychology, 15,* 215-225.

DeFleur, L. (1975). Biasing influences on drug arrest records: Implications for deviance research. *American Sociological Review, 40,* 88-103.

DeFleur, M. L., & Quinney, R. (1966). A reformulation of Sutherland's differential association theory and a strategy for empirical verification. *Journal of Research in Crime and Delinquency, 3,* 1-22.

DeFries, J. C., & Plomin, R. (1978). Behavioral genetics. *Annual Reviews in Psychology, 29,* 473-515.

de Haan, W. (1986). Abolitionism and the politics of bad conscience. In H. Bianchi & R. van Swaaningen (Eds.), *Abolitionism: Towards a non-repressive approach to crime.* Amsterdam: Free Press.

Dekeseredy, W., & MacLean, B. (1990). Researching women abuse in Canada: A realistic critique of the conflict tactics scale. *Canadian Review of Social Policy, 25,* 19-27.

Dekeseredy, W., & MacLean, B. (in press). Exploring the gender, class, and race dimension of victimization: A realist critique of the Canadian urban victimization survey. *International Journal of Offender Therapy and Comparative Criminology.*

Délacoste, F., & Alexander, P. (Eds.). (1987). *Sex work: Writings by women in the sex industry.* San Francisco: Cleis.

de Lauretis, T. (1990). Upping the anti [*sic*] in feminist theory. In M. Hirsch & E. F. Keller (Eds.), *Conflicts in feminism* (pp. 255-270). New York: Routledge.

Deleuze, G., & Guattari, F. (1987). *A thousand plateaus.* Minneapolis: University of Minnesota Press.

Delgado, R. (1989). Storytelling for oppositionists and others: A plea for narrative. *Michigan Law Review, 87,* 2411-2441.

Della Fave, L. R. (1974). Success values: Are they universal or class-differentiated? *American Journal of Sociology, 80,* 153-169.

Della Fave, L. R. (1980). The meek shall not inherit the earth: Self-evaluations and the legitimacy of stratification. *American Sociological Review, 45,* 955-971.

Della Fave, L. R., & Klobus, P. (1976). Success values and the value stretch: A biracial comparison. *Sociological Quarterly, 17,* 491-502.

Del Olmo, R. (1999). The development of criminology in Latin America. *Social Justice, 26*(2), 19-45.

Demsky, L. S. (1984). The use of Depo-Provera in the treatment of sex offenders. *The Journal of Legal Medicine, 5,* 295-322.

Dennis, D. (1989). Richard Quinney: An interview, 8/1/89. *Critical Criminologist, 1*(Summer), 11-14.

Denno, D. W. (1988). Human biology and criminal responsibility: Free will or free ride? *University of Pennsylvania Law Review, 137,* 615-671.

Dentler, R. A., & Erikson, K. T. (1959). The functions of deviance in groups. *Social Problems, 7,* 98-107.

Denzin, N. K. (1989). *Interpretive interactionism.* Newbury Park, CA: Sage.

Depue, R., & Collins, P. (1999). Neurobiology of the structure of personality: Dopamine, facilitation of incentive motivation, and extraversion. *Behavioral and Brain Sciences, 22,* 491-569.

Derrida, J. (1973). *Speech and phenomena.* Evanston, IL: Northwestern University Press.

Derrida, J. (1981). *Positions.* Chicago: University of Chicago Press.

Deutsch, M. (1975). Equity, equality, and need: What determines which value will be used as the basis of distributive justice. *Journal of Social Issues, 31,* 137-149.

Deykin, E. Y., Levy, J. C., & Wells, V. (1986). Adolescent depression, alcohol and drug abuse. *American Journal of Public Health, 76,* 178-182.

DiLalla, L., & Gottesman, I. (1989). Heterogeneity of causes for delinquency and criminality: Lifespan perspectives. *Development and Psychopathology, 1,* 339-349.

di Leonardo, M. (1991). Introduction. In M. di Leonardo (Ed.), *Gender at the crossroads of knowledge: Feminist anthropology in the postmodern era* (pp. 1-48). Berkeley: University of California Press.

Dill, B. T. (1983). Race, class, and gender: Prospects for an all-inclusive sisterhood. *Feminist Studies, 9,* 131-150.

Dinitz, S., Scarpitti, F. R., & Reckless, W. C. (1962). Delinquency vulnerability: A cross-group and longitudinal analysis. *American Sociological Review, 27,* 515-517.

Dishion, T. J., French, D. C., & Patterson, G. R. (in press). The development and ecology of antisocial behavior. In D. Cicchetti & D. Cohen (Eds.), *Manual of developmental psychopathology.* New York: John Wiley.

di Stefano, C. (1990). Dilemmas of difference: Feminism, modernity, and postmodernism. In L. J. Nicholson (Ed.), *Feminism/postmodernism* (pp. 63-82). New York: Routledge.

Dobash, R. E., & Dobash, R. P. (1984). The nature and antecedents of violent events. *British Journal of Criminology, 24,* 269-288.

Dodge, K. A., Coie, J. D., & Brakke, N. P. (1982). Behavior patterns of socially rejected and neglected preadolescents: The roles of social approach and aggression. *Journal of Abnormal Child Psychology, 10,* 389-410.

Dodge, K. A., & Frame, C. L. (1982). Social cognitive biases and deficits in aggressive boys. *Child Development, 53,* 629-635.

Dodge, K. A., & Newman, J. P. (1981). Biased decision-making processes in aggressive boys. *Journal of Abnormal Psychology, 90,* 375-379.

Dohrenwend, B. P. (1974). Problems in defining and sampling the relevant population of stressful life events. In B. S. Dohrenwend & B. P. Dohrenwend (Eds.), *Stressful life events: Their nature and effects.* New York: John Wiley.

Dohrenwend, B. S., & Dohrenwend, B. P. (1974). Overview and prospects for research on stressful life events. In B. S. Dohrenwend & B. P. Dohrenwend (Eds.), *Stressful life events: Their nature and effects.* New York: John Wiley.

Doleschal, E. (1970). Hidden crime. *Crime and Delinquency Literature, 2,* 546-572.

Dollard, J., Doob, L. W., Miller, N. E., Mowrer, O. H., Sears, R. R., Ford, C. S., Hovland, C. I., & Sollenberger, R. T. (1939). *Frustration and aggression.* New Haven, CT: Yale University Press.

Donnerstein, E., & Hatfield, E. (1982). Aggression and equity. In J. Greenberg & R. L. Cohen (Eds.), *Equity and justice in social behavior.* New York: Academic Press.

Douglas, J. D. (1970). Deviance and respectability: The social construction of moral meanings. In J. D. Douglas (Ed.), *Deviance and respectability* (pp. 3-30). New York: Basic Books.

Downes, D., & Rock, P. (1982). *Understanding deviance: A guide to the sociology of crime and rule breaking.* Oxford, UK: Clarendon.

Drigotas, S., & Udry, R. (1993). Biosocial models of adolescent problem behavior: Extensions to panel design. *Social Biology, 40,* 1-7.

Durkheim, E. (1938). *The rules of sociological method* (G. E. G. Catlin, Ed.). Chicago: University of Chicago Press.

Durkheim, E. (1951). *Suicide: A study of sociology.* Glencoe, IL: Free Press.

Durkheim, E. (1965). *The division of labor in society.* New York: Free Press.

Durkheim, E. (1982). *The rules of the sociological method.* New York: Macmillan.

Dworkin, A. (1987). *Intercourse.* New York: Free Press.

Eaton, M. (1983). Mitigating circumstances: Familiar rhetoric. *International Journal of the Sociology of Law, 11,* 385-400.

Eaton, M. (1985). Documenting the defendant: Placing women in social inquiry reports. In J. Brophy & C. Smart (Eds.), *Women in law: Explorations in law, family, and sexuality* (pp. 117-138). Boston: Routledge & Kegan Paul.

Eaton, M. (1986). *Justice for women? Family, court and social control.* Philadelphia: Open University Press.

Eaton, M. (1987). The question of bail: Magistrates responses to applications for bail on behalf of men and women defendants. In P. Carlen & A. Worrall (Eds.), *Gender, crime and justice* (pp. 95-107). Philadelphia: Open University Press.

Eberle, P., & Eberle, S. (1986). *The politics of child abuse.* Secaucus, NJ: Lyle Stuart.

Edmunds, G., & Kendrick, D. C. (1980). *The measurement of human aggressiveness.* New York: John Wiley.

Edsall, T. B. (1992, February). Willie Horton's message. *New York Review, 13,* 7-11.

Einstadter, W. (1989, August). *Asymmetries of control: Technologies of surveillance in the theft of privacy.* Paper presented to the Society for the Study of Social Problems, San Francisco, CA.

Elkins, S. M. (1968). *Slavery: A problem in American institutional and intellectual life* (2nd ed.). Chicago: University of Chicago Press.

Elliott, D. S. (1962). Delinquency and perceived opportunity. *Sociological Inquiry, 32,* 216-227.

Elliott, D. S. (1985). The assumption that theories can be combined with increased explanatory power: Theoretical integrations. In R. F. Meier (Ed.), *Theoretical methods in criminology.* Beverly Hills, CA: Sage.

Elliott, D. S., Ageton, S. S., & Canter, R. J. (1979). An integrated theoretical perspective on delinquent behavior. *Journal of Research on Crime and Delinquency, 16,* 3-27.

Elliott, D. S., Ageton, S. S., Huizinga, D., Knowles, B. A., & Canter, R. J. (1983). *The prevalence and incidence of delinquent behavior: 1976-1980* (The National Youth Survey Report No. 26). Boulder, CO: Behavioral Research Institute.

Elliott, D. S., Huizinga, D., & Ageton, S. S. (1985). *Explaining delinquency and drug use.* Beverly Hills, CA: Sage.

Elliott, D. S., Huizinga, D., & Menard, S. (1989). *Multiple problem youth: Delinquency, substance use, and mental health problems.* New York: Springer-Verlag.

Elliott, D., & Menard, S. (in press). Delinquent friends and delinquent behavior: Temporal and developmental patterns. In D. Hawkins (Ed.), *Some current theories of deviance and crime.* New York: Springer-Verlag.

Elliott, D. S., & Voss, H. (1974). *Delinquency and dropout.* Lexington, MA: D. C. Heath.

Ellis, L. (1996a). Arousal theory and the religiosity-criminality relationship. In P. Cordella & L. Siegel (Eds.), *Readings in contemporary criminological theory.* Boston: Northeastern University Press.

Ellis, L. (1996b). A discipline in peril: Sociology's future hinges on curing its biophobia. *American Sociologist, 27,* 21-41.

Ellis, L., & Ames, M. A. (1987). Neurohormonal functioning and sexual orientation: A theory of homosexuality-heterosexuality. *Psychological Bulletin, 101,* 233-258.

Elshtain, J. B. (1985). Invasion of the child savers: How we succumb to hype and hysteria. *The Progressive, 49,* 23-26.

Empey, L. (1956). Social class and occupational aspiration: A comparison of absolute and relative measurement. *American Sociological Review, 21,* 703-709.

Empey, L. (1982). *American delinquency: Its meaning and construction.* Homewood, IL: Dorsey.

Enloe, C. H. (1983). *Does khaki become you? The militarization of women's lives.* Boston: South End.

Enloe, C. H. (1987). Feminists thinking about war, militarism, and peace. In B. B. Hess & M. M. Feree (Eds.), *Analyzing gender* (pp. 526-547). Newbury Park, CA: Sage.

Epstein, S. (1994). A queer encounter: Sociology and the study of sexuality. *Sociological Theory, 12,* 188-202.

Erickson, M. L., Gibbs, J. P., & Jensen, G. F. (1977). Deterrence and the perceived certainty of legal punishment. *American Sociological Review, 42,* 305-317.

Erickson, M. L., Stafford, M. C., & Galliher, J. M. (1984). The normative erosion hypothesis: The latent consequences of juvenile justice practices. *The Sociological Quarterly, 25,* 373-384.

Erikson, E. H. (1960). Youth and the life cycle. *Children Today, 7,* 187-194.

Eron, L. D. (1963). Relationship of TV viewing habits and aggressive behavior in children. *Journal of Abnormal and Social Psychology, 67,* 193-196.

Eve, R. (1977). *The efficacy of strain, culture conflict and social control theories for explaining rebelliousness among high school students.* Unpublished manuscript, University of Texas at Arlington.

Ewick, P., & Silbey, S. S. (1995). Subversive stones and hegemonic tales: Toward a sociology of narrative. *Law & Society Review, 29,* 197-226.

Eysenck, H. J. (1962). Conditioning and personality. *British Journal of Psychology, 53,* 299-305.

Eysenck, H. J. (1964). *Crime and personality.* Boston: Houghton Mifflin.

Eysenck, H. (1977). *Crime and personality* (Rev. ed.). London: Paladin.

Faris, E. (1914). The origin of punishment. *International Journal of Ethics, 25,* 54-67.

Farnworth, M., & Leiber, M. J. (1989). Strain theory revisited: Economic goals, educational means, and delinquency. *American Sociological Review, 54*, 263-274.

Farrington, D. P. (1977). The effects of public labelling. *British Journal of Criminology, 17*, 112-125.

Farrington, D. P. (1986a). Age and crime. In M. Tonry & N. Morris (Eds.), *Crime and justice* (Vol. 7, pp. 29-90). Chicago: University of Chicago Press.

Farrington, D. P. (1986b). Stepping stones to adult criminal careers. In D. Olweus, J. Block, & M. R. Yarrow (Eds.), *Development of antisocial and prosocial behavior* (pp. 359-383). New York: Academic Press.

Farrington, D. P. (1991). Antisocial personality from childhood to adulthood. *The Psychologist, 4*, 389-394.

Farrington, D. (1996). The explanation and prevention of youthful offending. In J. D. Hawkins (Ed.), *Delinquency and crime: Current theories.* Cambridge, UK: Cambridge University Press.

Farrington, D. P., Ohlin, L. E., & Wilson, J. Q. (1986). *Understanding and controlling crime.* New York: Springer-Verlag.

Faunce, W. A. (1989). Occupational status-assignment systems: The effect of status on self-esteem. *American Journal of Sociology, 95*, 378-400.

Felson, M. (1980). Human chronography. *Sociology and Social Research, 65*, 1-9.

Felson, M. (1981). Social accounts based on map, clock and calendar. In T. Juster & K. Land (Eds.), *Social accounting systems: Essays in the state of the art.* New York: Academic Press.

Felson, M. (1983). Ecology of crime. In *Encyclopedia of crime and justice.* New York: Macmillan.

Felson, M. (1985). Crime at any point on the city map. In R. M. Figlio, S. Hakim, & G. F. Rengert (Eds.), *Metropolitan crime patterns.* Monsey, NY: Criminal Justice Press.

Felson, M. (1986). Routine activities, social controls, rational decisions and criminal outcomes. In D. Cornish & R. V. Clarke (Eds.), *The reasoning criminal.* New York: Springer-Verlag.

Felson, M. (1998). *Crime and everyday life* (2nd ed.). Thousands Oaks, CA: Pine Forge.

Felson, M. (2000). The routine activity approach as a general crime theory. In S. S. Simpson (Ed.), *Of crime and criminality.* Thousands Oaks, CA: Pine Forge.

Felson, M., & Cohen, L. E. (1981). Modeling crime rate trends—A criminal opportunity perspective. *Journal of Research in Crime and Delinquency, 18*, 138-164.

Felson, M., & Gottfredson, M. (1984). Adolescent activities near peers and parents. *Journal of Marriage and the Family, 46*, 709-714.

Feshbach, S. (1961a). The influence of drive arousal and conflict upon fantasy behavior. In J. Kagan (Ed.), *Contemporary issues in thematic apperceptive methods.* Springfield, IL: Charles C Thomas.

Feshbach, S. (1961b). The stimulating versus cathartic effects of a vicarious aggressive activity. *Journal of Abnormal and Social Psychology, 63*, 381-385.

Festinger, L. (1957). *A theory of cognitive dissonance.* Stanford, CA: Stanford University Press.

Figueira-McDonough, J., & Selo, E. (1980). A reformulation of the equal opportunity explanation of female delinquency. *Crime and Delinquency, 26*, 333-343.

Findlay, M. (1999). *The globalisation of crime: Understanding transnational relationships in context.* Cambridge, UK: Cambridge University Press.

Fineman, M. (1994). Feminist legal scholarship and women's gendered lives. In M. Cain & C. B. Harrington (Eds.), *Lawyers in a postmodern world* (pp. 229-246). Buckingham: Open University Press.

Finestone, H. (1976). *Victims of change: Juvenile delinquents in American society.* Westport, CT: Greenwood Press.

Finnegan, W. (1990a, September). Out there, I. *The New Yorker, 51-86.*

Finnegan, W. (1990b, November). Out there, II. *The New Yorker, 60-90.*

Fishbein, D. (1990). Biological perspectives in criminology. *Criminology, 28*, 27-75.

Fishbein, D. (1992). The psychobiology of female aggression. *Criminal Justice and Behavior, 19*, 99-126.

Fishbein, D. (1998). Building bridges. *Academy of Criminal Justice Sciences: ACJS Today, 17*, 1-5.

Fisher, S. (1972). Stigma and deviant careers in school. *Social Problems, 20*, 78-83.

Fitzhugh, G. (1954). *Sociology for the South.* Richmond, VA: Morris.

Fitzpatrick, P. (1984). Law and societies. *Osgood Hall Law Journal, 22*, 115-138.

Fitzpatrick, P. (1988). The rise and rise of informalism. In R. Matthews (Ed.), *Informal justice.* London: Sage.

Flax, J. (1990). Postmodernism and gender relations in feminist theory. In L. Nicholson (Ed.), *Feminism/ postmodernism* (pp. 39-62). New York: Routledge.

Folger, R. (1984). Emerging issues in the social psychology of justice. In R. Folger (Ed.), *The sense of injustice: Social psychological perspective.* New York: Plenum.

Folger, R. (1986). Rethinking equity theory: A referent cognitions model. In H. W. Bierhoff, R. L. Cohen, & J. Greenberg (Eds.), *Justice in social relations.* New York: Plenum.

Folkman, S. (1991). Coping across the life-span: Theoretical issues. In E. M. Cummings, A. L. Greene, & K. H. Karraker (Eds.), *Life-span developmental psychology: Perspectives on stress and coping.* Hillsdale, NJ: Lawrence Erlbaum.

Foster, J. D., Dinitz, S., & Reckless, W. C. (1972). Perceptions of stigma following public intervention for delinquent behavior. *Social Problems, 20*, 202-209.

Foucault, M. (1965). *Madness and civilization.* New York: Random House.

Foucault, M. (1973). *The birth of the clinic*. New York: Pantheon.

Foucault, M. (1977). *Discipline and punish*. New York: Pantheon.

Foucault, M. (1978). *The history of sexuality* (Vol. 1). New York: Pantheon.

Franks, C. N. (1955-1956). Recidivism, psychopathy and personality. *British Journal of Delinquency, 6*, 192-201.

Freedman, E. B. (1981). *Their sisters keepers: Women's prison reform in America, 1830-1930*. Ann Arbor: University of Michigan Press.

Frick, P. J., Lahey, B. B., Loeber, R., Tannenbaum, L., Van Horn, Y., Christ, M. A. G., Hart, E. A., & Hanson, K. (1993). Oppositional defiant disorder and conduct disorder: A meta-analytic review of factor analyses and cross-validation in a clinic sample. *Clinical Psychology Review, 13*, 319-340.

Friedrichs, D. (1986). Critical legal studies and the critique of criminal justice. *Criminal Justice Review, 112*, 11-15.

Friedrichs, D. (1989). Critical criminology and critical legal studies. *The Critical Criminologist, 1*(Summer), 7.

Gallop, J., Hirsch, M., & Miller, N. K. (1990). Criticizing feminist criticism. In M. Hirsch & E. F. Keller (Eds.), *Conflicts in feminism* (pp. 349-369). New York: Routledge.

Garfinkel, H. (1956). Conditions of successful degradation ceremonies. *American Journal of Sociology, 61*, 420-424.

Garfinkel, H. (1967). *Studies in ethnomethodology*. Englewood Cliffs, NJ: Prentice Hall.

Garland, D. (1994). Of crime and criminals: The development of criminology in Britain. In M. Maguire, R. Morgan, & R. Reiner (Eds.), *The Oxford handbook of criminology* (pp. 17-68). Oxford, UK: Clarendon Press.

Garmezy, N., & Rutter, M. (Eds.). (1983). *Stress, coping, and development in children*. New York: McGraw-Hill.

Garrett, J., & Libby, W. L., Jr. (1973). Role of intentionality in mediating responses to inequity in the dyad. *Journal of Personality and Social Psychology, 28*, 21-27.

Gatens, M. (1996). *Imaginary bodies: Ethics, power, and corporeality*. New York: Routledge.

Gauthier, M. (1959). The psychology of the compulsive forger. *Canadian Journal of Corrections, 1*, 62-69.

Gebhard, P. H., et al. (1965). *Sex offenders*. New York: Harper & Row.

Gehlke, C. E., & Biehl, K. (1934). Certain effects of grouping upon the size of the correlation in census tract material. *Journal of the American Statistical Association, Proceedings, 29*(Suppl.), 169-170.

Gelsthorpe, L., & Morris, A. (1988). Feminism and criminology in Britain. *British Journal of Criminology, 28*, 93-110.

Gelwick, R. (1977). *The way of discovery*. New York: Oxford University Press.

Gersten, J. C., Langer, T. S., Eisenberg, J. G., & Ozek, L. (1974). Child behavior and life events: Undesirable change or change per se. In B. S. Dohrenwend & B. P. Dohrenwend (Eds.), *Stressful life events: Their nature and effects*. New York: John Wiley.

Gersten, J. C., Langer, T. S., Eisenberg, J. G., & Smith-Fagon, O. (1977). An evaluation of the etiological role of stressful life-change events in psychological disorders. *Journal of Health and Social Behavior, 18*, 228-244.

Gibbons, D. C. (1977). *Society, crime and criminal careers* (3rd ed.). Englewood Cliffs, NJ: Prentice Hall.

Gibbs, J. P. (1975). *Crime, punishment, and deterrence*. New York: Elsevier.

Gibbs, J. P. (1985a). The methodology of theory construction in criminology. In R. F. Meier (Ed.), *Theoretical methods in criminology* (pp. 23-50). Beverly Hills, CA: Sage.

Gibbs, J. P. (1985b). Review essay. *Criminology, 23*, 381-388.

Gibbs, J. P., & Martin, W. T. (1958). A theory of status integration and its relationship to suicide. *American Sociological Review, 23*, 140-147.

Giddens, A. (1984). *The constitution of society: Outline of the theory of structuration*. Oxford, UK: Polity Press.

Giedd, J., Blumenthal, J., Jeffries, N., Castelano, F., Lui, H., Zijdenbos, A., Paus, T., Evans, A., & Rapoport, J. (1999). Brain development during childhood and adolescence: A longitudinal MRI study. *Nature Neuroscience, 2*, 861-863.

Gilman, C. P. (1898). *Women and economics*. Boston: Small, Maynard.

Giordano, P. C. (1978). Girls, guys and gangs: The changing social context of female delinquency. *Journal of Criminal Law and Criminology, 69*, 126-132.

Giordano, P., Kerbel, S., & Dudley, S. (1981). The economics of female criminality: An analysis of police blotters, 1890-1975. In L. H. Bowker (Ed.), *Women and crime in America* (pp. 65-82). New York: Macmillan.

Glaser, D. (1956). Criminality theories and behavioral images. *American Journal of Sociology, 5*, 433-444.

Glick, T. F. (Ed.). (1987). The comparative reception of relativity. Dordrecht, The Netherlands: D. Reidel.

Glueck, S. (1941). Crime causation. *National Probation Association Yearbook*, 86-108.

Glueck, S., & Glueck, E. (1950). *Unraveling juvenile delinquency*. Cambridge, MA: Harvard University Press.

Glueck, S., & Glueck, E. (1956). *Physique and delinquency*. New York: Harper.

Glueck, S., & Glueck, E. (1970). Working mothers and delinquency. In M. E. Wolfgang, L. Savitz, & N. Johnston (Eds.), *The sociology of crime and delinquency* (2nd ed., pp. 496-498). New York: Wiley.

Goddard, H. H. (1921). *Juvenile delinquency.* New York: Dodd, Mead.

Goetzmann, W. H. (1992). Exploration and the culture of science: The long goodbye of the twentieth century. In L. S. Luedtke (Ed.), *Making America: The society and culture of the United States* (pp. 413-431). Chapel Hill: University of North Carolina Press.

Goffman, E. (1961). *Asylums: Essays in the social situation of mental patients and other inmates.* Garden City, NY: Anchor.

Goffman, E. (1974). *Frame analysis.* New York: Harper & Row.

Goffman, E. (1981). *Forms of talk.* Oxford, UK: Basil Blackwell.

Gold, M. (1958). Suicide, homicide and the socialization of aggression. *American Journal of Sociology, 63,* 651-661.

Gold, M. (1963). *Status forces in delinquent boys.* Ann Arbor: University of Michigan, Institute for Social Research.

Gold, M. (1966). Undetected delinquent behavior. *Journal of Research in Crime and Delinquency, 3,* 27-46.

Gold, M. (1970). *Delinquent behavior in an American city.* Belmont, CA: Wadsworth.

Gold, M., & Reimer, D. J. (1974). *Changing patterns of delinquent behavior among Americans 13 to 16 years old—1972* (Report No. 1 of the National Survey of Youth). Ann Arbor: University of Michigan, Institute for Social Research.

Goldman, N. (1963). *The differential selection of juvenile offenders for court appearance.* Washington, DC: National Council on Crime and Delinquency.

Goldman-Racik, P., Bourgeois, J.-P., & Racik, P. (1997). Synaptic substrate of cognitive development: Life-span analysis of synaptogenesis in the prefrontal cortex of the non-human primate. In N. Krasnegor, G. R. Lyon, & P. Goldman-Racik (Eds.), *The development of the prefrontal cortex: Evolution, neurobiology, and behavior.* Baltimore: Paul Brooks.

Goldsmith, H. H. (1993). Nature-nurture issues in the behavioral genetics context: Overcoming barriers to communication. In R. Plomin & G. McClearn (Eds.), *Nature, nurture, and psychology.* Washington, DC: American Psychological Association.

Goldsmith, H. H., Bradshaw, D. L., & Rieser-Danner, L. A. (1986). Temperament as a potential developmental influence on attachment. In J. V. Lerner & R. M. Lerner (Eds.), *Temperament and social interaction during infancy and childhood* (pp. 5-34). San Francisco: Jossey-Bass.

Goldstein, A. P. (1990). *Delinquents on delinquency.* Champaign, IL: Research Press.

Goode, W. J. (1960). Norm commitment and conformity to role status obligation. *American Journal of Sociology, 64,* 246-258.

Goodrich, P. (1984). Law and language: An historical and critical introduction. *Journal of Law and Society, 11,* 173-206.

Goonatilake, S. (1998). *Toward a global science: Mining civilizational knowledge.* Bloomington: Indiana University Press.

Gottesman, I., & Goldsmith, H. H. (1994). Developmental psychopathology of antisocial behavior: Inserting genes into its ontogenesis and epigenesis. In C. Nelson (Ed.), *Threats to optimal development: Integrating biological, psychological, and social risk factors.* Hillsdale, NJ: Lawrence Erlbaum.

Gottfredson, H., & Hirschi, T. (1987). The methodological adequacy of longitudinal research on crime. *Scientology, 25,* 581-614.

Gottfredson, L. (1996). Social consequences of the g factor in employment. *Journal of Vocational Behavior, 29,* 379-410.

Gottfredson, M. (1984). *Victims of crime: The dimensions of risk.* London: HMSO.

Gottfredson, M. R., & Hirschi, T. (1986). The true value of lambda would appear to be zero. *Criminology, 24,* 213-233.

Gottfredson, M. R., & Hirschi, T. (Eds.). (1987a). *Positive criminology.* Newbury Park, CA: Sage.

Gottfredson, M. R., & Hirschi, T. (1987b). The positive tradition. In M. R. Gottfredson & T. Hirschi (Eds.), *Positive criminology* (pp. 9-22). Newbury Park, CA: Sage.

Gottfredson, M. R., & Hirschi, T. (1988). Science, public policy, and the career paradigm. *Criminology, 26,* 37-56.

Gottfredson, M., & Hirschi, T. (1990). *A general theory of crime.* Stanford, CA: Stanford University Press.

Gottfredson, S. (1986). Statistical and actual considerations. In F. Dutile & C. Foust (Eds.), *The prediction of criminal violence.* Springfield, IL: Charles C Thomas.

Gough, H. G. (1948). A sociological theory of psychopathy. *American Journal of Sociology, 53,* 359-366.

Gould, L. C. (1969). Who defines delinquency: A comparison of self-reported and officially reported incidences of delinquency for three racial groups. *Social Problems, 16,* 325-336.

Gove, W. R. (1985). The effect of age and gender on deviant behavior: A biopsychosocial perspective. In A. S. Rossi (Ed.), *Gender and the life course* (pp. 115-144). New York: Aldine.

Grassberg, J. M. (1964). Behavior therapy: A review. *Psychological Bulletin, 62,* 73-88.

Grau, J., Fagan, J., & Wexler, S. (1984). Restraining orders for battered women: Issues of access and efficacy. *Women and Politics, 4*(3), 13-28.

Greenberg, D. F. (1977). Delinquency and the age structure of society. *Contemporary Crises, 1,* 189-223.

Greenberg, D. F. (Ed.). (1981). *Crime and capitalism.* Stanford, CA: Mayfield.

Greimas, A. (1987). *On meaning*. Minneapolis: University of Minnesota Press.

Grosz, E. (1990). A note on essentialism and difference. In S. Gunew (Ed.), *Feminist knowledge: Critique and construct* (pp. 332-344). London: Routledge.

Grosz, E. (1994). *Volatile bodies: Toward a corporeal feminism*. St. Leonards, New South Wales, Australia: Allen and Unwin.

Grosz, E. (1995). *Space, time and perversion: The politics of bodies*. St. Leonards, New South Wales, Australia: Allen and Unwin.

Gruder, C. L. (1977). Choice of comparison persons in evaluating oneself. In J. M. Suls & R. L. Miller (Eds.), *Social comparison processes*. New York: Hemisphere.

Grusec, J. E. (1992). Social learning theory and developmental psychology: The legacies of Robert Sears and A. Bandura. *Developmental Psychology, 28,* 776-786.

Habermas, J. (1984). *The theory of communicative action: Vol. 1. Reason and the rationalization of society*. Boston: Beacon Press.

Habermas, J. (1987). *The theory of communicative action: Vol. 2. Lifeworld and system: A critique of functionalist reason*. Boston: Beacon Press.

Haen Marshall, I. (1998). Internationalisering van de criminologie. *Tijdschrift voor Criminologie, 40,* 176-184.

Haen Marshall, I. (1999). Steeds Meer Amerikaanse Toestanden in Nederland? Het Zal Wel Meevallen! In G. J. N. Bruinsma, H. G. van de Bunt, & G. B. Rovers (Eds.), *Vooruitzichten in de Criminologie* (pp. 19-42). Amsterdam: Vrije Universiteit.

Hagan, J. (1989). *Structural criminology*. New Brunswick, NJ: Rutgers University Press.

Hagan, J., & Albonetti, C. (1982). Race, class, and the perception of criminal injustice in America. *American Journal of Sociology, 88,* 329-355.

Hagan, J., Gillis, A. R., & Simpson, J. (1985). The class structure of gender and delinquency: Toward a power-control theory of common delinquent behavior. *American Journal of Sociology, 90,* 1151-1178.

Hagan, J., & Parker, P. (1985). White collar crime and punishment: The class structure and legal sanctioning of securities violations. *American Sociological Review, 50,* 302-316.

Hagan, J., Simpson, J., & Gillis, A. R. (1979). The sexual stratification of social control: A gender-based perspective on crime and delinquency. *British Journal of Sociology, 30,* 25-38.

Hagan, J., Simpson, J., & Gillis, A. R. (1987). Class in the household: A power-control theory of gender and delinquency. *American Journal of Sociology, 92,* 788-816.

Hagedorn, J. (1988). *People and folks: Youth gangs, crime, and the underclass in a rustbelt city*. Chicago: Lake View.

Hall, J. (1940). Criminal attempts—A study of the foundations of criminal liability. *Yale Law Review, 49,* 789-840.

Hall, J. (1941). Prolegomena to a science of criminal law. *University of Pennsylvania Law Review, 89,* 549-580.

Hall, J. (1943). Interrelations of criminal law and torts. *Columbia Law Review, 43,* 735-779, 967-1001.

Hall, L. (1937). Statutory law of crimes, 1887-1936. *Harvard Law Review, 50,* 616-653.

Hamparin, D. M., Schuster, R., Dinitz, S., & Conrad, J. P. (1978). *The violent few: A study of dangerous juvenile offenders*. Lexington, MA: Lexington Books.

Hanushek, E. A., & Jackson, J. E. (1977). *Statistical methods for social scientists*. New York: Academic Press.

Harding, S. (1986). *The science question in feminism*. Ithaca, NY: Cornell University Press.

Harding, S. (1987). The instability of the analytical categories of feminist theory. In S. Harding & J. F. O'Barr (Eds.), *Sex and scientific inquiry* (pp. 283-302). Chicago: University of Chicago Press.

Harding, S. (1990). Feminism, science, and the anti-Enlightenment critiques. In L. J. Nicholson (Ed.), *Feminism/postmodernism* (pp. 83-106). New York: Routledge.

Hare, R. D. (1965). A conflict and learning theory analysis of psychopathic behavior. *Journal of Research in Crime and Delinquency, 2,* 12-19.

Hare, R. D., & Schalling, D. (1978). *Psychopathic behavior*. New York: John Wiley.

Harpur, T. J., & Hare, R. D. (1991). *The assessment of psychopathy as a function of age*. Unpublished manuscript, University of British Columbia, Vancouver, British Columbia, Canada.

Harre, R. (1985). *The philosophies of science*. New York: Oxford University Press.

Harrington, C. (1988). Moving from integrative to constitutive theories of law. *Law and Society Review, 22,* 963-967.

Harrington, C., & Merry, S. (1988). Ideological production: The making of community mediation. *Law and Society Review, 22,* 709-735.

Harrington, C., & Yngvesson, B. (1990). Interpretive sociolegal research. *Law and Social Inquiry, 15,* 135-148.

Harris, A. R. (1977). Sex and theories of deviance: Toward a functional theory of deviant type-scripts. *American Sociological Review, 42,* 3-16.

Harris, J. (1995). Where is the child's environment? A group socialization theory of development. *Psychological Review, 102,* 458-489.

Harris, J. (1998). *The nurture assumption: Why children turn out the way they do*. New York: Free Press.

Harris, M. K. (1987). Moving into the new millennium: Toward a feminist vision of justice. *The Prison Journal, 67*(2), 27-38.

Hartmann, H., Kris, E., & Loewenstein, R. (1949). Notes on the theory of aggression. *Psychoanalytic Study of the Child, 3,* 9-36.

Hartsock, N. (1983). The feminist standpoint: Developing the ground for a specifically feminist historical materialism. In S. Harding & M. Hintikka (Eds.), *Discovering reality* (pp. 283-310). Dordrecht, The Netherlands: Reidel.

Hawkesworth, M. E. (1989). Knowers, knowing, known: Feminist theory and claims of truth. *Signs: Journal of Women in Culture and Society, 14,* 533-557.

Hawkins, J. D., & Lishner, D. M. (1987). Schooling and delinquency. In E. H. Johnson (Ed.), *Handbook on crime and delinquency prevention.* New York: Greenwood.

Hawkins, J. D., Lishner, D. M., Catalano, R. F., & Howard, M. O. (1986). Childhood predictors of adolescent substance abuse: Toward an empirically grounded theory. *Journal of Children in Contemporary Society, 8,* 11-40.

Hawley, A. (1950). *Human ecology: A theory of community structure.* New York: Ronald.

Hayes, D., & Hogrefe, R. (1964, March). *Group sanction and restraints related to use of violence in teenagers.* Paper presented at the 41st annual meeting of the American Orthopsychiatric Association, Chicago, IL.

Healy, W., & Bonner, A. F. (1969). *New light on delinquency and its treatment.* New Haven, CT: Yale University Press.

Hearn, C. R. (1977). *The American dream in the Great Depression.* Westport, CT: Greenwood.

Hebb, D. O. (1966). *Psychology.* Philadelphia: Saunders.

Hegtvedt, K. A. (1987). When rewards are scarce: Equal or equitable distributions. *Social Forces, 66,* 183-207.

Hegtvedt, K. A. (1990). The effects of relationship structure on emotional responses to inequity. *Social Psychology Quarterly, 53,* 214-228.

Hegtvedt, K. A. (1991a). Justice processes. In M. Foschi & E. J. Lawler (Eds.), *Group processes: Sociological analyses.* Chicago: Nelson-Hall.

Hegtvedt, K. A. (1991b). Social comparison processes. In E. F. Borgotta & M. E. Borgotta (Eds.), *Encyclopedia of sociology.* New York: Macmillan.

Heidensohn, F. M. (1968). The deviance of women: A critique and an enquiry. *British Journal of Sociology, 19,* 160-176.

Heidensohn, F. M. (1985). *Women and crime: The life of the female offender.* New York: New York University Press.

Heidensohn, F. M. (1986). Models of justice: Portia or Persephone? Some thoughts on equality, fairness and gender in the field of criminal justice. *International Journal of the Sociology of Law, 14,* 287-298.

Heidensohn, F. M. (1987). Women and crime: Questions for criminology. In P. Carlen & A. Worrall (Eds.), *Gender, crime and justice* (pp. 16-27). Philadelphia: Open University Press.

Heilbroner, R. (1991, November). A pivotal question unanswered. *The World & I: A Chronicle of Our Changing Era,* 538-540.

Heimer, C. A., & Staffen, L. R. (1995). Interdependence and reintegrative social control. *American Sociological Review, 60,* 635-654.

Heise, D. R. (1975). *Causal analysis.* New York: Wiley.

Held, D., McGrew, A., Goldblatt, D., & Perraton, J. (1999). *Global transformations: Politics, economics and culture.* Stanford, CA: Stanford University Press.

Henry, A. F., & Short, J. F., Jr. (1954). *Suicide and homicide.* Glencoe, IL: Free Press.

Henry, S. (1983). *Private justice.* London: Routledge & Kegan Paul.

Henry, S. (1985). Community justice, capitalist society and human agency: The dialectics of collective law in the cooperative. *Law and Society Review, 19,* 301-325.

Henry, S. (1987). Private justice and the policing of labor: The dialectics of industrial discipline. In C. Shearing & P. Stenning (Eds.), *Private policing.* Beverly Hills, CA: Sage.

Henry, S. (1988a). Can the hidden economy be revolutionary? Toward a dialectic analysis of the relations between formal and informal economies. *Social Justice, 15,* 29-60.

Henry, S. (1988b). Rules, rulers and ruled in egalitarian collectives: Deviance and social control in cooperatives. In J. G. Flanagan & Steve Rayner (Eds.), *Rules, decisions, and egalitarian societies.* Aldershot, UK: Avebury.

Henry, S. (1989a). Constitutive criminology: The missing link. *The Critical Criminologist, 1*(Summer), 9, 12.

Henry, S. (1989b). Justice on the margin: Can alternative justice be different. *The Howard Journal of Criminal Justice, 28,* 255-271.

Henry, S., & Milovanovic, D. (1996). *Constitutive criminology: Beyond postmodernism.* London: Sage.

Hepburn, J. R. (1976). Testing alternative models of delinquency causation. *Journal of Criminal Law and Criminology, 67,* 450-460.

Herrnstein, R. (1989). *Biology and crime* (National Institute of Justice Crime File, NCJ 97216). Washington, DC: U.S. Department of Justice.

Hetherington, E. M., & Klinger, E. (1964). Psychopathy and punishment. *Journal of Abnormal and Social Psychology, 69,* 112-115.

Hewitt, J. P., & Stokes, R. (1975). Disclaimers. *American Sociological Review, 40,* 1-11.

Hindelang, M. J. (1971). Age, sex, and the versatility of delinquent involvements. *Social Problems, 18,* 522-535.

Hindelang, M. J. (1974). Moral evaluations of illegal behaviors. *Social Problems, 21,* 370-384.

Hindelang, M., Hirschi, T., & Weis, J. (1981). *Measuring delinquency.* Beverly Hills, CA: Sage.

Hirschi, T. (1969). *Causes of delinquency.* Berkeley: University of California Press.

Hirschi, T. (1979). Separate and unequal is better. *Journal of Research in Crime and Delinquency, 16,* 34-38.

Hirschi, T. (1986). On the compatibility of rational choice and social control theories. In D. Cornish & R. V. Clarke (Eds.), *The reasoning criminal: Rational choice perspectives on offending.* New York: Springer-Verlag.

Hirschi, T. (1987, May). *Exploring alternatives to integrated theory.* Paper presented at the Albany Conference, Department of Sociology, State University of New York at Albany.

Hirschi, T., & Gottfredson, M. R. (1980). Introduction: The Sutherland tradition in criminology. In T. Hirschi & M. Gottfredson (Eds.), *Understanding crime* (pp. 7-19). Beverly Hills, CA: Sage.

Hirschi, T., & Gottfredson, M. (1983). Age and the explanation of crime. *American Journal of Sociology, 89,* 552-584.

Hirschi, T., & Gottfredson, M. (1986). The distinction between crime and criminality. In T. F. Hartnagel & R. A. Silverman (Eds.), *Critique and explanation.* New Brunswick, NJ: Transaction Books.

Hirschi, T., & Gottfredson, M. (1987). Causes of white-collar crime. *Criminology, 25,* 949-974.

Hirschi, T., & Hindelang, M. J. (1977). Intelligence and delinquency: A revisionist review. *American Sociological Review, 42,* 571-587.

Hochschild, J. (1995). *Facing up to the American Dream: Race, class, and the soul of the nation.* Princeton, NJ: Princeton University Press.

Hochschild, J. L. (1981). *What's fair: American beliefs about distributive justice.* Cambridge, MA: Harvard University Press.

Hollinger, D. A. (1985). *In the American province: Studies in the history and historiography of ideas.* Bloomington: Indiana University Press.

Homans, G. (1967). *The nature of social science.* New York: Harcourt, Brace.

Homans, G. C. (1961). *Social behavior: Its elementary forms.* New York: Harcourt, Brace.

hooks, b. (1981). *Ain't I a woman? Black women and feminism.* Boston: South End Press.

hooks, b. (1984). *Feminist theory: From margin to center.* Boston: South End Press.

Hooten, E. A. (1939). *The American criminal: An anthropological study.* Cambridge, MA: Harvard University Press.

Hope, T. J. (1982). *Burglary in schools: The prospects for prevention* (Research and Planning Unit Paper 11). London: HMSO, Home Office.

Houchon, G. (1962, October). *Définition et éléments constitutifs de l'état dangereux prédélictuel.*

General Report to the Third French Congress of Criminology, Aix-en-Provence, France.

House, J. S. (1981). *Work stress and social support.* Reading, MA: Addison-Wesley.

Howe, A. (1990). Prologue to a history of women's imprisonment: In search of a feminist perspective. *Social Justice, 17*(2), 5-22.

Howe, A. (1994). *Discipline and critique: Towards a feminist analysis of penality.* New York: Routledge.

Huber, J. (1976). Toward a socio-technological theory of the women's movement. *Social Problems, 23,* 371-388.

Huesmann, L. R., Eron, L. D., Lefkowitz, M. M., & Walder, L. O. (1984). Stability of aggression over time and generations. *Developmental Psychology, 20,* 1120-1134.

Huff, C. R. (1988). *Youth gangs and public policy in Ohio: Findings and recommendations.* Paper presented at the Ohio Conference on Youth Gangs and the Urban Underclass, Ohio State University, Columbus.

Huizinga, D., & Elliott, D. S. (1986). *The Denver high-risk delinquency project.* Proposal submitted to the Office of Juvenile Justice and Delinquency Prevention.

Hunt, A. (1987). The critique of law: What is critical about critical legal theory? *Journal of Law and Society, 14,* 5-19.

Hur, Y.-M., & Bouchard, T. (1997). The genetic correlation between impulsivity and sensation-seeking traits. *Behavior Genetics, 27,* 455-463.

Hurst, C. (1995). *Social inequality: Forms, causes, and consequences.* Boston: Allyn & Bacon.

Hyman, H. (1953). The value systems of the different classes: A social-psychological contribution to the analysis of stratification. In R. Bendix & S. M. Lipset (Eds.), *Class, status, and power.* New York: Free Press.

Ianni, F. A. J., & Reuss-Ianni, E. (1973). *A family business: Kinship and social control in organized crime.* New York: New American Library.

Illinois Law Enforcement Commission. (1984). *Crime in Illinois.* Springfield, IL: Author.

Jackson, B. (1985). *Semiotics and legal theory.* New York: Routledge & Kegan Paul.

Jackson, B. (1988). *Law, fact and narrative coherence.* Merseyside, UK: Deborah Charles Publications.

Jacobs, J. (1961). *The life and death of great American cities.* New York: Random House.

Jacobs, J. B., & Gouldin, L. P. (1999). Cosa nostra: The final chapter? In M. Tonry (Ed.), *Crime and justice: A review of research* (Vol. 25, pp. 129-190). Chicago: University of Chicago Press.

Jacobs, P. A., Brunton, M., Melville, M. M., Brittain, R. P., & McClemont, W. (1965). Aggressive behaviour, mental sub-normality, and the XYY male. *Nature, 108,* 1351-1352.

Jaggar, A. (1983). *Feminist politics and human nature.* Totowa, NJ: Rowman & Allenheld.

Jaggar, A., & Rothenberg, P. (Eds.). (1993). *Feminist frameworks* (3rd ed.). New York: McGraw-Hill.

Jakobson, R. (1971). Two aspects of language and two types of aphasic disorders. In R. Jakobson & M. Halle (Eds.), *Fundamentals of language.* Paris: Mouton.

Jasso, G. (1980). A new theory of distributive justice. *American Sociological Review, 45,* 3-32.

Jasso, G., & Rossi, P. H. (1977). Distributive justice and earned income. *American Sociological Review, 42,* 639-651.

Jefferson, T. (1990). *The case for paramilitary policing.* Milton Keynes, UK: Open University Press.

Jefferson, T. (1994). Theorizing masculine subjectivity. In T. Newburn & E. A. Stanko (Eds.), *Just boys doing business? Men, masculinities and crime* (pp. 10-31). New York: Routledge.

Jeffery, C. R. (1965). Criminal behavior and learning theory. *Journal of Criminal Law, Criminology and Police Science, 56,* 294-300.

Jensen, A. (1998). *The g factor.* Westport, CT: Praeger.

Jensen, G. (1986). *Dis-integrating integrated theory: A critical analysis of attempts to save strain theory.* Paper presented at the annual meeting of the American Society of Criminology, Atlanta, GA.

Jensen, G. F. (1972). Delinquency and adolescent self-conceptions: A study of the personal relevance of infraction. *Social Problems, 20,* 84-103.

Jensen, G. F., Erickson, M. L., & Gibbs, J. P. (1978). Perceived risk of punishment and self-reported delinquency. *Social Forces, 57,* 57-78.

Jessop, B. (1982). *The capitalist state.* New York: New York University Press.

Jessor, R., & Jessor, S. L. (1977). *Problem behavior and psychosocial development: A longitudinal study of youth.* San Diego, CA: Academic Press.

Jessor, R., et al. (1968). *Society, personality and deviant behavior: A study of a tri-ethnic community.* New York: Holt, Rinehart & Winston.

Joe, K. A., & Chesney-Lind, M. (1995). "Just every mother's angel": An analysis of gender and ethnic variations in youth gang membership. *Gender & Society, 9,* 408-430.

Johnson, J. M. (1985). Symbolic salvation: The changing meanings of the child maltreatment movement. *Studies in Symbolic Interaction, 6,* 289-305.

Johnson, R. E. (1979). *Juvenile delinquency and its origins.* Cambridge, UK: Cambridge University Press.

Jones, T., MacLean, B., & Young, J. (1986). *The Islington Crime Survey: Crime, victimization, and policing in inner-city London.* Aldershot, UK: Gower Press.

Jordan, J. (1985). Report from the Bahamas. In J. Jordan (Ed.), *On call: Political essays* (pp. 39-49). Boston: South End Press.

Kadzin, A. E. (1987). Treatment of antisocial behavior in children: Current status and future directions. *Psychological Bulletin, 102,* 187-203.

Kahn, A. J. (1953). *A court for children.* New York: Columbia University Press.

Kandel, D. (1980). Drug and drinking behavior among youth. *Annual Review of Sociology, 6,* 235-285.

Kandel, D. B., & Logan, J. A. (1984). Patterns of drug use from adolescence to young adulthood: I. Periods of risk for initiation, continued risk and discontinuation. *American Journal of Public Health, 74,* 660-667.

Kaplan, H. B. (1980). *Deviant behavior in defense of self.* New York: Academic Press.

Kaplan, H. B., Robbins, C., & Martin, S. S. (1983). Toward the testing of a general theory of deviant behavior in longitudinal perspective: Patterns of psychopathology. In J. R. Greenley & R. G. Simmons (Eds.), *Research in community and mental health.* Greenwich, CT: JAI.

Katz, J. (1988). *Seductions of crime: Moral and sensual attractions of doing evil.* New York: Basic Books.

Kellam, S. G., Branch, J. D., Agrawal, D. C., & Ensminger, M. E. (1975). *Mental health and going to school: The Woodlawn program of assessment, early intervention and evaluation.* Chicago: University of Chicago Press.

Kellam, S. G., Ensminger, M. E., & Simon, M. B. (1980). Mental health in first grade and teenage drug, alcohol, and cigarette use. *Drug and Alcohol Dependence, 5,* 273-304.

Kelly, D. H. (1977). The effects of legal processing upon a delinquent's public identity: An analytical and empirical critique. *Education, 97,* 280-289.

Kemper, T. D. (1978). A social interactional theory of emotions. New York: John Wiley.

King, D. K. (1988). Multiple jeopardy, multiple consciousness: The context of a black feminist ideology. *Signs: Journal of Women in Culture and Society, 14,* 42-72.

Kinsey, R., Lea, J., & Young, J. (1986). *Losing the fight against crime.* London: Basil Blackwell.

Kirk, R. (1993). *America's British culture.* New Brunswick, NJ: Transaction.

Kitsuse, J. I. (1962). Societal reaction to deviant behavior: Problems of theory and method. *Social Problems, 9*(Winter), 247-256.

Kitsuse, J. I., & Cicourel, A. V. (1963). A note on the uses of official statistics. *Social Problems, 11*(Fall), 131-138.

Klare, K. (1979). Law making as praxis. *TELOS, 40,* 123-135.

Klein, D. (1973). The etiology of female crime: A review of the literature. *Issues in Criminology, 8,* 3-30.

Klein, D. (1982). The dark side of marriage: Battered wives and the domination of women. In N. H. Rafter & E. A. Stanko (Eds.), *Judge, lawyer, victim, thief* (pp. 83-107). Boston: Northeastern University Press.

Klein, M. (1984). Offense specialization and versatility among juveniles. *British Journal of Criminology, 24,* 185-194.

Klein, M. W. (1986). Labelling theory and delinquency policy. *Criminal Justice and Behavior, 13*, 47-79.

Klockars, C. (1974). *The professional fence*. London: Tavistock.

Klockars, C. (1980). The contemporary crisis of Marxist criminology. In J. A. Inciardi (Ed.), *Radical criminology*. Beverly Hills, CA: Sage.

Kluegel, J. R., & Smith, E. R. (1986). *Beliefs about inequality*. New York: Aldine de Gruyter.

Knight, B. J., & West, D. J. (1975). Temporary and continuing delinquency. *British Journal of Criminology, 15*, 43-50.

Knorr-Cetina, K., & Cicourel, A. (1981). Advances in social theory and methodology: Toward an integration of macro- and micro-sociologies. London: Routledge & Kegan Paul.

Kochanska, G. (1991). Socialization and temperament in the development of guilt and conscience. *Child Development, 62*, 1379-1392.

Kohn, M. (1976). Looking back—A 25-year review and appraisal of social problems research. *Social Problems, 24*, 94-112.

Kohn, M. (1977). *Class and conformity* (2nd ed.). Chicago: University of Chicago Press.

Kohn, M., Slomczynski, K., & Schoenbach, C. (1986). Social stratification and the transmission of values in the family: A cross-national assessment. *Sociological Forum, 1*, 73-102.

Kornhauser, R. P. (1978). *Social sources of delinquency*. Chicago: University of Chicago Press.

Kozol, J. (1991). *Savage inequalities: Children in America's schools*. New York: Crown.

Kozol, J. (1992, September). Whittle and the privateers. *The Nation, 21*, 272-278.

Kregarman, J. J., & Worchel, P. (1961). Arbitrariness of frustration and aggression. *Journal of Abnormal and Social Psychology, 63*, 183-187.

Kreuz, L. E., & Rose, R. M. (1971). Assessment of aggressive behavior and plasma testosterone in a young criminal population. *Psychosomatic Medicine, 34*, 321-332.

Krohn, M. D., & Massey, J. (1980). Social and delinquent behavior: An examination of the elements of the social bond. *Sociological Quarterly, 21*, 529-543.

Kuhn, T. (1970). *The structure of scientific revolutions*. Chicago: University of Chicago Press.

Kuperman, S., & Stewart, M. (1987). Use of propranolol to decrease aggressive outbursts in younger patients. *Psychosomatics, 28*, 315-319.

Labouvie, E. W. (1986a). Alcohol and marijuana use in relation to adolescent stress. *International Journal of the Addictions, 21*, 333-345.

Labouvie, E. W. (1986b). The coping function of adolescent alcohol and drug use. In R. K. Silbereisen, K. Eyfeth, & G. Rudinger (Eds.), *Development as action in context*. New York: Springer.

Lacan, J. (1977). *Ecrits* (A. Sheridan, Trans.). New York: Norton.

LaFrenier, P., & Sroufe, L. A. (1985). Profiles of peer competence in the preschool: Interrelations between measures, influence of social ecology, and relation to attachment history. *Developmental Psychology, 21*, 56-69.

LaGrange, R. L., & White, H. R. (1985). Age differences in delinquency. *Criminology, 23*, 19-45.

Lane, R. E. (1953). Why businessmen violate the law. *Journal of Criminal Law, Criminology, and Police Science, 44*, 151-165.

Larder, D. L. (1962). Effect of aggressive story content on nonverbal play behavior. *Psychological Reprints, 11*, 1, 14.

Larson, C. J. (1984). *Crime, justice and society*. New York: General Hall.

Laub, J. H. (1987). Data for positive criminology. In M. R. Gottfredson & T. Hirschi (Eds.), *Positive criminology* (pp. 56-70). Newbury Park, CA: Sage.

Lauritsen, J. L., Sampson, R. J., & Laub, J. (1991). The link between offending and victimization among adolescents. *Criminology, 29*, 265-292.

Lawson, R. (1965). *Frustration, the development of a scientific concept*. New York: Macmillan.

Leader, A. L. (1941). A differential theory of criminality. *Sociology and Social Research, 26*, 45-53.

LeBlanc, M. (1983). Delinquency as an epiphenomenon of adolescence. In R. Corrado, M. LeBlanc, & J. Trepanier (Eds.), *Current issues in juvenile justice* (pp. 31-48). Toronto, Ontario, Canada: Butterworths.

LeBlanc, M. (1994). Family, school, delinquency, and criminality: The predictive power of an elaborated social control theory for males. *Criminal Behaviour and Mental Health, 4*, 101-117.

LeBlanc, M., & Loeber, R. (1993). Precursors, causes, and the development of offending. In D. F. Hay & A. Angold (Eds.), *Precursors and causes in development and psychopathology* (pp. 233-263). London: Wiley.

Lecerle, J.-J. (1985). *Philosophy through the looking glass: Language, nonsense, desire*. London: Hutchinson.

Lejeune, R. (1977). The management of a mugging. *Urban Life, 6*(2), 123-148.

Lemert, C. C. (1994). Post-structuralism and sociology. In S. Seidman (Ed.), *The postmodern turn: New perspectives on social theory* (pp. 265-281). New York: Cambridge University Press.

Lemert, E. M. (1951). *Social pathology*. New York: McGraw-Hill.

Lemert, E. M. (1953). An isolation and closure theory of naive check forgery. *Journal of Criminal Law, Criminology and Police Science, 44*, 296-307.

Lemert, E. M. (1967). *Human deviance, social problems, and social controls*. Englewood Cliffs, NJ: Prentice Hall.

Lemert, E. M. (1969). Records in juvenile court. In S. Wheeler (Ed.), *On record: Files and dossiers in American life* (pp. 355-389). New York: Russell Sage Foundation.

Leonard, E. B. (1983). Judicial decisions and prison reform: The impact of litigation on women prisoners. *Social Problems, 31*(1), 45-58.

Lerman, L. G. (1980). Protection of battered women: A survey of state legislation. *Women's Rights Law Reporter, 6,* 271-284.

Lerner, M. J. (1977). The justice motive: Some hypotheses as to its origins and forms. *Journal of Personality, 45,* 1-52.

Leventhal, G. S. (1976). The distribution of rewards and resources in groups and organizations. In L. Berkowitz & E. Walster (Eds.), *Advances in experimental social psychology: Equity theory: Toward a general theory of social interaction.* New York: Academic Press.

Leventhal, G. S., Karuzajr, J., & Fry, W. R. (1980). Beyond fairness: A theory of allocation preferences. In G. Mikula (Ed.), *Justice and social interaction.* New York: Springer-Verlag.

Lewin, K. (1935). *A dynamic theory of personality.* New York: McGraw-Hill.

Lewis, D. O., Moy, E., Jackson, L. D., Aaronson, R., Restifo, N., Serra, S., & Simos, A. (1985). Biopsychosocial characteristics of children who later murder: A prospective study. *American Journal of Psychiatry, 142,* 1161-1167.

Lewis, D. O., Pincus, J. H., Bard, B., Richardson, E., Prichep, L. S., Feldman, M., & Yeager, C. (1988). Neuropsychiatric, psychoeducational, and family characteristics of 14 juveniles condemned to death in the United States. *American Journal of Psychiatry, 145,* 584-589.

Lewis, D. O., Pincus, J. H., Feldman, M., Jackson, L., & Bard, B. (1986). Psychiatric, neurological, and psychoeducational characteristics of 15 death row inmates in the United States. *American Journal of Psychiatry, 143,* 838-845.

Lewis, D. O., Shanok, S. S., & Balla, D. A. (1979). Perinatal difficulties, head and face trauma and child abuse in the medical histories of serious youthful offenders. *American Journal of Psychiatry, 136,* 419-423.

Lewis, D. O., Shanok, S. S., & Pincus, J. N. (1981). The neuropsychiatric status of violent male delinquents. In D. O. Lewis (Ed.), *Vulnerabilities of delinquency.* New York: Spectrum.

Lind, E. A., & Tyler, T. R. (1988). *The social psychology of procedural justice.* New York: Plenum.

Linden, E., & Hackler, J. C. (1973). Affective ties and delinquency. *Pacific Sociological Review, 16*(1), 27-46.

Linsky, A. S., & Straus, M. A. (1986). *Social stress in the United States.* Dover, MA: Auburn House.

Lion, J. R. (1974). Diagnosis and treatment of personality disorders. In J. R. Lion (Ed.), *Personality disorders: Diagnosis and treatment.* Baltimore: Williams & Wilkins.

Lion, J. R. (1979). Benzodiazepines in the treatment of aggressive patients. *Journal of Clinical Psychiatry, 40,* 70-71.

Lipset, S. M. (1991). American exceptionalism reaffirmed. In B. E. Shafter (Ed.), *Is America different? A new look at American exceptionalism* (pp. 1-45). Oxford: Clarendon Press.

Lipton, D., Martinson, R., & Wilks, J. (1975). *The effectiveness of correctional treatment: A survey of treatment evaluation studies.* New York: Praeger.

Liska, A., & Reed, M. (1985). Ties to conventional institutions and delinquency. *American Sociological Review, 50,* 547-560.

Liska, A. E. (1971). Aspirations, expectations and delinquency: Stress and additive models. *Sociological Quarterly, 12,* 99-107.

Liska, A. E. (1987). *Perspectives on deviance.* Englewood Cliffs, NJ: Prentice Hall.

Litwak, E. (1968). Technological innovation and theoretical functions of primary groups and bureaucratic structures. *American Journal of Sociology, 73,* 468-481.

Loeber, R. (1982). The stability of antisocial and delinquent child behavior: A review. *Child Development, 53,* 1431-1446.

Loeber, R. (1988). Natural histories of conduct problems, delinquency, and associated substance use. In B. B. Lahey & A. E. Kazdin (Eds.), *Advances in clinical child psychology* (pp. 73-124). New York: Plenum.

Loeber, R. (1991). Questions and advances in the study of developmental pathways. In D. Cicchetti & S. Toth (Eds.), *Rochester symposium on developmental psychopathology: III* (pp. 97-115). Rochester, NY: University of Rochester Press.

Loeber, R., & Baicker-McKee, C. (1989). *The changing manifestations of disruptive/antisocial behavior from childhood to early adulthood: Evolution or tautology?* Unpublished manuscript, Western Psychiatric Institute, University of Pittsburgh, Pittsburgh, PA.

Loeber, R., & Dishion, T. (1983). Early predictors of male delinquency: A review. *Psychological Bulletin, 94,* 68-99.

Loeber, R., & Farrington, D. P. (1994). Problems and solutions in longitudinal and experimental treatment studies of child psychopathology and delinquency. *Journal of Consulting and Clinical Psychology, 62,* 887-900.

Loeber, R., Green, S., Lahey, B., & Stouthamer-Loeber, M. (1990). Optimal informants on childhood disruptive behaviors. *Development and Psychopathology, 1,* 317-337.

Loeber, R., & Hay, D. F. (1994). Developmental approaches to aggression and conduct problems. In M. L. Rutter & D. F. Hay (Eds.), *Development through life: A handbook for clinicians* (pp. 488-516). Oxford, UK: Blackwell.

Loeber, R., Keenan, K., & Zhang, Q. (1994). *Boys experimentation and persistence in developmental pathways toward serious delinquency.* Unpublished manuscript, University of Pittsburgh,

Western Psychiatric Institute and Clinic, School of Medicine, Pittsburgh, PA.

Loeber, R., & Le Blanc, M. (1990). Toward a developmental criminology. In N. Morris & M. Tonry (Eds.), *Crime and justice* (pp. 375-473). Chicago: University of Chicago Press.

Loeber, R., & Schmaling, K. B. (1985). Empirical evidence for overt and covert patterns of antisocial conduct problems: A metaanalysis. *Journal of Abnormal Child Psychology, 13,* 337-353.

Loeber, R., & Stouthamer-Loeber, M. (1986). Family factors as correlates and predictors of juvenile conduct problems and delinquency. In N. Morris & M. Tonry (Eds.), *Crime and justice: An annual review of research.* Chicago: University of Chicago Press.

Loeber, R., & Stouthamer-Loeber, M. (1987). Prediction. In H. C. Quay (Ed.), *Handbook of juvenile delinquency* (pp. 325-382). New York: John Wiley.

Loeber, R., & Stouthamer-Loeber, M. (1994, July). *The interrelation and impact of protective and risk factors on juvenile delinquency.* Paper presented at the meeting of the International Society for the Study of Behavioral Development, Amsterdam, The Netherlands.

Loeber, R., Wung, P., Keenan, K., Giroux, B., Stouthamer-Loeber, M., Van Kammen, W. B., & Maughan, B. (1993). Developmental pathways in disruptive child behavior. *Development and Psychopathology, 5,* 101-132.

Loehlin, J. C. (1989). Partitioning environmental and genetic contributions to behavioral development. *American Psychologist, 44,* 1285-1292.

Lombroso, C. (1918). *Crime: Its causes and remedies.* Boston: Little, Brown.

Long, E. (1985). *The American dream and the popular novel.* Boston: Routledge & Kegan Paul.

Lopreato, J. (1968). Authority relations and class conflict. *Social Forces, 47,* 70-79.

Lorde, A. (1984). *Sister Outsider.* Trumansburg, NY: The Crossing Press.

Lottier, S. F. (1942). Tension theory of criminal behavior. *American Sociological Review, 7,* 840-848.

Lovaas, O. I. (1961). Effect of exposure to symbolic aggression on aggressive behavior. *Child Development, 32,* 37-44.

Lubiano, W. (1992). Black ladies, welfare queens, and state minstrels: Ideological war by narrative means. In T. Morrison (Ed.), *Race-ing justice, engender-ing power* (pp. 323-363). New York: Pantheon.

Lugones, M. C. (1991). On the logic of pluralist feminism. In C. Card (Ed.), *Feminist ethics* (pp. 35-44). Lawrence: University Press of Kansas.

Luhmann, N. (1985). *A sociological theory of law.* Boston: Routledge & Kegan Paul.

Lykken, D. (1995). *The antisocial personalities.* Hillsdale, NJ: Lawrence Erlbaum.

Lykken, D. T. (1957). A study of anxiety in the sociopathic personality. *Journal of Abnormal and Social Psychology, 55,* 6-10.

Lyman, S. M., & Scott, M. B. (1970). *A sociology of the absurd.* New York: Appleton-Century-Crofts.

Lynn, R. (1996). *Dysgenics: Genetic deterioration in modern populations.* Westport, CT: Greenwood Press.

Lytton, H. (1990). Child and parent effects in boys conduct disorder: A reinterpretation. *Developmental Psychology, 26,* 683-697.

Maccoby, E., & Martin, J. (1983). Socialization in the context of family: Parent-child interaction. In P. Mussen & E. Heatherington (Eds.), *Handbook of child psychology, socialization, personality, and social development* (4th ed.). New York: Wiley.

MacIver, R. M. (1950). *The ramparts we guard.* New York: Macmillan.

MacKinnon, C. (1982). Feminism, Marxism, method, and the state: An agenda for theory. *Signs: Journal of Women in Culture and Society, 7,* 515-544.

MacKinnon, C. (1983). Feminism, Marxism, method, and the state: Toward feminist jurisprudence. *Signs: Journal of Women in Culture and Society, 8,* 635-658.

MacKinnon, C. A. (1987). *Feminism unmodified: Discourses on life and law.* Cambridge, MA: Harvard University Press.

MacLean, B. (1991). In partial defense of socialist realism. *Crime, Law and Social Change: An International Journal, 15.*

MacLeod, J. (1987). *Ain't no makin it.* Boulder, CO: Westview Press.

Maher, L. (1995). *Dope girls: Gender, race and class in the drug economy.* Unpublished doctoral dissertation, Rutgers University, New Brunswick, New Jersey.

Maher, L., & Daly, K. (1996). Women in the street-level drug economy: Continuity or change? *Criminology, 34.*

Makkai, T., & Braithwaite, J. (1994). Reintegrative shaming and compliance with regulatory standards. *Criminology, 32,* 361-383.

Manning, P. (1986). Signwork. *Human Relations, 39,* 283-308.

Manning, P. (1987). *Semiotics and fieldwork.* Newbury Park, CA: Sage.

Manning, P. (1988). *Symbolic communication: Signifying calls and the police response.* Cambridge, MA: MIT Press.

Manning, P. (1990). Semiotics and postmodernism. In D. Dickens & A. Fontana (Eds.), *Post modernism and sociology.* Chicago: University of Chicago Press.

Marcus, S. (1992). Fighting bodies, fighting words: A theory and politics of rape prevention. In J. Butler & J. W. Scott (Eds.), *Feminists theorize the political* (pp. 385-403). New York: Routledge.

Margolin, L. (1990). When vocabularies of motive fail: The example of fatal child abuse. *Qualitative Sociology, 13,* 373-385.

Mark, M. M., & Folger, R. (1984). Responses to relative deprivation: A conceptual framework. In P. Shaver (Ed.), *Review of personality and social psychology* (Vol. 5). Beverly Hills, CA: Sage.

Martin, J. (1986). When expectations and justice do not coincide: Blue collar visions of a just world. In H. Weiner Bierhoff, R. L. Cohen, & J. Greenberg (Eds.), *Justice in social relations.* New York: Plenum.

Martin, J., & Murray, A. (1983). Distributive injustice and unfair exchange. In D. M. Messick & K. S. Cook (Eds.), *Equity theory: Psychological and social perspectives.* New York: Praeger.

Martin, J., & Murray, A. (1984). Catalysts for collective violence: The importance of a psychological approach. In R. Folger (Ed.), *The sense of injustice: Social psychological perspectives.* New York: Plenum.

Martin, J. R. (1994). Methodological essentialism, false difference, and other dangerous traps. *Signs: Journal of Women in Culture and Society, 19,* 630-657.

Martin, S. E., & Jurik, N. C. (1996). *Doing justice, doing gender.* Newbury Park, CA: Sage.

Marx, G. (1988). *Undercover: Policy surveillance in America.* Berkeley: University of California Press.

Marx, K. (1984). *The eighteenth brumaire of Louis Bonaparte.* In E. Kamenka (Ed.), *The portable Marx.* New York: Penguin.

Masserman, J. H. (1959). The biodynamic approaches. In S. Arieti (Ed.), *American handbook of psychiatry* (Vol. 2, p. 1684). New York: Basic Books.

Massey, J. L., & Krohn, M. (1986). A longitudinal examination of an integrated social process model of deviant behavior. *Social Forces, 65,* 106-134.

Matarazzo, J. (1992). Psychological testing and assessment in the 21st century. *American Psychologist, 47,* 1007-1018.

Mathy, J.-P. (2000). French resistance: The French-American culture wars. Minneapolis: University of Minnesota Press.

Matsueda, R. (1982). Testing social control theory and differential association. *American Sociological Review, 47,* 489-504.

Matthews, R. (1987). Taking realist criminology seriously. *Contemporary Crisis, 11,* 371-401.

Matthews, R., & Young, J. (Eds.). (1986). *Confronting crime.* London: Sage.

Matza, D. (1964). *Delinquency and drift.* New York: Wiley.

Matza, D., & Sykes, G. M. (1961). Juvenile delinquency and subterranean values. *American Sociological Review, 26,* 712-719.

Mausner, B., & Platt, E. S. (1971). *Smoking: A behavioral analysis.* Elmsford, NY: Pergamon Press.

Mawson, A. R. (1987). *Criminality: A model of stress-induced crime.* New York: Praeger.

McCaldon, R. J. (1964). Aggression. *Journal of the Canadian Psychiatric Association, 6,* 502-511.

McCardle, L., & Fishbein, D. H. (1989). The self-reported effects of PCP on human aggression. *Addictive Behaviors, 4,* 465-472.

McCary, J. L. (1949-1950). Ethnic and cultural reactions to frustration. *Journal of Personality, 18,* 321-326.

McCary, J. L. (1951). Reactions to frustration by some cultural and racial groups. *Personality: Symposia in Topical Issues, 1,* 84-102.

McClelland, K. (1990). The social management of ambition. *Sociological Quarterly, 31,* 225-251.

McConaghy, N. (1962). The inhibitory index in relation to extraversion-introversion. *American Journal of Psychiatry, 119,* 527-533.

McCord, J. (1979). Some child-rearing antecedents of criminal behavior in adult men. *Journal of Personality and Social Psychology, 37,* 1477-1486.

McCord, W., & McCord, J. (1959). *Origins of crime: A new evaluation of the Cambridge-Somerville Study.* New York: Columbia University Press.

McCormack, A., Janus, M.-D., & Wolbert Burgess, A. (1986). Runaway youths and sexual victimization: Gender differences in an adolescent runaway population. *Child Abuse and Neglect, 10,* 387-395.

McGue, M. (1994). Why developmental psychopathology should find room for behavior genetics. In C. Nelson (Ed.), *Threats to optimal development: Integrating biological, psychological, and social risk factors.* Hillsdale, NJ: Lawrence Erlbaum.

McGue, M., Bacon, S., & Lykken, D. (1993). Personality stability and change in early adulthood: A behavioral genetic analysis. *Developmental Psychology, 29,* 96-109.

McKinley, D. G. (1964). *Social class and family life.* New York: Free Press.

McLanahan, S. (1985). Family structure and the reproduction of poverty. *American Journal of Sociology, 90,* 873-901.

McNeil, E. B. (1959). Psychology and aggression. *Journal of Conflict Resolution, 3,* 195-293.

Mead, G. H. (1918). The psychology of punitive justice. *American Journal of Sociology, 23,* 577-602.

Mednick, S. A., Gabrelli, W. F., Jr., & Hutchings, B. (1984). Genetic influences in criminal convictions: Evidence from an adoption cohort. *Science, 224,* 891-894.

Mednick, S. A., Moffitt, T. E., & Stack, S. A. (1987). *The causes of crime: New biological approaches.* New York: Cambridge University Press.

Meehan, A. J. (1986). Record-keeping practices in the policing of juveniles. *Urban Life, 15,* 70-102.

Meier, R. F. (1985). *Theoretical methods in criminology.* Beverly Hills, CA: Sage.

Menaghan, E. (1982). Measuring coping effectiveness: A panel analysis of marital problems and coping efforts. *Journal of Health and Social Behavior, 23,* 220-234.

Menaghan, E. (1983). Individual coping efforts: Moderators of the relationship between life stress and mental health outcomes. In H. B. Kaplan (Ed.), *Psychosocial stress: Trends in theory and research.* New York: Academic Press.

Menninger, K. (1942). *Love against hate.* New York: Harcourt, Brace.

Merton, R. K. (1938). Social structure and anomie. *American Sociological Review, 3,* 672-682.

Merton, R. K. (1957). *Social theory and social structure.* Glencoe, IL: Free Press.

Messerschmidt, J. D. (1986). *Capitalism, patriarchy and crime: Toward a socialist feminist criminology.* Lanham, MD: Rowman and Littlefield.

Messerschmidt, J. W. (1993). *Masculinities and crime: Critique and reconceptualization of theory.* Lanham, MD: Rowman and Littlefield.

Messick, D. M., & Sentis, K. (1979). Fairness and preference. *Journal of Experimental Social Psychology, 15,* 418-434.

Messick, D. M., & Sentis, K. (1983). Fairness, preference, and fairness biases. In D. M. Messick & K. S. Cook (Eds.), *Equity theory: Psychological and sociological perspectives.* New York: Praeger.

Messner, S. F., & Rosenfeld, R. (1997). *Crime and the American Dream* (2nd ed.). Belmont, CA: Wadsworth.

Michael, J. (1973). Positive and negative reinforcement, a distinction that is no longer necessary; or a better way to talk about bad things. In E. Ramp & G. Semb (Eds.), *Behavior analysis: Areas of research and application.* Englewood Cliffs, NJ: Prentice Hall.

Michael, J., & Adler, M. J. (1933). *Crime, law, and social science.* New York: Harcourt, Brace.

Mickelson, R. A. (1990). The attitude-achievement paradox among black adolescents. *Sociology of Education, 63,* 44-61.

Mikula, G. (1980). *Justice and social interaction.* New York: Springer-Verlag.

Mikula, G. (1986). The experience of injustice: Toward a better understanding of its phenomenology. In H. W. Bierhoff, R. L. Cohen, & J. Greenberg (Eds.), *Justice in social relations.* New York: Plenum.

Miller, D., & Swanson, G. (1958). *The changing American parent.* New York: Wiley.

Miller, E. M. (1986). *Street woman.* Philadelphia: Temple University Press.

Miller, L. (1987). Neuropsychology of the aggressive psychopath: An integrative review. *Aggressive Behavior, 13,* 119-140.

Miller, N. E. (1951). Comment on theoretical models illustrated by the development of a theory of conflict behavior. *Journal of Personality, 20,* 82-100.

Miller, W. B. (1958). Lower class culture as a generating milieu of gang delinquency. *Journal of Social Issues, 14*(3), 5-19.

Mills, C. W. (1940). Situated actions and vocabularies of motive. *American Sociological Review, 5,* 904-913.

Milovanovic, D. (1986). Juridico-linguistic communicative markets: Towards a semiotic analysis. *Contemporary Crises, 10,* 281-304.

Milovanovic, D. (1988a). Jailhouse lawyers and jailhouse lawyering. *International Journal of the Sociology of Law, 16,* 455-475.

Milovanovic, D. (1988b). *Primer in the sociology of law.* Albany, NY: Harrow and Heston.

Milovanovic, D. (1988c). Review essay: Critical legal studies and the assault on the bastion. *Social Justice, 15,* 161-172.

Milovanovic, D. (1989). Critical criminology and the challenge of post modernism. *The Critical Criminologist, 1*(Winter), 9-10, 17.

Milovanovic, D. (1991a). Images of unity and disunity in the juridic subject and the movement to the peacemaking community. In H. Pepinsky & R. Quinney (Eds.), *Criminology as peacemaking.* Bloomington: Indiana University Press.

Milovanovic, D. (1991b). *Law, semiotics and reality construction.* Unpublished manuscript, Northeastern Illinois University.

Milovanovic, D. (in press). Rethinking subjectivity in law and ideology. In D. Currie & B. MacLean (Eds.), *Struggle for equality: Rethinking the administration of justice.* Toronto, Ontario, Canada: Garamond Press.

Milovanovic, D., & Thomas, J. (1989). Overcoming the absurd: Prisoner litigation as primitive rebellion. *Social Problems, 36,* 48-60.

Mirowsky, J. (1985). Depression and marital power: An equity model. *American Journal of Sociology, 91,* 557-592.

Mirowsky, J., & Ross, C. E. (1990). The consolation-prize theory of alienation. *American Journal of Sociology, 95,* 1505-1535.

Mischel, W. (1968). *Personality and assessment.* New York: Wiley.

Moffitt, T. E. (1990a). Juvenile delinquency and attention-deficit disorder: Developmental trajectories from age 3 to 15. *Child Development, 61,* 893-910.

Moffitt, T. E. (1990b). The neuropsychology of delinquency: A critical review of theory and research. In N. Morris & M. Tonry (Eds.), *Crime and justice* (Vol. 12, pp. 99-169). Chicago: University of Chicago Press.

Moffitt, T. (1993). Adolescent-limited and life-course persistent antisocial behavior: A developmental taxonomy. *Psychological Review, 100,* 674-701.

Moffitt, T. (1996). The neuropsychology of conduct disorder. In P. Cordella & L. Siegal (Eds.), *Readings in contemporary criminological theory.* Boston: Northeastern University Press.

Moffitt, T., Brammer, G., Caspi, A., Fawcett, J. P., Raleigh, M., Yuwiler, A., & Silva, P. (1998). Whole blood serotonin relates to violence in an epidemiological study. *Biological Psychiatry, 43,* 446-457.

Moffitt, T. E., & Henry, B. (1989). Neuropsychological assessment of executive functions in self-reported delinquents. *Development and Psychopathology, 1,* 105-118.

Moffitt, T. E., & Henry, B. (1991). Neuropsychological studies of juvenile delinquency and violence: A review. In J. Milner (Ed.), *The neuropsychology of aggression* (pp. 67-91). Norwell, MA: Kluwer Academic.

Moffitt, T. E., Mednick, S. A., & Gabrielli, W. F., Jr. (1989). Predicting careers of criminal violence: Descriptive data and predispositional factors. In D. A. Brizer & M. Crowner (Eds.), *Current approaches to the prediction of violence.* Washington, DC: American Psychiatric Press.

Moffitt, T. E., & Silva, P. A. (1988a). Neuro-psychological deficit and self-reported delinquency in an unselected birth cohort. *Journal of the American Academy of Child and Adolescent Psychiatry, 27,* 233-240.

Moffitt, T. E., & Silva, P. A. (1988b). Self-reported delinquency: Results from an instrument for New Zealand. *Australian and New Zealand Journal of Criminology, 21,* 227-240.

Monahan, J. (1981). *The clinical prediction of violent behavior.* Rockville, MD: U.S. Department of Health and Human Services.

Monahan, T. P. (1957). Family status and the delinquent child: A reappraisal and some new findings. *Social Forces, 35,* 250-258.

Moore, J. W. (1978). *Homeboys: Gangs, drugs, and prison in the barrios of Los Angeles.* Philadelphia: Temple University Press.

Moraga, C., & Anzaldua, G. (Eds.). (1983). *This bridge called my back: Writings by radical women of color* (2nd ed.). New York: Kitchen Table Press.

Morgan, R. L., & Heise, D. (1988). Structure of emotions. *Social Psychology Quarterly, 51,* 19-31.

Morris, A. (1987). *Women, crime and criminal justice.* New York: Blackwell.

Morris, A., & Giller, H. (1987). *Understanding juvenile justice.* London: Croom Helm.

Morrissey, E. R. (1985). Power and control through discourse: The case of drinking and drinking problems among women. *Contemporary Crisis, 10,* 57-79.

Mowrer, O. H. (1960). *Learning theory and behavior.* New York: Wiley.

Moyer, A. E. (1992). *A scientist's voice in American culture: Simon Newcomb and the rhetoric of scientific method.* Berkeley: University of California Press.

Moyer, I. L. (1985). Crime, conflict theory, and the patriarchal society. In I. L. Moyer (Ed.), *The changing roles of women in the criminal justice system* (pp. 1-29). Prospect Heights, IL: Waveland.

Moynihan, M. (1968). Social mimicry: Character convergence versus character displacement. *Evolution, 22,* 315-331.

Mueller, C. W. (1983). Environmental stressors and aggressive behavior. In R. G. Geen & E. I. Donnerstein (Eds.), *Aggression: Theoretical and empirical reviews* (Vol. 2). New York: Academic Press.

Mussen, P., & Rutherford, E. (1961). Effects of aggressive cartoons on children's aggressive play. *Journal of Abnormal and Social Psychology, 62,* 461-464.

Naffine, N. (1994). Introduction. In N. Naffine (Ed.), *Gender, crime and feminism* (pp. xi-xxx). Brookfield, VT: Dartmouth Publishing Company.

Nagel, I. H., & Hagan, J. (1983). Gender and crime: Offense patterns and criminal court sanctions. In M. H. Tonry & N. Morris (Eds.), *Crime and justice: An annual review of research* (Vol. 4, pp. 91-144). Chicago: University of Chicago Press.

Nasby, W., Hayden, B., & DePaulo, B. M. (1980). Attributional bias among aggressive boys to interpret unambiguous social stimuli as displays of hostility. *Journal of Abnormal Psychology, 89,* 459-468.

Neisser, U., Boodoo, G., Bouchard, T., Boykin, A. W., Brody, N., Ceci, S., Halpern, D., Loehlin, J., Perloff, R., Sternberg, R., & Urbina, S. (1995). *Intelligence: Knowns and unknowns: Report of a task force established by the board of scientific affairs of the American Psychological Association.* Washington, DC: American Psychological Association.

Nettler, G. (1984). *Explaining crime.* New York: McGraw-Hill.

Newcomb, M. D., & Harlow, L. L. (1986). Life events and substance use among adolescents: Mediating effects of perceived loss of control and meaninglessness in life. *Journal of Personality and Social Psychology, 51,* 564-577.

Newman, O. (1972). *Defensible space: Crime prevention through urban design.* New York: Macmillan.

Newman, O. (1975). *Community of interest.* New York: Anchor.

Nicholson, L. (Ed.). (1990). *Feminism/postmodernism.* New York: Routledge.

Norris, C. (1992). *Uncritical theory: Postmodernism, intellectuals and the Gulf War.* London: Lawrence & Wishart.

Novy, D. M., & Donohue, S. (1985). The relationship between adolescent life stress events and delinquent conduct including conduct indicating a need for supervision. *Adolescence, 78,* 313-321.

Nye, F. I. (1958). *Family relationships and delinquent behavior.* New York: Wiley.

O'Connor, T., Deater-Deckard, K., Fulker, D., Rutter, M., & Plomin, R. (1998). Genotype-environment correlations in late childhood and early adolescence: Antisocial behavioral problems and coercive parenting. *Developmental Psychology, 34,* 970-981.

Olweus, D. (1979). Stability of aggressive reaction patterns in males: A review. *Psychological Bulletin, 86,* 852-857.

Olweus, D., Mattsson, A., Schalling, D., & Low, H. (1988). Circulating testosterone levels and aggression in adolescent males: A causal analysis. *Psychosomatic Medicine, 50,* 261-272.

Orcutt, J. D. (1987). Differential association and marijuana use. *Criminology, 25,* 341-358.

Orru, M. (1990). Merton's instrumental theory of anomie. In J. Clark, C. Modgil, & S. Modgil (Eds.), *Robert K. Merton: Consensus and controversy* (pp. 231-240). London: Falmer.

Osborne, J. A. (1984). Rape law reform: A new cosmetic for Canadian women. *Women and Politics, 4*(3), 49-64.

Osgood, C. E. (1962). *An alternative to war or surrender.* Urbana: University of Illinois Press.

Outrive, L. van, & Robert, P. (1999). Un tableau d'ensemble. In *GERN, crime et justice en Europe depuis 1990: Etat des recherches, evaluation et recommandations.* Paris: L'Harmattan.

Palmer, T. (1984). Treatment and the role of classification: A review of basics. *Crime and Delinquency, 30,* 245-267.

Parisi, N. (1982). Are females treated differently? A review of the theories and evidence on sentencing and parole decisions. In N. H. Rafter & E. A. Stanko (Eds.), *Judge, lawyer, victim, thief* (pp. 205-220). Boston: Northeastern University Press.

Parsons, T. (1951). *The social system.* New York: Free Press.

Passas, N. (1990). Anomie and corporate deviance. *Contemporary Crises, 14,* 157-178.

Pastore, N. (1952). The role of arbitrariness in the frustration-aggression hypothesis. *Journal of Abnormal and Social Psychology, 47,* 728-731.

Paternoster, R., Saltzman, L. E., Chiricos, T. G., & Waldo, G. P. (1983). Perceived risk and social control: Do sanctions really deter? *Law and Society Review, 17,* 457-479.

Paternoster, R., Saltzman, L. E., Waldo, G. P., & Chiricos, T. G. (1982). Perceived risk and deterrence: Methodological artifacts in perceptual deterrence research. *Journal of Criminal Law and Criminology, 73,* 1238-1258.

Patterson, G. (1960). A nonverbal technique for the assessment of aggression in children. *Child Development, 31,* 643-653.

Patterson, G. R. (1980). Children who steal. In T. Hirschi & M. Gottfredson (Eds.), *Understanding crime* (pp. 73-90). Beverly Hills, CA: Sage.

Patterson, G. R. (1982). *Coercive family interactions.* Eugene, OR: Castalia.

Patterson, G. R., & Dishion, T. S. (1985). Contributions of families and peers to delinquency. *Criminology, 23,* 63-80.

Payne, J. W., Braunstein, M. L., & Carroll, J. S. (1978). Exploring predecisional behavior: An alternative approach to decision research. *Organizational Behavior and Human Performance, 22,* 17-44.

Pearlin, L. I. (1982). The social contexts of stress. In L. Goldberger & S. Berznitz (Eds.), *Handbook of stress.* New York: Free Press.

Pearlin, L. I. (1983). Role strains and personal stress. In H. Kaplan (Ed.), *Psychosocial stress: Trends in theory and research.* New York: Academic Press.

Pearlin, L. I., & Lieberman, M. A. (1979). Social sources of emotional distress. In R. G. Simmons (Ed.), *Research in community and mental health* (Vol. 1). Greenwich, CT: JAI.

Pearlin, L. I., Menaghan, E. G., Lieberman, M. A., & Mullan, J. T. (1981). The stress process. *Journal of Health and Social Behavior, 22,* 337-356.

Pearlin, L. I., & Schooler, C. (1978). The structure of coping. *Journal of Health and Social Behavior, 19,* 2-21.

Pells, R. (1997). *Not like us: How Europeans have loved, hated, and transformed American culture since World War II.* New York: Basic Books.

Pepinsky, H. (1986). This can't be peace: A pessimist looks at punishment. In W. B. Groves & G. Newman (Eds.), *Punishment and privilege.* New York: Harrow and Heston.

Pepinsky, H. (1989). Peacemaking in criminology. *Critical Criminologist, 1*(Summer), 6-10.

Pepinsky, H., & Quinney, R. (Eds.). (1991). *Criminology as peacemaking.* Bloomington: Indiana University Press.

Pepitone, A. (1963). *Attraction and hostility.* New York: Atherton.

Petersilia, J. (1980). Criminal career research: A review of recent evidence. In M. Tonry & N. Morris (Eds.), *Crime and justice: An annual review of research* (Vol. 2, pp. 321-379). Chicago: University of Chicago Press.

Pfohl, S. J. (1985). Toward a sociological deconstruction of social problems. *Social Problems, 32,* 228-232.

Piliavin, I., & Briar, S. (1964). Police encounters with juveniles. *American Sociological Review, 70,* 206-214.

Piliavin, I., Thornton, C., Gartner, R., & Matsueda, R. (1986). Crime, deterrence, and rational choice. *American Sociological Review, 51,* 101-119.

Piven, F. F., & Cloward, R. A. (1971). *Regulating the poor: The functions of public welfare.* New York: Pantheon.

Platt, A. M. (1969). *The child savers: The invention of delinquency.* Chicago: University of Chicago Press.

Platt, A. M. (1993). Beyond the canon, with great difficulty. *Social Justice, 20,* 72-81.

Platt, J. R. (1964). Strong inference. *Science, 146,* 347-353.

Plomin, R. (1989). Environment and genes: Determinants of behavior. *American Psychologist, 44,* 105-111.

Plomin, R. (1990). The role of inheritance in behavior. *Science, 248,* 183-188.

Plomin, R. (1995). Genetics and children's experiences in the family. *Journal of Child Psychology and Psychiatry, 36,* 33-68.

Plomin, R., & Bergeman, C. S. (1990). The nature of nurture: Genetic influence on environmental measures. *Behavioral and Brain Sciences, 14,* 373-386.

Plomin, R., Chipuer, H. M., & Loehlin, J. C. (1990). Behavioral genetics and personality. In L. A. Pervin (Ed.), *Handbook of personality theory and research* (pp. 225-243). New York: Guilford Press.

Plomin, R., & Daniels, D. (1987). Why are children in the same family so different from one another? *Behavioral and Brain Sciences, 10,* 1-16.

Plomin, R., DeFries, J. C., & Loehlin, J. C. (1977). Genotype-environment interaction and correlation in the analysis of human behavior. *Psychological Bulletin, 88,* 245-258.

Plomin, R., DeFries, J. C., & McClearn, G. E. (1980). *Behavioral genetics: A primer.* San Francisco: W. H. Freeman.

Plomin, R., McClearn, G., Smith, D., Vignetti, S., Chorney, M., Chorney, K., Venditti, C., Kasarda, S., Thompson, L., Detterman, D., Daniels, J., Owen, M., & McGuffin, P. (1994). DNA markers associated with high versus low IQ: The IQ quantitative trait loci (QTL) project. *Behavior Genetics, 24,* 107-118.

Plomin, R., Nitz, K., & Rowe, D. C. (1990). Behavioral genetics and aggressive behavior in childhood. In M. Lewis & S. M. Miller (Eds.), *Handbook of developmental psychopathology.* New York: Plenum.

Polanyi, K. (1957). *The great transformation: The political and economic origins of our time.* Boston: Beacon.

Polanyi, M. (1958). *Personal knowledge.* Chicago: University of Chicago Press. (Original work published 1944)

Polk, K., Adler, C., Bazemore, G., Blake, G., Cordray, S., Coventry, G., Galvin, J., & Temple, M. (1981). *Becoming adult: An analysis of maturational development from age 16 to 30 of a cohort of young men* (Final Report of the Marion County Youth Study). Eugene: University of Oregon.

Pollak, O. (1964). Our social values and juvenile delinquency. *The Quarterly of the Pennsylvania Association on Probation, Parole and Correction, 21,* 12-22.

Pollner, M. (1987). *Mundane reason: Reality in everyday and sociological discourse.* Cambridge, UK: Cambridge University Press.

Poole, E. D., & Regoli, R. M. (1979). Parental support, delinquent friends and delinquency: A test of interactional effects. *Journal of Criminal Law and Criminology, 70,* 188-193.

Popper, K. (1968). *The logic of scientific discovery.* New York: Harper & Row.

Powell, E. H. (1958). Occupational status and suicide: Toward a redefinition of anomie. *American Sociological Review, 23,* 131-139.

Poyner, B. (1983). *Design against crime: Beyond defensible space.* London: Butterworths.

Pratt, M. B. (1984). Identity: Skin blood heart. In E. Bulkin, M. B. Pratt, & B. Smith (Eds.), *Yours in struggle* (pp. 11-63). Ithaca, NY: Firebrand Books.

Price, B. H., Daffner, K. R., Stowe, R. M., & Mesulam, M. M. (1990). The comportmental learning disabilities of early frontal lobe damage. *Brain, 113,* 1383-1393.

Price, B. R., & Sokoloff, N. J. (Eds.). (1995). *The criminal justice system and women* (2nd ed.). New York: McGraw-Hill.

Pride, M. (1986). *The child abuse industry.* Westchester, IL: Crossway.

Quarm, D., & Schwartz, M. D. (1984). Domestic violence in criminal court: An examination of new legislation in Ohio. *Women and Politics, 4*(3), 29-46.

Quicker, J. (1974). The effect of goal discrepancy on delinquency. *Social Problems, 22,* 76-86.

Quinney, R. (1970). *Social reality of crime.* Boston: Little, Brown.

Quinney, R. (1974). *Critique of legal order.* Boston: Little, Brown.

Quinney, R. (1977). *Class, state, and crime.* New York: McKay.

Quinney, R. (1988, November). *The theory and practice of peacemaking in the development of radical criminology.* Paper presented to the American Society of Criminology, Chicago, IL.

Rada, R. T., Laws, D. R., Kellner, R., Stivastava, L., & Peake, G. (1983). Plasma androgens in violent and nonviolent sex offenders. *Bulletin of the American Academy of Psychiatry Law, 11,* 149-158.

Radford, J., Kelly, L., & Hester, M. (1996). Introduction. In M. Hester, L. Kelly, & J. Radford (Eds.), *Women, violence and male power* (pp. 1-16). Philadelphia: Open University Press.

Rafter, N. H. (1985). *Partial justice: Women in state prisons, 1800-1935.* Boston: Northeastern University Press.

Raine, A. (1993). *The psychopathology of crime: Criminal behavior as a clinical disorder.* San Diego, CA: Academic Press.

Rankin, J. H., & Wells, L. E. (1990). The effect of parental attachments and direct controls on delinquency. *Journal of Research in Crime and Delinquency, 27,* 140-165.

Reckless, W. (1943). *The etiology of delinquent and criminal behavior.* New York: Social Science Research Council.

Reckless, W. C. (1961a). *The crime problem* (3rd ed.). New York: Appleton-Century-Crofts.

Reckless, W. C. (1961b). A new theory of delinquency and crime. *Federal Probation, 25,* 42-46.

Reckless, W. C. (1962). A non-causal explanation: Containment theory. *Excerpta Criminologica, 2,* 131-134.

Redl, F., & Wineman, D. (1951). *Children who hate.* Glencoe, IL: Free Press.

Reichel, P. L. (1994). *Comparative criminal justice systems: A topical approach.* Englewood Cliffs, New Jersey: Prentice Hall.

Reiss, A. J., Jr. (1951). Delinquency as the failure of personal and social controls. *American Sociological Review, 16,* 196-207.

Reiss, A. J., Jr. (1961). The social integration of queers and peers. *Social Problems, 9,* 102-120.

Reiss, A. J., Jr. (1986). Co-offender influences on criminal careers. In A. Blumstein, J. Cohen, J. A. Roth, & C. Visher (Eds.), *Criminal careers and career criminals* (pp. 121-160). Washington, DC: National Academy Press.

Reppetto, T. A. (1976). Crime prevention and the displacement phenomenon. *Crime and Delinquency, 22,* 166-177.

Resnik, J., & Shaw, N. (1980). Prisoners of their sex: Health problems of incarcerated women. In I. Robbins (Ed.), *Prisoners rights sourcebook: Theory, litigation and practice* (Vol. 2, pp. 319-413). New York: Clark Boardman.

Reuter, P., Rubenstein, J., & Wynn, S. (1983). *Racketeering in legitimate industries: Two case studies.* Washington, DC: National Institute of Justice.

Rhode, D. (1987). Justice, gender, and the justices. In L. L. Crites & W. L. Hepperle (Eds.), *Women, the courts, and equality* (pp. 13-34). Newbury Park, CA: Sage.

Rich, A. (1979). Disloyal to civilization: Feminism, racism, gynophobia. In A. Rich (Ed.), *On lies, secrets, and silence* (pp. 275-310). New York: Norton.

Rich, A. (1980). Compulsory heterosexuality and lesbian existence. *Signs: Journal of Women in Culture and Society, 5,* 631-660.

Richardson, L. (1990). Narrative and sociology. *Journal of Contemporary Ethnography, 19,* 116-135.

Richman, N., Stevenson, J., & Graham, P. J. (1982). *Pre-school to school: A behavioural study.* London: Academic Press.

Ritzer, G. (1975). *Sociology.* Boston: Allyn & Bacon.

Rivera, B., & Widom, C. S. (1990). Childhood victimization and violent offending. *Violence and Victims, 5,* 19-35.

Rivera, R. J., & Short, J. F., Jr. (1967a). Occupational goals: A comparative analysis. In M. W. Klein (Ed.), *Juvenile gangs in context: Theory, research and action.* Englewood Cliffs, NJ: Prentice Hall.

Rivera, R. J., & Short, J. F., Jr. (1967b). Significant adults, caretakers and structures of opportunity: An exploratory study. *Journal of Research in Crime and Delinquency, 4,* 76-97.

Robert, P. (1991). The sociology of crime and deviance in France. *British Journal of Criminology, 31,* 27-38.

Robert, P., & van Outrive, L. (Eds.). (1995). *Research, crime, and justice in Europe: An assessment and some recommendations.* Centre for Criminology Research.

Robin, G. (1974). The American customer: Shopper or shoplifter? *Police, 8,* 6-14.

Robins, L. (1978). Aetiological implications in studies of childhood histories relating to antisocial personality. In R. Hare & D. Schalling (Eds.), *Psychopathic behavior* (pp. 255-271). New York: Wiley.

Robins, L. N. (1966). *Deviant children grown up.* Baltimore: Williams & Wilkins.

Robins, L. N. (1978). Sturdy childhood predictors of adult antisocial behaviour: Replications from longitudinal studies. *Psychological Medicine, 8,* 611-622.

Robins, L. N. (1985). Epidemiology of antisocial personality. In J. O. Cavenar (Ed.), *Psychiatry* (Vol. 3, pp. 1-14). Philadelphia: J. B. Lippincott.

Robinson, R. V., & Kelly, J. (1979). Class as conceived by Marx and Dahrendorff: Effects on income inequality, class consciousness, and class conflict in the United States and Great Britain. *American Sociological Review, 44,* 38-57.

Rock, P. (Ed.). (1994). *History of criminology.* Brookfield, VT: Darthmouth.

Rock, P., & Holdaway, S. (1998). Thinking about criminology: Facts are bits of biography. In S. Holdaway & P. Rock (Eds.), *Thinking about criminology.* Toronto, Ontario, Canada: University of Toronto Press.

Rodman, H. (1967). Marital power in France, Greece, Yugoslavia, and the United States: A cross-national discussion. *Journal of Marriage and the Family, 29,* 320-324.

Rojek, D., & Erickson, M. (1982). Delinquent careers. *Criminology, 20,* 5-28.

Roncek, D. W., & Lobosco, A. (1983). The effect of high schools on crime in their neighborhoods. *Social Science Quarterly, 64,* 598-613.

Rosen, L. (1970). The broken home and male delinquency. In M. E. Wolfgang, L. Savitz, & N. Johnston (Eds.), *The sociology of crime and delinquency* (2nd ed., pp. 484-495). New York: Wiley.

Rosenbaum, M. (1981). *Women on heroin.* New Brunswick, NJ: Rutgers University Press.

Rosenberg, M. (1979). *Conceiving the self.* New York: Basic.

Rosenberg, M. (1990). Reflexivity and emotions. *Social Psychology Quarterly, 53,* 3-12.

Roseneil, S. (1995). The coming of age of feminist sociology: Some issues of practice and theory for the next twenty years. *British Journal of Sociology, 46,* 191-205.

Rosenhan, D. L. (1973). On being sane in insane places. *Science, 179,* 250-258.

Rosenzweig, S. (1938a). Frustration as an experimental problem: Part I. The significance of frustration as a problem of research. *Character and Personality, 7,* 126-128.

Rosenzweig, S. (1938b). Frustration as an experimental problem: Part VI. A general outline of frustration. *Character and Personality, 7,* 151-160.

Rosenzweig, S. (1944). An outline of frustration theory. In J. McV. Hunt (Ed.), *Personality and the behavior disorders.* New York: Ronald Press.

Rosenzweig, S., & Rosenzweig, L. (1952). Aggression in problem children and normals as evaluated by the Rosenzweig P-F study. *Journal of Abnormal and Social Psychology, 47,* 683-687.

Ross, M., Thibaut, J., & Evenback, S. (1971). Some determinants of the intensity of social protest. *Journal of Experimental Social Psychology, 7,* 401-418.

Rothaus, P., & Worchel, P. (1960). The inhibition of aggression under nonarbitrary frustration. *Journal of Personality, 28,* 108-117.

Rothbart, M., & Ahadi, S. (1994). Temperament and the development of personality. *Journal of Abnormal Psychology, 101,* 55-66.

Rothbart, M. K., & Derryberry, D. (1981). Development of individual differences in temperament. In M. E. Lamb & A. L. Brown (Eds.), *Advances in developmental psychology* (Vol. 1, pp. 37-66). Hillsdale, NJ: Lawrence Erlbaum.

Rotter, J. B. (1954). *Social learning and clinical psychology.* Englewood Cliffs, NJ: Prentice Hall.

Rowe, D. (1994). *The limits of family influence: Genes, experience, and behavior.* New York: Guilford Press.

Rowe, D., & Gulley, B. (1992). Sibling effects on substance use and delinquency. *Criminology, 30,* 217-233.

Rowe, D. C., & Osgood, D. W. (1984). Heredity and sociological theories of delinquency: A reconsideration. *American Sociological Review, 49,* 526-540.

Rubington, E. R., & Weinberg, M. S. (Eds.). (1968). *Deviance: The interactionist perspective.* New York: Macmillan.

Ruggiero, V., South, N., & Taylor, I. (Eds.). (1998). *The new European criminology: Crime and social order in Europe.* London: Routledge.

Ruiz, V. L., & DuBois, E. C. (Eds.). (1994). *Unequal sisters* (2nd ed.). New York: Routledge.

Russell, K. K. (1992). Development of a black criminology and role of the black criminologist. *Justice Quarterly, 9,* 667-683.

Rutter, M. (1977). Brain damage syndromes in childhood: Concepts and findings. *Journal of Child Psychology and Psychiatry, 18,* 1-22.

Rutter, M. (Ed.). (1983). *Developmental neuropsychiatry.* New York: Guilford Press.

Rutter, M., & Giller, H. (1984). *Juvenile delinquency: Trends and perspectives.* New York: Guilford.

Sameroff, A., & Chandler, M. (1975). Reproductive risk and the continuum of caretaking casualty. In F. Horowitz, M. Hetherington, S. Scarr-Salapatek, & G. Siegel (Eds.), *Review of child development research* (Vol. 4, pp. 187-244). Chicago: University of Chicago Press.

Sampson, R. (1987). Does an intact family reduce burglary risk for its neighbors? *Sociology and Social Research, 71,* 204-207.

Sampson, R. J., & Groves, W. B. (1989). Community structure and crime. *American Journal of Sociology, 94,* 774-802.

Sampson, R. J., & Laub, J. H. (1993). *Crime in the making: Pathways and turning points through life.* Cambridge, MA: Harvard University Press.

Sampson, R. J., & Wilson, W. (1995). Toward a theory of race, crime and urban inequality. In J. Hagan & R. Peterson (Eds.), *Crime and inequality* (pp. 37-54). Stanford, CA: Stanford University Press.

Sapolsky, R. (1992). *Stress, the aging brain, and the mechanisms of neuron death.* Cambridge, MA: MIT Press.

Sargeant, L. (Ed.). (1981). *Women and revolution: A discussion of the unhappy marriage of Marxism and feminism.* Boston: South End Press.

Sarnecki, J. (1986). *Delinquent networks.* Stockholm, Sweden: National Council for Crime Prevention.

Saul, L. S. (1956). *The hostile mind.* New York: Random House.

Savitz, L. (1970). Delinquency and migration. In M. E. Wolfgang, L. Savitz, & N. Johnston (Eds.), *The sociology of crime and delinquency* (2nd ed., pp. 473-480). New York: Wiley.

Scarr, S. (1992). Developmental theories for the 1990s: Development and individual differences. *Child Development, 63,* 1-19.

Scarr, S., & McCartney, K. (1983). How people make their own environments: A theory of genotype environment effects. *Child Development, 54,* 424-435.

Schiavi, R. C., Theilgaard, A., Owen, D. R., & White, D. (1984). Sex chromosome anomalies, hormones, and aggressivity. *Archives of General Psychiatry, 41,* 93-99.

Schneider, H. J. (1987). *Kriminologie.* Berlin, Germany: Walter de Gruyter.

Schoenberg, R. J. (1975). *A structural model of delinquency.* Unpublished doctoral dissertation, University of Washington, Seattle.

Schoenfeld, W. N. (1965). Learning theory and social psychology. In O. Klineberg & R. Christie (Eds.), *Perspectives in social psychology* (pp. 117-135). New York: Holt, Rinehart & Winston.

Schultz, L. G. (1962). Why the Negro carries weapons. *Journal of Criminal Law, Criminology and Police Science, 53,* 476-483.

Schur, E. M. (1971). *Labeling deviant behavior.* New York: Harper & Row.

Schur, E. M. (1973). *Radical non-intervention.* Englewood Cliffs, NJ: Prentice Hall.

Schur, E. M. (1984). *Labeling women deviant: Gender, stigma, and social control.* New York: Random House.

Schutz, A. (1967). *The phenomenology of the social world.* Evanston, IL: Northwestern University Press.

Schutz, A., & Luckmann, T. (1973). *The structures of the life-world* (R. M. Zaner & H. T. Engelhardt, Jr., Trans.). Evanston, IL: Northwestern University Press.

Schwartz, B. (1994a). *The costs of living: How market freedom erodes the best things in life.* New York: Norton.

Schwartz, B. (1994b). On morals and markets. *Criminal Justice Ethics, 13,* 61-69.

Schwartz, M. (1989). The undercutting edge of criminology. *The Critical Criminologist, 1*(Spring), 1-2, 5-6.

Schwartz, M. D., & Friedrichs, D. O. (1994). Postmodern thought and criminological discontent: New metaphors for understanding violence. *Criminology, 32,* 221-246.

Schwartz, M. D., & Milovanovic, D. (Eds.). (1995). *Race, gender, and class in criminology: The intersections.* New York: Garland.

SchWeber, C. (1982). The government's unique experiment in salvaging women criminals: Cooperation and conflict in the administration of a women's prison—The case of the Federal Industrial Institution for Women at Alderson. In N. H. Rafter & E. A. Stanko (Eds.), *Judge, lawyer, victim, thief* (pp. 277-303). Boston: Northeastern University Press.

Schwendinger, J., & Schwendinger, H. (1983). *Rape and inequality.* Newbury Park, CA: Sage.

Schwendinger, J., & Schwendinger, H. (1985). *Adolescent subcultures and delinquency.* New York: Praeger.

Schwinger, T. (1980). Just allocations of goods: Decisions among three principles. In G. Mikula (Ed.), *Justice and social interaction.* New York: Springer-Verlag.

Scott, J. P. (1958). *Aggression.* Chicago: University of Chicago Press.

Scott, J. W. (1992). Experience. In J. Butler & J. W. Scott (Eds.), *Feminists theorize the political* (pp. 22-40). New York: Routledge.

Scott, M. B., & Lyman, S. M. (1968). Accounts. *American Sociological Review, 22,* 664-670.

Sears, R. R. (1943). *Survey of objective studies of psychoanalytical concepts* (Bulletin 51). New York: Social Science Research Council.

Sechrest, L., White, S. O., & Brown, E. D. (Eds.). (1979). *The rehabilitation of criminal offenders: Problems and prospects.* Washington, DC: National Academy of Sciences.

Seeman, M. (1959). On the meaning of alienation. *American Sociological Review, 24,* 783-791.

Seidman, S. (1994). Introduction. In S. Seidman (Ed.), *The post-modern turn: New perspectives on social theory* (pp. 1-23). New York: Cambridge University Press.

Seligman, D. (1992). *A question of intelligence: The IQ debate in America.* New York: Birch Lane.

Selva, L., & Bohm, B. (1987). Law and liberation: Toward an oppositional legal discourse. *Legal Studies Forum, 113,* 243-266.

Selvin, H. C. (1958). Durkheim's *Suicide* and problems of empirical research. *American Journal of Sociology, 63,* 607-619.

Severy, L. J. (1973). Exposure to deviance committed by valued peer groups and family members. *Journal of Research in Crime and Delinquency, 10,* 35-46.

Shafter, B. E. (Ed.). (1991a). *Is America different? A new look at American exceptionalism.* Oxford, UK: Clarendon Press.

Shafter, B. E. (1991b). What is the American Way? Four themes in search of their next incarnation. In B. E. Shafter (Ed.), *Is America different? A new look at American exceptionalism* (pp. 222-261). Oxford, UK: Clarendon Press.

Shank, G. (1999). Looking back: Radical criminology and social movements. *Social Justice, 26,* 114-134.

Shapland, J. (1991). Criminology in Europe. In F. Heidensohn & M. Farrell (Eds.), *Crime in Europe.* London: Routledge.

Shaw, C., & McKay, H. D. (1931). *Report on the causes of crime: Vol. 2. Social factors in juvenile delinquency* (Report No. 13, National Commission on Law Observance and Enforcement). Washington, DC: U.S. Government Printing Office.

Shaw, C., & McKay, H. D. (1942). *Juvenile delinquency and urban areas.* Chicago: University of Chicago Press.

Shaw, C., Zorbaugh, F., McKay, H., & Cottrell, L. (1929). *Delinquency areas.* Chicago: University of Chicago Press.

Shaw, G. (1931). *Delinquency areas.* Chicago: University of Chicago Press.

Sheldon, W. H. (1949). *Varieties of delinquent youth.* New York: Harper & Row.

Shelley, E. L. V., & Toch, H. (1962). The perception of violence as an indicator of adjustment in institutionalized offenders. *Journal of Criminal Law, Criminology and Police Science, 53,* 463-469.

Shepelak, N. J. (1987). The role of self-explanations and self-evaluations in legitimating inequality. *American Sociological Review, 52,* 495-503.

Shepelak, N. J., & Alwin, D. (1986). Beliefs about inequality and perceptions of distributive justice. *American Sociological Review, 51,* 30-46.

Sherman, L. W. (1993). Defiance, deterrence, and irrelevance: A theory of the criminal sanction. *Journal of Research in Crime and Delinquency, 30,* 445-473.

Shonfeld, I. S., Shaffer, D., O'Connor, P., & Portnoy, S. (1988). Conduct disorder and cognitive functioning: Testing three causal hypotheses. *Child Development, 59,* 993-1007.

Short, J. F., Jr. (1964). Gang delinquency and anomie. In M. B. Clinard (Ed.), *Anomie and deviant behavior* (pp. 98-127). New York: Free Press.

Short, J. F., Jr. (1965). Social structure and group processes in explanations of gang delinquency. In M. Sherif & C. W. Sherif (Eds.), *Problems of youth.* Chicago: Aldine.

Short, J. F., Jr. (1997). *Poverty, ethnicity and violent crime.* Boulder, CO: Westview Press.

Short, J. F., Jr., & Nye, F. I. (1957). Reported behavior as a criterion of deviant behavior. *Social Problems, 5,* 207-213.

Short, J. F., Jr., & Nye, F. I. (1958). Extent of unrecorded juvenile delinquency: Tentative conclusions. *Journal of Criminal Law, Criminology and Police Science, 49,* 296-302.

Short, J. F., Jr., Rivera, R., & Tennyson, R. A. (1965). Perceived opportunities, gang membership and delinquency. *American Sociological Review, 30,* 56-67.

Short, J. F., Jr., & Strodtbeck, F. L. (1965). *Group process and gang delinquency.* Chicago: University of Chicago Press.

Shover, N., & Bryant, K. M. (1993). Theoretical explanations of corporate crime. In M. B. Blankenship (Ed.), *Understanding corporate criminality* (pp. 141-176). New York: Garland.

Silbereisen, R. K., & Noack, P. (1988). On the constructive role of problem behavior in adolescence. In N. Bolger, A. Caspi, G. Downey, & M. Moorehouse (Eds.), *Persons in context: Developmental processes* (pp. 152-180). Cambridge, UK: Cambridge University Press.

Silbert, M., & Pines, A. M. (1981). Sexual child abuse as an antecedent to prostitution. *Child Abuse and Neglect, 5,* 407-411.

Simon, H. A. (1978). Rationality as process and product of thought. *American Economic Review, 8*(2), 1-11.

Simon, W., & Gagnon, J. H. (1976). The anomie of affluence: A post Mertonian conception. *American Journal of Sociology, 82,* 356-378.

Simpson, S. S. (1991). Caste, class, and violent crime: Explaining differences in female offending. *Criminology, 29,* 115-135.

Simpson, S. S., & Elis, L. (1995). Doing gender: Sorting out the caste and crime conundrum. *Criminology, 33,* 47-81.

Skogan, W. G. (1977). Dimensions of the dark figure of unreported crime. *Crime & Delinquency, 23,* 41-50.

Skogan, W. G. (1979). Crime in contemporary America. In H. D. Graham & T. R. Gurr (Eds.), *Violence in America: Historical and comparative perspectives* (pp. 375-391). Beverly Hills, CA: Sage.

Skogan, W. G. (1990). *Disorder and decline.* New York: Free Press.

Slaby, R. G., & Guerra, N. G. (1988). Cognitive mediators of aggression in adolescent offenders: 1. *Developmental Psychology, 24,* 580-588.

Smart, C. (1985). Legal subjects and sexual objects: Ideology, law and female sexuality. In J. Brophy & C. Smart (Eds.), *Women in law: Explorations in law, family and sexuality* (pp. 50-70). Boston: Routledge & Kegan Paul.

Smart, C. (1989). *Feminism and the power of law.* New York: Routledge.

Smart, C. (1990a). Feminist approaches to criminology, or postmodern woman meets atavistic man. In L. Gelsthorpe & A. Morris (Eds.), *Feminist perspectives in criminology* (pp. 70-84). Philadelphia: Open University Press.

Smart, C. (1990b). Law's power, the sexed body, and feminist discourse. *Journal of Law and Society, 17,* 194-210.

Smart, C. (1992). The woman of legal discourse. *Social and Legal Studies, 1,* 29-44.

Smart, C. (1995). *Law, crime and sexuality: Essays in feminism.* London: Sage.

Smith, D. (1987). *The everyday world as problematic: A feminist sociology.* Toronto, Ontario, Canada: University of Toronto Press.

Smith, D. A., & Paternoster, R. (1987). The gender gap in theories of deviance: Issues and evidence. *Journal of Research in Crime and Delinquency, 24,* 140-172.

Smith, D. E. (1974). The social construction of documentary reality. *Sociological Inquiry, 44,* 257-268.

Smith, D. E. (1979). A sociology for women. In J. A. Sherman & E. T. Beck (Eds.), *The prism of sex: Essays in the sociology of knowledge* (pp. 135-187). Madison: University of Wisconsin Press.

Smith, R. J. (1961). The Japanese world community: Norms, sanctions, and ostracism. *American Anthropologist, 63,* 522-533.

Smith, W. (1975). The spirit of American philosophy. In W. Smith (Ed.), *Essays in American intellectual history* (pp. 473-479). Hinsdale, IL: Dryden Press.

Snyder, J., & Patterson, G. (1987). Family interaction and delinquent behavior. In H. Quay (Ed.), *Handbook of juvenile delinquency* (pp. 216-243). New York: Wiley.

Snyder, J., & Patterson, G. (in press). Family interactions and delinquent behavior. *Child Development.*

Snyderman, M., & Rothman, S. (1988). *The IQ controversy, the media and public policy.* New Brunswick, NJ: Transaction.

Sokoloff, N. J. (1980). *Between money and love: The dialectics of women's home and market work.* New York: Praeger.

Soubrie, P. (1986). Reconciling the role of central serotonin neurons in human and animal behavior. *Behavioral and Brain Sciences, 9,* 319-364.

Sowell, E., Thompson, P., Holmes, C., Jernigan, T., & Toga, A. (1999). In vivo evidence of post-adolescent brain maturation in frontal and striatal regions. *Nature Neuroscience, 2,* 859-869.

Spencer, C. C. (1987). Sexual assault: The second victimization. In L. L. Crites & W. L. Hepperle (Eds.), *Women, the courts, and equality* (pp. 54-73). Newbury Park, CA: Sage.

Spergel, I. (1967). Deviant patterns and opportunities of pre-adolescent Negro boys in three Chicago neighborhoods. In M. W. Klein (Ed.), *Juvenile gangs in context: Theory, research and action* (pp. 38-54). Englewood Cliffs, NJ: Prentice Hall.

Spivak, G. C. (1992). French feminism revisited: Ethics and politics. In J. Butler & J. W. Scott (Eds.), *Feminists theorize the political* (pp. 54-85). New York: Routledge.

Sprecher, S. (1986). The relationship between inequity and emotions in close relationships. *Social Psychology Quarterly, 49,* 309-321.

Srole, L. (1956a). Anomie, authoritarianism and prejudice. *American Journal of Sociology, 62,* 63-67.

Srole, L. (1956b). Social integration and certain corollaries: An exploratory study. *American Sociological Review, 21,* 709-716.

Staats, A. (1975). *Social behaviorism.* Homewood, IL: Dorsey.

Stafford, M., & Warr, M. (1993). A reconceptualization of general and specific deterrence. *Journal of Research in Crime and Delinquency, 30,* 123-135.

Stafford, M. C., & Ekland-Olson, S. (1982). On social learning and deviant behavior: A reappraisal of the findings. *American Sociological Review, 47,* 167-169.

Stagner, R. (1956). *Psychology of industrial conflict.* New York: Wiley.

Stagner, R. (1957). Le teorie della personalità. *Rassegna di Psicologia Generale e Clinica, 2,* 34-48.

Stagner, R. (1961). *Psychology and personality* (3rd ed.). New York: McGraw-Hill.

Stagner, R. (1965). The psychology of human conflict. In E. B. McNeil (Ed.), *The nature of human conflict* (pp. 60-61). Englewood Cliffs, NJ: Prentice Hall.

Stark, R., Kent, L., & Doyle, D. P. (1982). Religion and delinquency: The ecology of a lost relationship. *Journal of Research in Crime and Delinquency, 19,* 4-24.

Stattin, H., & Klackenberg-Larsson, I. (1993). Early language and intelligence development and their relationship to future criminal behavior. *Journal of Abnormal Psychology, 102,* 369-378.

Steffensmeier, D. J. (1983). Organizational properties and sex-segregation in the underworld: Building a sociological theory of sex differences in crime. *Social Forces, 61,* 1010-1032.

Steffensmeier, D. J., & Terry, R. M. (1973). Deviance and respectability: An observational study of reactions to shoplifting. *Social Forces, 51,* 417-426.

Steinberg, L., Fegley, S., & Dornbusch, S. M. (1993). Negative impact of part-time work on adolescent adjustment: Evidence from a longitudinal study. *Developmental Psychology, 29,* 171-180.

Stenning, P. C., & Shearing, C. D. (1980). The quiet revolution: The nature, development, and general legal implications of private security in Canada. *Criminal Law Quarterly, 22,* 220-248.

Stephenson, G. M., & White, J. H. (1968). An experimental study of some effects of injustice on children's moral behavior. *Journal of Experimental Social Psychology, 4,* 460-469.

Stivers, C. (1993). Reflections on the role of personal narrative in social science. *Signs: Journal of Women in Culture and Society, 18,* 408-425.

Stouthamer-Loeber, M., Loeber, R., Farrington, D. P., Zhang, Q., Van Kammen, W. B., & Maguin, F. (1993). The double edge of protective and risk factors for delinquency: Interrelations and developmental patterns. *Development and Psychopathology, 5,* 683-701.

Straus, M. (1991). Discipline and deviance: Physical punishment of children and violence and other crimes in adulthood. *Social Problems, 38,* 133-154.

Strictland, D. E. (1982). Social learning and deviant behavior: A specific test of a general theory: A comment and critique. *American Sociological Review, 47,* 162-167.

Sudman, S., & Bradburn, N. M. (1991). *Asking questions: A practical guide to questionnaire design.* San Francisco: Jossey-Bass.

Sudnow, D. (1965). Normal crimes: Sociological features of the penal code in a public defender office. *Social Problems, 12,* 255-276.

Suedfeld, P., & Landon, P. B. (1978). Approaches to treatment. In R. Hare & D. Schalling (Eds.), *Psychopathic behaviour* (pp. 347-376). New York: Wiley.

Sullivan, M. L. (1989). *Getting paid.* Ithaca, NY: Cornell University Press.

Suls, J. M. (1977). Social comparison theory and research: An overview from 1954. In J. M. Suls & R. L. Miller (Eds.), *Social comparison processes.* New York: Hemisphere.

Suls, J. M., & Wills, T. A. (1991). *Social comparison: Contemporary theory and research.* Hillsdale, NJ: Lawrence Erlbaum.

Surette, R. (1992). *Media, crime, and criminal justice: Images and realities.* Pacific Grove, CA: Brooks/Cole.

Sutherland, E. H. (1940). White collar criminality. *American Sociological Review, 5,* 1-12.

Sutherland, E. H. (1941). Crime and business. *Annals of the American Academy of Political and Social Science, 217,* 112-118.

Sutherland, E. H. (1942). The development of the concept of differential association. *Ohio Valley Sociologist, 15,* 3-4.

Sutherland, E. H. (1947). *Criminology.* Philadelphia: J. B. Lippincott.

Sutherland, E. H. (1949). *White collar crime.* New York: Dryden.

Sutherland, E. H., & Cressey, D. R. (1960). *Principles of criminology* (6th ed.). Chicago: J. B. Lippincott.

Swaaningen, R. van. (1995). Sociale Controle met een Structureel Tekort: Pleidooi voor een Sociaal Rechtvaardig Veiligheidsbeleid. *Justitiele Verkenningen, 3,* 63-87.

Swaaningen, R. van. (1997a). *Critical criminology: Visions from Europe.* London: Sage.

Swaaningen, R. van. (1997b). De positie van de criminologie aan Nederlandse universiteiten in vergelijking met Belgie en Engeland. *Nieuws voor Criminologen, 8*(3), 5-23.

Swigert, V., & Farrell, R. (1977). Normal homicides and the law. *American Sociological Review, 42,* 16-32.

Sykes, G. M., & Matza, D. (1957). Techniques of neutralization: A theory of delinquency. *American Sociological Review, 22,* 664-670.

Sykes, G., & Matza, D. (1961). Juvenile delinquency and subterranean values. *American Sociological Review, 26,* 712-719.

Sztompka, P. (1994). *The sociology of social change.* Oxford, UK: Blackwell.

Tarter, R. E., Alterman, A. I., & Edwards, K. L. (1985). Vulnerability to alcoholism in men: A behavior-genetic perspective. *Journal of Studies on Alcoholism, 46,* 329-356.

Tavris, C. (1984). On the wisdom of counting to ten. In P. Shaver (Ed.), *Review of personality and social psychology.* Beverly Hills, CA: Sage.

Taylor, I., Walton, P., & Young, J. (1973). *The new criminology.* New York: Harper & Row.

Tennyson, R. A. (1967). Family structure and delinquent behavior. In M. W. Klein (Ed.), *Juvenile gangs in context: Theory, research, and action.* Englewood Cliffs, NJ: Prentice Hall.

Terrill, R. J. (1999). *World criminal justice systems: A survey.* Cincinnati, OH: Anderson.

Thibaut, J. W., & Kelley, H. H. (1959). *The social psychology of groups.* New York: Wiley.

Thoits, P. (1983). Dimensions of life events that influence psychological distress: An evaluation and synthesis of the literature. In H. B. Kaplan (Ed.), *Psychosocial stress: Trends in theory and research.* New York: Academic Press.

Thoits, P. (1984). Coping, social support, and psychological outcomes: The central role of emotion. In P. Shaver (Ed.), *Review of personality and social psychology.* Beverly Hills, CA: Sage.

Thoits, P. (1989). The sociology of emotions. In W. R. Scott & J. Blake (Eds.), *Annual review of sociology* (Vol. 15). Stanford, CA: Annual Reviews.

Thoits, P. (1990). Emotional deviance research. In T. D. Kemper (Ed.), *Research agendas in the sociology of emotions.* Albany: State University of New York Press.

Thoits, P. (1991a). On merging identity theory and stress research. *Social Psychology Quarterly, 54,* 101-112.

Thoits, P. (1991b). Patterns of coping with controllable and uncontrollable events. In E. M. Cummings, A. L. Greene, & K. H. Karraker (Eds.), *Life-span developmental psychology: Perspectives on stress and coping.* Hillsdale, NJ: Lawrence Erlbaum.

Thomas, A., & Chess, S. (1977). *Temperament and development.* New York: Brunner/Mazel.

Thomas, C. W. (1977). *The effect of legal sanctions on juvenile delinquency: A comparison of the labeling and deterrence perspectives* (Final Report, LEAA Grants 75-NI-99-0031 and 76-NI-99-0050). Bowling Green, OH: Bowling Green State University.

Thomas, J. (1988). *Prisoner litigation: The paradox of the jailhouse lawyer.* Totowa, NJ: Rowman and Littlefield.

Thomas, J., & O'Maochatha, A. (1989). Reassessing the critical metaphor: An optimistic revisionism view. *Justice Quarterly, 6,* 143-172.

Thomas, W. I., & Thomas, D. S. (1928). *The child in America: Behavior problems and programs.* New York: Knopf.

Thomas, W. I., & Znaniecki, F. (1927). *The Polish peasant in Europe and America.* New York: Knopf.

Thornberry, T. P. (1987a). *Reflections on the advantages and disadvantages of theoretical integration.* Paper presented at the Albany Conference on Theoretical Integration in the Study of Crime and Deviance.

Thornberry, T. P. (1987b). Towards an interactional theory of delinquency. *Criminology, 25,* 863-891.

Thornberry, T. P., & Christenson, R. L. (1984). Unemployment and criminal involvement: An investigation of reciprocal causal structures. *American Sociological Review, 49,* 398-411.

Thornberry, T. P., Farnworth, M., & Lizotte, A. (1986). *A panel study of reciprocal causal model of delinquency* (Proposal submitted to the Office of Juvenile Justice and Delinquency Prevention).

Thornberry, T. P., Lizotte, A. J., Krohn, M. D., Farnworth, M., & Jang, S. J. (1994). Delinquent peers, beliefs, and delinquent behavior: A longitudinal test of interactional theory. *Criminology, 32,* 47-83.

Thornberry, T. P., Moore, M., & Christenson, R. L. (1985). The effect of dropping out of high school on subsequent delinquent behavior. *Criminology, 23,* 3-18.

Thorne, B. (1995). Symposium participant. *Gender & Society, 9,* 497-499.

Thrasher, F. M. (1937). *The gang.* Chicago: University of Chicago Press.

Thurston, J. R., Feldhusen, N. F., & Benning, J. J. An approach to theory explaining classroom aggression. In *Eau Claire County Youth Study* (NIMH Grant No. 5-RII MH 00672-03). Wisconsin State Department of Public Welfare;

U.S. Department of Health, Education, and Welfare; National Institute of Health.

Tinsley, B. R., & Parke, R. D. (1983). The person-environment relationship: Lessons from families with preterm infants. In D. Magnusson & V. L. Allen (Eds.), *Human development: An interactional perspective* (pp. 93-110). San Diego, CA: Academic Press.

Tittle, C. (1995). *Control balance: Toward a general theory of deviance.* Boulder, CO: Westview Press.

Tittle, C. R., Villemez, W. J., & Smith, D. A. (1978). The myth of social class and criminology. *American Sociological Review, 43,* 643-656.

Toby, J. (1957). The differential impact of family disorganization. *American Sociological Review, 22,* 505-512.

Toch, H. H. (1961). The stereoscope: A new frontier in psychological research. *The Research Newsletter, 3*(3-4), 18-22.

Toch, H. H., & Schulte, R. (1961). Readiness to perceive violence as a result of police training. *British Journal of Psychology, 52,* 389.

Tonry, M., Ohlin, L. E., & Farrington, D. P. (1991). Human development and criminal behavior. New York: Springer-Verlag.

Tooby, J., & Cosmides, L. (1992). The psychological foundations of culture. In J. Barkow, L. Cosmides, & J. Tooby (Eds.), *The adapted mind: Evolutionary psychology and the generation of culture.* New York: Oxford University Press.

Tornblum, K. Y. (1977). Distributive justice: Typology and propositions. *Human Relations, 30,* 1-24.

Trasler, G. (1962). *The explanation of criminality.* London: Routledge & Kegan Paul.

Tunc, A. (1968). Law and judicial system. In A. N. J. den Hollander & S. Skard (Eds.), *American civilisation: An introduction* (pp. 198-223). London: Longman.

Turk, A. T. (1969). *Criminality and legal order.* Chicago: Rand McNally.

Udry, J. R. (1995). Sociology and biology: What biology do sociologists need to know? *Social Forces, 73,* 1267-1278.

Umbreit, M., & Coates, R. (1993). Cross-site analysis of victim-offender mediation in four states. *Crime and Delinquency, 39,* 565-585.

Utne, M. K., & Kidd, R. (1980). Equity and attribution. In G. Mikula (Ed.), *Justice and social interaction.* New York: Springer-Verlag.

Van Houten, R. (1983). Punishment: From the animal laboratory to the applied setting. In S. Axelrod & J. Apsche (Eds.), *The effects of punishment on human behavior.* New York: Academic Press.

Vaux, A. (1988). *Social support: Theory, research, and intervention.* New York: Praeger.

Vaux, A., & Ruggiero, M. (1983). Stressful life change and delinquent behavior. *American Journal of Community Psychology, 11,* 169-183.

Veblen, T. (1934). *The theory of the leisure class.* New York: Mentor.

Veldman, D. J., & Worchel, P. (1961). Defensiveness and self-acceptance in the management of hostility. *Journal of Abnormal and Social Psychology, 63,* 319-325.

Venables, P. (1987). Autonomic nervous system factors in criminal behavior. In S. Mednick, T. Moffitt, & S. Stack (Eds.), *The causes of crime: New biological approaches.* Cambridge, UK: University of Cambridge Press.

Vila, B. (1994). A general paradigm for understanding criminal behavior: Extending evolutionary ecological theory. *Criminology, 32,* 311-360.

Vitaro, F., Gagnon, C., & Tremblay, R. E. (1990). Predicting stable peer rejection from kindergarten to grade one. *Journal of Clinical Child Psychology, 19,* 257-264.

Vogel, L. (1983). *Marxism and the oppression of women: Toward a unitary theory.* New Brunswick, NJ: Rutgers University Press.

Vogel, L. (1991). Telling tales: Historians of our own lives. *Journal of Women's History, 2,* 89-101.

Vogel, L. (in press). Debating difference: The problem of special treatment of pregnancy in the workplace. *Feminist Studies.*

Vold, G. B., & Bernard, T. J. (1986). *Theoretical criminology.* New York: Oxford University Press.

Volosinov, V. (1986). *Marxism and the philosophy of language.* Cambridge, MA: Harvard University Press.

Voss, H. L. (1966). Socio-economic status and reported delinquent behavior. *Social Problems, 13,* 314-324.

Waegel, W. B. (1981). Case routinization in investigative police work. *Social Problems, 28,* 263-275.

Waelder, R. (1956). Critical discussion of the concept of an instinct of destruction. *Bulletin of the Philadelphia Psychoanalytic Association, 6,* 97-109.

Wagner, D. G. (1992). Daring modesty: On metatheory, observation, and theory growth. In S. Seidman & D. G. Wagner (Eds.), *Postmodernism and social theory* (pp. 199-220). Cambridge, MA: Blackwell.

Wahler, R. (1980). The insular mother: Her problems in parent-child treatment. *Journal of Applied Behavior Analysis, 13,* 207-219.

Walker, S., & Brown, M. (1995). A pale reflection of reality: The neglect of racial and ethnic minorities in introductory criminal justice textbooks. *Journal of Criminal Justice Education, 6,* 61-83.

Walkowitz, J. R. (1980). *Prostitution and Victorian society: Women, class and the state.* New York: Cambridge University Press.

Waller, I. (1979). *What reduces residential burglary: Action and research in Seattle and Toronto.* Paper presented at the Third International Symposium on Victimology, Munster, West Germany.

Walsh, A. (1991). *Intellectual imbalance, love deprivation, and violent delinquency: A biosocial perspective*. Springfield, IL: Charles C Thomas.

Walsh, A. (1995). *Biosociology: An emerging paradigm*. New York: Praeger.

Walsh, A., & Ellis, L. (1999). Political ideology and American criminologists explanations for criminal behavior. *The Criminologist, 24,* 1-27.

Walster, E., Berscheid, E., & Walster, G. W. (1973). New directions in equity research. *Journal of Personality and Social Psychology, 25,* 151-176.

Walster, E., Walster, G. W., & Berscheid, E. (1978). *Equity: Theory and research*. Boston: Allyn & Bacon.

Walters, G. D., & White, T. W. (1989). Heredity and crime: Bad genes or bad research? *Criminology, 27,* 455-486.

Walters, R. H., Thomas, E. L., & Acker, C. W. (1962). Enhancement of punitive behavior by audiovisual display. *Science, 136,* 872-873.

Wang, A. Y., & Richarde, R. S. (1988). Global versus task-specific measures of self-efficacy. *Psychological Record, 38,* 533-541.

Waring, N. W. (1986). Coming to terms with pornography: Towards a feminist perspective on sex, censorship, and hysteria. In S. Spitzer & A. T. Scull (Eds.), *Research in law, deviance and social control* (Vol. 8, pp. 85-112). Greenwich, CT: JAI.

Warr, M., & Stafford, M. (1991). The influence of delinquent peers: What they think or what they do? *Criminology, 29,* 851-866.

Warren, M. Q. (1982). Delinquency causation in female offenders. In N. H. Rafter & E. A. Stanko (Eds.), *Judge, lawyer, victim, thief* (pp. 181-202). Boston: Northeastern University Press.

Weber, M. (1947). *The theory of social and economic organizations* (A. M. Henderson & T. Parsons, Trans.). New York: Free Press.

Weiher, A., Huizinga, D., Lizotte, A. J., & Van Kammen, W. B. (1991). The relationship between sexual activity, pregnancy, delinquency, and drug abuse. In D. Huizinga, R. Loeber, & T. Thornberry (Eds.), *Urban delinquency and substance abuse: A technical report*. Washington, DC: Office of Juvenile Justice and Delinquency Prevention.

Weiner, B. (1982). The emotional consequences of causal attributions. In M. S. Clark & S. T. Fiske (Eds.), *Affect and cognition: The seventeenth annual Carnegie Symposium on Cognition*. Hillsdale, NJ: Lawrence Erlbaum.

Weis, J. G., & Sederstrom, J. (1981). *The prevention of serious delinquency: What to do?* Washington, DC: U.S. Department of Justice.

Weiss, R. P. (1987). From slugging detectives to labor relations. In C. D. Shearing & P. C. Stenning (Eds.), *Private policing*. Beverly Hills, CA: Sage.

Wellford, C. F. (1987). Delinquency prevention and labeling. In J. Q. Wilson & G. C. Loury (Eds.), *Families, schools, and delinquency prevention*. New York: Springer-Verlag.

Wells, L. E., & Rankin, J. H. (1988). Direct parental controls and delinquency. *Criminology, 26,* 263-285.

Welter, B. (1966). The cult of the true womanhood, 1820-1860. *American Quarterly, 18,* 151-174.

Wender, P. H. (1971). *Minimal brain dysfunction in children*. New York: Wiley.

Wenk, E. A., Robison, J. O., & Smith, G. W. (1972). Can violence be predicted? *Crime and Delinquency, 18,* 393-402.

Weppner, R. S. (Ed.). (1977). *Street ethnography: Selected studies of crime and deviance in a natural setting*. Beverly Hills, CA: Sage.

West, C., & Fenstermaker, S. (1995). Doing difference. *Gender & Society, 9,* 8-37.

West, C., & Zimmerman, D. H. (1987). Doing gender. *Gender & Society, 1,* 125-151.

West, D., & Farrington, D. (1973). *Who becomes delinquent?* London: Heinemann.

West, D., & Farrington, D. (1977). *The delinquent way of life*. London: Heinemann.

West, D. J. (1982). *Delinquency*. Cambridge, MA: Harvard University Press.

Wexler, R. (1985). Invasions of the child savers: No one is safe in the war against abuse. *The Progressive, 49,* 19-22.

Wheeler, S. (1976). Trends and problems in the sociological study of crime. *Social Problems, 23,* 525-534.

White, J., Moffitt, T. E., Earls, F., Robins, L. N., & Silva, P. A. (1990). How early can we tell? Preschool predictors of boys conduct disorder and delinquency. *Criminology, 28,* 507-533.

Widom, C. S. (1978). Toward an understanding of female criminality. *Progress in Experimental Personality Research, 8,* 245-308.

Wilbanks, W. (1987). *The myth of a racist criminal justice system*. Monterey, CA: Brooks/Cole.

Wilkinson, K. (1974). The broken family and juvenile delinquency: Scientific explanation or ideology. *Social Problems, 21,* 726-739.

Williams, C. L., & Uchiyama, C. (1989). Assessment of life events during adolescence: The use of self-report inventories. *Adolescence, 24,* 95-118.

Williams, J. R., & Gold, M. (1972). From delinquent behavior to official delinquency. *Social Problems, 20,* 209-229.

Williams, K. R., & Hawkins, R. (1986). Perceptual research on general deterrence: A review. *Law & Society Review, 20,* 545-572.

Williams, P. J. (1991). *The alchemy of race and rights: Diary of a law professor*. Cambridge, MA: Harvard University Press.

Willis, C., Evans, T. D., & LaGrange, R. L. (1999). Down home criminology: The place of indigenous theories of crime. *Journal of Criminal Justice, 27,* 227-238.

Willis, P. (1977). *Learning to labor*. Farnborough, UK: Saxon House.

Wilson, J. Q., & Herrnstein, R. J. (1985). *Crime and human nature.* New York: Simon & Schuster.

Winchester, S. W. C., & Jackson, H. (1982). *Residential burglary: The limits of prevention* (Home Office Research Studies No. 74). London: HMSO.

Wolfgang, M. E. (1958). *Patterns in criminal homicide.* Philadelphia: University of Pennsylvania Press.

Wolfgang, M. E., & Ferracuti, F. (1967). *The subculture of violence: Towards an integrated theory in criminology.* Beverly Hills, CA: Sage.

Wolfgang, M. E., Figlio, R. M., & Sellin, T. (1972). *Delinquency in a birth cohort.* Chicago: University of Chicago Press.

Wolfgang, M. E., Figlio, R. M., & Thornberry, T. P. (1978). *Evaluating criminology.* New York: Elsevier.

Wolfgang, M. E., Thornberry, T. P., & Figlio, R. M. (1987). *From boy to man—From delinquency to crime: Followup to the Philadelphia Birth Cohort of 1945.* Chicago: University of Chicago Press.

Wolpe, J., Salter, A., & Reyna, L. J. (1964). *The conditioning therapies: The challenge in psychotherapy.* New York: Holt, Rinehart & Winston.

Worchel, P. (1958). Personality factors in the readiness to express aggression. *Journal of Clinical Psychology, 14,* 355-359.

Worchel, P. (1961). Status restoration and the reduction of hostility. *Journal of Abnormal and Social Psychology, 63,* 443-445.

Worchel, P., & McCormick, B. L. (1963). Self-concept and dissonance reduction. *Journal of Personality, 31,* 588-599.

Worrall, A. (1987). Sisters in law? Women defendants and women magistrates. In P. Carlen & A. Worrall (Eds.), *Gender, crime and justice* (pp. 108-124). Philadelphia: Open University Press.

Worrall, A. (1990). *Offending women.* New York: Routledge.

Wright, E. O., & Perrone, L. (1977). Marxist class categories and income inequality. *American Sociological Review, 42,* 32-55.

Wright, R., & Miller, J. M. (1998). Taboo until today? The coverage of biological arguments in criminology textbooks 1961 to 1970 and 1987 to 1996. *Journal of Criminal Justice, 26,* 1-19.

Wylie, R. (1979). *The self-concept* (Vol. 2). Lincoln: University of Nebraska Press.

Yablonsky, L. (1962). *The violent gang.* New York: Macmillan.

Yates, A. J. (1962). *Frustration and conflict.* London: Methuen.

Yeatman, A. (1995). Interlocking oppressions. In B. Caine & R. Pringle (Eds.), *Transitions: New Australian feminisms* (pp. 42-56). Sydney, Australia: Allen and Unwin.

Yochelson, S., & Samenow, S. E. (1976). *The criminal personality.* New York: Aronson.

Young, A. (1990). *Femininity in dissent.* London: Routledge.

Young, A. (1996). *Imagining crime.* London: Sage.

Young, I. M. (1994). Gender as seriality: Thinking about women as a social collective. *Signs: Journal of Women in Culture and Society, 19,* 713-738.

Young, J. (1987). The tasks facing a realist criminology. *Contemporary Crisis, 11,* 337-356.

Young, J. (1988). Radical criminology in Britain: The emergence of a competing paradigm. *British Journal of Criminology, 28,* 159-183.

Young, J. (1989). *Realist criminology.* London: Sage.

Young, V. D., & Greene, H. T. (1995). Pedagogical reconstruction: Incorporating African-American perspectives into the curriculum. *Journal of Criminal Justice Education, 6,* 85-104.

Yudofsky, S. C., Silver, J. M., & Schneider, S. E. (1987). Pharmacologic treatment of aggression. *Psychiatric Annals, 17,* 397-406.

Zietz, D. (1981). *Women who embezzle or defraud: A study of convicted felons.* New York: Praeger.

Zillman, D. (1979). *Hostility and aggression.* Hillsdale, NJ: Lawrence Erlbaum.

Zimmerman, D. H. (1969). Record-keeping and the intake process in a public welfare agency. In S. Wheeler (Ed.), *On record: Files and dossiers in American life* (pp. 319-354). New York: Russell Sage Foundation.

Zimmerman, D. H. (1974). Fact as a practical accomplishment. In R. Turner (Ed.), *Ethnomethodology* (pp. 128-143). Middlesex, UK: Penguin Books.

Zimring, F. E., & Hawkins, G. (1968). Deterrence and marginal groups. *Journal of Research in Crime and Delinquency, 5,* 100-114.

Zipf, G. (1950). *The principle of least effort.* Reading, MA: Addison Wesley.

Znaniecki, F. (1928a). Social research in criminology. *Sociology and Social Research, 12,* 307-322.

Znaniecki, F. (1928b). Suggestions for criminological research. *Sociology and Social Research, 12,* 411-413.

Zuckerman, M. (1990). The psychophysiology of sensation-seeking. *Journal of Personality, 58,* 314-345.

INDEX

ABOUT THE EDITOR

Suzette Cote, PhD, is Assistant Professor in the Division of Criminal Justice at California State University, Sacramento, where she teaches undergraduate and graduate courses that primarily deal with criminological theory; sex offenses and offenders; and family violence, child abuse, and elder abuse. She received her law degree with a concentration in family law from the State University of New York at Buffalo School of Law in 1998.

Cote's dissertation, *Modernity, Risk, and Contemporary Crime Control Strategies as Risk Management: An Analysis of Sex Offender Statutes and the Shift Toward a Risk Society,* focuses on the shift in penal practices away from rehabilitation and treatment of individual criminals and toward the management of dangerous classes of offenders. A forthcoming publication, "Megan's Law in California: The CD-ROM and the Changing Nature of Crime Control," will be published in *Sexual Violence: Policies, Practices, and Challenges*, edited by Debra S. Kelley and James Hodgson.

Cote's current research interests include the impact of law on society and on certain groups within communities, namely the sex offender laws and sexual violence against women in intimate relationships; crime, criminal justice, and the media; and fear of crime and the roles of knowledge, empowerment, and trust in relation to fear and risk.